Less managing. More teaching. Greater learning.

 INSTRUCTORS...

Would you like your **students** to show up for class **more prepared**?

(Let's face it, class is much more fun if everyone is engaged and prepared…)

Want an **easy way to assign** homework online and track student **progress**?

(Less time grading means more time teaching…)

Want an **instant view** of student or class performance?

(No more wondering if students understand…)

Need to **collect data and generate reports** required for administration or accreditation?

(Say goodbye to manually tracking student learning outcomes…)

Want to **record and post your lectures** for students to view online?

(The more students can see, hear, and experience class resources, the better they learn…)

A: With **McGraw-Hill's Connect,®**

INSTRUCTORS GET:

- Simple **assignment management**, allowing you to spend more time teaching.
- **Auto-graded** assignments, quizzes, and tests.
- **Detailed visual reporting** where student and section results can be viewed and analyzed.
- Sophisticated **online testing** capability.
- A **filtering and reporting** function that allows you to easily assign and report on materials that are correlated to learning objectives and Bloom's taxonomy.
- An easy-to-use **lecture capture** tool.
- The option to **upload course documents** for student access.

Business
A Changing World

FIFTH CANADIAN EDITION

O.C. Ferrell
University of New Mexico—Albuquerque

Geoffrey A. Hirt
DePaul University

Linda Ferrell
University of New Mexico—Albuquerque

Suzanne Iskander
Humber College and University of Guelph at Humber

Peter Mombourquette
Mount Saint Vincent University

 McGraw-Hill
Ryerson

BUSINESS: A CHANGING WORLD
Fifth Canadian Edition

ISBN-13: 978-0-07-133883-7
ISBN-10: 0-07-133883-7

1 2 3 4 5 6 7 8 9 10 TCP 1 9 8 7 6 5 4

Printed and bound in Canada.

Care has been taken to trace ownership of copyright material contained in this text; however, the publisher will welcome any information that enables them to rectify any reference or credit for subsequent editions.

Director of Product Management: Rhondda McNabb
Group Product Manager: Kim Brewster
Marketing Manager: Cathie Lefebvre
Product Developer: Tracey Haggert
Senior Product Team Associate: Christine Lomas
Supervising Editor: Jessica Barnoski
Photo/Permissions Researcher: Alison Lloyd Baker
Copy Editor: Evan Turner
Proofreader: Laurel Sparrow
Plant Production Coordinator: Michelle Saddler
Manufacturing Production Coordinator: Lena Keating
Cover Design: Brett Miller
Cover Image: Fotolia.com (RF)
Interior Design: Sarah Orr
Page Layout: Artplus Limited/Valerie Van Volkenburg
Printer: Transcontinental Printing Group

Library and Archives Canada Cataloguing in Publication

Ferrell, O. C., author
    Business : a changing world / O.C. Ferrell, Geoffrey
A. Hirt, Linda Ferrell, Suzanne Iskander, Peter Mombourquette.
—Fifth Canadian edition.

Includes bibliographical references and index.
ISBN 978-0-07-133883-7

1. Business—Textbooks. 2. Management--Textbooks.
I. Mombourquette, Peter, author II. Iskander, Suzanne, author
III. Title.

HF1008.B88 2014   650   C2013-905923-7

DEDICATION

To Simon Iskander — S.I.

To the memory of Autumn Lea Mombourquette — P.M.

O.C. Ferrell

O.C. Ferrell is Professor of Management and Creative Enterprise Scholar in the Anderson Schools of Management, University of New Mexico. He recently served as the Bill Daniels Distinguished Professor of Business Ethics at the University of Wyoming, and the Chair of the Department of Marketing and the Ehrhardt, Keefe, Steiner, and Hottman P. C. Professor of Business Administration at Colorado State University. He also has held faculty positions at the University of Memphis, University of Tampa, Texas A&M University, Illinois State University, and Southern Illinois University, as well as visiting positions at Queen's University (Ontario, Canada), University of Michigan (Ann Arbor), University of Wisconsin (Madison), and University of Hannover (Germany). He has served as a faculty member for the Master's Degree Program in Marketing at Thammasat University (Bangkok, Thailand). Dr. Ferrell received his B.A. and M.B.A. from Florida State University and his Ph.D. from Louisiana State University. His teaching and research interests include business ethics, corporate citizenship, and marketing.

Dr. Ferrell is widely recognized as a leading teacher and scholar in business. His articles have appeared in leading journals and trade publications. In addition to *Business: A Changing World*, he has two other textbooks, *Marketing: Concepts and Strategies* and *Business Ethics: Ethical Decision Making and Cases*, that are market leaders in their respective areas. He also has co-authored other textbooks for marketing, management, business and society, and other business courses, as well as a trade book on business ethics. He chaired the American Marketing Association (AMA) ethics committee that developed its current code of ethics. He was the vice president of marketing education and president of the Academic Council for the AMA. Currently he is vice president of publications for the Academy of Marketing Science.

Dr. Ferrell's major focus is teaching and preparing learning material for students. He has taught the Introduction to Business course using this textbook. This gives him the opportunity to develop, improve, and test the book and ancillary materials on a first-hand basis. He has travelled extensively to work with students and understands the needs of instructors of introductory business courses. He lives in Albuquerque, New Mexico, and enjoys skiing, golf, and international travel.

Geoffrey A. Hirt

Geoffrey A. Hirt is currently Professor of Finance at DePaul University and a Mesirow Financial Fellow. From 1987 to 1997 he was Chairman of the Finance Department at DePaul University. He teaches investments, corporate finance, and strategic planning. He developed and was director of DePaul's M.B.A. program in Hong Kong and has taught in Poland, Germany, Thailand, and Hong Kong. He received his Ph.D. in Finance from the University of Illinois at Champaign–Urbana, his M.B.A. from Miami University of Ohio, and his B.A. from Ohio-Wesleyan University. Dr. Hirt has directed the Chartered Financial Analysts Study program for the Investment Analysts Society of Chicago since 1987.

Dr. Hirt has published several books, including *Foundations of Financial Management* published by McGraw-Hill/Irwin. Now in its thirteenth edition, this book is used at more than 600 colleges and universities worldwide. It has been used in more than 31 countries and has been translated into more than 10 different languages. Additionally, Dr. Hirt is well known for his text, *Fundamentals of Investment Management*, also published by McGraw-Hill/Irwin, and now in its ninth edition. He plays tennis and golf, is a music lover, and enjoys travelling with his wife, Linda.

Linda Ferrell

Dr. Linda Ferrell is Associate Professor and Creative Enterprise Scholar in the Anderson Schools of Management at the University of New Mexico. She completed her Ph.D. in Business Administration, with a concentration in management, at the University of Memphis. She has taught at the University of Tampa, Colorado State University, University of Northern Colorado, University of Memphis, and the University of Wyoming. She also team teaches a class at Thammasat University in Bangkok, Thailand, as well as an online Business Ethics Certificate course through the University of New Mexico.

Her work experience as an account executive for McDonald's and Pizza Hut's advertising agencies supports her teaching of advertising, marketing management, marketing ethics, and marketing principles. She has published in the *Journal of Public Policy and Marketing, Journal of Business Research, Journal of Business Ethics, Journal of Marketing Education, Marketing Education Review, Journal of Teaching Business Ethics,* and *Case Research Journal,* and is co-author of *Business Ethics: Ethical Decision Making and Cases* (Seventh Edition) and *Business and Society* (Third Edition). She is the ethics content expert for the AACSB Ethics Education Resource Center (**www.aacsb.edu/eerc**) and was co-chair of the 2005 AACSB Teaching Business Ethics Conference in Boulder, CO.

Dr. Ferrell is the Vice President of Programs for the Academy of Marketing Science, Vice President of Development for the Society for Marketing Advances, and the past president for the Marketing Management Association. She is a member of the college advisory board for Petco Vector. She frequently speaks to organizations on "Teaching Business Ethics," including the Direct Selling Education Foundation's training programs and AACSB International Conferences. She has served as an expert witness in cases related to advertising, business ethics, and consumer protection.

Suzanne Iskander

Suzanne Iskander is a faculty member of University of Guelph–Humber and the Business School at Humber Institute of Technology & Advanced Learning. Suzanne teaches the undergraduate Introduction to Business courses at the University of Guelph-Humber and finance and economics courses in the Humber Degree and Diploma Programs. At Humber, she served as Chair, Academic Council, and member, Degree Council. She holds an M.B.A. from Schulich School of Business and is a holder of the Chartered Financial Analyst designation. She has broad experience in business and in the financial services industry.

Peter Mombourquette

Peter S. Mombourquette is an Associate Professor and Chair of the Department of Business and Tourism and Hospitality Management at Mount Saint Vincent University, where he teaches Introduction to Business, Strategic Management, and Entrepreneurship and Small Business. In addition to teaching and research, Peter founded and manages the Entrepreneurship Skills Program (ESP), a highly intensive, multi-disciplinary entrepreneurship program aimed at encouraging entrepreneurship propensity among university graduates. Peter has also founded and chairs the highly successful Social Enterprise for a Day (SE4D) conference where students and community leaders learn about social enterprise and start and run social ventures. Over Peter's time as chair of the department he has worked with his colleagues in creating an engaging environment for students and provided them with an opportunity to give back to society while learning about career opportunities. Peter has worked collaboratively to create a highly successful Learning Passport program for students, an annual Career Week, a job clubs, a mentorship program with community leaders, an annual Social Enterprise Study Tour, a quarterly newsletter, an annual sustainable business tour, and so forth. Peter was recognized for his efforts by Mount Saint Vincent University when he received the Innovative Teaching Award. Peter has also been nominated on two separate occasions by Mount Saint Vincent University for the Atlantic Canadian Leadership Award in teaching.

Peter has completed his D.B.A. from the University of Southern Queensland and previous to that he graduated with an M.B.A. from Saint Mary's University, a B.Ed. from Saint Francis Xavier University, and a B.A. from Cape Breton University. His research interests include human resource practices in small firms, teaching methodologies, student engagement, and Internet use by small and medium-sized businesses. He has published and/or presented over 35 pieces of scholarly work, co-authored six books, and been a keynote speaker at a number of conferences. At Mount Saint Vincent University he serves on the team that is managing the implementation of the university's strategic plan, is a member of the University's Senate, chairs the Senate Committee on Teaching and Learning, is a member of the University Curriculum Planning Committee, and sits on the Pension Governance Board, the University Investment Committee, and several other boards and committees. Peter currently resides in Halifax with his wife, Amanda, and they have had the immense pleasure of having three children, their wonderful son, Jack, a beautiful baby girl, Autumn, who tragically passed away shortly before her first birthday, and a young baby girl, April Autumn.

BRIEF CONTENTS

CONTENTS

PART 2
Starting and Growing a Business

Chapter 8:   Managing Service and
Manufacturing Operations   182

PART 4
Creating the Human Resource Advantage

Chapter 9:   Motivating the Workforce   204

PART 6
Financing the Enterprise

Chapter 14: Accounting and Financial Statements 332

Chapter 15: Money and the Financial System 356

Welcome

This new edition reflects many dynamic changes in the business environment related to how managers make decisions. It is important for students to understand how the functional areas of business have to be coordinated as the economy, technology, global competition, and consumer decision making continue to evolve. All of these changes are presented in concepts that entry-level students can understand. Our book contains all of the essentials that most students should learn in a semester. *Business: A Changing World* has, since its inception, been a concise presentation of the essential material needed to teach the Introduction to Business course. From our experience in teaching the course, we know that the most effective way to engage a student is by making business exciting, relevant, and current. Our teachable, from-the-ground-up approach involves a variety of media, application exercises, and subject matter, including up-to-date content supplements, boxed examples, video cases, PowerPoint presentations, and testing materials that work for entry-level business students. We have worked hard to make sure that the content of this edition is as up to date as possible in order to best reflect today's dynamic world of business. We cover major changes in our economy related to sustainability, digital marketing, and social networking.

The Fifth Canadian Edition

The Fifth Canadian Edition represents one of our most thorough revisions. This is because so many recent events and changes in the environment relate to the foundational concepts in business. Economic and financial instability have resulted in an economy sometimes called the New Normal. This means that an Introduction to Business textbook has to provide adequate coverage of these changes as they relate to traditional business concepts. Businesses must adapt to be successful. Therefore, we have listened to your feedback and incorporated needed changes in content, boxes, opening and closing cases, team exercises, and other features.

In this edition we are launching a chapter on digital marketing and social networking in business, a dynamic area which continues to change the face of business. Entrepreneurs and small businesses have to be able to increase sales and reduce costs by using social networking to communicate and develop relationships with customers.

While the title of our book remains *Business: A Changing World,* we could have changed the title to *Business: A Green World.* Throughout the book, we recognize the importance of sustainability and "green" business. By using the philosophy "Reduce, reuse, and recycle," we believe every business can be more profitable and contribute to a better world through green initiatives. There are new "Going Green" boxes that cover these environmental changes. Our "Entrepreneurship in Action" boxes also discuss many innovations and opportunities to use green business for success. We have been careful to continue our coverage of global business, ethics and social responsibility, and information technology as it relates to the foundations important in an introduction to business course. Our co-author team has a diversity of expertise in these important areas.

The foundational areas of introduction to business, entrepreneurship, small business management, marketing, accounting, and finance have been completely revised. Examples have been provided to which students can easily relate. An understanding of core functional areas of business is presented so students get a holistic view of the world of business. Box examples related to "Responding to Business Challenges," "Entrepreneurship in Action," and "Going Green" help provide real-world examples in these areas.

Our goal is to make sure that the content and teaching package for this book are of the highest quality possible. We wish to seize this opportunity to gain your trust, and we appreciate feedback to help us continually improve these materials. We hope that the real beneficiary of all of our work will be well-informed students who appreciate the role of business in society and take advantage of the opportunity to play a significant role in improving our world. As students understand how our free enterprise system operates and how we fit into the global competitive environment, they will develop the foundation for creating their own success and improving our quality of life.

Chapter-by-Chapter Changes

Chapter 1

- New Destination CEO profile on Christine Day of Lululemon with discussion questions
- New boxed features: Going Green, Entrepreneurship in Action, Responding to Business Challenges
- Updated Team Exercise
- Updated content in "So You Want a Job in the Business World" box at the end of the chapter to offer valuable advice on a wide spectrum of business career choices
- Inclusion of numerous new examples in the text including but not limited to the Japanese nuclear disaster, student protests in Quebec, HootSuite.com, BlackBerry
- Expanded discussions on the Canadian economy including the trend of large corporations stockpiling large sums of cash or dead money, the impact of the Economic Action Plan going forward, and the role of government in the economy
- New in-chapter case on Dutch Disease, which is the impact the high Canadian dollar created by a boom in oil and natural gas on the manufacturing industry in Canada
- Expanded discussion on the role of entrepreneurship in Canada including profiles of young entrepreneurs
- New closing case: Is the Recession Over? It Depends on Whom You Ask

Chapter 2

- New Destination CEO profile on Russell Girling of TransCanada Corporation with discussion questions
- New boxed features: Going Green, Responding to Business Challenges
- Updated Team Exercise
- Updated content in "So You Want a Job in Business Ethics and Social Responsibility" box at the end of the chapter to offer valuable advice on a wide spectrum of business career choices
- Updated Team Exercise
- Inclusion of six in-chapter discussion cases on relevant topics to encourage student participation. Cases include: The Occupy Movement; Are Social Media Sites Fair Game for Employers?; When Is Organic Really Organic?; Is Helping People Download Music and Videos Wrong?; Canada, the Counterfeiters' Safe Haven; and Are Energy Drinks Safe?
- New in-chapter content on recent ethical and social responsibility issues including Keystone XL, SNC Lavalin, Robocall, XL Foods, BP Oil, probiotic yogurt, and so forth
- New closing case: Social Media and Privacy

Chapter 3

- Updated Destination CEO profile on Jim Treliving of Boston Pizza and *Dragons' Den* with discussion questions
- New boxed features: Going Green, Entrepreneurship in Action, Responding to Business Challenges
- Updated Team Exercise
- Updated content in "So You Want a Job in Global Business" box at the end of the chapter to offer valuable advice on a wide spectrum of business career choices
- Expanded information on the relation of Canada to the global economy
- Updated information on the European financial crisis and bailouts
- New section on offshoring
- New closing case: China's Money and Hollywood Films Make for a Partnership

Chapter 4

- New Destination CEO profile on Heather Reisman of Chapters-Indigo with discussion questions
- New boxed features: Going Green, Entrepreneurship in Action, Responding to Business Challenges
- Updated Team Exercise
- Updated content in "So You Want to Start a Business" box at the end of the chapter to offer valuable advice on a wide spectrum of business career choices
- Updated Team Exercise
- New information on IPOs including Facebook
- New information on joint ventures including information on Tim Hortons and Stone Cold Creamery, and Joe Fresh and Loblaws (as well as Joe Fresh and JC Penney in the United States)
- Expanded discussion on mergers and acquisitions including information on Royal Bank, TD Canada Trust, and the Bank of Nova Scotia making significant acquisitions
- New information on the role of government approval and regulations in approving acquisitions with discussion on Bell Canada's purchase of Astral Media and the attempted purchase of Rona by Lowes
- New closing case: Canadian Acquisitions—Not as Easy as They Once Were, which discusses acquisitions in the oilsands

Chapter 5

- New Destination CEO profile on Kevin O'Leary of O'Leary Funds and *Dragon's Den* with discussion questions
- New boxed features: Going Green, Entrepreneurship in Action, Responding to Business Challenges
- Updated Team Exercise
- Updated content in "So You Want to be an Entrepreneur or Small-Business Owner" box at the end of the chapter to offer valuable advice on a wide spectrum of business career choices
- New box insert discussing the differences between an entrepreneur and a small business owner
- New student questionnaire on determining if they have what it takes to be an entrepreneur
- Updated information on idea generation and ideas on current trends in business
- Numerous new examples on social media and digital companies started by young entrepreneurs
- New creativity questionnaire
- Expanded discussion on raising money to start a business including a new in-chapter case on crowdfunding in Canada
- New closing case: Finding a Niche in the Golf Apparel Business

Chapter 6

- New Destination CEO profile on Joyce Groote of Holeys with discussion questions
- New boxed features: Going Green, Entrepreneurship in Action, Responding to Business Challenges
- Updated content in "So You Want to be a Manager: What Kind?" box at the end of the chapter to offer valuable advice on a wide spectrum of business career choices
- Updated Team Exercise
- New information on the role of vision statements, mission statements and value in an organization
- Updated information including a more thorough discussion on the role of planning in an organization using example of BlackBerry and CEO Thorsten Heins
- New information on crisis management including a discussion on the different practices and resulting outcomes of crisis management at Maple Leaf Foods and XL Foods
- Enhanced information pertaining to leadership
- New in-chapter case on Walmart's decision to introduce smaller stores in Canada
- New closing case: Lululemon Practises Crisis Management and Perhaps Marketing All at the Same Time

Chapter 7

- Updated Destination CEO profile on Cora Mussely Tsouflidou of Chez Cora with discussion questions
- New boxed features: Going Green, Entrepreneurship in Action, Responding to Business Challenges
- Updated Team Exercise
- Updated content in "So You Want in Global Business: Managing Organizational Culture, Teamwork, and Communication" box at the end of the chapter to offer valuable advice on a wide spectrum of business career choices
- New closing case: Ford Develops All-Women Team to Green Its Vehicles

Chapter 8

- Updated Destination CEO profile on Gary Kusin of Fedex–Kinko's with discussion questions
- New boxed features: Going Green, Entrepreneurship in Action, Responding to Business Challenges
- Updated Team Exercise
- Updated content in "So You Want a Job in Operations Management" box at the end of the chapter to offer valuable advice on a wide spectrum of business career choices
- New section on Sustainability and Manufacturing
- New closing case: Shell Uses New Refinery to Support Sustainability

Chapter 9

- Updated Destination CEO profile on Jim Pattison of the Jim Pattison Group with discussion questions
- New boxed features: Going Green, Responding to Business Challenges
- Updated Team Exercise
- Updated content in "So You Want Think You May be Good at Motivating a Workforce" box at the end of the chapter to offer valuable advice on a wide spectrum of business career choices
- New closing case: Is It Possible Your Dog Could Increase Business Productivity?

Chapter 10

- Updated Destination CEO profile on Jack Welch of GE with discussion questions
- New Going Green boxed feature
- Updated Team Exercise
- Updated content in "So You Want to Work in Human Resources" box at the end of the chapter to offer valuable advice on a wide spectrum of business career choices
- New closing case: Challenges of Working at Home

Chapter 11

- New Destination CEO profile on Ronnen Harary and Anton Rabie of Spin Master Toys with discussion questions
- New boxed features: Going Green, Entrepreneurship in Action, Responding to Business Challenges
- Updated Team Exercise
- Updated content in "So You Want a Job in Marketing" box at the end of the chapter to offer valuable advice on a wide spectrum of business career choices
- Updated information on the marketing concept and the need by consumers to be heard and engaged; the impact of social media and digital marketing is also discussed
- Introduction of the social media era
- New information on the marketing mix including new trends emerging in pricing and place/location strategies including information on digital and social media
- New in-chapter case on Walmart battling Target for market share in Canada
- New in-chapter case on the role of Yelp in business in Canada
- New closing case: New "Places" Have Emerged to Sell Wedding Gowns and Rings—Helping Couples Lower Wedding Costs

Chapter 12

- New Destination CEO profile on Thorsten Heins of BlackBerry with discussion questions
- New boxed features: Going Green, Entrepreneurship in Action
- Updated Team Exercise
- Updated content in "So You Want to be a Marketing Manager" box at the end of the chapter to offer valuable advice on a wide spectrum of business career choices
- Updated and enhanced information on pricing
- New in-chapter case on Tim Hortons increasing its cup size to make more money
- New in-chapter case on the PlasmaCar in Canada
- Enhanced information on the promotional mix including in-depth coverage of digital media and social media, including new examples of Canadian companies using Facebook, LinkedIn, Pinterest, Tumblr, Twitter, and so forth
- New material on mobile marketing
- Updated in-chapter case: Lululemon's Unconventional Marketing
- New closing case: Finding the Real Green Products

Chapter 13 (New Chapter)

- New chapter on digital marketing and social networking
- Detailed discussion of digital marketing
- New discussion on social networking and social media
- New discussion on the impact of digital marketing
- New information on the legal and social issues of digital marketing
- Destination CEO profile on Arlene Dickinson of Venture Communications with discussion questions
- New boxed features: Going Green, Entrepreneurship in Action, Responding to Business Challenges
- New Team Exercise
- New content in "So You Want to be a Digital Marketer" box at the end of the chapter to offer valuable advice on a wide spectrum of business career choices
- New in-chapter case on Canadian company Mobovivo, the first company to produce video for iPods
- Enhanced in-chapter case: Going Viral
- New in-chapter case on Pinterest
- New in-chapter case on companies engaging in social media monitoring
- New closing case: Facebook and Twitter Offer Businesses Both Opportunities and Challenges

Chapter 14

- Updated Destination CEO profile on Clarence Otis of Darden Restaurants with discussion questions
- New boxed features: Going Green, Entrepreneurship in Action
- Updated Team Exercise
- Updated content in "So You Want to be an Accountant" box at the end of the chapter to offer valuable advice on a wide spectrum of business career choices
- Updated information on the financial information and ratios of Tim Hortons
- Significant updates to industry analysis section
- New information about accounting standards and principles
- New closing case: Recession Encouraged United Parcel Service (UPS) to Rethink the Budgeting Process

Chapter 15

- Updated Destination CEO profile on Jack Dorsey of Twitter with discussion questions
- New boxed features: Going Green, Entrepreneurship in Action
- Updated Team Exercise
- Updated content in "So You Want to Know About Economics" box at the end of the chapter to offer valuable advice on a wide spectrum of business career choices
- New closing case: Are Credit Unions a Better Deal Than Banks?

Chapter 16

- Updated Destination CEO profile on Michael Lee-Chin of AIC Advantage Mutual Fund with discussion questions
- New boxed features: Entrepreneurship in Action, Responding to Business Challenges
- Updated Team Exercise
- Updated content in "So You Want to Work in Financial Management or Securities" box at the end of the chapter to offer valuable advice on a wide spectrum of business career choices
- Expanded coverage concerning capital budgeting
- New closing case: Hershey Foods: Melts in Your Mouth and May Melt Your Heart

Created From the Ground Up

Business: A Changing World was built from the ground up—that is, developed and written expressly for faculty and students who value a brief, flexible, and affordable textbook with the most up-to-date coverage available. With market-leading teaching support and fresh content and examples, *Business: A Changing World* offers just the right mix of currency, flexibility, and value that you need. What sets this book by Ferrell/Hirt/Ferrell/Iskander/Mombourquette apart from the competition is an unrivalled mixture of current content, topical depth, and the best teaching support around.

The Freshest Topics and Examples

Business: A Changing World reflects the very latest developments in the business world, from the growth of outsourcing to Asia and Southeast Asia to Toyota's business strategy. In addition, ethics continues to be a key issue and Ferrell et al. use pedagogical boxes with the topic of Ashley Madison dating service to start a discussion about ethical conduct in business.

Just Enough of a Good Thing

It's easy for students taking their first steps into business to become overwhelmed. *Business: A Changing World* carefully builds just the right mix of coverage and applications to give students a firm grounding in business principles. Instead of sprinting through the semester to get everything in, Ferrell et al. allows for time to explore topics and incorporate other activities that are important to teachers and students.

Teaching Assistance That Makes a Difference

The first and often most serious hurdle in teaching is engaging students' interest, making them understand how textbook material plays a very real role in real business activities. The instructor's material for *Business: A Changing World* is full of helpful resources, including detailed teaching notes and additional material in the Instructor's Manual. The Instructor's Manual contains a matrix to help teachers decide which exercise to use with which chapter.

There's much more to *Business: A Changing World*, and much more it can do for the Introduction to Business course. To learn about this book's great pedagogical features and top-notch ancillaries, keep reading.

Getting a Handle on Business

Business: A Changing World's pedagogy helps students get the most out of their reading, from Learning Objectives at the beginning of the chapter to the Learning Objectives Summary at the end of it.

Learning Objectives

These appear at the beginning of each chapter to provide goals for students to reach in their reading. The objectives are then used in the **Learning Objectives Summary** at the end of each chapter, and help the students gauge whether they've learned and retained the material.

DESTINATION CEO

Christine Day just left a meeting wearing stretch yoga pants and a blazer. This is not typical meeting attire for a CEO, but then again Christine is not managing a typical company. If you haven't guessed, Christine is CEO of Lululemon, a Canadian retailer that continues to grow and thrive in the face of increasing competition.

Lululemon, which became known for $100 yoga pants and innovative marketing ideas such as putting chalkboards next to fitting rooms to get customer feedback, continues to expand both in Canada and in the United States. Day, who became CEO in 2010, brought with her 20 years of retail experience selling premium coffee at Starbucks, which became famous for getting customers to spend upwards of five dollars on what is essentially a dollar drink. Much like Starbucks, Lululemon wants to sell its customers, or guests as they are called, on an overall experience. Shoppers who visit a store are greeted with a warm, lively atmosphere where customers and employees are sharing a commitment to living a healthy life. Day considers Lululemon to be "part of, and contributing to, a bigger macro-trend that affects consumers from their early teens to their 70s. Investing in your health will pay dividends for individuals and society...elevating the world from mediocrity to greatness." Day wants her customers to feel special, to want to be part of the Lululemon culture. Lululemon is selling a lifestyle right down to its shopping bags, which feature inspirational and motivational quotes such as, "Do one thing a day that scares you" and "Friends are more important than money."[1]

Lululemon's strategy is paying off as it currently boasts 122 stores in Canada and the United States with plans to open 100 more. But growth also comes with challenges. For example, one of the unique selling qualities of Lululemon products is they are unique. Women do not want to go to the gym and see other women wearing the exact same clothes. To counter this, Lululemon engages in what experts refer to as the "scarcity model" of stocking shelves, which roughly translates into limiting the size and colour of popular items so they remain in demand. Day has admitted to using the "scarcity model" as part of the company's overall marketing strategy to keep products in demand and customers coming back.

The other pressing challenge for the company is increasing competition from large global players such as Nike, who are willing to sell yoga pants for a substantially lower price than the $100 Lululemon charges. Day's response to large competitors entering the marketplace is to focus on the unique experience and culture her stores offer their guests. Day believes that the experience of shopping at Lululemon will not easily be duplicated. Lululemon's customers are very loyal, and the company will continue to succeed as a result.[2]

Introduction

We begin our study of business by examining the fundamentals of business and economics in this chapter. First, we introduce the nature of business, including its goals, activities, and participants. Next, we describe the basics of economics and apply them to the Canadian economy. Finally, we establish a framework for studying business in this text.

Destination CEO

Each chapter opens with an introduction to one of the key leaders in industry, by detailing their personal journey, how they got to the top, and what it took to get there.

Pedagogical Boxes

An important feature of the book is the "Consider the Following" pedagogical boxes demonstrating real-world examples to drive home the applied lessons to students. These features provide an excellent vehicle for stimulating class discussions.

Consider the Following: The Occupy Movement

The Occupy Movement can be described as a global protest against social and economic inequality. The protestors believe that global corporations, especially financial institutions and wealthy individuals, have an unfair influence in politics leading to economic and social problems that undermine democracy. The movement, which originated in New York, spread quickly throughout North America as protestors built camps in highly visible areas such as in public parks or in front of government buildings. Critics of the movement have said that many of the protestors didn't understand the issues they were protesting, could not even name the companies they were upset with, and were taking over public space to run unsanitary camps. Early in the movement, politicians and law enforcement agencies let the camps exist, but as time passed, tolerance for the protestors started to wane. Citing concerns about the health and safety of the protestors and a desire to return public space back to the public, law enforcement agencies eventually tore down many camps throughout North America. Often the protestors refused to move and were arrested as a result. Today, people in the movement claim they are still strong and are determined to end economic and social inequality, but they appear to suffer from a lack of leadership and clear goals.

1. Some people in the Occupy Movement argued the practice of business itself is unethical. Do you agree or disagree?

2. Do you think law enforcement agencies were right to tear down camps? Why or why not?

3. Some protestors fought back when police officers came to evict them from their camps, including physically confronting officers and throwing objects. Do you think protestors were acting ethically? Why or why not?

RESPONDING TO
BUSINESS CHALLENGES | Nobody Wants Dutch Disease

Dutch Disease simply does not sound pleasant. In fact, some may think it sounds awful. The disease, which has been around since 1977, does not infect people. Rather, it infects countries. The term "Dutch Disease" refers to a country's rapid increase in production of natural resources...say, for instance, oil in Canada. The increase in production normally drives up the price of the country's currency, in this case the Canadian dollar. The result of the increase in the dollar increases the price of manufacturing goods and eventually a decline in manufacturing jobs occurs.

Many economists think Canada may have a case of Dutch Disease with the steady growth in oil production in recent years. As a result, the dollar has risen in value compared to other currencies, thus raising the price of Canadian goods in the global marketplace. The end result of the rise in currency is that many manufacturing jobs, particularly in Ontario and Quebec, have disappeared while new jobs have been created in oil-rich Alberta. Thomas Mulcair, leader of the New Democratic Party, claims Canada has lost a half-million manufacturing jobs in the past six years as a result of the petro-fuelled dollar. Mulcair's supporters note that the Canadian dollar has risen 55percent against the U.S. dollar in the past decade, hurting Canada's manufacturing companies. Mulcair's answer to Dutch Disease is to create a carbon tax, a special tax on oil and gas producers, which will create revenue to invest in companies that have been hurt by the rising dollar.

Not everyone agrees that Canada has a full-blown case of Dutch Disease. Many economists state that Canada's manufacturing industry failed to invest in new technologies over the past decade and, as a result, some of them cannot compete against global firms. These economists charge that a carbon tax will increase the price of fuel, and ask why Canadians should pay because manufacturing firms failed to remain competitive. Additionally, critics of Mulcair's ideas note that people who have lost their jobs in manufacturing have an opportunity to move and find work in the growing oil and gas business.[24]

DISCUSSION QUESTIONS

1. If Dutch Disease creates jobs in one part of the country at the expense of another, should the government step in and try to help struggling companies?

2. While Canada as a whole may not have lost jobs because of the increase in the dollar, there is little doubt the increase has resulted in a loss of jobs in Ontario and Quebec. Should the government come up with a plan to redistribute some of the oil and gas profits to manufacturing firms in central Canada? What would some of the advantages and disadvantages be?

3. What do you think of economists who state that Canadians should just move where the jobs are? What are the advantages and disadvantages of this and is it reasonable?

The **Responding to Business Challenges** boxes illustrate how businesses overcome tough challenges and many also highlight the importance of ethical conduct and how unethical conduct hurts investors, customers, and indeed the entire business world.

The **Entrepreneurship in Action** boxes spotlight successful entrepreneurs and the challenges they have faced on the road to success.

ENTREPRENEURSHIP
IN ACTION | Student Success: Selling Candy to a Baby (Boomer)

Joseph Moncada
Founded: 2006
The Business: Sweet Tooth Candy Emporium
Success: Joseph Moncada, a student at York University, started Sweet Tooth Candy Emporium—retailing over 2,700 different types of candy through its stores and kiosks. The business, which is only a few years old, employs over 25 people and boasts annual income in excess of $700,000.

In 2006, Joseph Moncada borrowed $10,000 from his parents to start a candy store with a "difference." The difference was not the product, but who Moncada planned on targeting with his sugary treats—adults. Moncada felt that there was a market for retro candy and wanted to offer Baby Boomers treats from when they were young. Moncada describes a visit to his store as "a walk down memory lane." His unique concept actually encourages parents to bring their children to a candy store. The concept appears to be working as

Candy is big business for university student Joseph Moncada. The entrepreneur retails over 2,700 different types of candy from his stores.

the company has three permanent stores as well as seasonal kiosks, and Moncada is currently eyeing an expansion plan that includes franchising his concept throughout Canada.[36]

GOING
GREEN | EarthCraft Houses—Crafted for Earth

These days, almost everyone seems to be going green. However, most people seek easy solutions such as purchasing local organic produce, buying chemical-free household products, or driving a hybrid car. Most of us probably believe that not many people live in homes that are entirely "green." Although it may not be page-one news, the green trend is growing in today's housing market. Among those companies promoting green living is EarthCraft House. Founded in 1999 by the Atlanta Home Builders Association and Southface Home, EarthCraft aims to build comfortable homes that reduce utility costs while at the same time benefiting the environment.

As of 2007, EarthCraft House had certified more than 4,000 single-family homes and 1,500 multifamily dwelling units within the Atlanta metro area. Atlanta also boasts six EarthCraft communities. EarthCraft House has expanded beyond Georgia to South Carolina, Alabama, Tennessee, and Virginia. All are supported by local state agencies and home-builders' associations. Similar organizations exist in Florida (Green Building Coalition) and North Carolina (Healthy Built Homes).

So, what is an EarthCraft house? The house can be newly constructed or renovated, and can be tailored to fit price point. To be certified by EarthCraft, a house must meet certain guidelines in energy efficiency, durability, indoor air quality, resource efficiency, waste management, and water conservation. All new homes must meet ENERGY STAR certification criteria and must score at least 150 points on an EarthCraft scoring sheet. Those homes that score 200 or 230 points are awarded *select* or *premium* status, respectively.

So, how does an EarthCraft house benefit the environment, and how does it benefit the homeowner? To answer these questions, a little background information is required. Construction and maintenance of homes and offices are major sources of CO_2 emissions. EarthCraft houses, on the other hand, can reduce emissions by more than 1,100 pounds of greenhouse gases per home each year. EarthCraft homes also use as many recycled and renewable materials as possible, as well as conserving water and reducing storm water pollution.

Homeowner benefits are twofold. One of the aims of EarthCraft is to create a healthier home. For example, an EarthCraft home can reduce levels of mould, mildew, and dust. Therefore EarthCraft homes can benefit our bodies in addition to reducing our carbon footprint. An EarthCraft home can also benefit our wallets. EarthCraft home buyers can take advantage of two different kinds of mortgage incentives. The Energy Efficient Mortgage increases the buyer's purchasing power due to the lower operating costs of an energy-efficient home. The Energy Improvement Mortgage can be used to finance energy-efficient upgrades on an existing home. All in all, EarthCraft and similar companies predicted that by 2010, 10 percent of all homes would be green.[61]

DISCUSSION QUESTIONS

1. In addition to reducing carbon dioxide emissions, what are other reasons to build an energy-efficient, "green" house?

2. What type of incentive would cause you to pay extra for an energy-efficient house?

3. What additional incentives might convince people to go green when building or remodelling their homes?

The **Going Green** boxes show how issues of sustainability affect all levels of domestic business, and these boxes encourage students to keep their eyes on how "business as usual" now includes an environmentally responsible element.

End-of-Chapter Material

The end-of-chapter material provides a great opportunity to reinforce and expand upon the chapter content.

Key Terms Important terms, highlighted in bold face throughout the text with an accompanying definition on the page, are listed in alphabetical order for ease of reference.

KEY TERMS

bribes
business ethics
codes of ethics
consumerism
corporate citizenship

ethical issue
plagiarism
social responsibility
whistleblowing

SO YOU WANT A JOB *in Business Ethics and Social Responsibility*

In the words of Kermit the Frog, "It's not easy being green." It may not be easy, but green business opportunities abound. A popular catch phrase, "Green is the new black," indicates how fashionable green business is becoming. Consumers are more in tune with and concerned about green products, policies, and behaviours by companies than ever before. Companies are looking for new hires to help them see their business creatively and bring insights to all aspects of business operations. The American Solar Energy Society estimates that the number of green jobs could rise to 40 million in North America by 2030. Green business strategies not only give a firm a commercial advantage in the marketplace, but help lead the way toward a greener world. The fight to reduce our carbon footprint in an attempt to reverse climate change has opened up opportunities for renewable energy, recycling, conservation, and increasing overall efficiency in the way resources are used. New businesses that focus on hydro, wind, and solar power are on the rise and will need talented businesspeople to lead them. Carbon emissions trading is gaining popularity as large corporations and individuals alike seek to decrease their footprints. A job in this growing field could be similar to that of a stock trader, or you could lead the search for carbon-efficient companies in which to invest.

In the ethics arena, current trends in business governance strongly support the development of ethics and compliance departments to help guide organizational integrity. This alone is a billion-dollar business, and there are jobs in developing organizational ethics programs, developing company policies, and training employees and management. An entry-level position might be as a communication specialist or trainer for programs in a business ethics department. Eventually there's an opportunity to become an ethics officer with typical responsibilities of meeting with employees, the board of directors, and top management to discuss and advise on ethics issues in the industry; developing and distributing a code of ethics; creating and maintaining an anonymous, confidential service to answer questions about ethical issues; taking actions on possible ethics code violations; and reviewing and modifying the code of ethics of the organization.

There are also opportunities to support initiatives that help companies relate social responsibility to stakeholder interests and needs. These jobs could involve coordinating and implementing philanthropic programs that give back to others important to the organization or developing a community volunteering program for employees. In addition to the human relations function, most companies develop programs to assist employees and their families to improve their quality of life. Companies have found that the healthier and happier employees are, the more productive they will be in the workforce.

Social responsibility, ethics, and sustainable business practices are not a trend; they are good for business and the bottom line. New industries are being created and old ones are adapting to the new market demands, opening up many varied job opportunities that will lead not only to a paycheque, but to the satisfaction of making the world a better place.[95]

So You Want a Job These end-of-chapter features offer valuable advice on a wide spectrum of business career choices.

Build Your Business Plan The end-of-chapter feature **Build Your Business Plan** and the opening chapter's **Guidelines for the Development of the Business Plan** help students through the development of their business plan by relating the steps to the content of each chapter. Additional information and resources can be found in the Instructor's Manual.

BUILD YOUR BUSINESS PLAN

Business Ethics and Social Responsibility
Think about which industry you are considering competing in with your product/service. Are there any kind of questionable practices in the way the product has been traditionally sold? Produced? Advertised? Have there been any recent accusations regarding safety within the industry? What about any environmental concerns?

For example, if you are thinking of opening a lawn care business, you need to consider what possible effects the chemicals you are using will have on the client and the environment. You have a responsibility not to threaten your customers' health or safety. You also have the social responsibility to let the community know of any damaging effect you may be directly or indirectly responsible for.

Supplements

McGraw-Hill Connect™ is a web-based assignment and assessment platform that gives students the means to better connect with their coursework, with their instructors, and with the important concepts that they will need to know for success now and in the future.

With Connect, instructors can deliver assignments, quizzes, and tests online. Instructors can edit existing questions and author entirely new problems. Track individual student performance—by question, by assignment, or in relation to the class overall—with detailed grade reports. Integrate grade reports easily with Learning Management Systems (LMS).

By choosing Connect, instructors provide students with a powerful tool for improving academic performance and truly mastering course material. Connect allows students to practise important skills at their own pace and on their own schedule. Importantly, students' assessment results and instructors' feedback are all saved online—so students can continually review their progress and plot their course to success.

Connect also provides 24/7 online access to an eBook—an online edition of the text—to aid them in successfully completing their work, wherever and whenever they choose.

Key Features

Simple Assignment Management With Connect, creating assignments is easier than ever, so instructors can spend more time teaching and less time managing.

- Create and deliver assignments easily with selectable end-of-chapter questions and test bank material to assign online.

- Streamline lesson planning, student progress reporting, and assignment grading to make classroom management more efficient than ever.

- Go paperless with the eBook and online submission and grading of student assignments.

Smart Grading When it comes to studying, time is precious. Connect helps students learn more efficiently by providing feedback and practice material when they need it, where they need it.

- Automatically score assignments, giving students immediate feedback on their work and side-by-side comparisons with correct answers.

- Access and review each response, manually change grades, or leave comments for students to review.

- Reinforce classroom concepts with practice tests and instant quizzes.

Instructor Library The Connect Instructor Library is your course creation hub. It provides all the critical resources you'll need to build your course, just how you want to teach it.

- Assign eBook readings and draw from a rich collection of textbook-specific assignments.

- Access instructor resources, including ready-made PowerPoint presentations and media to use in lectures.

- View assignments and resources created for past sections.

- Post personal resources for students to use.

eBook Connect reinvents the textbook learning experience for the modern student. Every Connect subject area is seamlessly integrated with Connect eBooks, which are designed to keep students focused on the concepts key to their success.

- Provide students with a Connect eBook, allowing for anytime, anywhere access to the textbook.

- Merge media, animation, and assessments with the text's narrative to engage students and improve learning and retention.

- Pinpoint and connect key concepts in a snap using the powerful eBook search engine.

- Manage notes, highlights, and bookmarks in one place for simple, comprehensive review.

LearnSmart **LEARNSMART**

No two students are alike. Why should their learning paths be? LearnSmart uses revolutionary adaptive technology to build a learning experience unique to each student's individual needs. It starts by identifying the topics a student knows and does not know. As the student progresses, LearnSmart adapts and adjusts the content based on his or her individual strengths, weaknesses, and confidence, ensuring that every minute spent studying with LearnSmart is the most efficient and productive study time possible.

SmartBook **SMARTBOOK**

As the first and only adaptive reading experience, SmartBook is changing the way students read and learn. SmartBook creates a personalized reading experience by highlighting the most important concepts a student needs to learn at that moment in time. As a student engages with Smart-Book, the reading experience continuously adapts by highlighting content based on what each student knows and doesn't know. This ensures that he or she is focused on the content needed to close specific knowledge gaps, while it simultaneously promotes long-term learning.

Instructors' Resources

Business: A Changing World, Fifth Edition, offers a complete, integrated supplements package for instructors to address all your needs.

- **Instructor's Manual:** The Instructor's Manual, prepared by the Canadian text authors, Suzanne Iskander and Peter Mombourquette, accurately represents the text's content and supports instructors' needs. Each chapter includes the learning objectives, glossary of key terms, a chapter synopsis, complete lecture outline, and solutions to the end-of-chapter discussion questions.

- **EZ Test Computerized Test Bank:** This flexible and easy to use electronic testing program allows instructors to create tests from book specific items. Created by Sandra Wellman, Seneca College, the test bank has undergone a rigorous auditing and revision process for the Fifth Canadian Edition. It contains a broad selection of multiple choice, true/false, and essay questions and instructors may add their own questions as well. Each question identifies the relevant page reference and difficulty level. Multiple versions of the test can be created and printed.

- **PowerPoint™ Presentations:** Prepared by Nicole Rourke, St. Clair College, these robust presentations offer high quality visuals from the text and highlight key concepts from each chapter to bring key business concepts to life.

Business Plan Pro

The Business Plan Pro is available as a bundled option that includes more than 250 sample business plans and 400 case studies to give you a wide variety of examples as you create your own plan. It helps you set up your business by answering questions that help the software customize your plan. Then you enter your financial data to generate financial worksheets and statements.

Superior Learning Solutions and Support

The McGraw-Hill Ryerson team is ready to help you assess and integrate any of our products, technology, and services into your course for optimal teaching and learning performance. Whether it's helping your students improve their grades, or putting your entire course online, the McGraw-Hill Ryerson team is here to help you do it. Contact your Learning Solutions Consultant today to learn how to maximize all of McGraw-Hill Ryerson's resources!

For more information on the latest technology and Learning Solutions offered by McGraw-Hill Ryerson and its partners, please visit us online: www.mcgrawhill.ca/he/solutions.

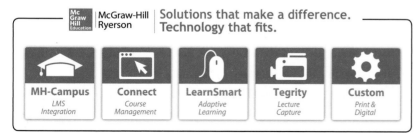

Acknowledgements

The Fifth Canadian Edition of *Business: A Changing World* would not have been possible without the commitment, dedication, and patience of our excellent task masters and guides at McGraw-Hill Ryerson: Kim Brewster, Group Product Manager; Tracey Haggert, Developmental Editor; Jessica Barnoski, Supervising Editor; Michelle Saddler, Production Coordinator; Evan Turner, Copy Editor; and Laurel Sparrow, Proofreader.

Many others have assisted us with their helpful comments, recommendations, and support throughout this and previous editions. We'd like to express our thanks to the following reviewers who were among the instructors who helped us shape the Fifth Canadian Edition:

Glen Kobussen, St. Peter's College—University of Saskatchewan
Kayrod Niamir, Dawson College
Dustin Quirk, Red Deer College
Frank Saccucci, Grant MacEwan University
Brian Turford, Fanshawe College

—*Suzanne Iskander and Peter Mombourquette*

The Dynamics of Business and Economics

LEARNING OBJECTIVES

LO1 Define basic concepts such as business, product, and profit.

LO2 Identify the main participants and activities of business, and explain why studying business is important.

LO3 Define economics and compare the four types of economic systems.

LO4 Describe the role of supply, demand, and competition in a free-enterprise system.

LO5 Specify why and how the health of the economy is measured.

LO6 Trace the evolution of the Canadian economy, and discuss the role of the entrepreneur in the economy.

DESTINATION CEO

Christine Day just left a meeting wearing stretch yoga pants and a blazer. This is not typical meeting attire for a CEO, but then again Christine is not managing a typical company. If you haven't guessed, Christine is CEO of Lululemon, a Canadian retailer that continues to grow and thrive in the face of increasing competition.

Lululemon, which became known for $100 yoga pants and innovative marketing ideas such as putting chalkboards next to fitting rooms to get customer feedback, continues to expand both in Canada and in the United States. Day, who became CEO in 2010, brought with her 20 years of retail experience selling premium coffee at Starbucks, which became famous for getting customers to spend upwards of five dollars on what is essentially a dollar drink. Much like Starbucks, Lululemon wants to sell its customers, or guests as they are called, on an overall experience. Shoppers who visit a store are greeted with a warm, lively atmosphere where customers and employees are sharing a commitment to living a healthy life. Day considers Lululemon to be "part of, and contributing to, a bigger macro-trend that affects consumers from their early teens to their 70s. Investing in your health will pay dividends for individuals and society…elevating the world from mediocrity to greatness." Day wants her customers to feel special, to want to be part of the Lululemon culture. Lululemon is selling a lifestyle right down to its shopping bags, which feature inspirational and motivational quotes such as, "Do one thing a day that scares you" and "Friends are more important than money."[1]

Lululemon's strategy is paying off as it currently boasts 122 stores in Canada and the United States with plans to open 100 more. But growth also comes with challenges. For example, one of the unique selling qualities of Lululemon products is they are unique. Women do not want to go to the gym and see other women wearing the exact same clothes. To counter this, Lululemon engages in what experts refer to as the "scarcity model" of stocking shelves, which roughly translates into limiting the size and colour of popular items so they remain in demand. Day has admitted to using the "scarcity model" as part of the company's overall marketing strategy to keep products in demand and customers coming back.

The other pressing challenge for the company is increasing competition from large global players such as Nike, who are willing to sell yoga pants for a substantially lower price than the $100 Lululemon charges. Day's response to large competitors entering the marketplace is to focus on the unique experience and culture her stores offer their guests. Day believes that the experience of shopping at Lululemon will not easily be duplicated. Lululemon's customers are very loyal, and the company will continue to succeed as a result.[2]

Introduction

We begin our study of business by examining the fundamentals of business and economics in this chapter. First, we introduce the nature of business, including its goals, activities, and participants. Next, we describe the basics of economics and apply them to the Canadian economy. Finally, we establish a framework for studying business in this text.

The Nature of Business

A **business** tries to earn a profit by providing products that satisfy people's needs. The outcomes of its efforts are **products** that have both tangible and intangible characteristics that provide satisfaction and benefits. When you purchase a product, what you are buying is the benefits and satisfaction you think the product will provide. A Subway sandwich, for example, may be purchased to satisfy hunger; a Porsche Cayenne sport utility vehicle, to satisfy the need for transportation and the desire to present a certain image.

Most people associate the word *product* with tangible goods—an automobile, computer, loaf of bread, coat, or some other tangible item. However, a product can also be a service, which results when people or machines provide or process something of value to customers. Dry cleaning, photo processing, a check-up by a doctor, a performance by a movie star or hockey player—these are examples of services. A product can also be an idea. Consultants and attorneys, for example, generate ideas for solving problems.

Business individuals or organizations who try to earn a profit by providing products that satisfy people's needs

Product a good or service with tangible and intangible characteristics that provide satisfaction and benefits

Profit the difference between what it costs to make and sell a product and what a customer pays for it

Nonprofit organizations groups that may provide goods or services but do not have the fundamental purpose of earning profits

The Goal of Business

The primary goal of all businesses is to earn a **profit,** the difference between what it costs to make and sell a product and what a customer pays for it. If a company spends $2.00 to manufacture, finance, promote, and distribute a product that it sells for $2.75, the business earns a profit of 75 cents on each product sold. Businesses have the right to keep and use their profits as they choose—within legal limits—because profit is the reward for the risks they take in providing products. Not all organizations are businesses. **Nonprofit organizations,** such as the Canadian Cancer Society, Special Olympics, and other charities and social causes, do not have the fundamental purpose of earning profits, although they may provide goods or services.

To earn a profit, a person or organization needs management skills to plan, organize, and control the activities of the business and to find and develop employees so that it can make products consumers will buy. A business also needs marketing expertise to learn what products consumers need and want and to develop, manufacture, price, promote, and distribute those products. Additionally, a business needs

A not-for-profit student group—Association pour une solidarité syndicate étudiante (ASSÉ)—was the focus of attention when the Quebec government tried to raise tuition rates. The governing Liberals eventually lost the election and the tuition increases were scrapped by the incoming Parti Québécois.

financial resources and skills to fund, maintain, and expand its operations. Other challenges for businesspeople include abiding by laws and government regulations; acting in an ethical and socially responsible manner; and adapting to economic, technological, and social changes. Even nonprofit organizations engage in management, marketing, and finance activities to help reach their goals.

To achieve and maintain profitability, businesses have found that they must produce quality products, operate efficiently, and be socially responsible and ethical in dealing with customers, employees, investors, government regulators, the community, and society. Because these groups have a stake in the success and outcomes of a business, they are sometimes called **stakeholders.** Many businesses, for example, are concerned with

Stakeholders groups that have a stake in the success and outcomes of a business

how stakeholders view the impact that a business's waste has on the environment and their surrounding communities. Jim Reid, President of Green Solutions Inc., a North American reuse and recycling company in Bridgewater, Nova Scotia, noticed this trend in environmental responsibility and decided he could build a business and help the economy at the same time. Reid's company takes office furniture, electronic equipment such as laptops, and smartphones from companies that would otherwise be throwing them out and diverts them from landfills. He then finds charities that are in need of such products and distributes them for free. When Reid first started the company, naysayers told him that corporations wouldn't pay for such a service, but Reid has proven them wrong by signing up some of Canada's largest companies including the Royal Bank and TD Canada Trust. Reid notes, "Green Solutions recognizes the need for a simple, turnkey, cost-effective way to eliminate and re-purpose no-longer-needed facility assets . . . and we are seeing a large increase in organizations across the board wanting to be part of what we do."[3] Other businesses are concerned about the quality of life in the communities in which they operate. For example, both CIBC and Canadian Western Bank have recently made donations to the Streettohome Foundation in Vancouver to build housing for homeless youth. Mike Stevenson, Senior Vice President, Retail Markets at CIBC, says, "We're proud to support organizations like Streettohome in helping youth in Vancouver build a better future off the streets."[4] Streettohome Foundation has also received support from BC Hydro in its "Seeing is Believing" program, which is aimed at further assisting homeless people in Vancouver. Jae Kim, former president of the Streettohome Foundation, says, "By engaging key business executives we have an opportunity to discuss solutions."[5] Wendy Campbell, Director of Programs at the Canadian Business for Social Responsibility (CBSR), states, "Business has the skill and resources to make a real contribution to alleviate homelessness.... The direct interaction between business leaders and community members fostered by the Seeing is Believing program has inspired organizations to leverage their resources towards creative solutions."[6] Some businesses are concerned with promoting careers among minority groups. Petro-Canada sponsors a "Stay in School" program aimed at Aboriginal communities, and created a human resource strategy to encourage students to meet the company's employment and business requirements. Other companies are concerned with social responsibility in times of natural disasters. Canadian Pacific, a Calgary-based transportation company with operations primarily in North America, donated $1 million to help victims of Hurricane Sandy, a major storm which caused hundreds of millions of dollars in damage in sixteen U.S. states.[7] Other Canadian companies have also donated money to assist in the clean-up after the 2012 Japanese Fukushima Daiichi nuclear disaster or the 2005 tsunami in Indonesia. Talisman Energy Inc., a Calgary-based oil company, has helped to support reconstruction efforts in the village of Lamreh, Indonesia, following the tsunami. The project has included, among other things, the construction of homes and schools.[8] In Canada, the emphasis on social responsibility has led to the formation of such groups as the above-mentioned CBSR, which is a network of Canadian companies that are intent on focusing on environmental, social, and economic solutions that lead to better business and a better world.

LO2 Identify the main participants and activities of business, and explain why studying business is important.

The People and Activities of Business

Figure 1.1 shows the people and activities involved in business. At the centre of the figure are owners, employees, and customers; the outer circle includes the primary business activities—management, marketing, and finance. Owners have to put up resources—money or credit—to start a business. Employees are responsible for the work that goes on within a business. Owners can manage the business themselves or hire employees to accomplish this task. The president of Shoppers Drug Mart, for example, does not own the drug store but is an employee who is responsible for managing all the other employees in a way that earns a profit for investors, who are the real owners. Finally, and most importantly, a business's major role is to satisfy the customers who buy its goods or services. Note also that people and forces beyond an organization's control—such as legal and regulatory forces, the economy, competition, technology, and ethical and social concerns—all have an impact on the daily operations of businesses. You will learn more about these participants in business activities throughout this book. Next, we will examine the major activities of business.

Management. Notice that in Figure 1.1 management and employees are in the same segment of the circle. This is because management involves coordinating employees' actions to achieve the firm's goals, organizing people to work

Many of Canada's largest corporations are reaching out to assist their communities. Petro-Canada contributes to Aboriginal communities, assists the Canadian Cancer Society, and contributes to environmentally friendly initiatives.

> "Managers plan, organize, staff, and control the tasks required to carry out the work of the company or nonprofit organization."

efficiently, and motivating them to achieve the business's goals. For example, Montreal-based Bombardier—a manufacturer of airplanes and trains—has been a family-run business except for a very brief period of time since its inception. Current CEO Pierre Beaudoin is following in the footsteps of his father-in-law in providing leadership for the company by expanding the business into the manufacturing of larger planes and faster high-speed trains. Under Beaudoin's leadership, the company, which traditionally made regional jets for fewer than 100 passengers, has expanded its fleet to include planes that seat 110 and 130 people respectively. Some business experts question if the expansion into larger planes—known as the CSeries—is a good idea, but Beaudoin has stated that it is essential for the company to meet its goals. The strategy appears to be paying off. Bombardier has recently reported sales of the CSeries in excess of $2.5 billion to Latvian airline AirBaltic and Delta Airlines in the United States.[9] Management is also concerned with acquiring, developing, and using resources (including people) effectively and efficiently. For example, management at CGI Group, a Montreal-based IT service firm, is constantly looking to hire IT specialists, who are often in scarce supply, as the company grows.[10] Other examples of people or worker shortages include the oil industry in Canada. Even though unemployment rates in Canada have risen in recent years, oil and gas companies continue to cite a shortage of labour

One of the challenges for BlackBerry is finding enough skilled workers to fill jobs at the company's Waterloo offices.

as a barrier to meeting their goals. As a result many oil and gas managers have increased compensation levels to attract more workers, offered incentives to older workers to stay on the job rather than retire, and brought in foreign workers to fill the gap in the labour force. In Alberta alone, the Petroleum Human Resources Council has predicted up to 130,000 new workers will be needed in the coming ten years.[11] Many projects remain stalled in Western Canada due to a lack of skilled tradespeople.[12]

Production and manufacturing is another element of management. In essence, managers plan, organize, staff, and control the tasks required to carry out the work of the company or nonprofit organization. We take a closer look at management activities in Parts 3 and 4 of this text.

To illustrate the importance of management, consider a small hypothetical retailer, owned and managed by the El-Skior family, which provides excellent service in the community. Among the many management activities the El-Skior family engages in are finding, training, scheduling, and motivating staff; locating and purchasing high-quality products; and planning advertising and promotion campaigns. If a large corporate retailer such as Walmart or Target opens nearby, the El-Skior family will have to decide how to respond to the new competition—change prices, advertise, or make some other response. Consequently, making decisions to ensure the business achieves its short and long-term goals is a vital part of management.

Marketing. Marketing and consumers are in the same segment of Figure 1.1 because the focus of all marketing activities is satisfying customers. Marketing includes all the activities designed to provide goods and services that satisfy

figure 1.1 Overview of the Business World

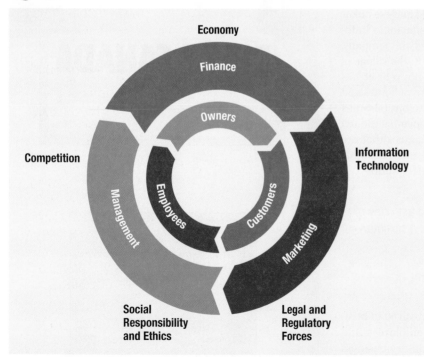

consumers' needs and wants. Marketers gather information and conduct research to determine what customers want. Using information gathered from marketing research, marketers plan and develop products and make decisions about how much to charge for their products and when and where to make them available. For example, prior to starting

their frozen organic baby food company—Sweetpea Baby Food—the founders, Eryn Green and Tamar Wagman from Toronto, conducted research to see if the idea had merit, what types of products customers would buy, and who their potential competition might be. The pair visited retailers to see who was selling similar products, interviewed potential

GOING GREEN | The Potential for a Canadian Game Changer

"Game changers" in the sports world are athletes who have redefined the way a game is played. Think about the impact that Bobby Orr, the first offensive defenceman, has had on how hockey is played; how Canadian Steve Nash re-introduced the fast break to basketball. In business "game changers" are new advances in technology that drastically change how business is conducted. Examples of such game changers include the Internet, smartphones, and tablets. The battery-powered car has the potential to be such a game changer in the automobile industry. Currently, gas combustion engines dominate car sales but sales of hybrid cars, which combine gas engines with lithium batteries, have risen in popularity in recent years due to the rapid run-up in the price of gas and improvements in hybrid technology. Large multinational auto companies such as Toyota, General Motors, and Nissan are all trying to further develop hybrid technology with the hope of getting to the point where the gas combustion engine is a thing of the past.

Interestingly, a small Canadian company, ZENN Motor Company, which stands for "zero emissions, no noise," is trying to participate in this industry. A few years ago, former ZENN CEO Ian Clifford took a chance and invested in EEStor, a Texas-based company that is trying to replace the current lithium battery with a new energy storage device based on ultracapacitor technology. ZENN originally invested $2.5 million for 3.8 percent of the company but more importantly, ZENN was given exclusive rights to use the technology in vehicles up to 1,400 kilograms, or most small and midsize cars. ZENN has since upped its stake in EEStor to 10.7 percent as results from EEStor's testing of the ultracapacitor have exceeded expectations. One industry analyst noted that a functional ultracapacitor could generate $2 billion in annual revenue for the company. Other technology experts are not convinced that EEStor can build such a device, noting that no one in the past has come close to successfully building such a battery based on the ultracapacitor technology. ZENN has already experienced one significant setback as they attempted to manufacture ZENN City, a micro car powered solely by a battery. The car, which was supposed to be able to travel over 640 kilometres on a single two- to three-minute charge at speeds in excess of 125 kilo-

The ZENN car pictured here may be the answer to rising oil prices.

metres per hour, never resonated with consumers and had problems meeting regulatory requirements based on its size and speed. ZENN noted that once the price of gas went down, and the 2008–09 recession occurred, people seemed less willing to spend excess dollars on a small, environmentally friendly car. ZENN ended manufacturing of the car after two years of production and is focusing all its efforts on its partnership with EEStor and its ultracapacitor technology—essentially becoming a manufacturer of automobile components.[15]

DISCUSSION QUESTIONS

1. Do you think ZENN will ultimately be successful?

2. What do you see as some of the challenges for a company like ZENN? Would managers have a difficult time convincing prospective employees to work for the firm? Why or why not?

3. One of the challenges for ZENN is they are actually spending more money a month than they are making. If you were a banker or an investor, would you lend money to ZENN based on its past history and future prospects?

4. Should ZENN consider selling its technology to larger automobile companies? Do you think this is a wise strategy? Do you think anyone would buy the technology?

One of the most successful marketing efforts in Canada is Tim Hortons' "Roll up the Rim to Win," which has been described as a national obsession.

customers to see if they would consider purchasing frozen organic food, reviewed birth data from Statistics Canada, used an online consumer survey to select the company's name, and made financial projections based on research from the food industry. A few short years after starting the business, the pair have annual sales in excess of $500,000 and are eyeing an expansion into the lucrative U.S. market.[13] Business and nonprofit organizations use promotion—advertising, personal selling, sales promotion (coupons, games, sweepstakes, movie tie-ins), and publicity—to communicate the benefits and advantages of their products to consumers and increase sales. One of the best-known Canadian marketing initiatives of all time is Tim Hortons' "Roll up the Rim to Win" campaign. The simple idea was developed by Tim Hortons executive Ron Buist, in partnership with previous owner Ron Joyce, who both felt their cup with the company's name and logo was one of the company's best marketing tools. Buist says they developed the idea as a way to gain even more marketing leverage (strength) from their paper cup and to increase sales. The simple advertising campaign has been described by *The Globe and Mail* as, "an obsession that lures customers year after year as the saying 'Rrrroll up the Rim to Win' echoes across the country."[14] We will examine marketing activities in Part 5 of this text.

Finance. Owners and finance are in the same part of Figure 1.1 because, although management and marketing have to deal with financial considerations, it is the primary responsibility of the owners to provide financial resources for the operation of the business. Moreover, the owners have the most to lose if the business fails to make a profit. Finance refers to all activities concerned with obtaining money and using it effectively. People who work as accountants, stockbrokers, investment advisors, or bankers are all part of the financial world. Owners sometimes have to borrow money to get started or attract additional owners who become partners or shareholders. One of the biggest challenges in Canada's economy in recent years is the difficulty both large and small companies are having in borrowing money, often called *capital*. The inability of businesses and consumers to

borrow money is referred to as a *credit crunch*. Banks and other lenders are hesitant to lend money because many of them either have lost millions of dollars making bad loans to people who could not afford them in the U.S. sub-prime housing crisis, or are worried that the state of the economy is so bad that any loans may not be paid. Since companies need to borrow money to pay their bills and expand, the impact of the credit crunch caused a global recession—defined as a period of poor economic activity that includes rising unemployment. While the recession is over in Canada and the United States at the time of writing this book, many banks are mindful that problems still exist in other parts of the world—particularly in Europe—and have been hesitant to lend money fearing that another global recession could occur. Additionally, many large companies have been slow to spend money, preferring to save their profits just in case another recession occurs or problems in Europe spread to North America. This cash savings has been termed *dead money*, meaning the money is just sitting in an account and not being used to produce any positive economic activity. For example, the Bank of Nova Scotia has approximately $54 billion in cash reserves, and Suncor Energy, a Canadian Oil Sands company, has stockpiled $6.5 billion. Both Finance Minister Jim Flaherty and Prime Minister Stephen Harper have been urging companies to invest the cash, which some estimate is as much as $600 billion, or pay some of the profits to investors or shareholders.[16] Sneh Seetal, a spokesman for Suncor, says they are just being financially prudent: "In any uncertain economic environment with volatile commodity pricing, we think it's prudent to have cash on the balance sheet."[17] The banks' unwillingness to lend money coupled with corporations opting to save their cash rather than invest the proceeds has led to a prolonged period of slow growth in North America. *Canadian Business*, the leading national business publication, recently stated that the economy is in "stalled speed" and questioned if another recession could occur as a result.[18] Governments in many countries, including Canada, have taken action to encourage banks and lenders to lend money in order to avoid another recession. An example of a company that was highly influenced by the credit crunch was Teck Resources, a large Canadian mining company. Teck borrowed a great deal of money to acquire Fording Coal and its valuable coal resources. Because of this purchase, Teck needed to borrow money and access credit during the height of the credit crunch and industry analysts thought the company might be forced to close due to a lack of available credit. Fortunately for Teck and its thousands of employees, the Canadian government's intervention into the credit markets started to work and the company successfully renegotiated its loan portfolio. The result was that Teck shares went from a low of $3.37 to over $35 a share within a year.[19] As of 2013, the Canadian economy appears to be recovering, but other challenges have arisen including the European Debt Crisis and the possibility of rising *inflation*—a term defined in more detail later in the chapter. Part 6 of this text discusses financial management.

Studying business can also help you better understand the many business activities that are necessary to provide satisfying goods and services—and that these activities carry a price tag. For example, if you pay to download a song, about half of the price goes toward activities related to distribution and the studio's expenses and profit margins and only a small portion goes to the artist. Most businesses charge a reasonable price for their products to ensure that they cover their production costs, pay their employees, provide their owners with a return on their investment, and perhaps give something back to their local communities. For example, the Royal Bank of Canada (RBC) donated

When a Carly Rae Jepsen song is downloaded on iTunes the amount of money going to the musician is often much smaller than the selling price.

over $64 million to charities in 2011 and has committed to donating $50 million over 10 years for the development of clean water initiatives. RBC is also actively involved in supporting scholarships for university students, developing programs to help the mentally challenged, and supporting emerging artists.[20] Canadian Jeff Skoll, former president and first employee of eBay, has donated approximately $1 billion to the Skoll Foundation, an organization he founded to support a sustainable world. Skoll's foundation invests heavily in "social entrepreneurs," who can be defined as people who are using entrepreneurial skills such as creativity and risk taking to solve some of society's problems. Canadian hockey player Wayne Gretzky has also been actively involved in charities, most notably the Wayne Gretzky Foundation which helps underprivileged children participate in sports. The foundation has grown to support the Heart and Stroke Foundation, the Canadian National Sledge Hockey team, and various minor hockey programs.[21] Thus, learning about business can help you become a well-informed consumer and member of society.

Business activities help generate the profits that are essential not only to individual businesses and local economies but also to the health of the global economy. Without profits, businesses find it difficult, if not impossible, to buy more raw materials, hire more employees, attract more capital, and create additional products that in turn make more profits and fuel the world economy. Understanding how our free-enterprise economic system allocates resources and provides incentives for industry and the workplace is important to everyone.

LO3 Define economics and compare the four types of economic systems.

The Economic Foundations of Business

To continue our introduction to business, it is useful to explore the economic environment in which business is conducted. In this section, we examine economic systems, the free-enterprise system, the concepts of supply and demand, and the role of competition. These concepts play important roles in determining how businesses operate in a particular society.

Economics is the study of how resources are distributed for the production of goods and services within a social system. As evident in the examples below, the Canadian economy has many of the resources needed for the successful production of goods and services. You are already familiar with the types of resources available. Land, forests, minerals, water, and other things that are not made

> **Economics** the study of how resources are distributed for the production of goods and services within a social system

Canada's abundant natural resources include vast quantities of oil. As of 2013, Canada surpassed Iran to become the fifth-largest oil producer in the world.

by people are **natural resources.** Canada has an abundance of natural resources including vast supplies of fresh water, large areas of forest, nickel, copper, uranium, and large deposits of oil and natural gas. In fact some oil experts estimate that Canada may have the second-largest oil reserves in the world, and it was recently announced that Canada has become the fifth-largest global producer of oil. Michael McCullogh, in a recent article in *Canadian Business,* says, "...Canada is now an oil nation." Patricia Mohr, a vice-president and economist from the Bank of Nova Scotia, states, "Canadian oil production creates jobs and wealth from Newfoundland to British Columbia." Canada also has an abundance of natural gas, with the latest U.S. geological survey estimating Canada has 44 billion barrels of gas in the ground or enough natural gas to last 100 years.[22] Mike Dawson, president of the Canadian Society for Unconventional Gas, noted, "The magnitude of these numbers may blow you away... . We have an awful lot of natural gas potential lying within the country."[23] **Human resources,** or labour, refer to the physical and mental abilities that people use to produce goods and services. As previously discussed, some Canadian companies have had challenges finding enough workers in recent years. This trend is likely to continue as the Baby Boomers, who make up roughly one-third of Canada's population, retire. **Financial resources,** or capital, are the funds used to acquire the natural and human resources needed to provide products. Until recently Canadian companies have been able to readily access capital. But as discussed in this chapter, accessing money has been challenging in recent years. Because natural, human, and financial resources are used to produce goods and services, they are sometimes called *factors of production.*

Natural resources land, forests, minerals, water, and other things that are not made by people

Human resources the physical and mental abilities that people use to produce goods and services; also called labour

Financial resources the funds used to acquire the natural and human resources needed to provide products; also called capital

Economic Systems

An **economic system** describes how a particular society distributes its resources to produce goods and services. A central issue of economics is how to fulfill an unlimited demand for goods and services in a world with a limited supply of resources. Different economic systems attempt to resolve this central issue in numerous ways, as we shall see.

Although economic systems handle the distribution of resources in different ways, all economic systems must address three important issues:

1. What goods and services, and how much of each, will satisfy consumers' needs?

2. How will goods and services be produced, who will produce them, and with what resources will they be produced?

3. How are the goods and services to be distributed to consumers?

Communism, socialism, and capitalism, the basic economic systems found in the world today (Table 1.1), have fundamental differences in the way they address these issues.

Communism. Karl Marx (1818–1883) first described **communism** as a society in which the people, without regard to class, own all the nation's resources. In his ideal political-economic system, everyone contributes according to ability and receives benefits according to need. In a communist economy, the people (through the government) own and operate all businesses and factors of production. Central government planning determines what goods and services satisfy citizens' needs, how the goods and services are produced, and how they are distributed. However, no true communist economy exists today that satisfies Marx's ideal.

Economic system a description of how a particular society distributes its resources to produce goods and services

Communism first described by Karl Marx as a society in which the people, without regard to class, own all the nation's resources

On paper, communism appears to be efficient and equitable, producing less of a gap between rich and poor. In practice, however, communist economies have been marked by low standards of living, critical shortages of consumer goods, high prices, and little freedom. Russia, Poland, Hungary, and other Eastern European nations have turned away from communism and toward economic systems governed by supply and demand rather than by central planning. However, their experiments with alternative economic systems have been fraught with difficulty and hardship. China and Cuba continue to apply communist principles to their economies, but these countries are also enduring economic and political change. The Chinese economy has in fact grown more than any other country's over the past 30 years and the government attributes this to its ability to combine central planning with free economy

Dutch Disease simply does not sound pleasant. In fact, some may think it sounds awful. The disease, which has been around since 1977, does not infect people. Rather, it infects countries. The term "Dutch Disease" refers to a country's rapid increase in production of natural resources...say, for instance, oil in Canada. The increase in production normally drives up the price of the country's currency, in this case the Canadian dollar. The result of the increase in the dollar increases the price of manufacturing goods and eventually a decline in manufacturing jobs occurs.

Many economists think Canada may have a case of Dutch Disease with the steady growth in oil production in recent years. As a result, the dollar has risen in value compared to other currencies, thus raising the price of Canadian goods in the global marketplace. The end result of the rise in currency is that many manufacturing jobs, particularly in Ontario and Quebec, have disappeared while new jobs have been created in oil-rich Alberta. Thomas Mulcair, leader of the New Democratic Party, claims Canada has lost a half-million manufacturing jobs in the past six years as a result of the petro-fuelled dollar. Mulcair's supporters note that the Canadian dollar has risen 55 percent against the U.S. dollar in the past decade, hurting Canada's manufacturing companies. Mulcair's answer to Dutch Disease is to create a carbon tax, a special tax on oil and gas producers, which will create revenue to invest in companies that have been hurt by the rising dollar.

Not everyone agrees that Canada has a full-blown case of Dutch Disease. Many economists state that Canada's manufacturing industry failed to invest in new technologies over the past decade and, as a result, some of them cannot compete against global firms. These economists charge that a carbon tax will increase the price of fuel, and ask why Canadians should pay because manufacturing firms failed to remain competitive. Additionally, critics of Mulcair's ideas note that people who have lost their jobs in manufacturing have an opportunity to move and find work in the growing oil and gas business.[24]

DISCUSSION QUESTIONS

1. If Dutch Disease creates jobs in one part of the country at the expense of another, should the government step in and try to help struggling companies?

2. While Canada as a whole may not have lost jobs because of the increase in the dollar, there is little doubt the increase has resulted in a loss of jobs in Ontario and Quebec. Should the government come up with a plan to redistribute some of the oil and gas profits to manufacturing firms in central Canada? What would some of the advantages and disadvantages be?

3. What do you think of economists who state that Canadians should just move where the jobs are? What are the advantages and disadvantages of this and is it reasonable?

---

or capitalist reforms. The Chinese government continues to maintain a great deal of central control over the economy but has allowed for a great deal of individual economic freedom. Economic experts generally agree that communism is declining and its future as an economic system is uncertain.

Socialism.   Closely related to communism is **socialism,** an economic system in which the government owns and operates basic industries—postal service, telephone, utilities, transportation, health care, banking, and some manufacturing—but individuals own most businesses. Central planning determines what basic goods and services are produced, how they are produced, and how they are distributed. Individuals and small businesses provide other goods and services based on consumer demand and the availability of resources. As with

Socialism an economic system in which the government owns and operates basic industries but individuals own most businesses

communism, citizens are dependent on the government for many goods and services.

Most socialist nations, such as Denmark, Sweden, India, and Israel, are democratic and recognize basic individual freedoms. Citizens can vote for political offices, but central government planners usually make decisions about what is best for the nation. People are free to go into the occupation of their choice, but they often work in government-operated organizations. Socialists believe their system permits a higher standard of living than other economic systems, but the difference often applies to the nation as a whole rather than to its individual citizens. Socialist economies profess egalitarianism—equal distribution of income and social services. They believe their economies are more stable than those of other nations. Although this may be true, taxes and unemployment are generally higher in socialist countries. Perhaps as a result, many socialist countries are also experiencing economic turmoil.

table 1.1 Comparisons of Communism, Socialism, Capitalism, and Mixed Economy

	Communism	Socialism	Capitalism	Mixed Economy
Business ownership	Most businesses are owned and operated by the government.	The government owns and operates major industries; individuals own small businesses.	Individuals own and operate all businesses.	Individuals own most of the businesses, although the government may operate some.
Competition	None. The government owns and operates everything.	Restricted in major industries; encouraged in small business.	Encouraged by market forces and government regulations.	Encouraged by market forces and government regulations.
Profits	Excess income goes to the government.	Profits earned by small businesses may be reinvested in the business; profits from government-owned industries go to the government.	Individuals are free to keep profits and use them as they wish.	Individuals are free to keep profits and use them as they wish.
Product availability and price	Consumers have a limited choice of goods and services; prices are usually high.	Consumers have some choice of goods and services; prices are determined by supply and demand.	Consumers have a wide choice of goods and services; prices are determined by supply and demand.	Consumers have a wide choice of goods and services; prices are determined by supply and demand.
Employment options	Little choice in choosing a career; most people work for government-owned industries or farms.	Some choice of careers; many people work in government jobs.	Unlimited choice of careers.	Unlimited choice of careers.

SOURCE: "Gross Domestic Product or Expenditure, 1930–2002," *InfoPlease* (n.d.), www.infoplease.com/ipa/A0104575.html (accessed February 16, 2004).

Capitalism. **Capitalism, or free enterprise,** is an economic system in which individuals own and operate the majority of businesses that provide goods and services. Competition, supply, and demand determine which goods and services are produced, how they are produced, and how they are distributed. Canada, the United States, Japan, and Australia are examples of economic systems based on capitalism.

There are two forms of capitalism: pure capitalism and modified capitalism. In pure capitalism, also called a **free-market system,** all economic decisions are made without government intervention. This economic system was first described by Adam Smith in *The Wealth of Nations* (1776). Smith, often called the father of capitalism, believed that the "invisible hand of competition" best regulates the economy. He argued that competition should determine what goods and services people need. Smith's system is also called *laissez-faire* ("leave it alone") *capitalism* because the government does not interfere in business.

Capitalism, or free enterprise an economic system in which individuals own and operate the majority of businesses that provide goods and services

Free-market system pure capitalism, in which all economic decisions are made without government intervention

Modified capitalism differs from pure capitalism in that the government intervenes and regulates business to some extent. One of the ways in which the Canadian and the United States governments regulate business is through laws. Laws such as the Privacy Act in Canada, which protects consumers' private information, and the Federal Trade Commission Act in the United States, which created the Federal Trade Commission to enforce antitrust laws, illustrate the importance of the government's role in the economy.

Mixed Economies. No country practises a pure form of communism, socialism, or capitalism, although most tend to favour one system over the others. Most nations operate as **mixed economies,** which have elements from more than one economic system. In Canada, most businesses are owned and operated by private individuals, yet a number of government-owned businesses or crown corporations exist including the Canada Post Corporation, the Bank of Canada, and the Canadian Dairy Commission. While Canada's economy can still be classified as a mixed economy, the trend in recent years is towards a more capitalist system. Many Canadian crown corporations have been taken private, where the government sells its stake in the business and allows private citizens to manage the company. For example, over the last number of years, Canadian National Railway, Petro-Canada, and NS Power have all been converted to private enterprises. The trend towards greater capitalism has been aided in Canada by deregulation, which is a reduction in the number of laws and rules that govern the economy.

Mixed economies economies made up of elements from more than one economic system

"Demand is the number of goods and services that consumers are willing to buy at different prices at a specific time."

The Free-Enterprise System

Many economies—including those of Canada, the United States, and Japan—are based on free enterprise, and many communist and socialist countries, such as China, are applying more principles of free enterprise to their own economic systems. Free enterprise provides an opportunity for a business to succeed or fail on the basis of market demand. In a free-enterprise system, companies that can efficiently manufacture and sell products that consumers desire—such as Apple, Rogers Communications, and Lululemon—will probably succeed. Inefficient businesses and those that sell products that do not offer needed benefits will likely fail as consumers take their business to firms that have more competitive products. For example, during the Internet boom from 1995 to 2000, Nortel Networks was considered a great Canadian company. But from 2000 to 2009 the company failed to properly meet the needs of its consumers and was plagued by inefficiencies. The once-great Canadian company declared bankruptcy in 2009,[25] something that would have been considered unimaginable ten years previously. Currently another well-known Canadian tech company, BlackBerry—formerly known as Research In Motion—has fallen on difficult times. BlackBerry, which was once the largest global manufacturer of smartphones, saw its market share plunge in recent years as more popular and consumer friendly products such as the iPhone and the Galaxy were introduced to the market. BlackBerry has since introduced a number of new smartphones with the hopes of gaining back lost customers. Some technology experts think it may be too late for the company and they are predicting the company's demise.

A number of basic individual and business rights must exist for free enterprise to work. These rights are the goals of many countries that have recently embraced free enterprise.

1. Individuals must have the right to own property and to pass this property on to their heirs. This right motivates people to work hard and save to buy property.

2. Individuals and businesses must have the right to earn profits and to use the profits as they wish, within the constraints of their society's laws and values.

3. Individuals and businesses must have the right to make decisions that determine the way the business operates. Although there is government regulation, the philosophy in countries like Canada and Australia is to permit maximum freedom within a set of rules of fairness.

4. Individuals must have the right to choose what career to pursue, where to live, what goods and services to purchase, and more. Businesses must have the right to choose where to locate, what goods and services to produce, what resources to use in the production process, and so on.

Consumers are less sensitive to the price of milk (left) than to steak (right). When the price of milk goes up, demand does not fall significantly because people still need to buy milk. However, if the price of steak rises beyond a certain point, people will buy less because they can turn to the many substitutes for steak.

Without these rights, businesses cannot function effectively because they are not motivated to succeed. Thus, these rights make possible the open exchange of goods and services.

LO4 Describe the role of supply, demand, and competition in a free-enterprise system.

The Forces of Supply and Demand

In Canada and in other free-enterprise systems, the distribution of resources and products is determined by supply and demand. **Demand** is the number of goods and services that consumers are willing to buy at different prices at a specific time. From your own experience, you probably recognize that consumers are usually willing to buy more of an item as its price falls because they want to save money. Consider handmade rugs, for example. Consumers may be willing to buy six rugs at $350 each, four at $500 each, or only two at $650 each. The relationship between the price and the number of rugs consumers are willing to buy can be shown graphically, with a *demand curve* (see Figure 1.2).

Supply is the number of products that businesses are willing to sell at different prices at a specific time. In general, because the potential for profits is higher, businesses are willing to supply more of a good or service at higher prices. For example, a company that sells rugs may be willing to sell six at $650 each, four at $500 each, or just two at $350 each. The relationship between the price of rugs and the quantity the company is willing to supply can be shown graphically with a *supply curve* (see Figure 1.2).

In Figure 1.2, the supply and demand curves intersect at the point where supply and demand are equal. The price at which the number of products that businesses are willing to supply equals the amount of products that consumers are willing to buy at a specific point in time is the **equilibrium price.** In our

> **Demand** the number of goods and services that consumers are willing to buy at different prices at a specific time
>
> **Supply** the number of products—goods and services—that businesses are willing to sell at different prices at a specific time
>
> **Equilibrium price** the price at which the number of products that businesses are willing to supply equals the amount of products that consumers are willing to buy at a specific point in time

figure 1.2 Equilibrium Price of Handmade Rugs

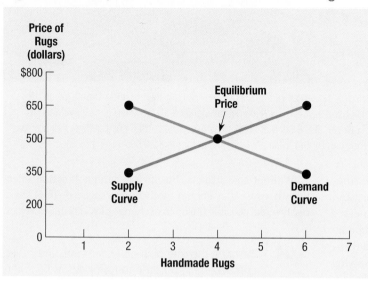

Critics of supply and demand say the system does not distribute resources equally. The forces of supply and demand prevent participation in the market by sellers who have to sell at higher prices (because their costs are high) and buyers who cannot afford to buy goods at the equilibrium price. According to critics, the wealthy can afford to buy more than they need, but the poor are unable to buy enough of what they need to survive.

The Nature of Competition

Competition, the rivalry among businesses for consumers' dollars, is another vital element in free enterprise. According to Adam Smith, competition fosters efficiency and low prices by forcing producers to offer the best products at the most reasonable price; those who fail to do so are not able to stay in business. Thus, competition should improve the quality of the goods and services available or reduce prices. For example, smartphone manufacturer BlackBerry had captured a large share of the business market in North America. Over the last number of years, several firms, including Apple who manufactures the iPhone, have entered the market with their sights set on eroding BlackBerry's market share. The results of competition have been an improvement in smartphone technology and a reduction in price for the popular devices.

Within a free-enterprise system, there are four types of competitive environments: pure competition, monopolistic competition, oligopoly, and monopoly.

Pure competition exists when there are many small businesses selling one standardized product, such as agricultural commodities like wheat, corn, and cotton. No one business sells enough of the product to influence the product's price. And, because there is no difference in the products, prices are determined solely by the forces of supply and demand. For example, Atlantic Canadian lobster prices are set by the forces of supply and demand. In recent years, demand has slowed as people are less likely to spend large amounts of money on premium seafood during periods of economic uncertainty. The low prices have forced some fishermen out of business. Other fishermen have taken a more entrepreneurial route and have started to sell directly to the consumer and eliminated the middleman to maximize their earnings.

Monopolistic competition exists when there are fewer businesses than in a pure-competition environment and the differences among the goods they sell are small. Clothes, pain killers, soft drinks, and coffee are examples

rug example, the company is willing to supply four rugs at $500 each, and consumers are willing to buy four rugs at $500 each. Therefore, $500 is the equilibrium price for a rug at that point in time, and most rug companies will price their rugs at $500. As you might imagine, a business that charges more than $500 (or whatever the current equilibrium price is) for its rugs will not sell many and might not earn a profit. On the other hand, a business that charges less than $500 accepts a lower profit per rug than could be made at the equilibrium price.

> ## "Competition, the rivalry among businesses for consumers' dollars, is another vital element in free enterprise."

If the cost of making rugs goes up, businesses will not offer as many at the old price. Changing the price alters the supply curve, and a new equilibrium price results. This is an on-going process, with supply and demand constantly changing in response to changes in economic conditions, availability of resources, and degree of competition. For example, gasoline prices rose sharply in 2006 in response to a shrinking supply of gasoline and crude oil and rising demand.[26] On the other hand, the world's largest music company, Universal Music Group, slashed the suggested retail price for CDs of popular artists in response to declining demand for music CDs. Sales of CDs have declined by 30 percent over the past few years, partly due to increased downloading of music from the Internet and increased competition from companies such as Apple and Walmart, which sell individual songs for $0.99 or lower.[27] Prices for goods and services vary according to these changes in supply and demand. This concept is the force that drives the distribution of resources (goods and services, labour, and money) in a free-enterprise economy.

Competition the rivalry among businesses for consumers' dollars

Pure competition the market structure that exists when there are many small businesses selling one standardized product

Monopolistic competition the market structure that exists when there are fewer businesses than in a pure-competition environment and the differences among the goods they sell are small

of such goods. These products differ slightly in packaging, warranty, name, and other characteristics, but all satisfy the same consumer need. Businesses have some power over the price they charge in monopolistic competition because they can make consumers aware of product differences through advertising. Consumers value some features more than others and are often willing to pay higher prices for a product with the features they want. For example, a brewed cup of coffee satisfies the same need for consumers—a caffeinated hot drink. Yet Tim Hortons, Second Cup, and Starbucks have managed to differentiate their product by offering consumers a different taste and in-store experience. As a result of this differentiation, Starbucks has been successful in charging a significant premium for its products compared to its closest Canadian rivals. Another example is Advil, a non-prescription pain reliever that contains ibuprofen instead of aspirin. Consumers who cannot take aspirin or who believe ibuprofen is a more effective pain reliever may not mind paying a little extra for the ibuprofen in Advil.

Oligopoly the market structure that exists when there are very few businesses selling a product

Monopoly the market structure that exists when there is only one business providing a product in a given market

An **oligopoly** exists when there are very few businesses selling a product. In an oligopoly, individual businesses have control over their products' price because each business supplies a large portion of the products sold in the marketplace. Nonetheless, the prices charged by different firms stay fairly close because a price cut or increase by one company will trigger a similar response from another company. In the airline industry, for example, when one airline cuts fares to boost sales, other airlines quickly follow with rate decreases to remain competitive. This commonly occurs in the Canadian air travel business, which is dominated by Air Canada and WestJet. As soon as one airline drops its prices the other quickly follows. The same thing usually occurs when one of the airlines raises its prices. Oligopolies exist when it is expensive for new firms to enter the marketplace. Not just anyone can acquire enough financial capital to build an automobile production facility or purchase enough airplanes and related resources to build an airline.

When there is one business providing a product in a given market, a **monopoly** exists. Utility companies that supply electricity, natural gas, and water are monopolies. The government permits such monopolies because the cost of creating the good or supplying the service is so great that new producers cannot compete for sales. Government-granted monopolies are subject to government-regulated prices. Some monopolies exist because of technological developments that are protected by patent laws. Patent laws grant the developer of new technology a period of time (usually 20 years) during which no other producer can use the same technology without the agreement of the original developer. Canada granted the first national patent in 1869, and the patent office received approximately 35,000 patent applications last year.[28] This monopoly allows the developer to recover research, development, and production

With the decline in lobster prices many fishermen have decided to cut out the middleman and sell directly to consumers. What do you think are the pros and cons of such an approach?

expenses and to earn a reasonable profit. Examples of this type of monopoly include the drug release process developed by Biovail, a Canadian pharmaceutical company that now operates as Valeant Pharmaceuticals International, Inc. after they purchased the company in 2010 and opted to assume its name. The patented drug release system allows for a gradual release of drugs into a patient's body. Other examples include the dry-copier process developed by Xerox and the self-developing photographic technology created by Polaroid. Because of their technology, the companies operated for significant periods of time without competition and could charge premium prices because no alternative products existed to compete with their products.

LO5 Specify why and how the health of the economy is measured.

Economic Cycles and Productivity

Expansion and Contraction. Economies are not stagnant; they expand and contract. **Economic expansion** occurs when an economy is growing and people are spending more money. Their purchases stimulate the production of goods and services, which in turn stimulates employment. The standard of living rises because more people are employed and have money to spend. Rapid expansions of the economy, however, may result in **inflation,** a continuing rise in prices. Inflation can be harmful if individuals' incomes do not increase at the same pace as rising prices, reducing their buying power. Zimbabwe has the highest inflation rate at 66,212 percent.[29]

Economic contraction occurs when spending declines. Businesses cut back on production and lay off workers, and the

Economic expansion the situation that occurs when an economy is growing and people are spending more money; their purchases stimulate the production of goods and services, which in turn stimulates employment

Inflation a condition characterized by a continuing rise in prices

Economic contraction a slowdown of the economy characterized by a decline in spending and during which businesses cut back on production and lay off workers

Recession a decline in production, employment, and income

Unemployment the condition in which a percentage of the population wants to work but is unable to find jobs

Depression a condition of the economy in which unemployment is very high, consumer spending is low, and business output is sharply reduced

economy as a whole slows down. Contractions of the economy lead to **recession**—a decline in production, employment, and income. Recessions are often characterized by rising levels of **unemployment,** which is measured as the percentage of the population that wants to work but is unable to find jobs. Figure 1.3 shows the overall unemployment rate in the civilian labour force from 2000 to 2013, while Figure 1.4 shows the impact the recent recession has had on unemployment from 2007 to 2010. Rising unemployment levels tend to stifle demand for goods and services, which can have the effect of forcing prices downward, a condition known as *deflation.* Canada has experienced numerous recessions, including 1990–1992, 2001–2003, and 2008–2009, which was discussed earlier in the chapter. As the Canadian economy is so dependent on the United States to purchase a large supply of our resources and products, our recessions have typically followed their recessions. A severe recession may turn into a **depression,** in which unemployment is very high, consumer spending is low, and business output is sharply reduced, such as occurred in Canada and the United States in the early 1930s.

Economies expand and contract in response to changes in consumer, business, and government spending. War also can affect an economy, sometimes stimulating it (as in Canada during World War I and II) and sometimes stifling it (as during the Persian Gulf wars). Although fluctuations in the economy are inevitable, and to a certain extent predictable, their effects—inflation and unemployment—disrupt lives and thus governments try to minimize them. As noted above, the last part of the past decade has been characterized by a strong global recession that resulted from a global tightening of credit also known as a credit crunch. The credit crunch was a direct result of the sub-prime mortgage crisis where banks, primarily in the United States, lent consumers money at attractive rates with the hope that the value of their homes would continue to escalate and consumers could make their payments. When interest rates increased and the value of homes started to decline at record rates, many homeowners couldn't make their mortgage payments and lost their homes. As more and more consumers failed to make their payments some large global finance companies including Lehman Brothers and Washington Mutual actually declared bankruptcy, causing further chaos in the global economic system. The economic impact spread around the globe as banks started to limit the money they were willing to lend to businesses and consumers. Consumers, perhaps fuelled by their lack of borrowing power, started to save more and spend less. As previously noted, capital is a resource that all economies need and as banks restricted capital, economic growth slowed or stopped completely. In Canada and many other countries, this resulted in higher unemployment. Globally, almost every government took measures to ensure that businesses and consumers could access capital and started to invest in infrastructure projects to create jobs. Canada's economy fared slightly better than the rest of the world as it was quite strong when the crisis began, thus allowing the government to enact financial measures to slow or limit the recession. Furthermore, Canada's banking system, which is consistently recognized as one of the best in the world by the World Economic Forum, remained strong during the recession, helping stabilize the country and providing much needed consumer confidence. Additionally, the Canadian economy ultimately benefited from demand for its natural resources from large countries such as China and India, which started to grow again in 2009 despite global economic conditions. From an economic perspective Canada has fully recovered from the recession in the summer of 2009 and while 400,000 jobs were lost during the slump, 600,000 have been created during the recovery. In the short term conditions have improved, but economists are worried about the long-term impact of the government's strategy which involved spending money on infrastructure—things like roads and sewage systems that we need to live. Historically, periods of inflation have followed instances when governments have invested heavily in infrastructure and encouraged lending by banks. This ultimately slowed growth and sometimes led to another recession.

figure 1.3 Unemployment Rate in Canada, 2000–2013

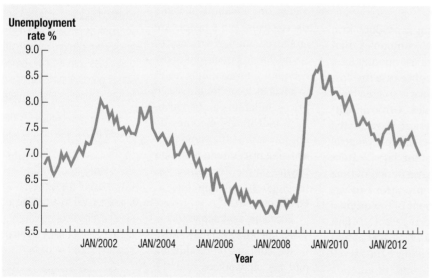

figure 1.4 Impact of the Recession on the Unemployment Rate

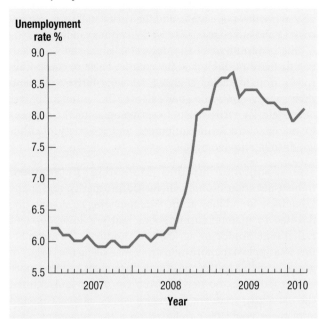

SOURCE: http://www.statcan.gc.ca/subjects-sujets/labour-travail/lfs-epa/lfs-epa-eng.htm.

Gross domestic product (GDP) the sum of all goods and services produced in a country during a year

Budget surplus the condition in which a nation spends less than it takes in from taxes

Budget deficit the condition in which a nation spends more than it takes in from taxes

Measuring the Economy. Countries measure the state of their economies to determine whether they are expanding or contracting and whether corrective action is necessary to minimize the fluctuations. One commonly used measure is **gross domestic product (GDP)**—the sum of all goods and services produced in a country during a year. GDP measures only those goods and services made within a country and, therefore, does not include profits from companies' overseas operations; it does include profits earned by foreign companies within the country being measured. However, it does not take into account the concept of GDP in relation to population (GDP per capita). According to Statistics Canada, the total GDP for the country was $1.6 trillion and GDP growth for 2012 was positive at 0.10 percent, a sharp decline from 2.7 percent in 2007. The decline can mostly be attributed to a decrease in exports, capital investment, and personal spending. Declines in exports are particularly worrisome to the Canadian economy as total trade represented roughly 45 percent of GDP in 2012.[30] As discussed in this chapter, the economy in the United States experienced severe problems from 2007 to 2011 and accounts for approximately 75 percent of Canadian export sales. While the American economy appears to be back on the upswing, consumers and businesses are still purchasing fewer products and services than before the recession. As such, the Canadian economy has experienced slow growth.

Another important indicator of a nation's economic health is the relationship between its spending and income (from taxes). When a nation spends less than it takes in from taxes it has a **budget surplus**, and when it spends more than it takes in from taxes, it has a **budget deficit.** In the 1990s, the Canadian government eliminated its long-standing budget deficit by balancing the money spent for social, defence, and other programs with the amount of money taken in from taxes. Since 1997, it has been common policy for the government of Canada to accumulate large budget surpluses. Much of the extra money or surplus was used to pay down the government's debt, the amount of money that the nation owes its lenders. By 1997, Canada's debt had risen to $563 billion, but due to the government surpluses it had been reduced to roughly $460 billion in 2008 but has risen sharply since 2008 to $600 billion in 2013. Much of the increase in debt can be attributed to Canada's Economic Action Plan which consisted of a $62 billion injection into the economy during the last recession. The Economic Action Plan included infrastructure spending of $8 billion, tax relief of $20 billion over five years, incentives of $7.8 billion to generate jobs in housing projects, in excess of $15 billion to help the unemployed, and $50 billion in spending on programs to encourage and promote lenders to grant Canadians access to credit. This extra spending has increased Canada's debt and may result in long-term financial hardship. TD Bank has actually predicted that the result of the spending in the Economic Action Plan will increase Canada's debt to $630 billion by 2014.[31] While the recession is over, Canada is still projecting an annual deficit of $15 billion in 2013 as the government continues to support a slow economy by investing in projects to create economic growth. This figure is especially worrisome because, to reduce the debt to a manageable level, the government has to either increase its revenues (through taxes) or reduce spending on social, defence, and legal programs, none of which are politically popular. Some economists argue that the spending is not that worrisome as the $600 billion may seem high, on a per capita basis, and in comparison to its GDP, Canada's debt level is better than most other industrialized countries'. Table 1.2 describes some of the other ways we evaluate our nation's economy.

The Canadian Economy

As we said previously, Canada is a mixed economy based on free enterprise. The answers to the three basic economic issues are determined primarily by competition and the forces of supply and demand, although the federal government does intervene in economic decisions to a certain extent. To understand the current state of the Canadian economy and its effect on business practices, it is helpful to examine its history and the roles of the entrepreneur and the government.

table 1.2 How Do We Evaluate Our Nation's Economy?

Unit of Measure	Description
Trade balance	The difference between our exports and our imports. If the balance is positive, as it has been for much of the last ten years, it is called a trade surplus. Recently the balance has been negative; when this occurs it is called a trade deficit and is generally viewed as unhealthy for our economy.
Consumer Price Index	Measures changes in prices of goods and services purchased for consumption by typical urban households.
Per capita income	Indicates the income level of "average" Canadians. Useful in determining how much "average" consumers spend and how much money Canadians are earning.
Unemployment rate	Indicates how many working age Canadians are not working who otherwise want to work.
Inflation	Monitors price increases in consumer goods and services over specified periods of time. Used to determine if costs of goods and services are exceeding worker compensation over time.
Worker productivity	The amount of goods and services produced for each hour worked.

LO6 Trace the evolution of the Canadian economy, and discuss the role of the entrepreneur in the economy.

A Brief History of the Canadian Economy

The Early Economy. Before the colonization of North America, Native Americans lived as hunter/gatherers and farmers, with some trade among tribes. The first European settlements on the east coast of what was to become Canada came because of the fishing industry. The settlers operated primarily as an agricultural economy. Abundant natural resources nourished industries such as farming, fishing, shipping, and the fur trade. The fur trade was also important to Canada's early development as it began in the 16th century and remained a major industry for almost 300 years. The first major business competitors in Canada were the North West Trading Company and the Hudson Bay Company, which remained active in the fur trade until the 1980s.[33]

The Industrial Revolution. The 19th century and the Industrial Revolution brought the development of new technology and factories. The factory brought together all the resources needed to make a product—materials, machines, and workers. Work in factories became specialized as workers focused on one or two tasks. As work became more efficient, productivity increased, making more goods available at lower prices. Industrialization was not as widespread in Canada as in the United States and mostly occurred in Central Canada. Due to the size of the country, its relatively small population, and the richness of its resources, most Canadians continued to work in primary industries.[34]

The government of the day established the Canadian Pacific Railway and linked the country coast to coast. Railroads brought major changes, allowing farmers to send their surplus crops and goods all over the nation for barter or for sale. Factories began to spring up along the railways to manufacture farm equipment and a variety of other goods to be shipped by rail.

The Manufacturing and Marketing Economies. Industrialization brought increased prosperity, and many Canadians found jobs in the *manufacturing economy*—one devoted to manufacturing goods and providing services rather than producing agricultural products. The assembly line was applied to more industries, increasing the variety of goods available to the consumer. Businesses became more concerned with the needs of the consumer and entered the *marketing economy.* Expensive goods such as cars and appliances could be purchased on a time-payment plan. Companies conducted research to find out what products consumers needed and wanted. Advertising made consumers aware of differences in products and prices.

Because these developments occurred in a free-enterprise system, consumers determined what goods and services were produced. They did this by purchasing the products they liked at prices they were willing to pay. Canada prospered, and Canadian citizens had one of the highest standards of living in the world.

The Service and Internet-Based Economy. After World War II, with the increased standard of living, Canadians had more money and more time. They began to pay others to perform services that made their lives easier. Beginning in the 1960s, more and more women entered the workforce. The profile of the family changed: Today there are more single-parent families and individuals living alone, and in two-parent families, both parents often work. One result of this trend is that time-pressed Canadians are increasingly paying others to do tasks they used to do at home, like cooking, laundry, landscaping, and child care. These trends have gradually changed Canada to a *service economy*—one devoted to the production of services that make life easier for busy consumers. Service industries such as restaurants, banking, medicines, child care, auto repair, leisure-related industries, and even education are growing rapidly and employ over 75 percent of Canadians. These trends continue with advanced technology contributing to new service products such as overnight mail, electronic banking, and shopping through cable television networks and the Internet. More about the Internet and e-commerce can be found throughout the text.[35]

DID YOU KNOW? 60% of adult women work outside the home.[32]

Joseph Moncada

Founded: 2006

The Business: Sweet Tooth Candy Emporium

Success: Joseph Moncada, a student at York University, started Sweet Tooth Candy Emporium—retailing over 2,700 different types of candy through its stores and kiosks. The business, which is only a few years old, employs over 25 people and boasts annual income in excess of $700,000.

In 2006, Joseph Moncada borrowed $10,000 from his parents to start a candy store with a "difference." The difference was not the product, but who Moncada planned on targeting with his sugary treats—adults. Moncada felt that there was a market for retro candy and wanted to offer Baby Boomers treats from when they were young. Moncada describes a visit to his store as "a walk down memory lane." His unique concept actually encourages parents to bring their children to a candy store. The concept appears to be working as

Candy is big business for university student Joseph Moncada. The entrepreneur retails over 2,700 different types of candy from his stores.

the company has three permanent stores as well as seasonal kiosks, and Moncada is currently eyeing an expansion plan that includes franchising his concept throughout Canada.[36]

The Role of the Entrepreneur

An entrepreneur is an individual who risks his or her wealth, time, and effort to develop for profit a product or service that he or she can sell. For example, Ryan Holmes of Vancouver, British Columbia, founded www.HootSuite.com in 2008 with the idea that marketers should be able to manage multiple social media campaigns from one central website. HootSuite allows companies to send messages to a variety of social media sites including Twitter, Facebook, LinkedIn, Google+, Foursquare, MySpace, WordPress, and Mixi. HootSuite can also be used with YouTube, Instagram, MailChimp, Reddit, Storify, Tumblr, and Vimeo. The company currently has 5 million users, ranks among the 200 most popular sites in the world, and has been estimated to be worth $500 million in 2013. While Holmes has been quite successful, he did take on the risks of entrepreneurship including investing his money and time with no guarantee of success. We will learn more about starting a new business in Chapter 5.

The free-enterprise system provides the conditions necessary for entrepreneurs to succeed. In the past, entrepreneurs were often inventors who brought all the factors of production together to produce a new product. Joseph-Armand Bombardier, who invented the snowmobile, and Alexander Graham Bell, who invented the telephone, are early Canadian entrepreneurs. Over the past century, Canadian entrepreneurs have succeeded by offering consumers both services and products. For example,

The Irving Group based in New Brunswick retails gasoline, sells hardware supplies, owns sports teams, and manufactures products such as paper and tissue, and is heavily invested in the oil and gas business.[38] Garfield Weston Ltd., which was started in the late 19th century, now controls a great deal of the retail food business in Canada through its controlling interest in Loblaws.[39] Entrepreneurship is essential to a free-enterprise system and a growing area of interest as people are attracted to being their own boss and being in charge of their own destiny. Years ago most students studied business with the hope of gaining a job upon graduation. Now, many students plan to start a business, and some do not even wait until they graduate. For example, Brian Scudamore, owner of 1-800-GOT-JUNK?— a Vancouver-based junk removal company with over 300 locations in three countries—started the business as a student with a pickup truck when he couldn't find a summer job.[40] Every year, Enactus, formerly known as Advancing Canadian Entrepreneurship (ACE), a nonprofit group that encourages youth entrepreneurship, recognizes outstanding student entrepreneurs who started businesses while attending college or university. Enactus Canada's 2012 Student Entrepreneur National Champion was Brett Sheffield, a University of Manitoba student who owns and operates two businesses in addition to attending school full-time. Brett not only runs his family farm which he has grown from 160 acres to 1700 acres in a few short years, but he also owns Stay Fit Health Club. Both businesses net over six figures a year and Brett finished third at the

Jimmy Wales

Business: Wikipedia

Founded: 2001

Success: Wikipedia currently ranks among the ten most visited sites worldwide.

Almost everyone uses Wikipedia, the multilingual, Web-based, free content encyclopaedia project launched in 2001 as a nonprofit based on user donations. It is written collaboratively by volunteers from all around the world, and almost all of its articles can be edited by anyone with access to the Internet. Since its creation in 2001, Wikipedia has rapidly grown into one of the largest reference websites in the world. It has more than 8.2 million articles in 253 languages, while the English Wikipedia edition has more than 2 million articles. Since its creation, it has been rising in popularity and currently ranks among the top 10 most-visited websites worldwide. Wikipedia has more than 160 million unique visitors monthly, and this number continues to increase. Jimmy Wales, Wikipedia's founder, has enjoyed success as an entrepreneur based on his understanding of rapid changes in the marketing environment and utilizing emerging technologies to develop new products. He has made transparency a core principle; his collaborative products capture social networking and the desire to have information accessible in an efficient and inexpensive way.[37]

2012 Global Student Entrepreneur Awards. Other recent award winners include Ryan Flood, a Memorial University student who created 6am Software, and Simon Fraser University student Milun Tesovic, who co-founded Metroleap Media Inc. Flood's company provides school administrators with software tools including its most successful product: the Online Parent–Teacher Interview Scheduler, which allows parents, teachers, and administrators the opportunity to schedule online meetings. Tesovic's business, www.metrolyrics.com, provides music lovers with the written lyrics to their favourite songs and has grown to become one of the most popular lyric websites worldwide, boasting the most comprehensive database of legal lyrics in the world with over 700,000 titles.[41] We will examine the importance of entrepreneurship further in Chapter 5.

The Role of Government in the Canadian Economy

The Canadian economic system is best described as a mixed economy because entrepreneurs and citizens control many of the factors of production and own the majority of businesses, but the government is still active in the economic system through its ownership of crown corporations and the regulations it maintains to preserve competition and protect consumers and employees. Federal and provincial governments intervene in the economy with laws and regulations designed to promote competition and to protect consumers, employees, and the environment. Many of these laws are discussed in Appendix A.

Additionally, government agencies such as Industry Canada and the Department of Finance measure the health of the economy (GDP, productivity, etc.). Furthermore, the government—through the Bank of Canada, tax policy, and, when necessary, spending—takes steps to minimize the disruptive effects of economic fluctuations, and reduce unemployment. When the economy is contracting and unemployment is rising, the federal government tries to spur growth so that consumers will spend more money and businesses will hire more employees. To accomplish this, it may, through the Bank of Canada, reduce interest rates or increase its own spending for goods and services. When the economy expands so fast that inflation results, the government may intervene to reduce inflation by slowing down economic growth. This can be accomplished by raising interest rates to discourage spending by businesses and consumers. Techniques used to control the economy are discussed in Chapter 14.

Brian Scudamore, the owner of 1-800-GOT-JUNK?, started the business as a university student with a pickup truck when he couldn't find a summer job. Now, it bills itself as the world's largest junk removal company and is an international franchise.

The Role of Ethics and Social Responsibility in Business

In the past few years, you may have read about a number of ethical issues at several well-known corporations, including Maple Leaf, XL Foods, and SNC-Lavalin. In a few cases, misconduct by individuals within these firms had an adverse effect on current and retired employees, investors, and others associated with these firms. In some cases, individuals may go to jail for their actions. For example, former SNC-Lavalin CEO Pierre Duhaime has been arrested by the RCMP after it was revealed that $56 million was unaccounted for and appears to have been illegally paid to commercial agents. Perhaps a better-known case occurred in the U.S. where Martha Stewart

---

RESPONDING TO BUSINESS CHALLENGES | Kicking Horse Back on Track

Kicking Horse, founded in the Canadian Rockies town of Invermere, British Columbia, by Elena Rosenfeld and Leo Johnson, eventually ran into trouble after going through a series of successes and challenges. The former Torontonians had already worked in restaurants, opened a fruit stand, and bought a café before starting the trendy company in 1996. Inspired by the fact that they could not obtain organic coffee for their café, the couple spent a year travelling and researching the idea of starting a fair-trade coffee company before founding Kicking Horse. Fair trade is an assurance that the farmers and workers harvesting the beans are paid a fair salary. Both the organic and fair-trade accreditations mean that Kicking Horse and the growers have to be audited every quarter.

The husband and wife team chose to compete in the organic fair-trade niche, a relatively untapped market, because it suited their ethical values. They import raw, organic coffee beans from countries like Sumatra, Nicaragua, and Cuba to their roasting plant in British Columbia. There the beans are roasted, blended, packaged, and distributed with unique names like Hoodoo Jo and 454 High Octane, which make the most of the local legends surrounding Kicking Horse Pass.

Initially, they focused on building a local client base among cafés, gourmet food stores, grocery chains, and restaurants, before pursuing a broader market. By 2005, sales of Kicking Horse Coffee's fair-trade beans had soared ahead of even Starbucks in terms of national grocery-store sales of super-premium coffee. However, the company's expansion eastward, combined with 40 percent annual growth in existing accounts in Western Canada, left it unable to supply the coffee its clients demanded. Like many entrepreneurs, the couple had been so focused on day-to-day operations they had neglected to develop the organization, infrastructure, and resources needed to scale their firm to keep up with booming sales. In late 2005, the Business Development Bank of Canada awarded Kicking Horse $5,000 worth of consulting as part of its Ongoing Achievement Award for a firm that sustains growth well past its start-up. As a result of those recommendations, Kicking Horse went back to the planning stage and developed detailed sales forecasts and determined future capital needs. That allowed it to adopt a more systematic approach to anticipating its space, people, and equipment requirements. The recommendations paid off, and Kicking Horse celebrated its 13th straight year as Canada's #1 seller of Organic Fair Trade Coffee. The company continues to grow and has constructed 40,000 ft^2 of additional production space resulting in new homes for Hoodoo Jo and 454 High Octane.

Today, the company sells 10,000 kg of coffee per week, in 30 blends, to grocery stores and restaurants in Canada, the United States, and Holland. Recently, the founders opted to sell a stake in their business with Rosenfeld remaining as CEO and Johnson exiting the company. The investor in the company, Branch Brook Holdings, is a partnership between Swander Pace Capital, Jefferson Capital Partners, and United National Foods that invests in North American organic and natural consumer product companies. The group of investors brings significant American retail experience to Kicking Horse but potential customers won't find the coffee in Walmarts everywhere in the U.S. as a result. Rosenfeld states, "The company must grow slowly in the highly competitive U.S. market, as many Canadians have tried to enter the American market only to spend millions with very little to show for their investment." Rosenfeld's strategy is to stay away from mass retailers, and focus on smaller chains and independent stores. Kicking Horse's strategy appears to be working as the firm is now in 400 U.S. stores and looking to continue to expand its organic coffee business.

Future plans are to export to other European countries and to diversify by opening cafés in 10 Canadian cities.[42]

DISCUSSION QUESTIONS

1. Why was Kicking Horse so successful?

2. How did Kicking Horse run into trouble and what was done to save Kicking Horse?

3. Why do you think the company is trying to go slow with its U.S. expansion? What do you think of its strategy to stay out of mass merchants such as Walmart?

was convicted of obstructing justice and lying to federal investigators. She was sentenced to five months in jail and five months of home detention for making false statements. Martha Stewart agreed to pay $195,000 and accept a five-year ban on serving as a director of a public company to settle civil insider-trading charges with the Securities and Exchange Commission.[43] Scandals such as that at SNC-Lavalin undermined public confidence in Canada's free-enterprise system and sparked a new debate about ethics in business. Business ethics generally refer to the standards and principles used by society to define appropriate and inappropriate conduct in the workplace. In many cases, these standards have been codified as laws prohibiting actions deemed unacceptable.

Society is increasingly demanding that businesspeople behave ethically and socially responsibly toward not only their customers but also their employees, suppliers, investors, government regulators, communities, and the natural environment. For example, Just Us Coffee, a growing Nova Scotia coffee roaster and retailer, has pledged to pay above-market prices for coffee beans to farmers in Central and South America to help boost the quality of life in those regions.[44] Thus, social responsibility relates to the impact of business on society.

One of the primary lessons from the scandals of the 2000s has been that the reputations of business organizations depend not just on bottom-line profits, but also on ethical conduct and concern for the welfare of others. Consider that in the aftermath of these scandals, the reputations of all companies suffered regardless of their association with the scandals.[45] While progress is being made in business ethics, as employees become more sensitive to ethical issues, reporting of ethical misconduct has increased over the past few years. The fact that employees continue to report observing misconduct and experiencing pressure to engage in unethical or illegal acts remains troubling and suggests that companies need to continue their efforts to raise ethical standards. We take a closer look at ethics and social responsibility in business in Chapter 2.

Can You Learn Business in a Classroom?

Obviously, the answer is yes, or there would be no purpose for this textbook! To be successful in business, you need knowledge, skills, experience, and good judgment. The

figure 1.5 The Organization of This Book

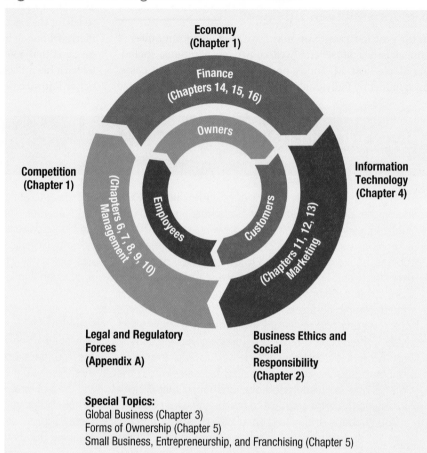

Economy
(Chapter 1)

Finance
(Chapters 14, 15, 16)

Owners

Competition
(Chapter 1)

Information
Technology
(Chapter 4)

Employees

Customers

(Chapters 6, 7, 8, 9, 10)
Management

(Chapters 11, 12, 13)
Marketing

Legal and Regulatory
Forces
(Appendix A)

Business Ethics and
Social
Responsibility
(Chapter 2)

Special Topics:
Global Business (Chapter 3)
Forms of Ownership (Chapter 5)
Small Business, Entrepreneurship, and Franchising (Chapter 5)

topics covered in this chapter and throughout this book provide some of the knowledge you need to understand the world of business. The boxes and examples within each chapter describe experiences to help you develop good business judgment. The interactive exercises and assignments found on Connect will help you develop skills that may be useful in your future career.

> ## "Business ethics generally refers to the standards and principles used by society to define appropriate and inappropriate conduct in the workplace."

However, good judgment is based on knowledge and experience plus personal insight and understanding. Therefore, you need more courses in business, along with some practical experience in the business world, to help you develop the special insight necessary to put your personal stamp on knowledge as you apply it. The challenge in business is in the area of judgment, and judgment does not develop from memorizing an introductory business textbook. If you are observant in your daily experiences as an employee, as a student, and as a consumer, you will improve your ability to make good business judgments.

Figure 1.5 is an overview of how the chapters in this book are linked together and how the chapters relate to the participants, the activities, and the environmental factors found in the business world. The topics presented in the chapters that follow are those that will give you the best opportunity to begin the process of understanding the world of business.

TEAM EXERCISE

Major economic systems—including capitalism, socialism, and communism, as well as mixed economies—were discussed in this chapter. Assuming that you want an economic system that is best for the majority, not just a few members of society, defend one of the economic systems as the best system. Form groups and try to reach agreement on one economic system. Defend why you supported the system you advanced.

LEARNING OBJECTIVES SUMMARY

LO1 Define basic concepts such as business, product, and profit.

Business can be defined as individuals or organizations who try to earn a profit by providing products that satisfy people's needs. A product is a good or service with tangible and intangible characteristics that provide satisfaction and benefits. Profit is the difference between what it costs to make and sell a product and what a customer pays for it.

LO2 Identify the main participants and activities of business, and explain why studying business is important.

The main participants in business are owners, employees, and customers; the primary business activities are management, marketing, and finance. Studying business can help you develop skills and acquire knowledge to prepare for your future career, regardless of whether you plan to work for a multinational *Fortune* 500 firm, start your own business, work for a government agency, or manage or volunteer at a nonprofit organization. The field of business offers a variety of interesting and challenging career opportunities throughout the world, such as human resources management, information technology, finance, production and operations, wholesaling and retailing, and many more. Studying business can also help you better understand the many business activities that are necessary to provide satisfying goods and services, and learning about business can help you become a well-informed consumer and member of society.

LO3 Define economics and compare the four types of economic systems.

Economics is the study of how resources are distributed for the production of goods and services within a social system. The four economic systems are as follows:

- Communism: a society in which the people, without regard to class, own all the nation's resources
- Socialism: an economic system in which the government owns and operates basic industries but individuals own most businesses
- Free market: pure capitalism, in which all economic decisions are made without government intervention
- Mixed economies: economies made up of elements from more than one economic system

LO4 Describe the role of supply, demand, and competition in a free-enterprise system.

Competition, supply, and demand determine which goods and services are produced, how they are produced, and how they are distributed.

LO5 Specify why and how the health of the economy is measured.

Economies are not stagnant; they expand and contract. Economic expansion occurs when an economy is growing and people are spending more money. Economic contraction occurs when spending declines. Businesses cut back on production and lay off workers, and the economy as a whole slows down.

Countries measure the state of their economies to determine whether they are expanding or contracting and whether corrective action is necessary to minimize the fluctuations. Commonly used measures include: (1) Gross domestic product (GDP): The sum of all goods and services produced in a country during a year. GDP measures only those goods and services made within a country and therefore does not include profits from companies' overseas operations; it does include profits earned by foreign companies within the country being measured; (2) Deficits/surplus: Another important indicator of a nation's economic health is the relationship between its spending and income (from taxes). When a nation spends less than it takes in from taxes it has a budget surplus, and when it spends more than it takes in from taxes, it has a budget deficit; (3) Trade balance: The difference between a nation's exports and imports. If the balance is positive, as it has been for much of the last ten years, it is called a trade surplus; (4) Consumer Price Index: Measures changes in prices of goods and services purchased for consumption by typical urban households; (5) Per capita income: Indicates the income level of "average" Canadians; useful in determining how much "average" consumers spend and how much money Canadians are earning; (6) Unemployment rate: Indicates how many working age Canadians are not working who otherwise want to work; (7) Inflation: Monitors price increases in consumer goods and services over specified periods of time; used to determine if costs of goods and services are exceeding worker compensation over time; and (8) Worker productivity: The amount of goods and services produced for each hour worked.

LO6 Trace the evolution of the Canadian economy, and discuss the role of the entrepreneur in the economy.

Before the colonization of North America, Native Americans lived as hunter/gatherers and farmers, with some trade among tribes. The first European settlements on the east coast of what was to become Canada came because of the fishing industry. The settlers operated primarily as an agricultural economy; abundant natural resources nourished industries such as farming, fishing, shipping, and the fur trade. The 19th century and the Industrial Revolution brought the development of new technology and factories. Industrialization brought increased prosperity, and many Canadians found jobs in the *manufacturing economy*—one devoted to manufacturing goods and providing services rather than producing agricultural products. After World War II, with the increased standard of living, Canadians had more money and more time. They began to pay others to perform services that made their lives easier. Canadians are increasingly paying others to do tasks they used to do at home, like cooking, laundry, landscaping, and child care. These trends have gradually changed Canada to a *service economy*—one devoted to the production of services that make life easier for busy consumers.

An entrepreneur is an individual who risks his or her wealth, time, and effort to develop a business for profit. Entrepreneurship is essential to a free-enterprise system and a growing area of interest as people are attracted to being their own boss and being in charge of their own destiny.

KEY TERMS

budget deficit
budget surplus
business
capitalism, or free enterprise
communism
competition
demand
depression
economic contraction
economic expansion
economic system
economics
equilibrium price
financial resources
free-market system
gross domestic product (GDP)

human resources
inflation
mixed economies
monopolistic competition
monopoly
natural resources
nonprofit organizations
oligopoly
product
profit
pure competition
recession
socialism
stakeholders
supply
unemployment

1. How do you think Christine Day's experience at Starbucks has helped her at Lululemon?

2. What do you think of Lululemon's marketing strategy of limiting the size and colour availability of popular products? Is this a wise strategy not to have what customers are looking for? Could this practice be considered unethical?

3. If large competitors continue to enter the marketplace selling similar products at lower prices, will Lululemon continue to be as successful as it is today? Will it be able to sell $100 yoga pants when other retailers are selling similar items for a lower price?

4. Do you think customers, or guests as Day calls them, will continue to pay a premium for yoga clothes to be part of the Lululemon experience?

SO YOU WANT A JOB *in the Business World*

The only thing certain anymore is that the world is constantly changing, and this applies to future career options for you and your classmates. The traditional career track that earlier generations followed, in which a person started working at one company upon graduation and worked his or her way up until retirement, is passé. In fact, the average large corporation replaces the equivalent of its entire workforce every four years. Moreover, constantly evolving technology means today's graduates and workers need to be computer literate and able to adapt to new technologies. The globalization of business suggests that you be fluent in a second or even third language, for there is a good chance that you'll be working with people from around the world, and you may even do a stint overseas yourself. Changes in the makeup of the workforce mean more doors opening for women and minorities as companies recognize the need to understand and cater to the desires of a diverse customer base. Changes in organizational structure may require you to work in teams, where communication is a crucial skill, or they may leave you out of the corporate hierarchy altogether, and instead put you in an entrepreneurial role as a self-employed contractor or small-business owner.

Because of these and other changes taking place in the business world that we discuss throughout this book, when you enter the workforce full time, you are far more likely to define yourself by what you do ("I create winning social media campaigns") than by your employer ("I work for Lululemon"). And, you're more likely to think in terms of short-term projects, such as launching a product or reengineering a process, rather than a long-term career track like the one your grandfather may have followed.

This business course and textbook, including the boxes, cases, and skills-building exercises, will help you learn the basic knowledge, skills, and trends that you can use whether you work for a corporation or run your own small business, whether you work in upper management or on the shop floor. Along the way, we'll introduce you to some specific careers and offer advice on developing your own job opportunities in career boxes in various chapters. You may want to start talking to people in careers or fields you are interested in to find out how they earned their job or what they actually do on a day to day basis. You will likely learn a great deal by asking these simple questions.

BUSINESS PLAN DEVELOPMENT

Guidelines for the Development of the Business Plan

These guidelines are to assist you in creating a hypothetical business plan for a product/service/business of your choice. You should assume you have $25,000 to start this new business in your community.

At the end of every chapter there will be a section entitled "Build Your Business Plan" to assist you in the development of your plan.

Phase 1: Development of the Business Proposal

You are encouraged to submit your idea for approval to your instructor as soon as possible. This will eliminate wasted effort on an idea that is not feasible in the instructor's view. Business plan proposals will be evaluated based on their thoroughness and your ability to provide support for the idea.

The business proposal consists of:

Business Description. This consists of an overview of the existing product/service or the product/service/business you will be starting (manufacturer, merchandiser, or service provider). This includes developing a mission (reason for existence; overall purpose of the firm) and a rationale for why you believe this business will be a success. What is your vision for this proposed product/business?

Brief Marketing Plan. (The marketing plan will be further developed as the plan evolves.) A description of your business/product/service is required. Identify the target market and develop a strategy for appealing to it. Justify your proposed location for this business. Describe how you will promote the new business and provide a rationale for your pricing strategy. Select a name for this business. The name should be catchy yet relate to the competencies of the business.

Competitive Analysis. Identify the competition as broadly as possible. Indicate why this business will be successful given the market.

Phase 2: Final Written Business Plan

Executive Summary. The executive summary appears first, but should be written last.

Business Description. This section requires fleshing out the body of the business plan including material from your revised preliminary proposal with more data, charts, and appendices. Include a description of the proposed form of organization, either a partnership or corporation, and the rationalization of the form chosen.

Industry and Market Analysis. An analysis of the industry including the growth rate of the industry and number of new entrants into this field is necessary. Identify uncontrollable variables within the industry. Determine an estimate of the proposed realistic size of the potential market. This will require interpretation of statistics from federal sources such as Statistics Canada as well as local sources such as the Chamber of Commerce.

Competitive Analysis. Include an exhaustive list of the primary and secondary competition, along with the competitive advantage of each.

Marketing Strategy. Target market specifics need to be developed.
Decisions on the marketing mix variables need to be made:
- Price (at the market, below market, above market).
- Promotion (sales associates, advertising budget, use of sales promotions, and publicity/goodwill).
- Distribution—Rationale of choice and level of distribution.
- Product/Service—A detailed rationale of the perceived differential advantage of your product/service offering.

Operational Issues. How will you make or provide your product/service? Location rationale, facility type, leasing considerations, and sources of suppliers need to be detailed. Software/hardware requirements necessary to maintain operations must be determined.

Human Resource Requirement. Determine the number and description of personnel needed, including realistic required education and skills.

Financial Projections. Statement of cash flows must be prepared for the first twelve months of the business. This must include start-up costs, opening expenses, and an estimation of cash inflows and outflows. A breakeven analysis should be included along with an explanation of all financial assumptions.

Appendices

Phase 3: Oral Presentation
Specific separate guidelines on the oral presentation will be provided.

BUILD YOUR BUSINESS PLAN

The Dynamics of Business and Economics

Have you ever thought about owning your business? If you have, how did your idea come about? Is it your experience with this particular field? Or might it be an idea that evolved from your desires for a particular product or service not being offered in your community. For example, perhaps you and your friends have yearned for a place to go have coffee, relax, and talk. Now is an opportunity to create the café bar you have been thinking of!

Whether you consider yourself a visionary or a practical thinker, think about your community. What needs are not being met? While it is tempting to suggest a new restaurant (maybe near campus), easier-to-implement business plans can range from a lawn care business or a designated driver business, to a placement service agency for teenagers.

Once you have an idea for a business plan, think about how profitable this idea might be. Is there sufficient demand for this business? How large is the market for this particular business? What about competitors? How many are there?

To learn about your industry you should do a thorough search of your initial ideas of a product/service on the Internet.

Statistics Canada and the Canadian government both highlight 2010 as the end of the 2008–2009 recession, which many economic experts claimed was going to lead to another great Depression. The federal government states that the country's Gross Domestic Product (GDP) is growing, albeit slowly, and the economy has created 600,000 new jobs to replace the 400,000 jobs lost in the recession. Statistics Canada and the federal government use GDP growth to determine if the country is in fact in a recession or experiencing a period of economic growth.

So, one would expect Canadians to be happy with the current state of the economy. Well ... the Canadian population appears to disagree with the government's economic outlook as 70 percent of Canadians believe the economy is in fact in a recession. This belief is troublesome, as people who are worried about the state of the economy are less likely to spend money, which can harm the economy and in some cases actually cause an economic downturn. Some economists argue that people are worried for good reason. While GDP is growing again, it is only one measure of the state of the economy and if you consider other factors perhaps Canadians are worse off than in 2008. For example, Canadians' net worth, which can be defined simply as all your assets (things you own) minus what you owe to creditors, is lower today when adjusted for inflation than in 2008. Looking at employment figures, while Canada did create roughly 600,000 jobs to replace the 400,000 jobs that were lost, more young people became of working age over the past three years and immigration continued to rise. The result of this is employment below pre-recession levels and the economy would have to create another 750,000 jobs to reach 2008 employment numbers. Jim Stanford, an economist with the Canadian Auto Workers, argues that Canadians are worse off today than they were prior to 2008. He describes the situation by saying, "...we've fixed one-fifth of the damage, and four-fifths of the damage is still with us. That is why it is still recessionary conditions." Philip Cross, the chief economic analyst for Statistics Canada, says that he gets questioned every time he states the recession is over and more or less admits the economy is only headed in the right direction and has yet to fully recover from 2008–2009. Cross notes, "Invariably when we say the recession is over, I get a great deal of abuse because people say the level of economic activity is still rotten. When we say the recession is over, what we're saying is the period of things getting worse by the day is over. The level of economic activity could still be unacceptable, but at least you are going in the right direction, rather than the wrong direction."

Other factors contributing to Canadians' perception about the economy may be the constant discussion in the press about poor or worrisome economic news. In the winter of 2013, national newspapers and magazines ran prominent articles about the fear of a Canadian housing crisis. For example, the cover of *Canadian Business* asked the question, "How Low Will House Prices Go?" and underneath the title stated real estate values will plummet 20 percent and stay down for years.[46] Nothing makes people cringe more than thinking their most valuable asset may decline in value. In the same edition, the magazine predicted the Canadian economy would fall back into a recession in the coming year. Additionally, the European debt crisis has become a major news story. Investors are worried that many European countries may not be able to pay back the money they have borrowed, which could cause another global recession. As well, stories continue to pour in from the United States about debt levels, inability to meet budget payments, and so forth. Some people in government have claimed that the media is going to talk the country into another recession as people will continue to hear and read all the poor economic news and stop spending money. Members of the media claim that they are informing the public about things they have a right to know, and that they do not make the news—they just report it.

DISCUSSION QUESTIONS

1. How would you describe the state of the economy today? Do you feel confident that you will be able to land a job or kick-start your career based on the current economic conditions? Why or why not?

2. Do you think Statistics Canada is correct in claiming the recession is over?

3. If people's homes declined significantly in value, what do you think the result would be for the economy? If time permits, use an Internet search engine such as Google and conduct some research on the state of the Canadian housing market.

4. Do you think negative news stories can persuade people to think the economy is in a recession? What are the potential pitfalls of this happening?

5. Using Internet resources, identify any national or global economic developments that have occurred since 2010 and indicate their impact, if any, on the Canadian economy.

connect | **LEARNSMART** | **SMARTBOOK**

For more information on the resources available from McGraw-Hill Ryerson, go to www.mcgrawhill.ca/he/solutions.

Business Ethics and Social Responsibility

LEARNING OBJECTIVES

LO1 Define business ethics and social responsibility, and examine their importance.

LO2 Detect some of the ethical issues that may arise in business.

LO3 Specify how businesses can promote ethical behaviour.

LO4 Explain the four dimensions of social responsibility.

LO5 Debate an organization's social responsibilities to owners, employees, consumers, the environment, and the community.

DESTINATION CEO

Russell K. Girling is past co-chair of the 2012 United Way Campaign, director of the Willow Park Charity Golf Classic, and a winner of Canada's Top 40 Under 40 award. To many in the business community Girling is a respected CEO with a proven track record.

To others, Russell Girling is public enemy number one. Girling's company, TransCanada Corporation, is the firm trying to build the controversial Keystone XL project which will transport oil from Canada's oil sands in Alberta to Steele City, Nebraska. While Phases I and II of the Keystone Project have been built and Phase III has been approved, it is the controversial fourth phase that has been getting all the attention. For example, Global Exchange, an environmental group supporting a sustainable earth, has Girling's company on the list of the worst "Corporate Human Rights Violators,"[1] while Greenpeace Canada describes the project as "...an act of aggression to the plants, wildlife, and people who live in its path."[2]

Girling admits to being a bit surprised by the opposition and the negative impact on the project to date. Critics of how Girling has handled the approval say he underestimated the opposition. Girling counters the critics and opponents of the pipeline stating, "There is literally two and a half million (miles) of pipeline traversing the ground. You would think, based on the arguments coming up, that this was the first pipeline that has ever been built and that we have to start from scratch. We have been at this for more than 100 years."[3] Girling's arguments have been focused consistently on facts, but some business pundits think the company hasn't been able to sell the project because of its reliance on repeating facts and not connecting with people, especially Nebraskans.

The original proposed pipeline was to travel through Sand Hills, a large wetland, and Ogallala Aquifer, one of the largest sources of fresh water in the world. The aquifer provides drinking water for eight states and supports a $20 billion agricultural industry. When TransCanada was presented with opposition about the pipeline going through these environmentally sensitive areas, it opted to offer no alternative route. Instead, the company repeated facts about the safety of the pipeline and argued no other feasible route existed. This lack of flexibility seemed to galvanize opposition, including from editors of *The New York Times,* who argued that the pipeline could damage the environment if an oil spill occurred and that oil coming from Alberta's oil sands produces roughly 12 percent more greenhouse gas than conventional production.

Girling's response was to change the route of the pipeline away from the two environmentally sensitive areas cited above and to continue to argue for the merits of the Keystone Project, which include the creation of thousands of jobs and millions, if not billions, in economic spinoffs. Girling further says the U.S. needs access to the oil from Canada and getting oil from a friendly North American company is better than alternatives. Girling states, "Importing oil from a friendly, stable, reliable neighbour that shares the interests and values of the United States with respect to environmental management and safety of workers is far better than importing from other jurisdictions around the world that don't share those same values. ... The U.S. needs 10 million barrels a day of imported oil and the debate over the proposed pipeline is not a debate of oil versus alternative energy. This is a debate

Determining what is ethical is often difficult. Both advocates and opponents of the Keystone XL Pipeline no doubt feel they are acting ethically while their opposition is acting unethically.

about whether you want to get your oil from Canada or Venezuela or Nigeria."[4]

Changing the route has led to an approval from the Nebraska state government and now TransCanada is waiting for final approval from the Office of the President. President Barack Obama originally turned down the proposal in 2011 when he was given a 60-day deadline by Congress to make a decision on the issue. Obama cited a lack of time to fully consider the proposal as a determining factor in his decision. Most political pundits believe Obama delayed his final decision as he didn't want to approve or fully reject the project close to an election.

Introduction

Auto manufacturers that make hybrid cars have taken on the challenge of positively contributing to society through their business activities. At the other extreme, wrongdoing by some businesses has focused public attention and government involvement to encourage more acceptable business conduct. Almost any business decision may be judged as right or wrong, ethical or unethical, depending on who is doing the judging. For example, the Keystone XL project, which we discussed in the opening Destination CEO Profile, has many proponents and opponents. Canadians in favour of the project argue that Canada's oil sand companies need the pipeline to ship oil to refineries in the U.S. They state that Alberta's oil currently sells at a discount because there is a lack of means to transport the oil to refineries and as a result tax dollars and jobs are being lost. If the pipeline is approved, Canadian companies will be able to get more money for their oil, resulting in more jobs and additional tax dollars. These tax dollars support health care, scientific research, education,

and a number of positive initiatives. Many politicians including Prime Minister Stephen Harper have supported the project. In addition, many labour groups support the proposed pipeline for the thousands of jobs it will create, and shareholders favour the deal as it will lead to further profits for the company. Opponents of the deal, including many people in the general public and some politicians, say the oil sands produce more greenhouse gas than traditional oil production and should be discouraged—not encouraged. Furthermore, with any pipeline there is a danger of a spill that can harm the environment. Another example of a business proposal that attracted both supporters and detractors is BlackBerry (formerly Research In Motion (RIM)), which urged the government to stop the sale of Nortel Networks' assets to foreign companies. BlackBerry argued that technology developed in Canada should stay in Canada and that the government had a moral and ethical duty to intervene. Shareholders and creditors, on the other hand, wanted the assets sold to the highest bidder regardless of the buyer's location. The Canadian government opted not to interfere with the sale, which resulted in many of Nortel's prized assets being bought by Ericsson, the Swedish telecommunications manufacturer.[5]

In this chapter, we take a look at the role of ethics and social responsibility in business decision making. First we define business ethics and examine why it is important to understand the role of ethics in business. Next we explore a number of business ethics issues to help you learn to recognize such issues when they arise. Finally, we consider steps businesses can take to improve ethical behaviour in their organizations. The second half of the chapter focuses on social responsibility. We survey some important responsibility issues and detail how companies have responded to them.

LO1 Define business ethics and social responsibility, and examine their importance.

Business Ethics and Social Responsibility

In this chapter, we define **business ethics** as the principles and standards that determine acceptable conduct in business organizations. The acceptability of behaviour in business is determined by customers, competitors, government regulators, interest groups, and the public, as well as each individual's personal moral principles and values. Readers should realize that determining ethical behaviour is not as easy as one may think and often depends on which stakeholder group an individual belongs to. Reconsider the Keystone XL project that was discussed above. Advocates of the pipeline, including the management of the company, shareholders, and some people in the public including the government, likely believe their arguments are ethical. People opposing the deal, including some government officials both in Canada and the U.S., environmental groups, and some labour unions, have stated that approving the pipeline would constitute unethical behaviour. You may also want to consider the situation with General Motors (GM), Ford, and Chrysler, which all maintain manufacturing facilities in Canada. Due to the recent recession, these companies laid off thousands of workers and essentially tore up contracts that they had negotiated with their employees, claiming that this was the only way to ensure that any manufacturing jobs were left in the local economies.[6] GM went a step further and entered into bankruptcy protection in the United States, enabling the company to avoid paying some creditors, to pass off some expenses to government, and essentially to destroy any shareholder value. Ford opted not to enter into bankruptcy protection but did receive some government support. During the recession, the companies continued to manufacture cars, offered consumers better warranties, and attempted to introduce more environmentally friendly automobiles to the marketplace, including the GM Volt which may be the most environmentally friendly car in the world. If you worked for these companies in the past couple of years, would you consider them ethical? As a consumer, would your opinions differ from employees'? One of the reasons Ford avoided bankruptcy was its ability to drastically reduce wages, thus allowing its shareholders to avoid losing everything they had invested. Would

> **Business ethics** principles and standards that determine acceptable conduct in business

Facebook has millions of active users and has become an important business tool for networking, marketing, sourcing suppliers, finding employers and employees, and much more—but the site has led to some ethical dilemmas especially with regards to privacy.

shareholders and employees have a different opinion of Ford? Another interesting ethical dilemma is any action that has a perceived negative environmental impact, such as tree-cutting by the Irving Group's forestry division. While one may presume that the cutting of trees is unethical behaviour, the Irving Group is the largest private planter of trees in the country. Does knowing this affect your opinion of the company and its business practices?

At other times, determining ethical behaviour is much easier. For example, the Quebec police have charged Pierre Duhaime, former CEO of SNC-Lavalin, for engaging in fraud. Research indicates that most unethical activities within organizations are supported by an organizational culture that encourages employees to bend the rules.[7]

Many people—including entrepreneurs, employees, consumers, and social advocates—believe that businesses should not only make a profit but also consider the social implications of their activities. For example, the employees at the Montreal law firm Stikeman Elliott LLP formed a green committee to ensure that the company was minimizing its impact on the environment.[8] These employees are apparently not on their own, according to Nicholas Lamm, co-founder of Green Workplace, a Vancouver-based consulting firm. Lamm says, "As the go-green message increasingly gains footing, Canadians are looking for ways to make an environmental impact on their job."[9] Business owners may want to take note about the growing importance of acting in a socially responsible manner. In a recent poll, 78 percent of Canadians said that they would quit their jobs to work at a company that was more environmentally friendly.[10]

> "Many people including entrepreneurs, employees, consumers, and social advocates believe that businesses should not only make a profit but also consider the social implications of their activities."

We define **social responsibility** as a business's obligation to maximize its positive impact and minimize its negative impact on society. Although many people use the terms *social responsibility* and *ethics* interchangeably,

they do not mean the same thing. Business ethics relate to an *individual's* or a *work group's* decisions that society evaluates as right or wrong, whereas social responsibility is a broader concept that concerns the impact of the *entire business's* activities on society. From an ethical perspective, for example, we may be concerned about a drug company overcharging the government for its medications. From a social responsibility perspective, we might be concerned about the impact that this overcharging will have on the ability of the health care system to provide adequate services for all citizens.

The most basic ethical and social responsibility concerns have been codified as laws and regulations that encourage businesses to conform to society's standards, values, and attitudes. For example, in the early 2000s, corporate scandals involving Nortel, Atlas Cold Storage, Enron, WorldCom, Global Crossing, and Tyco, as well as several major auditing firms, including Arthur Andersen, resulted in hundreds of billions of dollars in corporate and investor losses and shook public confidence in the integrity of the public markets. To help restore confidence in corporations and markets, the U.S. Congress passed the Sarbanes-Oxley Act[11] and the Ontario government proclaimed Bill C-198, which criminalized securities fraud and stiffened penalties for corporate fraud. At a minimum, managers are expected to obey all laws and regulations. Yet even obeying laws is open to interpretation. In Canada, Rogers Communications was running advertisements noting that it offered consumers the fastest and most reliable cell phone service.

Telus, one of Rogers' competitors, disagreed with the claim and brought the matter before the courts. Telus ultimately succeeded in getting Rogers to stop running the ads, but Rogers did not admit to any wrongdoing.[12] Essentially both businesses felt that they were obeying the laws at the time. Most legal issues arise as choices that society deems unethical, irresponsible, or otherwise unacceptable. However, all actions deemed unethical by society are not necessarily illegal, and both legal and ethical concerns change over time (see Table 2.1). Business law refers to the laws and regulations that govern the conduct of business. Many problems and conflicts in business can be avoided if owners, managers, and employees know more about business law and the legal system. Together, business ethics, social responsibility, and legislation act as a compliance system requiring that businesses and employees act responsibly in society. In this chapter, we explore ethics and social responsibility; Appendix A addresses business law, including securities regulations.

The Role of Ethics in Business

You only have to pick up the *National Post* or *The Globe and Mail's Report on Business* to see examples of the growing concern about legal and ethical issues in business. XL Foods, for example, sold tainted meat products to Canadians. Other examples include Ontario-based Premier Fitness's advertising and collection methods, which included luring people in for free fitness trials and then charging them for mandatory physical assessments or continuing to bill clients after they cancelled their memberships. Additionally, the rent-to-own store Aarons installed spy software on people's laptops, which enabled Aarons to record pictures and video of users at home or work without their knowledge. Regardless of what an individual believes about a particular action, if society judges it to be unethical or wrong, whether correctly

table 2.1 A Timeline of Ethical and Socially Responsible Concerns

1960s	1970s	1980s	1990s	2000s
• Environmental issues	• Employee militancy	• Bribes and illegal contracting practices	• Sweatshops and unsafe working conditions in third-world countries	• Employee benefits
• Civil rights issues	• Human rights issues	• Influence peddling		• Privacy issues
• Increased employee–employer tension	• Covering up rather than correcting issues	• Deceptive advertising	• Rising corporate liability for personal damages (e.g., cigarette companies)	• Financial mismanagement
• Honesty	• Discrimination	• Financial fraud (e.g., savings and loan scandal)		• Abusive behaviour
• Changing work ethic	• Harassment			• Cyber crime
• Rising drug use		• Transparency issues	• Financial mismanagement and fraud	• Intellectual property theft

SOURCE: Adapted from "Business Ethics Timeline," Copyright © 2003, *Ethics Resource Center* (n.d.), www.ethics.org, updated 2006. Used with permission.

The Occupy Movement can be described as a global protest against social and economic inequality. The protestors believe that global corporations, especially financial institutions and wealthy individuals, have an unfair influence in politics leading to economic and social problems that undermine democracy. The movement, which originated in New York, spread quickly throughout North America as protestors built camps in highly visible areas such as in public parks or in front of government buildings. Critics of the movement have said that many of the protestors didn't understand the issues they were protesting, could not even name the companies they were upset with, and were taking over public space to run unsanitary camps. Early in the movement, politicians and law enforcement agencies let the camps exist, but as time passed, tolerance for the protestors started to wane. Citing concerns about the health and safety of the protestors and a desire to return public space back to the public, law enforcement agencies eventually tore down many camps throughout North America. Often the protestors refused to move and were arrested as a result. Today, people in the movement claim they are still strong and are determined to end economic and social inequality, but they appear to suffer from a lack of leadership and clear goals.

1. Some people in the Occupy Movement argued the practice of business itself is unethical. Do you agree or disagree?

2. Do you think law enforcement agencies were right to tear down camps? Why or why not?

3. Some protestors fought back when police officers came to evict them from their camps, including physically confronting officers and throwing objects. Do you think protestors were acting ethically? Why or why not?

---

or not, that judgment directly affects the organization's ability to achieve its business goals.[13]

Well-publicized incidents of unethical and illegal activity—from accounting fraud to using the Internet to steal another person's credit-card number, from deceptive advertising of food and diet products to unfair competitive practices in the computer software industry—strengthen the public's perception that ethical standards and the level of trust in business need to be raised. Author David Callahan has commented, "[People] who wouldn't so much as shoplift a pack of chewing gum are committing felonies at tax time, betraying the trust of their patients, misleading investors, ripping off their insurance companies, lying to their clients, and much more."[14] Often, such charges start as ethical conflicts but evolve into legal disputes when cooperative conflict resolution cannot be accomplished. For example, Shirley Slesinger Lasswell, whose late husband acquired the rights to Winnie the Pooh and his friends from creator A. A. Milne in 1930, filed a lawsuit against the Walt Disney Company over merchandising rights to the characters. Although Lasswell granted rights to use the characters to Walt Disney, she contended that the company cheated her and her family out of millions of dollars in royalties on video sales for two decades. Disney asserted that video sales were not specified in its agreement with Lasswell and declined to pay her a percentage of those sales. A California Superior Court judge dismissed the case after 13 years of negotiations and proceedings, effectively siding with Disney.[15] Indeed, many activities deemed unethical by society have been outlawed through legislation.

However, it is important to understand that business ethics go beyond legal issues. Ethical conduct builds trust among individuals and in business relationships, which validates and promotes confidence in business relationships. Establishing trust and confidence is much more difficult in organizations that have established reputations for acting unethically. If you were to discover, for example, that a manager had misled you about company benefits when you were hired, your trust and confidence in that company would probably diminish. And, if you learned that a colleague had lied to you about something, you probably would not trust or rely on that person in the future.

Ethical issues are not limited to for-profit organizations, as the recent national election in Canada is being investigated by Elections Canada and the RCMP. The scandal, commonly referred to as Robocall, involved people being called and told the place where they would cast their ballot had been changed—when this was not the case. Additionally, some of the callers pretended to be from the Liberal Party of Canada, and called late at night or used rude and/or racist statements. The calls were an attempt to dissuade people from voting for a Liberal candidate in the election. Originally, the scandal was thought

> "Ethical conduct builds trust among individuals and in business relationships, which validates and promotes confidence in business relationships."

Consider the Following: Are Social Media Sites Fair Game for Employers?

1. In a recent survey, 40 percent of employers admitted to visiting social media sites to pre-screen applicants who are applying for a job. Of the employers who pre-screen candidates, over 70 percent of them will not allow prospective applicants to explain questionable behaviour they see online. These companies simply remove the person from the pool of candidates they are considering for a job. While most people know that having pictures of yourself engaging in illegal activity is likely not a good idea for your Facebook page, employers are going even further than quickly reviewing photos. Many businesses are reading people's online posts to pre-determine if they have a good attitude and are friendly. Do you think it's ethical for companies to screen potential employees by viewing their social media sites such as Facebook, Twitter, and Instagram? Why or why not?

2. Tom comes to work and looks exhausted during a presentation he is giving to clients. Tom's boss later visits Tom's Facebook page where she discovers he was out partying the night before the presentation. How should she handle the situation? Should she have visited Tom's profile to determine what he was doing the day before the presentation? Why or why not?

3. A salesperson comes back from a tropical vacation. On her Facebook page she creates a folder with the title, "Close friends only! My vacation pics." In order to see the vacation pics you have to click on the folder. Her employer logs onto Facebook and visits the salesperson's profile. She notices the folder and clicks on it to view the pictures. She is outraged by the apparent lack of judgment by one of her employees engaging in questionable behaviour and then posting the pictures of this behaviour online. Was it right for her to view the pictures? Would it be right for her to discipline the employee?

4. An employee notes on his Facebook page that his boss is an idiot. The boss finds out about this through the office grapevine. How should the boss handle the situation?

---

to be limited to a few areas, but the media has reported that up to 100 ridings may have been impacted. Other government scandals include the federal sponsorship scandal. In 2004, Auditor General Sheila Fraser released a report saying taxpayer dollars were mismanaged during the federal sponsorship program.[16] Forensic accountants later said the government had spent $355 million on sponsorships to promote Canadian unity at sporting and cultural events in Quebec. A government-appointed commission was set up and Judge John Gomery, its chair, looked at how the scheme was abused for political ends, and in particular at how $147 million paid in fees and commissions to a dozen advertising and public relations firms found its way into the coffers of the Quebec Liberal Party. Five crown corporations and agencies—the RCMP, VIA Rail, the Old Port of Montreal, the Business Development Bank of Canada, and Canada Post—were cited as involved in transferring money through dubious means since 1995. Stephen Harper's government later introduced the Accountability Act to crack down on unethical actions and make government transparent. More recently a number of Nova Scotia politicians landed in hot water when the provincial auditor general reviewed their expense reports. He discovered a number of questionable claims and referred the actions of four members to the RCMP for criminal investigation.[17]

In government, several politicians and some high-ranking officials have been forced to apologize and/or resign in disgrace over ethical indiscretions. For example, Nova Scotia politician Richard Hulbert resigned in 2010 after the above-mentioned review by the Nova Scotia auditor general revealed that he bought a $9,000 generator using provincial money. Hulbert had actually installed the generator in his home.[18] Irv Lewis "Scooter" Libby, a White House advisor, was indicted on five counts of criminal charges: one count of obstruction of justice, two counts of perjury, and two counts of making false statements. In 2007, he was convicted on four of those counts. Each count carried a $250,000 fine and maximum prison term of 30 years.[19] Several scientists have been accused of falsifying research data, which could invalidate later research based on their data and jeopardize trust in all scientific research. Hwang Woo-Suk was found to have faked some of his famous stem cell research, in which he claimed to have created 30 cloned human embryos and made stem cell lines from skin cells of 11 people, as well as to have produced the world's first cloned dog. He also apologized for using eggs from his own female researchers, which was in breach of guidelines, but he still denied fabricating his research.[20] Even sports can be subject to ethical lapses. At many universities, for example, coaches and athletic administrators have been put on administrative leave after allegations of improper recruiting practices by team members came to light.[21] In some cases, even

> **"Many business issues may seem straightforward and easy to resolve, but in reality,** a person often needs several years of experience in business to understand what is acceptable or ethical."

Nobody likes a cheater, not even in the sports business. Although Mark McGwire broke baseball's home run record in 1998, he later admitted to taking steroids.

an entire team of athletes have engaged in ethical misconduct. Dalhousie University, the largest university in Atlantic Canada, recently suspended the majority of the players on its women's hockey team for engaging in unethical behaviour. The result was the team had to default the remainder of the season. In other examples, Jimmy Johnson's crew chief, Chad Knaus, was thrown out of the Daytona 500 for illegal modifications made to Johnson's car during NASCAR pole qualifying. Although Johnson finished fifth in qualifying, he had to start from the rear of the field and then went on to win the Daytona 500.[22] Thus, whether made in science, politics, sports, or business, most decisions are judged as right or wrong, ethical or unethical. Negative judgments can affect an organization's ability to build relationships with customers and suppliers, attract investors, and retain employees.[23]

Although we will not tell you in this chapter what you ought to do, others—your superiors, co-workers, and family—will make judgments about the ethics of your actions and decisions. Learning how to recognize and resolve ethical issues is an important step in evaluating ethical decisions in business.

LO2 Detect some of the ethical issues that may arise in business.

Recognizing Ethical Issues in Business

Learning to recognize ethical issues is the most important step in understanding business ethics. An **ethical issue** is an identifiable problem, situation, or opportunity that requires a person to choose from among several actions that may be evaluated as right or wrong, ethical or unethical. In business, such a choice often involves weighing monetary profit against what a person considers appropriate conduct. The best way to judge the ethics of a decision is to look at a situation from a customer's or competitor's viewpoint:

> **Ethical issue** an identifiable problem, situation, or opportunity that requires a person to choose from among several actions that may be evaluated as right or wrong, ethical or unethical

Consider the Following: When Is Organic Really Organic?

The organic food industry boasts that sales have surpassed $2.6 billion with supermarkets and specialty stores often charging a premium price for products labelled as organic. In Canada, food with the organic label must be certified by the Canadian Food Inspection Agency (CFIA). Once certified, a company's products do not undergo any laboratory testing to confirm they are free of pesticides. The industry operates on what amounts to an honour system. The CFIA states that testing may be done as part of its annual monitoring program but specific lab tests to confirm products are organic are not used. In one recent spot test, CFIA documents showed that 24 percent of organic apples contained pesticide residue. The CFIA theorized that many of the tainted apples likely resulted from inadver-

tent contamination. The CFIA states that while it is not opposed to testing of products, it is not a proponent of excessive tests, arguing that too much testing will increase the price of organic food—something it says consumers do not want to see happen.[24]

1. Do you think the Canadian Food Inspection Agency is doing enough to ensure foods labelled as organic are actually organic?

2. Would you trust producers not to use pesticides in their operations? Why or why not?

3. Do you think consumers would be willing to pay more for organic food if a testing program ensured the food truly was organic? Why or why not?

Should liquid-diet manufacturers make unsubstantiated claims about their products? Should an engineer agree to divulge her former employer's trade secrets to ensure that she gets a better job with a competitor? Should a salesperson omit facts about a product's poor safety record in his presentation to a customer? Such questions require the decision maker to evaluate the ethics of his or her choice.

Many business issues may seem straightforward and easy to resolve, but in reality, a person often needs several years of experience in business to understand what is acceptable or ethical. For example, if you are a salesperson, when does offering a gift—such as season basketball tickets—to a customer become a bribe rather than just a sales practice? Clearly, there are no easy answers to such a question. But the size of the transaction, the history of personal relationships within the particular company, as well as many other factors may determine whether an action will be judged as right or wrong by others.

Bullying, which was once something that occurred on the playground, has become a problem at work as abusive or intimidating behaviour continues to plague employees.

RESPONDING TO BUSINESS CHALLENGES | Spouses' Cheating—Ethical or Unethical?

The title for this section seems rather straightforward. Most people would agree that spouses' cheating is unethical and not something that should be encouraged in business or society. Then again, most people aren't Noel Biderman, CEO of Avid Life Media and owner of the famous or infamous Toronto-based website AshleyMadison.com, which facilitates extramarital affairs for its users. In fact, the company's popular saying is, "Life is short, have an affair." The company, which reports millions in profits, has recently discovered that all is not fair in love and business. First, the company wanted to go public and sell shares on the Toronto Stock Exchange to raise money for further expansion, but in order to do so it had to find investment firms to sell shares to large institutional investors. After a prolonged effort, the company announced it would not be pursuing its plans as no investment firm would work with the company. A short time later, AshleyMadison.com tried to run advertisements on Toronto buses, but was turned down by the local authorities. Some may question if Biderman's company is being treated fairly. After all, many investment banks and public transit services work with companies that produce military equipment, produce or promote the use and sale of alcohol and cigarettes, and promote gambling and/or other vices. Yet others argue that AshleyMadison.com has exactly the kind of content that reputable investment banks and companies should avoid.[26]

AshleyMadison.com has had its business rejected by advertisers and investors. Yet the company continues to grow and profit.

DISCUSSION QUESTIONS

1. Investment bankers are, by their very nature, capitalists and rarely, some people would state, consider ethics in their decision making. Why do you think investment bankers were hesitant to work with AshleyMadison.com when many have previously worked with companies that sell or produce military equipment, alcohol, and cigarettes, or promote gambling?

2. Should Toronto have allowed the advertisements on the buses? What about if the city allows other "vice" products or companies to advertise?

3. Would you invest in AshleyMadison.com? Why or why not?

4. Do you think Avid Life Media is an ethical business? Why or why not?

> ## "Bullying is associated with a hostile workplace when someone considered a target (or a group) is threatened, harassed, belittled, or verbally abused or overly criticized."

Ethics is also related to the culture in which a business operates. In Canada, for example, it would be inappropriate for a businessperson to bring an elaborately wrapped gift to a prospective client on their first meeting—the gift could be viewed as a bribe. In Japan, however, it is considered impolite *not* to bring a gift. Experience with the culture in which a business operates is critical to understanding what is ethical or unethical.

To help you understand ethical issues that perplex businesspeople today, we will take a brief look at some of them in this section. The vast number of news-format investigative programs has increased consumer and employee awareness of organizational misconduct. In addition, the multitude of cable channels and Internet resources has improved the awareness of ethical problems among the general public. The National Business Ethics Survey of more than 3,000 U.S. employees found that workers witness many instances of ethical misconduct in their organizations (see Table 2.2). The most common types of observed misconduct were abusive/intimidating behaviour, lying, and placing employee interests over organizational interests.[25]

One of the principal causes of unethical behaviour in organizations is overly aggressive financial or business objectives. Many of these issues relate to decisions and concerns that managers have to deal with daily. It is not possible to discuss every issue, of course. However, a discussion of a few issues can help you begin to recognize the ethical problems with which businesspersons must deal. Many ethical issues in business can be categorized in the context of their relation with abusive and intimidating behaviour, conflicts of interest, fairness and honesty, communications, and business associations.

Abusive or Intimidating Behaviour. Abusive or intimidating behaviour is the most common ethical problem for employees. The concepts can mean anything from physical threats, false accusations, being annoying, profanity, insults, yelling, harshness, or ignoring someone, to unreasonableness, and the meaning of these words can differ by person—you probably have some ideas of your own. Abusive behaviour can be placed on a continuum from a minor distraction to a workplace disruption. For example, what one person may define as yelling might be another's definition of normal speech. Civility in our society has been a concern, and the workplace is no

exception. The productivity level of many organizations has been damaged by the time spent unravelling abusive relationships.

Abusive behaviour is difficult to assess and manage because of diversity in culture and lifestyle. What does it mean to speak profanely? Is profanity only related to specific words or other such terms that are common in today's business world? If you are using words that are normal in your language but others consider profanity, have you just insulted, abused, or disrespected them?

Within the concept of abusive behaviour, intent should be a consideration. If the employee was trying to convey a compliment but the comment was considered abusive, then it was probably a mistake. The way a word is said (voice inflection) can be important. Add to this the fact that we now live in a multicultural environment—doing business and working with many different cultural groups—and the businessperson soon realizes the depth of the ethical and legal issues that may arise. There are problems of word meanings by age and within cultures. For example an expression such as "Did you guys hook up last night?" can have various meanings, including some that could be considered offensive in a work environment.

Bullying is associated with a hostile workplace when someone considered a target (or a group) is threatened, harassed, belittled, or verbally abused or overly criticized. While bullying may create what some may call a hostile environment, this term is generally associated with sexual harassment. Although sexual harassment has legal recourse, bullying has little legal recourse at this time. Bullying can cause psychological damage that can result in health endangering consequences to the target. As Table 2.3 indicates, bullying can use a mix of verbal, nonverbal, and manipulative threatening expressions to damage workplace productivity. One may wonder why workers tolerate such activities; the problem is that 81 percent of workplace bullies are supervisors. A top officer at Boeing cited an employee survey indicating 26 percent had observed abusive or intimidating behaviour by management.[27]

table 2.2 Types and Incidences of Observed Misconduct

Type of Conduct Observed	Employees Observing It
Abusive or intimidating behaviour toward employees	21%
Lying to employees, customers, vendors, or the public	19
Situations placing employee interests over organizational interests	18
Violations of safety regulations	16
Misreporting of actual time worked	16
Discrimination on the basis of race, colour, gender, age, or similar categories	12
Stealing or theft	11
Sexual harassment	9

SOURCE: "National Business Ethics Survey 2005," "Survey Documents State of Ethics in the Workplace," and "Misconduct," Ethics Resource Center (n.d.), www.ethics.org/ (accessed April 11, 2006).

Conflict of Interest. A conflict of interest exists when a person must choose whether to advance his or her own personal interests or those of others. For example, a manager in a corporation is supposed to ensure that the company is profitable so that its shareholder-owners receive a return on their investment. In other words, the manager has a responsibility to investors. If she instead makes decisions that give her more power or money but do not help the company, then she has a conflict of interest—she is acting to benefit herself at the expense of her company and is not fulfilling her responsibilities. To avoid conflicts of interest, employees must be able to separate their personal financial interests from their business dealings. For example, a $1 million donation by Citigroup to the 92nd Street Y nursery school represents a possible conflict of interest. Jack Grubman, an analyst for Salomon Smith Barney, upgraded his rating for AT&T stock after Sanford Weill, the CEO of Citigroup (the parent company of Salomon Smith Barney), agreed to use his influence to help Grubman's twins gain admission to the elite Manhattan nursery school. During the late 1990s, Weill, an AT&T board member, had been upset that Citigroup wasn't getting any of AT&T's business. Grubman changed his AT&T rating to buy. A year later he bragged in an e-mail that he had made the switch to placate Weill in exchange for Weill's help in getting Grubman's children into the exclusive 92nd Street Y nursery school. Grubman denied elevating his rating for AT&T's stock to gain admission to the school, but his children were enrolled. Industry leaders still avoid him, publicly anyway, but on the fringes of telecom, Grubman has had no trouble finding people who are willing to overlook his past or are simply unaware of it. According to a *Fortune* article, although Grubman was "banned from Wall Street, the former Telecom King wants to prove that he wasn't a huckster."[28]

As mentioned earlier, it is considered improper to give or accept **bribes**—payments, gifts, or special favours intended to influence the outcome of a decision. A bribe is a conflict of interest because it benefits an individual at the expense of an organization or society. Companies that do

> **Bribes** payments, gifts, or special favours intended to influence the outcome of a decision

table 2.3 Actions Associated With Bullies

1. Spreading rumours to damage others
2. Blocking others' communication in the workplace
3. Flaunting status or authority to take advantage of others
4. Discrediting others' ideas and opinions
5. Use of e-mails to demean others
6. Failing to communicate or return communication
7. Insults, yelling, and shouting
8. Using terminology to discriminate by gender, race, or age
9. Using eye or body language to hurt others or their reputation
10. Taking credit for others' work or ideas

SOURCE: © O. C. Ferrell, 2011.

RESPONDING TO BUSINESS CHALLENGES | What Is Ethical When Bribes Are the Norm?

For years, bribes and corruption in foreign countries were customary and considered acceptable, meaning a Canadian company operating in a part of the world where bribery was the norm would be forgiven for following local customs and could pay bribes. This attitude started to change in 1999, when both the U.S. and Canadian governments started to pass tougher rules governing how North American companies conducted business globally. Like most of what happens in business though, things are not always straightforward. While large bribes are no longer considered acceptable, it still isn't clear about small bribes, often referred to as "facilitation payments," that get people to perform their jobs. For example, in some European countries it is not unusual for the mailman to knock on your door at Christmas looking for a cash gift. The norm is that you pay the gift or you don't get your mail anymore.

DISCUSSION QUESTIONS

1. Do you think it is ethical to pay a bribe in a country where it is a cultural norm? Why or why not?

2. Do you think "facilitation payments" should be considered bribes? If you ran a company in a country where these payments were the norm, would you pay them?

3. Do you think Canada's legal system should be investigating crimes such as bribes which occur in other countries? Why or why not?

table 2.4 Least Corrupt Countries

Rank	Country	2012 CPI Score*
1	Denmark	90
1	Finland	90
1	New Zealand	90
4	Sweden	88
5	Singapore	87
6	Switzerland	86
7	Australia	85
7	Norway	85
9	Canada	84
9	Netherlands	84
11	Iceland	82
12	Luxembourg	80
13	Germany	79
14	Hong Kong	77
15	Barbados	76
16	Belgium	75
17	Japan	74
17	United Kingdom	74
19	United States	73
20	Chile	72
20	Uruguay	72

*CPI score relates to perceptions of the degree of corruption as seen by businesspeople and country analysts and ranges between 100 (highly clean) and 0 (highly corrupt).

SOURCE: This information is 'extracted from' the CPI and the CPI is measuring perceived public sector corruption. © Transparency International 2012. All Rights Reserved. For more information, visit http://www.transparency.org.

Consumers are flocking to buy products with added probiotics hoping to improve their health. Unfortunately, research by the European Food Safety Authority and the U.S. Food and Drug Safety Administration does not support any of these claims. Are companies pushing consumers to purchase probiotic products ethical?

business overseas should be aware that bribes are a significant ethical issue and are in fact illegal in many countries. For example, Acres International of Oakville, Ontario, was convicted by the Lesotho High Court in Africa of bribing a local official to secure contracts.[29] Bribery is more prevalent in some countries than in others. For example, bribes are standard practice in Bangladesh, where Niko Resources, a Calgary-based company recently experienced trouble when it was caught purchasing a $190,000 car for a government official.[30] Transparency International has developed a Corruption Perceptions Index (Table 2.4). Note there are 13 countries perceived as less corrupt than Canada.

Fairness and Honesty. Fairness and honesty are at the heart of business ethics and relate to the general values of decision makers. At a minimum, businesspersons are expected to follow all applicable laws and regulations. But beyond obeying the law, they are expected not to harm customers, employees, clients, or competitors knowingly through deception, misrepresentation, coercion, or discrimination. As discussed throughout the chapter, issues of ethics are not always clear, as in the case of probiotics, one of the trendiest health products over the past decade. Probiotics are being put into yogurt, sports drinks, and other food products with claims that they improve the digestive system. Advocates of the bacteria cite incidents of people's health improving as a result of ingesting the bacteria. Yet scientific research does not support these claims. The European Food Safety Authority (EFSA) has studied hundreds of health claims associated with probiotics and rejected them all. The EFSA is moving forward with plans to ban the use of the word *probiotics* on food labels. Yet some companies that produce these products point to research which they state proves their claim that probiotics are good for you. Other examples are a bit more clear cut, such as when Suzy Shier Inc. and The Forzani Group, owners and operators of Sport-Chek and Sports Smart stores, ended up on the receiving end of a number of consumer complaints as consumer groups noted that the stores frequently overstated the regular selling price on items to make the sales price look more attractive. The result was consumers felt that they were getting a larger bargain and spent more or bought items that they normally would not have bought. The Canadian Competition Bureau, an independent law enforcement agency that protects and promotes consumers, brought the matter before the courts; the result was fines of $1 million for Suzy Shier Inc. and total fines and court costs of $1.7 million for The Forzani Group.[31]

figure 2.1 Most Popular Office Supplies Employees Pilfer

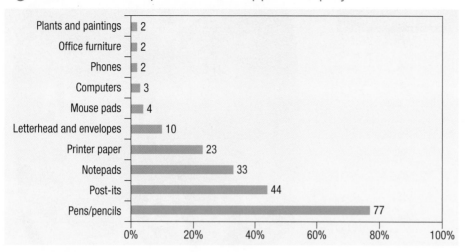

Plants and paintings	2
Office furniture	2
Phones	2
Computers	3
Mouse pads	4
Letterhead and envelopes	10
Printer paper	23
Notepads	33
Post-its	44
Pens/pencils	77

SOURCE: "More Employees Taking Supplies," *The (Wilmington, Del.) News Journal*, using data from Lawyers.com, April 1, 2007, http://www.usatoday.com/money/industries/retail/2007-03-30-supply_N.htm (accessed June 1, 2007).

Vault.com found that 67 percent of employees have taken office supplies from work to use for matters unrelated to their job. Most employees do not view taking office supplies as stealing or dishonest, with 97 percent saying they have never gotten caught and it would not matter if they were found out. In addition, only 3.7 percent say they have taken items like keyboards, software, and memory sticks. Still, an employee should be aware of policies on taking items and recognize how these decisions relate to ethical behaviour.[32] Figure 2.1 above provides an overview of the most pilfered office supplies.

One aspect of fairness relates to competition. Although numerous laws have been passed to foster competition and make monopolistic practices illegal, companies sometimes gain control over markets by using questionable practices that harm competition. Bullying can also occur between companies that are in intense competition. Even respected companies such as Intel have been accused of monopolistic bullying. A competitor, Advanced Micro Devices (AMD), claimed in a lawsuit that 38 companies, including Dell and Sony, were strong-arming customers (such as Apple) into buying Intel chips rather than those marketed by AMD. The AMD lawsuit seeks billions of dollars and will take years to litigate. In many cases, the alleged misconduct not only can have monetary and legal implications but can threaten reputation, investor confidence, and customer loyalty. A front-cover *Forbes* headline stated "Intel to AMD: Drop Dead." An example of the intense competition and Intel's ability to use its large size won it the high-profile Apple account, displacing IBM and Free-scale. AMD said it had no opportunity to bid because Intel offered to deploy 600 Indian engineers to help Apple software run more smoothly on Intel chips.[33]

Another aspect of fairness and honesty relates to disclosure of potential harm caused by product use. For example, Maple Leaf Foods announced a series of recalls in 2008 after it discovered that some of its products were tainted with *Listeria monocytogenes*, a bacterium that can cause serious illness and even death if ingested. While a number of people did become ill and some in fact died, Maple Leaf CEO Michael McCain's handling of the situation was recognized as positive by the business press and many Canadians. McCain claimed full responsibility for the recall and was in constant communication with the public and the press. Right from the start of the outbreak Maple Leaf reached out to the public using press conferences, Web postings, and commercials to keep consumers informed. Testifying before a parliamentary committee on food safety McCain noted, "This tragedy was a defining moment for Maple Leaf Foods and for those that worked there. We are determined to make a terrible wrong, right."[34] Maple Leaf's efforts not only helped consumers realize they may have purchased tainted products but also helped the company's image and bottom line as the decline in the firm's value has not been as significant as industry experts thought it would be as a result of the recall. Toyota had to deal with an even larger issue in 2009 and 2010 when the company had to recall millions of cars and trucks due to problems with unintended acceleration, and again in 2013 when it had to recall 1.7 million vehicles, 75,000 of them in Canada, due to problems with airbags.[35] Toyota, much like Maple Leaf Foods, addressed the problem in the media and worked to find a solution.

Compare the responses of those companies to that of XL Foods, a Canadian beef processing plant where testing for *E. coli* was not stringent enough. The lack of testing resulted in infected food reaching the marketplace, causing consumers to become ill and requiring the company to institute a large recall of products. Rather than address the problem directly, the company basically went into a media blackout, ignoring requests for additional information. The result was no one trusted the few statements they heard from XL and rumours ran rampant in the press. A similar event occurred

Toyota had to recall 9 million cars globally including the popular hybrid Prius after problems were uncovered with the accelerator.

with Mitsubishi Motors, Japan's number-four automaker, which faced criminal charges and negative publicity after executives admitted that the company had systematically covered up customer complaints about tens of thousands of defective automobiles over a 20-year period to avoid expensive and embarrassing product recalls.[36] Consumers seem willing to accept that mistakes, even deadly mistakes, will happen in the manufacturing of consumer goods. What upsets consumers, however, is when companies attempt to avoid the truth to limit financial damage. Both Toyota and Maple Leaf benefitted from being honest with their customers.

While corrupt business practices in Canada are an issue, the country has recently improved its standing according to the Corruption Perceptions Index from Transparency International, which annually ranks countries based on perceptions of corruption in business and government circles.[37] As of 2012, Canada is ranked ninth in the world, an improvement from our 14th place ranking a few years ago. Lying was the most observed form of misconduct in the National Business Ethics Survey. Other examples of dishonesty include piracy. The Canadian Recording Industry Association has reported that net music sales in Canada have declined significantly in the past decade. The CRIA said the decline reflects an almost 15 year spiral paralleling the rise of music file sharing on the Internet, and continues unabated due to the failure of the Canadian government to enact much overdue copyright reform.[38] The music industry has been calling on the Canadian government to modernize copyright laws in this country in order to stem illegal downloading, and in June 2010, the government responded with Bill C-32. Research group Pollara says an estimated 1.6 billion illegal music files are shared online annually in Canada. The situation is so bad that Canada is now cited by the OECD as having the largest online piracy rate per capita in the world. Interestingly, a study released in March 2004 by Harvard Business School claims that Internet music piracy not only does not hurt legitimate CD sales, but may even boost sales of some types of music. The study provides evidence that file sharing cannot explain the decline in music sales in the last couple of years. In addition, music sales appear to have increased as file sharing

has become even more popular. Even the Recording Industry Association of America (RIAA) now states that file sharing is only "one factor, along with economic conditions and competing forms of entertainment that is displacing legitimate sales."[39] The contradictory evidence on the impact of file sharing reinforces the discussion at the start of the chapter that it can be difficult to judge ethical behaviour.

Dishonesty is not found only in business. According to the first major study of academic misconduct in Canada, cheating, deceit, and plagiarism were found to be serious problems. Julia Christensen Hughes of the University of Guelph and Donald McCabe of Rutgers University surveyed 14,913 undergraduate students, 1,318 graduate students, 683 teaching assistants, and 1,902 faculty from 11 Canadian post-secondary institutions across five provinces.

Students admitted to having engaged in some form of misconduct while completing their academic work. Seventy-three percent admitted to "serious" cheating while in high school and 53 percent of undergrads admitted they are still cheating in university.[41] If today's students are tomorrow's leaders, there is likely to be a correlation between acceptable behaviour today and tomorrow, adding to the argument that the leaders of today must be prepared for the ethical risks

Seventy-three percent of high school students and 53 percent of university students admitted to serious cheating.

associated with this downward trend. According to a poll by Deloitte Touche of teenagers aged 13 to 18, when asked if people who practise good business ethics are more successful than those who don't, 69 percent of teenagers agreed.[42] The same poll found only 12 percent of teens think business leaders today are ethical. On the other hand, another survey indicated that many students do not define copying answers from another student's paper or downloading music or content for classroom work as cheating.[43]

Communications. Communications is another area in which ethical concerns may arise. False and misleading advertising, as well as deceptive personal-selling tactics, anger consumers and can lead to the failure of a business. Truthfulness about product safety and quality is also important to consumers. As discussed above, manufacturers of products with probiotics are starting to come under increased government scrutiny in Europe and the U.S. The bacteria was largely ignored in North America until Danone, producers of Activia yogurt, started spending upwards of $130 million annually to promote the health benefits of the product. The issue is that the benefits are not supported by any scientific research.[44] Claims about dietary supplements and weight-loss products can be particularly problematic. For example, Canada, Mexico, and the United States recently announced actions taken to fight weight-loss fraud: they had taken 734 compliance actions to combat companies promoting bogus and misleading weight-loss schemes. Canadian investigative news shows *Marketplace* and *W5* have spent considerable effort studying some of the claims of the weight loss industry with surprising results. CBC's *Marketplace* investigated Herbal Magic, one of the biggest weight loss companies in Canada—with more than 300 stores nationwide. The journalists discovered that Herbal Magic clients were being told to purchase two expensive dietary supplements to encourage weight loss. CBC brought the supplements to laboratories for independent testing and discovered that there was not enough scientific evidence to justify the claims. Since the airing of the show, Herbal Magic has announced it will replace the supplements with different formulations.[45] *W5* also uncovered questionable behaviour in its investigation of PhytoPharma, which became known for many weight-loss products including the popular Plant Macerate and Apple Cider Vinegar capsules by Naturalab. *W5* determined that there was no scientific evidence to support the claim that the products assisted in weight loss.[46]

Unscrupulous activity is not limited to just the diet industry. Governments in Canada, Mexico, and the United States launched 177 compliance and enforcement actions against companies promoting bogus diabetes products and services. Actions include prosecutions, recalls, seizures, import refusals, warnings, and other enforcement programs against false and misleading advertising and labelling, as well as the promotion of industry compliance.[47]

Some companies fail to provide enough information for consumers about differences or similarities between products. For example, driven by high prices for medicines, many consumers are turning to the Internet, Mexico, and overseas sources for drugs to treat a variety of illnesses and conditions. However, research suggests that a significant percentage of these imported pharmaceuticals may not actually contain the labelled drug, and the counterfeit drugs could even be harmful to those who take them. The issue of drug importation is particularly problematic in the United States where millions of people do not have health insurance. Unfortunately, as stated above, people do not always know what they are getting. In a recent FDA seizure it was discovered that 85 percent of the drugs that were purported to be sold from Canada in fact came from other countries.[48]

Another important aspect of communications that may raise ethical concerns relates to product labelling. In Canada, anti-tobacco legislation requires cigarette manufacturers to include graphic pictures, health warnings, health information messages, and toxic emissions/constituents statements on their packages. The U.S. Surgeon General currently requires cigarette manufacturers to indicate clearly on cigarette packaging that smoking cigarettes is harmful to the smoker's health. In Europe, at least 30 percent of the front side of product packaging and 40 percent of the back needs to be taken up by the warning. The use of descriptors such as "light" or "mild" has been banned.[49] However, labelling of other products raises ethical questions when it threatens basic rights, such as freedom of speech and expression. This is the heart of the controversy surrounding the movement to require warning labels on movies and videogames, rating their content, language, and appropriate audience age. Although people in the entertainment industry believe that such labelling violates their rights, other consumers—particularly parents—believe that such labelling is needed to protect children from harmful influences. Internet regulation, particularly that designed to protect children and the elderly, is at the forefront in consumer protection legislation. Because of the debate surrounding the acceptability of these business activities, they remain major ethical issues. The Canadian Radio-television and Telecommunications Commission, the body responsible for regulating broadcasting and telecommunications in Canada, does not regulate the Internet. However, certain obligations must be met under consumer protection laws when doing business with consumers on the Internet. Another highly polarized debate concerns the labelling of genetically modified (GM) foods in Canada. Currently, disclosure of GM foods among Canadian food

Cigarette labels now have to warn about health risks.

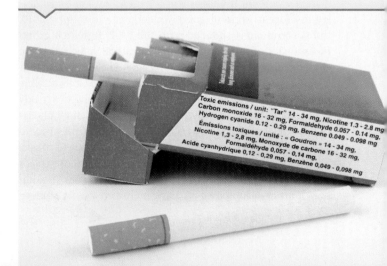

manufacturers and retailers is not required, even though GM foods are said to be present in 60 to 70 percent of all processed foods on the market, according to the Food and Consumer Products Manufacturers of Canada.[50]

Opponents of GM foods argue that they might pose health risks for certain people (for example, foods could become metabolically dangerous or even toxic from the introduction of a fish gene in a plant). Proponents assert that GM foods will promise many health benefits (for example, farmers typically produce GM crops using fewer pesticides, herbicides, and fertilizers). Other arguments against GM crops are that the technology will hurt small farmers and harm the environment, that modification goes against nature, that the industry suffers from poor oversight and regulation, and that biotech companies are profit-driven with little concern for potential risks to people or nature. Proponents maintain that farmers will reap great benefits from biotechnology; that the technology helps the environment, is completely natural, and uses the most thoroughly tested and highly regulated food plants; and that GM crops hold the greatest hope for adequately feeding a rapidly expanding population. Because of the debate surrounding the acceptability of these business activities, they remain major ethical issues.

Business Relationships. The behaviour of businesspersons toward customers, suppliers, and others in their workplace may also generate ethical concerns. Ethical behaviour within a business involves keeping company secrets, meeting obligations and responsibilities, and avoiding undue pressure that may force others to act unethically.

Managers, in particular, because of the authority of their position, have the opportunity to influence employees' actions. For example, a manager can influence employees to use pirated computer software to save costs. The use of illegal software puts the employee and the company at legal risk, but employees may feel pressured to do so by their superior's authority. The Canadian Alliance Against Software Theft (CAAST) and the Business Software Alliance (BSA), watchdog groups that represent the world's leading software manufacturers, announced that some 11 Canadian companies from diverse industries have recently agreed to pay a total of $252,093 to settle claims that they were using unlicensed software. According to a study, 33 percent of software installed on computers in Canada was pirated, representing a loss of $943 million. It is estimated that, globally, software piracy resulted in a loss of $41 billion.[51]

It is the responsibility of managers to create a work environment that helps the organization achieve its objectives and fulfill its responsibilities. However, the methods that managers use to enforce these responsibilities should not compromise employee rights. Organizational pressures may encourage a person to engage in activities that he or she might otherwise view as unethical, such as invading others' privacy or stealing a competitor's secrets. For example, in 2004, when Air Canada

Air Canada and WestJet have both engaged in questionable practices as they fight for market share in Canada.

found that WestJet had gained access to its internal website to acquire commercially sensitive data, it launched a $220 million lawsuit against the company. In return, WestJet filed a $5 million countersuit claiming that Air Canada had hired private investigators to pilfer the garbage of WestJet's co-founder, Mark Hill. After two years of arguments, WestJet apologized and admitted that its online snooping was unethical. It agreed to pay Air Canada $5.5 million to settle the allegations of corporate espionage, and to donate $10 million to children's charities in the name of both airlines. In return, Air Canada accepted WestJet's apologies and withdrew the legal claims.[52] Another example includes Betty Vinson, an accounting executive at WorldCom, who protested when her superiors asked her to make improper accounting entries to cover up the company's deteriorating financial condition. She acquiesced only after being told that it was the only way to save the troubled company. She, along with several other WorldCom accountants, pleaded guilty to conspiracy and fraud charges related to WorldCom's bankruptcy after the accounting improprieties came to light.[53] Alternatively, the firm may provide only vague or lax supervision on ethical issues, providing the opportunity for misconduct. Managers who offer no ethical direction to employees create many opportunities for manipulation, dishonesty, and conflicts of interest.

Plagiarism—taking someone else's work and presenting it as your own without mentioning the source—is another ethical issue. As a student, you may be familiar

> "In Canada, corporate espionage is estimated to cost the economy upwards of $100 billion a year as secrets and confidential information is stolen."[54]

> **Plagiarism** the act of taking someone else's work and presenting it as your own without mentioning the source

with plagiarism in school; for example, copying someone else's term paper or quoting from a published work or Internet source without acknowledging it. In business, an ethical issue arises when an employee copies reports or presents the work or ideas of others as his or her own. At *USA Today,* for example, an internal investigation into the work of veteran reporter Jack Kelley identified dozens of stories in which Kelley appeared to have plagiarized material from competing newspapers. The investigation also uncovered evidence Kelley fabricated significant portions of at least eight major stories and conspired to cover up his lapses in judgment. The newspaper later apologized to its readers, and Kelley resigned.[55] A manager attempting to take credit for a subordinate's ideas is engaging in another type of plagiarism.

> "It is the responsibility of managers to create a work environment that helps the organization achieve its objectives and fulfill its responsibilities."

Making Decisions About Ethical Issues

Although we've presented a variety of ethical issues that may arise in business, it can be difficult to recognize specific ethical issues in practice. Whether a decision maker recognizes an issue as an ethical one often depends on the issue itself. Managers, for example, tend to be more concerned about issues that affect those close to them, as well as issues that have immediate rather than long-term consequences. Thus, the perceived importance of an ethical issue substantially affects choices, and only a few issues receive scrutiny, while most receive no attention at all.[56]

Table 2.5 lists some questions you may want to ask yourself and others when trying to determine whether an action is ethical. Open discussion of ethical issues does not eliminate ethical problems, but it does promote both trust and learning in an organization.[57] When people feel that they cannot discuss what they are doing with their co-workers or superiors, there is a good chance that an ethical issue exists. Once a person has recognized an ethical issue and can openly discuss it with others, he or she has begun the process of resolving the ethical issue.

LO3 Specify how businesses can promote ethical behaviour.

Improving Ethical Behaviour in Business

Understanding how people make ethical choices and what prompts a person to act unethically may reverse the current trend toward unethical behaviour in business. Ethical decisions in an organization are influenced by three key factors: individual moral standards, the influence of managers and co-workers, and the opportunity to engage in misconduct (Figure 2.2). While you have great control over your personal ethics outside the workplace, your co-workers and superiors exert significant control over your choices at work through authority and example. In fact, the activities and

examples set by co-workers, along with rules and policies established by the firm, are critical in gaining consistent ethical compliance in an organization. If the company fails to provide good examples and direction for appropriate conduct, confusion and conflict will develop and result in the opportunity for misconduct. If your boss or co-workers leave work early, you may be tempted to do so as well. If you see co-workers making personal long-distance phone calls at work and charging them to the company, then you may be more likely to do so also. In addition, having sound personal values contributes to an ethical workplace.

Because ethical issues often emerge from conflict, it is useful to examine the causes of ethical conflict. Business managers and employees often experience some tension between their own ethical beliefs and their obligations to the organizations in which they work. Many employees utilize different ethical standards at work than they do at home. This conflict increases when employees feel that their company is encouraging unethical conduct or exerting pressure on them to engage in it.

It is difficult for employees to determine what conduct is acceptable within a company if the firm does not have ethics policies and standards. And without such policies and standards, employees may base decisions on how their peers and superiors behave. Professional **codes of ethics** are formalized rules and standards that describe what the company expects of its employees. Codes of ethics do not have to be so detailed that they take into account every situation, but they should provide guidelines and principles that can help employees achieve organizational objectives and address risks in an acceptable and ethical way. The development of a code of ethics should include not only a firm's executives and board of directors, but also legal staff and employees from all areas of a firm.[58] Table 2.6 lists some key things to consider when developing a code of ethics.

> **Codes of ethics** formalized rules and standards that describe what a company expects of its employees

table 2.5 Questions to Consider in Determining Whether an Action Is Ethical

Are there any potential legal restrictions or violations that could result from the action?
Does your company have a specific code of ethics or policy on the action?
Is this activity customary in your industry? Are there any industry trade groups that provide guidelines or codes of conduct that address this issue?
Would this activity be accepted by your co-workers? Will your decision or action withstand open discussion with co-workers and managers and survive untarnished?
How does this activity fit with your own beliefs and values?

figure 2.2 Three Factors That Influence Business Ethics

"Many employees utilize different ethical standards at work **than they do at home.**"

Codes of ethics, policies on ethics, and ethics training programs advance ethical behaviour because they prescribe which activities are acceptable and which are not, and they limit the opportunity for misconduct by providing punishments for violations of the rules and standards. According to the National Business Ethics Survey (NBES), employees in organizations that have written standards of conduct, ethics training, ethics offices or hotlines, and systems for anonymous reporting of misconduct are more likely to report misconduct when they observe it. The survey also found that such programs are associated with higher employee perceptions that they will be held accountable for ethical infractions.[59] The enforcement of such codes and policies through rewards and punishments increases the acceptance of ethical standards by employees.

One of the most important components of an ethics program is a means through which employees can report observed misconduct anonymously. The NBES found that although employees are increasingly reporting illegal and unethical activities they observe in the workplace, 59 percent of surveyed employees indicated they are unwilling to report misconduct because they fear that no corrective action will be taken or that their report will not remain confidential.[60] The lack of anonymous reporting mechanisms may encourage **whistleblowing,** which occurs when an employee exposes an employer's wrongdoing to outsiders, such as the media or government regulatory agencies. However, more companies are establishing programs to encourage employees to report illegal or unethical practices internally so that they can take steps to remedy problems before they result in legal action or generate negative publicity. The Federal Accountability Act, among other measures, provides public-sector workers legal protection against reprisals for reporting government wrongdoing. The legislation is "part of the government's broader commitment to ensure transparency, accountability, financial responsibility and ethical conduct."[61] Currently, whistleblowers in Canada also have special protection in respect of environmental and health and safety matters and there is a requirement for public companies to have confidential whistleblower

Whistleblowing the act of an employee exposing an employer's wrongdoing to outsiders, such as the media or government regulatory agencies

table 2.6 Key Things to Consider in Developing a Code of Ethics

- Create a team to assist with the process of developing the code (include management and non-management employees from across departments and functions).
- Solicit input from employees from different departments, functions, and regions to compile a list of common questions and answers to include in the code document.
- Make certain that the headings of the code sections can be easily understood by all employees.
- Avoid referencing specific Canadian laws and regulations or those of specific countries, particularly for codes that will be distributed to employees in multiple regions.
- Hold employee group meetings on a complete draft version (including graphics and pictures) of the text using language that everyone can understand.
- Inform employees that they will receive a copy of the code during an introduction session.
- Let all employees know that they will receive future ethics training which will, in part, cover the important information contained in the code document.

SOURCE: Adapted from William Miller, "Implementing an Organizational Code of Ethics," *International Business Ethics Review* 7 (Winter 2004), pp. 1, 6–10.

hotlines and established procedures for anonymous reporting. Unfortunately, whistleblowers are often treated negatively in organizations.

The current trend is to move away from legally based ethical initiatives in organizations to cultural- or integrity-based initiatives that make ethics a part of core organizational values. Organizations recognize that effective business ethics programs are good for business performance. Firms that develop higher levels of trust function more efficiently and effectively and avoid damaged company reputations and product images. Organizational ethics initiatives have been supportive of many positive and diverse organizational objectives, such as profitability, hiring, employee satisfaction, and customer loyalty.[62] Conversely, lack of organizational ethics initiatives and the absence of workplace values such as honesty, trust, and integrity can have a negative impact on organizational objectives. According to one report on employee loyalty and work practices, 79 percent of employees who questioned their bosses' integrity indicated that they felt uncommitted or were likely to quit soon.[63]

"The Canadian government is hoping to encourage whistleblowers to inform them about tax cheats. Revenue Canada is offering whistleblowers a 15 percent commission on money collected as a result of tips."

The Nature of Social Responsibility

There are four dimensions of social responsibility: economic, legal, ethical, and voluntary (including philanthropic) (Figure 2.3).[64] Earning profits is the economic foundation of the pyramid in Figure 2.3, and complying with the law is the next step. However a business whose *sole* objective is to maximize profits is not likely to consider its social responsibility, although its activities will probably be legal. (We looked at ethical responsibilities in the first half of this chapter.) Finally, voluntary responsibilities are additional activities that may not be required but which promote human welfare or goodwill. Legal and economic concerns have long been acknowledged in business, but voluntary and ethical issues are more recent concerns.

> **Corporate citizenship** the extent to which businesses meet the legal, ethical, economic, and voluntary responsibilities placed on them by their stakeholders

Corporate citizenship is the extent to which businesses meet the legal, ethical, economic, and voluntary responsibilities placed on them by their various stakeholders. It involves the activities and organizational processes adopted by businesses to meet their social responsibilities. A commitment to corporate citizenship by a firm indicates a strategic focus on fulfilling the social responsibilities expected of it by its stakeholders.

Corporate citizenship involves action and measurement of the extent to which a firm embraces the corporate citizenship philosophy and then follows through by implementing citizenship and social responsibility initiatives. Nexen, a Canadian-based, global energy company, follows the Imagine Canada guidelines, committing 1 percent of pre-tax earnings to community investment. The company recently donated $7.2 million. Nexen Inc. is rated one of the "Top 50 Companies to Work For in Canada"[65] and spearheaded the development of the "International Code of Ethics for Canadian Business" in 1997 as a template for Canadian businesses to follow when conducting business at home and abroad. Nexen received an award from the federal government for this initiative.[66] Nexen was recently taken over by Hong Kong-based CNOOC Limited.

Most companies today consider being socially responsible a cost of doing business. Corporate Knights, a Canadian-based media company with a focus on corporate responsibility, publishes an annual list of Canada's Best 50 Corporate Citizens based on 13 key indicators, such as: reducing factory emissions, paying CEOs a fair wage relative to earnings, providing leadership opportunities to women and visible minorities, paying their fair share of taxes, avoiding work stoppages, and making sure workers' pension funds are properly funded.[67]

Although the concept of social responsibility is receiving more and more attention, it is still not universally accepted. Table 2.7 lists some of the arguments for and against social responsibility.

"Organizations recognize that effective business ethics programs are good for business performance."

Social Responsibility Issues

As with ethics, managers consider social responsibility on a daily basis as they deal with real issues. Among the many social issues that managers must consider are their firms' relations with owners and shareholders, employees, consumers, the environment, and the community.

figure 2.3 The Pyramid of Social Responsibility

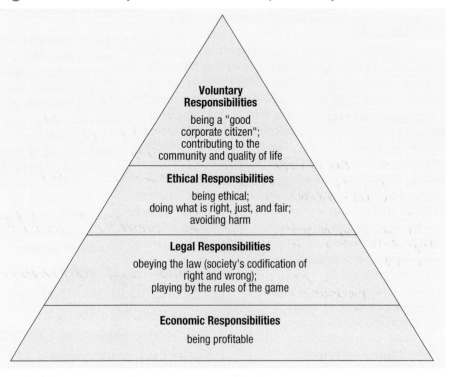

SOURCE: Reprinted with permission from A. B. Carroll, "The Pyramid of Corporate Social Responsibility: Toward the Moral Management of Organizational Stakeholders," *Business Horizons*, July/August 1991. Copyright © 1991 by the Board of Trustees at Indiana University, Kelley School of Business.

Social responsibility is a dynamic area with issues changing constantly in response to society's desires. There is much evidence that social responsibility is associated with improved business performance. Consumers are refusing to buy from businesses that receive publicity about misconduct. A number of studies have found a direct relationship between social responsibility and profitability, as well as that social responsibility is linked to employee commitment and customer loyalty—major concerns of any firm trying to increase profits.[68] This section highlights a few of the many social responsibility issues that managers face; as managers become aware of and work toward the solution of current social problems, new ones will certainly emerge.

| **L05** | Debate an organization's social responsibilities to owners, employees, consumers, the environment, and the community. |

Relations With Owners and Shareholders. Businesses must first be responsible to their owners, who are primarily concerned with earning a profit or a return on their investment in a company. In a small business, this responsibility is fairly easy to fulfill because the owner(s) personally manages the business or knows the managers well. In larger businesses, particularly corporations owned by thousands of shareholders, ensuring responsibility to the owners becomes a more difficult task.

A business's responsibilities to its owners and investors, as well as to the financial community at large, include maintaining proper accounting procedures, providing all relevant information to investors about the current and projected performance of the firm, and protecting the owners' rights and investments. In short, the business must maximize the owners' investment in the firm.

Employee Relations. Another issue of importance to a business is its responsibilities to employees, for without employees a business cannot carry out its goals. Employees expect businesses to provide a safe workplace, pay them adequately for their work, and tell them what is happening in their company. They want employers to listen to their grievances and treat them fairly. As noted at the start of the chapter, sometimes it is difficult to determine if businesses are acting ethically and responsibly to their employees as their motives often differ. Businesses usually want to maximize value for their

shareholders while employees often want to maximize their own earnings. Thus there is often an ongoing debate about what is considered adequate pay. In Canada's auto sector, assembly workers earned approximately $80 an hour including benefits and received numerous other perks. When General Motors and Ford attempted to cut labour costs, the Canada Auto Workers Union (CAW) fought strongly against the move.[69] In order to engage employees, many business such as WestJet and Royal Bank offer employees an opportunity to own shares in their company.[70] The result is employees who feel more engaged and interested in the performance of the company. Employee ownership programs are not just limited to large businesses. *Profit* magazine, a Canadian publication that covers small- and mid-size businesses in Canada, has discovered that many small firms are encouraging employees to become shareholders in their company.

The Canadian government has passed several laws regulating safety in the workplace. Labour unions have also made significant contributions to achieving safety in the workplace and improving wages and benefits. Most organizations now recognize that the safety and satisfaction of their employees are critical ingredients in their success, and many strive to go beyond what is expected of them by the law. Healthy, satisfied employees supply more than just labour to their employers, however. Employers are beginning to realize the importance of obtaining input from even the lowest-level employees to help the company reach its objectives.

A major social responsibility for business is providing equal opportunities for all employees regardless of their sex, age, race, religion, or nationality. Women and minorities have been slighted in the past in terms of education,

table 2.7 The Arguments For and Against Social Responsibility

For:

1. Business helped to create many of the social problems that exist today, so it should play a significant role in solving them, especially in the areas of pollution reduction and cleanup.

2. Businesses should be more responsible because they have the financial and technical resources to help solve social problems.

3. As members of society, businesses should do their fair share to help others.

4. Socially responsible decision making by businesses can prevent increased government regulation.

5. Social responsibility is necessary to ensure economic survival: If businesses want educated and healthy employees, customers with money to spend, and suppliers with quality goods and services in years to come, they must take steps to help solve the social and environmental problems that exist today.

Against:

1. It sidetracks managers from the primary goal of business—earning profits. Every dollar donated to social causes or otherwise spent on society's problems is a dollar less for owners and investors.

2. Participation in social programs gives businesses greater power, perhaps at the expense of particular segments of society.

3. Some people question whether business has the expertise needed to assess and make decisions about social problems.

4. Many people believe that social problems are the responsibility of government agencies and officials, who can be held accountable by voters.

If you search the Internet for information regarding Nestlé, you are likely to come across a large amount of documentation referring to a 30-year-old scandal involving infant formula and poor handling of the resolution of debt owed by Ethiopia. Critics argue that Nestlé's socially responsible activities serve only as cover-ups for these scandals. Whatever the truth may be, Nestlé appears to be a company learning from its past mistakes—sometimes, the errors of the past can be great motivators to do good in the future. In the past few years, Nestlé has been working to promote itself as a company focused more on wellness, and for many years—although perhaps overshadowed by negative publicity—the company has been heavily focused on helping to improve the lives of people in Africa.

Nestlé opened the first of 27 African factories in South Africa in 1927. Since that time, African consumers have come to view Nestlé products as familiar parts of their lives. The company employs around 11,500 people in Africa; only 120 of those people are from other countries. Companies working with Nestlé provide about 50,000 additional jobs. In 2004, the dean of the University of Ibadan's Faculty of Social Sciences found that in Nigeria, Nestlé employees earn above-average manufacturing wages. It was noted that more than 75 percent of those employees would decline to change jobs if given the option. Nestlé is reputed to be a large supporter of bettering the standard of living in African communities.

Nestlé does not own farmland in Africa, but it does work to help local farmers improve the quality of their crops and often their incomes. For example, Nestlé is the largest direct buyer of coffee in the world. The company also invests highly in research on how to help farmers improve the quality of their coffee crops. By improving the quality, the farmers can become more competitive in the global market.

In Africa, Nestlé is committed to improving the labour standards of farming, promoting local African products, preserving water, creating less waste, and offering nutritional education. Nestlé is also contributing to the United Nations' Millennium Development Goals in Africa to wipe out extreme poverty and hunger; ensure universal primary education; promote gender equality and empower women; reduce child mortality; improve maternal health; fight HIV/AIDS, malaria, and other diseases; and work toward environmental sustainability. Nestlé is committed, in a wide variety of ways, to helping people in Africa lead high-quality, healthy lives.[71]

DISCUSSION QUESTIONS

1. Do you think that Nestlé's socially responsible activities today have made up for possible mistakes involving infant formula in the past?

2. What has Nestlé done to improve its image in Africa?

3. What can Nestlé do to improve its commitment to Africa?

employment, and advancement opportunities; additionally, many of their needs have not been addressed by business. For example, as many as 1.6 million current and former female Walmart employees filed a class-action discrimination lawsuit accusing the giant retailer of paying them lower wages and salaries than men in comparable positions. Pretrial proceedings uncovered not only discrepancies between the pay of men and women, but also the fact that men dominate higher-paying store manager positions while women occupy more than 90 percent of cashier jobs, most of which pay about $14,000 a year. Walmart faces fines and penalties in the millions of dollars if found guilty of sexual discrimination.[72] Women, who continue to bear most child-rearing responsibilities, often experience conflict between those responsibilities and their duties as employees. Consequently, day care has become a major employment issue for women, and more companies are providing day care facilities as part of their effort to recruit and advance women in the workforce. In addition, companies are considering alternative scheduling such as flex-time and job sharing to accommodate employee concerns. Telecommuting has grown significantly over the past 5 to 10 years, as well. Many Canadians today believe business has a social obligation to provide special opportunities for women and minorities to improve their standing in society.

Consumer Relations. A critical issue in business today is business's responsibility to customers, who look to business to provide them with satisfying, safe products and to respect their rights as consumers. The activities that independent individuals, groups, and organizations undertake to protect their rights as consumers are known as **consumerism.** To achieve their objectives, consumers and their advocates

> **Consumerism** the activities that independent individuals, groups, and organizations undertake to protect their rights as consumers

write letters to companies, lobby government agencies, make public service announcements, and boycott companies whose activities they deem irresponsible.

Many of those involved in the consumer movement argue that consumers should have four specific rights. The *right to safety* means that a business must not knowingly sell anything that could result in personal injury or harm to consumers. Defective or dangerous products erode public confidence in the ability of business to serve society. They also result in expensive litigation that ultimately increases the cost of products for all consumers. The right to safety also means businesses must provide a safe place for consumers to shop. In recent years, many large retailers have been under increasing pressure to improve safety in their large warehouse-type stores. At Home Depot, for example, three consumer deaths and numerous serious injuries have been caused by falling merchandise. One lawsuit brought against the company over injuries received in one of its stores resulted in a $1.5 million

judgment. To help prevent further deaths, injuries, and litigation, Home Depot now has a corporate safety officer and has hired 130 safety managers to monitor store compliance with new safety measures.[73]

The *right to be informed* gives consumers the freedom to review complete information about a product before they buy it. This means that detailed information about ingredients, risks, and instructions for use are to be printed on labels and packages.

The *right to choose* ensures that consumers have access to a variety of products and services at competitive prices. The assurance of both satisfactory quality and service at a fair price is also a part of the consumer's right to choose. Some consumers are not being given the right to choose. Many are being billed for products and services they never ordered.

The *right to be heard* assures consumers that their interests will receive full and sympathetic consideration when the government formulates policy. It also ensures the fair treatment of consumers who voice complaints about a purchased product.

The role of provincial and federal governments is to protect consumers against unfair, deceptive, or fraudulent practices. Canada's Office of Consumer Affairs, a part of Industry Canada, works with both the public and private sectors, using information, research, and policy to complement and support consumer protection regulation.[74]

Environmental Issues. Environmental responsibility has become a leading issue as both business and the public acknowledge the damage done to the environment in the past. Today's consumers are increasingly demanding that businesses take a greater responsibility for their actions and how they impact the environment.

Animal Rights One area of environmental concern in society today is animal rights. Probably the most controversial business practice in this area is the testing of cosmetics and drugs on animals who may be injured or killed as a result. Animal-rights activists, such as People for the Ethical Treatment of Animals, say such research is morally wrong because it harms living creatures. Consumers who share this sentiment may boycott companies that test products on animals and take their business instead to companies such as The Body Shop and John Paul Mitchell Systems, which do not use animal testing. However, researchers in the cosmetics and pharmaceutical industries argue that animal testing is necessary to prevent harm to human beings who will eventually use the products. Business practices that harm wildlife and their habitats are another environmental issue. The seal hunt is one such controversial issue in Canada and around the world. Many Canadians argue that hunting seals is the same as farming beef cows or pigs, while animal rights groups argue that it is unethical and cruel. The hunt of 25-day-old seals takes place every March in the waters off the coast of Newfoundland. The federal government says the landed value of seals was $26.5 million in 2006 when 350,000 seals were killed, and provides a "significant" source of income for thousands of sealers.[75] The International Fund for Animal Welfare (IFAW) describes the contribution of sealing to Newfoundland's GDP as "trivial" and says after costs and indirect subsidies are taken into account, Canadians would "likely find that the hunt actually costs the Canadian taxpayer money." It is a pointless activity, in the view of the IFAW, which says, "the only economically valuable part of the seal is its fur, a non-essential luxury product that no one really needs."[76] Most of the pelts are exported to Russia and China where demand is strong and growing. IFAW and other interest groups including many consumers recently struck a blow to the sealing industry when the European Union banned imported seal products. This

ban, along with mild weather which prevents sealers from going on the ice, has seriously limited the seal hunt in recent years.

Pollution. Another major issue in the area of environmental responsibility is pollution. Water pollution results from dumping toxic chemicals and raw sewage into rivers and oceans, oil spills, and the burial of industrial waste in the ground where it may filter into underground water supplies. Water pollution and oil spills dominated the news in 2010, with the BP oil spill overshadowing other disasters. The blowout of the Deep Horizon oil rig resulted in the release of almost 5 million barrels of oil into the Gulf of Mexico, and its effects have been felt around the world. Environmentalists and governments are worried about the long-term impact of the spill on marine life and small industries such as fishing that rely on the Gulf waters.[77] The spill has also impacted oil drilling in Canada. At the time of the spill, the Nova Scotia government was deciding whether it should allow deep-water oil drilling on George's Bank, an area known for its vast undersea wildlife. The government opted not to allow drilling for exploration wells until at least 2015 in order to give science more time to study the impact of underwater exploration. While the Nova Scotia government did not cite the BP oil spill in its news release announcing the moratorium, political pundits all agreed that it influenced the decision.[78] Fertilizers and insecticides used in farming and grounds maintenance also run off into water supplies with each rainfall. Water pollution problems are especially notable in heavily industrialized areas. Medical waste—such as used syringes, vials of blood, and AIDS-contaminated materials—has turned up on beaches in Toronto, Halifax, and Vancouver, as well as other places. In May of 2000, the water supply of Walkerton, Ontario, was contaminated with *E. coli* bacteria. The result was that seven people died and 2,300 were made ill. The suspected cause of the contamination was untreated manure from a dairy farm being carried into a municipal well by spring runoff. A judicial inquiry held that no regulations were broken by the farmer. As a result of such occurrences, society is demanding that regulations be enacted and enforced to safe-guard clean, healthful water supplies. The inquiry resulted in 93 recommendations of which 50 were included in the Ontario Safe Drinking Water Act of 2002.[79]

Air pollution is usually the result of smoke and other pollutants emitted by manufacturing facilities, as well as carbon monoxide and hydrocarbons emitted by motor vehicles. In addition to the health risks posed by air pollution, when some chemical compounds emitted by manufacturing facilities react with air and rain, acid rain results. Acid rain has contributed to the deaths of many valuable forests and lakes in North America as well as in Europe. Air pollution may also contribute to global warming in which

> "Related to the problem of land pollution is the larger issue of how to dispose of waste in an environmentally responsible manner."

carbon dioxide collects in the earth's atmosphere, trapping the sun's heat and preventing the earth's surface from cooling. Chlorofluorocarbons also harm the earth's ozone layer, which filters out the sun's harmful ultraviolet light; this too may be a cause of the greenhouse effect.

In 1997, 39 of the world's richest countries agreed to curb greenhouse-gas emissions at the Kyoto Climate Change Conference. However, the resulting Kyoto Protocol, enacted in February 2005, had little impact because it did not require developing countries to cut their emissions, and because the U.S. was not a party to it. Although Canada, under the Liberals, was one of the countries to sign the Kyoto Protocol in 1998, the Conservative government reneged on that agreement to meet greenhouse-gas targets with the introduction of the Clean Air Act to regulate industrial pollutants. The legislation took effect in January 2010. At present, rich countries emit more CO_2 than developing countries. Nevertheless, developing countries as a whole will shortly overtake rich countries, and China, the most populous of the emerging economies, will become the world's biggest greenhouse-gas emitter by 2015. Every year, China builds 60 gigawatts of power-generation capacity, and four-fifths of Chinese power is generated by coal, the dirtiest source of electricity. China currently uses 40 percent of the world's coal—more than the U.S., Europe, and Japan put together.[80]

Land pollution is tied directly to water pollution because many of the chemicals and toxic wastes that are dumped on the land eventually work their way into the water supply.

GOING GREEN | EarthCraft Houses—Crafted for Earth

These days, almost everyone seems to be going green. However, most people seek easy solutions such as purchasing local organic produce, buying chemical-free household products, or driving a hybrid car. Most of us probably believe that not many people live in homes that are entirely "green." Although it may not be page-one news, the green trend is growing in today's housing market. Among those companies promoting green living is EarthCraft House. Founded in 1999 by the Atlanta Home Builders Association and Southface Home, Earth-Craft aims to build comfortable homes that reduce utility costs while at the same time benefiting the environment.

As of 2007, EarthCraft House had certified more than 4,000 single-family homes and 1,500 multifamily dwelling units within the Atlanta metro area. Atlanta also boasts six EarthCraft communities. EarthCraft House has expanded beyond Georgia to South Carolina, Alabama, Tennessee, and Virginia. All are supported by local state agencies and home-builders' associations. Similar organizations exist in Florida (Green Building Coalition) and North Carolina (Healthy Built Homes).

So, what is an EarthCraft house? The house can be newly constructed or renovated, and can be tailored to fit price point. To be certified by EarthCraft, a house must meet certain guidelines in energy efficiency, durability, indoor air quality, resource efficiency, waste management, and water conservation. All new homes must meet ENERGY STAR certification criteria and must score at least 150 points on an EarthCraft scoring sheet. Those homes that score 200 or 230 points are awarded *select* or *premium* status, respectively.

So, how does an EarthCraft house benefit the environment, and how does it benefit the homeowner? To answer these questions, a little background information is required. Construction and maintenance of homes and offices are major sources of CO_2 emissions. EarthCraft houses, on the other hand, can reduce emissions by more than 1,100 pounds of greenhouse gases per home each year. EarthCraft homes also use as many recycled and renewable materials as possible, as well as conserving water and reducing storm water pollution.

Homeowner benefits are twofold. One of the aims of EarthCraft is to create a healthier home. For example, an EarthCraft home can reduce levels of mould, mildew, and dust. Therefore EarthCraft homes can benefit our bodies in addition to reducing our carbon footprint. An EarthCraft home can also benefit our wallets. Earth-Craft home buyers can take advantage of two different kinds of mortgage incentives. The Energy Efficient Mortgage increases the buyer's purchasing power due to the lower operating costs of an energy-efficient home. The Energy Improvement Mortgage can be used to finance energy-efficient upgrades on an existing home. All in all, EarthCraft and similar companies predicted that by 2010, 10 percent of all homes would be green.[81]

DISCUSSION QUESTIONS

1. In addition to reducing carbon dioxide emissions, what are other reasons to build an energy-efficient, "green" house?

2. What type of incentive would cause you to pay extra for an energy-efficient house?

3. What additional incentives might convince people to go green when building or remodelling their homes?

Land pollution results from the dumping of residential and industrial waste, strip mining, forest fires, and poor forest conservation. In Brazil and other South American countries, rain forests are being destroyed—at a rate of one hectare every two minutes—to make way for farms and ranches, at a cost of the extinction of the many animals and plants (some endangered species) that call the rain forest home. Large-scale deforestation also depletes the oxygen supply available to humans and other animals.

Related to the problem of land pollution is the larger issue of how to dispose of waste in an environmentally responsible manner. One specific solid waste problem is being created by rapid innovations in computer hardware that make many computers obsolete after just 18 months. By 2005, 350 million computers had reached obsolescence, and at least 55 million were expected to end up in landfills.[83] Computers contain toxic substances such as lead, mercury, and polyvinyl chloride, which can leach into the soil and contaminate the groundwater when disposed of improperly. In Europe, the Waste of Electrical and Electronic Equipment (WEEE) legislation aims to reduce the waste arising from this equipment. The key elements are that users recycle equipment free of charge, while producers (manufacturers, sellers, and distributors) are responsible for financing the collection, treatment, recovery, and disposal of WEEE from the recycling facilities.[84]

Response to Environmental Issues.   Partly in response to laws and partly due to consumer concerns, businesses are responding to environmental issues. Many small and large companies, including the Irving Group, Suncor, Black-Berry, Walt Disney Company, Chevron, and Scott Paper, have created new positions to help them achieve their business goals in an environmentally responsible manner. A survey indicated that 83.5 percent of *Fortune* 500 companies have a written environmental policy, 74.7 percent engage in recycling efforts, and 69.7 percent have made investments in waste-reduction efforts.[85] Many companies, including Alcoa, Dow Chemical, Phillips Petroleum, and Raytheon, now link executive pay to environmental performance.[86] Some companies are finding that environmental consciousness can save them money. DuPont saved more than $3 billion through energy conservation by replacing natural gas with methane in its industrial boilers in many of its plants.[87]

Many firms are trying to eliminate wasteful practices, the emission of pollutants, and/or the use of harmful chemicals. For example, Toronto-based Delta hotels

DID YOU KNOW?

It takes one barrel of oil to produce six barrels of oil from the Athabasca Tar Sands in Alberta.[82]

is in the process of introducing Delta Greens, a national sustainability program aimed at improving environmental practices. Marriott Hotels of Canada have also engaged in similar environmentally friendly practices by using low-energy light bulbs and low-flow showerheads in their guest rooms.[88] Other companies are seeking ways to improve their products to minimize the environmental impact. Lush Fresh Handmade Cosmetics, a Vancouver-based cosmetic retailer, has averted 6 million plastic bottles from landfills by selling shampoo in bars.[89] Utility providers, for example, are increasingly supplementing their services with alternative energy sources, including solar, wind, and geothermal power. Many businesses have turned to *recycling*, the reprocessing of materials—aluminum, paper, glass, and some plastic—for reuse. The above-mentioned Lush Fresh Handmade Cosmetics uses recycled material in its packaging 90 percent of the time. Such efforts to make products, packaging, and processes more environmentally friendly have been labelled "green" business or marketing by the public and media. Lumber products at Home Depot may carry a seal from the Forest Stewardship Council to indicate that they were harvested from sustainable forests using environmentally friendly methods.[90] Likewise, most Chiquita bananas are certified through the Better Banana Project as having been grown with more environmentally and labour friendly practices.[91]

It is important to recognize that, with current technology, environmental responsibility requires trade-offs. Society must weigh the huge costs of limiting or eliminating pollution against the health threat posed by the pollution. Environmental responsibility imposes costs on both business and the public. Although people certainly do not want oil fouling beautiful waterways and killing wildlife, they insist on low-cost, readily available gasoline and heating oil. People do not want to contribute to the growing garbage-disposal problem, but they often refuse to pay more for "green" products packaged in an environmentally friendly manner, to recycle as much of their own waste as possible, or to permit the building of additional waste-disposal facilities (the "not in my backyard," or NIMBY, syndrome). Managers must coordinate environmental goals with other social and economic ones.

Community Relations.   A final, yet very significant, issue for businesses concerns their responsibilities to the general welfare of the communities and societies in which they operate. Many businesses want to make their

British Petroleum (BP) has become synonymous with the worst oil leak disaster in U.S. waters to date. Simply put, BP failed to adequately prepare for a worst-case scenario. When the Deepwater Horizon oil rig exploded, killing eleven workers and pouring millions of litres of oil into the Gulf of Mexico, BP had no effective contingency plan. The crisis immediately spun out of control.

Not only did BP underestimate the risks, but some suggest it willfully cut corners to save money. A rig technician accused BP of knowing that the rig's blow-out preventer was leaking weeks prior to the explosion. Similar accusations of risky or negligent behaviour soon followed. Two months into the disaster, it was revealed that one-third of BP's deep water oil rig designs were deemed risky by government inspectors—a higher percentage than those of other oil companies.

Effective business ethics requires firms to identify risks and educate employees to deal with issues related to the risks. BP did not adequately acknowledge the risks despite warnings from industry experts. It also had no effective crisis management plan in place. BP did have a spill-response plan; however, its plan proved ineffective to handle the situation.

The disaster has undermined BP's reputation, and its ethics and social responsibility have been questioned by stakeholders. Many consumers responded by boycotting BP gas stations and products. The disaster has overshadowed BP's positive multimillion dollar investments in renewable energy. BP has implemented a $20 billion Deepwater Horizon Oil Spill Trust to pay out claims and a $500 million Gulf of Mexico Research Initiative to fund the study of the impacts of the disaster,

British Petroleum (BP) has become synonymous with the worst oil leak disaster in U.S. waters to date.

among other initiatives. BP has a long history of environmental disasters and safety violations. What will it take to improve the reputation of BP?[92]

DISCUSSION QUESTIONS

1. Are BP's attempts at compensation enough to change the company's reputation in the eyes of consumers?

2. What are the ethical considerations that BP failed to recognize in its management of risks?

3. How important is BP's reputation for business success?

"Many businesses want to make their communities better places for everyone to live and work."

communities better places for everyone to live and work. The most common way that businesses exercise their community responsibility is through donations to local and national charitable organizations. Nationally, Statistics Canada reports that millions of individual and corporate donors contributed a record high $10 billion in 2007. The number did drop sharply to just over $8 billion in 2008 as the economic crisis appeared to be hindering donations. However, corporate donations are once again on the rise. Examples of donations include Delta Hotels' support of Habitat for Humanity Canada, CIBC's sponsorship of MADD Canada, and significant contributions by Pfizer Canada and Boardwalk Realty to the Canadian Mental Health Association.[93]

Turn the clock back: imagine it's 2008 and the Canadian government is being asked to supply the Big Three automakers—Ford, General Motors (GM), and Chrysler—with approximately $3 billion in bailout money. The car companies are arguing that if they cease operations, it will cost the country more than 100,000 jobs.

The three automakers have had their business hurt in the recent recession and have made numerous management missteps that have added to their economic pain. All three auto companies failed to foresee rising consumer demand for fuel-efficient vehicles and continued to produce much larger cars than consumers wanted. The three companies also produce too many similar cars. For example, up until 2008, GM manufactured Saturn, GM, Saab, Cadillac, Hummer, and Pontiac brands and operated too many dealerships in the same geographic region. The three companies are hampered by high wages, with employee costs coming in at approximately $80 an hour, and they also suffer from a significant pension shortfall (meaning that they do not have enough money to pay their past employees their contracted pension). While their market share has continued to drop throughout the 1990s and 2000s, their competitors including Honda, Toyota, and Hyundai have increased their market share by producing cars that people want.

As the automakers were pressing their case for government money, arguing that thousands of jobs would be lost without the injection of funds, another Canadian giant was going through a financial crisis of its own. Nortel Networks Corp., a technology company that was once the darling of Canada's Internet boom, was seriously hurt by the downturn in the economy and years of financial mismanagement. Nortel managers, like senior executives from the car companies, were meeting with government officials and looking for bailout money to the tune of $3 billion. Nortel managers were no doubt pointing out to government officials in Ottawa that the tech giant still employs thousands of people in Canada, that it is the biggest corporate spender on research and development in the country, and that Nortel's spending may in fact be paying off as its next-generation Long Term Evolution, or LTE, wireless technology is expected to deliver top broadband speeds of 100 megabits per second for voice and data transmission to mobile phones—over 14 times quicker than the top networks currently operating across Canada.

Turn the clock to 2009 and you would discover that the Canadian government did supply General Motors and Chrysler with roughly $3 billion between them and gave Ford an operating line of credit. In addition, management has attempted to lower costs by renegotiating contracts with labour unions, reducing the number of cars that they manufacture, and focusing on building the fuel-efficient cars that consumers want. Industry analysts are still unsure if the companies will be successful even with the changes. Nortel, on the other hand, did not receive a government bailout and the company was forced into bankruptcy in 2009. The company's assets were then auctioned off, including the licensing rights to LTE technology, which were sold to Ericsson (a Swedish company) for approximately $1.1 billion.[94]

DISCUSSION QUESTIONS

1. What are some of the potential pitfalls with bailouts? Do you think the government is acting ethically when it spends taxpayers' dollars on bailouts? Why or why not?

2. Do you think Ford, General Motors, and Chrysler will survive in the coming years?

3. Did the government have an ethical obligation to invest in Nortel for the betterment of Canada's scientific community?

TEAM EXERCISE

Sam Walton, founder of Walmart, had an early strategy for growing his business related to pricing. The "Opening Price Point" strategy used by Walton involved offering the introductory product in a product line at the lowest point in the market. For example, a minimally equipped microwave oven would sell for less than anyone else in town could sell the same unit. The strategy was that if consumers saw a product, such as the microwave, and saw it as a good value, they would assume that all of the microwaves were good values. Walton also noted that most people don't buy the entry-level product; they want more features and capabilities and often trade up.

Form teams and assign the role of defending this strategy or casting this strategy as an unethical act. Present your thoughts on either side of the issue.

LO1 Define business ethics and social responsibility and examine their importance.

Business ethics refers to principles and standards that define acceptable business conduct. Acceptable business behaviour is defined by customers, competitors, government regulators, interest groups, the public, and each individual's personal moral principles and values. Social responsibility is the obligation an organization assumes to maximize its positive impact and minimize its negative impact on society. Socially responsible businesses win the trust and respect of their employees, customers, and society and, in the long run, increase profits. Ethics is important in business because it builds trust and confidence in business relationships. Unethical actions may result in negative publicity, declining sales, and even legal action.

LO2 Detect some of the ethical issues that may arise in business.

An ethical issue is an identifiable problem, situation, or opportunity requiring a person or organization to choose from among several actions that must be evaluated as right or wrong. Ethical issues can be categorized in the context of their relation with conflicts of interest, fairness and honesty, communications, and business associations.

LO3 Specify how businesses can promote ethical behaviour by employees.

Businesses can promote ethical behaviour by employees by limiting their opportunity to engage in misconduct. For-mal codes of ethics, ethical policies, and ethics training programs reduce the incidence of unethical behaviour by informing employees of what is expected of them and providing punishments for those who fail to comply.

LO4 Explain the four dimensions of social responsibility.

The four dimensions of social responsibility are economic (being profitable), legal (obeying the law), ethical (doing what is right, just, and fair), and voluntary (being a good corporate citizen).

LO5 Debate an organization's social responsibilities to owners, employees, consumers, the environment, and the community.

Businesses must maintain proper accounting procedures, provide all relevant information about the performance of the firm to investors, and protect the owners' rights and investments. In relations with employees, businesses are expected to provide a safe workplace, pay employees adequately for their work, and treat them fairly. Consumerism refers to the activities undertaken by independent individuals, groups, and organizations to protect their rights as consumers. Increasingly, society expects businesses to take greater responsibility for the environment, especially with regard to animal rights, as well as water, air, land, and noise pollution. Many businesses engage in activities to make the communities in which they operate better places for everyone to live and work.

KEY TERMS

bribes
business ethics
codes of ethics
consumerism
corporate citizenship

ethical issue
plagiarism
social responsibility
whistleblowing

1. The Keystone Project has been in the news for the past few years. Prior to reading the opening case, what was your opinion and knowledge of the issues at hand? After reading the case, do you think TransCanada Corp. has acted ethically throughout the process?

2. TransCanada Corp. has been relying on facts to argue the merits of Keystone XL while many opponents have been making emotional arguments. What are some of the advantages and disadvantages of TransCanada's approach?

3. Given what you have read in the opening case, do you think Keystone XL will be approved for development?

SO YOU WANT A JOB *in Business Ethics and Social Responsibility*

In the words of Kermit the Frog, "It's not easy being green." It may not be easy, but green business opportunities abound. A popular catch phrase, "Green is the new black," indicates how fashionable green business is becoming. Consumers are more in tune with and concerned about green products, policies, and behaviours by companies than ever before. Companies are looking for new hires to help them see their business creatively and bring insights to all aspects of business operations. The American Solar Energy Society estimates that the number of green jobs could rise to 40 million in North America by 2030. Green business strategies not only give a firm a commercial advantage in the marketplace, but help lead the way toward a greener world. The fight to reduce our carbon footprint in an attempt to reverse climate change has opened up opportunities for renewable energy, recycling, conservation, and increasing overall efficiency in the way resources are used. New businesses that focus on hydro, wind, and solar power are on the rise and will need talented businesspeople to lead them. Carbon emissions trading is gaining popularity as large corporations and individuals alike seek to decrease their footprints. A job in this growing field could be similar to that of a stock trader, or you could lead the search for carbon-efficient companies in which to invest.

In the ethics arena, current trends in business governance strongly support the development of ethics and compliance departments to help guide organizational integrity. This alone is a billion-dollar business, and there are jobs in developing organizational ethics programs, developing company policies, and training employees and management. An entry-level position might be as a communication specialist or trainer for programs in a business ethics department. Eventually there's an opportunity to become an ethics officer with typical responsibilities of meeting with employees, the board of directors, and top management to discuss and advise on ethics issues in the industry; developing and distributing a code of ethics; creating and maintaining an anonymous, confidential service to answer questions about ethical issues; taking actions on possible ethics code violations; and reviewing and modifying the code of ethics of the organization.

There are also opportunities to support initiatives that help companies relate social responsibility to stakeholder interests and needs. These jobs could involve coordinating and implementing philanthropic programs that give back to others important to the organization or developing a community volunteering program for employees. In addition to the human relations function, most companies develop programs to assist employees and their families to improve their quality of life. Companies have found that the healthier and happier employees are, the more productive they will be in the workforce.

Social responsibility, ethics, and sustainable business practices are not a trend; they are good for business and the bottom line. New industries are being created and old ones are adapting to the new market demands, opening up many varied job opportunities that will lead not only to a paycheque, but to the satisfaction of making the world a better place.[95]

Business Ethics and Social Responsibility

Think about which industry you are considering competing in with your product/service. Are there any kind of questionable practices in the way the product has been traditionally sold? Produced? Advertised? Have there been any recent accusations regarding safety within the industry? What about any environmental concerns?

For example, if you are thinking of opening a lawn care business, you need to consider what possible effects the chemicals you are using will have on the client and the environment. You have a responsibility not to threaten your customers' health or safety. You also have the social responsibility to let the community know of any damaging effect you may be directly or indirectly responsible for.

CASE | Social Media and Privacy

As more and more people establish profile pages on social networking sites to kindle friendships (Facebook), create professional networks (LinkedIn), and inform people about the happenings in their day-to-day lives (Twitter), the line between public and private information has become blurred. While ten years ago much of this information may have only been shared with a small number of close friends, people now maintain online relationships that number in the thousands. This large network of contacts often includes professional relationships and employers.

Today, it is not uncommon to see someone post risqué photos on Facebook, state their opinion about their job or employer, and update their online friends about their sexual orientation and drinking habits. Unfortunately for some people, employers or potential employers, family members, and friends have accessed online information to help in evaluating a person's performance or potential performance; learn their opinions about work; determine who their friends are; and/or discover where they were the night before. The people who access and then use this information will often argue that the material is posted online in the public domain. For example, an employer may feel that they have just cause to discipline or fire an employee who criticizes their boss on Facebook or displays risqué photos of themselves from their recent vacation. Some social media users object to this behaviour and note that the information is not intended for public consumption. This begs the question, how can some people consider Facebook sites public and others consider them private? A recent exploratory study by Dr. Amy Thurlow, a professor at Halifax-based Mount Saint Vincent University, on the acceptable use of online information may shed

some light on the opposing viewpoints. During the course of the study she discovered that older people thought all information in the public domain including information on social media sites was public content and it was fair to use such information any way that they see fit. Others, in particular younger students, indicated that it was not the poster's responsibility to control what they put on their social media site, rather the visitor of the site should be expected to know what is private and what is intended for public viewing. For example, if someone posts risqué photos or private information about themselves on their Facebook profile, the view of the students was that people likely know who this information is intended for and visitors to Facebook should not view or use information that was not meant for their use.[96]

DISCUSSION QUESTIONS

1. Do you think employers should look at people's social media pages as part of the hiring process? Do you think employers should monitor employees' social media sites?

2. Who is responsible for privacy on social media sites—the person who posts the information or the person who visits the site?

3. Facebook, Twitter, and LinkedIn are valuable business tools. List some of the advantages and disadvantages that social media offers to: (1) students looking for a job; (2) businesses that are trying to market their products; (3) charities that are raising money.

connect LEARNSMART SMARTBOOK

For more information on the resources available from McGraw-Hill Ryerson, go to www.mcgrawhill.ca/he/solutions.

THE LEGAL AND REGULATORY ENVIRONMENT

Business law refers to the rules and regulations that govern the conduct of business. Problems in this area come from failure to keep promises, misunderstandings, disagreements about expectations, or, in some cases, attempts to take advantage of others. The regulatory environment offers a framework and enforcement system in order to provide a fair playing field for all businesses. The regulatory environment is created based on inputs from competitors, customers, employees, special interest groups, and the public's elected representatives. Lobbying by pressure groups who try to influence legislation often shapes the legal and regulatory environment.

Sources of Law

Canada's Constitution, including the Charter of Rights and Freedoms, is the foundation for Canada's legal system. The constitution stipulates the divisions of power between the provincial and the federal governments while the Charter outlines individual rights and freedoms. There are three basic sources of laws in Canada:

- Statutory law: developed by provincial or federal governments

- Administrative law: developed by regulatory agencies

- Common law: based on previous court decisions

Quebec only follows Canada's common law for criminal matters. For non-criminal matters, Quebec follows a codified system of civil law.

Courts and the Resolution of Disputes

The primary method of resolving conflicts and business disputes is through **lawsuits,** where one individual or organization takes another to court. The legal system, therefore, provides a forum for businesspeople to resolve disputes based on our legal foundations. The courts may decide when harm or damage results from the actions of others.

Because lawsuits are so frequent in the world of business, it is important to understand more about the court system where such disputes are resolved. Both financial restitution and specific actions to undo wrongdoing can result from going before a court to resolve a conflict. All decisions made in the courts are based on statutory, administrative, or common law except in Quebec where civil law is routinely used in business disputes.

A businessperson may win a lawsuit in court and receive a judgment, or court order, requiring the loser of the suit to pay monetary damages. However, this does not guarantee that the victor will be able to collect those damages. If the loser of the suit lacks the financial resources to pay the judgment—for example, if the loser is a bankrupt business—the winner of the suit may not be able to collect the award. Most business lawsuits involve a request for a sum of money, but some lawsuits request that a court specifically order a person or organization to do or to refrain from doing a certain act, such as scamming telephone customers.

"The primary method of resolving conflicts and business disputes is through lawsuits, where one individual or organization takes another to court."

Alternative Dispute Resolution Methods

Although the main remedy for business disputes is a lawsuit, other dispute resolution methods are becoming popular. The schedules of courts are often crowded; long delays between the filing of a case and the trial date are common. Further, complex cases can become quite expensive to pursue. As a result, many businesspeople are turning to alternative methods of resolving business arguments: mediation and arbitration, the mini-trial, and litigation in a private court.

Mediation is a form of negotiation to resolve a dispute by bringing in one or more third-party mediators, usually chosen by the disputing parties, to help reach a settlement. The mediator suggests different ways to resolve a dispute between the parties. The mediator's resolution is nonbinding—that is, the parties do not have to accept the mediator's suggestions; they are strictly voluntary.

Arbitration involves submission of a dispute to one or more third-party arbitrators, usually chosen by the disputing parties, whose decision usually is final. Arbitration differs from mediation in that an arbitrator's decision must be followed, whereas a mediator merely offers suggestions and facilitates negotiations. Cases may be submitted to arbitration because a contract—such as a labour contract—requires it or because the parties agree to do so. Arbitration can be an attractive alternative to a lawsuit because it is often cheaper and quicker, and the parties frequently can choose arbitrators who are knowledgeable about the particular area of business at issue.

Important Elements of Business Law

To avoid violating laws, as well as to discourage lawsuits from consumers, employees, suppliers, and others, businesspeople need to be familiar with laws that address business practices.

The Canadian Criminal Code

The Canadian Criminal Code is the codification of almost all of the criminal offences in Canada. The code is based on common law and is applicable throughout Canada including Quebec.

Sales Agreements. The Sales of Goods Act notes that sales transactions (excluding services) are a special type of contract. The Act also clarifies the use of warranties, which may be expressed and/or implied. An **express warranty** stipulates the specific terms the seller will honour. Many automobile manufacturers, for example, provide three-year or 60,000 km warranties on their vehicles, during which period they will fix any and all defects specified in the warranty. An **implied warranty** is imposed on the producer or seller by law, although it may not be a written document provided at the time of sale.

The Law of Torts and Fraud

A **tort** is a noncriminal act other than breach of contract. For example, a tort can result if the driver of a Boston Pizza delivery car loses control of the vehicle and damages property or injures a person. In the case of the delivery car accident, the injured persons might sue the driver and the owner of the company—Boston Pizza in this case—for damages resulting from the accident.

Fraud is a purposeful unlawful act to deceive or manipulate in order to damage others. Thus, in some cases, a tort may also represent a violation of criminal law. Insurance fraud has become a major issue in the courts.

An important aspect of tort law involves **product liability**—businesses' legal responsibility for any negligence in the design, production, sale, and consumption of products. Product liability laws have evolved from both common and statutory law.

The Law of Contracts

Virtually every business transaction is carried out by means of a **contract,** a mutual agreement between two or more parties that can be enforced by law. If you rent an apartment or house, for example, your lease is a contract. If you have borrowed money under a student loan program, you have a contractual agreement to repay the money. A "handshake deal" is in most cases as fully and completely binding as a written, signed contract agreement. Indeed, construction contractors have for years agreed to take on projects on the basis of such handshake deals. Some provinces stipulate that contracts involving the transfer of goods over a certain value must however be signed.

Only those contracts that meet certain requirements—called *elements*—are enforceable by the courts. A person or business seeking to enforce a contract must show that it contains the following elements: voluntary agreement, consideration, contractual capacity of the parties, and legality.

For any agreement to be considered a legal contract, all persons involved must agree to be bound by the terms of the contract. *Voluntary agreement* typically comes about when one party makes an offer and the other accepts. If both the offer and the acceptance are freely, voluntarily, and knowingly made, the acceptance forms the basis for the contract. If, however, either the offer or the acceptance is the result of fraud or force, the individual or organization subject to the fraud or force can void, or invalidate, the resulting agreement or receive compensation for damages.

The second requirement for enforcement of a contract is that it must be supported by *consideration*—that is, money or something of value must be given in return for fulfilling a contract. As a general rule, a person cannot be forced to abide by the terms of a promise unless that person receives a consideration. The something-of-value could be money, goods, services, or even a promise to do or not to do something.

Contractual capacity is the legal ability to enter into a contract. As a general rule, a court cannot enforce a contract if either party to the agreement lacks contractual capacity. A person's contractual capacity may be limited or nonexistent if he or she is a minor (under the age of 18), mentally unstable, or intoxicated.

Legality is the state or condition of being lawful. For an otherwise binding contract to be enforceable, both the purpose of and the consideration for the contract must be legal. A contract in which a bank loans money at a rate of interest prohibited by law, a practice known as usury, would be an illegal contract, for example. The fact that one of the parties may commit an illegal act while performing a contract does not render the contract itself illegal, however.

Breach of contract is the failure or refusal of a party to a contract to live up to his or her promises. In the case of an apartment lease, failure to pay rent would be considered breach of contract. The breaching party—the one who fails to comply—may be liable for monetary damages that he or she causes the other person.

The Law of Agency

An **agency** is a common business relationship created when one person acts on behalf of another and under that person's control. Two parties are involved in an agency relationship: The **principal** is the one who wishes to have a specific task accomplished; the **agent** is the one who acts on behalf of the principal to accomplish the task. Authors, movie stars, and athletes often employ agents to help them obtain the best contract terms.

The Law of Property

Property law is extremely broad in scope because it covers the ownership and transfer of all kinds of real, personal, and intellectual property. **Real property** consists of real estate

"An agency is a common business relationship created when one person acts on behalf of another and under that person's control."

and everything permanently attached to it; **personal property** basically is everything else. Personal property can be further subdivided into tangible and intangible property. *Tangible property* refers to items that have a physical existence, such as automobiles, business inventory, and clothing. *Intangible property* consists of rights and duties; its existence may be represented by a document or by some other tangible item. For example, accounts receivable, stock in a corporation, goodwill, and trademarks are all examples of intangible personal property. **Intellectual property** refers to property, such as musical works, artwork, books, and computer software, that is generated by a person's creative activities. The Canadian Intellectual Property Office administers intellectual property in Canada. Canadian companies go to great lengths to protect their intellectual property, as illustrated by the company Canada Goose. Canada Goose's popularity has increased in recent years and the company is spending a great deal of money to ensure that counterfeit products do not reach the marketplace.

Copyrights, patents, and trademarks provide protection to the owners of property by giving them the exclusive right to use it. *Copyright* protects the ownership rights on material (often intellectual property) such as books, music, videos, photos, and computer software. The creators of such works, or their heirs, generally have exclusive rights to the published or unpublished works for the creator's lifetime, plus 70 years. *Patents* give inventors exclusive rights to their invention for 20 years.

A *trademark* is a brand (name, mark, or symbol) that is registered with the Canadian Intellectual Property Office and is thus legally protected from use by any other firm. In Canada trademarks can last forever but they must be renewed every 15 years. Companies are diligent about protecting their trademarks both to avoid confusion in consumers' minds and because a term that becomes part of everyday language can no longer be trademarked. The names *aspirin* and *nylon,* for example, were once the exclusive property of their creators but became so widely used as product names (rather than brand names) that now anyone can use them.

The Law of Bankruptcy

Although few businesses and individuals intentionally fail to repay (or default on) their debts, sometimes they cannot fulfill their financial obligations. Individuals may charge goods and services beyond their ability to pay for them. Businesses may take on too much debt in order to finance growth, or business events such as an increase in the cost of commodities can bankrupt a company. An option of last resort in these cases is bankruptcy, or legal insolvency.

Individuals or companies may ask a bankruptcy court to declare them unable to pay their debts and thus release them from the obligation of repaying those debts. The debtor's assets may then be sold to pay off as much of the debt as possible. In the case of a personal bankruptcy, although the individual is released from repaying debts and can start over with a clean slate, obtaining credit after bankruptcy proceedings is very difficult.

3 Business in a Borderless World

LEARNING OBJECTIVES

LO1 Explore some of the factors within the international trade environment that influence business.

LO2 Investigate some of the economic, legal-political, social, cultural, and technological barriers to international business.

LO3 Specify some of the agreements, alliances, and organizations that may encourage trade across international boundaries.

LO4 Summarize the different levels of organizational involvement in international trade.

LO5 Contrast two basic strategies used in international business.

DESTINATION CEO

Jim Treliving After burgers and fries, pizza is the most popular restaurant food in North America. Boston Pizza International Inc. is Canada's No. 1 casual dining brand. Currently, there are more than 390 restaurants across North America. There are additional restaurants in the pipeline for global expansion as the company is now looking toward Australia, the United Kingdom, and eventually Asia. It is clear that growth will only continue through global expansion of the franchise.

It was more than 40 years ago when Jim Treliving walked into the original Boston Pizza restaurant in Edmonton and tried his first pizza. It was love at first taste and in a very short time it was to be his future. As a true visionary, born entrepreneur, and risk-taker, Jim saw the potential in the pizza restaurant business and left the security of his position as an RCMP officer to become a Boston Pizza franchisee. He opened his first restaurant in 1968 in Penticton, B.C. In the ensuing few years, he became friends with a local accountant, George Melville, who became his business partner in 1973. Today, the two men share responsibility as co-owners and co-chairmen of Canada's No. 1 casual dining chain.

To Jim, one of the most important parts of running a successful business is creating and maintaining a strong culture of camaraderie. No matter where he is, Jim makes a point of stopping in to say hello at every Boston Pizza in town. When he visits a restaurant, he always shakes hands with the staff and thanks them for their hard work. According to Jim, "You take people in as franchisees and they become part of your family."[1]

Introduction

Consumers around the world can drink Coca-Cola and Pepsi; eat at McDonald's and Pizza Hut; see movies from Mexico, England, France, Australia, and China; and watch CBC and Much Music on Toshiba and Sony televisions. The products you consume today are just as likely to have been made in China, Korea, or Germany as in North America. Likewise, consumers in other countries buy Western electrical equipment, clothing, rock music, cosmetics, and toiletries, as well as computers, robots, and earth-moving equipment.

Many Canadian firms are finding that international markets provide tremendous opportunities for growth. Accessing these markets can promote innovation, while intensifying global competition spurs companies to market better and less expensive products. Today, the more than 7.1 billion people who inhabit the earth create one tremendous marketplace.

In this chapter, we explore business in this exciting global marketplace. First, we'll look at the nature of international business, including barriers and promoters of trade across international boundaries. Next, we consider the levels of organizational involvement in international business. Finally, we briefly discuss strategies for trading across national borders.

The Role of International Business

International business refers to the buying, selling, and trading of goods and services across national boundaries. Falling political barriers and new technology are making it possible for more and more companies to sell their products overseas as well as at home. And, as differences among nations continue to blur, the trend toward the globalization of business is becoming increasingly important. Starbucks, for example, serves millions of global customers a week at more than 17,000 coffee shops in 55 countries.[3] Amazon.com, an online retailer, has global fulfillment/distribution centres from Mississauga to Beijing that fill millions of orders a day and ship them to customers in every corner of the world. Proctor and Gamble's Febreze brand passed the $1 billion mark partially due to its strong growth overseas. While North American sales of air fresheners have fallen in recent years, global sales have seen an increase.[4] Indeed, most of the world's population and two-thirds of its total purchasing power are outside of North America.

When McDonald's sells a Big Mac in Moscow, Sony sells a stereo in Vancouver, or a small Swiss medical supply company sells a shipment of orthopaedic devices to a hospital in Monterrey, Mexico, the sale affects the economies of the countries involved. The Canadian market, with 35 million consumers, makes up only a small part of the more than 7.1 billion people in the world to whom global companies must consider marketing. Global marketing requires balancing your global brand with the needs of local consumers.[5] To begin our study of international business, we must first consider some economic issues: why nations trade, exporting and importing, and the balance of trade.

> **International business**
> the buying, selling, and trading of goods and services across national boundaries

Why Nations Trade

Nations and businesses engage in international trade to obtain raw materials and goods that are otherwise unavailable to them or are available elsewhere at a lower price than that at which they themselves can produce. A nation, or individuals and organizations from a nation, sell surplus materials and goods to acquire funds to buy the goods, services, and ideas its people need. Poland and Hungary, for example, want to trade with Western nations so that they can acquire new technology and techniques to revitalize their formerly communist economies. Which goods and services a nation sells depends on what resources it has available.

Some nations have a monopoly on the production of a particular resource or product. Such a monopoly, or **absolute advantage,** exists when a country is the only source of an item, the only producer of an item, or the most efficient producer of an item. Because South Africa has the largest deposits of diamonds in the world, one company, De Beers Consolidated Mines, Ltd., controls a major portion of the world's diamond trade and uses its control to maintain high prices for gem-quality diamonds. The United States, until recently, held an absolute advantage in oil-drilling equipment. But an absolute advantage not based on the availability of natural resources rarely lasts, and Japan and Russia are now challenging the United States in the production of oil-drilling equipment.

Most international trade is based on **comparative advantage,** which occurs when a country specializes in products that it can supply more efficiently or at a lower cost than it can produce other items. Canada has a comparative advantage in wood products, minerals, and hydroelectric generation. Until recently, the United States had a comparative advantage in manufacturing automobiles, heavy machinery, airplanes, and weapons; other countries now hold the comparative advantage for many of these products. Other countries, particularly India and Ireland, are also gaining a comparative advantage in the provision of some services, such as call-centre operations, engineering, and software programming. The *opportunity cost* of a decision refers to what must be given up as a result of that decision. For example, if Canada has a choice between catching 10 fish or producing 10 apples, the opportunity cost of producing one apple is one fish. If Mexico can catch eight fish or produce four apples, then the opportunity cost of two fish is one apple. In this example, Canada has a comparative advantage in

> **DID YOU KNOW?**
> Subway has surpassed McDonald's as the largest global restaurant chain with over 33,000 locations.[2]

> **Absolute advantage** a monopoly that exists when a country is the only source of an item, the only producer of an item, or the most efficient producer of an item
>
> **Comparative advantage** the basis of most international trade, when a country specializes in products that it can supply more efficiently or at a lower cost than it can produce other items

> "Falling political barriers and new technology are making it possible for more and more companies to sell their products overseas as well as at home."

Companies such as KFC have become widely popular in China. Some are making more sales in China than they are in North America.

Outsourcing the transferring of manufacturing or other tasks—such as data processing—to countries where labour and supplies are less expensive

Exporting the sale of goods and services to foreign markets

Importing the purchase of goods and services from foreign sources

producing apples and Mexico has a comparative advantage in catching fish. Opportunity cost is the key to understanding comparative advantage: individuals and nations gain by producing goods at relatively low costs and exchanging their outputs for different goods produced by others at relatively low cost. As a result, companies are increasingly **outsourcing,** or transferring manufacturing and other tasks to countries where labour and supplies are less expensive. Outsourcing has become a controversial practice because many jobs have moved overseas where those tasks can be accomplished for lower costs. For example, the Philippines has surpassed India as the popular choice for call-centre jobs. Call-centre jobs are appealing to many Filipinos because the pay is almost as much as the average family income within the country. English is also one of the country's official languages, which makes it easier to communicate with English–speaking customers.[6]

"Outsourcing has become a controversial practice in [many Western nations]"

Trade Between Countries

To obtain needed goods and services and the funds to pay for them, nations trade by exporting and importing. **Exporting** is the sale of goods and services to foreign markets. Canada exported more than $457 billion in goods and services in 2011.[7] Canadian businesses export many goods and services, particularly energy products, industrial goods and materials (metals, chemicals, and fertilizers, etc.), and machinery and equipment products. **Importing** is the purchase of goods and services from foreign sources. Many of the goods you buy in Canada are likely to be imports or to have some imported components. Sometimes, you may not even realize they are imports. As shown in Table 3.1, Canada imported more than $456 billion in goods and services in 2011.[8]

Balance of Trade

You have probably read or heard about the fact that in some years Canada has a trade deficit. But what is a trade deficit? A nation's **balance of trade** is the difference in value between its exports and imports. Because some nations import more products than they export, they have a negative balance of trade, or **trade deficit.** Table 3.2 shows Canada's principal trading partners and whether Canada has a trade deficit or a trade surplus with them. In 2011, Canada had a trade surplus of about $1.0 billion, recovering from a trade deficit of $10.8 billion The trade deficit fluctuates according to such factors as the economic health of Canada and other countries, productivity, perceived quality, and exchange rates. In 2011, Canada had a $4.9 billion trade surplus with the United States and a $31.4 billion trade deficit with China.[9] Trade deficits are harmful because they can mean the failure of businesses, the loss of jobs, and a lowered standard of living.

Of course, when a nation exports more goods than it imports, it has a favourable balance of trade, or trade surplus. Until 2008, Canada had a trade surplus due to trade in automotive products, machinery and equipment, and an abundance of natural resources, including crude oil and related energy products.[10]

The difference between the flow of money into and out of a country is called its **balance of payments.** A country's balance of trade, foreign investments, foreign aid, loans, military expenditures, and money spent by tourists comprise its balance of payments. As you might expect, a country with a trade surplus generally has a favourable balance of payments because it is receiving more money from trade with foreign

Balance of trade the difference in value between a nation's exports and its imports

Trade deficit a nation's negative balance of trade, which exists when that country imports more products than it exports

Balance of payments the difference between the flow of money into and out of a country

table 3.1 Canada's Trade Balance, 2006–2011 (in millions of dollars)

	2006	2007	2008	2009	2010	2011
Exports	451,971	461,385	487,261	367,429	403,071	456,518
Imports	404,510	415,790	443,592	373,984	413,847	455,606
Balance	47,461	45,595	43,669	−6,554	−10,776	912

SOURCE: Adapted from Statistics Canada, "Imports, exports and trade balance of goods on a balance-of-payments basis, by country or country grouping," http://www.statcan.gc.ca/tables-tableaux/sum-som/l01/cst01/gblec02a-eng.htm (accessed January 7, 2012).

table 3.2 Canada's Top 5 Trading Partners (2011)

Export Destinations	Import Sources
1. United States	United States
2. United Kingdom	China
3. China	Mexico
4. Japan	Japan
5. Mexico	Germany

SOURCE: Adapted from Statistics Canada, Exports, top five countries of destination in 2011, customs basis, http://www.statcan.gc.ca/daily-quotidien/120404/t120404a001-eng.htm, Imports, top five countries of origin in 2011, customs basis, http://www.statcan.gc.ca/daily-quotidien/120404/t120404a002-eng.htm (accessed January 7, 2012).

countries than it is paying out. When a country has a trade deficit, more money flows out of the country than into it. If more money flows out of the country than into it from tourism and other sources, the country may experience declining production and higher unemployment, because there is less money available for spending.

LO2 Investigate some of the economic, legal-political, social, cultural, and technological barriers to international business.

International Trade Barriers

Completely free trade seldom exists. When a company decides to do business outside its own country, it will encounter a number of barriers to international trade. Any firm considering international business must research the other country's economic, legal, political, social, cultural, and technological background. Such research will help the company choose an appropriate level of involvement and operating strategies, as we will see later in this chapter.

Economic Barriers

When looking at doing business in another country, managers must consider a number of basic economic factors, such as economic development, infrastructure, and exchange rates.

Economic Development. When considering doing business abroad, businesspeople need to recognize that they cannot take for granted that other countries offer the same things as are found in *industrialized nations*—economically advanced countries such as Canada, Japan, Great Britain, and the United States. Many countries in Africa, Asia, and South America, for example, are in general poorer and less economically advanced than those in North America and Europe; they are often called *less-developed countries*

(LDCs). LDCs are characterized by low per-capita income (income generated by the nation's production of goods and services divided by the population), which means that consumers are less likely to purchase nonessential products. Nonetheless, LDCs represent a potentially huge and profitable market for many businesses because they may be buying technology to improve their infrastructures, and much of the population may desire consumer products. For example, pharmaceutical companies offer infant vaccines in LDCs at a fraction of what they cost in developed countries. As emerging economies such as China and India have begun to prosper, more citizens are demanding health care. With China now the third-largest vaccine market in the world, pharmaceutical manufacturers like Novartis are partnering with Chinese companies to offer medicines at affordable prices and increase their share in this lucrative industry.[11]

A country's level of development is determined in part by its **infrastructure,** the physical facilities that support its economic activities, such as railroads, highways, ports, airfields, utilities and power plants, schools, hospitals, communication systems, and commercial distribution systems. When doing business in LDCs, for example, a business may need to compensate for rudimentary distribution and communication systems, or even a lack of technology.

Exchange Rates. The ratio at which one nation's currency can be exchanged for another nation's currency is the **exchange rate.** Exchange rates vary daily and can be found in newspapers and through many sites on the Internet. Familiarity with exchange rates is important because they affect the cost of imports and exports.

> **Infrastructure** the physical facilities that support a country's economic activities, such as railroads, highways, ports, airfields, utilities and power plants, schools, hospitals, communication systems, and commercial distribution systems
>
> **Exchange rate** the ratio at which one nation's currency can be exchanged for another nation's currency

When the value of the Canadian dollar declines relative to other currencies, such as the euro, the price of imports becomes relatively expensive for Canadian consumers. On the other hand, Canadian exports become relatively cheap for international markets—in this example, the European Union.

Occasionally, a government may alter the value of its national currency. Devaluation decreases the value of currency in relation to other currencies. If the Canadian government were to devalue the dollar, it would lower the cost of Canadian goods abroad and make trips to Canada less expensive for foreign tourists. Thus, devaluation encourages the sale of domestic goods and tourism. Mexico has repeatedly devalued the peso for this reason. Revaluation, which increases the value of a currency in relation to other currencies, occurs rarely.

"Devaluation decreases the value of currency in relation to other currencies."

China has made great strides in sustainability. The country has become the largest producer of wind turbines worldwide and has captured more than half of the market for solar technology. However, with 1.3 billion consumers and a growing middle class, pollution in China has also grown—with sometimes catastrophic results. The Ministry of Environmental Protection in Beijing has estimated that one-sixth of China's river water is dangerously polluted. Acid rain is also common in China, and less than one-fifth of its hazardous waste is properly treated each year. Perhaps most tragically, many cities located near factories have reported high incidences of cancer and other diseases.

The situation has prompted the Chinese government to take action. The government is closing many of the country's worst-polluting factories, is adopting stringent environmental laws, and has announced its intention of implementing a cap-and-trade system. Although most people would applaud China's attempt to reduce pollution, serious economic disadvantages come with better environmental enforcement. The loss of jobs that occurs when factories close is a major drawback. For example, one older steel mill employed 6,000 workers, many of whom were laid off when the factory closed. Additionally,

because the majority of China is still powered by coal (a dirtier source of energy), the nation is opening up new power plants even as it is closing less-efficient older ones. Finally, although China releases the most greenhouse gas emissions, each person in China is responsible for only one-third of the carbon emissions attributable to the average North American. Therefore, China's pollution problem not only involves the clash between economics and the environment but also brings up the issue of fairness. [12]

DISCUSSION QUESTIONS

1. Describe the environmental issues that China is facing.

2. Describe the clash between China's economic situation and the environment. Why is this such a major concern?

3. Do you feel that it is fair for China to receive attention for greenhouse gas emissions when North American people's activities cause more greenhouse gas emissions per capita?

Ethical, Legal, and Political Barriers

A company that decides to enter the international marketplace must contend with potentially complex relationships among the different laws of its own nation, international laws, and the laws of the nation with which it will be trading; various trade restrictions imposed on international trade; changing political climates; and different ethical values. Legal and ethical requirements for successful business are increasing globally. BlackBerry (formerly Research In Motion (RIM)) ran into legal barriers in Saudi Arabia and the United Arab Emirates. The two countries announced a countrywide ban of the company's devices out of a concern that data on the devices was encrypted and could not be monitored. Additionally, because information on BlackBerrys was routed through the company's overseas suppliers, the countries felt this could allow outside parties access to personal data. The bans were lifted after BlackBerry agreed to make some changes. As part of the agreement with Saudi Arabia, BlackBerry agreed to use local data servers. [13]

Laws and Regulations.   Canada has a number of laws and regulations that govern the activities of Canadian firms engaged in international trade. For example, the Customs Act and the Reporting of Exported Goods Regulations require Canadian firms to report their exports. The three main

objectives of the export reporting program are the following: to control the export of strategic and dangerous goods, as well as other controlled and regulated goods; to collect accurate information on Canadian exports; and to control the outbound movement of goods in transit through Canada. [14] Canada is a member of the World Trade Organization which administers the rules governing trade among its 153 members. Canada also has a variety of international trade agreements with other nations, ranging from Free Trade Agreements, Foreign Investment Promotion and Protection Agreements (FIPAs), and other types of agreements. These agreements allow business to be transacted among citizens of the specified countries. Some agreements also eliminate tariffs in a range of sectors, including for industrial, agricultural, forestry, fish and seafood products.

Once outside Canadian borders, businesspeople are likely to find that the laws of other nations differ from those of Canada. Many of the legal rights that Canadians take for granted do not exist in other countries, and a firm doing business abroad must understand and obey the laws of the host country. Some countries have strict laws limiting the amount of local currency that can be taken out of the country and the amount of foreign currency that can be brought in; others forbid foreigners from owning real property outright. In Mexico, for example, foreigners cannot directly own property in what is known as the "Restricted Zone." The Restricted Zone includes land within 100 kilometres of Mexico's international borders along with land within 50 kilometres of Mexico's oceans and beaches. Foreigners who wish to use property in these areas must obtain a title through a bank title transfer or through a corporation.[15]

Some countries have copyright and patent laws that are less strict than those of Canada and some countries fail to honour Canada's laws. Because copying is a tradition in China and Vietnam and laws protecting copyrights and intellectual property are weak and minimally enforced, those countries are flooded with counterfeit videos, movies, CDs, computer software, furniture, and clothing. Companies are angry because the counterfeits harm not only their sales, but also their reputations if the knockoffs are of poor quality. Such counterfeiting is not limited to China or Vietnam. It is estimated that nearly half of all software installed on personal computers worldwide is illegally pirated or copied, amounting to more than $50 billion in global revenue losses annually.[16] In countries where these activities occur, laws against them may not be sufficiently enforced, if counterfeiting is deemed illegal. Thus, businesses engaging in foreign trade may have to take extra steps to protect their products because local laws may be insufficient to do so.

Tariffs and Trade Restrictions.   Tariffs and other trade restrictions are part of a country's legal structure but may be established or removed for political reasons. An **import tariff** is a tax levied by a nation on goods imported into the country. A *fixed tariff* is a specific amount of money levied on each unit of a product brought into the country, while an *ad valorem tariff* is based on the value of the item. Most countries allow citizens travelling abroad to bring home a certain amount of merchandise without paying an import tariff. A Canadian citizen may bring up to $200 worth of merchandise into Canada duty free after each absence of 24 hours, up to $800 worth of goods after each absence of 48 hours. After that, Canadian citizens must pay duty rates according to the goods imported, the country where the goods were made, and the country from which they are imported. Thus, identical items purchased in different countries might have different tariffs.

Countries sometimes levy tariffs for political reasons, as when they impose sanctions against other countries to protest their actions. However, import tariffs are more commonly imposed to protect domestic products by raising the price of imported ones. Such protective tariffs have become controversial, as governments become increasingly concerned over their trade deficits. Protective tariffs allow more expensive domestic goods to compete with foreign ones. For example, Canada has protectionist tariff walls sheltering poultry and dairy farmers from foreign competition.[18] The United States has had tariffs on imported sugar for almost two centuries. The European Union levies tariffs on many products, including some seafood imports.

Critics of protective tariffs argue that their use inhibits free trade and competition. Supporters of protective tariffs say they insulate domestic industries, particularly new ones, against well-established foreign competitors. Once an industry matures, however, its advocates may be reluctant to let go of the tariff that protected it. Tariffs also help when, because of low labour costs and other advantages, foreign competitors can afford to sell their products at prices lower than those charged by domestic companies. Some protectionists argue that tariffs should be used to keep domestic wages high and unemployment low.

Exchange controls restrict the amount of currency that can be bought or sold. Some countries

> **Import tariff** a tax levied by a nation on goods imported into the country

> **Exchange controls** regulations that restrict the amount of currency that can be bought or sold

---

Consider the Following: Is There Room for Entrepreneurs in Cuba?

For the first time in its communist history, the entrepreneur may become part of Cuba's business landscape. However, it will come at a cost. Cuba will lay off over a half million state workers to make way for private-sector jobs.

This marks a major shift in a country traditionally viewed as the enemy of entrepreneurship. Cuban entrepreneurs are subjected to high taxes, advertising bans, no access to bank or foreign credit exchange, hiring restrictions, and more. Creating private-sector job growth will require major economic reforms. According to the Cuban union, the government has announced it will increase the job options available, distribute more licences to allow citizens to find work on their own, and lease more land.

These changes seem promising to other countries. A more privatized Cuban economy might enable more foreign investment. There is already talk of extending microloans to Cuba to support small-business growth. However, the willingness of the government to lift restrictions on private enterprise will largely determine whether entrepreneurship in Cuba will take off.[17]

control their foreign trade by forcing businesspeople to buy and sell foreign products through a central bank. If John Deere, for example, receives payments for its tractors in a foreign currency, it may be required to sell the currency to that nation's central bank. When foreign currency is in short supply, as it is in many less-developed and Eastern European countries, the government uses foreign currency to purchase necessities and capital goods and produces other products locally, thus limiting its need for foreign imports.

A **quota** limits the number of units of a particular product that can be imported into a country. A quota may be established by voluntary agreement or by government decree. In Canada, the Export and Import Controls Bureau is responsible for issuing permits and certificates for various products included on the Import Controls List. Products subject to quotas include agricultural products, firearms, textiles and clothing, and steel.[19]

An **embargo** prohibits trade in a particular product. Embargoes are generally directed at specific goods or countries and may be established for political, economic, health, or religious reasons. While the United States maintains a trade embargo with Cuba, European and Canadian hotel chains are engaged in a building boom on the Caribbean island, where tourism is the number-one industry. U.S. hotel chains are eager to build in Cuba but have no opportunity until the embargo is lifted. Even U.S. tourists are forbidden by the U.S. government to vacation in Cuba, although the push to lift the government embargo is growing stronger all the time. If permitted, cruise ships would likely be the first type of U.S. tourism to reach the island since the early 1960s. You may be surprised to know that U.S. farmers export hundreds of millions of dollars' worth of commodities to Cuba each year, based on a 2000 law that provided permission for some trade to the embargoed country.[20] Health embargoes prevent the importing of various pharmaceuticals, animals, plants, and agricultural products. Other nations forbid the importation of alcoholic beverages on religious grounds.

One common reason for setting quotas or tariffs is to prohibit **dumping,** which occurs when a country or business sells products at less than what it costs to produce them.

The European Union, for example, recently announced that it had opened the largest antidumping investigation ever, into imports of Chinese solar panels worth $26.5 billion last year. China retaliated by filing a case with the World Trade Organization accusing some European Union member countries of violating free trade rules.[21] A company may dump its products for several reasons. Dumping permits quick entry into a market. Sometimes dumping occurs when the domestic market for a firm's product is too small to support an efficient level of production. In other cases, technologically obsolete products that are no longer saleable in the country of origin are dumped overseas. Dumping is relatively difficult to prove, but even the suspicion of dumping can lead to the imposition of quotas or tariffs.

Political Barriers. Unlike legal issues, political considerations are seldom written down and often change rapidly. Nations that have been subject to economic sanctions for political reasons in recent years include Cuba, Iran, Syria, and North Korea. While these were dramatic events, political considerations affect international business daily as governments enact tariffs, embargoes, or other types of trade restrictions in response to political events.

Businesses engaged in international trade must consider the relative instability of countries such as Iraq, Haiti, and Venezuela. Political unrest in countries such as Pakistan, Somalia, and the Democratic Republic of the Congo may create a hostile or even dangerous environment for foreign businesses. Natural disasters, like the Haitian or Chilean earthquakes in 2010, can cripple a country's government, making the region even more unstable. Even Japan, a developed country, had its social, economic, and political institutions stressed by the 2011 earthquake and tsunamis. Finally, a sudden change in power can result in a regime that is hostile to foreign investment. Some businesses have been

The vegetable cutter in the bottom photo is a knockoff distributed by the NingHai Well International Trade Co. in China. The dubious honour is given to the "best" product knockoffs by the organization Action Plagiarius in an effort to shame their makers. (The Veggi Cut Revolution, top photo, manufactured by swizzzProzzz AG in Switzerland, is the original item.)

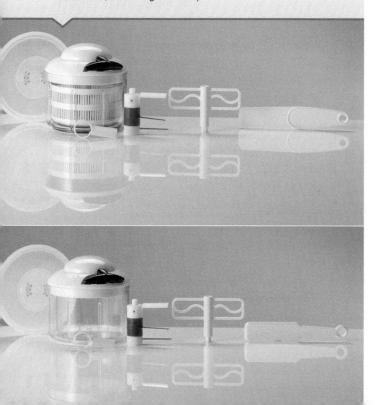

Cartel a group of firms or nations that agree to act as a monopoly and not compete with each other, in order to generate a competitive advantage in world markets

forced out of a country altogether, as when Hugo Chávez conducted a socialist revolution in Venezuela to force out or take over foreign oil companies. Whether they like it or not, companies are often involved directly or indirectly in international politics.

Political concerns may lead a group of nations to form a **cartel,** a group of firms or nations that agree to act as a monopoly and not compete with each other, to generate a competitive advantage in world markets. Probably the most famous cartel is OPEC, the Organization of Petroleum Exporting Countries, founded in the 1960s to increase the price of petroleum throughout the world and to maintain high prices. By working to ensure stable oil prices, OPEC hopes to enhance the economies of its member nations.

Social and Cultural Barriers

Most businesspeople engaged in international trade underestimate the importance of social and cultural differences; but these differences can derail an important transaction. For example, when Big Boy opened a restaurant in Bangkok, it quickly became popular with Western tourists, but the local Thais refused to eat there. Instead, they placed gifts of rice and incense at the feet of the Big Boy statue (a chubby boy holding a hamburger) because it reminded them of Buddha. In Japan, customers were forced to tiptoe around a logo painted on the floor at the entrance to an Athlete's Foot store because in Japan, it is considered taboo to step on a crest.[22] And in Russia, consumers found the Western-style energetic happiness of McDonald's employees insincere and offensive when the company opened its first stores there.[23] Unfortunately, cultural norms are rarely written down, and what is written down may well be inaccurate.

Cultural differences include differences in spoken and written language. Although it is certainly possible to translate words from one language to another, the true meaning is sometimes misinterpreted or lost. Consider some translations that went awry in foreign markets:

- Scandinavian vacuum manufacturer Electrolux used the following in an American campaign: "Nothing sucks like an Electrolux."

- The Coca-Cola name in China was first read as "Ke-kou-ke-la," meaning "bite the wax tadpole."

- In Italy, a campaign for Schweppes Tonic Water translated the name into Schweppes Toilet Water.[24]

Translators cannot just translate slogans, advertising campaigns, and website language; they must know the cultural differences that could affect a company's success.

Differences in body language and personal space also affect international trade. Body language is nonverbal, usually unconscious communication through gestures, posture, and facial expression. Personal space is the distance at which one person feels comfortable talking to another. Canadians tend to stand a moderate distance away from the person with whom they are speaking. Arab businessmen tend to stand face-to-face with the object of their conversation. Additionally, gestures vary from culture to culture, and gestures considered acceptable in Canadian society—pointing, for example—may be considered rude in others. Table 3.3 shows some of the behaviours considered rude or unacceptable in other countries. Such cultural differences may generate uncomfortable feelings or misunderstandings when businesspeople of different countries negotiate with each other.

Family roles also influence marketing activities. Many countries do not allow children to be used in advertising, for example. Advertising that features people in non-traditional social roles may or may not be successful either. One airline featured advertisements with beautiful flight attendants serving champagne on a flight. The ad does not seem unusual in Western markets, but there was a major backlash in the Middle East. Saudi Arabia even considered restricting the airline from flights in that country. Not only is alcohol usage forbidden among Muslims, but unveiled women are not allowed to interact with men—especially without their husbands around. Some in Saudi Arabia saw the airline as being insensitive to their religious beliefs and customs.[25]

The people of other nations quite often have a different perception of time as well. Canadians value promptness; a business meeting scheduled for a specific time seldom starts more than a few minutes late. In Mexico and Spain, however, it is not unusual for a meeting to be delayed half an hour or more. Such a late start might produce resentment in a Canadian negotiating in Spain for the first time.

Companies engaged in foreign trade must observe the national and religious holidays and local customs of the host country. In many Islamic countries, for example, workers expect to take a break at certain times of the day to observe

table 3.3 Cultural Behavioural Differences

Region	Gestures Viewed as Rude or Unacceptable
Japan, Hong Kong, Middle East	Summoning with the index finger
Middle and Far East	Pointing with index finger
Thailand, Japan, France	Sitting with soles of shoes showing
Brazil, Germany	Forming a circle with fingers (e.g., the "O.K." sign in North America)
Japan	Winking means "I love you"
Buddhist countries	Patting someone on the head

SOURCE: Adapted from Judie Haynes, "Communicating with Gestures," *EverythingESL* (n.d.), www.everythingesl.net/inservice/body_language.php (accessed March 2, 2004).

religious rites. Companies also must monitor their advertising to guard against offending customers. In Thailand and many other countries, public displays of affection between the sexes are unacceptable in advertising messages; in many Middle Eastern nations, it is unacceptable to show the soles of one's feet.[26] In Russia, smiling is considered appropriate only in private settings, not in business.

With the exception of the United States, most nations use the metric system. This lack of uniformity creates problems for both buyers and sellers in the international marketplace. American sellers, for instance, must produce goods destined for foreign markets in litres or metres, and Japanese sellers must convert to the imperial system if they plan to sell a product in the United States. Tools also must be calibrated in the correct system if they are to function correctly. Hyundai and Honda service technicians need metric tools to make repairs on those cars.

The literature dealing with international business is filled with accounts of sometimes humorous but often costly mistakes that occurred because of a lack of understanding of the social and cultural differences between buyers and sellers. Such problems cannot always be avoided, but they can be minimized through research on the cultural and social differences of the host country.

Technological Barriers

Many countries lack the technological infrastructure found in North America, and some marketers are viewing such barriers as opportunities. For instance, marketers are targeting many countries such as India and China and some African nations where there are few private phone lines. Citizens of these countries are turning instead to wireless communication through cell phones. Technological advances, such as the Internet, are creating additional global marketing opportunities. Along with opportunities, changing technologies also create new challenges and competition. For example, although Apple is making strides in the tablet industry, its market share in the PC market remains low compared to competitors. In fact, out of the top five global PC companies—Hewlett-Packard, Dell, Acer, Lenovo, and Toshiba—three are from Asian countries.[27]

LO3 Specify some of the agreements, alliances, and organizations that may encourage trade across international boundaries.

Trade Agreements, Alliances, and Organizations

Although these economic, political, legal, and sociocultural issues may seem like daunting barriers to international trade, there are also organizations and agreements—such as the General Agreement on Tariffs and Trade, the World Bank, and the International Monetary Fund—that foster international trade and can help companies get involved in and succeed in global markets. Various regional trade agreements, such as the North American Free Trade Agreement and the European Union, also promote trade among member nations by eliminating tariffs and trade restrictions. In this section, we'll look briefly at some of these agreements and organizations.

General Agreement on Tariffs and Trade (GATT)

During the Great Depression of the 1930s, nations established so many protective tariffs covering so many products that international trade became virtually impossible. By the

---

ENTREPRENEURSHIP IN ACTION | Entrepreneurs Make Money in an Unusual Way

David Auerbach, Ani Vallabhaneni, and Lindsay Stradley

Business: Sanergy

Founded: 2011, in Kenya

Success: The idea for Sanergy won the three student entrepreneurs the $100,000 grand prize in MIT's annual Business Plan Competition, enabling them to start their Kenyan business.

Making money off human waste seems like an unusual (and disgusting) idea. But for recent MBA graduate David Auerbach, it is an opportunity to make money and meet critical needs in developing countries. According to the World Health Organization, 2.6 billion people lack proper sanitation facilities, a situation Auerbach witnessed when visiting China. Auerbach partnered with fellow students Ani Vallabhaneni and Lindsay Stradley to submit a business plan for a sanitation business in Kenya. They won MIT's annual Business Plan Competition and received $100,000 to start Sanergy.

Sanergy involves a four-step process. First, it builds the sanitation facilities, which include showers and toilets. The centres are then franchised to other entrepreneurs, who charge five cents for each use. The waste is collected daily and finally converted into electricity and fertilizer and sold. In this way, Sanergy can make a profit, create clean sanitation facilities for Kenyans, and generate jobs simultaneously.[28]

end of World War II, there was considerable international momentum to liberalize trade and minimize the effects of tariffs. The **General Agreement on Tariffs and Trade (GATT),** originally signed by 23 nations in 1947, provided a forum for tariff negotiations and a place where international trade problems could be discussed and resolved. More than 100 nations abided by its rules. GATT sponsored rounds of negotiations aimed at reducing trade restrictions. The Uruguay Round (1988–1994), further reduced trade barriers for most products and provided new rules to prevent dumping. The most recent round, the Doha Development Round, which was started in 2001, collapsed in 2008 after failing to agree on major issues. The main stumbling block was farm import rules, which allow countries to protect poor farmers by imposing a tariff on certain goods in the event of a drop in prices or a surge in imports.[29]

The **World Trade Organization (WTO),** an international organization dealing with the rules of trade between nations, was created in 1995 by the Uruguay Round. Key to the World Trade Organization are the WTO agreements, which are the legal ground rules for international commerce. The agreements were negotiated and signed by most of the world's trading nations and ratified by their parliaments. The goal is to help producers of goods and services and exporters and importers conduct their business. In addition to administering the WTO trade agreements, the WTO presents a forum for trade negotiations, monitors national trade policies, provides technical assistance and training for developing countries, and cooperates with other international organizations. Based in Geneva, Switzerland, the WTO has also adopted a leadership role in negotiating trade disputes among nations.[30] For example, the WTO investigated Chinese accusations of unfair treatment against the European Union after the EU levied tariffs against Chinese-manufactured steel fasteners. The EU claimed that China was dumping its steel fasteners and imposed a tariff of 63 to 87 percent. The WTO ruled in favour of China, claiming that the tariff discriminated against Chinese exporters.[31]

The North American Free Trade Agreement (NAFTA)

The **North American Free Trade Agreement (NAFTA),** which went into effect on January 1, 1994, effectively merged Canada, the United States, and Mexico into one market of more than 440 million consumers. NAFTA was designed to eliminate

The WTO facilitates trade among nations through the development of trade policies.

virtually all tariffs on goods produced and traded among Canada, Mexico, and the United States to create a free trade area. The estimated annual output for this trade alliance is $14 trillion. NAFTA makes it easier for Canadian businesses to invest in the U.S. and Mexico; provides protection for intellectual property (of special interest to high-technology and entertainment industries); expands trade by requiring equal treatment of Canadian firms in both countries; and simplifies country-of-origin rules, hindering Japan's use of Mexico as a staging ground for penetration into Canadian and U.S. markets.

> ## "NAFTA makes it easier for Canadian businesses to invest in the U.S. and Mexico."

The United States' 300 million consumers are extremely affluent, with a per capita GDP of $48,000.[32] Trade between the United States and Canada totals approximately $550 billion. About 70 percent of Canada's exports go to the United States, including gold, oil, and uranium.[33] In fact, Canada is the single largest trading partner of the United States.[34]

With a per capita GDP of $14,266, Mexico's 111 million consumers are less affluent than Canadian consumers.[35] However, they bought $6 billion worth of Canadian products in 2011, making Mexico Canada's fifth-largest trading market. Mexico is on a course of a market economy, rule of law, respect for human rights, and responsible public policies. There is also a commitment to the environment and sustainable human development. Many Canadian and U.S. companies have taken advantage of Mexico's low labour costs and proximity to set up production facilities, sometimes called *maquiladoras*. Mexico is also attracting major technological industries, including electronics, software, and aerospace. Companies as diverse as Bombardier, Celestica, and Ford have set up facilities in Mexican states. With the maquiladoras and the influx of foreign technological industries, Mexico became the world's 12th-largest economy.[36]

However, there is great disparity within Mexico. The country's southern states cannot seem to catch up with the more affluent northern states on almost any socioeconomic indicator. For example, 47 percent of rural Mexicans in the south are considered extremely poor, compared with just 12 percent in the north. The disparities are growing, as can be seen comparing the south to the northern industrial capital of Monterrey, which is beginning to seem like south Texas.[37] However, drug gang wars threaten the economic stability and tourist industry of Mexico, especially in the northern states.

Mexico's membership in NAFTA links it, along with Canada and the U.S., to other Latin American countries, providing additional opportunities to integrate trade among all the nations in the Western Hemisphere. Indeed, a free trade agreement among the nations of North and South America was expected to be completed by 2005, and like NAFTA, the Free Trade Area of the Americas (FTAA) will progressively eliminate trade barriers and create the world's largest free trade zone with 800 million people.[38] However, opposition and demonstrations have hampered efforts to move forward with the proposed plan. Although the deadline was missed and it is not in place yet, there is still a chance for the FTAA to become a reality.

Despite its benefits, NAFTA has been controversial and disputes continue to arise over the implementation of the trade agreement. While many Canadians feared the agreement would erase jobs in Canada, Mexicans have been disappointed that the agreement failed to create more jobs. Moreover, Mexico's rising standard of living has increased the cost of doing business there; some 850 *maquiladoras* have closed their doors and transferred work to China and other nations where labour costs are cheaper. Indeed, China has become Canada's third-largest importer. On the other hand, high transportation costs, intellectual property theft, quality failures, and the difficulty management often incurs in controlling a business so far away and under a communist regime are now causing some manufacturers to reconsider opting for Mexican factories over China, even going so far as to relocate from China back to Mexico.[39]

Although NAFTA has been controversial, it has become a positive factor for North American firms wishing to engage in international marketing. Because licensing requirements have been relaxed under the pact, smaller businesses that previously could not afford to invest in Mexico and Canada will be able to do business in those markets without having to locate there. NAFTA's long phase-in period provides ample time for adjustment by those firms affected by reduced tariffs on imports. Furthermore, increased competition should lead to a more efficient market, and the long-term prospects of including most countries in the Western Hemisphere in the alliance promise additional opportunities for North American marketers.

The European Union (EU)

The **European Union (EU),** also called the *European Community* or *Common Market,* was established in 1958 to promote trade among its members, which initially included Belgium, France, Italy, West Germany, Luxembourg, and the Netherlands. East and West Germany united in 1991, and by 1995 the United Kingdom, Spain, Denmark, Greece, Portugal, Ireland, Austria, Finland, and Sweden had joined as well. Cyprus, the Czech Republic, Estonia, Hungary, Latvia, Lithuania, Malta, Poland, Slovakia, and Slovenia joined in 2004. In 2007 Bulgaria and Romania also became members, which brought total membership to 27. Croatia, the former Yugoslav Republic of Macedonia, and Turkey are candidate countries that hope to join the European Union soon.[40] Until 1993 each nation functioned as a separate market, but at that time the members officially unified into one of the largest single world markets.

To facilitate free trade among members, the EU is working toward standardization of business regulations and requirements, import duties, and value-added taxes; the elimination of customs checks; and the creation of a standardized currency for use by all members. Many European nations (Austria, Belgium, Finland, France, Germany, Ireland, Italy, Luxembourg, the Netherlands, Portugal, and Spain) link their exchange rates together to a common currency, the *euro;* however, several EU members have rejected use of the euro in their countries. Although the common currency requires many marketers to modify their pricing strategies and will subject them to increased competition, the use of a single currency frees companies that sell goods among European countries from the nuisance of dealing with complex exchange rates.[41] The long-term goals are to eliminate all trade barriers within the EU, improve the economic efficiency of the EU nations, and stimulate economic growth, thus making the union's economy more competitive in global markets, particularly against Japan and other Pacific Rim nations, and North America. However, several disputes and debates still divide the member nations, and many barriers to complete free trade remain. Consequently, it may take many years before the EU is truly one deregulated market.

The prosperity of the EU has suffered in recent years. EU members experienced a severe economic crisis in 2010 that required steep bailouts from the International Monetary Fund (IMF). The first country to come to the forefront was Greece, which had so much debt that it risked default. With an increase in Greek bond yields and credit risks—along with a severe deficit and other negative economic factors—the country's economy plummeted. Since Greece uses the euro as its currency, the massive downturn served to decrease the euro's value. This had a profound effect on other countries in the Euro zone (the Euro zone refers collectively to European member countries that have adopted the euro as their form of currency). Ireland, Spain, and Portugal were particularly vulnerable as they had some of the region's largest deficits.[42] Ireland began experiencing problems similar to Greece's, including a debt crisis, failing economic health, and rising bond yields.[43] It too required a bailout package from the IMF. Spain's housing bust and a collapse in the construction sector negatively affected its economy as well.[44]

Much as the United States created new agencies to ensure the future stability of U.S. financial markets, the European Union created the European Financial Stability

Facility (EFSF) to "safeguard financial stability in the Euro zone." EFSF will be able to raise funds through the issuing of capital such as bonds in order to finance loans for European Union member countries.[45] It is hoped that this organization will maintain stability in the region and prevent such a crisis from reoccurring in the future.

Asia-Pacific Economic Cooperation (APEC)

Asia-Pacific Economic Cooperation (APEC), established in 1989, promotes open trade and economic and technical cooperation among member nations, which initially included Australia, Brunei Darussalam, Canada, Indonesia, Japan, Korea, Malaysia, New Zealand, the Philippines, Singapore, Thailand, and the United States. Since then the alliance has grown to include China, Hong Kong, Chinese Taipei, Mexico, Papua New Guinea, Chile, Peru, Russia, and Vietnam. The 21-member alliance represents approximately 41 percent of the world's population, 44 percent of world trade, and 54 percent of world GDP. APEC differs from other international trade alliances in its commitment to facilitating business and its practice of allowing the business/private sector to participate in a wide range of APEC activities.[46]

The APEC countries have become increasingly competitive and sophisticated in global business in the last three decades. The Japanese and South Koreans in particular have made tremendous inroads on world markets for automobiles, motorcycles, watches, cameras, and audio and video equipment. Products from Samsung, Sony, Sanyo, Toyota, Daewoo, Mitsubishi, Suzuki, and Toshiba are sold all over the world and have set standards of quality by which other products are often judged. The People's Republic of China, a country of 1.3 billion people, has launched a program of economic reform to stimulate its economy by privatizing many industries, restructuring its banking system, and increasing public spending on infrastructure (including railways and telecommunications).[47] As a result, China has become a manufacturing powerhouse, with an estimated economic growth rate of 8 to 10 percent a year.[48] China's export market has consistently outpaced its import growth in recent years and its GDP is the world's second-largest behind the United States. As China continues to prosper, working conditions are also beginning to improve. Strikes and calls for unions are increasing among Chinese factory workers, prompting the government to improve wages and labour standards. On the other hand, this rise in labour costs concerns some international companies. Minimum wage increases are estimated to push labour costs up 5 to 15 percent on average, which may be passed on to consumers in the form of higher prices. This brings up a key ethical concern for consumers and businesses: Would they be willing to accept higher priced items if it meant better conditions for workers in different countries?[49]

Increased industrialization has also caused China to become the world's largest emitter of greenhouse gases as of 2008. China mainly uses coal-fired power plants; in fact,

"The IMF is the closest thing the world has to an international central bank."

it builds a new one every 10 days, so it has become the world's largest emitter of carbon dioxide. As companies transfer their manufacturing to China, they increase their CO_2 emissions because China emits 22 percent more than the global average of carbon per kilowatt-hour.[50] On the other hand, China has also begun a quest to become a world leader in green initiatives and renewable energy. This is an increasingly important quest as the country becomes more polluted.

Less visible Pacific Rim regions, such as Thailand, Singapore, Taiwan, Vietnam, and Hong Kong, have also become major manufacturing and financial centres. Vietnam, with one of the world's most open economies, has bypassed its communist government with private firms moving ahead despite bureaucracy, corruption, and poor infrastructure. In a country of 85 million barely able to feed themselves, Vietnamese firms now compete internationally with an agricultural miracle, making the country one of the world's main providers of farm produce. Coach, Inc. wants to increase its presence in Vietnam, while Guess, Inc. is considering an expansion of its production facilities in Vietnam along with Cambodia and Indonesia.[51]

World Bank

The **World Bank,** more formally known as the International Bank for Reconstruction and Development, was established in 1946 to loan money to underdeveloped and developing countries.

It loans its own funds or borrows funds from member countries to finance projects ranging from road and factory construction to the building of medical and educational facilities. The World Bank and other multilateral development banks (banks with international support that provide loans to developing countries) are the largest source of advice and assistance for developing nations. The International Development Association and the International Finance Corporation are associated with the World Bank and provide loans to private businesses and member countries.

International Monetary Fund

The **International Monetary Fund (IMF)** was established in 1947 to promote trade among member nations by eliminating trade barriers and fostering financial cooperation. It also makes short-term loans to member countries that have balance-of-payment deficits and provides foreign currencies to member nations. The International Monetary

Asia-Pacific Economic Cooperation (APEC) community established in 1989 to promote international trade and facilitate business; as of 2013, has 21 member countries

World Bank an organization established by the industrialized nations in 1946 to loan money to underdeveloped and developing countries; formally known as the International Bank for Reconstruction and Development

International Monetary Fund (IMF) organization established in 1947 to promote trade among member nations by eliminating trade barriers and fostering financial cooperation

In 2008, Howard Schultz returned as CEO to re-anchor Starbucks after years of expansion. After closing almost 1,000 stores and cutting expenses, Starbucks is back on track. The company has become more discerning about where and how to expand by focusing on its international markets.

Starbucks operates in more than 50 countries, but its primary focus is on expansion in China. Starbucks first entered China in 1999. It now runs about 450 stores and plans to grow to 1,500 by 2015. Finding the right approach in China is challenging. Some have complained that Starbucks' early entrance was invasive and accused the company of pushing American culture along with its products. At one point, Starbucks closed its Forbidden City location after complaints circulated throughout the media. This time around, Schultz is adapting stores to incorporate Chinese cultural expectations. Stores will offer Chinese-inspired food items and more coffee-free beverages, because the Chinese are less drawn to coffee. In recent meetings with Chinese

managers, Schultz has been honest about the company's challenges, thereby creating an impression of trust. The company has also opened a coffee farm and processing facilities in China. Schultz believes China might become the company's largest market. Therefore, he is changing the company's structure to include a China and Asia Pacific division. Will this focus on global expansion be Starbucks' recipe for further success?[52]

DISCUSSION QUESTIONS

1. What are some of the cultural barriers Starbucks encountered in its China expansion?

2. How has CEO Howard Schultz been able to resolve some of the differences between Chinese and American culture?

3. What are some ways that Starbucks is creating trust with its Chinese stakeholders?

Fund also tries to avoid financial crises and panics by alerting the international community about countries that will not be able to repay their debts. The IMF's Internet site provides additional information about the organization, including news releases, frequently asked questions, and members.

The IMF is the closest thing the world has to an international central bank. If countries get into financial trouble, they can borrow from the World Bank. However, the global economic crisis created many challenges for the IMF as it was forced to significantly increase its loans to both emerging economies and more developed nations. Ireland accepted a bailout package worth up to £77 billion (C$120 billion) from the IMF and the EU. Similarly, the IMF also loaned 30 billion euros (C$39 billion) to help rescue Greece's struggling economy.[53] The usefulness of the IMF for developed countries is limited because these countries use private markets as a major source of capital.[54]

LO4 Summarize the different levels of organizational involvement in international trade.

Getting Involved in International Business

Businesses may get involved in international trade at many levels—from a small Kenyan firm that occasionally exports African crafts to a huge multinational corporation such as

Shell Oil that sells products around the globe. The degree of commitment of resources and effort required increases according to the level at which a business involves itself in international trade. This section examines exporting and importing, trading companies, licensing and franchising, contract manufacturing, joint ventures, direct investment, and multinational corporations.

Exporting and Importing

Many companies first get involved in international trade when they import goods from other countries for resale in their own businesses. For example, a grocery store chain may import bananas from Honduras and coffee from Colombia. A business may get involved in exporting when it is called upon to supply a foreign company with a particular product. Such exporting enables enterprises of all sizes to participate in international business. Exporting to other countries becomes a necessity for established countries that seek to grow continually. Products often have higher sales growth potential in foreign countries than they have in the parent country. For example, Heinz exports its ketchup to other countries, including Mexico, Africa, and the Middle East, because there exists much greater potential for growth. Retail sales of packaged food have risen 32 percent in Asian-Pacific countries and 27 percent in Africa, while rising only a mere 4 percent in Europe and declining 1 percent in North America. Mexico in particular has become a crucial part of Heinz's growth strategy because Mexicans consume more

The ship *Cosco Ran* transports cargo from one side of the globe to the other.

An advantage of trading through an agent instead of directly is that the company does not have to deal with foreign currencies or the red tape (paying tariffs and handling paperwork) of international business. A major disadvantage is that, because the export agent must make a profit, either the price of the product must be increased or the domestic company must provide a larger discount than it would in a domestic transaction.

Trading Companies

A **trading company** buys goods in one country and sells them to buyers in another country. Trading companies handle all activities required to move products from one country to another, including consulting, marketing research, advertising, insurance, product research and design, warehousing, and foreign exchange services to companies interested in selling their products in foreign markets. Trading companies are similar to export agents, but their role in international trade is larger. By linking sellers and buyers of goods in different countries, trading companies promote international trade. Canada has a few trading companies but one of the oldest is the Canadian Commercial Corporation (CCC), a federal crown corporation in existence since 1946. Its primary goal is to promote and facilitate international trade on behalf of Canadian industry, particularly with government markets.[56] Export Development Canada (EDC) is another crown corporation and Canada's export credit agency. It helps Canadian exporters and investors expand their international business among other services.[57]

> **Trading company** a firm that buys goods in one country and sells them to buyers in another country
>
> **Licensing** a trade agreement in which one company—the licensor—allows another company—the licensee—to use its company name, products, patents, brands, trademarks, raw materials, and/or production processes in exchange for a fee or royalty

ketchup than all but eight other nations.[55] Table 3.4 shows the number of Canadian exporters and the export value by company size, while Figure 3.1 shows the major export markets for Canadian companies.

Exporting sometimes takes place through **countertrade agreements,** which involve bartering products for other products instead of for currency. Such arrangements are fairly common in international trade, especially between Western companies and Eastern European nations. An estimated 40 percent or more of all international trade agreements contain countertrade provisions.

Although a company may export its wares overseas directly or import goods directly from their manufacturer, many choose to deal with an intermediary, commonly called an *export agent*. Export agents seldom produce goods themselves; instead, they usually handle international transactions for other firms. Export agents either purchase products outright or take them on consignment. If they purchase them outright, they generally mark up the price they have paid and attempt to sell the product in the international marketplace. They are also responsible for storage and transportation.

> **Countertrade agreements** foreign trade agreements that involve bartering products for other products instead of for currency

Licensing and Franchising

Licensing is a trade arrangement in which one company—the *licensor*—allows another company—the *licensee*—to use its company name, products, patents, brands, trademarks, raw materials, and/or production processes in exchange for a fee or royalty. The Coca-Cola Company and PepsiCo frequently use licensing as a means to market their soft drinks, apparel, and other merchandise in other countries. Licensing is an attractive alternative to direct investment when the political stability of a foreign country is in doubt or when resources are unavailable for direct investment. Licensing is especially advantageous for small manufacturers wanting to launch a well-known brand

table 3.4 Canadian Exporters and Value by Company Size, 2009

	No. of Exporters	%	Value (C$ millions)	%
< 50 employees	36,585	76.80	100,147	30.4
50–99	5,125	10.8	47,258	14.4
100–199	3,151	6.6	36,147	11.0
200 and over	2,776	5.8	145,567	44.2

SOURCE: Adapted from Statistics Canada, "A Profile of Canadian Exporters, 1996 to 2009," http://www.statcan.gc.ca/pub/65-507-m/65-507-m2010010-eng.pdf (accessed January 7, 2013).

table 3.5 Top Global Franchises

Franchise	Country	Ranking
Subway	United States	1
7Eleven	United States	2
Intercontinental Hotels Group	United Kingdom	10
Tim Hortons	Canada	18
Kumon	Japan	27
Cartridge World	Australia	61
VOM FASS	Germany	86
Pita Pit	Canada	87
Naturhouse	Spain	91
Jamba Juice	United States	100

SOURCE: "Top 100 Global Franchises—Ranking," Franchise Direct, www.franchisedirect.com/top100globalfranchises/rankings/ (accessed June 24, 2013).

The Canadian frozen yogurt franchise Yogen Fruz has operations on four continents.

> **Franchising** a form of licensing in which a company—the franchiser—agrees to provide a franchisee a name, logo, methods of operation, advertising, products, and other elements associated with a franchiser's business, in return for a financial commitment and the agreement to conduct business in accordance with the franchiser's standard of operations

internationally. Yoplait is a French yogurt that is licensed for production in Canada.

Franchising is a form of licensing in which a company—the *franchiser*—agrees to provide a *franchisee* a name, logo, methods of operation, advertising, products, and other elements associated with the franchiser's business, in return for a financial commitment and the agreement to conduct business in accordance with the franchiser's standard of operations. Subway, McDonald's, Pizza Hut, and Holiday Inn are well-known franchisers with international visibility. Table 3.5 lists a selection of the top 100 global franchises for 2013 as ranked by *Franchise Direct*.

Licensing and franchising enable a company to enter the international marketplace without spending large sums of money abroad or hiring or transferring personnel to handle overseas affairs. They also minimize problems associated with shipping costs, tariffs, and trade restrictions. And, they allow the firm to establish goodwill for its products in a foreign market, which will help the company if it decides to produce or market its products directly in the foreign country at some future date. However, if the licensee (or franchisee) does not maintain high standards of quality, the product's image may be hurt; therefore, it is important for the licensor to monitor its products overseas and to enforce its quality standards.

Contract Manufacturing

> **Contract manufacturing** the hiring of a foreign company to produce a specified volume of the initiating company's product to specification; the final product carries the domestic firm's name

Contract manufacturing occurs when a company hires a foreign company to produce a specified volume of the firm's product to specification; the final product carries the domestic firm's name. Spalding, for example, relies on contract manufacturing for its sports equipment; Reebok uses Korean contract manufacturers to manufacture many of its athletic shoes.

Outsourcing

Earlier, we defined outsourcing as transferring manufacturing or other tasks (such as information technology operations) to companies in countries where labour and supplies are less expensive. Many international firms have outsourced tasks to India, Ireland, Mexico, and the Philippines, where there are many well-educated workers and significantly

figure 3.1 Major Export Markets for Canadian Companies

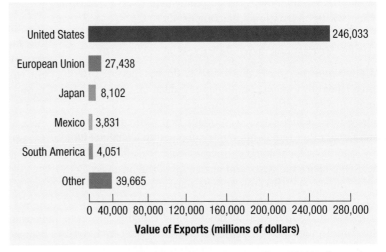

Market	Value of Exports (millions of dollars)
United States	246,033
European Union	27,438
Japan	8,102
Mexico	3,831
South America	4,051
Other	39,665

SOURCE: Adapted from Statistics Canada, "A Profile of Canadian Exporters, 1996 to 2009," http://www.statcan.gc.ca/pub/65-507-m/65-507-m2010010-eng.pdf (accessed January 7, 2013).

lower labour costs. Experts estimate that 80 percent of *Fortune* 500 companies have some relationship with an offshore company.[58]

Although outsourcing has become politically controversial in recent years amid concerns over jobs lost to overseas workers, foreign companies transfer tasks and jobs to North American companies—sometimes called *insourcing*. However, some firms are bringing their outsourced jobs back after concerns that foreign workers were not adding enough value. For example, some of the bigger banks are now choosing to set up offshore operations themselves rather than outsource. This has to do with increased regulations in foreign countries and concerns over data security. One instance of fraud at the Indian outsourcer Satyam amounted to more than $1 billion.[59]

Offshoring

Offshoring is the relocation of a business process by a company, or a subsidiary, to another country. Offshoring is different from outsourcing: the company retains control of the process because it is not subcontracting to a different company. Companies may choose to offshore for a number of reasons, ranging from lower wages, skilled labour, or taking advantage of time zone differences in order to offer services around the clock. Some banks have chosen not to outsource because of concerns about data security in other countries. These institutions may instead engage in offshoring, which allows a company more control over international operations because the offshore office is an extension of the company. Barclays Bank, for instance, has an international offshore banking unit called Barclays Wealth International. This branch helps the company better serve wealthy clients with international banking needs.[60]

Joint Ventures and Alliances

Many countries, particularly LDCs, do not permit direct investment by foreign companies or individuals. A company may also lack sufficient resources or expertise to operate elsewhere. In such cases, a company that wants to do business in another region or country may set up a **joint venture** by finding a local partner (occasionally, the host nation itself) to share the costs and operation of the business (see also Chapter 4). The French hypermarket chain Carrefour, for example, has a joint venture with Majid al Futtaim (MAF), a group of companies that has become a highly successful Middle Eastern business. The venture between Carrefour and MAF resulted in the expansion of MAF–Carrefour hypermarkets in the United Arab Emirates, Qatar, Oman,

Saudi Arabia, and Egypt. The partnership has allowed Carrefour to become one of the most popular retailers in Egypt.[61]

In some industries, such as automobiles and computers, strategic alliances are becoming the predominant means of competing. A **strategic alliance** is a partnership formed to create competitive advantage on a worldwide basis. In such industries, international competition is so fierce and the costs of competing on a global basis are so high that few firms have the resources to go it alone, so they collaborate with other companies. An example of a strategic alliance is the partnership between Australian airlines Virgin Blue and Skywest. By forming an alliance, the two airlines hope to tap into the increased demand from the mining industry for flights to distant mining sites. As part of the agreement, Skywest can use as many as 18 Virgin Blue turbo-prop aircraft for 10 years. In addition to penetrating a lucrative market, Virgin Blue hopes the alliance will help it extend its influence into regional markets and steal market share from its competitor QantasLink.[62]

Direct Investment

Companies that want more control and are willing to invest considerable resources in international business may consider **direct investment,** the ownership of overseas facilities. Direct investment may involve the development and operation of new facilities—such as when Starbucks opens a new coffee shop in Japan—or the purchase of all or part of an existing operation in a foreign country. India's Tata Motors purchased Jaguar and Land Rover from Ford Motor Company. Tata, a maker of cars and trucks, is attempting to broaden its global presence, including manufacturing these vehicles in the United Kingdom.[63]

The highest level of international business involvement is the **multinational corporation (MNC),** a corporation, such as IBM or ExxonMobil, that operates on a worldwide scale, without significant ties to any one nation or region. Table 3.6 lists the 10 largest multinational corporations. MNCs are more than simple corporations. They often have greater assets than some of the countries in which they do business. General Motors, ExxonMobil, Ford Motors, and General Electric, for example, have sales higher than the GDP of many of the countries in which they operate. Nestlé, with headquarters in Switzerland, operates more than 300 plants around the world and receives revenues from Europe; North, Central, and South America; Africa; and Asia. The Royal Dutch/Shell Group, one of the world's major oil producers, is another MNC. Its main offices are located in The Hague and London. Other MNCs include BASF, British Petroleum, Cadbury Schweppes, Matsushita, Mitsubishi, Siemens, Texaco, Toyota, and Unilever. Many MNCs have been targeted

table 3.6 Top 10 Largest Global Corporations

Company	Revenue (in millions)	Country
1. Walmart Stores	$421,849	U.S.
2. Royal Dutch Shell	$378,152	Netherlands
3. Exxon Mobil	$354,674	U.S.
4. BP	$308,928	Britain
5. Sinopec Group	$273,422	China
6. China National Petroleum	$240,294	China
7. State Grid	$226,294	China
8. Toyota Motor	$221,760	Japan
9. Japan Post Holdings	$203,958	Japan
10. Chevron	$196,337	U.S.

SOURCE: "Global 500: *Fortune*'s Annual Ranking of the World's Largest Corporations," CNNMoney, http://money.cnn.com/magazines/fortune/global500/2011/full_list/ (accessed July 20, 2011).

by antiglobalization activists at global business forums, and some protests have turned violent. The activists contend that MNCs increase the gap between rich and poor nations, misuse and misallocate scarce resources, exploit the labour markets in LDCs, and harm their natural environments.[64]

LO5   Contrast two basic strategies used in international business.

International Business Strategies

Planning in a global economy requires businesspeople to understand the economic, legal, political, and sociocultural realities of the countries in which they will operate. These factors will affect the strategy a business chooses to use outside its own borders.

Developing Strategies

Companies doing business internationally have traditionally used a **multinational strategy,** customizing their products, promotion, and distribution according to cultural, technological, regional, and national differences. To succeed in India, for example, McDonald's had to adapt its products to respect religious customs. McDonald's India does not serve beef or pork products and also has vegetarian dishes for its largely vegetarian consumer base. Many soap and detergent manufacturers have adapted their products to local water conditions, washing equipment, and washing habits. For customers in some less-developed countries, Colgate-Palmolive Co. has developed an inexpensive, plastic, hand-powered washing machine for use in households that have no electricity. Even when products are standardized, advertising often has to be modified to adapt to language and cultural differences. Also, celebrities used in advertising in the North America may be unfamiliar to foreign consumers and thus would not be effective in advertising products in other countries.

More and more companies are moving from this customization strategy to a **global strategy (globalization),** which involves standardizing products (and, as much as possible, their promotion and distribution) for the whole world, as if it were a single entity. As it has become a global brand, Starbucks has standardized its products and stores. Starbucks was ranked as the world's most engaged brand in terms of online activities, even surpassing Coca-Cola, which is another global brand. Starbucks communicates with fans around the world via Facebook, Twitter, YouTube, and its company website.

Before moving outside their own borders, companies must conduct environmental analyses to evaluate the potential of and problems associated with various markets and to determine what strategy is best for doing business in those markets. Failure to do so may result in losses and even negative publicity. Some companies rely on local managers to gain greater insights and faster response to changes within a country. Astute businesspeople today "think globally, act locally." That is, while constantly being aware of the total picture, they adjust their firms' strategies to conform to local needs and tastes.

Multinational strategy
a plan, used by international companies, that involves customizing products, promotion, and distribution according to cultural, technological, regional, and national differences

Global strategy (globalization)
a strategy that involves standardizing products (and, as much as possible, their promotion and distribution) for the whole world, as if it were a single entity

---

TEAM EXERCISE

Visit Transparency International's Country Corruption Index website: www.transparency.org/. Form groups and select two countries. Research some of the economic, ethical, legal, regulatory, and political barriers that would have an impact on international trade. Be sure to pair a fairly ethical country with a fairly unethical country (e.g., Sweden with Myanmar, Ireland with Haiti). Report your findings.

Managing the Challenges of Global Business

As we've pointed out in this chapter, many past political barriers to trade have fallen or been minimized, expanding and opening new market opportunities. Managers who can meet the challenges of creating and implementing effective and sensitive business strategies for the global marketplace can help lead their companies to success. For example, the Canadian Trade Commissioner Service is the global business solutions unit of Foreign Affairs and International Trade Canada that offers Canadian firms wide and deep practical knowledge of international markets and industries, a network of international business professionals, market intelligence, financial support, and expert advice.[65] As mentioned previously, Canadian Commercial Corporation (CCC) promotes and facilitates international trade on behalf of Canadian industry, and Export Development Canada provides Canadian exporters with financing, insurance, and bonding services as well as foreign market expertise. A major element of the assistance that these governmental organizations can provide firms (especially for small- and medium-sized firms) is knowledge of the internationalization process. Small businesses, too, can succeed in foreign markets when their managers have carefully studied those markets and prepared and implemented appropriate strategies. Being globally aware is therefore an important quality for today's managers and will become a critical attribute for managers of the 21st century.

LEARNING OBJECTIVES SUMMARY

LO1 Explore some of the factors within the international trade environment that influence business.

International business is the buying, selling, and trading of goods and services across national boundaries. Importing is the purchase of goods and services from another nation; exporting is the sale of goods and services to foreign markets. A nation's balance of trade is the difference in value between its exports and imports; a positive balance of trade is a trade surplus and a negative balance of trade is a trade deficit. The difference between the flow of money into and out of a country is called the balance of payments. An absolute or comparative advantage in trade may determine what products a company from a particular nation will export.

LO2 Investigate some of the economic, legal-political, social, cultural, and technological barriers to international business.

Companies engaged in international trade must consider the effects of economic, legal, political, social, and cultural differences between nations. Economic barriers are a country's level of development (infrastructure) and exchange rates. Wide-ranging legal and political barriers include differing laws (and enforcement), tariffs, exchange controls, quotas, embargoes, political instability, and war. Ambiguous cultural and social barriers involve differences in spoken and body language, time, holidays and other observances, and customs.

LO3 Specify some of the agreements, alliances, and organizations that may encourage trade across international boundaries.

Among the most important promoters of international business are the General Agreement on Tariffs and Trade (GATT), the World Trade Organization (WTO), the North American Free Trade Agreement (NAFTA), the European Union (EU), the Asia-Pacific Economic Cooperation (APEC), the World Bank, and the International Monetary Fund (IMF).

LO4 Summarize the different levels of organizational involvement in international trade.

A company may be involved in international trade at several levels, each requiring a greater commitment of resources and effort, ranging from importing/exporting to multinational corporations. Countertrade agreements occur at the import/export level and involve bartering products for other products instead of currency. At the next level, a trading company links buyers and sellers in different countries to foster trade. In licensing and franchising, one company agrees to allow a foreign company the use of its company name, products, patents, brands, trademarks, raw materials, and production processes, in exchange for a flat fee or royalty. Contract manufacturing occurs when a company hires a foreign company to produce a specified volume of the firm's product to specification; the final product carries the domestic firm's name. A joint venture is a partnership in which companies from different countries agree to share the costs and operation of the business. The purchase of overseas production and marketing facilities is direct investment. Outsourcing, a form of direct investment, involves transferring manufacturing to countries where labour and supplies are cheap. A multinational corporation is one that operates on a worldwide scale, without significant ties to any one nation or region.

LO5 Contrast two basic strategies used in international business.

Companies typically use one of two basic strategies in international business. A multinational strategy customizes products, promotion, and distribution according to cultural, technological, regional, and national differences. A global strategy (globalization) standardizes products (and, as much as possible, their promotion and distribution) for the whole world, as if it were a single entity.

KEY TERMS

absolute advantage
Asia-Pacific Economic Cooperation (APEC)
balance of payments
balance of trade
cartel
comparative advantage
contract manufacturing
countertrade agreements
direct investment
dumping
embargo
European Union (EU)
exchange controls
exchange rate
exporting
franchising
General Agreement on Tariffs and Trade (GATT)
global strategy (globalization)

importing
import tariff
infrastructure
international business
International Monetary Fund (IMF)
joint venture
licensing
multinational corporation (MNC)
multinational strategy
North American Free Trade Agreement (NAFTA)
offshoring
outsourcing
quota
strategic alliance
trade deficit
trading company
World Bank
World Trade Organization (WTO)

DESTINATION CEO DISCUSSION QUESTIONS

1. Why do you think that expansion opportunities for the Boston Pizza franchise are global rather than domestic?

2. To what does Jim Treliving attribute his success as a manager?

3. Does technology play a role in the global expansion of Boston Pizza?

Have you always dreamt of travelling the world? Whether backpacking your way through Central America or sipping espressos at five-star European restaurants is your style, the increasing globalization of business might just give you your chance to see what the world has to offer. Most new jobs will have at least some global component, even if located within Canada, so being globally aware and keeping an open mind to different cultures is vital in today's business world. Think about the 1.3 billion consumers in China who have already purchased 500 million mobile phones. In the future, some of the largest markets will be in Asia.

Many jobs discussed in chapters throughout this book tend to have strong international components. For example, product management and distribution management are discussed as marketing careers in Chapter 12. As more and more companies sell products around the globe, their function, design, packaging, and promotions need to be culturally relevant to many different people in many different places. Products very often cross multiple borders before reaching the final consumer, both in their distribution and through the supply chain to produce the products.

Jobs exist in export and import management, product and pricing management, distribution and transportation, and advertising. Many "born global" companies such as Google operate virtually and consider all countries their market. Many companies sell their products through eBay and other Internet sites and never leave Canada. Today, communication and transportation facilitates selling and buying products worldwide with delivery in a few days. You may have sold or purchased a product on eBay outside Canada without thinking about how easy and accessible international markets are to business. If you have, welcome to the world of global business.

To be successful you must have an idea not only of differing regulations from country to country, but of different languages, ethics, and communication styles and varying needs and wants of international markets. From a regulatory side, you may need to be aware of laws related to intellectual property, copyrights, antitrust, advertising, and pricing in every country. Translating is never only about translating the language. Perhaps even more important is ensuring that your message gets through. Whether on a product label or in advertising or promotional materials, the use of images and words varies widely across the globe.

BUILD YOUR BUSINESS PLAN

Business in a Borderless World

Think about the product/ service you are contemplating for your business plan. If it is an already established product or service, try to find out if the product is currently being sold internationally. If not, can you identify opportunities to do so in the future? What countries do you think would respond most favourably to your product? What problems would you encounter if you attempted to export your product to those countries?

If you are thinking of creating a new product or service for your business plan, think about the possibility of eventually marketing that product in another country. What countries or areas of the world do you think would be most responsive to your product?

Does Canada have trade agreements or alliances with countries that would make your entry into the market easier? What would be the economic, social, cultural, and technological barriers you would have to recognize before entering the prospective country(ies)? Think about the specific cultural differences that would have to be considered before entering the prospective market.

China and Hollywood are forging a deepening bond thanks to money and market demand. Hollywood, which relies heavily on investors, has recently discovered the deep pockets of both the Chinese government and individual Chinese investors. At the same time, China, determined to grow its own film industry, is looking toward Hollywood for knowledge and audience expansion.

China's economy is booming, creating a new market heavy on capital and enthusiasm for film. Recent endeavours include government-backed China Film Group Corporation's $5 million investment in *The Karate Kid* remake and Orange Sky Golden Harvest Entertainment's $25 million investment in Legendary Pictures (known for *The Dark Knight* and other blockbusters) for a 3.3 percent stake in the company. In addition, China's movie audience is growing, up 80 percent from 2009, and the government is driving a large expansion in movie theatre construction. With China getting more in-depth knowledge of the movie-making industry and Hollywood receiving more capital to make its movies, the situation appears to be a win-win for both parties.

However, as with any partnership, there is often a certain degree of conflict. The Chinese government, for instance, prefers to show Chinese-made movies within China and currently permits only 20 foreign films into the country each year. This makes co-producing more ideal as co-produced films do not fall under this ruling and give Chinese filmmakers more international exposure. Yet with China gaining more expertise in filmmaking, is there a possibility that China could one day become a competitor with Hollywood? Rumour has it that China may be looking into direct investment by purchasing a Hollywood film studio to solidify the partnership. Time will tell whether the increased knowledge that Chinese filmmakers will receive from co-production will one day lead to the creation of China's own Hollywood.[66]

DISCUSSION QUESTIONS

1. Why are the Chinese investing in Hollywood films?

2. How is the Chinese government limiting opportunities for the U.S. film industry?

3. Should Hollywood movie companies be concerned about competition from Chinese filmmakers?

connect **LEARNSMART** **SMARTBOOK**

For more information on the resources available from McGraw-Hill Ryerson, go to www.mcgrawhill.ca/he/solutions.

4 Options for Organizing Business

LEARNING OBJECTIVES

LO1 Define and examine the advantages and disadvantages of the sole proprietorship form of organization.

LO2 Identify three types of partnership, and evaluate the advantages and disadvantages of the partnership form of organization.

LO3 Describe the corporate form of organization, and cite the advantages and disadvantages of corporations.

LO4 Define and debate the advantages and disadvantages of mergers, acquisitions, and leveraged buyouts.

DESTINATION CEO

Heather Reisman If you walk into any Chapters or Indigo bookstore in Canada, you are likely to see some books flagged as "Heather's Picks." Heather, in case you don't know, is Heather Reisman, founder of Indigo Books and Music and the current CEO of Canada's largest retail chain of bookstores, Indigo, which includes Chapters, Indigo, and Coles branded stores. Reisman maintains she has always had a deep love of books and she had originally intended to be a major investor in bringing Borders, an American bookstore, to Canada. Borders' attempts to enter the Canadian market failed to gain approval from the Canadian government and Reisman opted to start her own book retailer.

During Indigo's early years, the company battled for market share with what at the time was its main rival, Chapters. This competitive rivalry changed dramatically in 2001 when Indigo, under Reisman's leadership, launched a hostile takeover of Chapters. While Chapters' management tried to prevent the sale of the company to Indigo, Reisman was ultimately successful. The acquisition, or merger, gave Indigo a virtual monopoly of retail bookstores in Canada.

Since the successful merger, Indigo has had to deal with the emergence of both online retailers, including Amazon.ca, and e-books, which have hurt sales of traditional store-bought printed books. Indigo has responded by improving its online presence and shifting its merchandise mix to include household items, giftware, stationery, baby gifts, and toys with the hopes of increasing its revenue. Reisman is confident that this strategy will pay off and her new merchandise mix will lead to continued success.[1]

Introduction

The legal form of ownership taken by a business is seldom of great concern to you as a customer. When you eat at a restaurant, you probably don't care whether the restaurant is owned by one person (a sole proprietorship), has two or more owners who share the business (a partnership), or is an entity owned by many shareholders (a corporation); all you want is good food. If you buy a foreign car, you probably don't care whether the company that made it has laws governing its form of organization that are different from those for businesses in Canada. You are buying the car because it is well made, fits your price range, or appeals to your sense of style. Nonetheless, a business's legal form of ownership affects how it operates, how much tax it pays, and how much control its owners have.

This chapter examines three primary forms of business ownership—sole proprietorship, partnership, and corporation—and weighs the advantages and disadvantages of each. These forms are the most often used whether the business is a traditional "bricks and mortar" company, an online-only one, or a combination of both. We also take a look at cooperatives and discuss some trends in business ownership. You may wish to refer to Table 4.1 to compare the various forms of business ownership mentioned in the chapter.

Sole Proprietorships

Sole proprietorships, businesses owned and operated by one individual, are the most common form of business organization in Canada. Common examples include many restaurants, hair salons, flower shops, doggie day cares, and independent retail stores. For example, stay-at-home mom Sandra Wilson of Vancouver started making form-fitted leather shoes for toddlers when she was unable to find traditional shoes that would stay on her son's feet. Wilson made 20 pairs of shoes in her basement and started selling them at local trade shows. The company, which shares its name with the shoes—Robeez—was eventually sold for $27.5 million.[2] While most sole proprietors stay small, stories like Wilson's are not uncommon. Where Wilson's tale is unique is that most sole proprietors focus on services—small retail stores, financial counselling, appliance repair, child care, and the like—rather than on the manufacture of goods, which often requires large amounts of money not available to small businesses.

> **Sole proprietorships** businesses owned and operated by one individual; the most common form of business organization in Canada

Sole proprietorships are typically small businesses employing fewer than 50 people. (We'll look at small businesses in greater detail in Chapter 5.) There are approximately 2.3 million businesses in Canada, of which the majority are sole proprietorships.

> ## "Common examples include many restaurants, hair salons, flower shops, doggie day cares, and independent retail stores."

Advantages of Sole Proprietorships

Sole proprietorships are generally managed by their owners. Because of this simple management structure, the owner/manager can make decisions quickly. This is just one of many advantages of the sole proprietorship form of business.

Ease and Cost of Formation.   Forming a sole proprietorship is relatively easy and inexpensive. In some instances all the entrepreneur has to do is to start selling a product or service. For example, when Chris Neville of Sydney, Nova Scotia, started his online business, www.lifeofsports.com, he simply started running his business online. Neville now owns and operates several online companies, including University Poker Championship. Neville is no doubt trying to follow in the footsteps of other entrepreneurs who made it big starting with a small company. For example, Frank Stronach of Magna International Inc. and Brian Scudamore of 1-800-GOT-JUNK? both started small companies in Canada, and grew them into large successful enterprises. Other proprietorships, such as barbershops and restaurants, may require provincial and local licences and permits because of the nature of the business. The cost of these permits may run from $25 to $1,000. No lawyer is needed to create such enterprises, and the owner can usually take care of the required paperwork.

Of course, an entrepreneur starting a new sole proprietorship must find a suitable site from which to operate the business. Some sole proprietors look no farther than their garage or a spare bedroom that they can convert into a workshop or office. Among the more famous businesses that sprang to life in their founders' homes are Robeez (which we discussed above), SpinMaster (Canada's largest private toy company, which can trace its origins to a poster business in a dorm room), Google, Dell, eBay, and Mattel.[3] Computers, personal copiers, fax machines, and other high-tech gadgets have been a boon for home-based businesses, permitting them to interact quickly with customers, suppliers, and others. Many independent salespersons and contractors can perform their work using a tablet computer or smart phone as they travel. E-mail and cell phones have made it possible for many proprietorships to develop in the services area. Internet connections also allow small businesses to establish websites to promote their products and even to make low-cost long-distance phone calls with voice over Internet protocol (VOIP) technology such as Skype.

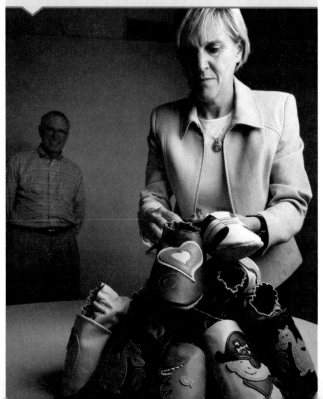

While most sole proprietorships stay small, some experience tremendous success. Sandra Wilson sold her business, Robeez, for $27 million.

table 4.1 Various Forms of Business Ownership

Structure	Ownership	Taxation	Liability	Use
Sole Proprietorship	1 owner	Individual income taxed	Unlimited	Individual starting a business and easiest way to conduct business
Partnership	2 or more owners	Individual owners' income taxed	Unlimited (unless it is a limited partnership)	Easy way for two individuals to conduct business
Private Corporation	Any number of shareholders	Corporate and shareholder income taxed	Varies between limited and unlimited	A legal entity with shareholders or stakeholders
Public Corporation	Any number of shareholders	Corporate and shareholder income taxed	Limited	A legal entity with shareholders or stakeholders

Secrecy. Sole proprietorships allow for the greatest degree of secrecy. The proprietor, unlike the owners of a partnership or corporation, does not have to share his or her operating plans, minimizing the possibility that competitors can obtain trade secrets. Financial reports need not be disclosed, as do the financial reports of publicly owned corporations. For example, when David Reynolds of Halifax, Nova Scotia, founded his sole proprietorship QuickSnap, selling a unique shoe-fastening device that was later featured on CBC's hit TV series *Dragons' Den*, he did not have to share information on how the product was constructed or his financial results with anyone.

Distribution and Use of Profits. All profits from a sole proprietorship belong exclusively to the owner. He or she does not have to share them with any partners or shareholders. The owner alone decides how the profits are used, which could include to expand the business, to increase salaries, or to find new customers.

Flexibility and Control of the Business. The sole proprietor has complete control over the business and can make decisions on the spot without anyone else's approval. This control allows the owner to respond quickly to competitive business conditions or to changes in the economy. Jim Pattison, one of Canada's most successful entrepreneurs and owner of the Pattison Group (www.jimpattison.com), a private corporation that is managed very much like a sole proprietorship, has frequently stated that his company has remained private as it allows him to make quick decisions that focus on the long term without having to answer to a board of directors or shareholders like publicly owned corporate operators.

Government Regulation. Sole proprietorships have the most freedom from government regulation. Many government regulations—federal, provincial, and local—apply only to businesses that have a certain number of employees, and securities laws apply only to corporations that issue shares. Nonetheless, sole proprietors must ensure that they follow all laws that do apply to their business.

Taxation. Profits from the business are considered personal income to the sole proprietor and are taxed at individual tax rates. The owner pays one income tax. In addition, owners of sole proprietorships can deduct losses from their business against other forms of income. For example, Bill, a high school teacher, starts a part-time business sealing driveways and loses $10,000 in his first year of operations. He can now deduct $10,000 from the $80,000 he makes as an educator and only pay tax on $70,000. A sole proprietor who works from his or her home can also deduct expenses such as their home office from their business income. Another tax benefit is that a sole proprietor is allowed to establish a tax-exempt retirement account. Such accounts are exempt from current income tax, but payments taken after retirement are taxed when they are received.

> "Sole proprietorships have the most freedom from government regulation."

Closing the Business. A sole proprietorship can be dissolved easily. No approval of co-owners or partners is necessary. When Mary Drain of Sudbury, Ontario, closed her home-based craft business, she only told her friends and family she was closing. No other formal notice was required.

Disadvantages of Sole Proprietorships

What is seen as an advantage by one person may turn out to be a disadvantage to another. The goals and talents of the individual owner are the deciding factors in determining the success of a sole proprietorship. For profitable businesses managed by capable owners, many of the following factors do not cause problems. On the other hand, proprietors starting out with little management experience and little money are likely to encounter many of the disadvantages.

Unlimited Liability. The sole proprietor has unlimited liability in meeting the debts of the business. In other words, if the business cannot pay its creditors, the owner may be forced to use personal, non-business holdings such as a car or a home to pay off the debts. Furthermore, the sole proprietor may also be legally responsible for any claims made against the business. For example if a person walks into a retail store and slips, he or she will be able to personally sue the sole proprietor for the accident. The more wealth an individual has, the greater is the disadvantage of unlimited liability.

Limited Sources of Funds. Among the relatively few sources of money available to the sole proprietorship are banks, friends, family, some government programs, and/or his or her own funds. The owner's personal financial condition determines his or her credit standing. Additionally, sole proprietorships may have to pay higher interest rates on funds borrowed from banks than do large corporations because they are considered greater risks. Often, the only way a sole proprietor can borrow for business purposes is to pledge a house, other real estate, or other personal assets to guarantee the loan. If the business fails, the owner may lose the personal assets as well as the business. Publicly owned corporations, in contrast, not only can obtain funds from banks but can sell shares and bonds to the public to raise money. If a public company goes out of business, the owners do not lose personal assets.

Limited Skills. The sole proprietor must be able to perform many functions and possess skills in diverse fields such as management, marketing, finance, accounting, bookkeeping, and personnel. Business owners can rely on specialized professions for advice and services, such as accountants and attorneys. Musicians, for example, can turn to agents for assistance in navigating through the complex maze of the recording business. One start-up firm specializing in this type of assistance for online musicians and bands is the Digital Artists Agency, which researches, markets, and cultivates online music talent in exchange for a commission on their online sales of music, tickets, and merchandise.[4] In the end, however, it is up to the owner to make the final decision in all areas of the business, and not everyone has the skills to be successful on their own.

> "The sole proprietor has unlimited liability in meeting the debts of the business."

Lack of Continuity. The life expectancy of a sole proprietorship is directly related to that of the owner and his or her ability to work. The serious illness of the owner could result in failure if competent help cannot be found.

It is difficult to arrange for the sale of a proprietorship and at the same time assure customers that the business will continue to meet their needs. For instance, how does one sell a veterinary practice? A veterinarian's major asset is patients. If the vet dies suddenly, the equipment can be sold, but the patients will not necessarily remain loyal to the office. On the other hand, a veterinarian who wants to retire could take in a younger partner and sell the practice to the partner over time.

Consider the Following: Microlending Helps Small Entrepreneurs Start Businesses

Sending food and money to disadvantaged communities meets immediate needs, but ending long-term poverty is more difficult. Kiva.org is one business that seeks to tackle this problem head on. Founded by Stanford University graduates with an interest in business and technology, Kiva was first designed to lend money to impoverished Ugandan entrepreneurs. It soon expanded its reach to include other developing countries. Kiva is a microfinance business, which means it provides small loans—as little as $25 for equipment, for example—to individuals to start their own businesses.

Kiva partners with microfinance institutions worldwide. These field partners approve entrepreneurs and send their profiles to Kiva. The entrepreneurs' profiles are then posted on Kiva's website, and people who want to lend to an entrepreneur send their donations through the site. Kiva's field partners distribute the loans, work with the entrepreneurs, and collect repayments. Kiva.org does not earn returns on investments for lenders, but it does charge interest rates of between 23 and 48 percent. These interest rates cover loan costs, transaction costs, defaults, and inflation rates—and are much lower than rates charged by informal lenders or predatory lenders who typically supply loans to those who do not qualify for bank loans.

Kiva and over 560,000 lenders have succeeded in providing loans to over half a million entrepreneurs since 2005. The company has given $200 million in worldwide loans, but Kiva wants to go even further. It has established a five-year plan, aiming to reach $1 billion in global loans, help 2 million entrepreneurs, and achieve organizational sustainability. The buzz about Kiva is positive, and Kiva.org's future looks bright as microlending continues to receive favourable press.[5]

DISCUSSION QUESTIONS

1. Kiva.org has been very successful at extending microlending to entrepreneurs in need. What about Kiva.org has helped make it so successful?

2. What is unique about the way Kiva.org is organized that sets it apart from more traditional businesses?

3. Do you think the Kiva.org model of giving loans would work for larger loans, or even for other kinds of businesses?

Taxation. Although we listed taxation as an advantage for sole proprietorships, it can also be a disadvantage, depending on the proprietor's income. Under current tax rates, sole proprietors pay a higher marginal tax rate than do small corporations. This means sole proprietors may pay more in tax than small corporations.

> **LO2** Identify three types of partnership, and evaluate the advantages and disadvantages of the partnership form of organization.

Partnerships

One way to minimize the disadvantages of a sole proprietorship and maximize its advantages is to have more than one owner. For example, Mississauga-based Dekalam Hire Learning—a provider of online training to help people with pre-employment exams for policing, the public service and so forth—was founded by three partners who brought complementary skills to the business: Adam Cooper had testing experience, Kalpesh Rathod brought IT experience, and Deland Jessop worked in law enforcement. Cooper says, "We went into business together because our skill set was so complementary."[6]

In Canada, partnerships are formed when two or more people fill out simple forms registering their business with the provincial governments to form partners. The partnership would then be governed by the Partnership Act (see Table 4.2), which outlines the rights and duties of partners toward one another. The rules of the Partnership Act apply unless the partners have signed a *partnership agreement*. A **partnership** can be defined as "an association of two or more persons who carry on as co-owners of a business for profit." Partnerships are the least used form of business organization in Canada. They are typically larger than sole proprietorships but smaller than corporations.

> **Partnership** a form of business organization defined as "an association of two or more persons who carry on as co-owners of a business for profit"
>
> **General partnership** a partnership that involves a complete sharing in both the management and the liability of the business

Types of Partnership

There are three basic types of partnership: general partnership, limited partnership, and a limited liability partnership. A **general partnership** involves a complete sharing in the management of a business. In a general partnership,

---

ENTREPRENEURSHIP IN ACTION | Business Ownership—An Ever-Changing Structure Story

David Reynolds

Business: Quicksnap

Founded: 2003

Success: Since his appearance on Season III of *Dragons' Den*, sales have risen more than twofold, with online orders originating from as far away as Australia and New Zealand.

When David Reynolds of Halifax, Nova Scotia, started university he was like most students, unsure about what he wanted to do with his life. Reynolds notes, "I had no idea why I was even enrolled in university other than it was what everyone does." Shortly after attending a lecture on entrepreneurship, Reynolds became enthralled with the idea of starting his own company, saying, "I loved the idea of being my own boss, thoughts of getting rich with something I created." Reynolds searched for an idea and a short time later found one as he was getting tired of waiting for his friend to tie his shoes. Reynolds states, "People hate tying their shoes. What if they didn't have to do this? What if there was a way to clip the laces together?" A short time later Quicksnap (www.Quicksnap.ca), a shoe-fastening device, was

born. When the company first started, it was structured as a sole proprietorship; as Reynolds quips, "It was just me and my idea." A short time later, Reynolds realized he needed some help managing his business as well as some extra funding, and recruited two friends to join his company. Thus, the sole proprietor became a partner. Reynolds says that forming a partnership was cheaper and easier than forming a corporation. "We drafted a partnership agreement, we all signed it, and we became partners." Like most start-ups, the business eventually needed more funding and Reynolds found himself looking for outside investors. Reynolds notes, "At this time I knew that we needed a formal structure and the business went through the process of incorporating. We needed the advantages of a private corporation, we needed to be able to issue shares to investors, ensure that everyone involved in the ownership group had limited liability and so forth." As of 2010, the business has been featured on the hit CBC series *Dragons' Den* and the product is being sold nationally in various stores. Reynolds is no longer CEO, but still owns shares in the business that he founded as a 19-year-old with an idea he had while watching his friend struggle to tie his shoes.[7]

table 4.2 The Partnership Act

The following rules can be found in the Ontario statute of the Partnership Act, which is similar to those of other provinces:

- All partners are entitled to share equally in the capital and profits of the business and must contribute equally toward the losses, whether of capital or otherwise, sustained by the firm

- All money or property brought into or acquired by the partnership becomes partnership property

- No partner should be entitled to remuneration for acting in the partnership of the business

- No person may be introduced as a partner without the consent of existing partners

Limited partnership a business organization that has at least one general partner, who assumes unlimited liability, and at least one limited partner, whose liability is limited to his or her investment in the business

Limited liability partnership (LLP) a partnership agreement where partners are not responsible for losses created by other partners

Partnership agreement document that sets forth the basic agreement between partners

each partner has unlimited liability for the debts of the business. For example, Cirque du Soleil grew from a group of Quebec street performers, who acted as partners, into a half-billion–dollar global company.[8] Professionals such as lawyers, accountants, and architects often join together in general partnerships.

A **limited partnership** has at least one general partner, who assumes unlimited liability, and at least one limited partner, whose liability is limited to his or her investment in the business. Limited partnerships exist for risky investment projects where the chance of loss is great. The general partners accept the risk of loss; the limited partners' losses are limited to their initial investment. Limited partners do not participate in the management of the business, but share in the profits in accordance with the terms of a partnership agreement. Usually the general partner receives a larger share of the profits after the limited partners have received their initial investment back. Popular examples are oil-drilling partnerships and real estate partnerships. A **limited liability partnership (LLP)** is a unique partnership agreement where non-negligent partners are not personally responsible for losses created by other partners. This type of partnership is only available in some provinces and is popular among legal and accounting firms.

Partnership Agreement

A **partnership agreement** is a legal document that sets forth the basic agreement between partners. Unless partners sign a partnership agreement, their partnership will be bound by the rules outlined in their provincial Partnership Act. While not legally required, it makes good sense for partners to sign and follow such an agreement. Partnership agreements usually list the money or assets that each partner

has contributed (called *partnership capital*), state each partner's individual management role or duty, specify how the profits and losses of the partnership will be divided among the partners, and describe how a partner may leave the partnership, as well as any other restrictions that might apply to the agreement. Table 4.3 lists some of the issues and provisions that should be included in articles of partnership.

Advantages of Partnerships

Law firms, accounting firms, and investment firms with several hundred partners have partnership agreements that are quite complicated in comparison with the partnership agreement among two or three people owning a computer repair shop. The advantages must be compared with those offered by other forms of business organization, and not all apply to every partnership.

Ease of Organization. Starting a partnership requires little more than filling out some basic forms with the provincial government including the registration of the business's name. While a partnership agreement is highly recommended, it is not required as the provincial Partnership Act provides rules for the business to follow. As evident in "Business Ownership—An Ever-Changing Structure Story," forming a partnership is relatively simple.

Combined Knowledge and Skills. Successful partners acknowledge each other's talents and avoid confusion and conflict by specializing in a particular area of expertise such as marketing, production, accounting, or service. The diversity of skills in a partnership makes it possible for the business to be run by a management team of specialists instead of by a generalist sole proprietor. For example, Mike Lazaridis (founder of Research In Motion—better known as RIM, and now called BlackBerry, and manufacturer of the BlackBerry line of smart phones) brought Jim Balsillie in as partner. Lazaridis notes, "I asked Jim to join RIM in 1992 because I needed a partner with finance expertise. The decision to go with a co-CEO structure is based on a trust of each other's strengths and an appreciation for the complexity of running a fast-growing global company."[9] Lazaridis and Balsillie successfully ran the company under this structure for over nine years before being replaced in 2012. Service-oriented partnerships in fields such as law, financial planning, and accounting may attract customers because clients may think that the service offered by a diverse team is of higher quality than that provided by one person. Larger law firms, for example, often have individual partners who specialize in certain areas of the law—such as family, bankruptcy, corporate, entertainment, and criminal law.

> "When a business has several partners, it has the benefit of a combination of talents."

Availability of Capital and Credit. When a business has several partners, it has the benefit of a combination of talents and skills and pooled financial resources. The pooling of financial resources is particularly attractive to new firms as they are heavily dependent on the personal investment of the owner for start-up financing. As discussed in Chapter 5, personal investment of the owner is responsible for 66 percent of the money raised by new ventures. Partnerships tend to be larger than sole proprietorships and therefore have greater earning power and better credit ratings.

Decision Making. Small partnerships can react more quickly to changes in the business environment than can large partnerships and corporations. Such fast reactions are possible because the partners are involved in day-to-day operations and can make decisions quickly after consultation. Examples of this quick decision making can often be seen by partners on CBC's hit series *Dragons' Den* or ABC's *Shark Tank* where entrepreneurs are looking to raise money for a fledging business or idea. Often partners are given very little time to make decisions about selling a percent of their business for much needed capital. This was the situation in which the owners of Atomic Tea, a Calgary-based specialty tea store, found themselves while pitching on the show. The sister and brother—Jessica and Russell Bohrson—were offered a $120,000 investment for 50.1 percent of their business. The pair had to make the decision in minutes and opted to accept the money and give up a large percent of their business.[10] While the Bohrsons' decision-making process was obviously more dramatic because it occurred on television, viewers did get to see how quickly small partners can react to changes in their environment.

Regulatory Controls. Like a sole proprietorship, a partnership has fewer regulatory controls affecting its activities than does a corporation. A partnership does, however, have to abide by all laws relevant to the industry or profession

table 4.3 Issues and Provisions in Articles of Partnership

1. Name, purpose, location
2. Duration of the agreement
3. Authority and responsibility of each partner
4. Character of partners (i.e., general or limited, active or silent)
5. Amount of contribution from each partner
6. Division of profits or losses
7. Salaries of each partner
8. How much each partner is allowed to withdraw
9. Death of partner
10. Sale of partnership interest
11. Arbitration of disputes
12. Required and prohibited actions
13. Absence and disability
14. Restrictive covenants
15. Buying and selling agreements

SOURCE: Adapted from "Partnership Agreement Sample," State of New Jersey, http://www.state.nj.us/njbusiness/start/biztype/partner/agreement_sample.shtml (accessed June 13, 2007).

in which it operates, as well as provincial and federal laws relating to hiring and firing, food handling, and so on, just as the sole proprietorship does.

Disadvantages of Partnerships

Partnerships have many advantages compared to sole proprietorships and corporations, but they also have some disadvantages. Limited partners have no voice in the management of the partnership, and they may bear most of the risk of the business while the general partner reaps a larger share of the benefits. There may be a change in the goals and objectives of one partner but not the other, particularly when the partners are multinational organizations. This can cause friction, giving rise to an enterprise that fails to satisfy both parties or even forcing an end to the partnership. Many partnership disputes wind up in court or require outside mediation. For example, a quarrel among the partners who owned the Montreal Expos baseball team moved to U.S. District Court after new general partner Jeffrey Loria moved the team to Florida and renamed it the Florida Marlins. Twelve of the team's limited partners sued Loria, accusing him of buying the Expos with the intent of moving the team, diluting their share in the team, and effectively destroying "the economic viability of baseball in Montreal."[11] In such cases, the ultimate solution may be dissolving the partnership. Major disadvantages of partnerships include the following.

Disagreements Among Partners. A partnership is similar to any relationship including a close friendship or a marriage. Partners often work together on a daily basis and disagreements are inevitable. Smaller firms are more likely to suffer from such disagreements as their size

Mike Lazaridis, on the right, and Jim Balsillie, on the left, were likely the most famous Canadian business partners in recent years. The former co-CEOs of Research In Motion combined their expertise to build one of the top technology companies in the world. The pair was recently replaced by Thorsten Heins.

table 4.4 Keys to Success in Business Partnerships

1. Keep profit sharing and ownership at 50/50, or you have an employer/employee relationship.

2. Partners should have different skill sets to complement one another.

3. Honesty is critical.

4. Maintain face-to-face communication in addition to phone and e-mail.

5. Maintain transparency, sharing more information over time.

6. Be aware of funding constraints and do not put yourself in a situation where neither you nor your partner can secure additional financial support.

7. To be successful, you need experience.

8. Whereas family should be a priority, be careful to minimize the number of associated problems.

9. Do not become too infatuated with "the idea" as opposed to its implementation.

10. Couple optimism with realism in sales and growth expectations and planning.

SOURCE: Abstracted from J. Watananbe, "14 Reasons Why 80 Percent of New Business Partnerships Would Fail Within Their First 5 Years of Existence," http://ezinearticles.com/?14-Reasons-Why-80-Percent-Of-New-Business-Partnerships-Would-Fail-Within-Their-First-5-Years-Of-Exis&id=472498 (accessed June 20, 2013).

often prevents a clear distinction of duties that can be found in larger partnerships. Often disagreements are minor and about day-to-day occurrences, but sometimes they can spell the end of a partnership, a friendship, and a business. This is what happened to the highly successful partnership of Michel Boucher and Chuck Buchanan. The pair operated Flightexec, a London, Ontario-based company which went from bankruptcy to $20 million in annual sales in 10 years. But when the two partners differed over the long-term strategy for the company, it ended the partnership and Buchanan was forced to leave the business. Partnership disputes can occur in large companies as well. One of the most talked about disputes in Canadian business history was the succession battle at the multibillion dollar McCain Foods frozen food empire. Harrison and Wallace McCain co-managed the business for years with Harrison looking after sales and growth and his brother Wallace dealing with managing the manufacturing facilities. When the pair started to look for a successor, Wallace was insistent that his son Michael receive the job while Harrison objected to the idea. The succession battle ended with Harrison removing Wallace as his co-CEO, the brothers' relationship being in tatters, and Wallace buying a large interest in Maple Leaf Foods where his son Michael was eventually named CEO. Table 4.4 lists some suggestions for building a successful partnership.

Unlimited Liability. In general partnerships, the general partners have unlimited liability for the debts incurred by

> "All partners are responsible for the business actions of all others."

the business, just as the sole proprietor has unlimited liability for his or her business. Such unlimited liability can be a distinct disadvantage to one partner if his or her personal financial resources are greater than those of the others. A potential partner should make sure that all partners have comparable resources to help the business in times of trouble. This disadvantage is eliminated for limited partners, who can lose only their initial investment.

Business Responsibility. All partners are responsible for the business actions of all others. Partners may have the ability to commit the partnership to a contract without approval of the other partners. A bad decision by one partner may put the other partners' personal resources in jeopardy. Personal problems such as a divorce can eliminate a significant portion of one partner's financial resources and weaken the financial structure of the whole partnership.

Life of the Partnership. A partnership is terminated when a partner dies or withdraws. In a two-person partnership, if one partner withdraws, the firm's liabilities would be paid off and the assets divided between the partners. Obviously, the partner who wishes to continue in the business would be at a serious disadvantage. The business could be disrupted, financing would be reduced, and the management skills of the departing partner would be lost. The remaining partner would have to find another partner or reorganize the business as a sole proprietorship. In very large partnerships such as those found in law firms and investment banks, the continuation of the partnership may be provided for in the articles of partnership. The provision may simply state the terms for a new partnership agreement among the remaining partners. In such cases, the disadvantage to the other partners is minimal.

Selling a partnership interest has the same effect as the death or withdrawal of a partner. It is difficult to place a value on a partner's share of the partnership. No public value is placed on the partnership, as there is on publicly owned corporations. What is a law firm worth? What is the local hardware store worth? Coming up with a fair value to which all partners can agree is not easy. For example, in the McCain partnership dispute discussed above, Wallace maintained 35 percent ownership in the business even after being fired as co-CEO because he could not sell his stake in the company. No buyer wanted to purchase his minority stake in the company and he and his brother Harrison could never agree on a price for the shares.[12] Selling a partnership interest is easier if the articles of partnership specify a method of valuation. Even if there is not a procedure for selling one partner's interest, the old partnership must still be dissolved and a new one created. In contrast, in the corporate form of business, the departure of owners has little effect on the financial resources of the business, and the loss of managers does not cause long-term changes in the structure of the organization.

Distribution of Profits. Profits earned by the partnership are distributed to the partners in the proportions specified in the articles of partnership. This may be a disadvantage if the division of the profits does not reflect the work each partner puts into the business. You may have encountered this disadvantage while working on a student group project: You may have felt that you did most of the work and that the other students in the group received grades based on your efforts. Even the perception of an unfair profit-sharing agreement may cause tension between the partners, and unhappy partners can have a negative effect on the profitability of the business.

Limited Sources of Funds. As with a sole proprietorship, the sources of funds available to a partnership are limited. Because no public value is placed on the business (such as the current trading price of a corporation's shares), potential partners do not know what one partnership share is worth. Moreover, because partnership shares cannot be bought and sold easily in public markets, potential owners may not want to tie up their money in assets that cannot be readily sold on short notice, as is evident in the McCain dispute. Accumulating enough funds to operate a national business, especially a business requiring intensive investments in facilities and equipment, can be difficult. Partnerships also may have to pay higher interest rates on funds borrowed from banks than do large corporations because partnerships may be considered greater risks.

Taxation of Partnerships

Partnerships do not pay taxes when submitting the partnership tax return to the Canada Revenue Agency. Partners must report their share of profits on their individual tax returns and pay taxes at the income tax rate for individuals. Much like sole proprietors, partners can deduct losses from their partnership against other sources of income, but often pay more in taxes compared to corporations due to their tax rate.

RESPONDING TO BUSINESS CHALLENGES | Should Partners Have a Shotgun?

"Should partners have a shotgun?" Perhaps the question makes you think of the Old West or organized crime movies, but the term *shotgun* has a very different meaning in partnership agreements.

Essentially the term is used to describe a clause where one business partner can make a cash offer for the other partner's share of the business. The person being offered the money for their share of the business is usually left with only two choices: (1) Accept the offer and take the money; or (2) Match the partner's offer and assume the partner's share of the business.

People's opinions of shotgun clauses in partnerships differ. Some argue that they are useful tools, which allow for a quick end to a partnership that is no longer working. Furthermore, the cash offer is usually at a premium as the person making the offer risks getting removed from the business if they make a low offer. Others argue that shotgun clauses are often used too quickly when other dispute resolutions could be used to save partnerships, and that shotguns favour the partner with the most resources.

Joyce Groote, owner of Vancouver-based Holey Soles Holding Limited (http://holeys.com), did not start the business that she currently runs with her husband. Groote, who was very successful in the pharmaceutical industry, was asked to join the company to offer the founders managerial assistance. Groote eventually invested some cash in the business and ultimately exercised a shotgun clause to oust the founding partners. Groote noted that while her partners were good at starting a company, they were often too slow at making decisions, which negatively impacted growth.

The use of shotgun clauses is not limited to small business, as evident in the case of Tim Hortons and its partner, the Swiss specialist bakery conglomerate Aryzta AG. Tim Hortons and Aryzta AG had formed a partnership whereby the companies jointly owned a baking facility in Brantford, Ontario, that supplied all of the Tim Hortons stores with baked goods. Unexpectedly, the Swiss firm exercised a shotgun clause forcing Tim Hortons to either pay a substantial amount of money for a key production facility that is essential to its operation or allow Aryzta AG to assume control over an essential part of Tim Hortons' business. Tim Hortons eventually accepted the $475 million offer after Aryzta agreed to continue to supply product to the company until 2016.[13]

DISCUSSION QUESTIONS

1. If you were ever to join a partnership, would you want to have a shotgun clause?

2. What are some of the advantages and disadvantages of a shotgun clause?

3. What alternatives would you suggest to using a shotgun clause?

4. Would exercising the shotgun clause negatively impact Aryzta AG's ability to form partnerships in the future? Why or why not?

Corporations

When you think of a business, you probably think of a huge corporation such as Bell Canada, Tim Hortons, Shoppers Drug Mart, or the Royal Bank because most of your consumer dollars go to such corporations. A **corporation** is a legal entity, created under law either provincially or federally, whose assets and liabilities are separate from its owners'. As a legal entity, a corporation has many of the rights, duties, and powers of a person, such as the right to receive, own, and transfer property. Corporations can enter into contracts with individuals or with other legal entities, and they can sue and be sued in court.

Corporations account for the majority of Canadian sales and employment. Thus, most of the dollars you spend as a consumer probably go to incorporated businesses (see Table 4.5 for the largest corporations in Canada). Not all corporations are mega-companies like Encana Corp. or Manulife; even small businesses can incorporate and share in many of the advantages of being an incorporated company.

> **Corporation** a legal entity, whose assets and liabilities are separate from its owners'
>
> **Shares** shares of a corporation that may be bought or sold
>
> **Dividends** profits of a corporation that are distributed in the form of cash payments to shareholders

Corporations are typically owned by many individuals and organizations who own **shares** of the business sometimes referred to as stocks (thus, corporate owners are often called *shareholders* or *stockholders*). Shareholders can buy, sell, give or receive as gifts, or inherit their shares of stock. As owners, the shareholders are entitled to all profits that are left after all the corporation's other obligations have been paid. These profits may be distributed in the form of cash payments called **dividends.** For example, if a corporation earns $100 million after expenses and taxes and decides to pay the owners $40 million in dividends, the shareholders receive 40 percent of the profits in cash dividends. However, not all after-tax profits are paid to shareholders in dividends. In this example, the corporation retained $60 million of profits to finance expansion.

Creating a Corporation

A corporation is created, or incorporated, under the laws of the provincial or federal government. A business that is incorporated provincially does so under its provincial corporations legislation and can only conduct business in the province in which it is incorporated. Businesses that are incorporated federally do so under the Canada Business Corporations Act and can conduct business in all provinces and territories provided that they register their corporation in all the provinces where they carry on business. The main advantages of incorporating federally are the ability to operate anywhere in Canada and to use the same company name. Federal corporations do cost more to start than provincial corporations and have extra paperwork, including filings required by the federal Directors of Corporations Branch and all the filings required by the provinces.

The individuals creating the corporation are known as *incorporators.* Each provincial and the federal government has specific procedures, sometimes called *chartering the corporation,* for incorporating a business. The first step is often choosing the name of the company, which must have:

- Distinctive portion to identify the business
- Descriptive portion that assists in identifying the activities of the company
- Legal element that identifies the business as a corporation including Limited, Incorporated, or Corporation

After a name is chosen, a search is conducted to determine if the name is original and suitable.

The incorporators must then file legal documents including: the *Memorandum,* which lays out the rules for the company's conduct; the *Articles of Incorporation,* which are the rules and regulations that the company's members and directors must follow; and the *Notice of Officers,* which states the location of the required offices for the company—the registered office and the records office. Corporations that are incorporating under federal law must also prepare a *Notice of Directors* with the appropriate provincial or federal government. The following information is necessary when filing for a corporation.

1. Name and address of the corporation.
2. Address for the Registered and Records Office.
3. Description of the classes of shares and the maximum number of shares that will be issued, as well as a clear description of the rights, privileges, and restrictions for each class of share.

table 4.5 Market Cap: Top 10 Snapshot

The largest corporations in Canada by market cap from largest to smallest are as follows.[14] Since the information in the table can change quickly, students may want to use Internet resources to see what companies have moved up or down the list.

TD Bank

Bank of Nova Scotia

Royal Bank

Barrick Gold

Suncor Energy

Imperial Oil

Bank of Montreal

CIBC

Potash Corp. of Saskatchewan

Teck Resources

4. Restrictions on share transfers, which must specify whether shares can be sold or transferred.

5. Number of directors.

6. Restrictions on the company's business activities.

7. Other provisions. (While there is no requirement to include this, some incorporators do so to satisfy requirements from other provinces or regulatory agencies.)

Based on the information in the articles of incorporation, the provincial or federal government approves the corporation by issuing a **certificate of incorporation.** After securing approval, the owners hold an organizational meeting at which they establish the corporation's bylaws and elect a board of directors. The bylaws might set up committees of the board of directors and describe the rules and procedures for their operation.

Types of Corporations

A corporation may be privately or publicly owned. A **private corporation** is owned by just one or a few people who are closely involved in managing the business. These people, sometimes a family, own the majority if not all of the corporation's shares, and shares are not sold on any of the public stock exchanges. Shares in private corporations can be sold but the details of the transactions usually remain private. Many corporations are quite large, yet remain private, including the Irving Group of New Brunswick. Irving is one of the largest and most diversified companies in Canada with interests in shipbuilding, newspapers, tissue paper, transportation, and oil and gas, yet it remains a large private corporation. Privately owned corporations are not required to disclose financial information publicly, but they must, of course, pay taxes.

"A corporation may be privately or publicly owned."

A **public corporation** is one whose shares anyone may buy, sell, or trade on a public stock exchange such as the Toronto Stock Exchange (www.tmx.com). In large public corporations, such as the Royal Bank, the shareholders are often far removed from the management of the company. In other public corporations, the managers are often the founders and the majority shareholders. For example, the late Ted Rogers, founder of Rogers Communications, ran Rogers Communications right up until the time of his death. Other Canadian companies that have been or still are controlled by their founders include Magna International (Frank Stronach), Power Corporation of Canada

Certificate of incorporation a legal document that the provincial or federal government issues to a company based on information the company provides in the articles of incorporation

Private corporation a corporation owned by just one or a few people who are closely involved in managing the business

Public corporation a corporation whose shares anyone may buy, sell, or trade

Facebook CEO Mark Zuckerberg saw the company's share price fall shortly after taking the company public. The share price has recovered as Facebook has managed to increase its revenue through mobile advertising.

"Privately owned corporations are not required to disclose financial information publicly, but they must, of course, pay taxes."

(Paul Desmarais), and Onex Corporation (Gerald Schwartz). Publicly owned corporations must disclose financial information to the public under specific laws that regulate the trade of stocks and other securities.

A private corporation sometimes goes public to obtain more financing through the sale of shares, to allow the founders of the company to realize the value of the business, to raise money to pay off debt, to invest the proceeds in the firm, or to enhance the company's ability to raise capital in the future. A company goes public through an **initial public offering (IPO),** that is, becoming a public corporation by selling its shares so that it can be traded in public markets. For example, Google, the popular Internet search engine, went public with an initial public offering in 2004 and raised US$1.66 billion.[15] Facebook's recent IPO surpassed Google's, and raised US$16 billion, valuing the company at US$104.2 billion. As a result of the IPO, Facebook founder Mark Zuckerberg became the 19th-richest person on Earth, with a net worth of roughly US$19 billion. Unfortunately for Zuckerberg, and many of the company's initial investors, Facebook's share price did not increase dramatically in value after its IPO and actually declined.[16] The stock has since recovered as Facebook has managed to make more money from mobile advertising than was originally expected. Pizza Pizza Ltd., one of Canada's largest fast-food restaurants, went public and raised in excess of C$150 million. The owners of Pizza Pizza took the company public so they could realize some of the value in the company. They initially sold 75 percent of the shares in the business. Shoppers Drug Mart raised C$540 million when it went

Initial public offering (IPO) selling a corporation's shares on public markets for the first time

public and used a large amount of the money to pay off the company's debt. Hudson's Bay Company (HBC) has recently become a public corporation again after being taken private a short time ago by an American firm. HBC raised roughly $350 million in its IPO, of which 20 percent will be used to pay down debt; the rest of the money will be re-invested in improving stores in the face of increased competition from Target. Sometimes, privately owned firms are forced to go public with share offerings when a majority owner dies and the company's family members cannot decide on how best to manage the company or settle a large tax bill due as a result of the owner's death. The Irving Group discussed above has a long history of being a "very private" corporation—meaning very little information about the company was ever shared with the outside world. The family-owned business is currently controlled by the three sons of founder KC Irving, but they are apparently considering taking the company public in order to assist in long-term planning for the business and to ensure that all family members are properly compensated. Another example occurred at Adolph Coors Inc. When brewer Adolph Coors died, his business went public and his family sold shares of stock to the public to pay the estate taxes. Interestingly enough, KC Irving actually changed his place of residence from Canada to Bermuda to avoid paying large estate taxes.

Often when students see the letters IPO they may recall media stories describing the large amounts of money investors were willing to pay for the initial public offerings of companies such as Facebook, Hudson's Bay Company, Google, Boston Pizza, or Tim Hortons. But these figures are not always the norm. In fact, sometimes the money raised is not as significant as you might imagine and often the companies are not well known. Listed below are some of the companies that completed IPOs in Canada between 2010 and 2013. How many of these have you heard of? Consider using the Internet to find out how much money their IPOs raised and what they did with the proceeds.

- Canadian Chartered Banc Split Corp.

- Canadian Convertible Debenture Fund

- Canadian Real Estate Split Corp

- Dollarama Inc.

- Groppe-Middlefield Energy Fund

- Harvest Banks & Buildings Income Fund

- Horizons BetaPro Double Gold Bullion Fund

- Marret Investment Grade Bond Fund

- North American Financials Capital Securities Trust

- O'Leary Canadian Income Opportunities Fund

On the other hand, public corporations can be "taken private" when one or a few individuals (perhaps the management of the firm) purchase all the firm's shares so that it can no longer be sold publicly. For example, the founder and CEO of Hollywood Video, Mark Wattles, took the video rental chain private in 2004 by buying up all the shares for $14 each.[17] Taking a corporation private may be desirable when new owners want to exert more control over the firm, or they want to avoid the necessity of public disclosure of future activities for competitive reasons. For example, Frank Stronach opted to privatize two Canadian auto component manufacturing companies he owns, Intier and Decoma, to avoid the increased scrutiny public companies are now facing in North America. Michael Dell, the founder of computer company Dell Inc., is currently attempting to take the computer company that bears his name private. Dell, who resumed duties as CEO when the company's fortunes continued to fade in recent years, believes that increased pressure from investors for short-term results is negatively impacting the company's ability to innovate and plan for long-term success. Taking a corporation private is also one technique for avoiding a takeover by another corporation.

Two other types of corporations are crown corporations and nonprofit corporations. **Crown corporations** are owned by the provincial or federal government, such as Canada Post, and focus on providing a service to citizens, such as mail delivery, rather than earning a profit. Examples of federal crown corporations include the Royal Canadian Mint and Via Rail Canada Inc. Provincial examples often include providers of electricity such as BC Hydro, lottery corporations, and liquor boards, such as the LCBO in Ontario.

Like crown corporations, **nonprofit corporations** focus on providing a service rather than earning a profit, but they are not owned by a government entity. Organizations such as the Children's Wish Foundation, the United Way, the Canadian Cancer Society, museums, and private schools provide services without

Crown corporations corporations owned and operated by government (federal or provincial)

Nonprofit corporations corporations that focus on providing a service rather than earning a profit but are not owned by a government entity

After the accounting scandals of the early 2000s and the passage of much tougher regulations, directors on public corporations' boards are expected to be more involved in the running of the company and highly scrutinize management decisions.

Board of directors a group of individuals, elected by the shareholders to oversee the general operation of the corporation, who set the corporation's long-range objectives

a profit motive. To fund their operations and services, nonprofit organizations sometimes charge for their services (private schools), solicit donations from individuals and companies, and apply for grants from the government and other charitable foundations.

Elements of a Corporation

The Board of Directors. A **board of directors,** elected by the shareholders to oversee the general operation of the corporation, sets the long-range objectives of the corporation. It is the board's responsibility to ensure that the objectives are achieved on schedule. Board members are legally liable for the mismanagement of the firm or for any misuse of funds. An important duty of the board of directors is to hire corporate officers, such as the president and the chief executive officer (CEO), who are responsible to the directors for the management and daily operations of the firm. The role and expectations of the board of directors took on greater significance after the accounting scandals of the early 2000s and the passage of much tougher regulation in Canada by the provincial regulatory boards and the Sarbanes-Oxley Act in the United States.[18] As a result, the duties and the workload of board members has increased substantially along with their accountability. Allen Shaw, chairman and CEO of the Shaw Group and a director at the Bank of Nova Scotia, says, "Fifteen years ago, it wouldn't have been unusual for very little paper to be sent out before a meeting. Directors could prepare for lots of meetings in an hour. Today it is not unusual to spend a day or more reading documents and studying financial statements while preparing for board meetings."[19] An example of this increased accountability and scrutiny occurred when former Newfoundland premier Brian Tobin recruited Kevin O'Leary, a well-known TV personality and investor, along with former Ontario premier Mike Harris, Nova Scotia seafood king John Risley, and Toronto governance expert Timothy Rowley to serve on the board at Environmental Management Solutions Inc. (EMS), today known as EnGlobe Corp. Tobin had agreed to assist then CEO Frank D'Addario in building a board and quickly built what many would consider an All-Star team of directors. The public reacted strongly to the move and the company's shares soared. Unfortunately, the new directors quickly learned about what they characterized as financial misdeeds by D'Addario and were forced to fire him from his post. Some of the new board members considered leaving the company due to the financial mess they inherited, but after hearing from their lawyers that they could be held responsible for the mismanagement of the company, the board stayed on and dealt with the company's problems.

Directors can be employees of the company (*inside directors*) or people unaffiliated with the company (*outside directors*). Inside directors are usually the officers responsible for

Habitat for Humanity is a nonprofit, nondenominational Christian housing organization that builds simple, decent, affordable houses in partnership with those who lack adequate shelter. Chosen families work alongside volunteers to build their own home.

running the company. For example, when Frank Stronach of Magna sat on the board of directors and acted as CEO he would have been considered an inside director. Outside directors are often top executives from other companies, lawyers, bankers, or even professors. Directors today are increasingly chosen for their expertise, competence, and ability to bring diverse perspectives to strategic discussions. Outside directors are also thought to bring more independence to the monitoring function because they are not bound by past allegiances, friendships, a current role in the company, or some other issue that may create a conflict of interest. Many of the corporate scandals uncovered in recent years might have been prevented if each of the companies' boards of directors had been better qualified, more knowledgeable, and more independent. A survey by *USA Today* found that corporate boards have considerable overlap. More than 1,000 corporate board members sit on four or more company boards, and of the nearly 2,000 boards of directors, more than 22,000 board members are linked to boards of more than one company.[20] According to Phil Purcell, CEO of Morgan Stanley, "Some director overlap is inevitable when shareholders demand the highest-calibre directors for their board."[21] This overlap creates the opportunity for conflicts of interest in decision making and limits the independence of individual boards of directors. For example, the telecommunications firm Verizon, which shares four board members with prescription-drug producer Wyeth, withdrew from nonprofit organization Business for Affordable Medicine, which had been criticized by Wyeth because of its stance on bringing generic drugs to market sooner.[22]

Share Ownership. Corporations issue two types of shares: preferred and common. Owners of **preferred shares** are a special class of owners because, although they generally do not have any say in running the company, they have a claim to any profits before any other shareholders do. Other shareholders do not receive any dividends unless the preferred shareholders have already been paid. Dividend payments on preferred shares are usually a fixed percentage of the initial issuing price (set by the board of directors). For example, if a preferred share originally cost $100 and the dividend rate was stated at 7.5 percent, the dividend payment will be $7.50 per share per year. Dividends are usually paid quarterly. Most preferred shares carry a cumulative claim to dividends. This means that if the company does not pay preferred-share dividends in one year because of losses, the dividends accumulate to the next year. Such dividends unpaid from previous years must also be paid to preferred shareholders before other shareholders can receive any dividends.

> **Preferred shares** a special type of share whose owners, though not generally having a say in running the company, have a claim to profits before other shareholders do
>
> **Common shares** shares whose owners have voting rights in the corporation, yet do not receive preferential treatment regarding dividends

Although owners of **common shares** do not get such preferential treatment with regard to dividends, they do get some say in the operation of the corporation. Their ownership gives them the right to vote for members of the board of directors and on other important issues. Common share dividends may vary according to the profitability of the business, and some corporations do not issue dividends at all, but instead plow their profits back into the company to fund expansion.

Common shareholders are the voting owners of a corporation. They are usually entitled to one vote per share. During an annual shareholders' meeting, common shareholders elect a board of directors. Because they can choose the board of directors, common shareholders have some say in how the company will operate. Common shareholders may vote by *proxy,* which is a written authorization by which shareholders assign their voting privilege to someone else, who then votes for his or her choice at the shareholders' meeting. It is a normal practice for management to request proxy statements from shareholders who are not planning to attend the annual meeting. Most owners do not attend annual meetings of the very large companies, such as Encana or Suncor, unless they live in the city where the meeting is held.

Common shareholders have another advantage over preferred shareholders. Sometimes when the corporation decides to sell new common shares in the marketplace, common shareholders have the first right, called a *preemptive right,* to purchase new shares from the corporation. A preemptive right is often included in the articles of incorporation. This right is important because it allows shareholders to purchase new shares to maintain their original positions. For example, if a shareholder owns 10 percent of a corporation that decides to issue new shares, that shareholder has the right to buy enough of the new shares to retain the 10 percent ownership.

Advantages of Corporations

Because a corporation is a separate legal entity, it has some very specific advantages over other forms of ownership. The biggest advantage may be the limited liability of the owners.

Limited Liability. Because the corporation's assets (money and resources) and liabilities (debts and other obligations including legal) are separate from its owners', in most cases the shareholders are not held responsible for the firm's debts if it fails. Their liability or potential loss is limited to the amount of their original investment. Although a creditor can sue a corporation for not paying its debts, even forcing the corporation into bankruptcy, it cannot make the shareholders pay the corporation's debts out of their personal assets. This advantage is rarely extended to small private corporations when borrowing money. Most banks and credit unions will insist that the owners of a private corporation pledge personal assets to secure a loan for the corporation unless the business has a long successful history; this would be most unusual for a public corporation. The main advantage of limited liability to small business is against loss to trade creditors/suppliers who granted the business credit and against legal liability.

> "Corporations issue two types of shares: preferred and common."

Ease of Transfer of Ownership. Shareholders in public corporations can sell or trade shares to other people without causing the termination of the corporation, and they can do this without the prior approval of other shareholders. The transfer of ownership (unless it is a majority position) does not affect the daily or long-term operations

RBC is currently Canada's third-largest public corporation.

of the corporation. Private corporations also allow shareholders to sell or transfer shares, but the transfer is not always easy, as is evident from the discussion about McCain Foods Ltd. Private corporations often face the same hurdles as partnerships when people are trying to sell shares or a stake in the business.

Perpetual Life. A corporation usually is chartered to last forever unless its articles of incorporation stipulate otherwise. The existence of the corporation is unaffected by the death or withdrawal of any of its shareholders. It survives until the owners sell it or liquidate its assets. However, in some cases, bankruptcy ends a corporation's life. Bankruptcies occur when companies are unable to compete and earn profits. Eventually, uncompetitive businesses must close or seek protection from creditors in bankruptcy court while the business tries to reorganize.

External Sources of Funds. Of all the forms of business organization, the public corporation finds it easiest to raise money. When a corporation needs to raise more money, it can sell more shares or issue bonds (corporate "IOUs," which pledge to repay debt), attracting funds from anywhere in North America and even overseas. The larger a corporation becomes, the more sources of financing are available to it. We take a closer look at some of these in Chapter 16. Research has indicated that a private corporation's ability to raise funds has more to do with the history of the company than its business structure. A private corporation such as the Irving Group or Chapman's Ice Cream (Canada's largest ice cream seller) would have little trouble raising money. A small corporation with an unproven business record would likely face the same hurdles in raising funds that a sole proprietor or partnership would have.

Expansion Potential. Because large public corporations can find long-term financing readily, they can easily expand into national and international markets. And, as a legal entity, a corporation can enter into contracts without as much difficulty as a partnership.

> "Of all the forms of business organization, the public corporation finds it easiest to raise money."

Tax Advantages. Corporations have a number of tax advantages. Public corporations pay a lower tax rate than sole proprietorships and partnerships. Smaller private corporations also pay a lower tax rate, and their owners can often defer tax by leaving money in the corporation, splitting income through payment of dividends to spouses or children, and, if the business is sold, realizing tax-free capital gains of up to $750,000.

Disadvantages of Corporations

Corporations have some distinct disadvantages resulting from tax laws and government regulation.

Double Taxation. As a legal entity, the corporation must pay taxes on its income just like you do. When after-tax corporate profits are paid out as dividends to the shareholders, the dividends are taxed a second time as part of the individual owner's income. This process creates double taxation for the shareholders of dividend-paying corporations. Often, the disadvantage of double taxation is offset by the Dividend Tax Credit program, a tax credit that allows the Canada Revenue Agency to tax dividend income at a lower rate than personal income. For example, if a private corporation earns $200,000, the money is taxed at 16 percent, which creates a $32,000 tax bill. If the owner then pays himself the remaining $168,000 as dividends, which are taxed at 15 percent, his take-home pay will be $142,800. If the owner of the business was a sole proprietor, all of the $200,000 would be taxed at personal rates, which can be as high as 49 percent. Double taxation does not occur with the other forms of business organization.

Forming a Corporation. The formation of a corporation can be costly. There are filing fees associated with forming a corporation, and often a lawyer is needed. The total costs of forming a corporation are usually in excess of $1,000.

Disclosure of Information and Regulations. Corporations must make information available to their owners, usually through an annual report to shareholders. The annual report contains financial information about the firm's profits, sales, facilities and equipment, and debts, as well as descriptions of the company's operations, products, and plans for the future. Public corporations must also file reports with the public stock exchanges and the various provincial exchange commissions. As discussed above, tougher corporate governance laws and increased scrutiny in Canada and the United States means corporations are faced with increased paperwork and regulations. In fact, some of Canada's most prominent business leaders, including Paul Desmarais, owner of Power Corp., and Dominic D'Allessandro, former CEO of Manulife, have stated that the increased regulations have hindered corporate growth by draining time and money away from the company. Frank Stronach, former CEO of the publicly traded Canadian automobile component manufacturing company Magna, notes, "The time we spend complying with regulations is now enormous."[23]

Impact on Management Decisions. Shareholders of publicly traded companies are becoming much more aggressive in demanding share appreciation and short-term results from management teams. As a result, management sometimes feels pressure to make decisions that are beneficial in the short term, but are not good long-term decisions. When Rogers Communications invested hundreds of millions of

> "Common shareholders are the voting owners of a corporation."

dollars in 3G technology, shareholders and stock market analysts questioned the decision and some attempted to pressure management to halt the costly project. As a result of the investment, Rogers became the technological leader among cell phone companies in Canada. This leadership position is what allowed the company to be the first cell phone provider to sell the popular iPhone in Canada, giving Rogers a substantial advantage over its competitors, but this shareholder pressure is why some owners prefer to remain private. Jim Pattison of Jim Pattison Group sums up the advantages of remaining private: "We can make better decisions as the owner of a private enterprise where we don't have to worry about daily share prices and analysts' expectations."[24]

Employee–Owner Separation. Many employees are not shareholders of the company for which they work. This separation of owners and employees may cause employees to feel that their work benefits only the owners. Employees without an ownership stake do not always see how they fit into the corporate picture and may not understand the importance of profits to the health of the organization. If managers are part owners but other employees are not, management–labour relations take on a different, sometimes difficult, aspect from those in partnerships and sole proprietorships. However, this situation is changing as more corporations establish employee share ownership plans (ESOPs), which give employees shares in the company. Such plans build a partnership between employee and employer and can boost productivity because they motivate employees to work harder so that they can earn dividends from their hard work as well as from their regular wages. In fact, of the 100 fastest-growing businesses in Canada identified by *Profit* magazine, 47 percent run ESOPs.[25]

Other Types of Ownership

In this section we will take a brief look at joint ventures, and cooperatives—businesses formed for special purposes.

Joint Ventures

A **joint venture** is a partnership established for a specific project, often for a limited time. The partners in a joint venture may be individuals or organizations, as in the case of the international joint ventures discussed in Chapter 3. Control of a joint venture may be shared equally, or one partner may control decision making. Joint ventures are especially popular in situations that call for large investments, such as extraction of natural resources, and are quite common in the Alberta oil patch. For example, Husky Energy and BP plc formed a 50/50 joint venture in the Athabasca Oil Sands in Alberta. BP plc agreed to bring its excess refinery capacity to the agreement and Husky Energy brought its reserves from the oil patch. Joint ventures are also common in the development of new products. Ballard Power, a B.C-based alternative energy company, has been in various joint ventures and strategic partnerships with such companies as Ford and Mercedes-Benz as they strive to replace traditional car engines. One of the more successful retail joint ventures in recent years is the partnership between Tim Hortons and Cold Stone Creamery. Tim Hortons and Cold Stone have agreed to include Cold Stone ice cream in over 100 stores in Canada and Tim Hortons' coffee in some of the more prominent Cold Stone stores in the United States. The venture allowed Cold Stone to quickly gain access to the Canadian market through a proven retailer, and Tim Hortons is able to offer a product with strong summer sales to its customers and franchise owners. Tim Hortons also gains access to some of Cold Stone's U.S. locations as a result of the arrangement.[26] Successful retail partnerships are not limited to the food industry, as illustrated by the partnership between Loblaws and Joe Fresh, the Canadian clothing company. The partnership allows Joe Fresh to sell its products in 300 supermarket locations, and Loblaws gets access to a popular consumer brand. Joe Fresh is hoping to create the same type of relationship in the U.S., and has recently announced a partnership with JC Penney to carry its line in stores throughout America.[27] Other examples include MovieLink, a joint venture of the film studios MGM, Paramount, Sony, Universal, and Warner Bros. that was developed as a competitor to Netflix, the popular online movie-rental source.[28] While the theory supporting joint ventures such as the pooling of resources and/or the sharing of expertise is sound in principle, many studies indicate that over 50 percent of joint ventures fail and most will not last five years.

Cooperatives

Another form of organization in business is the **cooperative or co-op,** an organization composed of individuals or small businesses that have banded together to reap the benefits of belonging to a larger organization. In cooperatives, the owners usually are limited to one share per person—although the share structure can be altered to reflect the level of a member's contribution to the co-op. There are currently over 8,800 co-ops in Canada that provide services to 17 million members. Well-known Canadian co-ops include Farmers Dairy, which is a co-operative of milk producers in Atlantic Canada; The Toronto Renewable Energy Co-operative (TREC), which was Canada's first green power community co-operative; SSQ Groupe Financier in Quebec, which stands out in the financial services industry as its clients are also the company's owners; and Community Health Co-operative Federation in Saskatchewan, which aims to reform health policy and provide community-oriented alternatives to traditional care. A co-op is set up not to make money as an entity but so that its members can become more profitable

> **Cooperative or co-op** an organization composed of individuals or small businesses that have banded together to reap the benefits of belonging to a larger organization

> **Joint venture** a partnership established for a specific project or for a limited time involving the sharing of the costs and operation of a business, often between a foreign company and a local partner

As people become more and more concerned about the state of the environment, *sustainable*, *local*, and *green* are just some of the words being tossed around with increasing frequency. Individuals are looking for ways to reduce their carbon footprint, protect the land, and take better care of their own health. To this end, community-supported agriculture (CSA) is becoming a popular alternative to large-chain grocery stores. The CSA is not a new idea. It originated in Japan around 30 years ago and was adopted in Canada in the 1980s.

A CSA is a way for local farmers to bypass the bureaucracy of traditional corporate grocery stores and to conduct business directly with consumers. Under this model, a farmer first creates a budget for the growing season that includes all costs (such as land payments, seeds, salaries, equipment, and so on). The farmer then divides this budget into the number of shares of crops available for purchase. Usually a CSA share is designed to feed a family of four for a week. People become members of a farm's CSA by purchasing shares. They will then receive a portion of local, often organic, produce each week during the growing season. The CSA creates a sustainable relationship in which members receive quality produce and farmers have a reliable method for distributing their crops.

How does the CSA benefit the environment and contribute to health? The farms offering CSAs are usually small and dedicated to ecologically sound farming practices, such as permaculture and avoiding chemical pesticides. Because the cost of distribution is lower for these farmers, members often receive produce at prices competitive with conventional produce sold in grocery stores. Farmers, knowing that their basic costs are covered, can focus their full attention on growing high-quality produce rather than searching for distributors. In addition, because deliveries are made locally, produce is fresher. The local aspect of delivery also cuts down on pollution because the products do not need to travel great distances.

Farmers and consumers are embracing community-supported agriculture, in which consumers invest in farms and get paid in produce.

In a world where people are looking to take better care of themselves and the environment, as well as to understand where their food came from, the CSA is becoming a popular alternative to traditional stores.[29] While Agriculture Canada has yet to determine the number of CSAs in existence, an Internet search reveals that they exist in every province and news articles indicate that they are growing in popularity with consumers.

DISCUSSION QUESTIONS

1. What are some of the benefits farmers gain by switching to the CSA model?

2. Why are people opting to use CSAs over traditional grocery stores?

3. Can you think of any drawbacks to the CSA model?

or save money. Co-ops are generally expected to operate without profit or to create only enough profit to maintain the co-op organization. For example, Mountain Equipment Co-op is the largest retailer co-operative in Canada, and its goal is to provide accessible and fairly priced outdoor gear to its members. At the end of the year any surplus money is returned to shareholders.

Many cooperatives exist in small farming communities. The co-op stores can market grain; order large quantities of fertilizer, seed, and other supplies at discounted prices; and reduce costs and increase efficiency with good management. A co-op can purchase supplies in large quantities and pass the savings on to its members. It also can help distribute the products of its members more efficiently than each could on an individual basis. A cooperative can advertise its members' products and thus generate demand. Ace Hardware, a cooperative of independent hardware store owners, allows its members to share in the savings that result from buying supplies in large quantities; it also provides advertising, which individual members might not be able to afford on their own.

Jim Farmer, a lifelong livestock producer, wants his son and two daughters to be able to carry on the family farm. To help achieve this goal, he formed the Heartland Farm Foods Co-op with about three dozen beef producers to turn 1,000 cattle a year into canned beef. The co-op form of organization is not unusual for small businesses that band together to obtain the benefits of a larger organization. The co-op is not set up to make money as an organization, but rather so that all the ranchers involved can become more profitable or, in this case, continue to maintain a lifestyle that they enjoy. In the face of intense competition from large commercial feedlots, Farmer's idea was to offer a different kind of product and to market and support it through the co-op, which has the support of the local Beef Industry Council, and the Department of Agriculture.

The co-op's canned, precooked ground and chunked beef products contain just one ingredient—beef, with no preservatives, not even salt. Any harmful bacteria are removed through a pressure-cooking process. Each animal yields 400 to 500 cans of federally inspected beef from cattle raised without steroids, hormone additives, or routine antibiotics. The precooked beef is targeted at outdoor enthusiasts—from hikers and hunters to anglers and campers. Thanks to a shelf life of two to five years, the cans can be stowed in tackle boxes or backpacks, or even stored in storm shelters in case of a disaster.

The co-op has constructed a 415 square metre plant on 4 hectares to process the beef. Construction of this facility and first-year operating capital needs were estimated at approximately $750,000. Some of these expenses were partially offset by grants that the co-op received; co-ops that foster economic development in a region often receive grants or other financial support from provincial or federal development initiatives.

Currently, Heartland's canned beef is primarily available in local supermarkets and convenience stores and online at www.heartlandfarmfoods.com. Prices range from $2.69 to $3.99 on the website, although retailers sell the product for $4.99 per can. At this price, consumers surely demand a quality product, but Heartland believes the product's convenience and ingredients support sales. The co-op recently released five new products—Nacho Express, Zesty Beef'n Bean, Beef'n Bean Chili, Chili Con Queso, and Hearty Taco Beef—and is selling steaks to local restaurants and markets. Heartland's initiative offers an example of creativity in bringing back a product—canned meat—that was once a pantry staple before the era of refrigeration. The cooperative form of organization has made it possible for small ranchers to join together to make this product a reality.[30]

DISCUSSION QUESTIONS

1. Why did Heartland Foods employ a cooperative form of organization?

2. What are the advantages for ranchers who belong to the cooperative?

3. Can you think of any other industries where the cooperative form of business ownership would be beneficial?

LO4 Define and debate the advantages and disadvantages of mergers, acquisitions, and leveraged buyouts.

Trends in Business Ownership: Mergers and Acquisitions

Companies large and small achieve growth and improve profitability by expanding their operations, often by developing and selling new products or selling current products to new groups of customers in different geographic areas. Such growth, when carefully planned and controlled, is usually beneficial to the firm and ultimately helps it reach its goal of enhanced profitability. But companies also grow by merging with or purchasing other companies.

A **merger** occurs when two companies (usually corporations) combine to form a new company. An **acquisition** occurs when one company purchases another, generally by buying its shares. The acquired company may become a subsidiary of the buyer, or its operations and assets may be merged with those of the buyer. For example, in 2009 George Gillett sold the Montreal Canadiens, Bell Centre, and Gillett Entertainment to a group of investors led by the Molson family for $500 million. One of the better

Merger the combination of two companies (usually corporations) to form a new company

Acquisition the purchase of one company by another, usually by buying its shares

known recent acquisitions involved Disney purchasing Lucasfilm Ltd., including the rights to the *Star Wars* movies for $4.01 billion.[31] Disney has already announced plans to continue the successful movie franchise, ensuring children will be playing with light sabres for years to come.

Acquisitions and mergers are generally driven by: (1) economies of scale—where a larger company can reduce its costs and offer the same products or level or service at a lower cost; (2) increased market share—when the company is acquiring a competitor; (3) cross selling—where the acquired firm can sell different products to the same customer; (4) integration—where the acquired firm can act as a supplier or a distributor for the firms' products; (5) diversification—where a firm acquires another firm that operates in a different industry to hedge against an industry downturn. As previously discussed, even when one or more of these advantages are evident in an acquisition/merger, studies indicate that they are only successful 50 percent of the time. Common reasons cited for the lack of success include unanticipated expenses, overestimation of cost savings, and conflicting corporate cultures.

Recent examples of mergers and acquisitions in Canada include:

- The Bank of Nova Scotia's $3.1 billion acquisition of ING Direct (Canada)

- The $19.2 billion merger of Suncor Energy Inc. and Petro-Canada

- Teck Cominco Limited's $14.4 billion acquisition of Fording Canadian Coal Trust

- Valeant Pharmaceuticals' $2.6 billion acquisition of Medicis Pharmaceuticals

- Exxon Canada's $3.14 billion acquisition of Celtic Exploration Ltd.

When firms that make and sell similar products to the same customers merge, it is known as a *horizontal merger*, as when Toronto-Dominion Bank merged with another financial service company, Canada Trust, to form TD Canada Trust. Horizontal mergers, however, reduce the number of corporations competing within an industry, and for this reason usually are reviewed carefully by federal regulators before the merger is allowed to proceed. After the TD Canada Trust merger, a number of Canadian banks attempted to merge, including Royal Bank with the Bank of Montreal and CIBC with TD, but the federal government blocked these mergers noting that they would be unfair to consumers. Given that the federal government does not appear to be willing to allow any mergers or acquisitions between the largest banks in Canada, many of them have gone shopping for other companies. It is estimated that Canadian banks were involved in over 50 acquisitions between 2011 and 2013, and some examples include Royal Bank paying $4.1 billion for Ally,[32] a Canadian auto lending company, and TD Bank spending $6 billion for Target's credit card business.[33] Sometimes firms purchase other companies and allow them to continue operating under their brand and to maintain some form of independence. This often happens when the competitor's brand is strong, and it resonates with consumers. For example, the Bank of Nova Scotia/Scotiabank recently purchased ING Direct's Canadian operations for $3.1 billion. Scotia plans to continue to operate the company under the ING brand as it has 1.8 million loyal followers in Canada and 1,100 employees.[34]

Since most mergers and acquisitions result in larger companies and reduce the level of competition, the government through various regulatory agencies often has to approve mergers. As discussed above, and in the case at the end of the chapter, various regulatory boards review acquisitions to ensure that a level, competitive playing field exists, that consumers are not negatively impacted as a result of the merger, and (in the case of foreign takeovers of Canadian companies) that the result is of net benefit to Canada. Recently, the Canadian Radio-television and Telecommunications Commission (CRTC) rejected Bell Canada's proposed $3.4 billion takeover of Astral Media, saying it would place too much power in the hands of one company and threaten the competitive media landscape in Canada. Bell is currently opposing the rejection and likely to seek

One of the most discussed acquisitions in recent memory was the sale of the Montreal Canadiens to a group of investors led by the Molson family.

regulatory approval again in 2013 or 2014.[35] Perhaps, one of the stranger acquisition rejections was of a deal that never made its way before regulator review. Lowes, an American hardware retailer, launched a $1.8 billion takeover bid for Rona Inc., Canada's largest hardware store. The government of Quebec, where Rona maintains its head office, stated that Rona was of significant value to the province and the government would do everything in its power to block the bid. Lowes eventually walked away from the takeover, but many business analysts questioned the province's statements. Derek DeCloet, of *The Globe and Mail* stated, "Rona became a target for a reason. The company was plagued by poor management and its share price was underappreciated as a result."[36] Many journalists in the press agreed with DeCloet, arguing that the Quebec government was misguided and Lowes could have bought Rona and improved the company—with the end result being more Canadian jobs and lower prices for consumers.

When companies operating at different but related levels of an industry merge, it is known as a *vertical merger*. In many instances, a vertical merger results when one corporation merges with one of its customers or suppliers. For example, if Tim Hortons were to purchase a large coffee bean farm—to ensure a ready supply of beans for its coffee—a vertical merger would result. Vertical mergers allow for quick growth and were a key strategy used by KC Irving to grow the Irving Group. Irving noted that he started selling cars, and since cars needed gas, he opened a gas station. Since gas needed refined oil, he started an oil company, and since oil had to be transported, he entered into the transportation and shipping industry.

A *conglomerate merger* results when two firms in unrelated industries merge. For example, the purchase of the Toronto Blue Jays in the 1990s by brewer Labatt and the CIBC represents a conglomerate merger because the two companies are in different industries.

When a company (or an individual), sometimes called a *corporate raider*, wants to acquire or take over another company, it first offers to buy some or all of the other company's shares at a premium over its current price in a *tender offer*. Most such offers are "friendly," with both groups agreeing to the proposed deal, but some are "hostile," when the second company does not want to be taken over. For example, Potash Corp. of Saskatchewan, which is discussed in the case at the end of the chapter, opposed the US$38.6 billion hostile takeover bid by BHP Billiton Ltd. The bid was ultimately unsuccessful as the Canadian government refused to allow the takeover, arguing the bid was not in the best interest of Canadians. As discussed in the CEO profile at the start of the chapter, Indigo, a Canadian book retailer, made a hostile bid for Chapters, its largest Canadian competitor. Initially, management at Chapters tried to avert the bid using a number of techniques including looking for a white knight (see below), which they thought they found in Future Shop, but Indigo was persistent in its pursuit of the company and raised the initial offer price. Ultimately, Indigo successfully acquired Chapters.

To head off a hostile takeover attempt, a threatened company's managers may use one or more of several techniques. They may ask shareholders not to sell to the raider; file a lawsuit in an effort to abort the takeover; institute a *poison pill* (in which the firm allows shareholders to buy more shares at prices lower than the current market value) or *shark repellant* (in which management requires a large majority of shareholders to approve the takeover); or seek a *white knight* (a more acceptable firm that is willing to acquire the threatened company). In some cases, management may take the company private or even take on more debt so that the heavy debt obligation will "scare off" the raider. The result of companies taking actions such as these has been a reduction in the success rate of hostile bids—only 46 percent of hostile takeovers are successful.[37] As a result, the popularity of hostile takeovers has declined sharply since their heyday in the 1990s. From 2006 to 2011 only 5 percent of takeovers would be classified as hostile. In the case of the initial hostile bid by Sanofi for Aventis, for example, Aventis initially instituted several measures to thwart the takeover attempt, including asking a rival Swiss firm, Novartis, to bid for Aventis. Only when Sanofi significantly raised its offer did Aventis's board of directors recommend that its shareholders accept the revised offer from Sanofi.[38]

In a **leveraged buyout (LBO),** a group of investors borrows money from banks and other institutions to acquire a company (or a division of one), using the assets of the purchased company to guarantee repayment of the loan. In some LBOs, as much as 95 percent of the buyout price is paid with borrowed money, which eventually must be repaid. The new management then engages in a number of strategies including selling assets, cutting costs including termination of employees, and/or breaking up businesses to restore value to the acquired business. The company uses its improved balance sheet to pay off the debt and the business is often sold at a much higher price than the original purchase price. In Canada, Gerry Schwartz,

> **Leveraged buyout (LBO)** a purchase in which a group of investors borrows money from banks and other institutions to acquire a company (or a division of one), using the assets of the purchased company to guarantee repayment of the loan

CEO of Onex Corporation, has made billions by buying distressed businesses, making changes, and then selling the improved companies. Examples of Schwartz's work include Sky Chefs and Loews Cineplex, two companies that he bought at deep discounts using debt and eventually sold for millions in profit.

With the explosion of mergers, acquisitions, and leveraged buyouts in the 1980s and 1990s, some financial journalists coined the term *merger mania*. Many companies joined the merger mania simply to enhance their own operations by consolidating them with the operations of other firms. Mergers and acquisitions enabled these companies to gain a larger market share in their industries, acquire valuable assets, such as new products or plants and equipment, and lower their costs. Mergers also represent a means of making profits quickly, as was the case during the 1980s when many companies' shares were undervalued. Quite simply, such companies represent a bargain to other companies that can afford to buy them. Additionally, deregulation of some industries has permitted consolidation of firms within those industries for the first time, as is the case in the banking and airline industries.

Some people view mergers and acquisitions favourably, pointing out that they boost corporations' share prices and market value, to the benefit of their shareholders. In many instances, mergers enhance a company's ability to meet foreign competition in an increasingly global marketplace. And, companies that are victims of hostile takeovers generally streamline their operations, reduce unnecessary staff, cut costs, and otherwise become more efficient with their operations, which benefits their shareholders whether or not the takeover succeeds.

Critics, however, argue that mergers hurt companies because they force managers to focus their efforts on avoiding takeovers rather than managing effectively and profitably. Some companies have taken on a heavy debt burden to stave off a takeover, later to be forced into bankruptcy when economic downturns left them unable to handle the debt. Mergers and acquisitions also can damage employee morale and productivity, as well as the quality of the companies' products.

Many mergers have been beneficial for all involved; others have had damaging effects for the companies, their employees, and customers. No one can say if mergers will continue to slow, but many experts say the utilities, telecommunications, financial services, natural resources, computer hardware and software, gaming, managed health care, and technology industries are likely targets.

TEAM EXERCISE

Form groups and find examples of mergers and acquisitions. Mergers can be broken down into traditional mergers, horizontal mergers, and conglomerate mergers. When companies are found, note how long the merger or acquisition took, if there were any requirements by the government before approval of the merger or acquisition, and if any failed mergers or acquisitions were found that did not receive government approval. Report your findings to the class, and explain what the companies hoped to gain from the merger or acquisition.

LEARNING OBJECTIVES SUMMARY

LO1 Define and examine the advantages and disadvantages of the sole proprietorship form of organization.

Sole proprietorships—businesses owned and managed by one person—are the most common form of organization. Their major advantages are the following: (1) They are easy and inexpensive to form, (2) they allow a high level of secrecy, (3) all profits belong to the owner, (4) the owner has complete control over the business, (5) government regulation is minimal, (6) taxes are paid only once, and (7) the business can be closed easily. The disadvantages include: (1) The owner may have to use personal assets to borrow money, (2) limited source of external funds, (3) often owners have a limited skill set, (4) lack of continuity, and (5) successful sole proprietors pay a higher tax than they would under the corporate form of business.

LO2 Identify three types of partnership, and evaluate the advantages and disadvantages of the partnership form of organization.

Partnership is a form of business organization defined as "an association of two or more persons who carry on as co-owners of a business for profit." There are three basic types of partnership: general partnership, limited partnership, and limited liability partnership.

Partnerships offer the following advantages: (1) They are easy to organize, (2) partners can complement their skills, (3) they may have more access to capital, (4) partnerships can make decisions faster than larger businesses, and (5) government regulations are few. Partnerships also have several disadvantages: (1) All partnerships have to deal with disagreements, (2) general partners have unlimited liability for the debts of the partnership, (3) partners are responsible for each other's decisions, (4) the death or termination of one partner requires a new partnership agreement to be drawn up, (5) it is difficult to sell a partnership interest at a fair price, (6) the distribution of profits may not correctly reflect the amount of work done by each partner, and (7) partnerships may be taxed at a higher rate than corporations.

LO3 Describe the corporate form of organization, and cite the advantages and disadvantages of corporations.

A corporation is a legal entity created by the province or federal government, whose assets and liabilities are separate from those of its owners. Corporations have a board of directors made up of corporate officers or people from outside the company. Corporations, whether private or public, are owned by shareholders. Common shareholders have the right to elect the board of directors. Preferred shareholders do not have a vote but get preferential dividend treatment over common shareholders.

Advantages of the corporate form of business include: (1) The owners have limited liability, (2) ownership (stock) can be easily transferred, (3) corporations usually last forever, (4) raising money is easier than for other forms of business, and (5) expansion into new businesses is simpler because of the ability of the company to enter into contracts. Corporations also have disadvantages: (1) The company is taxed on its income, and owners pay a second tax on any profits received as dividends although the combined amount of tax paid may still be less than what would be paid by other forms of business, (2) forming a corporation can be expensive, (3) corporations have to disclose a great deal of information to the public (such as future plans) and comply with various government regulations, (4) corporations sometimes make decisions to appease shareholders' goals, and (5) owners and managers are not always the same and can have different goals.

LO4 Define and debate the advantages and disadvantages of mergers, acquisitions, and leveraged buyouts.

A merger occurs when two companies (usually corporations) combine to form a new company. An acquisition occurs when one company buys most of another company's stock. In a leveraged buyout, a group of investors borrows money to acquire a company, using the assets of the purchased company to guarantee the loan. They can help merging firms to gain a larger market share in their industries, acquire valuable assets such as new products or plants and equipment, and lower their costs. Consequently, they can benefit shareholders by improving the companies' market value and stock prices. However, they also can hurt companies if they force managers to focus on avoiding takeovers at the expense of productivity and profits. They may lead a company to take on too much debt and can harm employee morale and productivity.

acquisition
board of directors
certificate of incorporation
common shares
cooperative or co-op
corporation
crown corporations
dividends
general partnership
initial public offering (IPO)
joint venture
leveraged buyout (LBO)

limited liability partnership (LLP)
limited partnership
merger
nonprofit corporations
partnership
partnership agreement
preferred shares
private corporation
public corporation
shares
sole proprietorships

DESTINATION CEO DISCUSSION QUESTIONS

1. What do you think would be some of the advantages and disadvantages of Indigo taking over Chapters from a business perspective?

2. From a consumer perspective, what is the danger of Indigo having a virtual monopoly of retail bookstores in Canada? Should the Canadian government have stepped in and prevented the takeover?

3. How do you think Indigo will do as they face ever-increasing competition from both online stores such as Amazon and traditional retailers like Walmart and Target who are allocating significant shelf space to books?

4. Do you think Reisman's strategy of shifting the merchandising mix to include household items, giftware, stationery, baby gifts, and toys will be successful? Why or why not?

SO YOU WANT TO *Start a Business*

If you have a good idea and want to turn it into a business, you are not alone. Small businesses are popping up all over Canada and the concept of entrepreneurship is hot. Entrepreneurs seek opportunities and creative ways to make profits. Business emerges in a number of different organizational forms, each with its own advantages and disadvantages. Sole proprietorships are the most common form of business organization in Canada. They tend to be small businesses and can take pretty much any form—anything from a hair salon to a scuba shop, from an organic produce provider to a financial advisor. Proprietorships are everywhere serving consumers' wants and needs. Proprietorships have a big advantage in that they tend to be simple to manage—decisions get made quickly when the owner and the manager are the same person and they are fairly simple and inexpensive to set up. Rules vary by province, but at most all you will need is a licence from the province.

Many people have been part of a partnership at some point in their life. Group work in school is an example of a partnership. If you ever worked as a DJ on the weekend with your friend and split the profits, then you have experienced a partnership. Partnerships can be either general or limited. General partnerships have unlimited liability and share completely in the management, debts, and profits of the business. Limited partners, on the other hand, consist of at least one general partner and one or more limited partners who do not participate in the management of the company, but share in the profits. This form of partnership is used more often in risky investments where the limited partner stands only to lose his or her initial investment. Real estate limited partnerships are an example of how investors can minimize their financial exposure. Although it has its advantages, partnership is the least utilized form of business. Part of the reason is that all partners are responsible for the actions and decisions of all other partners, whether or not all of the partners were involved. Usually, partners will have to write up articles of partnership that outline respective responsibilities in the business. Unlike a corporation, proprietorships and partnerships both expire upon the death of one or more of those involved.

Corporations tend to be larger businesses, but do not need to be. A corporation can consist of nothing more than a small group of family members. In order to become a corporation, you have to file in the province in which you wish to incorporate. Each province has its own procedure for incorporation, meaning there are no general guidelines to follow. You can make your corporation private or public, meaning the company issues stocks and shareholders are the owners. While incorporating is a popular form of organization because it gives the company an unlimited lifespan and limited liability (meaning that if your business fails you cannot lose personal funds to make up for losses), there is a downside. You will be taxed as a corporation and as an individual, resulting in double taxation. No matter what form of organization suits your business idea best, there is a world of options out there for you if you want to be or experiment with being an entrepreneur.

BUILD YOUR BUSINESS PLAN

Options for Organizing a Business

As discussed above, there are a variety of legal structures for organizing your own business. In addition to reviewing the material in this chapter, students may want to talk to some small-business owners and see what structure they selected and why. Students should ask these entrepreneurs if they are happy with their form of business organization and what they see as its advantages and disadvantages. Students could also describe their business to the entrepreneur and ask them what form of business they would recommend.

CASE | Canadian Acquistions—Not as Easy as They Once Were

Foreign companies looking to complete an acquisition in Canada are starting to learn that regulatory approval is not as easy to obtain as it once was.

Prime Minister Stephen Harper's Conservative government and the Liberal government it replaced both were advocates of free trade and foreign investment in Canada and regularly approved foreign takeovers of Canadian companies. However, from 2005 to 2007, after a series of deals saw Canadian mining firms, such as Inco, Falconbridge, and Alcan, taken over by large global players, public sentiment about foreign firms buying Canadian companies started to turn negative.

A significant turning point in public perception was Australia-based BHP Billiton Ltd.'s US$38.6 billion hostile bid for Potash Corp. of Saskatchewan. Potash, which is used in fertilizers, is a rare resource, and Potash Corp. owns vast reserves in Saskatchewan. Saskatchewan's premier, Brad Wall, rallied support against the deal when he stated, "The people of Saskatchewan are justifiably proud of Potash Corp. and the success it has achieved here and around the world. Do we want to add Potash Corp. to that list of once-proud Canadian companies that are now under foreign control?"[39] While BHP stated it would keep the company's head office in Saskatchewan, it would allow global prices (not the provincial marketing board) to set the price for potash, likely resulting in lower prices and less tax revenue for the province. Other provinces quickly supported Saskatchewan's position, as did the opposition parties in Ottawa. The federal government, citing the Investment Act, opted to block the deal in 2010. One of the rules governing foreign takeovers in the Act is that the result must offer Canadians a positive net benefit, and the federal government determined this was not the case in the BHP bid. This marked only the second time a foreign takeover failed to meet the standards in the Act.

The arguments against foreign investment include keeping Canadian companies in the hands of Canadians who will protect Canadian interests (which include jobs and access to resources) and ensure that Canada's rules and regulations govern operations. Proponents of foreign investment in Canada counter that Canada really is a country built on foreign investment; Canadian companies often need the capital injection that foreign investment brings; and shareholders ultimately should decide whether they sell the company, not government. Furthermore, research indicates that countries which are open to foreign investment usually have economies that outperform countries who limit such investments.

Foreign takeovers became a hot button topic again in 2012–13 when Chinese giant CNOOC Ltd. successfully bought Canadian oil and gas company Nexen, and the Malaysian state-owned company Petronas purchased Alberta's Progress Energy for $6 billion. Public sentiment across the country was decidedly negative to the deals as many Canadians argued that Canada's greatest natural resource—the oil sands—would soon be controlled by foreign governments. The proponents of the takeover stated that both Canadian companies were poorly run and needed the injection of capital that could come from the foreign firms, and that the true owners of the company—the shareholders—were in favour of the deals. While the federal government eventually approved these takeovers, Stephen Harper noted that this was not the beginning of a trend but the end of one. Harper stated, "While Canada is open for business, we do not mean that Canada is for sale to foreign governments.... To be blunt, Canadians have not spent years reducing ownership of sectors of the economy by our own governments only to see them bought and controlled by foreign governments instead,"[40] As part of this pledge, Harper has made changes to the Investment Act, where foreign investors have to do more than prove a net benefit to Canada as a result of a takeover in the oil sands. Foreign companies, especially those controlled by governments, will only be granted approval to take over oil sand companies in exceptional circumstances. These new rules seem to make everyone unhappy. People opposed to foreign investment in the country stated that they did not go far enough and that tougher rules should apply to all takeovers, not just those in the oil sands. Those opposed to government interference in foreign takeovers felt that these new rules amounted to unneeded government interference into private industry.[41]

DISCUSSION QUESTIONS

1. What do you think are some of the advantages and disadvantages of foreign takeovers?

2. Why do you think Stephen Harper and the Conservative government changed their opinion on foreign takeovers and drafted stricter regulations?

3. Given that shareholders own the company, if they approve a takeover, should the government have the ability to step in and block the approved takeover? Is this ethical or unethical?

4. Some people have argued that the new takeover rules do not go far enough and that foreign takeovers of resource companies should be banned. What would be some of the advantages and disadvantages of barring such takeovers?

5 Small Business, Entrepreneurship, and Franchising

LEARNING OBJECTIVES

LO1 Define entrepreneurship and small business.

LO2 Investigate the importance of small business in the Canadian economy and why certain fields attract small business.

LO3 Specify the advantages of small-business ownership.

LO4 Summarize the disadvantages of small-business ownership, and analyze why many small businesses fail.

LO5 Describe how you go about starting a small business and what resources are needed.

LO6 Evaluate the demographic, technological, and economic trends that are affecting the future of small business.

LO7 Explain why many large businesses are trying to "think small."

Kevin O'Leary "You may lose your wife, you may lose your dog, [and] your mother may hate you. None of those things matter. What matters is that you achieve success and become free. Then you can do whatever you like."[1]

Kevin O'Leary
CBC's *Dragons' Den*

Chances are if you watch CBC or perhaps ABC you likely have seen and formed an opinion about Kevin O'Leary. O'Leary, while not being Canada's richest entrepreneur, is likely one of the best known and perhaps the brashest. In Canada, O'Leary is almost famous for being famous, as he stars in CBC's hit show *Dragons' Den* and appears on his daily new show, *The Lang and O'Leary Exchange*. O'Leary is also a regular on U.S. television as he stars on ABC's *Shark Tank*. In *Dragons' Den* and *Shark Tank*, O'Leary plays the role of a smart investor who will provide business owners with money and his much sought after advice in exchange for a part of their company. During both shows, entrepreneurs stand in front of a panel and describe their business, hoping one of the Dragons or Sharks will invest in their company. While O'Leary is not the most active investor in either show, he made himself famous by his somewhat brutal assessment of what he perceives as poor business ideas and the entrepreneurs behind them. O'Leary has occasionally asked guests if they are nuts; called them cockroaches; informed entrepreneurs that their product is ugly and a bad idea; and even told crying guests that there is no value in their tears and that they mean nothing. O'Leary is clear: His sole mandate on the show is to make money and he won't waste his time or hard earned dollars on bad ideas. On the nightly news show he co-hosts with Amanda Lang, viewers get more of the same where O'Leary comments on the stock market and stories that appear in the news, always with a right wing, capitalistic edge. This is something Chris Hedges, a *New York Times* correspondent, found out when he was on the show defending the Occupy Movement, which was a global protest against big business and government. O'Leary's response was to call the protestors "nothing burgers who couldn't name the companies they were upset with" and to tell Hedges he sounded like "a left-wing nutbar" for defending the protestors.

O'Leary's first successful entrepreneurial venture was SoftKey Software Products Inc., a company he co-founded in his basement with a $10,000 investment from his mother. O'Leary and his partner eventually moved the company to Boston where he kick-started sales by selling the company's software in big box stores at a deep discount compared to what other companies were selling their products for in computer stores. While the practice did not make O'Leary any friends in the computer industry, he did manage to grow revenue and eventually expanded his company into educational products. SoftKey eventually purchased The Learning Centre (TLC), another software company, and started operating under its name. TLC grew to become the biggest educational software company in the world, with sales of $800 million. In 1999, toy giant Mattel purchased TLC for $4 billion and asked O'Leary to stay on and manage the educational software business. While the two parted ways a short time later, O'Leary had his first major success under his belt.

O'Leary went on to other entrepreneurial ventures with a mixed degree of success, and in 2003 he called the Business News Network (BNN) and offered his own self-assessment that he would be good on TV. BNN felt O'Leary was a natural and eventually gave him his own nightly news show. While popular with viewers of BNN, O'Leary really hit the big time when he was cast in *Dragons' Den* in 2006. O'Leary quickly became "villain judge"... the person all either love or love to hate. After all, how often do you hear comments like, "Business is war. I go out there, [and] I want to kill the competitors. I want to make their lives miserable. I want to steal their market share. I want them to fear me and I want everyone on my team thinking we're going to win."[2] O'Leary's on-air presence eventually captured the eye of Mark Burnett, who created the hit reality TV show *Survivor*, and he cast O'Leary in *Shark Tank*—America's version of *Dragons' Den*.

O'Leary soon realized that while he was making money and creating a brand on TV he had a real opportunity to capitalize on his fame, and started to build businesses that he could personally brand. His first foray into creating a business to build on his brand was O'Leary Funds, a mutual fund for which he acted as the main spokesman whenever a camera was placed in front of him. While O'Leary did not personally manage the funds, he did a great job of promoting his new investment products and money poured into his company. Unfortunately for many investors, the performance of O'Leary Funds as an investment product has been mixed. O'Leary did not stop with O'Leary Funds and has since introduced O'Leary Mortgages and O'Leary Fine Wines, offers public speaking services, has authored two books, and is apparently developing other products and concepts. Whether you love him or love to hate him, O'Leary has come a long way from a $10,000 investment and a video game company he started in his basement.

Introduction

Although many business students go to work for large corporations upon graduation, others may choose to start their own business or find employment opportunities in small businesses with 500 or fewer employees. There are more than 2.3 million small businesses operating in Canada today.[3] Each small business represents the vision of its entrepreneurial owners to succeed by providing new or better products. Small businesses are the heart of the Canadian economic and social system because they offer opportunities and express the freedom of people to make their own destinies. *Profit* magazine's editor-in-chief, Ian Portsmouth, states, "Canada is in the middle of an entrepreneurial boom ... and Canada and the world [will be] full of opportunities ... in coming years."[4] Today, the entrepreneurial spirit is growing around the world, from India and China to Germany, Brazil, and Mexico.

This chapter surveys the world of entrepreneurship and small business. First we define entrepreneurship and small business and examine the role of small business in the Canadian economy. Then we explore the advantages and disadvantages of small-business ownership and analyze why small businesses succeed or fail. Next, we discuss how an entrepreneur goes about starting a small business and the challenges facing small business today. Finally, we look at entrepreneurship in larger businesses.

As you start to study this chapter, you may be asking yourself why you should study entrepreneurship. Research indicates students who study entrepreneurship are likely to experience the following benefits:

- Be three to four times more likely to start a business

- Earn 20 to 30 percent more than students studying in other fields

- Gain valuable entrepreneurial skills such as business planning, networking, and sales, which are valued by employers

- Improve their ability to think critically and become better problem solvers

- Improve their chance of landing their dream job because entrepreneurial students have many of the characteristics that employers are looking for

- Gain knowledge to supplement their income

Other reasons for studying entrepreneurship include:

- Entrepreneurs have unlimited earning potential.

- Many of society's problems today require entrepreneurial solutions. In fact, charity workers, nurses, and social workers often need to think entrepreneurially in order to solve problems. These people are sometimes referred to as social entrepreneurs.

- Ninety-nine percent of businesses in Canada are in fact small or medium enterprises (SMEs), so even if you don't start an SME you will probably end up working for one. By studying entrepreneurship you will understand how to succeed at such a firm.

The Nature of Entrepreneurship and Small Business

In Chapter 1, we defined an entrepreneur as a person who risks his or her wealth, time, and effort to develop for profit an innovative product or way of doing something. **Entrepreneurship** is the process of creating and managing a business to achieve desired objectives. Many large businesses you may recognize—Rogers Communications, Tim Hortons, 1-800-GOT-JUNK?, Magna International Inc., and Pizza Pizza all began as small businesses based on the entrepreneurial visions of their founders. Some entrepreneurs who start small businesses have the ability to see emerging trends; in response, they create a company to provide a product that serves customer needs. For example, rather than inventing a major new technology, an innovative company may take advantage of an existing technology to create markets that did not exist before, such as Amazon.com.[5] Or they may offer something familiar but improved or repackaged, such as what Vancouver-based 1-800-GOT-JUNK? did with junk removal. Prior to Brian Scudamore founding and subsequently franchising 1-800-GOT-JUNK?, most junk and garbage removal was done by small independent operators whose customer service practices were often questionable. Scudamore's approach was to first professionalize the service and then franchise the concept, which he has done successfully over 250 times in three different countries. The company that Scudamore started as a university student now generates millions of dollars in annual revenue. They may innovate by focusing on a particular market segment and delivering a combination of features that consumers in that segment could not find anywhere else (e.g., REI Outdoor Gear & Clothing for camping, hiking, backpacking, and more).[6]

Of course, smaller businesses do not have to evolve into such highly visible companies to be successful, but those

> **Entrepreneurship** the process of creating and managing a business to achieve desired objectives

entrepreneurial efforts that result in rapidly growing businesses become more visible with their success. Entrepreneurs who have achieved success—like Gerry Schwartz (Onex Corp.), Jim Pattison (Pattison Group), Mike Lazaridis (RIM), Ken Rowe (IMP Group), Michael Dell (Dell Inc.), and Bill Gates (Microsoft)—are the most visible.

The entrepreneurship movement is accelerating with many new, smaller businesses emerging. Technology once available only to the largest firms can now be acquired by a small business. The Internet and cloud computing have reshaped the business landscape and levelled the playing field between large and small businesses by allowing small businesses to offer products globally, present professional marketing campaigns, and conduct customer service at a fraction of what it used to cost. A recent article in the *National Post* sums this up when the author notes, "The Web has lowered the bar for people with skills and ideas. People don't need a development team or a big budget; they just need a good idea and a laptop."[7] For example, Mike McDerment of Toronto founded FreshBooks, an online accounting company aimed at servicing small businesses throughout North America. While the company is based in Ontario, it now boasts five million subscribers—most of them paying $19.95 a month for accounting services—and bills itself as the world's No. 1 cloud-based accounting specialist. FreshBooks has grown from four employees to over 100 who service clients from all over the world using the Internet. Vincent Cheung founded Shape Collage Inc. as a student at the University of Toronto. Cheung's website allows people to take hundreds of photos and, in seconds, automatically arrange them into a collage in any shape. His software has been downloaded over a million times so far. Not only has he managed to pay himself a full salary, but he also captured the 2010 Ontario Entrepreneur of the Year student award.[8] Much like Cheung, Cameron Laker started Vancouver-based Mindfield Group when he was in his 20s. Within three years the company had grown to be one of the leading retail human resource staffing firms in Canada. Laker notes that the Internet, in particular social media sites, is important to the company's success: "Social media has allowed us to get our name out there very quickly …. Every one of our deals, except for … one, has been attracted to us originally because

Consider the Following: What Is the Difference Between an Entrepreneur and a Small Business Person?

This common question can result in much discussion. The authors of the book think an entrepreneur is someone who is always looking to seize opportunities. Whether through expansion of a business or finding better ways to do things, an entrepreneur is consistently looking to create something new. A small business person is someone who works in a small business. They may have even started the company and engaged in one act of entrepreneurship, but if they do not continue to look for additional opportunities to create something new then they stop being an entrepreneur and become a manager. The question for you is: How would you define an entrepreneur and a small business person? Do you think they are different, as we believe?

Consider the Following: Should You Start Your Own Business?

Each day, thousands of individuals ask the difficult question, "Should I start my own business?" When queried, 85 percent of the populace said they would like to be in business for themselves. The driving force behind this desire to start a new venture is the desire to be one's own boss, to be independent. Since there is no definitive measurement developed that allows an individual to determine if he or she can be a successful entrepreneur, each individual needs to carefully appraise his or her situation through several different methods and self-assessment models. One way to determine whether you have what it takes to be an entrepreneur is to fill out the questionnaire below. If you find that you are answering "yes" to most of the questions, you might have all the qualities to be a great entrepreneur. If you answer "no" to many of the questions, it likely means you could still be an entrepreneur and do very well, but you may have to work on some of your weaknesses. There are many exceptions, and there is no such person as a "typical" entrepreneur.

1. Can you start a project and see it through to completion in spite of a myriad of obstacles? _____ Yes _____ No

2. Can you make a decision on a matter and then stick to the decision even when challenged? _____ Yes _____ No

3. Do you like to be in charge and be responsible? _____ Yes _____ No

4. Do other people you deal with respect and trust you? _____ Yes _____ No

5. Are you in good physical health? _____ Yes _____ No

6. Are you willing to work long hours with little immediate compensation? _____ Yes _____ No

7. Do you like meeting and dealing with people? _____ Yes _____ No

8. Can you communicate effectively and persuade people to go along with your dream? _____ Yes _____ No

9. Do others easily understand your concepts and ideas? _____ Yes _____ No

10. Have you had extensive experience in the type of business you wish to start? _____ Yes _____ No

11. Do you know the mechanics and forms of running a business (tax records, payroll records, income statements, balance sheets)? _____ Yes _____ No

12. Is there a need in your geographic area for the product or service you are intending to market? _____ Yes _____ No

13. Do you have skills in marketing and/or finance? _____ Yes _____ No

14. Are other firms in your industrial classification doing well in your geographic area? _____ Yes _____ No

15. Do you have a location in mind for your business? _____ Yes _____ No

16. Do you have enough financial backing for the first year of operation? _____ Yes _____ No

17. Do you have enough money to fund the start-up of your business or have access to it through family or friends? _____ Yes _____ No

18. Do you know the suppliers necessary for your business to succeed? _____ Yes _____ No

19. Do you know individuals who have the talents and expertise you lack? _____ Yes _____ No

20. Do you really want to start this business more than anything else? _____ Yes _____ No

SOURCE: Hisrich et al., *Entrepreneurship*, 2/C/e. McGraw-Hill Ryerson

of our use of social media."[9] The Internet also allows smaller companies to find great employees no matter where their head office is located. For example, Empire Avenue, an Edmonton-headquartered social media company, uses the Internet to link its employees together. The company's employees live all over the world, working collaboratively using the Internet to create value for clients. Empire Avenue CEO Duleepa Wijayawardhana says, "All of us are scattered all over the country. We run the company remotely." Other technological advances such as tablet computers, smart phones, high-speed printers, fax machines, copiers, voice mail, computer bulletin boards and networks, cellular phones, and even overnight delivery services enable small businesses to be more competitive with today's giant corporations. Small businesses can also form alliances with other companies to produce and sell products in domestic and global markets.

Entrepreneur Characteristics

While entrepreneurs can come from various backgrounds many of them share certain characteristics including:

- Strong desire to act independently

- High need for achievement

- Willingness to take some risks

- Energetic

Do you think you have some of these characteristics? Do you think entrepreneurs need all of them to be successful? Why or why not?

What Is a Small Business?

This question is difficult to answer because smallness is relative. While recent research has found that the most consistent determinant of business size is the number of employees, there is no consistency in identifying the actual number of employees that make up a small business. Furthermore, researchers and government agencies often consider other variables such as upper limits on revenue, limits on rank in the industry, and so forth when determining whether a business is small. In this book, we will define a **small business** as any independently owned and operated business that is not dominant in its competitive area and does not employ more than 500 people. A local Mexican restaurant may be the most patronized Mexican restaurant in your community, but because it does not dominate the restaurant industry as a whole, the restaurant can be considered a small business. This definition is similar to the one used by Statistics Canada, which uses 500 employees as the cut-off separating small and large businesses.[10] Interestingly the Canadian Federation of Independent Businesses (CFIB) also defines small business by the number of employees but uses less than 250 employees as

Small business any independently owned and operated business that is not dominant in its competitive area and does not employ more than 500 people

its cut-off. The CFIB website (www.cfib.ca) offers advice on starting a small business and offers a wealth of information to current and potential small-business owners.[11]

The Role of Small Business in the Canadian Economy

No matter how you define small business, one fact is clear: Small businesses are vital to the soundness of the Canadian economy. As you can see in Table 5.1, more than 99 percent of all Canadian firms are classified as small businesses, and they employ 48 percent of private workers.[12] Small firms are also important as exporters, representing roughly 97 percent of Canadian exporters of goods.[13] In addition, small businesses are largely responsible for fuelling job creation and innovation. Small businesses also provide opportunities for women to succeed in business. There are 910,000 women entrepreneurs in Canada with an ownership interest in approximately

Christine Magee is one of the better known female entrepreneurs in Canada. She co-founded Sleep Country Canada in 1994 and has grown the company from one store to 240 today.

one million small businesses.[14] For example, Christine Magee, co-founder and president of Sleep Country Canada, started the specialty store in 1994. The firm, which specializes in mattress sales, was purchased in 2008 for $356 million.[15] Today, Magee remains as president of the company, which has become famous for its slogan, "Why buy a mattress anywhere else?"

Job Creation. The energy, creativity, and innovative abilities of small-business owners have resulted in jobs for other people. In fact, in the last decade, between 60 and 80 percent of net new jobs annually were created by small businesses.[16] Table 5.2 indicates that 99.7 percent of all businesses employ fewer than 500 people.

Many small businesses today are being started because of encouragement from larger ones. Many jobs are being created by big-company/small-company alliances. Whether through formal joint ventures, supplier relationships, or product or marketing cooperative projects, the rewards of collaborative relationships are creating many jobs for small-business owners and their employees. Some publishing companies, for example, contract out almost all their editing and production to small businesses. Row House Publishing Services is a small business in Toronto, Ontario, that provides editorial services for educational publishers, and government and corporate clients.[17]

Innovation. Perhaps one of the most significant strengths of small businesses is their ability to innovate and bring significant changes and benefits to customers. Small firms produce approximately 55 percent of innovations.[18] Among important 20th century innovations by Canadian small firms are smart phones, insulin, and the snowmobile, pacemaker, washing machine, IMAX movie system, and television. Ballard Power, a British Columbia alternative energy company, may be working on one of the most important 21st century innovations: a car that runs without gas or oil. Although currently still in the testing phase, the company hopes one day to replace the oil combustion engine with one that is powered by batteries.[19]

table 5.1 Facts About Small Businesses

- Represent 99.7% of all employer firms.

- Employ 5 million people or 48% of all private sector employees.

- In 2008, small businesses created roughly 70,000 jobs, accounting for over 50% of the jobs created in Canada.

- Between 2002 and 2006, approximately 130,000 new small businesses were created each year.

- Approximately 15% of the population is self-employed.

- 75% of small businesses are in the service sector.

- Small firms spend approximately $4 billion on R&D annually.

SOURCES: http://www.ic.gc.ca/eic/site/sbrp-rppe.nsf/eng/rd01238.html and http://www.cfib-fcei.ca/cfib-documents/rr3093.pdf. Reproduced with the permission of the Minister of Public Works and Government Services, 2013.

The innovation of successful firms takes many forms. For example, a group of entrepreneurs and filmmakers noticed how popular multi-screen films were at EXPO '67 in Montreal and decided to build a system using a large screen and a powerful projector. The result of the invention was the IMAX screen and projection system.[20] As mentioned in Chapter 1, Ryan Holmes, CEO of Vancouver-based HootSuite, felt that companies should be able to manage their social media messages from one central location. Holmes created a social-media dashboard that is now being used by almost 80 out of the largest 100 companies in America.[21] Small-businessman Ray Kroc found a new way to sell hamburgers and turned his ideas into one of the most successful fast-food franchises in the world—McDonald's. Much like Kroc, Ron Joyce, long-time owner of Tim Hortons, found a way to sell doughnuts and coffee along with other quick-serve items from one store. Joyce's aggressive growth strategy resulted in Canada having more doughnut stores per capita than anywhere else in the world and the company name become a cultural icon.[22] James Dyson spent time from 1979 to 1984 developing a prototype of a dual-cyclone, bagless vacuum cleaner. As a matter of fact, he built more than 5,000 versions before manufacturing his G Force, which made the front cover of *Design* magazine in 1983. Today, the company outsells its leading rival, Hoover, by capturing 21 percent of the U.S. dollars spent on upright vacuum cleaners versus 16 percent for Hoover. Dyson's vacuums sell for $400 to $600 each, whereas Hoover's sell for $69 to $389. Hoover, however, still sells more overall units than Dyson. Dyson's designs are featured in the Metropolitan Museum of Art, New York; the Science Museum, London; and the Victoria and Albert Museum, London, to name a few.[23] Small businesses have become an integral part of our lives. They provide fresh ideas and usually have greater flexibility to change than do large companies.

Industries That Attract Small Business

Small businesses are found in nearly every industry, but retailing and wholesaling, services, manufacturing, and high technology are especially attractive to entrepreneurs

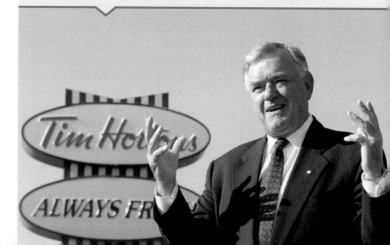

Ron Joyce, long-time owner of Tim Hortons, grew the company from a local coffee shop to a national chain. Joyce eventually sold the company to Wendy's in 1995.

table 5.2 Number of Businesses by Firm Size (Number of Employees), December 2008

Number of Employees	Cumulative Percent of Employer Businesses	TOTAL
Indeterminate		1,233,595
Employer Business Total	100.0	1,080,968
1–4	54.9	593,014
5–9	75.2	219,852
10–19	87.4	131,666
20–49	95.2	84,643
50–99	97.9	28,644
100–199	99.1	13,375
200–499	99.7	6,748
500+	100.0	3,026
TOTAL:		2,314,563

SOURCES: http://www.ic.gc.ca/eic/site/sbrp-rppe.nsf/eng/rd02300.html and http://www.cfib-fcei.ca/cfib-documents/rr3093.pdf. Reproduced with the permission of the Minister of Public Works and Government Services, 2013.

because they are relatively easy to enter and require low initial financing. Small-business owners also find it easier to focus on a specific group of consumers in these fields than in others, and new firms in these industries suffer less from heavy competition, at least in the early stages, than do established firms.

Retailing and Wholesaling. Retailers acquire goods from producers or wholesalers and sell them to consumers. Main streets, shopping strips, and shopping malls are lined with independent music stores, sporting-goods shops, dry cleaners, boutiques, drugstores, restaurants, caterers, service stations, and hardware stores that sell directly to consumers. Retailing attracts entrepreneurs because gaining experience and exposure in retailing is relatively easy. Additionally, an entrepreneur opening a new retailing store does not have to spend the large sums of money for the equipment and distribution systems that a manufacturing business requires. All that a new retailer needs is a lease on store space, merchandise, enough money to sustain the business, a knowledge about prospective customers' needs and desires, the ability to use promotion to generate awareness, and basic management skills. Some small retailers are taking their businesses online. For example, Jade Pearce of Winnipeg, who captured the eBay Young Entrepreneur award in 2007 with his company PNP Games, sells vintage video games and consoles through his eBay store and from his retail location in Winnipeg. At the time of the award Jade was selling over 400 games per week.[24]

Wholesalers supply products to industrial, retail, and institutional users for resale or for use in making other products. Wholesaling activities range from planning and negotiating for supplies, promoting, and distributing (warehousing and transporting) to providing management and merchandising assistance to clients. Wholesalers are extremely important for many products, especially consumer goods, because of the marketing activities they perform. Although it is true that wholesalers themselves can be eliminated, their functions must be passed on to some other organization such as the producer, or another intermediary, often a small business. For example, FouFou Dog was founded by Cheryl Ng from Richmond Hill, Ontario, to produce trendy, affordable, and high-quality pet clothes. After Ng started manufacturing and designing her own pet clothes, she expanded the business to act as a distributor for other manufacturers of similar products, including Rolf C. Hagen Inc., the world's largest pet products company.[25] Frequently, small businesses are closer to the final customers and know what it takes to keep them satisfied. Some smaller businesses start out manufacturing but find their real niche as a supplier or distributor of larger firms' products. One of the better-known Canadian success stories is Spin Master Toys, the firm founded by Ronnen Harary, Anton Rabie, and Ben Varadi after they graduated from university. They started manufacturing Earth Buddies, small pantyhose heads filled with grass seed, and built the business into the largest private toy company in Canada through in-house product development and by acting as a distributor/licensee for the Canadian market for large and small international toy firms. Today the company sells or distributes a variety of well-known toys including Air Hogs, Aqua Doodle, Bella Dancerella, Nano Speed, and the highly acclaimed Bakugan Battle Brawlers. Gerrick Johnson, an expert in the toy industry, notes, "They don't have to develop the toys themselves. If someone brings them the right idea, they'll develop it."[26] In fact, their latest hot toy, Bakugan Battle Brawlers, was acquired from an inventor who had no ties to the company. Anton Rabie states, "We have no ego about where the idea comes from. Lots of ideas come from in-house, but even more come from outside."[27]

Services. Services include businesses that work for others but do not actually produce tangible goods. They represent one of the fastest-growing sectors of the Canadian economy, accounting for 66 percent of the economy and employing roughly 75 percent of the workforce.[28] Real estate, insurance, and personnel agencies, barbershops, banks, television and computer repair shops, copy centres, dry cleaners, and accounting firms are all service businesses. Services also attract individuals—such as beauticians, morticians, jewellers, doctors, and veterinarians—whose skills are not usually

"Services include businesses that work for others but do not actually produce tangible goods."

required by large firms. Service businesses are attractive to start as the upfront costs are often quite low and potential profits can be quite high. If entrepreneurs are willing to complete the services themselves, then they don't even need employees. Of the 50 fastest-growing companies in Canada as identified in *Profit* magazine, nine of the top 10 are service-based businesses. *Profit* recently expanded its study of Canada's fastest-growing companies to 200 firms and discovered that 111 of the companies would be classified as service-based firms.[29] In 2006, four of the top five businesses had revenues less than $75,000.[30] Today, the top four service companies all have revenue in excess of $1 million. For example, Total Debt Freedom Inc., a Markham, Ontario, firm, assists consumers in getting rid of their debt by negotiating for settlements with various credit card holders. This service business, which promises to reduce unsecured debt by at least 40 percent, has grown from $300,000 to over $1 million in revenue in a few short years.[31]

Manufacturing. Manufacturing goods can provide unique opportunities for small businesses. While start-up costs can be higher for manufacturing businesses, entrepreneurs may be able to focus on a specific niche and keep costs down. Such products include custom artwork, jewellery, clothing, and furniture. For example, Canada Goose has carved a niche for itself by manufacturing warm stylish coats in Northern Canada. The company has managed to build a premium brand and sell its products at a premium through marketing and free celebrity endorsements. Other examples include Classic Cabinets Ltd., based in Medicine Hat, Alberta, and Fluidconcepts & Design Inc., from Mississauga, Ontario. Both companies focus on niche markets, with Classic Cabinets Ltd. manufacturing high-end cabinets specifically designed for customers. The company grew its revenue from slightly over $110,000 to $3.4 million in two years by focusing on the custom marketplace.[32] Fluidconcepts & Design Inc. designs and builds contemporary office furniture. The company, which had revenues of less than $400,000 in 2003, recently reported revenues in excess of $4 million.[33]

Technology. *Technology* was once a broad term used to describe businesses that depend heavily on advanced scientific and engineering knowledge. Today, the term also refers to businesses that make use of the Internet and cloud computing to create opportunities for entrepreneurs. As mentioned at the start of the chapter, the Internet has substantially levelled the playing field between large and small business. Whereas people previously needed substantial money to engineer new technology products, this is not the case anymore. People who can innovate or identify new markets in the fields of computers (smart phones and tablets), biotechnology, genetic engineering, robotics, and other markets have the opportunity to become today's high-tech giants. For example,

Toronto-based XMG Studios, creator of mobile games such as Cows vs. Aliens and Powder Monkeys, believes it is taking advantage of a growing niche in the gaming industry. XMG, which has grown from five employees to 35 in a few short years, has determined that there will be 1.5 billion smartphone users by 2015, most of whom will be people who would have some interest in casual games.[34] And unlike conventional video games, which can cost on average $20 million to create, casual games can be created for a fraction of this cost and offered for sale on an iPhone after paying Apple's $99 developer fee. Mike Lazaridis, founder of Research In Motion (RIM), managed to create a billion-dollar business when he took notice of the popularity of e-mail and designed a device (BlackBerry) to allow people to read and respond to e-mail on their telephones or smartphones. Other well-known examples include Michael Dell, who started building personal computers in his University of Texas dorm room at age 19. His Dell Inc. is now one of the leading PC companies in the world and the world's number-one direct-sale computer vendor with annual sales of more than $55 billion.[35] Apple Computer began in a garage. The Apple prototype was financed by the proceeds Steven Wozniak received from selling his Hewlett-Packard calculator and Steven Jobs got from selling his van.[36] In general, high-tech businesses require greater capital and have higher initial start-up costs than do other small businesses. The advent of the Internet is starting to change this, however, as the technology is reducing start-up costs and allowing entrepreneurs to reach consumers all over the globe. Jason DeZwirek of Toronto used the Internet to start an online media company, www.kaboose.com, which appealed to parents—specifically mothers. Within a few short years the company had a global audience and international advertisers. In 2009, Disney purchased the business for C$23.3 million.[37]

| **LO3** | Specify the advantages of small-business ownership. |

Advantages of Small-Business Ownership

There are many advantages to establishing and running a small business. These can be categorized as personal advantages and business advantages.

Independence

According to Statistics Canada, independence is the leading reason that entrepreneurs choose to go into business for themselves. Being a small-business owner means being your own boss. Many people start their own businesses because they believe they will do better for themselves than they could

DID YOU KNOW?
39 percent of high-tech jobs are in small businesses.[38]

Entrepreneurs do not just operate in business. The entrepreneurial spirit can also be found in the social sector. A social entrepreneur is someone who is driven to create social change by identifying and implementing solutions to social problems. Emphasis is being placed on the social entrepreneur as a necessary component for future economic growth. One of the most famous social entrepreneurs is Muhammad Yunus, founder of microfinance bank Grameen. Another example is Canadian Jeff Skoll, founder of the Skoll Foundation, which invests in social entrepreneurs who are helping solve some of the world's most pressing problems. The foundation is the world's largest organization of its type in the world and makes annual grants of $40 million to social entrepreneurs and organizations throughout the world.[39]

Although social entrepreneurship has long been privately funded, governments are recognizing its importance. For example, the Canadian government is in the process of implementing Social Impact Bonds (SIB). The bond would have private investors lend money to organizations who are trying to make improvements in society, such as increasing literacy rates for prisoners. If the organization succeeds, the government would then pay for the service and the organization could pay back its investors plus interest.

DISCUSSION QUESTIONS

1. What are the potential benefits of social entrepreneurship in our society?

2. What are some of the advantages and disadvantages of SIBs?

3. Should the government do more to encourage social enterprise? Why or why not?

4. If you were an investor, would you invest money in SIBs? Why or why not?

Mompreneur Victoria Turner of Toronto, creator of Pippalily baby slings, was attracted to entrepreneurship as a career choice as it enabled her to work at home with her child.

do by remaining with their current employer or by changing jobs. Kenzie MacDonald left his job as vice president at Colliers International, a global commercial real estate firm, to branch off and start his own company in Halifax. MacDonald stated the main reason for leaving his job was a strong desire to be his own boss: "I wanted to be in charge, to do things the way I wanted to do them ... when you work as an employee for years you always answer to someone ... its nice to be able to make all the decisions, to be in control."[40] Sometimes people who venture forth to start their own small business are those who simply cannot work for someone else. Such people may say that they just do not fit the "corporate mould."

More often, small-business owners just want the freedom to choose whom they work with, the flexibility to pick where and when to work, and the option of working in a family setting. The availability of the computer, copy machine, business telephone, and fax machine has permitted many people to work at home. Only a few years ago, most of them would have needed the support that an office provides. The desire for flexible work has given rise to a new type of entrepreneur or small-business owner—the *mompreneur*. Mompreneurs are mothers who are running a business either full-time or part-time and taking care of their children. Mompreneurs often start businesses rather than choose traditional employment as they can establish their own hours and schedule. Kathryn Bechthold, a mompreneur herself, founded *The Mompreneur*, a Canadian magazine dedicated to this niche group, noting that she wanted to assist other mompreneurs in balancing their family life and business.[41]

Enjoyment

One of the most commonly cited advantages of owning a business, whether big or small, is how much entrepreneurs enjoy their chosen careers. In fact, over 90 percent of Canadian entrepreneurs would start their business again if given the chance. Colin MacDonald, co-founder of Clearwater—a Halifax-based fish wholesale business that he founded out of the back of a pickup truck—notes that one of his biggest motivations in growing his business was how much he enjoyed working. "I really enjoyed the job, the responsibility, the growth," says MacDonald. Today, Clearwater is a publicly traded company and MacDonald says, "I still enjoy running the company ... there is good and bad but I truly enjoy it."[42] Young entrepreneur James Cuthbert, founder of the Port Moody, B.C.–based Rocky Point Kayak Ltd., echoes MacDonald's comments. "I love being an entrepreneur because it gives me the ability to earn a living in an area I love. It gives me an opportunity to be flexible with my time and pursue other personal and business interests."[43]

Financial Rewards

Often people are drawn to entrepreneurship with the hopes of earning a higher salary. Small-business owners know that their earnings are limited only by their skills as an entrepreneur. There is an old saying, "You can't get rich working for someone else." While there are no guarantees you will become wealthy by running your own business—you just may.

Low Start-Up Costs

As already mentioned, small businesses often require less money to start and maintain than do large ones. Obviously, a service firm with just five people will spend less money on wages and salaries, rent, utilities, and other expenses than does a firm employing tens of thousands of people in several large facilities. And, rather than maintain the expense and staff of keeping separate departments for accounting, advertising, and legal counselling, small businesses can hire other firms (often small businesses themselves) to supply these services as they are needed. Additionally, small-business owners trying to produce a difficult project can sometimes rely on the volunteer efforts of friends and family members in order to save money.

Management

Small businesses usually have only one layer of management—the owners. With small size comes the flexibility to adapt to changing market demands, the ability to build employee relations, and the capacity to create a strong corporate culture. Since decisions can be made and carried out quickly, small firms can change direction faster than larger businesses. For example, Targray Technology International Inc., a Quebec manufacturer of CD and DVD components, noticed the

Entrepreneurs like James Cuthbert, founder of Rocky Point Kayak Ltd., enjoy the freedom of being an entrepreneur.

trend toward green energy and started making inputs for solar panel makers. Solar power parts now account for more than half of the company's $225 million in revenue.[44] A similar situation occurred on a smaller scale for David Ciccarelli, who was acting as an agent and trying to market voice-over work for his wife. Ciccarelli noticed that no firms were offering what he thought was the appropriate level of service to voice-over artists. He quickly changed the focus of his work from drumming up business for his wife to building www.voices.com, a website that markets roughly 35,000 voice-over artists to *Fortune* 500 companies, advertising agencies, and various types of media.[45] If David had been working for a large marketing agency, this decision might have taken months if not years to come to fruition. In larger firms, decisions about even routine matters can take weeks because they must pass through two or more levels of management before action is authorized. When McDonald's introduces a new product, for example, it must first research what consumers want, then develop the product and test it carefully before introducing it nationwide, a process that sometimes takes years. An independent snack shop, however, can develop and introduce a new product (perhaps to meet a customer's request) in a much shorter time. Another advantage of being small is that business owners can build strong relationships with their employees, which can distinguish their business from larger competitors. Since managers/owners in smaller firms get to know their employees better than larger counterparts they can use this knowledge to differentiate themselves from larger competitors. Grant McKerarcher of Keen Technology Consulting, a Toronto-based IT staffing agency, states that by being small they get to know their employees, can monitor them more closely, and provide customers with better service: "It's easy to compete when your company is small. You can easily monitor the quality of work of people you are hiring and the work that's going on, because it's all happening right in front of you."[46] Small-business owners also get to create their company's corporate culture. In larger, more-established businesses, the culture of the business can be hard to influence and/or change. In smaller firms, especially new companies, the owner can create the culture that they desire and often use it to their advantage. For example, VersaPay Corp., a credit card and debt payment processing company based in Vancouver, uses its employee ownership program to motivate existing employees and to attract new talent. Michael Gokturk, the CEO, says he wanted to create employees that are owners of his company right from the start: "I went into this with a very Warren Buffett mindset. If you read his annual report ... employee ownership is one of the main reasons his subsidiary companies do so well. ... At our company we use our stock as currency to incentivize our current employees."[47]

Focus

Small firms can focus their efforts on a few key customers or on a precisely defined market niche—that is, a specific group of customers. Many large corporations must compete in the mass market or for large market segments. Smaller firms can develop products for particular groups of customers or to satisfy a need that other companies have not addressed. For example, Fatheadz focuses on producing sunglasses for people with big heads. To be an official "fathead" you need a ball cap size of at least 7⅝ and a head circumference above the ear of at least 23.5 inches. The idea arose when Rico Elmore was walking down the Las Vegas strip with his brother and realized that he had lost his sunglasses. He went to a nearby sunglass shop, and out of 300 pairs of glasses, he could not find one that fit. Customers include the entire starting line of the Indianapolis Colts, Rupert Boneham (of *Survivor* fame), and Tim Sylvia, former heavyweight title holder of Ultimate Fighting Championship.[48] By targeting small niches or product needs, small businesses can sometimes avoid fierce competition from larger firms, helping them to grow into stronger companies.

Reputation

Small firms, because of their capacity to focus on narrow niches, can develop enviable reputations for quality and service. For example, the above-mentioned VersaPay Corp. knew it was entering a market dominated by the large

Small-business owners, such as dentists, know that maintaining a high-quality reputation is essential to their success.

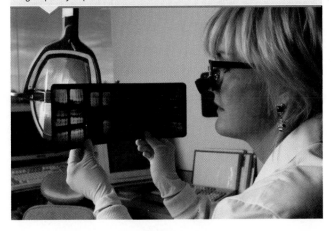

Canadian banks. The co-founders, Michael Gokturk and Kevin Short, felt that they could capture market share by offering superior customer service at lower fees—especially to smaller firms who frequently complain about how large banks treat them. The company's strategy appears to be paying off as it has grown from less than $50,000 in sales to $5.1 million in two years.[49] Another example of a small business with a formidable reputation is W. Atlee Burpee and Co., which has the U.S.'s premier bulb and seed catalogue. Burpee has an unqualified returns policy (complete satisfaction or your money back) that demonstrates a strong commitment to customer satisfaction.[50]

LO4 Summarize the disadvantages of small-business ownership, and analyze why many small businesses fail.

Disadvantages of Small-Business Ownership

The rewards associated with running a small business are so enticing that it's no wonder many people dream of it. However, as with any undertaking, small-business ownership has its disadvantages.

High Stress Level

A small business is likely to provide a living for its owner, but not much more (although there are exceptions, as some examples in this chapter have shown). There are always worries about competition, employee problems, new equipment, expanding inventory, rent increases, or changing market demand. In addition to other stresses, small-business owners tend to be victims of physical and psychological stress. The small-business person is often the owner, manager, sales force, shipping and receiving clerk, bookkeeper, and custodian. Figure 5.1 shows the five biggest challenges and goals of small- and medium-sized businesses. Many creative persons fail, not because of their business concepts, but rather because of difficulties in managing their business.

High Failure Rate

Despite the importance of small businesses to our economy, there is no guarantee of small-business success. Roughly 90 percent of all new businesses fail within the first five years.[51] Neighbourhood restaurants are a case in point. Look around your own neighbourhood and you can probably spot the locations of several restaurants that are no longer in business.

Small businesses fail for many reasons (see Table 5.3). A poor business concept—such as insecticides for garbage cans (research found that consumers are not concerned with insects in their garbage)—will produce disaster nearly every time. Expanding a hobby into a business may work if a genuine market niche exists, but all too often people start such

figure 5.1 Top Five Biggest Challenges, Concerns, and Goals of Small and Medium Businesses

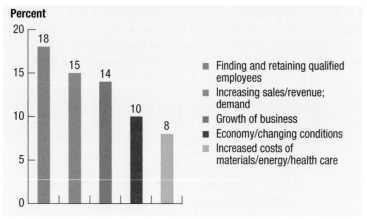

Percent

- ■ Finding and retaining qualified employees — 18
- ■ Increasing sales/revenue; demand — 15
- ■ Growth of business — 14
- ■ Economy/changing conditions — 10
- ■ Increased costs of materials/energy/health care — 8

SOURCE: "Entrepreneurial Challenges Survey Results," *Entrepreneur*, http://www.entrepreneur.com/encyclopedia/businessstatistics/article81812.html (accessed June 14, 2007).

a business without identifying a real need for the goods or services. Other notable causes of small-business failure include the burdens imposed by government regulation, insufficient funds to withstand slow sales, and vulnerability to competition from larger companies. However, four major causes of small-business failure deserve a close look: external shocks, undercapitalization, managerial inexperience or incompetence, and inability to cope with growth; roughly 90 percent of small-business failures can be attributed to these faults.[52]

External Shocks. Approximately 68 percent of businesses fail in Canada due to what is described as **external shocks.** These are events that occur in a company's external environment which the company could not control. Consider restaurants that operate in Windsor, Ontario, a region of the country that has seen a significant increase in the unemployment rate with the loss of numerous jobs in the auto sector. Dan Young, a food and beverage manager for a Windsor-based restaurant, notes, "We have managed to stay open, but many competitors have closed, revenue is down at almost every restaurant in town, and there is very little restaurant owners can do about it."[53] Examples of external shocks include: downturns in the economy, new competitors, customers going out of business, loss of suppliers, energy prices, and so forth.

Undercapitalization. The shortest path to failure in business is **undercapitalization,** the lack of funds to operate a business normally. Too many entrepreneurs think that all they need is enough money to get started, that the business can survive on cash generated from sales soon thereafter. But almost all businesses suffer from seasonal variations in sales, making cash tight, and few businesses make money

External shocks unanticipated events that occur in a firm's external environment that hurt the company's business

Undercapitalization the lack of funds to operate a business normally

from the start. Without sufficient funds, the best small-business idea in the world will fail.

Managerial Inexperience or Incompetence. Poor management is the cause of many business failures. Just because an entrepreneur has a brilliant vision for a small business does not mean he or she has the knowledge or experience to manage a growing business effectively. A person who is good at creating great product ideas and marketing them may lack the skills and experience to make good management decisions in hiring, negotiating, finance, and control. Moreover, entrepreneurs may neglect those areas of management they know little about or find tedious, at the expense of the business's success.

Inability to Cope With Growth. Sometimes, the very factors that are advantages turn into serious disadvantages when the time comes for a small business to grow. Growth often requires the owner to give up a certain amount of direct authority, and it is frequently hard for someone who has called all the shots to give up control.[54] For example, Rebecca MacDonald, founder of Toronto–based Energy Saving Income Fund, says that when she first started the business she did everything, but as the company grew she had to let other people do more and more. MacDonald notes that the transition was tough: "It was almost like letting a child leave home. It was hard for me. But I wanted to allow my talented people to do what they were hired to do."[55] Similarly, growth requires specialized management skills in areas such as credit analysis and promotion—skills that the founder may lack or not have time to apply. David Cynamon, CEO of KIK Corp., a private-label cleaning product producer, openly questions if he has the ability to manage the company as it grows: "It becomes a different game. ... At 700 people (current number of employees), it becomes difficult; 3,000 people might be beyond my capability." Cynamon has accepted that fact that his company may outgrow his ability to manage it. "Its not about the job (CEO), it's about the longevity and success of KIK forever. The status of the job means nothing to me."[56]

Poorly managed growth probably affects a company's reputation more than anything else, at least initially. And products that do not arrive on time or goods that are poorly made can quickly reverse a company's success.

The failure rate for small businesses is very high.

table 5.3 Most Common Mistakes Made by Start-Up Businesses

- Failing to spend enough time researching the business idea to see if it's viable.
- Miscalculating market size, timing, ease of entry, and potential market share.
- Underestimating financial requirements and timing.
- Overprojecting sales volume and timing.
- Making cost projections that are too low.
- Hiring too many people and spending too much on offices and facilities.
- Lacking a contingency plan for a shortfall in expectations.
- Bringing in unnecessary partners.
- Hiring for convenience rather than skill requirements.
- Neglecting to manage the entire company as a whole.
- Accepting that it's "not possible" too easily rather than finding a way.
- Focusing too much on sales volume and company size rather than profit.
- Seeking confirmation of your actions rather than seeking the truth.
- Lacking simplicity in your vision.
- Lacking clarity of your long-term aim and business purpose.
- Lacking focus and identity.
- Lacking an exit strategy.

SOURCE: John Osher, in Mark Henricks, "What Not to Do," *Entrepreneur*, February 2004, www.entrepreneur.com/article/0,4621,312661,00.html.

Starting a Small Business

We've told you how important small businesses are, and why they succeed and fail, but *how do you go about* starting your own business? To start any business, large or small, you must first have an idea. Sam Walton, founder of Walmart, had an idea for a discount retailing enterprise and spawned the world's largest retailing empire, also changing the way traditional companies look at their business. Next, you need to assess whether the idea is in fact an opportunity that is worth pursuing as a business—the two are not one and the same. You may have an idea to build an amusement park in space, but due to financial and resource limitations it is unlikely to be considered an opportunity for an entrepreneur. An opportunity is an idea that can be turned into a profitable company. Writing a business plan to guide planning and development in the business comes next. Finally, you must make decisions about form of ownership, the financial resources needed, and whether to buy an existing business, start a new one, or buy a franchise.

Idea Generation

Ideas can come from anywhere—past jobs and hobbies are two of the most common sources of business ideas, as 80 percent of new businesses in Canada can trace their beginnings to the entrepreneur's previous business experience. For example, Michelle Strum, owner of the Halifax Backpackers Hostel, came up with the idea of a locally owned hostel after travelling extensively overseas and staying and working in different countries.[57] Similarly, Costa

---

ENTREPRENEURSHIP IN ACTION | Alternative Outfitters Promotes High Fashion, Vegan Style

Jackie Horrick and Henny Hendra

Business: Alternative Outfitters

Founded: 2004

Success: The business has expanded to the point that the owners are looking to buy more warehouse space and to open a showroom.

In 2004, Jackie Horrick and Henny Hendra founded Alternative Outfitters—an online retail store featuring animal-free clothing, accessories, cosmetics, skin care products, and shoes. The two are firmly committed to selling only cruelty-free products that also happen to be fashionable. The idea for Alternative Outfitters came about due to personal need. Years ago, Horrick, a vegetarian and a vegan, began shopping for shoes,

bags, skin care products, cosmetics, and other items made without animal products. It was difficult for her to find the items she needed. Over time, Horrick began to realize that there were probably other individuals out there looking for the same items, and the concept for her business was born. The company has been hugely successful. In 2005, Alternative Outfitters won its second PETA (People for the Ethical Treatment of Animals) Proggy Award and *VegNews* magazine's Veggie Award. The company and its products have been featured in *People*, *Lucky*, and *InStyle*, among others. In early 2006, the company was expanding beyond its warehouse space and considering both additional space and the possibility of opening a Pasadena, California–based showroom.[58]

Elles, co-owner of Ela, a Greek restaurant that is expanding rapidly in Atlantic Canada, relied heavily on his 10-plus years of work experience in the food and beverage industry to shape the design and management of his restaurants.[59] Ideas can also come from watching television shows like CBC's *Dragons' Den*, observing consumers as they shop, or paying close attention to emerging trends by following reports by trend watchers such as www.wired.com, www.springwise.com, and www.trendwatching.com. For example, Jay Cho of Coma Food Truck, a gourmet Korean-Mexican-American food-truck operating in Vancouver, states he was inspired to open his business after seeing the popularity of the trucks in Los Angeles. Cho says he always wanted to open his own restaurant but could never come up with the start-up money. The food-truck business allows him to enter the restaurant business at much lower costs than opening a bricks-and-mortar establishment.[60] Coma Food Truck opened to rave reviews from customers, but Cho eventually closed the business after a dispute with the city. The growing number of tutoring companies, especially online tutoring, is a direct result of entrepreneurs watching trends and using the Internet to first reach customers and offer an improved experience. At one time, tutoring was used by struggling students to pass, but more and more parents are including tutoring as part of their children's extra-curricular activities with the hope that the extra attention will lead to long-term success. For example, Christopher Ide, co-founder of Pax Learning, is currently offering both in-home and online tutoring in Toronto; his selling point is personalized engagement. "I don't think we need a white paper to tell us that kids' lives are totally immersed in technology these days," he says. "Having a background in the educational-technology sector, I knew that tablets, computers and smartphones could make learning much more enjoyable for kids."[61] Other business ideas can come from a deliberate search, where entrepreneurs are engaging in formal methods to generate new ideas. For example, Dr. A.K. Kirumira of BioMedical, a Windsor, Nova Scotia–based diagnostic equipment company, says that when he needs new ideas he starts with a formal review of medical journals, old files, and research to look for opportunities that others may have missed.[62]

Opportunity Identification and Assessment

All entrepreneurs start with an idea that they hope can be an opportunity. An "opportunity" to an entrepreneur is an idea that can be turned into a profitable business. Prior to spending significant time on the development of an idea, an entrepreneur should first conduct an opportunity assessment. An opportunity assessment is a screening tool that can be used to determine if an entrepreneur should write a full business plan or go back to the drawing board and consider another idea. An opportunity assessment consists of:

1. Describing the business and the marketing mix (price, product, place, and promotion).
2. Assessing of his or her own skills. Does the potential entrepreneur know enough about the industry and have the skills necessary to run this type of business? Additionally, the entrepreneur should want to work in this type of industry.

3. Determining if there is a need for the business. While entrepreneurs do not have to engage in market research at this point, they may want to talk to friends, family, knowledgeable lawyers, accountants, and industry experts.
4. Identifying the competition and assess their strengths and weaknesses. Start to determine how they would react to a new competitor.
5. Calculating start-up costs, annual expenses, and potential revenue. Determine if the idea makes financial sense.
6. Determining if the entrepreneur has the ability to bring together the financial and human resources to start the company.

After completing a thorough opportunity assessment an entrepreneur should have enough facts to decide if the idea is still worth pursuing. If the idea looks promising, they will proceed and write a business plan.

The Business Plan

A key element of business success is a **business plan**—a precise statement of the rationale for the business and a step-by-step explanation of how it will achieve its goals. The business plan should include an explanation of the business, an analysis of the competition, estimates of income and expenses, and other information. It should establish a strategy for acquiring sufficient funds to keep the business going. Indeed, many financial institutions decide whether to loan small business money based on its business plan. However, the business plan should act as a guide and reference document—not a shackle to limit the business's flexibility and decision making. Finally, the business plan should be revised periodically to ensure that the firm's goals and strategies can adapt to changes in the environment. Julian Brass, founder and CEO of NotableTV.com, an online company that informs people about notable events and people in and around Toronto, sums up this sentiment: "Every entrepreneur needs to start with a business plan, and like when you're seeking advice and mentorship, it's an ongoing process. You can say, 'This is a golden plan and we're going to be rich in a year,' but often times when you hit the market things are very different than what you perceived before starting out. It's then that you have to return to the drawing board and tweak some things and go from there."[63]

Numerous websites provide information on how to write a business plan, including www.bdc.ca and www.scotiabank.com/cda/. The major points covered in a business plan include:

- Executive Summary
- Industry Analysis
- Description of the Venture
- Production Plan
- Operational Plan
- Marketing Plan
- Organizational Plan
- Assessment of Risk
- Financial Plan

> **Business plan** a precise statement of the rationale for a business and a step-by-step explanation of how it will achieve its goals

The entrepreneurial success stories in this chapter are about people who used their creative abilities to develop innovative products or ways of doing something that became the basis of a new business. Of course, being creative is not just for entrepreneurs or inventors; creativity is an important tool to help you find the optimal solutions to the problems you face on a daily basis.

Employees rely heavily on their creativity skills to help them solve daily workplace problems.

According to brain experts, the right-brain hemisphere is the source of creative thinking; and the creative part of the brain can "atrophy" from lack of use. Let's see how much "exercise" you're giving your right-brain hemisphere.

TASK:

1. Take the following self-test to check your Creativity Quotient.[64]

2. Write the appropriate number in the box next to each statement according to whether the statement describes your behaviour always (3), sometimes (2), once in a while (1), or never (0).

3. Check your score using the following scale:

30–36 High creativity. You are giving your right-brain hemisphere a regular workout.

20–29 Average creativity. You could use your creativity capacity more regularly to guard against "creativity atrophy."

10–19 Low creativity. You could benefit from reviewing the questions you answered "never" in the assessment and selecting one or two of the behaviours that you could start practising.

0–9 Undiscovered creativity. You have yet to uncover your creative potential.

	Always 3	Sometimes 2	Once in a While 1	Never 0
1. I am a curious person who is interested in other people's opinions.				
2. I look for opportunities to solve problems.				
3. I respond to changes in my life creatively by using them to redefine my goals and revising plans to reach them.				
4. I am willing to develop and experiment with ideas of my own.				
5. I rely on my hunches and insights.				
6. I can reduce complex decisions to a few simple questions by seeing the "big picture."				
7. I am good at promoting and gathering support for my ideas.				
8. I think farther ahead than most people I associate with by thinking long term and sharing my vision with others.				
9. I dig out research and information to support my ideas.				
10. I am supportive of the creative ideas from my peers and subordinates and welcome "better ideas" from others.				
11. I read books and magazine articles to stay on the "cutting edge" in my areas of interest. I am fascinated by the future.				
12. I believe I am creative and have faith in my good ideas.				
Subtotal for each column				
	Grand Total			

Many eco-responsible entrepreneurial companies are investigating the viability of new products that utilize recycling in some way. Eric Hudson, founder of Recycline, has even developed a toothbrush made out of recycled materials. The company makes a line of toothbrushes, tongue cleaners, and razors called "Preserve." In 2006, *Inc.* magazine recognized the company in its list of the top 50 sustainable businesses. Recycline already has sales deals with Target, Whole Foods, and Stop & Shop, and increased publicity helped sales jump 45 percent between 2005 and 2006.

Hudson also sends samples of his products to movie companies in hopes of enhancing the profile of the Preserve line. In 2006, he had the pleasure of discovering that Will Ferrell's character in the movie *Stranger Than Fiction* would be using a Recycline toothbrush. The company was able to leverage its increased visibility with promotional efforts at Target stores. Articles in newspapers, trade publications, and the movie itself helped promote the product. The company even offered free toothbrushes and movie tickets to volunteers who passed out postcards that read: "Meet Harold Crick's toothbrush." The cards directed moviegoers to visit a Target store in order to buy the product.

To make its toothbrushes and the handles of its razors, Recycline has developed a sustainable partnership with Stonyfield Farm. Recycline creates the plastic components of its products out of Stonyfield's waste yogurt containers. Many believe that this type of system, wherein one company's waste is another's raw materials, is the way of the future. Recycline has also launched a line of kitchen products, which it has introduced in Whole Foods Markets. The company hopes that it will become the brand that environmentally conscious consumers turn to for high-quality, innovative, and stylish personal care products.[65]

DISCUSSION QUESTIONS

1. What are the advantages for Recycline in partnering with Stonyfield Farm?

2. List some additional ways that Hudson could market his recycled-plastic toothbrushes and shavers.

3. How will the company have to change as it grows larger?

Forms of Business Ownership

After developing a business plan, the entrepreneur has to decide on an appropriate legal form of business ownership—whether it is best to operate as a sole proprietorship, partnership, or corporation—and examine the many factors that affect that decision, which we explored in Chapter 4.

Financial Resources

The old adage "It takes money to make money" holds true in developing a business enterprise. To make money from a small business, the owner must first provide or obtain money (capital) to start the business and keep it running smoothly. Often, the small-business owner has to put up a significant percentage of the necessary capital. Few new business owners have the entire amount, however, and must look to other sources for additional financing. Students should recognize that while finding money to start a business is hard, it is never impossible—the world is full of entrepreneurs who came up with creative fundraising techniques. For example, Susan Squires-Hutchings, owner of a St. John's, Newfoundland, pottery business, was turned down for financing on more than 50 occasions prior to convincing her landlord to lend her the money to get her company off the ground.[66] Jim Treliving and George Melville of Boston Pizza fame did not originally create the restaurant; rather they purchased the rights to be the franchisor from the original owner. The pair raised the funds needed by convincing two friends to lend them half the money and then persuading the founder to lend them the other half.[67]

Equity Financing. The most important source of funds for any new business is the owner. Many owners include among their personal resources ownership of a home or the accumulated value in a life-insurance policy or a savings account. A new business owner may sell or borrow against the value of such assets to obtain funds to operate a business. Gerry Schwartz, one of the richest men in Canada and founder of Onex Corp., says that people should invest in themselves—they shouldn't fear risking their assets if it means attempting to realize their dreams.[68]

"The most important source of funds for any new business is the owner."

Additionally, the owner may bring useful personal assets such as a computer, desks and other furniture, a car, or truck as part of his or her ownership interest in the firm. Such financing is referred to as *equity financing* because the owner uses real personal assets rather than borrowing funds from outside sources to get started in a new business. The owner can also provide working capital by reinvesting profits into the business or simply by not drawing a full salary. These thoughts are evident in the words of Michael Cerny, CEO of Creative Building Maintenance Inc. in Mississauga, Ontario, and Huck Owen, CEO of Toronto-based Owen Media Partners Inc. Cerny states, "The reality is that any grade-A financial institution is going to expect you to put up some kind of your own money up front to show your commitment and belief in your venture."[69] "Be prepared not to get paid,"[70] says Owen, who admits he is the last person in the company to get paid.

Small businesses can also obtain equity financing by finding investors for their operations. They may sell stock in the business to family members, friends, employees, or other investors. For example, when Eryn Green and Tamar Wagman—founders of Sweetpea Baby Food, an Ontario company that sells frozen organic baby food—needed money, they asked their family and friends to help out. The pair managed to raise $150,000 by selling a 10 percent stake in the company.[71]

Other sources of equity financing include the informal risk-capital market or business **angel investors** and venture capitalists. Angels are private, wealthy investors who typically invest anywhere from $10,000 to $500,000 in a business for an equity stake in the company. Angels in Canada are typically older males with entrepreneurship experience and most will want to invest in companies where they can provide some management assistance or mentoring. While little research has been done in Canada on the total value of dollars invested by angels, research in the U.S. has found that the amount far exceeds the total venture capital pool in the country. Examples of angel investors can be seen on CBC's *Dragons' Den* where entrepreneurs pitch their ideas to wealthy investors with hopes of receiving cash and business mentoring.[72] While the CBC version of angel investing has been spiced up for TV, it does provide some insight into what angel investors are looking for in a company—a motivated owner, strong business plan and presentation skills, an idea where they can add some expertise, and growth potential. A new trend in angel investing is the formation of angel groups or clubs. These are small organizations of investors who meet on a regular basis to hear pitches from aspiring entrepreneurs. Some of the better-known clubs in Canada include Atlantic Venture Networking Group, B.C. Angel Forum, Mindfirst Angels, and the Ottawa

Angel investors private investors who supply equity financing for businesses

Venture capitalists persons or organizations that agree to provide some funds for a new business in exchange for an ownership interest or stock

Members of the series *Dragons' Den* engage in a lively debate about the investment potential of an entrepreneur's idea.

Angel Alliance. **Venture capitalists** are businesses or organizations that agree to provide some funds for a new business in exchange for an ownership interest or stock. Venture capitalists hope to purchase the stock of a small business at a low price and then sell the stock for a profit after the business has grown successful. A teenage dance club that only exists online has been a real hit with venture capitalists. Doppelganger raised $11 million in one year from venture capitalists. What's so attractive about the site? Users to the club enter a three-dimensional, virtual world with custom characters meant to replicate their real-world counterparts. Entry is free, but inside they encounter plenty of advertising from marketers. The only public advertiser that Doppelganger has acknowledged is Vivendi Universal's Interscope Records.[73]

Although these forms of equity financing have helped many small businesses, they require that the small-business owner share the profits of the business—and sometimes control, as well—with the investors. The tradeoff in profits and control may well be worth the risk as research in Canada and the United States has found that businesses that make use of equity investors (angels/venture capitalists) are more financially successful, hire more employees, and bring more products to market than firms that do not use equity financing.

Debt Financing. Businesses often borrow the funds necessary to start and run their business. Banks are the main suppliers of external financing to small businesses. Business owners can also borrow money from some government sources such as the Business Development Centre or have some of their bank loans guaranteed by government programs such as the Canadian Small Business Financing Program. Other sources of debt financing can include family and friends and money borrowed from equity investors. If the business owner manages to borrow money from family or friends, he or she may be able to structure a favourable repayment schedule and sometimes negotiate an interest rate below current bank rates. If the business goes bad, however, the emotional losses for all concerned may greatly exceed the money involved. Anyone lending a friend or family member money for a venture should state the agreement clearly in writing.

The amount a bank or other institution is willing to loan depends on its assessment of the venture's likelihood of success and of the entrepreneur's ability to repay the loan. The bank will often require the entrepreneur to put up *collateral*, a financial interest in the property or fixtures of the business, to guarantee payment of the debt. Additionally, the small-business owner may have to offer some personal property as collateral, such as his or her home, in which case the loan is called a *mortgage*. If the small business fails to repay the loan, the lending institution may eventually claim and sell the collateral (or the owner's home, in the case of a mortgage) to recover its loss.

Banks and other financial institutions can also grant a small business a *line of credit*—an agreement by which a financial institution promises to lend a business a predetermined sum on demand. A line of credit permits an entrepreneur to take quick advantage of opportunities that require a

bank loan. Small businesses may obtain funding from their suppliers in the form of a *trade credit*—that is, suppliers allow the business to take possession of the needed goods and services and pay for them at a later date or in installments. Occasionally, small businesses engage in *bartering*—trading their own products for the goods and services offered by other businesses. For example, an accountant may offer accounting services to an office supply firm in exchange for printer paper and CDs.

Entrepreneurs know that being persistent is a requirement for raising money. If the idea is sound and an entrepreneur has a strong business plan, then raising debt and/ or equity is always possible. For example, when Christopher Frey, Kisha Ferguson, and Matt Robinson began searching for the $300,000 they needed to fund their Toronto-based, Canadian adventure travel magazine *Outpost*, they had to be determined. During a three-month period, the partners telephoned over 200 potential investors. While the trio were initially unsuccessful in raising all the money, they did manage to come up with $50,000—enough to get started. Two years later the company managed to raise $1 million

Consider the Following: Are These Angels From Heaven or Greedy Dragons?

"Stop the madness! You are a crazy chicken and this is a really bad idea," barks Kevin O'Leary at one entrepreneur. Jim Treliving tells another, "This idea is awful." Do these quotes sound like words from angels? Well, it depends on how you see the world. Both O'Leary and Treliving star on CBC's show, *Dragons' Den*, where entrepreneurs pitch their ideas to five angel investors in the hopes of receiving much-needed cash and business mentoring. Successful pitches may receive funding and often more than one new partner in their business, while unsuccessful pitches (poor products) are sometimes lambasted by the Dragons. Many viewers of the popular show are left to wonder if pitching ideas to angel investors even remotely resembles this process and if all investors are indeed as greedy as these so called angels appear to be.

The questions are not easy to answer. Yes, entrepreneurs may pitch their ideas to a group of angel investors in a relatively short time period as seen on the show. Yes, the investors will be mostly interested in the numbers, want a large return, and expect entrepreneurs to know their business inside and out. But the really poor ideas or the unprepared entrepreneurs often seen in the show would almost never get an opportunity to pitch to a group of angel investors. Almost all angel investors thoroughly pre-screen ideas (by reading a business plan) and would not consider listening to any of the poor, albeit entertaining, concepts that make their way onto the CBC. Furthermore, most angel inves-

tors do not want control of a company, whereas these investors almost always do. The question concerning greed is much more difficult to answer. Let's look at two examples, PeerFX and Atomic Tea. Both companies came looking for money and mentorship.

PeerFX, an online peer-to-peer currency exchange, allows customers to exchange money via the Internet at a substantially lower fee than traditional banks charge. At the time of their pitch to the Dragons, 22-year-old business students Robert Dunlop and Florence Leung were presenting an idea to make money, not operate a business. The pair had hoped to receive an investment of $200,000 for 25 percent of their business. What they ended up with was $200,000 but for 50.1 percent of their company and partners with the knowledge and contacts to bring the project to life. The Dragons, especially Kevin O'Leary, negotiated very strongly with the two students and perhaps bullied them a bit. But both students admitted later that they are soft spoken and may need a partner like O'Leary to get the business operating successfully. So, were the investors helpful angels or greedy dragons in this case? You decide.

Atomic Tea, an innovative tea company owned by Jessica and Russell Bohrson, presented the Dragons with an operating company and a vision of becoming the next Starbucks, albeit with teas. The brother and sister team hoped to raise $120,000 for 25 percent of their company and use the funds to franchise their business. During the

from BHVR Communications, a Montreal media and entertainment company.[74] See Table 5.4 for a list of funds that Canadian small and medium enterprises use.

Approaches to Starting a Small Business

Starting From Scratch Versus Buying an Existing Business. Although entrepreneurs often start new small businesses from scratch much as we have discussed in this section, they may elect instead to buy an already existing business. This has the advantage of providing a network of existing customers, suppliers, and distributors and reducing some of the guesswork inherent in starting a new business. However, an entrepreneur buying an existing business must also deal with whatever problems the business already has, such as human resource issues, declining business, and increasing competition. In addition, it is often difficult to determine a price for a business that satisfies both the buyer and seller.

Family Business. Another common method of starting a business is to engage in a family-run business. Entrepreneurs may join an existing family business, start their own family-orientated company, or inherit a firm. In Canada, family businesses account for 80 to 90 percent of all firms, create 50 percent of all new jobs, and represent 40 percent of the largest 100 companies.[75] The advantages of starting or joining a family business include: family businesses outperform non-family businesses in terms of profit and longevity; family members' strengths can be combined; family members tend to be more loyal to a firm than non-family members; owners of family businesses are often more driven to succeed than traditional business owners; and family members tend to trust each other more.

Even with these advantages, the long-term survival rate of family businesses is not as high as some people think—in fact, only one-third of family businesses survive to be passed on to the founder's children and fewer than 10 percent of those make it to the third generation. As the founder exits the business, the new owner(s) may not be as competent, the external environment can change, or issues may arise over succession planning that could result in the demise of the business. The Irving Group represents an example of

course of their pitch, the Dragons all stated that they loved Atomic Tea's products and all of them appeared interested in investing in the fledgling company. Jim Treliving spoke first, offering them $120,000 for 51 percent of the company. Laurence Lewin spoke next and offered to pair with Treliving and invest $75,000 each for a total of $150,000 for 50.1 percent of the business. Before the Bohrsons could respond, Dragon Robert Herjavec jumped in and stated that he believed Atomic Tea would need more money to franchise successfully and offered to join Treliving and Lewin in an investing syndicate that would invest $225,000 in the business for 50.1 percent equity in the company. While the three investors were contemplating their offer, fellow Dragon Arlene Dickinson offered the Bohrsons $120,000 for only 40 percent of the business. Meanwhile, the only Dragon not heard from, Kevin O'Leary, told the two Atomic Tea owners to go back behind the curtain and consider their options. The pair left thinking they were going to come back and choose between two offers—one for $225,000 for 50.1 percent of the company, and one for $120,000 for 40 percent of their company.

Back in the Den, the investors were listening to a pitch of a different kind from O'Leary that would see the investors withdraw both offers and counter with a new take-it-or-leave-it, single offer from all the Dragons. When the Atomic Tea owners reappeared in front of the Dragons, they were surprised to hear that both original offers were now gone and they could accept a one-time offer of $120,000 for 50.1 percent of their business. The Bohrsons tried to get the investors to revisit one of the previous offers and were told by O'Leary that they could "take or leave the new offer" as it was the only one that they would get. After some thought, the Bohrsons accepted the terms and shook on the deal. After the show, Internet chat rooms and blogs were filled with people questioning the ethics of the Dragons and stating the Bohrsons should have walked away from the offer. But the Bohrsons have since stated time and time again that they are happy with the terms and the Dragons' vast experience was worth giving up 50.1 percent of their company.

So, were the investors helpful angels or greedy dragons in this case? You decide.[76]

DISCUSSION QUESTIONS

1. If you represented PeerFX or Atomic Tea, would you have agreed to the deals proposed by the Dragons?

2. Did the investors act ethically?

3. Using Internet resources such as YouTube, review some *Dragons' Den* episodes. What were the pitches about? Were they successful? What were the terms of the offer? Communicate your findings to the class.

Entrepreneurs are starting to take advantage of a new source of obtaining capital—crowdfunding. Crowdfunding has entrepreneurs raising small amounts of money from a large number of investors rather than trying to find large sums of money from a few investors. The term is relatively new, though, and still means different things to different people. For example, crowdfunding sites have emerged on the Internet where people can invest money for equity and some promise of future returns. However, some see crowdfunding as a means to raise donations from people who are interested in helping you start or grow your business. For example, the Brooklyn Warehouse, a popular Halifax-based eatery, engaged in a crowdfunding campaign where they asked people for a donation to expand their business. In return, people received free meals and their picture on the wall of the restaurant.[77] The Canadian government is studying the concept of crowdfunding and is trying to establish some rules to protect investors. Others argue the government should provide some basic rules and stay out of the way of this emerging funding source as people should be able to decide what to do with their own money.

DISCUSSION QUESTIONS

1. Prior to reading this feature, did you know about crowdfunding?

2. Is it fair to call people investors if they do not have any opportunity to receive their money back or earn a return on their investment?

3. If crowdfunding grows, what are some of the advantages and potential pitfalls to this source of funds?

4. Should the government step in and provide and enforce a clear set of rules on crowdfunding?

5. Use the Internet and review the current state of the laws and regulations in Canada on crowdfunding. Report back to the class what you have found.

6. Use the Internet to find some crowdfunding opportunities. Report back to the class the type of opportunity, the amount of money they are trying to raise, if investors will receive their money back, and any other details.

what can happen to a family business over time. K.C. Irving, the original founder of the company, noted that his succession plan was rather simple. He had three male children and they would inherit the business equally with his oldest son in charge. While the eldest Irving's approach was rather traditional, it did work and the Irving Empire continued to grow into a multibillion dollar firm. Eventually, Irving's sons started to hand the company down to their children, but instead of three successors there were many more heirs. Still, the company remained relatively intact. Now, with the company going through another succession plan, there is loud talk that the firm will break up into separate companies as the family can no longer agree to a succession plan and there are too many shareholders at the table vying for their interests.[78] Besides the problems with succession planning, there are other disadvantages associated with family businesses including disputes among family members; family ties preventing people from being honest with one another; the inability of participants to separate work from home; problems in establishing fair remuneration policies; and difficulty in attracting qualified non-family workers. Still, even with these problems, people gravitate to starting or joining family businesses. For example, when Tyler Gompf of Winnipeg came up with the idea of a customer management company called Tell Us About Us Inc., he enlisted his brother Kirby to help start and eventually manage the business. The brothers have grown TUAU into a full-service customer-feedback research firm. The pair agree that there are advantages and disadvantages of working with family as they communicate easily and trust one another. But they admit that they do argue, which can strain family relations. Their solution was for Tyler to assume the role of CEO and for Kirby to become chief operating officer (COO).[79]

Franchise a licence to sell another's products or to use another's name in business, or both

Franchiser the company that sells a franchise

Franchisee the purchaser of a franchise

Franchising. Many small-business owners find entry into the business world through franchising. A licence to sell another's products or to use another's name in business, or both, is a **franchise.** The company that sells a franchise is the **franchiser.** Tim Hortons, Nurse Next Door, and Boston Pizza are well-known franchisers with national visibility. The purchaser of a franchise is called a **franchisee.**

"**Many** small-business owners find entry into the business world **through franchising.**"

The franchisee acquires the rights to a name, logo, methods of operation, national advertising, products, and other elements associated with the franchiser's business in return for a financial commitment and the agreement to conduct business in accordance with the franchiser's standard of operations. Depending on the franchise, the initial fee to join a system varies. In addition, franchisees buy equipment, pay for training, and obtain a mortgage or lease. The franchisee also pays the franchiser a monthly or annual fee based on a percentage of sales or profits. In return, the franchisee often receives building specifications and designs, site recommendations, management and accounting support, and perhaps most importantly, immediate name recognition. Visit the website of the International Franchise Association or the Canadian Franchise Association to learn more on this topic.

table 5.4 Types of Financial Instruments Used by SMEs

Start-up SMEs	Percentage Used	SMEs	Percentage Used
Personal savings	66%	Commercial loans and lines of credit	49%
Personal credit cards	32%	Trade credit from suppliers	39%
Commercial loans and lines of credit	29%	Personal savings of owners	35%
Personal loans of owners	23%	Personal credit cards of owners	33%
Trade credit from suppliers	18%	Business retained earnings	31%
Leasing	12%	Commercial credit cards	26%
Loans from friends and relatives	12%	Personal lines of credit	21%
Commercial credit cards	8%	Leasing	16%
Government loans and grants	5%	Personal loans of owners	14%
Other sources	5%	Loans from friends and relatives	10%
Loans from employees	3%	Other sources including factoring, loans from employees	8%
Loans and investment from other individuals	1%	Government loans and grants	7%
		Loans and investment from other individuals	4%

SOURCE: "Small- and Medium-Sized Enterprise Financing in Canada," Government of Canada publication, 2003, p. 58. Reproduced with the permission of the Minister of Public Works and Government Services, 2013.

The practice of franchising first began in the United States when Singer used it to sell sewing machines in the 19th century. It soon became commonplace in the distribution of goods in the automobile, gasoline, soft drink, and hotel industries. The concept of franchising grew especially rapidly during the 1960s, when it expanded to more diverse industries. Table 3.5 listed a selection of the top 100 global franchises for 2013.

There are both advantages and disadvantages to franchising for the entrepreneur. Franchising allows a franchisee the opportunity to set up a small business relatively quickly, and because of its association with an established brand, a franchise outlet often reaches the breakeven point faster than an independent business would. Franchisees often report the following advantages:

- Management training and support.
- Brand-name appeal.
- Standardized quality of goods and services.
- National advertising programs.
- Financial assistance.
- Proven products and business formats.
- Centralized buying power.
- Site selection and territorial protection.
- Greater chance for success.[80]

However, the franchisee must sacrifice some freedom to the franchiser. Furthermore, research has found that franchisees fail at the same rate as traditional small and medium firms. Some shortcomings experienced by some franchisees include:

- Franchise fees and profit sharing with the franchiser.
- Strict adherence to standardized operations.
- Restrictions on purchasing.
- Limited product line.
- Possible market saturation.
- Less freedom in business decisions.[81]

Strict uniformity is the rule rather than the exception. Entrepreneurs who want to be their own bosses are often frustrated with a franchise. In addition, entrepreneurs should recognize that not all franchises offer the same advantages to their franchisees. While there is value in the brand recognition and training of large franchises such as Tim Hortons, Quiznos, and Subway, an entrepreneur has to question if it is worthwhile to pay the extra costs and ongoing royalties associated with buying into a small, lesser-known company. Often times the entrepreneur could start a business from scratch and create a name and brand for less money than is required to purchase a franchise. For example, a Halifax woman purchased a Western Canada-based tanning franchise. She assumed that buying into a franchise would provide her with training and that she would receive some ongoing assistance for the royalties (fees) she paid to the franchiser. Soon after buying the franchise she received her training, which amounted to a small manual. She then learned that since all of the other franchisees were located in Western provinces, the franchise would not assist her in advertising her company until more franchises were sold in her region.[82]

Help for Small-Business Managers

Because of the crucial role that small business and entrepreneurs play in the Canadian economy, a number of organizations offer programs to improve the small-business owner's ability to compete. These include entrepreneurial training programs and programs sponsored by Industry Canada and the Business Development Centre. Such programs provide small-business owners with invaluable assistance in managing their businesses, often at little or no cost to the owner.

Entrepreneurs can learn critical marketing, management, and finance skills in seminars and university/college courses. In addition, knowledge, experience, and judgment are necessary for success in a new business. While knowledge can be communicated and some experiences can be simulated in the classroom, good judgment must be developed by the entrepreneur. Local chambers of commerce and provincial and federal economic development offices offer information and assistance helpful in operating a small business. National publications such as *Profit, Inc.*, and *Entrepreneur* share statistics, advice, tips, and success/failure stories. Additionally, many urban areas—including Halifax, Montreal, Ottawa, Toronto, Calgary, and Vancouver—have weekly or monthly business journals or newspapers that provide stories on local businesses as well as on business techniques that a manager or small business can use.

Additionally, the small-business owner can obtain advice from other small-business owners, suppliers, and even

> **"Entrepreneurs can learn critical marketing, management, and finance skills in seminars and university/college courses."**

customers. A customer may approach a small business it frequents with a request for a new product, for example, or a supplier may offer suggestions for improving a manufacturing process. Networking—building relationships and sharing information with colleagues—is vital for any businessperson, whether you work for a huge corporation or run your own small business. Communicating with other business owners is a great way to find ideas for dealing with employees and government regulation, improving processes, or solving problems. New technology is making it easier to network. For example, some regions are setting up computer bulletin boards for the use of their businesses to network and share ideas.

LO6 Evaluate the demographic, technological, and economic trends that are affecting the future of small business.

The Future for Small Business[83]

Although small businesses are crucial to the economy, they can be more vulnerable to turbulence and change in the marketplace than large businesses. Next, we take a brief look at the demographic, technological, and economic trends that will have the most impact on small business in the future.

Demographic Trends

Canada's baby boom started in 1946 and ended in 1964. The earliest Boomers are already past 65, and in the next few years, millions more will pass that mark. The Boomer generation numbers about 10 million, or 30 percent of Canadian citizens.[84] This segment of the population is probably the wealthiest, and the one that is often pursued by small businesses. For example, Atlantic Tours, a Halifax-based travel company, offers numerous tours aimed at this market. Industries such as travel, financial planning, and health care will continue to grow as Boomers age. Many experts think that this demographic is the market of the future. For example, Calgary-based Masterpiece Inc., a developer and operator of retirement homes, has enjoyed revenue growth of 7,710 percent over a five-year period.[85] Nurse Next Door, a new Canadian homecare franchiser, is hoping the trend of seniors' spending money on their care will grow significantly as the company embraces a major expansion campaign. The baby boom will also influence the labour market in Canada as many Boomers are considering retirement options. The results of this are a shortage of highly trained and skilled labour in various regions, which is a contributing factor to the growth in staffing agencies such as PEOPLEsource Staffing Solutions Inc. and MGA Computer Consulting Ltd., both in Toronto. In fact, when companies were surveyed for a recent *Profit* magazine poll they noted the lack of skilled workers as the biggest barrier to future growth.[86]

Curves is for women only. It's not a fast-food franchise—it's a fast-exercise franchise.

Another market with huge potential for small business is the echo generation who are the children of the Boomers. They are sometimes referred to as Millennials or Generation Y. Born between 1977 and 1994, there are about 6 million people in Canada in this age group. Typically, they shop frequently and spend lavishly on clothing, entertainment, and food.[87] Companies that have the most success with this group are ones that cater to the teens' and young adults' lifestyles. Some successful small businesses aimed at this market include Sylvan Learning Centre, a franchise that offers after-school tutoring, Alien Workshop (designs and distributes skateboards and apparel), Burton Snowboards (manufactures snowboards and accessories), and Femme Arsenal (develops and distributes cosmetics).

Yet another trend is the growing number of immigrants living in Canada, as 260,000 people immigrate to this country each year.[88] This vast number of people provides still another greatly untapped market for small businesses. Retailers who specialize in ethnic products, and service providers who offer bi- or multilingual employees, can find vast potential in this market. Table 5.5 ranks the top cities for doing business in Canada.

Technological and Economic Trends

Advances in technology have opened up many new markets to small businesses. As previously discussed, the Internet has revolutionized business and allows small firms to compete with larger counterparts. One of the hot areas will be the Internet infrastructure area that enables companies to improve communications with employees, suppliers, and customers.

Technological advances and an increase in service exports have created new opportunities for small companies to expand their operations abroad. Changes in communications and technology can allow small companies to customize their services quickly for international customers. Also,

table 5.5 Top Cities for Doing Business in Canada

1. Quebec
2. Charlottetown
3. Saguenay
4. Laval
5. St. John's
6. Saint John
7. Edmonton
8. Markham
9. Halifax
10. Sherbrooke

SOURCE: http://www.findmapping.com/canadian_business_cities/bestcitiesforbusiness.php.

free trade agreements and trade alliances are helping to create an environment in which small businesses have fewer regulatory and legal barriers.

In recent years, economic turbulence has provided both opportunities and threats for small businesses. As large information technology companies such as Cisco and Oracle had to recover from an economic slowdown and an oversupply of Internet infrastructure products, some smaller firms found new niche markets. Smaller companies can react quickly to change and can stay close to their customers. While many well-funded dot-coms were failing, many small businesses were learning how to use the Internet to promote their businesses and sell products online. For example, many arts and crafts dealers and makers of specialty products found they could sell their wares on existing websites, such as eBay. Service providers related to tourism, real estate, and construction also found they could reach customers through their own or existing websites.

Interest in alternative fuels and fuel conservation has spawned many small businesses. Earth First Technologies Inc. produces clean-burning fuel from contaminated water or sewage. Southwest Windpower Inc. manufactures and markets small wind turbines for producing electric power for homes, sailboats, and telecommunications. Solar Attic Inc. has developed a process to recover heat from home attics to use in heating hot water or swimming pools. As entrepreneurs begin to realize that worldwide energy markets are valued in the hundreds of billions of dollars, the number of innovative companies entering this market will increase. In addition, many small businesses have the desire and employee commitment to purchase such environmentally friendly products.

The future for small business remains promising. The opportunities to apply creativity and entrepreneurship to serve customers are unlimited. While large organizations such as Walmart, which has more than 1.8 million employees,[89] typically must adapt to change slowly, a small business can adapt to customer and community needs and changing trends immediately. This flexibility provides small businesses with a definite advantage over large companies.

LO7 Explain why many large businesses are trying to "think small."

Making Big Businesses Act "Small"

The continuing success and competitiveness of small businesses through rapidly changing conditions in the business world have led many large corporations to take a closer look at

Sirius created value for a product and a market that didn't previously exist.

what makes their smaller rivals tick. More and more firms are emulating small businesses in an effort to improve their own bottom line. Beginning in the 1980s and continuing through the present, the buzzword in business has been to *downsize,* or more recently, to *right-size;* to reduce management layers, corporate staff, and work tasks in order to make the firm more flexible, resourceful, and innovative like a smaller business. Many well-known Canadian companies—including Nortel, Bell Canada, and Air Canada—have downsized to improve their competitiveness, as have American, German, British, and Japanese firms. Other firms have sought to make their businesses "smaller" by making their operating units function more like independent small businesses, with each being responsible for its profits, losses, and resources. For example, when John Bell, CEO and president of an auto parts manufacturing business, assumed the role of board chair at Cambridge Hospital in Ontario, he managed to turn a $2 million deficit into a $3.5 million profit in one year. Bell first streamlined

services and eliminated 29 management jobs and then hired an entrepreneur—Julia Dumanian—to assume the day-to-day operations of the hospital. Under their joint leadership, the pair eliminated services that were provided elsewhere in the region for annual savings of $1.6 million.[90] Of course, some large corporations, such as WestJet Airlines, have acted like small businesses from their inception, with great success.

> **Intrapreneurs** individuals in large firms who take responsibility for the development of innovations within the organizations

Trying to capitalize on small-business success in introducing innovative new products, more and more companies are attempting to instill a spirit of entrepreneurship into even the largest firms. In major corporations, **intrapreneurs,** like entrepreneurs, take responsibility for, or "champion," the development of innovations of any kind *within* the larger organization.[91] Often, they use company resources and time to develop a new product for the company.

TEAM EXERCISE

Explore successful franchises. Go to the companies' websites and find the requirements for applying for three franchises. This chapter provides examples of successful franchises. What do these companies provide, and what is expected to be provided by the franchiser? Compare and contrast each group's findings for the franchises researched. For example, at Subway, the franchisee is responsible for the initial franchise fee, finding locations, leasehold improvements and equipment, hiring employees and operating restaurants, and paying an 8 percent royalty to the company and a fee into the advertising fund. The company provides access to formulas and operational systems, store design and equipment ordering guidance, a training program, an operations manual, a representative on-site during opening, periodic evaluations and ongoing support, and informative publications.

LEARNING OBJECTIVES SUMMARY

LO1 Define entrepreneurship and small business.

Entrepreneurship is the process of creating and managing a business to achieve desired objectives. Small business is any independently owned and operated business that is not dominant in its competitive area and does not employ more than 500 people.

LO2 Investigate the importance of small business in the Canadian economy and why certain fields attract small business.

No matter how you define small business, one fact is clear: Small businesses are vital to the soundness of the Canadian economy as more than 99 percent of all Canadian firms are classified as small businesses, and they employ 48 percent of private workers. Small firms are also important as export-

ers, representing roughly 97 percent of Canadian exported goods. In addition, small businesses are largely responsible for fuelling job creation and innovation.

LO3 Specify the advantages of small-business ownership.

Small-business ownership has many advantages including: (1) Independence—the leading reason that entrepreneurs choose to go into business for themselves; (2) Enjoyment of chosen career—one of the most commonly cited advantages of owning a business whether big or small; (3) Realization that earnings are limited only by their skills as an entrepreneur—they can become wealthy; (4) The requirement for less money to start and maintain a small business compared to a large one; (5) Small businesses usually have only one layer of management—the owners—which gives them flexibility to adapt to changing market demands, the ability to build strong employee relations, and the capacity to create a strong corporate culture; (6) The ability to focus efforts on a few key customers or on a precisely defined market niche—that is, a specific group of customers; (7) The ability, with that narrow focus, to develop enviable reputations for quality and service.

LO4 Summarize the disadvantages of small-business ownership, and analyze why many small businesses fail.

Small businesses have many disadvantages for their owners such as expense, physical and psychological stress, and a high failure rate. Small businesses fail for many reasons: undercapitalization, external shocks, management inexperience or incompetence, neglect, disproportionate burdens imposed by government regulation, and vulnerability to competition from larger companies.

LO5 Describe how you go about starting a small business and what resources are needed.

First you must have an idea for developing a small business. You must decide whether to start a new business from scratch, enter into a family business, buy an existing company, or buy a franchise operation. Next, you need to devise a business plan to guide planning and development of the business. Then you must decide what form of business ownership to use: sole proprietorship, partnership, or corporation. Small-business owners are expected to provide some of the funds required to start their businesses, but funds also

can be obtained from friends and family, financial institutions, other businesses in the form of trade credit, investors (angels and or venture capitalists), and government organizations.

LO6 Evaluate the demographic, technological, and economic trends that are affecting the future of small business.

Changing demographic trends that represent areas of opportunity for small businesses include more elderly people as Baby Boomers age, a large group known as echo boomers, Millennials, or Generation Y, and an increasing number of immigrants to Canada. Technological advances and an increase in service exports have created new opportunities for small companies to expand their operations abroad, while trade agreements and alliances have created an environment in which small business has fewer regulatory and legal barriers. Economic turbulence presents both opportunities and threats to the survival of small business.

LO7 Explain why many large businesses are trying to "think small."

More large companies are copying small businesses in an effort to make their firms more flexible, resourceful, and innovative, and generally to improve their bottom line. This effort often involves downsizing (reducing management layers, laying off employees, and reducing work tasks) and intrapreneurship, where an employee takes responsibility for (champions) developing innovations of any kind within the larger organization.

KEY TERMS

angel investors
business plan
entrepreneurship
external shocks
franchise
franchisee

franchiser
intrapreneurs
small business
undercapitalization
venture capitalists

DESTINATION CEO DISCUSSION QUESTIONS

1. Re-read the opening quote in the case. Would you live your life as described in the quote if you were guaranteed to be worth millions of dollars in the future?

2. How does O'Leary's sometimes "villainous" role help him sell himself and products to consumers? Would you buy products just because they were endorsed by a celebrity?

3. How did O'Leary try to capitalize on the brand he was building on TV? Some of the products and companies

he is branding are quite different—for example wine is very different from mortgages. What are some of the advantages and disadvantages of this?

4. After reading the opening profile, would you describe Kevin O'Leary's business practices as ethical?

5. Use the Internet to research O'Leary and his companies. Has he added his name to any new products? What is the status of his businesses?

In times when jobs are scarce, many people turn to entrepreneurship as a way to find employment. As long as there are unfulfilled needs from consumers, there will be a demand for entrepreneurs and small businesses. Entrepreneurs and small-business owners have been, and will continue to be, a vital part of the Canadian economy, whether in retailing, wholesaling, manufacturing, technology, or services. Creating a business around your idea has a lot of advantages. For many people, independence is the biggest advantage of forming their own small business, especially for those who do not work well in a corporate setting and like to call their own shots. Smaller businesses are also cheaper to start up than large ones in terms of salaries, infrastructure, and equipment. Smallness also provides a lot of flexibility to change with the times. If consumers suddenly start demanding new and different products or services, a small business is more likely to deliver quickly.

Starting your own business is not easy, especially in slow economic times. Even in a good economy, taking a good idea and turning it into a business has a very high failure rate. The possibility of failure can increase even more when money is tight. Reduced revenues and expensive material can hurt a small business more than a large one because small businesses have fewer resources. When people are feeling the pinch from rising food and fuel prices, they tend to cut back on other expenditures—which could potentially harm your small business. However, several techniques can help your company survive.

Set clear payment schedules for all clients. Small businesses tend to be worse about collecting payments than large ones, especially if the clients are acquaintances.

However, you need to keep cash flowing into the company in order to keep business going.

Take the time to learn about tax breaks. A lot of people do not realize all of the deductions they can claim on items such as equipment.

Focus on your current customers, and don't spend a lot of time looking for new ones. It is far less expensive for a company to keep its existing customers happy.

Although entrepreneurs and small-business owners are more likely to be friends with their customers, do not let this be a temptation to give things away for free. Make it clear to your customers what the basic price is for what you are selling and charge for extra features, extra services, etc.

Make sure the office has the conveniences employees need—like a good coffee maker and other drinks and snacks. This will not only make your employees happy, but it will also help maintain productivity by keeping employees closer to their desks.

Use your actions to set an example. If money is tight, show your commitment to cost cutting and making the business work by doing simple things like taking the bus to work and bringing your lunch every day.

Don't forget to increase productivity in addition to cutting costs. Try not to focus so much attention on cost cutting that you don't try to increase sales.

In unsure economic times, these measures should help new entrepreneurs and small-business owners sustain their businesses. Learning how to run a business on a shoestring is a great opportunity to cut the fat and establish lean, efficient operations.[92]

BUILD YOUR BUSINESS PLAN

Small Business, Entrepreneurship, and Franchising

Now you can get started writing your business plan! Refer to Guidelines for the Development of the Business Plan following Chapter 1, which provides you with an outline for your business plan. As you are developing your business plan, keep in mind that potential investors might be reviewing it. Or you might have plans to participate in some of the government opportunities aimed at supporting youth in entrepreneurship, such as the Canadian Youth Business Foundation loans program.

At this point in the process, you should think about collecting information from a variety of (free) resources. For example, if you are developing a business plan for a local business, product, or service, you might want to check out any of the following sources for demographic information: the local Chamber of Commerce, Economic Development Office, or the Statistics Canada website.

Go on the Internet and see if any recent studies or articles have focused on your specific type of business, especially in your area. Remember, you always want to explore any secondary data before trying to conduct your own research.

Like lots of golf enthusiasts, Linda Hipp loves to golf and played as much as she could. The more she played, though, the less she liked traditional women's golf apparel. Hipp notes that the clothes were mostly baggy shirts and shorts and the colours were bland. Hipp was certain that she could mesh the colours and styles from fashion runways into her own line of golf clothing. She started to do some research on the idea and discovered that a market was emerging for stylish golf clothing. "After doing research, I found that there was a huge upswing in younger women taking up the game and I thought there would be a demand for more fashionable apparel," says Hipp. Based on this market research, Hipp started manufacturing clothing under the brand name Hyp Golf in 1997.

Shortly into the 1998 season, Hipp started to realize that she was right; there was in fact a significant market for fashionable women's golf clothing. Retailers were signing up to sell her clothes and that year, Pearl Sinn became the first of many women on the LPGA tour to embrace the brand. "Our customers are women who are fit. They care about what they look like and they care about their health and well-being. They want to look good no matter what they're doing, whether taking kids to school, or out on a golf course or out to dinner."

Hipp, now armed with positive consumer reaction in Canada, started to look south of the border to the U.S. for expansion opportunities. She says, "We started off in Canada. We made sure that one, we could sell the product; and second, that we could manufacture and provide the goods completely and on time to customers." Hipp admits that she was hesitant to expand into the U.S. as many people advised her against the idea. "I had a lot of people tell me that we shouldn't [enter the U.S. market], that a Canadian company can never make it into the U.S." But Hipp could see the huge potential for her products, especially in the southern states where golf was played 12 months a year.

Rather than rush into the market, Hipp opted to spend considerable time conducting research and planning on the right market entry strategy. "To mitigate the risk, we spent a lot of time researching and finding the right people, and finding the right two or three markets that had the most potential." Hipp also designed a unique marketing program to help her break into new territories using a three-step approach. The first step is to identify market influencers in the geographical area such as golf pros and provide them with free clothes to create awareness for the brand. The second stage involves securing media coverage by targeting newspapers, radio, television, and Internet companies, providing them with free product, and encouraging them to write about the company. The final step involves a manager from head office contacting three to five key accounts and establishing a relationship with them and securing an initial order. Only once a relationship is established with key retailers, along with appropriate demand for the product, does the company find a sales representative to serve the area.

Hyp Golf's entry into the U.S. market has been a huge success and today the market accounts for more than 75 percent of the company's sales. Hipp has since rebranded her business and product line under the brand LIJA and expanded into tennis, running, and studio apparel.[93] LIJA has continued to expand globally and has launched its brand into Dubai, the United Arab Emirates, South Africa, and the United Kingdom.

DISCUSSION QUESTIONS

1. What are some of Linda Hipp's strengths as an entrepreneur? Does she have any apparent weaknesses?

2. Why do you think Hipp was advised to avoid the American market? What did she do to ensure that she would be successful?

3. What are some of the advantages and disadvantages of dropping the Hyp Golf name and rebranding her products under the LIJA name?

4. Given the company's success in America, what are some of the advantages of continuing to expand into other countries? What would some of the challenges be?

5. Hyp's original product, fashionable clothes for young female golfers, could be characterized as a niche product. She has now expanded her product line to include products that compete against much larger competitors such as Nike and Lululemon. Why do you think she diversified her product line? Do you think adding new products is a wise strategy?

---

connect **LEARNSMART** **SMARTBOOK**

For more information on the resources available from McGraw-Hill Ryerson, go to www.mcgrawhill.ca/he/solutions.

6 The Nature of Management

LEARNING OBJECTIVES

LO1 Define management, and explain its role in the achievement of organizational objectives.

LO2 Describe the major functions of management.

LO3 Distinguish among three levels of management and the concerns of managers at each level.

LO4 Specify the skills managers need to be successful.

LO5 Summarize the systematic approach to decision making used by many business managers.

DESTINATION CEO

Joyce Groote What are CROCS? Ask almost anyone and you will hear, "They are foam shoes." The CROCS company made millions between 2004 and 2007 when foam sandals became the "in" product. Now ask yourself, have you heard of Holeys? If you answered "yes" it means you are likely more familiar with the shoe industry than others. Holeys was, and to some extent is, the Canadian equivalent to CROCS. Holeys started at the same time as CROCS, and its shoes were produced by the same manufacturer. Much like CROCS, Holeys enjoyed strong growth as foam shoes became a must-have item. But as Joyce Groote, CEO of Holeys, would tell you, CROCS had a much larger marketing budget, built a stronger brand, and enjoyed greater growth. Today, after the popularity of foam shoes has tapered off, both companies are still active in footwear but to quote Groote, "We have gone in a different direction than CROCS."[1]

Joyce Groote, previously a president of an Ottawa-based biotech industry group, had recently relocated to Vancouver with her husband. When her neighbours asked for her help with their foam shoe company, Groote accepted the challenge and went to work as a full-time entrepreneur for Holey Soles. At that time, the garage-based business had $60,000 in annual sales, but had none of the underpinnings of a solid business. Joyce asked herself what vision and strategy the company was to have in order to build a business plan around those answers.

After formulating a business plan, she provided a loan to the business and took on the role of president. One thing led to another and she ultimately bought out the founder in late 2004. The strategy, along with a strong growth in the foam shoe business, paid off. Holey Soles went from a $60,000 business in 2002 to a multimillion dollar company operating out of a 7,900 square metre facility in Richmond, B.C. Holeys grew with the foam shoe industry and achieved sales growth over 6000 percent in 2006 and was named one of the fastest-growing companies in Canada in 2006 and 2007.

As the popularity of foam shoes started to wane, Groote opted to change the name of the company to Holeys. She then opted to take the company in another direction and not to focus on what was trendy but to develop shoes that performed a function. Holeys developed a new anti-slip technology called Sole-tek and worked to develop a new type of foam called SmartCel which could be used in a variety of products, not just foam shoes. Groote focused her company on several niche markets, including children's and gardening shoes as well as light boots. Holeys' appeal to parents is that their children do not need help tying their shoes and are safer due to their anti-slip soles, while the gardening shoes and boots are lighter and more functional then competitive brands. Holeys boasts that they have created the world's lightest multi-use boot, which you can clean with a garden hose. While Groote's company may not replicate the success it had during the foam shoe craze, she has developed a plan, which she believes will move the company forward.[2]

In interviews at the height of her company's growth, Groote's advice for other entrepreneurs was to dream big while emphasizing the importance of having a sound business plan and direction for the future of the company. She is apparently following her own advice as she has crafted a new plan for Holeys, which by all accounts is working.[3]

Introduction

For any organization—small or large, for profit or nonprofit—to achieve its objectives, it must have equipment and raw materials to turn into products to market, employees to make and sell the products, and financial resources to purchase additional goods and services, pay employees, and generally operate the business. To accomplish this, it must also have one or more managers to plan, organize, staff, direct, and control the work that goes on.

This chapter introduces the field of management. It examines and surveys the various functions, levels, and areas of management in business. The skills that managers need for success and the steps that lead to effective decision making are also discussed.

LO1 Define management, and explain its role in the achievement of organizational objectives.

The Importance of Management

Management is a process designed to achieve an organization's objectives by using its resources effectively and efficiently in a changing environment. *Effectively* means having the intended result; *efficiently* means accomplishing the objectives with a minimum of resources. **Managers** make decisions about the use of the organization's resources and are concerned with planning, organizing, staffing, directing, and controlling the organization's activities so as to reach its objectives (see Figure 6.1). When Dani Reiss became CEO of Snow Goose in 2001, he made two key decisions that impacted the company's long-term growth. The first was to change the company's name to Canada Goose. The other was to continue to manufacture in Canada at a time when most Canadian garment companies were leaving to produce goods in Asia. Reiss believed the "made in Canada" label could be a major selling point as customers would associate the label to their ideal view of Canada's wilderness. "My whole life was like a focus group," he says. "I realized people had an emotional response to 'made in Canada.' The experience of owning one of these jackets was like trying

> **Management** a process designed to achieve an organization's objectives by using its resources effectively and efficiently in a changing environment
>
> **Managers** those individuals in organizations who make decisions about the use of resources and who are concerned with planning, organizing, staffing, directing, and controlling the organization's activities to reach its objectives

on a piece of Canada."[4] The result of these two key decisions has been sales growth of 3000 percent over ten years and expansion throughout the U.S., Asia, and Europe. Gabe Magnotta, who passed away in 2010, and his wife, Rosanna, also found success by bucking industry trends. Together, the pair developed Ontario's third-largest winery by marketing Magnotta's wines through on-site stores. Known as mavericks in the Ontario wine industry, the Magnottas always insisted on selling their wines cheaper than anyone else. Their philosophy was to provide the highest possible quality at the lowest possible price. The first wines were priced at just $3.95 a bottle. This philosophy produced more than 180 products, including 100 wines (both blended and VQA), several ice wines, more than 10 brands of beer, and a number of spirits, the most famous of which is grappa. Magnotta's products have earned more than 2,300 awards, winning more international and highly regarded awards than any other country.[5] Management is universal. It takes place not only in businesses of all sizes, but also in government, the military, labour unions, hospitals, schools, and religious groups—any organization requiring the coordination of resources.

Every organization, in the pursuit of its objectives, must acquire resources (people, raw materials and equipment, money, and information) and coordinate their use to turn out a final good or service. The manager of a local movie theatre, for example, must make decisions about seating,

figure 6.1 The Functions of Management

projectors, sound equipment, screens, concession stands, and ticket booths. All this equipment must be in proper working condition. The manager must also make decisions about materials. There must be films to show, popcorn and candy to sell, and so on. To transform the physical resources into final products, the manager must also have human resources—employees to sell the tickets, run the concession stand, run the projector, and maintain the facilities. Finally, the manager needs adequate financial resources to pay for the essential activities; the primary source of funding is the money generated from sales of tickets and snacks. All these resources and activities must be coordinated and controlled if the theatre is to earn a profit. Organizations must have adequate resources of all types, and managers must carefully coordinate the use of these resources if they are to achieve the organization's objectives.

Dollarama is in the midst of a major expansion plan that provides direction for employees throughout the company.

LO2   Describe the major functions of management.

Management Functions

To coordinate the use of resources so that the business can develop, make, and sell products, managers engage in a series of activities: planning, organizing, staffing, directing, and controlling (Figure 6.1). Although we describe each separately, these five functions are interrelated, and managers may perform two or more of them at the same time.

Planning

Planning, the process of determining the organization's objectives and deciding how to accomplish them, is the first function of management. Planning is a crucial activity, for it designs the map that lays the groundwork for the other functions. It involves forecasting events and determining the best course of action from a set of options or choices. The plan itself specifies what should be done, by whom, where, when, and how. For example, Canada Goose CEO Dani Reiss was engaged in planning in the above-mentioned example when he opted to keep manufacturing his jackets in Canada. Reiss had a set of choices: he could move manufacturing to Asia and reduce costs, or he could continue to manufacture in Canada at higher costs but use this choice as part of the company's marketing. By making the decision to continue manufacturing in Canada and communicate this to customers, Reiss's plans provided direction to his entire organization. After making one successful decision to keep manufacturing in Canada, Reiss was faced with another decision—whether he should expand his growing company beyond winter jackets. Reiss once again considered his options and decided to start manufacturing spring and fall jackets along with accessories.

Dollarama, the Canadian dollar store, is in the midst of a major expansion plan. The company opened up 65–70 new stores in 2013 as it continues to grow across Canada.[6] When McDonald's CEO Jim Catalupo died suddenly of a heart attack in 2004, Charlie Bell took over as CEO and continued a three-year plan developed under Catalupo's leadership. Unfortunately, in November 2004 Bell learned that he had cancer and resigned, turning the position over to Jim Skinner. Bell died in early 2005 and Skinner continued the work of both previous CEOs in an effort to revitalize the company. The plans called for remodelling current restaurants, increasing emphasis on service quality, extending service hours, and increasing attention to offering nutritious menu items. The result for McDonald's was positive, with same-store sales in the United States up for 36 consecutive months. In addition, the company's stock price rose more than 30 percent over two years.[7] All businesses—from the smallest restaurant to the largest multinational corporation—need to develop plans for achieving success. But before an organization can plan a course of action, it must first determine what it wants to achieve.

> "Objectives: the ends or results desired by the organization."

Objectives.   Objectives, the ends or results desired by the organization, derive from the organization's **mission,** which describes its fundamental purpose and basic philosophy. When planning this philosophy, most companies start with a **vision statement** that explains why an organization exists and discusses the long-range goals or direction for the company and helps determine the organization's values. **Values** are guiding principles that direct an organization's decisions. The vision and values provide direction for the organization's planning process and help both managers and workers

Planning the process of determining the organization's objectives and deciding how to accomplish them; the first function of management

Mission the statement of an organization's fundamental purpose and basic philosophy

Vision statement the statement that explains why an organization exists and discusses its long-range goals

Values guiding principles that direct an organization's decisions

strive toward a purpose. For example, TELUS's vision statement is, "...to unleash the power of the Internet to deliver the best solutions to Canadians at home, in the workplace, and on the move." TELUS's values include: embrace change and initiate opportunity; have a passion for growth; believe in spirited teamwork; and have the courage to innovate.[8] When TELUS is crafting organizational plans, it does so with this vision and these values in mind. After an organization establishes its vision and values, the company will focus on its mission statement. A mission statement describes an organization's fundamental purpose and basic philosophy. A photo lab, for example, might say that its mission is to provide customers with memories. To carry out its mission, the photo lab sets specific objectives relating to its mission, such as reducing development defects to less than 2 percent, introducing a selection of photo albums and frames for customers' use in displaying their photos, providing customers' proofs or negatives over the Internet, providing technical assistance, and so on. Herbal tea marketer Celestial Seasonings says that its mission is "To create and sell healthful, naturally oriented products that nurture people's bodies and uplift their souls."[9]

A business's objectives may be elaborate or simple. Common objectives relate to profit, competitive advantage, efficiency, and growth. Organizations with profit as a goal want to have money and assets left over after paying off business expenses. Objectives regarding competitive advantage are generally stated in terms of percentage of sales increase and market share, with the goal of increasing those figures. Efficiency objectives involve making the best use of the organization's resources. The photo lab's objective of holding defects to less than 2 percent is an example of an efficiency objective. Growth objectives relate to an organization's ability to adapt and to get new products to the marketplace in a timely fashion. The mission of Loblaw Companies Ltd. is to be Canada's best food, health, and home retailer by exceeding customer expectations through innovative products at great prices. President's Choice (PC) "insiders" travel worldwide to investigate and bring back new product ideas. PC chefs and PC product developers also create new products and brands such as the successful PC Blue Menu. Other organizational objectives could include service, ethical, and community goals.

Plans.   There are three general types of plans for meeting objectives—strategic, tactical, and operational. A firm's highest managers develop its **strategic plans,** which establish the long-range objectives and overall strategy or course of action by which the firm fulfills its mission and vision statement while attempting to stay true to its values. Strategic plans generally cover periods ranging from 2 to 10 years or even longer. They include plans to add products, purchase companies, sell unprofitable segments of the business, issue stock, and move into international markets. For example, the recently appointed CEO of BlackBerry, Thorsten Heins, has developed a new strategic

> **Strategic plans** those plans that establish the long-range objectives and overall strategy or course of action by which a firm fulfills its mission

plan for the company that includes firming up business sales, which have always been a strength for the company, and aggressively expanding its consumer sales with BlackBerry 10, the company's latest smartphone. BlackBerry's sales have been declining for a number of years and Heins is attempting to turn the company around with new products and an aggressive marketing campaign. To help with strategic planning, managers use a technique known as a SWOT analysis. This framework is a simple but powerful tool for analyzing the strengths, weaknesses, opportunities, and threats the company faces or could potentially face in the future.

- *Strengths* are things the company does well or characteristics that give it an important capability, for example access to unique resources.

- *Weaknesses* are things the company does not have, does poorly, or conditions where it is at a disadvantage, for example a deteriorating financial position.

- *Opportunities* are found in the external environment and could potentially be an avenue for growth or a source of competitive advantage, for example, online sales through the Internet.

- *Threats* are also potentially present in the external environment, for example future demographic changes that would curtail demand for the product the company sells.

BlackBerry CEO Thorsten Heins has developed a new aggressive strategic plan for the company built around its new smartphone—the BlackBerry 10.

profits, brand, and reputation as a respected employer. Weaknesses could include the company's reliance on the Canadian market, and its main product, coffee. Under opportunities, there is the potential for global expansion, and new products and services such as the introduction of the Breakfast Sandwich. Threats could be changing consumer tastes, price increases of commodities like coffee, sugar, and milk, and the entry of new competition. Strategic plans must take into account the organization's capabilities and resources, the changing business environment, and organizational objectives. Plans should be market-driven, matching customers' desire for value with operational capabilities, processes, and human resources.[11]

Tactical plans are short-range plans designed to implement the activities and objectives specified in the strategic plan. These plans, which usually cover a period of one year or less, help keep the organization on the course established in the strategic plan. Because tactical plans permit the organization to react to changes in the environment while continuing to focus on the company's overall strategy, management must periodically review and update them. Declining performance or failure to meet objectives set out in tactical plans may be one reason for revising them. Other reasons for revision could be positive outcomes such as sales exceeding expectations or the emergence of other opportunities. As previously mentioned, BlackBerry is engaging in a new strategic plan, and part of the tactical plan is aggressive marketing with consumers as the company releases high-, mid- and low-cost smartphones. If sales exceed estimates, the company could alter its tactical plans and produce more phones or, if one type of phone sells better than the others, BlackBerry could change its marketing strategy as a result. When ImClone Systems failed to gain approval for its anticancer drug Erbitux, the stock fell from US$70 to the single digits. Former CEO and founder Sam Waksal was imprisoned for insider trading, and Martha Stewart served jail time for lying during the investigation. Six years after this hardship, ImClone received approval from federal regulators for many of its cancer treatments and reported total revenue of US$677.8 million. In a tactical plan to take advantage of the company's positive momentum, the company put itself on the marketplace to be sold for US$4.5 to $5 billion. However, with increased competition from similar products to Erbitux and the failure of "reasonable" bids to materialize, ImClone shifted back from its planned sale.[12]

A retailing organization with a five-year strategic plan to invest $5 billion in 500 new retail stores may develop five

Tactical plans short-range plans designed to implement the activities and objectives specified in the strategic plan

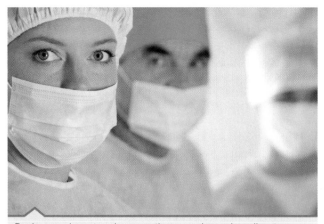
Businesses have to rely on contingency plans when disaster strikes.

tactical plans (each covering one year) specifying how much to spend to set up each new store, where to locate each new store, and when to open each new store. These five tactical plans could change depending on factors in the marketplace. For example, Dollarama has actually added more stores to the Canadian marketplace this year than originally planned. The dollar retailer had originally planned to open 55–60 stores, but is now on target for 65–70 as it is finding more opportunities for expansion than originally anticipated. Dollarama CEO Larry Rossy says, "It seems we're getting more opportunities, there's more construction in Canada, more big boxes being built across Canada, particularly in Western Canada, but even in Ontario."[13] Tactical plans are designed to execute the overall strategic plan. Because of their short-term nature, they are easier to adjust or abandon if changes in the environment or the company's performance so warrant.

Operational plans are very short term and specify what actions specific individuals, work groups, or departments need to accomplish to achieve the tactical plan and ultimately the strategic plan. They may apply to just one month, week, or even day. For example, a work group may be assigned a weekly production quota to ensure there are sufficient products available to elevate market share (tactical goal) and ultimately help the firm be number one in its product category (strategic goal). Returning to our retail store example, operational plans may specify the schedule for opening one new store, hiring new employees, obtaining merchandise, training new employees, and opening for actual business. BlackBerry has changed its operational planning to provide more structure and direction. The company now places developers and engineers on small teams, which focus on one project at a time. When the work team complete the project they move on to another. A previous challenge for the company was a failure to meet deadlines

and product development timelines cited in its tactical and strategic plans. By making these changes to operations, the company is hoping to be able to meet the timelines in its planning process.[14]

Another element in planning is the idea of contingency planning. Contingency planning is the process of creating alternative plans if the primary plan fails to deliver its objectives. For example, a company that releases a new product may plan for strong sales. If the sales fail to materialize, the company may increase marketing or drop prices to move products. For example RIM, now BlackBerry, was dealing with a surplus of PlayBook tablet computers in 2011. The company opted to significantly lower PlayBook's price in order to sell the tablet.[15] **Crisis management or contingency planning** is part of contingency planning and deals with sudden changes for the company such as potential disasters like product tampering, oil spills, fires, earthquakes, computer viruses, or even a reputation crisis due to unethical or illegal conduct by one or more employees.

Many companies have crisis management teams to deal specifically with problems, permitting other managers to continue to focus on their regular duties. Some companies even hold regular disaster drills to ensure that their employees know how to respond when a crisis does occur. Crisis management plans generally cover maintaining business operations throughout a crisis and communicating with the public, employees, and officials about the nature of the problem and the company's response to it. Communication is especially important to minimize panic and damaging rumours; it also demonstrates that the company is aware of the problem and plans to respond. Maple Leaf Foods, for example, saw its reputation and business suffer as a result of a listeriosis outbreak in 2008. The company issued a nationwide recall of meat products (worth approximately $30 million) and subsequently its stock dropped 21 percent. The company faced numerous class-action lawsuits in Ontario, Quebec, British Columbia, Alberta, and Saskatchewan. A Canada-wide settlement of up to $27 million has since been approved by the courts, providing financial compensation for people who purchased or consumed recalled meat products.[16] During the listeriosis crisis, Maple Leaf CEO Michael McCain was front and centre in the public eye. He addressed the media and his own employees frequently and stated the company would fix the problems and the processes that allowed infected meat to reach the marketplace. By being front and centre and openly engaging in discussion, McCain earned a great deal of respect among business leaders and consumers alike. As a result, McCain successfully restored trust in the Maple Leaf brand in Canada.[17] McCain's actions differed from Brian and Lee Nilsson, former co-CEOs of XL Foods, the second-largest beef producer in Canada. XL Foods wasn't testing properly for *E. Coli* and as a result a number of people became ill as

Crisis management or contingency planning an element in planning that deals with potential disasters such as product tampering, oil spills, fires, earthquakes, computer viruses, or airplane crashes

Operational plans very short-term plans that specify what actions individuals, work groups, or departments need to accomplish in order to achieve the tactical plan and ultimately the strategic plan

infected meat was distributed to grocery stores. The Nilssons were silent during much of the crisis even when the Canadian Food Inspection Agency shut down their plant. As a result of the silence rumours ran rampant about other problems in the company. A short time later, the Nilssons sold the company for $100 million, a figure that experts believe is considerably less than what it is worth.[18]

Incidents such as this highlight the importance of tactical planning for crises and the need to respond publicly and quickly when a disaster occurs. Businesses that have contingency and crisis management plans tend to respond more effectively when problems occur than do businesses that lack such planning.

Organizing

Rarely are individuals in an organization able to achieve common goals without some form of structure. **Organizing** is the structuring of resources and activities to accomplish objectives in an efficient and effective manner. Managers organize by reviewing plans and determining what activities are necessary to implement them; then, they divide the work into small units and assign it to specific individuals, groups, or departments. As companies reorganize for greater efficiency, more often than not, they are organizing work into teams to handle core processes such as new product development instead of organizing around traditional departments such as marketing and production. As previously noted, BlackBerry is now organizing employees into teams so they can focus on one thing at a time. The goal is to be more efficient and allow workers time to be creative.

> **Organizing** the structuring of resources and activities to accomplish objectives in an efficient and effective manner

Organizing is important for several reasons. It helps create synergy, whereby the effect of a whole system equals more than that of its parts. It also establishes lines of authority, improves communication, helps avoid duplication of resources, and can improve competitiveness by speeding up decision making. In an effort to reduce costs and improve efficiency, media giant Reuters Group PLC reorganized its product-based divisions into three key customer segments. The new business units are part of the company's strategy to get closer to clients using Internet technologies. The units focus on clients involved in financial products (sales and trading, enterprise solutions and research, and asset management), corporate products, and media products.[19] Because organizing is so important, we'll take a closer look at it in Chapter 7.

Staffing

Once managers have determined what work is to be done and how it is to be organized, they must ensure that the organization has enough employees with appropriate skills to do the work. Hiring people to carry out the work of the organization is known as **staffing.** Beyond recruiting people for positions within the firm, managers must determine what skills are needed for specific jobs, how to motivate and train employees to do their assigned jobs, how much to pay employees, what benefits to provide, and how to prepare employees for higher-level jobs in the firm at a later date. These elements of staffing will be explored in detail in Chapters 9 and 10.

Another aspect of staffing is **downsizing,** the elimination of significant numbers of employees from an organization, which has been a pervasive and much-talked-about trend. Whether it is called

> **Staffing** the hiring of people to carry out the work of the organization
>
> **Downsizing** the elimination of a significant number of employees from an organization

downsizing, rightsizing, trimming the fat, or the new reality in business, the implications of downsizing have been dramatic. Companies will generally downsize when they are failing to meet objectives in the strategic plan and it is often used as a measure to trim costs. For example, Best Buy Canada has recently laid off 900 workers and closed 15 stores as it deals with sagging sales. Best Buy hopes to reduce costs and focus sales efforts on its stronger locations.[20] The auto industry has just gone through the process of implementing a major North American restructuring. A slowing economy and changes in market demand resulted in falling sales, closing of assembly and component plants, and elimination of thousands of jobs. Many firms downsize by outsourcing production, sales, and technical positions to companies in other countries with lower labour costs. Downsizing has helped numerous firms reduce costs quickly and become more profitable (or become profitable after lengthy losses) in a short period of time.

Downsizing and outsourcing, however, have painful consequences. Obviously, the biggest casualty is those who lose their jobs, along with their incomes, insurance, and pensions. Some find new jobs quickly; others do not. Another victim is the morale of the employees at downsized

Best Buy has recently engaged in significant downsizing as store sales have fallen due to increased competition from online retailers.

firms who get to keep their jobs. The employees left behind in a downsizing often feel more insecure, angry, and sad, and their productivity may decline as a result, the opposite of the effect sought. Managers can expect that 70 to 80 percent of those surviving a downsize will take a "wait-and-see" attitude and need to be led. Ten to 15 percent will be openly hostile or try to sabotage change in an effort to return to the way things were before. The remaining 10 to 15 percent will be the leaders who will try proactively to help make the situation work.[21] A survey of workers who remained after a downsizing found that many felt their jobs demanded more time and energy.[22]

After a downsizing situation, an effective manager will promote optimism and positive thinking and minimize criticism and fault-finding. Management should also build teamwork and encourage positive group discussions. Honest communication is important during a time of change and will lead to trust. Truthfulness about what has happened and also about future expectations is essential.

> "Participation makes workers feel important, and the company benefits."

Directing

Once the organization has been staffed, management must direct the employees. **Directing** is motivating and leading employees to achieve organizational objectives. All managers are involved in directing, but it is especially important for lower-level managers who interact daily with the employees operating the organization. For example, a front-line manager or foreperson with Suncor, one of Canada's largest oil sand companies, must ensure that the workers know how to use their equipment properly and have the resources needed to carry out their jobs, and must motivate the workers to achieve their expected output.

Managers may motivate employees by providing incentives—such as the promise of a raise or promotion—for them to do a good job. But most workers want more than money from their jobs: They need to know that their employer values their ideas and input. Smart managers, therefore, ask workers to contribute ideas for reducing costs, making equipment more efficient, improving customer service, or even developing new products. This participation makes workers feel important, and the company benefits. For example, in 2006, Chrysler Group began using an online system called Dealer Scorecard. The "Scorecard" provides performance measurements along 37 different measures, covering all business activity from sales to financing and repair. Employee as well as dealership rewards are tied to exceptional service, and dealerships are able to recognize exemplary employee performance and employee deficiencies.[23] Recognition and appreciation are often the best motivators for employees. Employees

> **Directing** motivating and leading employees to achieve organizational objectives

who understand more about their effect on the financial success of the company may be motivated to work harder for that success, and managers who understand the needs and desires of workers can motivate their employees to work harder and more productively. The motivation of employees is discussed in detail in Chapter 9.

Controlling

Planning, organizing, staffing, and directing are all important to the success of an organization, whether its objective is earning a profit or something else. But what happens when a firm fails to reach its goals despite a strong planning effort? **Controlling** is the process of evaluating and correcting activities to keep the organization on course. Controlling involves five activities: (1) measuring performance, (2) comparing present performance with standards or objectives, (3) identifying deviations from the standards, (4) investigating the causes of deviations, and (5) taking corrective action when necessary.

> **Controlling** the process of evaluating and correcting activities to keep the organization on course

Controlling and planning are closely linked. Planning establishes goals and standards for performance. By monitoring performance and comparing it with standards, managers can determine whether performance is on target. When performance is substandard, management must determine why and take appropriate actions to get the firm back on course. In short, the control function helps managers assess the success of their plans. When plans have not been successful, the control process facilitates revision of the plans. ExxonMobil has run ads indicating that peak oil demand is decades away. This message conflicts with ads that Chevron is running, indicating that the world consumes two barrels of oil for every one that it finds. A strategy for dealing with concerns about depleting energy resources is for oil companies to invest in finding and developing new supplies of petroleum.[24]

The control process also helps managers deal with problems arising outside the firm. For example, if a firm is the subject of negative publicity, management should use the control process to determine why and to guide the firm's response.

LO3 Distinguish among three levels of management and the concerns of managers at each level.

Types of Management

All managers—whether the sole proprietor of a small video store or the hundreds of managers of a large company such as the CBC—perform the five functions just discussed. In

Sustainable products are usually great for business, but Nike discovered that going green doesn't always work. In 2005, the company launched "Considered," a line of eco-friendly shoes made from hemp. Quickly nicknamed "Air Hobbits," the line flopped. Nike customers wanted high-tech shoes to make them perform well, not to save the planet. However, the company still wanted to be more sustainable, so Nike is going green on the sly.

In 1993, Nike launched the Reuse-A-Shoe Program, which aimed to reduce the company's environmental footprint and decrease the waste Nike sent to landfills. Old shoes, along with excess materials from manufacturing, are recycled into "Nike Grind," a material used to create sports surfaces such as basketball courts and running tracks. The Reuse-A-Shoe Program is now linked to the National Recycling Coalition and has collected more than 20 million shoes.

Nike also has a corporate vision of eventually creating zero waste and providing products that can be continuously reused. Today, the company uses recycled and renewable materials as well as materials that reduce toxic output, such as organic cotton. Nike also uses environmentally friendly production techniques to produce its shoes. The Air Jordan is made using a faster, more efficient sewing machine that saves energy. The soles of Air Jordans are made from ground-up sneakers, and the manufacturing process prevents the use of excess plastic. The best part? The new Air Jordans sell so well that Nike now has a line of eco-friendly basketball, football, soccer, tennis, and running shoes.[25]

DISCUSSION QUESTIONS

1. Why did the "Considered" line fail?

2. Shoes and textiles are notoriously polluting industries. What has Nike done to improve its reputation as an environmentally friendly company?

3. What decisions have Nike managers made to improve the reputation of the company and increase sales?

---

the case of the video store, the owner handles all the functions, but in a large company with more than one manager, responsibilities must be divided and delegated. This division of responsibility is generally achieved by establishing levels of management and areas of specialization—finance, marketing, and so on.

Levels of Management

As we have hinted, many organizations have multiple levels of management—top management, middle management, and first-line, or supervisory management. These levels form a pyramid, as shown in Figure 6.2. As the pyramid shape implies, there are generally more middle managers than top managers, and still more first-line managers. Very small organizations may have only one manager (typically, the owner), who assumes the responsibilities of all three levels. Large businesses have many managers at each level to coordinate the use of the organization's resources. Managers at all three levels perform all five management functions, but the amount of time they spend on each function varies, as we shall see (Figure 6.3).

Top Management. In businesses, **top managers** include the president and other top executives, such as the chief executive officer (CEO), chief financial officer (CFO), and chief operations officer (COO), who have overall responsibility for the organization. Bradley Shaw, for example, is the chief executive officer of Shaw Communications Inc., which is one of Canada's biggest telecommunication companies offering phone, television, and Internet services. In public corporations, even chief executive officers such as Bradley Shaw have a boss—the firm's board of directors. With technological advances continuing and privacy concerns increasing, some companies are adding a new top management position—chief privacy officer (CPO). The number of CPOs is expected to rise over the next few years in response to growing concerns about privacy as well as a requirement in the Personal Information Protection and Electronic Documents Act (PIPEDA) that organizations appoint individuals to be accountable for their privacy practices. Among the companies that have appointed CPOs are Bell Canada, CIBC, Nexen, and Rogers Communications.[26] In government, top management refers to the prime minister, a premier, or a mayor or city manager; in education, a chancellor of a university or a school board's superintendent of education.

Top-level managers spend most of their time planning. They make the organization's strategic decisions, decisions that focus on an overall scheme or key idea for using resources

> **Top managers** the president and other top executives of a business, such as the chief executive officer (CEO), chief financial officer (CFO), chief operations officer (COO), and, more recently, chief privacy officer (CPO), who have overall responsibility for the organization

figure 6.2 Levels of Management

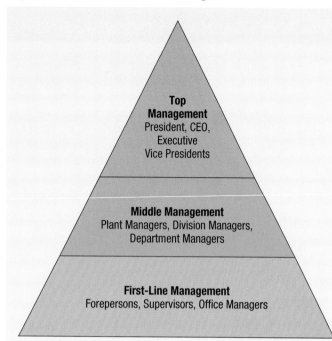

Top
Management
President, CEO,
Executive
Vice Presidents

Middle Management
Plant Managers, Division Managers,
Department Managers

First-Line Management
Forepersons, Supervisors, Office Managers

to take advantage of opportunities. They decide whether to add products, acquire companies, sell unprofitable business segments, and move into foreign markets. For example, when Target decided to enter the Canadian market, its CEO would have been involved in making the final decision. Top managers also represent their company to the public and to government regulators.

Given the importance and range of top management's decisions, top managers generally have many years of varied experience and command top salaries. In addition to salaries, top managers' compensation packages typically include bonuses, long-term incentive awards, stock, and stock options. Table 6.1 lists the 10 highest paid CEOs including bonuses, stock options, and other compensation.

Some people question the pay disparity between top executives and Canadian workers. According to a report by the Canadian Centre for Policy Alternatives, the average executive now earns 240 times as much as the average blue-collar worker.[27] Some CEOs, however, limit the level of compensation that they and other top managers can receive to minimize the disparity between the levels of employees and to show social responsibility with respect to their compensation.

Workforce diversity is an important issue in today's corporations. Effective managers at enlightened corporations have found that diversity is good for workers and for the bottom line. Putting together different kinds of people to solve problems often results in better solutions. In a recent interview, Gord Nixon, president and CEO of RBC, noted that the bank looks "at diversity through two different lenses. From an ethical perspective, it's extremely important and it's the right thing to do, but it also represents incredible business potential. To ignore the value offered by this huge part of Canada's workforce and potential client base is a missed business opportunity."[28] Unfortunately, lack of diversity continues to be a problem in Canada. For example, over 80 percent of Canadian organizations do not have a strategy to develop female leaders, and less than 5 percent of large corporations have women as CEOs.[29] Managers from companies devoted to workforce diversity devised six rules that make diversity work (see Table 6.2). Diversity is explored in greater detail in Chapter 10.

Middle Management. Rather than making strategic decisions about the whole organization, **middle managers** are responsible for tactical planning that will implement the general guidelines established by top management. Thus, their responsibility is more narrowly focused than that of top managers. Middle managers are involved in the specific operations of the organization and spend more time organizing than other managers. In business, plant managers, division

> **Middle managers** those members of an organization responsible for the tactical planning that implements the general guidelines established by top management

figure 6.3 Importance of Management Functions to Managers in Each Level

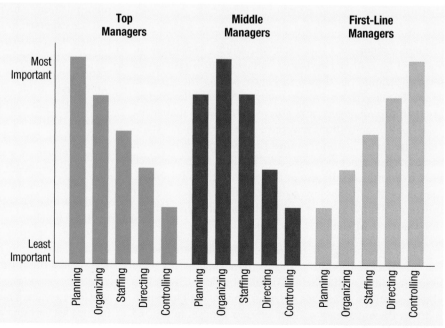

managers, and department managers make up middle management. The product manager for laundry detergent at a consumer products manufacturer, the department chairperson in a university, and the head of a regional public health department are all middle managers. The ranks of middle managers have been shrinking as more and more companies downsize to be more productive.

First-Line Management. Most people get their first managerial experience as **first-line managers,** those who supervise workers and the daily operations of the organization. They are responsible for implementing the plans established by middle management and directing workers' daily performance on the job. They spend most of their time directing and controlling. Common titles for first-line managers are foreperson, supervisor, and office manager.

"Most people get their first managerial experience as first-line managers."

Areas of Management

At each level, there are managers who specialize in the basic functional areas of business: finance, production and operations, human resources (personnel), marketing, and administration.

Financial Management. **Financial managers** focus on obtaining the money needed for the successful operation of the organization and using that money in accordance with organizational goals. Among the responsibilities of financial managers are projecting income and expenses over a specified period, determining short- and long-term financing needs and finding sources of financing to fill those needs, identifying and selecting appropriate ways to invest extra funds, monitoring the flow of financial resources, and protecting the financial resources of the organization. A financial manager at Subway, for example, may be asked to analyze the costs and revenues of a new sandwich product to determine its contribution to Subway's profitability. All organizations must have adequate financial resources to acquire the physical and human resources that are necessary to create goods and services. Consequently, financial resource management is of the utmost importance.

Production and Operations Management. **Production and operations managers** develop and administer the activities involved in transforming resources into goods, services, and ideas ready for the marketplace. Production and operations managers are typically involved in planning and designing production facilities, purchasing raw materials and supplies, managing inventory, scheduling processes to meet demand, and ensuring that products meet quality standards. Because no business can exist without the production of goods and services,

table 6.1 The 10 Highest-Paid CEOs

Rank	Name	Organization Name	Total Reported Compensation
1	J. Michael Pearson	Valeant Pharmaceuticals International, Inc.	$36,318,841
2	Bradley Shaw	Shaw Communications, Inc.	15,851,336
3	Donald J. Walker	Magna International, Inc.	14,841,085
4	Gerald W. Schwartz	Onex Corporation	14,137,644
5	Robert Friedland	Ivanhoe Mines Ltd.	12,577,811
6	Peter Marrone	Yamana Gold, Inc.	12,420,462
7	William A. Downe	Bank of Montreal	11,420,242
8	Edmund Clark	The Toronto-Dominion Bank	11,380,730
9	Charles A. Jeannes	Goldcorp Inc.	11,323,770
10	Gordon M. Nixon	Royal Bank of Canada	11,171,129

SOURCE: Adapted from TABLE Executive Compensation: Rankings for Canada's Top Earners, *The Globe and Mail*, June 8, 2012, http://www.theglobeandmail.com/report-on-business/careers/management/executive-compensation/executive-compensation-rankings-for-canadas-top-earners/article4243534/, August 6th, 2012.

table 6.2 Six Rules That Make Diversity Work

Rule	Action
1. Search for the best	Invest time and money in "affirmative recruiting."
2. Help newcomers fit in	Emphasize cooperation and teamwork.
3. Educate everyone	Address employees' fears of change and discomfort with people from diverse backgrounds; encourage minority employees to express their views; encourage others to listen.
4. Keep score	Hold managers accountable for diversity goals and progress.
5. Sweat the details	Pay attention to the smaller differences in diverse employees and address concerns.
6. See the future	Invest in potential employees of the future (e.g., develop programs that target minority groups in middle and high schools).

SOURCE: Annie Finnigan, "Different Strokes," *Working Woman*, April 2001, pp. 42–48.

First-line managers those who supervise both workers and the daily operations of an organization

Financial managers those who focus on obtaining needed funds for the successful operation of an organization and using those funds to further organizational goals

Production and operations managers those who develop and administer the activities involved in transforming resources into goods, services, and ideas ready for the marketplace

of the participants lost an average of 7.5 kilograms or 16 pounds, there was a 36 percent reduction in smoking (among those with high cardio-vascular risks), and participants reduced their 10-year cardiovascular risk from "moderate" at the beginning of the program to "low risk" at its end. The announcement of these results in 2006 led business analysts to indicate that DaimlerChrysler Canada could save more than $2 million in 10 years if this program were implemented across Canada.[32] However, in 2007, following the sale of Daimler interests by the Chrysler Group, the program was discontinued.

Top managers use online resources such as ceoexpress.com to gather economic, competitive, and other business information.

production and operations managers are vital to an organization's success. At Pfizer Global Research, for example, Robert Swanson works as an associate director of logistics and supply chain management, which makes him responsible for transporting and caring for lab equipment, protective gear, chemicals, and maintenance and office supplies, and shipping scientific documents, materials, and other equipment to other Pfizer facilities around the world.[31]

Human Resources Management. Human resources managers handle the staffing function and deal with employees in a formalized manner. Once known as personnel managers, they determine an organization's human resource needs; recruit and hire new employees; develop and administer employee benefits, training, and performance appraisal programs; and deal with government regulations concerning employment practices. For example, some companies recognize that their employees' health affects their health care costs. Therefore, more progressive companies provide health care facilities and outside health club memberships, encourage proper nutrition, and discourage smoking in an effort to improve employee health and lower the costs of providing health care benefits. In 2003, Pfizer of Canada and what was then DaimlerChrysler's Windsor Assembly Plant launched a program called "Turn Up Your Heart." The goal of the program is to assess and reduce the risks of heart disease among both employees and retirees and to increase quality of life and productivity while reducing health care costs. The results of the program after one year were dramatic. Almost half

DID YOU KNOW?

Women represent 6.9 percent of executive positions in Canadian companies and just 3 percent are CEOs.[30]

Marketing Management. Marketing managers are responsible for planning, pricing, and promoting products and making them available to customers through distribution. The marketing manager who oversees Sony televisions, for example, must make decisions regarding a new television's size, features, name, price, and packaging, as well as plan what type of stores to distribute the television through and the advertising campaign that will introduce the new television to consumers. Within the realm of marketing, there are several areas of specialization: product development and management, pricing, promotion, and distribution. Specific jobs are found in areas such as marketing research, advertising, personal selling, retailing, telemarketing, and Internet marketing.

Information Technology (IT) Management. Information technology (IT) managers are responsible for implementing, maintaining, and controlling technology applications in business, such as computer networks. OpenText, a fast-growing Waterloo-Ontario based firm that helps companies manage information and technology, employs more than 1,300 workers—many of whom have a strong background in IT. To maintain a positive and creative culture, Open-Text employees have access to outdoor barbecues, walking trails, a games room including a bar, ongoing development with tuition subsidies for job-related courses, and the opportunity to participate in various training programs. OpenText is likely basing some of its benefits on

Marketing managers those who are responsible for planning, pricing, and promoting products and making them available to customers

Information technology (IT) managers those who are responsible for implementing, maintaining, and controlling technology applications in business, such as computer networks

Human resources managers those who handle the staffing function and deal with employees in a formalized manner

Google's treatment of employees. Google, the online search engine, is one of the five most popular sites on the Internet and employs more than 5,500 people, many of whom are IT managers.[33] To maintain its creative and productive culture, Google employees have access to workout rooms, and roller hockey is played in the parking lot twice a week. The Google Café provides healthy lunches and dinners for all staff.[34] One major task in IT management is securing computer systems from unauthorized users while making the system easy to use for employees, suppliers, and others who have legitimate reason to access the system. Another crucial task is protecting the data, even during a disaster such as a fire. IT managers are also responsible for teaching and helping employees use technology resources efficiently through training and support. At many companies, some aspects of IT management are outsourced to third-party firms that can perform this function expertly and efficiently.

> "IT managers are also responsible for teaching and helping employees use technology resources efficiently through training and support."

OpenText, one of Canada's successful technology firms, is attempting to create a positive and creative culture by providing workers with the opportunity to hike outdoors while at work.

Consider the Following: Nick's Pizza & Pub Succeeds on "Trust and Track" System of Management

At Nick's Pizza & Pub, working with pizza is fun, rewarding, and challenging. Much of the company's success can be attributed to the strong management techniques of founder Nick Sarillo. When Sarillo started Nick's Pizza & Pub in 1995, he knew from the beginning that he wanted to create an environment with a dedicated workforce and a culture defined by honesty, loyalty, and excellent customer service. Sarillo rejected the traditional "command and control" management style in favour of creating a company culture in which he could trust his employees to work hard and behave ethically. The result is termed a "trust and track" management style.

Although Sarillo continually tracks what is going on inside the restaurant, he gives his employees responsibility over certain managerial functions. New hires at Nick's Pizza & Pub attend a two-day orientation, where they learn about the company's culture and are certified for particular jobs. Employees are expected to take responsibility for tasks that might traditionally be part of the supervisor's job. Sarillo wants his employees to feel like they are actively involved in the company's success and treats his mostly teenage workforce with respect. Nick's Pizza & Pub also cares for its customers. During the recession when unemployment was high, the restaurant gave customers half off on pizzas on Mondays and Tuesdays.

The result of the "trust and track" style is happier workers who choose to stick with the company. Whereas turnover is roughly 200 percent for the industry, Nick's Pizza & Pub experiences 20 percent. The annual operating profit rate is also high at 14 percent, compared to the 6.6 percent experienced by competitors. Sarillo's unusual but effective management style has created a corporate culture that translates into dedicated employees, satisfied customers, and over $7 million in annual sales.[35]

DISCUSSION QUESTIONS

1. Why is Nick Sarillo a good manager?

2. Of the basic functions in recruiting and staffing a pizza restaurant, which of the following do you think is most important and why: hiring, training, evaluating, or compensating?

3. How would you defend Nick Sarillo's management approach from a financial point of view?

Administrative Management. **Administrative managers** are not specialists; rather they manage an entire business or a major segment of a business, such as the Cadillac Division of General Motors. Such managers coordinate the activities of specialized managers, which in the GM Cadillac Division would include marketing managers, production managers, and financial managers. Because of the broad nature of their responsibilities, administrative managers are often called general managers. However, this does not mean that administrative managers lack expertise in any particular area. Many top executives have risen through the ranks of financial management, production and operations management, or marketing management; but most top managers are actually administrative managers, employing skills in all areas of management.

LO4	Specify the skills managers need to be successful.

Skills Needed by Managers

Managers are typically evaluated as to how effective and efficient they are. Managing effectively and efficiently requires certain skills—leadership, technical expertise, conceptual skills, analytical skills, and human relations skills. Table 6.3 describes some of the roles managers may fulfill.

Leadership

Leadership is the ability to motivate employees to work toward organizational goals. Strong leaders establish a vision or a shared set of goals, and then create an organizational culture to achieve these goals. For example, Brian Scudamore, CEO of 1-800-GOT-JUNK?, Canada's largest junk removal business states, "You need the right leadership, which is about people at all levels who see the vision, understand the business and are passionate about it."[36] Scudamore, who plans on reaching $200 million in sales by 2016, has created a corporate culture where employees feel they are part of a team, and he actively encourages employees to propose and develop ideas to improve the business. One of the more renowned books on leadership, *Leadership Challenge*, by James Kouzes and Barry Posner, states that strong leaders essentially do five things well. According to the authors' research, successful leaders act the way they want their employees to act; inspire a shared vision; challenge conventional processes;

> "Employees who have been involved in decision making generally require less supervision than those not similarly involved."

Administrative managers those who manage an entire business or a major segment of a business; they are not specialists but coordinate the activities of specialized managers

Leadership the ability to influence employees to work toward organizational goals

enable employees to act; and encourage people to act kindly toward others.[37] Scudamore, who is considered to be a highly effective leader, appears to follow Kouzes and Posner's leadership tenets. Scudamore openly engages in discussions with employees to encourage their ideas. He also removed the walls from the corporate office to allow for a team atmosphere, thus acting the way he wants his employees to act. He has created a vision for the company in terms of goals and culture, and he challenges conventional processes such as in basing the entire company on professional junk removal, which is very different from the industry norm. Finally, Scudamore has created a company where people can be kind and celebrate accomplishments, including morning huddles where employees come together to share goals and highlight personal achievements. While the ideas put forward by Kouzes and Posner appear simple enough, a recent survey of 150 senior executives indicated that 89 percent believe it is more challenging today to be a leader compared with five years ago.[38]

Managers often can be classified into three types based on their leadership style. *Autocratic leaders* make all the decisions and then tell employees what must be done and how to do it. They generally use their authority and economic rewards to get employees to comply with their directions. *Democratic leaders* involve their employees in decisions. The manager presents a situation and encourages his or her subordinates to express opinions and contribute ideas. The manager then considers the employees' points of view and makes the decision. *Free-rein leaders* let their employees work without much interference. The manager sets performance standards and allows employees to find their own ways to meet them. For this style to be effective, employees must know what the standards are, and they must be motivated to attain the standards. The free-rein style of leadership can be a powerful motivator because it demonstrates a great deal of trust and confidence in the employee.

The effectiveness of the autocratic, democratic, and free-rein styles depends on several factors. One consideration is the type of employees. An autocratic style of leadership is generally needed to stimulate unskilled, unmotivated employees; highly skilled, trained, and motivated employees may respond better to democratic or free-rein leaders. On the other hand, employees who have been involved in decision making generally require less supervision than those not similarly involved. Other considerations are the manager's abilities and the situation itself. When a situation requires quick decisions, an autocratic style of leadership may be best because the manager does not have to consider input from a lot of people. If a special task force must be set up to solve a quality-control problem, a normally democratic manager may give free rein to the task force. Many managers, however, are unable to use more than one style of leadership. Some are unable to allow their subordinates to participate in decision

table 6.3 Managerial Roles

Type of Role	Specific Role	Examples of Role Activities
Decisional	Entrepreneur	Commit organizational resources to develop innovative goods and services; decide to expand internationally to obtain new customers for the organization's products
	Disturbance handler	Move quickly to take corrective action to deal with unexpected problems facing the organization from the external environment, such as a crisis like an oil spill, or from the internal environment, such as producing faulty goods or services
	Resource allocator	Allocate organizational resources among different functions and departments of the organization; set budgets and salaries of middle and first-level managers
	Negotiator	Work with suppliers, distributors, and labour unions to reach agreements about the quality and price of input, technical, and human resources; work with other organizations to establish agreements to pool resources to work on joint projects
Informational	Monitor	Evaluate the performance of managers in different functions and take corrective action to improve their performance; watch for changes occurring in the external and internal environment that may affect the organization in the future
	Disseminator	Inform employees about changes taking place in the external and internal environment that will affect them and the organization; communicate to employees the organization's vision and purpose
	Spokesperson	Launch a national advertising campaign to promote new goods and services; give a speech to inform the local community about the organization's future intentions
Interpersonal	Figurehead	Outline future organizational goals to employees at company meetings; open a new corporate headquarters building; state the organization's ethical guidelines and the principles of behaviour employees are to follow in their dealings with customers and suppliers
	Leader	Provide an example for employees to follow; give direct commands and orders to subordinates; make decisions concerning the use of human and technical resources; mobilize employee support for specific organizational goals
	Liaison	Coordinate the work of managers in different departments; establish alliances between different organizations to share resources to produce new goods and services

SOURCE: Gareth R. Jones and Jennifer M. George, *Essentials of Contemporary Management* (Burr Ridge, IL: McGraw-Hill/Irwin, 2004), p. 14.

Technical expertise the specialized knowledge and training needed to perform jobs that are related to particular areas of management

making, let alone make any decisions. Thus, what leadership style is "best" depends on specific circumstances, and effective managers strive to adapt their leadership style as circumstances warrant.

Many organizations offer programs to develop leadership. Anne Mulcahy, former chief executive officer and president of Xerox, placed leadership development at the top of her agenda. She utilized team meetings and retreats with up-and-coming managers to plan strategy and identify talent. Xerox managers have access to online tools designed to help them help themselves. Mulcahy was named among *Fortune* magazine's "Most Powerful Women in Business," along with the CEOs of Kraft Foods, eBay, PepsiCo, and Avon Products.[39] In 2008, she was named "CEO of the Year" by *Chief Executive* magazine. She retired in May 2009. Table 6.4 presents some guidelines for successful leadership.

Technical Expertise

Managers need **technical expertise,** the specialized knowledge and training needed to perform jobs that are related

to their area of management. Accounting managers need to be able to perform accounting jobs, and production managers need to be able to perform production jobs. Although a production manager may not actually perform a job, he or she needs technical expertise to train employees, answer questions, provide guidance, and solve

table 6.4 Seven Tips for Successful Leadership

- Build effective and responsive interpersonal relationships.
- Communicate effectively—in person, print, e-mail, etc.
- Build the team and enable employees to collaborate effectively.
- Understand the financial aspects of the business.
- Know how to create an environment in which people experience positive morale and recognition.
- Lead by example.
- Help people grow and develop.

SOURCE: Susan M. Heçathfield, "Seven Tips About Successful Management," What You Need to Know About.com (n.d.), http://humanresources.about.com/cs/managementissues/qt/mg-mtsuccess.htm (accessed April 9, 2004).

problems. Technical skills are most needed by first-line managers and least critical to top-level managers.

Today, most organizations rely on computers to perform routine data processing, simplify complex calculations, organize and maintain vast amounts of information to communicate, and help managers make sound decisions. For this reason, most managers have found computer expertise to be an essential skill.

Conceptual Skills

Conceptual skills, the ability to think in abstract terms, and to see how parts fit together to form the whole, are needed by all managers, but particularly top-level managers. Top management must be able to evaluate continually where the company will be in the future. Conceptual skills

> **Conceptual skills** the ability to think in abstract terms and to see how parts fit together to form the whole

---

Consider the Following: CEO Leads Burger King Recovery

Burger King, founded in Miami in 1954 by James McLamore and David Edgerton, serves almost 12 million customers per day worldwide. However, over the years the profits and success of Burger King restaurants steadily declined. In 2004–05, in an attempt to revitalize the company, a new CEO joined the team.

After seeing 10 CEOs pass through Burger King in 14 years, CEO number 11, Greg Brenneman, turned things around. This charismatic, driven CEO raised sales 6.8 percent in restaurants open over a year—the largest increase in more than 10 years. The company's market share improved after years of decline.

Although Brenneman has an MBA from Harvard Business School, he attributes much of his success to growing up on a Kansas farm. While growing up, Brenneman developed a strong work ethic. For him, days began at 6 a.m. and ended late in the evening. He spent those days manicuring golf courses, working at a furniture warehouse, and hoisting bales into haylofts. Those who have worked with him view him as intelligent, aggressive, and quick. Even Edgerton, co-founder of Burger King, felt Brenneman was the first CEO who listened to everyone.

In approaching the issues facing Burger King, Brenneman took the simple path. His plan, called the "Go Forward Plan," existed on a single sheet of paper. His goals for the company were to earn money, bring in more customers/build enthusiasm in existing customers, and encourage BK employees. Among the changes he made to reach these goals were cutting the costs of building new Burger Kings and coming up with more ideas to take the company forward.

To cut the costs of building a new Burger King from $1.3 million to $970,000, Brenneman suggested making each new Burger King smaller. Research showed that many people ordered food to go, so the new Burger King prototype had about half the previous number of seats. The kitchens of these new stores were also smaller—making preparation more efficient. In addition, Brenneman wanted the new stores built with materials available at Home Depot. Doing all of this saved up to 50 percent on the price of land, which enabled franchisees to profit with greater speed.

When Brenneman took the helm of Burger King, the company had one project idea on the table. He wanted there always to be at least 30 project ideas in the works. Brenneman's first project was the Enormous Omelette Sandwich, which raised breakfast profits 20 percent.

While Brenneman achieved many of his goals before his departure, the company still had a long way to go to return to the successful levels of the 1990s. In 2006, Burger King launched a successful public offering of its stock and hired a new CEO, John Chidsey, to continue building on Brenneman's leadership ideas. Recently, however, the economic downturn that particularly affected Burger King's most important customer—young men—has caused the chain to struggle. In September 2010, the company was sold for $3.26 billion to private equity firm 3G.[40]

DISCUSSION QUESTIONS

1. How was Brenneman a strong leader in helping Burger King's recovery?

2. What areas of management do you think Brenneman emphasized in his attempt to re-establish Burger King as a fast-food leader?

3. What are the challenges for a new CEO when trying to ensure a company such as Burger King continues to stay successful?

also involve the ability to think creatively. Recent scientific research has revealed that creative thinking, which is behind the development of many innovative products and ideas, including fibre optics and compact disks, can be learned. As a result, IBM, AT&T, GE, Hewlett-Packard, Intel, and other top firms hire creative consultants to teach their managers how to think creatively.

Analytical Skills

Analytical skills refer to the ability to identify relevant issues and recognize their importance, understand the relationships between them, and perceive the underlying causes of a situation. When managers have identified critical factors and causes, they can take appropriate action. All managers need to think logically, but this skill is probably most important to the success of top-level managers.

Human Relations Skills

People skills, or **human relations skills,** are the ability to deal with people, both inside and outside the organization. Those who can relate to others, communicate well with others, understand the needs of others, and show a true appreciation for others are generally more successful than managers who lack human relations skills. People skills are especially important in hospitals, airline companies, banks, and other organizations that provide services.

Analytical skills the ability to identify relevant issues, recognize their importance, understand the relationships between them, and perceive the underlying causes of a situation

Human relations skills the ability to deal with people, both inside and outside the organization

Where Do Managers Come From?

Good managers are not born; they are made. An organization acquires managers in three ways: promoting employees from within, hiring managers from other organizations, and hiring managers who have recently graduated.

Promoting people within the organization into management positions tends to increase motivation by showing employees that those who work hard and are competent can advance in the company. Internal promotion also provides managers who are already familiar with the company's goals and problems. Procter & Gamble prefers to promote managers from within, which creates managers who are familiar with the company's products and policies and builds company loyalty. Promoting from within, however, can lead to problems: It may limit innovation.

"Good managers are not born; they are made."

WestJet Airlines has been able to successfully differentiate itself from its competitors by way of no-frills and low-price fares. But WestJet also is known for its human relations skills. Jovial flight crews often crack jokes over the intercom system to their captive audiences.

The new manager may continue the practices and policies of previous managers. Thus it is vital for companies—even companies committed to promotion from within—to hire outside people from time to time to bring new ideas into the organization.

Finding managers with the skills, knowledge, and experience required to run an organization or department is sometimes difficult. Specialized executive employment agencies—sometimes called headhunters, recruiting managers, or executive search firms—can help locate candidates from other companies. The downside is that even though outside people can bring fresh ideas to a company, hiring them may cause resentment among existing employees as well as involve greater expense in relocating an individual to another city or province.

Colleges and universities provide a large pool of potential managers, and entry-level applicants can be screened for their developmental potential. People with specialized management skills, such as those with an MBA (Master of Business Administration) degree, may be good candidates.

L05 Summarize the systematic approach to decision making used by many business managers.

Decision Making

Managers make many different kinds of decisions, such as what office hours to set, which employees to hire, what products to introduce, and what price to charge for a product. Decision making is important in all management functions at all levels, whether the decisions are on a strategic, tactical, or operational level. A systematic approach using these six steps usually leads to more effective decision making: (1) recognizing and defining the decision situation, (2) developing options to resolve the situation, (3) analyzing the options, (4) selecting the best option, (5) implementing

With thousands of Walmart stores across Canada and the United States, it is hard to imagine any region without the familiar big-box retailer. However, there is one market where Walmart is notably absent: urban areas. Many cities have been against the idea of Walmart Supercentres within their limits, and in others, Walmart could not find the space to build a giant super centre. This is becoming a problem for Walmart, as Target, its major competitor, has expanded to Canada where it hopes to repeat the success it has had in the U.S. where it has gained market share at Walmart's expense. With suburbs and smaller towns becoming increasingly saturated, Walmart is looking toward urban areas. In order to do so, Walmart is opening up stores on a smaller scale. "Canada has two very distinct physical areas: one is still northern and very rural where the idea of having a big, expansive Supercentre is terrific. But Canada is becoming more densely populated around our urban areas, and we need to find the best ways to serve those customers. As the population continues to urbanize, we will find ways to sell our products and bring low prices to those urban areas,"[41] chief executive Shelley Broader said in a recent news conference.

Smaller formats are not new to Walmart. In the United States, the company runs 152 Neighborhood Markets (at roughly 42,000 square feet) and four Marketside groceries, along with many smaller formats in Mexico. In Canada, Walmart has traditionally stuck with larger stores that average 130,000 square feet with some as large as 160,000–200,000 square feet. However, in its most recent expansion into urban areas, and its largest since it arrived in Canada, Walmart has opened 73 new stores with an average size of 81,000 square feet. These new stores are opening up in areas where people would have never seen a Walmart in the past, according to Jim Thompson, chief operating offi-

Walmart's recent building expansion in Canada has emphasized much smaller stores in urban areas compared to larger, rural and suburban Supercentres.

cer of Walmart Canada Corporation,[42] and are essential to the company's long-term success. In addition to being smaller, the stores are also customizing their merchandise to the tastes of the local marketplace. As noted by Broader above, Canada's population is becoming more urbanized and Walmart will have to have a presence in this marketplace.

DISCUSSION QUESTIONS

1. Do you think people will welcome Walmart into areas where they have not traditionally operated?

2. Will smaller stores help Walmart fend off its rival Target?

3. From an operations management point of view, what challenges will Walmart face running significantly smaller stores, and how could this impact the consumer?

the decision, and (6) monitoring the consequences of the decision (Figure 6.4).

Recognizing and Defining the Decision Situation

The first step in decision making is recognizing and defining the situation. The situation may be negative—for example, huge losses on a particular product—or positive—for example, an opportunity to increase sales.

Situations calling for small-scale decisions often occur without warning. Situations requiring large-scale decisions, however, generally occur after some warning signals. Effective managers pay attention to such signals. Declining profits, small-scale losses in previous years, inventory buildup, and retailers' unwillingness to stock a product are signals that may warn of huge losses to come. If managers pay attention to such signals, problems can be contained.

Once a situation has been recognized, management must define it. Huge losses reveal a problem—for example, a failing product. One manager may define the situation as a product quality problem; another may define it as a change in consumer preference. These two definitions may lead to vastly different solutions to the problem. The first manager,

figure 6.4 Steps in the Decision-Making Process

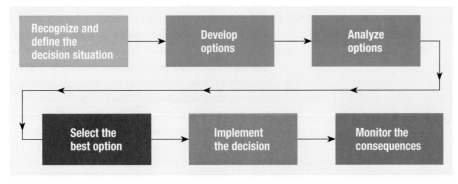

for example, may seek new sources of raw materials of better quality. The second manager may believe that the product has reached the end of its lifespan and decide to discontinue it. This example emphasizes the importance of carefully defining the problem rather than jumping to conclusions.

Developing Options

Once the decision situation has been recognized and defined, the next step is to develop a list of possible courses of action. The best lists include both standard courses of action and creative ones. As a general rule, more time and expertise are devoted to the development stage of decision making when the decision is of major importance. When the decision is of lesser importance, less time and expertise will be spent on this stage. Options may be developed individually, by teams, or through analysis of similar situations in comparable organizations. Creativity is a very important part of selecting the best option. Creativity depends on new and useful ideas, regardless of where the idea originates or the method used to create the ideas. The best option can range from a required solution to an identified problem to a volunteered solution to an observed problem by an outside work group member.[43]

Analyzing Options

After developing a list of possible courses of action, management should analyze the practicality and appropriateness of each option. An option may be deemed impractical because of a lack of financial resources to implement it, legal restrictions, ethical and social responsibility considerations, authority constraints, technological constraints, economic limitations, or simply a lack of information and expertise to implement the option. For example, a small computer manufacturer may recognize an opportunity to introduce a new type of computer but lack the financial resources to do so. Other options may be more practical for the computer company: It may consider selling its technology to another

> "After developing a list of possible courses of action, management should analyze the practicality and appropriateness of each option."

computer company that has adequate resources or it may allow itself to be purchased by a larger company that can introduce the new technology.

When assessing appropriateness, the decision maker should consider whether the proposed option adequately addresses the situation. When analyzing the consequences of an option, managers should consider the impact the option will have on the situation and on the organization as a whole. For example, when considering a price cut to boost sales, management must consider the consequences of the action on the organization's cash flow and consumers' reaction to the price change.

Selecting the Best Option

When all courses of action have been analyzed, management must select the best one. Selection is often a subjective procedure because many situations do not lend themselves to mathematical analysis. Of course, it is not always necessary to select only one option and reject all others; it may be possible to select and use a combination of several options.

Implementing the Decision

To deal with the situation at hand, the selected option or options must be put into action. Implementation can be fairly simple or very complex, depending on the nature of the decision. Effective implementation of a decision to abandon a product, close a plant, purchase a new business, or something similar requires planning. For example, when a product is dropped, managers must decide how to handle distributors and customers and what to do with the idle production facility. Additionally, they should anticipate resistance from people within the organization (people tend to resist change because they fear the unknown). Finally, management should be ready to deal with the unexpected consequences. No matter how well planned implementation is, unforeseen problems will arise. Management must be ready to address these situations when they occur.

Monitoring the Consequences

After managers have implemented the decision, they must determine whether the decision has accomplished the desired result. Without proper monitoring, the consequences of decisions may not be known quickly enough to make efficient changes. If the desired result is achieved, management can reasonably conclude that it made a good decision. If the desired result is not achieved, further analysis is warranted. Was the decision simply wrong, or did the situation change? Should some other option have been implemented?

If the desired result is not achieved, management may discover that the situation was incorrectly defined from the beginning. That may require starting the decision-making process all over again. Finally, management may determine that the decision was good even though the desired results have not yet shown up or it may determine a flaw in the decision's implementation. In the latter case, management would not change the decision but would change the way in which it was implemented.

The Reality of Management

Management is not a cut-and-dried process. There is no mathematical formula for managing an organization, although many managers passionately wish for one! Management is a widely varying process for achieving organizational goals. Managers plan, organize, staff, direct, and control, but management expert John P. Kotter says even these functions can be boiled down to two basic activities:

1. Figuring out what to do despite uncertainty, great diversity, and an enormous amount of potentially relevant information, and

2. Getting things done through a large and diverse set of people despite having little direct control over most of them.[44]

Managers spend as much as 75 percent of their time working with others—not only with subordinates but with bosses, people outside their hierarchy at work, and people outside the organization itself. In these interactions they discuss anything and everything remotely connected with their business.

Managers spend a lot of time establishing and updating an agenda of goals and plans for carrying out their responsibilities. An **agenda** contains both specific and vague items, covering short-term goals and long-term objectives. Like a calendar, an agenda helps the manager figure out what must be done and how to get it done to meet the objectives set by the organization. Technology tools such as personal digital assistants (PDAs) can help managers manage their agendas, contacts, and time.

Managers also spend a lot of time **networking**—building

> "Managers spend a lot of time establishing and updating an agenda of goals and plans for carrying out their responsibilities."

Agenda a calendar, containing both specific and vague items, that covers short-term goals and long-term objectives

Networking the building of relationships and sharing of information with colleagues who can help managers achieve the items on their agendas

relationships and sharing information with colleagues who can help them achieve the items on their agendas. Managers spend much of their time communicating with a variety of people and participating in activities that on the surface do not seem to have much to do with the goals of their organization. Nevertheless, these activities are crucial to getting the job done. Networks are not limited to immediate subordinates and bosses; they include other people in the company as well as customers, suppliers, and friends. These contacts provide managers with information and advice on diverse topics. Managers ask, persuade, and even intimidate members of their network in order to get information and to get things done. Networking helps managers carry out their responsibilities. Andrea Nierenberg, independent business consultant and founder of Nierenberg Group Inc., has been called a "networking success story" by *The Wall Street Journal*. She writes three notes a day: one to a client, one to a friend, and one to a prospective client. She maintains a database of 3,000 contacts. However, she believes that it isn't how many people you know, but how many you have helped and who know you well enough to recommend you that really count. Opportunity can knock almost anywhere with such extensive networking. Grateful for numerous referrals to her friends, Nierenberg's dentist introduced her to a Wall Street executive who happened to be in the dentist's office at the same time as Nierenberg. She followed up on the meeting and later landed four consulting projects at the executive's firm.[45] Her clients include Citigroup, Time Inc., TIAA–CREF, Food Network, Coach, and Tiffany.[46]

Finally, managers spend a great deal of time confronting the complex and difficult challenges of the business world today. Some of these challenges relate to rapidly changing technology (especially in production and information processing), increased scrutiny of individual and corporate ethics and social responsibility, the changing nature of the workforce, new laws and regulations, increased global competition and more challenging foreign markets, declining educational standards (which may limit the skills and knowledge of the future labour and customer pool), and time itself—that is, making the best use of it. But such diverse issues cannot simply be plugged into a computer program that supplies correct, easy-to-apply solutions. It is only through creativity and imagination that managers can make effective decisions that benefit their organizations.

TEAM EXERCISE

Form groups and research examples of crisis management implementation for companies dealing with natural disasters (explosions, fires, earthquakes, etc.), technology disasters (viruses, plane crashes, compromised customer data, etc.) or ethical or legal disasters. How did these companies communicate with key stakeholders? What measures did the company take to provide support to those involved in the crisis? Report your findings to the class.

LO1 Define management and explain its role in the achievement of organizational objectives.

Management is a process designed to achieve an organization's objectives by using its resources effectively and efficiently in a changing environment. Managers make decisions about the use of the organization's resources and are concerned with planning, organizing, staffing, directing, and controlling the organization's activities so as to reach its objectives.

LO2 Describe the major functions of management.

Planning is the process of determining the organization's objectives and deciding how to accomplish them. Organizing is the structuring of resources and activities to accomplish those objectives efficiently and effectively. Staffing obtains people with the necessary skills to carry out the work of the company. Directing is motivating and leading employees to achieve organizational objectives. Controlling is the process of evaluating and correcting activities to keep the organization on course.

LO3 Distinguish among three levels of management and the concerns of managers at each level.

Top management is responsible for the whole organization and focuses primarily on strategic planning. Middle management develops plans for specific operating areas and carries out the general guidelines set by top management. First-line, or supervisory, management supervises the workers and day-to-day operations. Managers can also be categorized as to their area of responsibility: finance, production and operations, human resources, marketing, or administration.

LO4 Specify the skills managers need in order to be successful.

To be successful, managers need leadership skills (the ability to influence employees to work toward organizational goals), technical expertise (the specialized knowledge and training needed to perform a job), conceptual skills (the ability to think in abstract terms and see how parts fit together to form the whole), analytical skills (the ability to identify relevant issues and recognize their importance, understand the relationships between issues, and perceive the underlying causes of a situation), and human relations (people) skills.

LO5 Summarize the systematic approach to decision making used by many business managers.

A systematic approach to decision making follows these steps: recognizing and defining the situation, developing options, analyzing options, selecting the best option, implementing the decision, and monitoring the consequences.

KEY TERMS

administrative managers
agenda
analytical skills
conceptual skills
controlling
crisis management or contingency planning
directing
downsizing
financial managers
first-line managers
human relations skills
human resources managers
information technology (IT) managers
leadership
management
managers

marketing managers
middle managers
mission
networking
operational plans
organizing
planning
production and operations managers
staffing
strategic plans
tactical plans
technical expertise
top managers
values
vision statement

DESTINATION CEO DISCUSSION QUESTIONS

1. Which function(s) of management are most clearly identified in this profile?

2. Holeys increased sales by 6000 percent from 2002 to 2006. What factors may account for this?

3. Did Joyce's background in biotech contribute to her success as a businesswoman?

4. CROCS continue to try to produce trendy shoes. Given what you know about Holeys and CROCS, why do you think Groote opted to focus on niche markets?

SO YOU WANT TO BE *a Manager: What Kind?*

Managers are needed in a wide variety of organizations. Experts suggest that employment will increase by millions of jobs by 2016. But the requirements for the jobs become more demanding with every passing year—with the speed of technology and communication increasing by the day, and the stress of global commerce increasing pressures to perform. However, if you like a challenge and if you have the right kind of personality, management remains a viable field. Even as companies are forced to restructure, management remains a vital role in business. In fact, government predicts that management positions in public relations, marketing, and advertising are set to increase around 12 percent overall between 2006 and 2016. Financial managers will be in even more demand, with jobs increasing 13 percent in the same time period. Computer and IT managers will continue to be in strong demand, with the number of jobs increasing 16 percent between 2006 and 2016.[47]

Salaries for managerial positions remain strong overall. While pay can vary significantly depending on your level of experience, the firm where you work, and the region of the country where you live, below is a list of the nationwide average incomes for a variety of different managers:

- Chief executives: $151,370
- Computer and information systems managers: $113,880
- Financial managers: $106,200
- Marketing managers: $113,400
- Human resources managers: $99,810
- Operations managers: $103,780
- Medical/health services managers: $84,980
- Administrative managers: $76,370
- Sales managers: $106,790[48]

In short, if you want to be a manager, there are opportunities in almost every field. There may be fewer middle-management positions available in firms, but managers remain a vital part of most industries and will continue to be long into the future—especially as navigating global business becomes ever more complex.

BUILD YOUR BUSINESS PLAN

The Nature of Management

The first thing you need to be thinking about is "What is the mission of your business? What is the shared vision your team members have for this business? How do you know if there is demand for this particular business?" Remember, you need to think about the customer's *ability and willingness* to try this particular product.

Think about the various processes or stages of your business in the creation and selling of your product or service.

What functions need to be performed for these processes to be completed? These functions might include buying, receiving, selling, customer service, and/or merchandising.

Operationally, if you are opening up a retail establishment, how do you plan to provide your customers with superior customer service? What hours will your customers expect you to be open? At this point in time, how many employees are you thinking you will need to run your business? Do you (or one of your partners) need to be there all the time to supervise?

Lululemon, the Burnaby, British Columbia-based, North American retailer of yoga clothes, recently engaged in a massive recall of its "Luon" yoga pants after determining the pants were too sheer in the backside area and could be seen through. According to the company, "The ingredients, weight and longevity qualities of the women's black Luon bottoms remain the same but the coverage does not, resulting in a level of sheerness in some of our women's black Luon bottoms that falls short of our very high standards." The recalled pants account for 17 percent of all women's pants in the stores, and may result in a $22 million shortfall in revenue for the year.

Lululemon, rather than just pulling the pants from store shelves, issued a number of press releases about the recall and produced a lengthy FAQ on its website. CEO Christine Day said that while regretting the inconvenience, the recall was necessary to protect "the quality of our fabrics." In a press release she also stated, "We will accept nothing less than the very highest quality we are known for." Lululemon appears to be following sound public relations advice as it has communicated openly with the public and has offered customers who bought the pants a full refund.[49]

Some marketing and public relations experts have even considered that Lululemon may be pushing the story as a way to garner free publicity from what others would classify as a problem. The story was covered by all major media outlets throughout North America and received in-depth TV coverage for what would be considered a relatively simple recall by a company. Unlike some recent recalls, think XL Foods or Maple Leaf, there were no potential health risks associated with the recall and it was surprising how much media attention the recall received. Many experts agree that the recall won't hurt the brand with its target market. For example, Simon Fraser University marketing professor Lindsay Meredith said a recall that ties the company to revealing clothing would do nothing to hurt the Lululemon brand with its target market—women aged 18–35.[50]

The recall story went "viral" on the Internet, receiving coverage from almost every online source of news, and people have been discussing the "Luon" pants on Twitter, Facebook, YouTube, and various other social media sites. Front and centre in most news stories is a quote or two from the company, bringing attention to the high quality of its products and its desire to offer consumers nothing but the best. These news stories often end with some company information stating how successful the retailer has been, the number of stores it has in North America, and that business analysts see this recall as just a blip.

DISCUSSION QUESTIONS

1. Do you think the recall will damage the image of the store with consumers?

2. After reading the chapter, especially the sections on contingency planning and crisis management, do you think Lululemon should have recalled the pants quietly? Why or why not?

3. Do you think it is possible that Lululemon has turned the recall into an opportunity for free publicity which will benefit the company in the long run? What are the pros and cons associated with doing this?

LEARNING OBJECTIVES

LO1 Define organizational structure, and relate how organizational structures develop.

LO2 Describe how specialization and departmentalization help an organization achieve its goals.

LO3 Determine how organizations assign responsibility for tasks and delegate authority.

LO4 Compare and contrast some common forms of organizational structure.

LO5 Distinguish between groups and teams, and identify the types of groups that exist in organizations.

LO6 Describe how communication occurs in organizations.

DESTINATION CEO

Cora Mussely Tsouflidou was born into a modest family in a little village in the Gaspé Peninsula. Cora had all the ingredients for success right from the very start. In 1960, she enrolled at Montreal's Cardinal Leger Institute, promising to pay for her education. There she studied Latin, Greek, literature, art, and other courses that would prepare her for a professional career. But destiny had other plans: Cora quit school during her final year to become a full-time mom. When her husband left her ten years later, Cora was suddenly a single mother with three children to support. Cora became a hostess in a well-known Montreal restaurant, where she worked her way up the ladder as a day manager, general manager, and junior partner. For the next five years, Cora perfected her knowledge of the food service industry until she mastered all aspects of the hospitality trade.

In 1977, Cora bought a snack bar in the Ville Saint-Laurent district of Montreal. After only a few months of operation, Cora transformed the little snack bar into a whole new breakfast concept in Quebec, which specialized in fruit, cheese, cereal, omelettes, pancakes, and French toast. Her philosophy: "Ingredients and a service of the highest quality. Offer your clientele the best and they will come back." Cora still remains up to date in the industry and regularly visits restaurants. She ensures that her standards of quality are being respected by remaining in contact with her customers, her main source of inspiration and motivation. The chain is operated across Canada under the Chez Cora and Cora's Breakfast and Lunch trademarks with over 100 franchise locations in eight provinces.[1]

Introduction

An organization's structure determines how well it makes decisions and responds to problems, and influences employees' attitudes toward their work. Even companies that operate within the same industry may utilize different organizational structures. For example, in the medical device industry, 3M is organized by line of business (health care products, office products, security tools), whereas Medtronic has similar business groups, but it also has top-level, functional units that focus on legal issues, strategy, and human resources operating above each of the lines of business.[2]

Because a business's structure can so profoundly affect its success, this chapter will examine organizational structure in detail. First, we discuss how an organization's culture affects its operations. Then we consider the development of structure, including how tasks and responsibilities are organized through specialization and departmentalization. Next, we explore some of the forms organizational structure may take. Finally, we consider communication within business.

Organizational Culture

One of the most important aspects of organizing a business is determining its **organizational culture,** a firm's shared values, beliefs, traditions, philosophies, rules, and role models for behaviour. Also called corporate culture, an organizational culture exists in every organization, regardless of size, organizational type, product, or profit objective. A firm's culture may be expressed formally through its mission statement, codes of ethics, memos, manuals, and ceremonies, but it is more commonly expressed informally. Examples of informal expressions of culture include dress codes (or the lack thereof), work habits, extracurricular activities, and stories. Employees often learn the accepted standards through discussions with co-workers.

> **Organizational culture** a firm's shared values, beliefs, traditions, philosophies, rules, and role models for behaviour

TOMS Shoes' organizational culture is determined by the founder's desire to provide as many shoes as possible to children in developing countries (where shoeless children walk for miles to get water, food, and medical care). Blake Mycoskie gives hundreds of thousands of shoes to children around the world each year, creating a strong organizational culture of giving back and corporate social responsibility. His company operates with a program that for every shoe purchased, a shoe will be donated to children in need.[3] Disneyland/DisneyWorld and McDonald's have organizational cultures focused on cleanliness, value, and service. At M5 Networks, a $32 million company that sells VoIP phone systems, employees are encouraged to learn how to play musical instruments as part of their company culture. The organization hires music instructors to come to the office in the afternoons. CEO Dan Hoffman believes that company bands will bring together workers from different areas of the firm who normally would not interact. He also sees this as a way to encourage his employees to learn new things, which he feels is essential for company growth.[4] When such values and philosophies are shared by all members of an organization, they will be expressed in its relationships with stakeholders. However, organizational cultures that lack such positive values may result in employees who are unproductive and indifferent and have poor attitudes, which will be reflected externally to customers. The corporate culture may have contributed to the misconduct at a number of well-known companies. For example, a survey found that executives in financial and technology companies are mostly cutthroat in collecting intelligence about competition, leading to unethical acts.[5]

GOING GREEN | Best Buy Emphasizes Teamwork and Communication to Promote Sustainability

After surveys indicated that customers wanted Best Buy to provide sustainable solutions to the electronic waste (e-waste) problem, the company set out to do just that. However, successfully implementing such a program requires collaboration among the company, employees, and partners.

Best Buy has a culture based on teamwork and open communication. The company also encourages employees to improve the company's products and operations. This cohesive work environment enables employees to work together to support Best Buy's green initiatives and come up with sustainable solutions. Communication of the company's sustainability goals is also essential. For this reason, Best Buy created a Sustainability and Corporate Responsibility Scorecard that provides employees with metrics enabling them to measure their progress toward the company's sustainability initiatives.

Best Buy's attempts to incorporate sustainability throughout its operations require employee participation as the company incorporates eco-friendly product lines and business practices. When Energy Star products were first introduced to Best Buy, employees underwent training so that they could educate consumers concerning Energy Star benefits. As part of Best Buy's energy conservation program, the company has set a goal to reduce operations emissions, which requires employees to change their behaviours by not leaving the engines of delivery trucks idling outside Best Buy locations.

Best Buy also teams up with recycling companies to tackle the problem of e-waste. Best Buy collects consumers' used electronics, and its partners work to give these products a "second life" by repairing them or using their parts for other products. Best Buy also monitors its recyclers to make sure they are following safe recycling practices. The collaboration among Best Buy, its employees, and its partners (including consumers) is reducing the e-waste in landfills one item at a time.[6]

DISCUSSION QUESTIONS

1. Why did Best Buy feel the need to embrace sustainability?

2. Why is communication so important in achieving Best Buy's sustainability goals?

3. Describe how Best Buy has used teamwork to increase sustainability within its operations.

Organizational culture helps ensure that all members of a company share values and suggests rules for how to behave and deal with problems within the organization. Table 7.1 confirms that executives in this study believe that corporate culture has a significant impact on organizational performance and the ability to retain good employees. The key to success in any organization is satisfying stakeholders, especially customers. Establishing a positive organizational culture sets the tone for all other decisions, including building an efficient organizational structure.

table 7.1 Impact of Corporate Culture on Business Performance

Culture has a strong or very strong impact on an organization's performance	82%
My corporate culture has a strong impact on the ability to retain top talent	68
My organization's culture drives sales and increases revenue	61
My organization's culture creates a sense of belonging	57
My organization's culture lowers turnover	53

SOURCE: "Ten Most Admired Corporate Cultures," February 10, 2010, http://cthrc.ca/en/member_area/member_news/ten_most_admired_corporate_cultures.aspx (accessed March 1, 2010).

LO1 Define organizational structure, and relate how organizational structures develop.

Developing Organizational Structure

Structure is the arrangement or relationship of positions within an organization. Rarely is an organization, or any group of individuals working together, able to achieve common objectives without some form of structure, whether that structure is explicitly defined or only implied. A professional baseball team such as the Toronto Blue Jays is a business organization with an explicit formal structure that guides the team's activities so that it can increase game attendance, win games, and sell souvenirs such as T-shirts. But even an informal group playing softball for fun has an organization that specifies who will pitch, catch, bat, coach, and so on. Governments and nonprofit organizations also have formal organizational structures to facilitate the achievement of their objectives. Getting people to work together efficiently and coordinating the skills of diverse individuals requires careful planning. Developing appropriate organizational structures is therefore a major challenge for managers in both large and small organizations.

> **Structure** the arrangement or relationship of positions within an organization

An organization's structure develops when managers assign work tasks and activities to specific individuals or work groups and coordinate the diverse activities required to reach the firm's objectives. When Sears, for example, has a sale, the store manager must work with the advertising department to make the public aware of the sale, with department managers to ensure that extra salespeople are scheduled to handle the increased customer traffic, and with merchandise buyers to ensure that enough sale merchandise is available to meet expected consumer demand. All the people occupying these positions must work together to achieve the store's objectives.

The best way to begin to understand how organizational structure develops is to consider the evolution of a new business such as a clothing store. At first, the business is a sole proprietorship in which the owner does everything—buys, prices, and displays the merchandise; does the accounting and tax records; and assists customers. As the business grows, the owner hires a salesperson and perhaps a merchandise buyer to help run the store. As the business continues to grow, the owner hires more salespeople. The growth and success of the business now require the owner to be away from the store frequently, meeting with suppliers, engaging in public relations, and attending trade shows. Thus, the owner must designate someone to manage the salespeople and maintain the accounting, payroll, and tax functions. If the owner decides to expand by opening more stores, still more managers will be needed. Figure 7.1 shows these stages of growth with three **organizational charts** (visual displays of organizational structure, chain of command, and other relationships).

> **Organizational chart** a visual display of the organizational structure, lines of authority (chain of command), staff relationships, permanent committee arrangements, and lines of communication

The organizational structure at TOMS Shoes consists of two parts. The for-profit component of the company manages overall operations. Its nonprofit component, Friends of TOMS, is responsible for volunteer activities and shoe donations.

Growth requires organizing—the structuring of human, physical, and financial resources to achieve objectives in an effective and efficient manner. Growth necessitates hiring people who have specialized skills. With more people and greater specialization, the organization needs to develop a formal structure to function efficiently. Consider Cirque du Soleil, which started in 1984 with 20 ambitious street artists. Today, with 3,000 employees and 40 nationalities, creativity and business must be balanced through some structure. Cirque returns 10 percent of its profits to employees, and the core team meets 10 times a year to recruit and keep the right people in a team-focused corporate culture.[7] As we shall see, structuring an organization requires that management assign work tasks to specific individuals and departments and assign responsibility for the achievement of specific organizational objectives.

> "Growth requires organizing—the structuring of human, physical, and financial resources to achieve objectives in an effective and efficient manner."

Henry Ford, the founder of Ford Motor Company, revolutionized manufacturing by creating assembly lines like this one to specialize the tasks his workers performed.

LO2 Describe how specialization and departmentalization help an organization achieve its goals.

Assigning Tasks

For a business to earn profits from the sale of its products, its managers must first determine what activities are required to achieve its objectives. At Celestial Seasonings, for example, employees must purchase herbs from suppliers, dry the herbs and place them in tea bags, package and label the tea, and then ship the packages to grocery stores around the country. Other necessary activities include negotiating with supermarkets and other retailers for display space, developing new products, planning advertising, managing finances, and managing employees. All these activities must be coordinated, assigned to work groups, and controlled. Two important aspects of assigning these work activities are specialization and departmentalization.

Specialization

After identifying all activities that must be accomplished, managers then break these activities down into specific tasks that can be handled by individual employees. This division of labour into small, specific tasks and the assignment

figure 7.1 The Evolution of a Clothing Store, Phases 1, 2, and 3

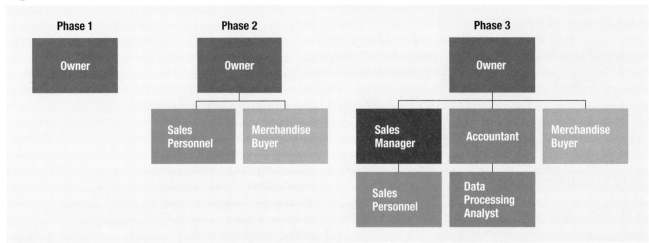

of employees to do a single task is called **specialization.**

The rationale for specialization is efficiency. People can perform more efficiently if they master just one task rather than all tasks. In *The Wealth of Nations,* 18th-century economist Adam Smith discussed specialization, using the manufacture of straight pins as an example. Individually, workers could produce 20 pins a day when each employee produced complete pins. Thus, 10 employees working independently of each other could produce 200 pins a day. However, when one worker drew the wire, another straightened it, a third cut it, and a fourth ground the point, 10 workers could produce 48,000 pins per day.[8] To save money and achieve the benefits of specialization, some companies outsource and hire temporary workers to provide key skills. Many highly skilled workers with diverse experience are available through temp agencies.[9]

Specialization means workers don't waste time shifting from one job to another, and training is easier. However, efficiency is not the only motivation for specialization. Specialization also occurs when the activities that must be performed within an organization are too numerous for one person to handle. Recall the example of the clothing store. When the business was young and small, the owner could do everything; but when the business grew, the owner needed help waiting on customers, keeping the books, and managing other business activities.

Overspecialization can have negative consequences. Employees may become bored and dissatisfied with their jobs, and the result of their unhappiness is likely to be poor quality work, more injuries, and high employee turnover. Although some degree of specialization is necessary for efficiency, because of differences in skills, abilities, and interests, all people are not equally suited for all jobs. We examine some strategies to overcome these issues in Chapter 9.

Departmentalization

After assigning specialized tasks to individuals, managers next organize workers doing similar jobs into groups to make them easier to manage. **Departmentalization** is the grouping of jobs into working units usually called

"Specialization means workers do not waste time shifting from one job to another, and training is easier."

departments, units, groups, or divisions. As we shall see, departments are commonly organized by function, product, geographic region, or customer (Figure 7.2). Most companies use more than one departmentalization plan to enhance productivity. For instance, many consumer goods manufacturers have departments for specific product lines (beverages, frozen dinners, canned goods, and so on) as well as departments dealing with legal, purchasing, finance, human resources, and other business functions. For smaller companies, accounting can be set up online, almost as an automated department. Accounting software can handle electronic transfers so you never have to worry about a late bill.[10] Many city governments also have departments for specific services (e.g., police, fire, waste disposal) as well as departments for legal, human resources, and other business functions. Figure 7.3 depicts the organizational chart for the city of Yellowknife, Northwest Territories, showing these departments.

figure 7.2 Departmentalization

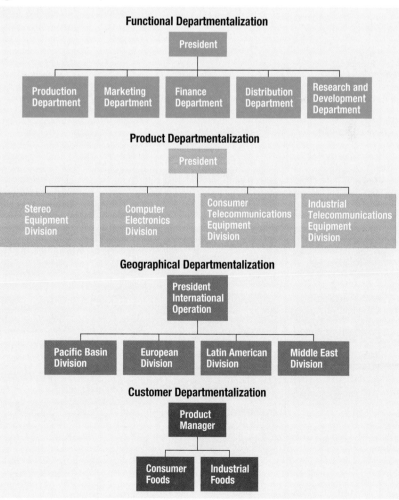

Functional Departmentalization. Functional departmentalization groups jobs that perform similar functional activities, such as finance, manufacturing, marketing, and human resources. Each of these functions is managed by an expert in the work done by the department—an engineer supervises the production department; a financial executive supervises the finance department. This approach is common in small organizations. A weakness of functional departmentalization is that, because it tends to emphasize departmental units rather than the organization as a whole, decision making that involves more than one department may be slow, and it requires greater coordination. Thus, as businesses grow, they tend to adopt other approaches to organizing jobs.

> **Functional departmentalization** the grouping of jobs that perform similar functional activities, such as finance, manufacturing, marketing, and human resources

Product Departmentalization. Product departmentalization, as you might guess, organizes jobs around the products of the firm. Procter & Gamble has global units, such as laundry and cleaning products, paper products, and health care products. Each division develops and implements its own product plans, monitors the results, and takes corrective action as necessary. Functional activities—production, finance, marketing, and others—are located within each product division. Consequently, organizing by products duplicates functions and resources and emphasizes the product rather than achievement of the organization's overall objectives. However, it simplifies decision making and helps coordinate all activities related to a product or product group. Campbell Soup Company is organized into four segments: (1) Soup, Sauces and Beverages, which includes Campbell's soups, Swanson broth,

> **Product departmentalization** the organization of jobs in relation to the products of the firm

figure 7.3 An Organizational Chart for the City of Yellowknife

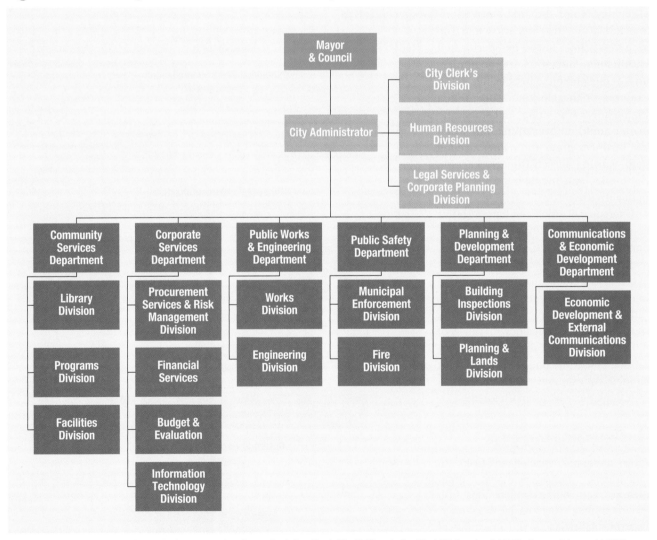

SOURCE: Yellowknife, "Organizational Chart of City Departments," http://www.yellowknife.ca/Assets/City+Hall/OrganizationalChartofCityDepartments2012.jpg (accessed January 14, 2013).

Prego pasta sauce, V8 juice and juice drinks, Campbell's tomato juice, and related products; (2) Baking and Snacking, which includes Pepperidge Farm cookies, crackers, bakery and frozen products, and Arnott's biscuits and salty snacks; (3) International Soup, Sauces and Beverages, which includes soup, sauces, and beverages sold outside the United States, and (4) North America Foodservice, which includes prepared food operations.[11]

Geographical Departmentalization. Geographical departmentalization groups jobs according to geographic location, such as a province, region, country, or continent. FritoLay, for example, is organized into four regional divisions, allowing the company to get closer to its customers and respond more quickly and efficiently to regional competitors. Multinational corporations often use a geographical approach because of vast differences between different regions. Coca-Cola, General Motors, and Caterpillar are organized by region. However, organizing by region requires a large administrative staff and control system to coordinate operations, and tasks are duplicated among the different regions.

> **Geographical departmentalization** the grouping of jobs according to geographic location, such as state, region, country, or continent
>
> **Customer departmentalization** the arrangement of jobs around the needs of various types of customers

Customer Departmentalization. Customer departmentalization arranges jobs around the needs of various types of customers. Banks, for example, typically have separate departments for commercial banking activities and for consumer or retail banking. This permits the bank to address the unique requirements of each group. Airlines, such as WestJet and Air Canada, provide prices and services customized for either business/frequent travellers or infrequent/vacationing customers. Customer departmentalization, like geographical departmentalization, does not focus on the organization as a whole and therefore requires a large administrative staff to coordinate the operations of the various groups.

LO3	Determine how organizations assign responsibility for tasks and delegate authority.

Assigning Responsibility

After all workers and work groups have been assigned their tasks, they must be given the responsibility to carry them out. Management must determine to what extent it will delegate responsibility throughout the organization and how many employees will report to each manager.

The Campbell Soup Company uses product departmentalization to organize its company. However, the firm also engages in a type of geographical departmentalization for various regions.

Delegation of Authority

Delegation of authority means not only giving tasks to employees but also empowering them to make commitments, use resources, and take whatever actions are necessary to carry out those tasks. Let's say a marketing manager at Nestlé has assigned an employee to design a new package that is less wasteful (more environmentally responsible) than the current package for one of the company's frozen dinner lines. To carry out the assignment, the employee needs access to information and the authority to make certain decisions on packaging materials, costs, and so on. Without the authority to carry out the assigned task, the employee would have to get the approval of others for every decision and every request for materials.

As a business grows, so do the number and complexity of decisions that must be made; no one manager can handle them all. Hotels such as Westin Hotels and Resorts and the Ritz-Carlton give authority to service providers, including front desk personnel, to make service decisions such as moving a guest to another room or providing a discount to guests who experience a problem at the hotel. Delegation of authority frees a manager to concentrate on larger issues, such as planning or dealing with problems and opportunities.

Delegation also gives a **responsibility,** or obligation, to employees to carry out assigned tasks satisfactorily and holds them accountable for the proper execution of their assigned work. The principle of **accountability**

> **Delegation of authority** giving employees not only tasks, but also the power to make commitments, use resources, and take whatever actions are necessary to carry out those tasks
>
> **Responsibility** the obligation, placed on employees through delegation, to perform assigned tasks satisfactorily and be held accountable for the proper execution of work
>
> **Accountability** the principle that employees who accept an assignment and the authority to carry it out are answerable to a superior for the outcome

means that employees who accept an assignment and the authority to carry it out are answerable to a superior for the outcome. Returning to the Nestlé example, if the packaging design prepared by the employee is unacceptable or late, the employee must accept the blame. If the new design is innovative, attractive, and cost-efficient, as well as environmentally responsible, or is completed ahead of schedule, the employee will accept the credit.

The process of delegating authority establishes a pattern of relationships and accountability between a superior and his or her subordinates. The president of a firm delegates responsibility for all marketing activities to the vice president of marketing. The vice president accepts this responsibility and has the authority to obtain all relevant information, make certain decisions, and delegate any or all activities to his or her subordinates. The vice president, in turn, delegates all advertising activities to the advertising manager, all sales activities to the sales manager, and so on. These managers then delegate specific tasks to their subordinates. However, the act of delegating authority to a subordinate does not relieve the superior of accountability for the delegated job. Even though the vice president of marketing delegates work to subordinates, he or she is still ultimately accountable to the president for all marketing activities.

Degree of Centralization

The extent to which authority is delegated throughout an organization determines its degree of centralization.

> **Centralized organization** a structure in which authority is concentrated at the top, and very little decision-making authority is delegated to lower levels

Centralized Organizations. In a **centralized organization,** authority is concentrated at the top, and very little decision-making authority is delegated to lower levels. Although decision-making authority in centralized organizations rests with top levels of management, a vast amount of responsibility for carrying out daily and routine procedures is delegated to even the lowest levels of the organization. Many government organizations, including the Canadian Armed Forces, Canada Post, and the Canada Revenue Agency, are centralized.

Businesses tend to be more centralized when the decisions to be made are risky and when low-level managers are not highly skilled in decision making. In the banking industry, for example, authority to make routine car loans is given to all loan managers, while the authority to make high-risk loans, such as for a large residential development, may be restricted to upper-level loan officers.

Overcentralization can cause serious problems for a company, in part because it may take longer for the organization as a whole to implement decisions and to respond to changes and problems on a regional scale. McDonald's, for example, was one of the last chains to introduce a chicken sandwich because of the amount of research, development, test marketing, and layers of approval the product had to go through.

Decentralized Organizations. A **decentralized organization** is one in which decision-making authority is delegated as far down the chain of command as possible. Decentralization is characteristic of organizations that operate in complex, unpredictable environments. Businesses that face intense competition often decentralize to improve responsiveness and enhance creativity. Lower-level managers who interact with the external environment often develop a good understanding of it and thus are able to react quickly to changes.

Delegating authority to lower levels of managers may increase the organization's productivity. Decentralization requires that lower-level managers have strong decision-making skills. In recent years the trend has been toward more decentralized organizations, and some of the largest and most successful companies, including GE, Sears, IBM, and Nestlé, have decentralized decision-making authority. McDonald's, realizing most of its growth outside North America, is becoming increasingly decentralized and "glocal," varying products in specific markets to better meet consumer demands. This change in organizational structure for McDonald's is fostering greater innovation and local market success. McDonald's, which was long known for the homogeneity of its products, has embraced local cuisine on a limited scale. In Italy, McDonald's introduced the McItaly, a burger made with only Italian products. The burger is designed with the red and green Italian flag in mind; customers can choose from artichoke spread and Asiago cheese or onion, lettuce, and pancetta.[12] Diversity and decentralization seem to be McDonald's keys to being better, not just bigger. Nonprofit organizations benefit from decentralization as well.

Span of Management

How many subordinates should a manager manage? There is no simple answer. Experts generally agree, however, that top managers should not directly supervise more than four to eight people, while lower-level managers who supervise routine tasks are capable of managing a much larger number of subordinates. For example, the manager of the finance department may supervise 25 employees, whereas the vice president of finance may supervise only five managers. **Span of management** refers to the number of subordinates who report to a particular manager.

> **Decentralized organization** an organization in which decision-making authority is delegated as far down the chain of command as possible
>
> **Span of management** the number of subordinates who report to a particular manager

A *wide span of management* exists when a manager directly supervises a very large number of employees. A *narrow span of management* exists when a manager directly supervises only a few subordinates (Figure 7.4). At Whole Foods, the best employees are recruited and placed in small teams in one of eight departments. Employees are empowered to discount, give away, and sample products, as well as to assist in creating a respectful workplace where goals are

John Earle

Business: Johnny Cupcakes

Founded: 2001, in Hull, Massachusetts

Success: Johnny Cupcakes has achieved a cult-like following with stores in Massachusetts, California, and the United Kingdom.

It might sound like a bakery, but Johnny Cupcakes is actually the name of a successful apparel retailer. Founded in 2001 by John Earle, Johnny Cupcakes sells limited edition clothing and accessories—all featuring cupcake designs. John began selling his first T-shirts out of the trunk of his car and the suitcase he used while touring with his band. As business accelerated, John's mother and sister began helping him fill orders. His parents' house became his warehouse. Along the road

to success, John turned down distribution offers from companies like Urban Outfitters, and instead, opened up his own stores in Hull, Massachusetts (his hometown), Los Angeles, Boston, and London, England. Customers often camp outside to score new designs and attend special events. At one event over 600 people waited in line for the grand opening of the Johnny Cupcakes Newbury Street (Boston) store with some customers driving 9 hours from Toronto! Through it all, John has been supported by his family and friends, who are also his co-workers. His mother serves as his chief financial officer, his sister runs human resources and customer service, his sister's best friend is training as bookkeeper, and his father assists with various aspects of the business. Although the creative inspiration rests with John, Johnny Cupcakes is truly a family affair.[13]

achieved, individual employees succeed, and customers are core in business decisions. This approach allows Whole Foods to offer unique and "local market" experiences in each of its stores. This level of customization is in contrast to more centralized national supermarket chains.[14]

Should the span of management be wide or narrow? To answer this question, several factors need to be considered. A narrow span of management is appropriate when superiors and subordinates are not in close proximity, the manager has many responsibilities in addition to the supervision, the interaction between superiors and subordinates is frequent, and problems are common. However, when superiors and subordinates are located close to one another, the manager has few responsibilities other than supervision, the level of interaction between superiors and subordinates is low, few problems arise, subordinates are highly competent, and a set of specific operating procedures governs the activities of managers and their subordinates, a wide span of management will be more appropriate. Narrow spans of management are typical in centralized organizations, while wide spans of management are more common in decentralized firms.

> "A company with many layers of managers is considered tall."

Organizational Layers

Complementing the concept of span of management are **organizational layers,** the levels of management in an organization.

A company with many layers of managers is considered tall; in a tall organization, the span of management is narrow (see Figure 7.4). Because each manager supervises only a few subordinates, many layers of management are necessary to carry out the operations of the business. McDonald's, for example, has a tall organization with many layers, including store managers, district managers, regional managers, and functional managers (finance, marketing, and so on), as well as a chief executive officer and many vice presidents. Because there are more managers in tall organizations than in flat organizations, administrative costs are usually higher. Communication is slower because information must pass through many layers.

Organizational layers the levels of management in an organization.

figure 7.4 Span of Management: Wide Span and Narrow Span

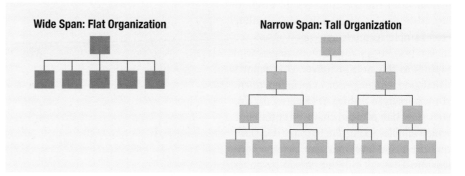

Wide Span: Flat Organization

Narrow Span: Tall Organization

figure 7.5 Line Structure

Convenience Store

Owner — Manager — Assistant Manager — Hourly Employee

Organizations with few layers are flat and have wide spans of management. When managers supervise a large number of employees, fewer management layers are needed to conduct the organization's activities. Managers in flat organizations typically perform more administrative duties than managers in tall organizations because there are fewer of them. They also spend more time supervising and working with subordinates.

Many of the companies that decentralized also flattened their structures and widened their spans of management, often by eliminating layers of middle management. Many corporations did so to reduce costs, speed decision making, and boost overall productivity.

> **LO4** Compare and contrast some common forms of organizational structure.

immediate supervisor. However, this structure requires that managers possess a wide range of knowledge and skills. They are responsible for a variety of activities and must be knowledgeable about them all. Line structures are most common in small businesses.

Line-and-Staff Structure

The **line-and-staff structure** has a traditional line relationship between superiors and subordinates, and specialized managers—called staff managers—are available to assist line managers (Figure 7.6). Line managers can focus on their area of expertise in the operation of the business, while staff

> **Line structure** the simplest organizational structure in which direct lines of authority extend from the top manager to the lowest level of the organization
>
> **Line-and-staff structure** a structure having a traditional line relationship between superiors and subordinates and also specialized managers—called staff managers—who are available to assist line managers

Forms of Organizational Structure

Along with assigning tasks and the responsibility for carrying them out, managers must consider how to structure their authority relationships—that is, what structure the organization itself will have and how it will appear on the organizational chart. Common forms of organization include line structure, line-and-staff structure, multidivisional structure, and matrix structure.

Line Structure

The simplest organizational structure, **line structure,** has direct lines of authority that extend from the top manager to employees at the lowest level of the organization. For example, a convenience store employee may report to an assistant manager, who reports to the store manager, who reports to a regional manager, or, in an independent store, directly to the owner (Figure 7.5). This structure has a clear chain of command, which enables managers to make decisions quickly. A mid-level manager facing a decision must consult only one person, his or her

figure 7.6 Line-and-Staff Structure

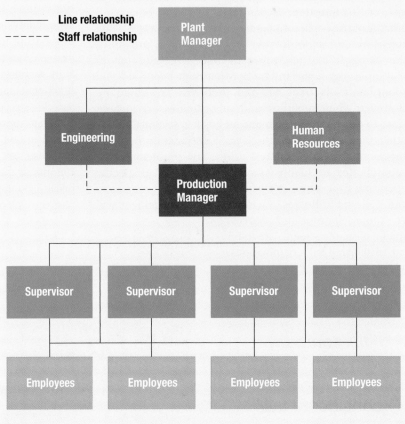

——— Line relationship
- - - - Staff relationship

Plant Manager

Engineering — Human Resources

Production Manager

Supervisor — Supervisor — Supervisor — Supervisor

Employees — Employees — Employees — Employees

managers provide advice and support to line departments on specialized matters such as finance, engineering, human resources, and the law. In the city of Yellowknife (Figure 7.3), for example, the City Administrator is a line manager who oversees groups of related departments. However, the heads of the Human Resources Division, Legal Services and Corporate Planning Division, Community Services Department, etc., are effectively staff managers who report directly to the City Administrator (the city equivalent of a business chief executive officer). Staff managers do not have direct authority over line managers or over the line manager's subordinates, but they do have direct authority over subordinates in their own departments. However, line-and-staff organizations may experience problems with overstaffing and ambiguous lines of communication. Additionally, employees may become frustrated because they lack the authority to carry out certain decisions.

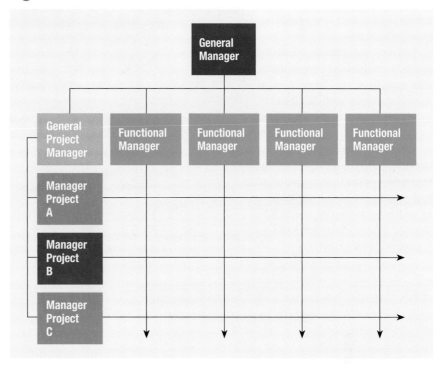

figure 7.7 Matrix Structure

Multidivisional Structure

As companies grow and diversify, traditional line structures become difficult to coordinate, making communication difficult and decision making slow. When the weaknesses of the structure—the "turf wars," miscommunication, and working at cross-purposes—exceed the benefits, growing firms tend to restructure, often into the divisionalized form. A **multidivisional structure** organizes departments into larger groups called divisions. Just as departments might be formed on the basis of geography, customer, product, or a combination of these, so too divisions can be formed based on any of these methods of organizing. Within each of these divisions, departments may be organized by product, geographic region, function, or some combination of all three. Indra Nooyi, CEO of PepsiCo, rearranged the company's organizational structure. Prior to her tenure, PepsiCo was organized geographically. She created new units—PepsiCo Americas Foods (PAF), PepsiCo Americas Beverages (PAB), PepsiCo Europe, and PepsiCo Asia, Middle East & Africa—that span international boundaries and make it easier for employees in different geographic regions to share business practices.[15]

Multidivisional structures permit delegation of decision-making authority, allowing divisional and department managers to specialize. They allow those closest to the action to make the decisions that will affect them. Delegation of authority and divisionalized work also mean that

better decisions are made faster, and they tend to be more innovative. Most importantly, by focusing each division on a common region, product, or customer, each is more likely to provide products that meet the needs of its particular customers. However, the divisional structure inevitably creates work duplication, which makes it more difficult to realize the economies of scale that result from grouping functions together.

Matrix Structure

Another structure that attempts to address issues that arise with growth, diversification, productivity, and competitiveness is the matrix. A **matrix structure,** also called a project-management structure, sets up teams from different departments, thereby creating two or more intersecting lines of authority (see Figure 7.7). The matrix structure superimposes project-based departments on the more traditional, function-based departments. Project teams bring together specialists from a variety of areas to work together on a single project, such as developing a new fighter jet. In this arrangement, employees are responsible to two managers—functional managers and project managers. Matrix structures are usually temporary: Team members typically go back to their functional or line department after a project is finished. However, more firms are becoming permanent matrix structures, creating and dissolving project teams as needed to meet customer needs. The aerospace industry was one of the first to apply the matrix structure,

Multidivisional structure a structure that organizes departments into larger groups called divisions

Matrix structure a structure that sets up teams from different departments, thereby creating two or more intersecting lines of authority; also called a project-management structure

but today it is used by universities and schools, accounting firms, banks, and organizations in other industries.

Matrix structures provide flexibility, enhanced cooperation, and creativity, and they enable the company to respond quickly to changes in the environment by giving special attention to specific projects or problems. However, they are generally expensive and quite complex, and employees may be confused as to whose authority has priority—the project manager's or the immediate supervisor's.

table 7.2 Differences Between Groups and Teams

Working Group	Team
Has strong, clearly focused leader	Has shared leadership roles
Has individual accountability	Has individual and group accountability
Has the same purpose as the broader organizational mission	Has a specific purpose that the team itself delivers
Creates individual work products	Creates collective work products
Runs efficient meetings	Encourages open-ended discussion and active problem-solving meetings
Measures its effectiveness indirectly by its effects on others (e.g., financial performance of the business)	Measures performance directly by assessing collective work products
Discusses, decides, and delegates	Discusses, decides, and does real work together

SOURCE: Robert Gatewood, Robert Taylor, and O. C. Ferrell, *Management: Comprehension Analysis and Application*, 1995, p. 427. Copyright © 1995 Richard D. Irwin, a Times Mirror Higher Education Group, Inc., company. Reproduced with permission of the McGraw-Hill Companies.

LO5 Distinguish between groups and teams, and identify the types of groups that exist in organizations.

The Role of Groups and Teams in Organizations

Regardless of how they are organized, most of the essential work of business occurs in individual work groups and teams, so we'll take a closer look at them now. Although some experts do not make a distinction between groups and teams, in recent years there has been a gradual shift toward an emphasis on teams and managing them to enhance individual and organizational success. Some experts now believe that highest productivity results only when groups become teams.[16]

Traditionally, a **group** has been defined as two or more individuals who communicate with one another, share a common identity, and have a common goal. A **team** is a small group whose members have complementary skills; have a common purpose, goal, and approach; and hold themselves mutually accountable.[17] All teams are groups, but not all groups are teams. Table 7.2 points out some important differences between them. Work groups emphasize individual work products, individual accountability, and even individual leadership. Salespeople working independently for the same company could be a work group. In contrast, work teams share leadership roles, have both individual and mutual accountability, and

create collective work products. In other words, a work group's performance depends on what its members do as individuals, while a team's performance is based on creating a knowledge centre and a competency to work together to accomplish a goal. To support sales of its extensive product lines, Procter & Gamble places teams of its employees in key retail customers' headquarters. For instance, Procter & Gamble teams assigned to Dollar General Stores work with the discount retailer to meet its customers' needs and even customize Procter & Gamble products to Dollar General's specification.[18]

The type of groups an organization establishes depends on the tasks it needs to accomplish and the situation it faces. Some specific kinds of groups and teams include committees, task forces, project teams, product-development teams, quality-assurance teams, and self-directed work teams. All of these can be *virtual teams*—employees in different locations who rely on e-mail, audio conferencing, fax, Internet, video-conferencing, or other technological tools to accomplish their goals. One survey found that almost 48 percent of workers have participated in virtual teams.[19]

Committees

A **committee** is usually a permanent, formal group that does some specific task. For example, many firms have a compensation or finance committee to examine the effectiveness of these areas of operation as well as the need for possible changes. Ethics committees are formed to develop and revise codes of ethics, suggest methods for implementing ethical standards, and review specific issues and concerns.

Task Forces

A **task force** is a temporary group of employees responsible for bringing about a particular change. They typically come

Group two or more individuals who communicate with one another, share a common identity, and have a common goal

Team a small group whose members have complementary skills; have a common purpose, goal, and approach; and hold themselves mutually accountable

Committee a permanent, formal group that performs a specific task

Task force a temporary group of employees responsible for bringing about a particular change from across all departments and levels of an organization. Task force membership is usually based on expertise rather than organizational position. Occasionally, a task force may be formed from individuals outside a company. When Toyota experienced a major product recall, the president, Akio Toyoda, formed and led a Global Quality Task Force to conduct quality improvements throughout the worldwide operations of the company. With massive recalls looming, the company focused on (1) improving the quality inspection process, (2) enhancing customer research, (3) establishing an automotive centre of quality excellence, (4) utilizing external industry experts, (5) increasing the frequency of communication with regional authorities, and (6) improving regional autonomy.[20]

Teams

Teams are becoming far more common in the Canadian workplace as businesses strive to enhance productivity and global competitiveness. In general, teams have the benefit of being able to pool members' knowledge and skills and make greater use of them than can individuals working alone. Team building is becoming increasingly popular in organizations, with around half of executives indicating their companies had team-building training. Teams require harmony, cooperation, synchronized effort, and flexibility to maximize their contribution.[22] Teams can also create more solutions to problems than can individuals. Furthermore, team participation enhances employee acceptance of, understanding of, and commitment to team goals. Teams motivate workers by providing internal rewards in the form of an enhanced sense of accomplishment for employees as they achieve more, and external rewards in the form of praise and certain perks. Consequently, they can help get workers more involved. They can help companies be more innovative, and they can boost productivity and cut costs.

According to psychologist Ivan Steiner, team productivity peaks at about five team members. People become less motivated and group coordination becomes more difficult after this size. Jeff Bezos, Amazon.com CEO, says that he has a "two-pizza rule": If a team cannot be fed by two pizzas, it is too large. Keep teams small enough that everyone gets a piece of the action.[23]

Project Teams. **Project teams** are similar to task forces, but normally they run

> "Teams are becoming far more common in the workplace as businesses strive to enhance productivity and global competitiveness."

DID YOU KNOW?

A survey of managers and executives found that they feel 28 percent of meetings are a waste of time and that information could be communicated more effectively using other methods.[21]

their operation and have total control of a specific work project. Like task forces, their membership is likely to cut across the firm's hierarchy and be composed of people from different functional areas. They are almost always temporary, although a large project, such as designing and building a new airplane at Boeing Corporation, may last for years.

Product-development teams are a special type of project team formed to devise, design, and implement a new product. Sometimes product-development teams exist within a functional area—research and development—but now they more frequently include people from numerous functional areas and may even include customers to help ensure that the end product meets the customers' needs.

Quality-Assurance Teams. **Quality-assurance teams (or quality circles)** are fairly small groups of workers brought together from throughout the organization to solve specific quality, productivity, or service problems. Although the *quality circle* term is not as popular as it once was, the concern about quality is stronger than ever. The use of teams to address quality issues will no doubt continue to increase throughout the business world.

Self-Directed Work Teams. A **self-directed work team (SDWT)** is a group of employees responsible for an entire work process or segment that delivers a product to an internal or external customer.[24] SDWTs permit the flexibility to change rapidly to meet the competition or respond to customer needs. The defining characteristic of an SDWT is the extent to which it is empowered or given authority to make and implement work decisions. Thus, SDWTs are designed to give employees a feeling of "ownership" of a whole job. With shared team responsibility for work outcomes, team members often have broader job assignments and cross-train to master other jobs, thus permitting greater team flexibility.

Project teams groups similar to task forces that normally run their operation and have total control of a specific work project

Product-development teams a specific type of project team formed to devise, design, and implement a new product

Quality-assurance teams (or quality circles) small groups of workers brought together from throughout the organization to solve specific quality, productivity, or service problems

Self-directed work team (SDWT) a group of employees responsible for an entire work process or segment that delivers a product to an internal or external customer

Communicating in Organizations

Communication within an organization can flow in a variety of directions and from a number of sources, each using both oral and written forms of communication. The success of communication systems within the organization has a tremendous effect on the overall success of the firm. Communication mistakes can lower productivity and morale.

Alternatives to face-to-face communications—such as meetings—are growing thanks to technology such as voicemail, e-mail, and online newsletters. Many companies use internal networks called intranets to share information with employees. Intranets increase communication across different departments and levels of management and help with the flow of everyday business activities. Companies can even integrate aspects of social media into their intranets, allowing employees to post comments and pictures, participate in polls, and create group calendars. However, increased access to the Internet at work has also created many problems, including employee abuse of company mail and Internet access.[25]

Formal Communication

Formal channels of communication are intentionally defined and designed by the organization. They represent the flow of communication within the formal organizational structure, as shown on organizational charts. Traditionally, formal communication patterns were classified as vertical and horizontal, but with the increased use of teams and matrix structures, formal communication may occur in a number of patterns (Figure 7.8).

Upward communication flows from lower to higher levels of the organization and includes information such as progress reports, suggestions for improvement, inquiries, and grievances. *Downward communication* refers to the traditional flow of information from upper organizational levels to lower levels. This type of communication typically involves directions, the assignment of tasks and responsibilities, performance feedback, and certain details about the organization's strategies and goals. Speeches, policy and procedures manuals, employee handbooks, company leaflets, telecommunications, and job descriptions are examples of downward communication.

Horizontal communication involves the exchange of information among colleagues and peers on the same organizational level, such as across or within departments. Horizontal information informs, supports, and coordinates activities both within the department and with other departments.

RESPONDING TO BUSINESS CHALLENGES | Creating a Corporate Culture . . . Virtually

It seems unlikely that businesses would encourage employees to engage in social networking, but clients of Yammer do just that. Yammer supplies internal social networking for organizations. These internal networks provide many benefits. For example, Yammer enables global employees to communicate easily in real time, cutting down significantly on e-mail. Yammer CEO David Sacks says employees using his service more easily develop relationships and a commitment to their companies—a claim bolstered by research. Although the networks are designed for conducting business, employees often share jokes, light banter, and personal information. Many companies also use Yammer and the equivalent to track ideas from conception through production and beyond in a streamlined fashion.

Despite advantages, internal social networking has pitfalls. Disadvantages primarily affect employees, who may be too free with their comments. Anything posted on an internal social network is potentially admissible during performance reviews, promotion decisions, and legal proceedings.

More than 100,000 companies currently use Yammer, and most love it. They do agree, however, that it's important to implement user guidelines to avoid trouble. For instance, the technology company Xerox states that employees should use discretion, professionalism, and common sense in the tone an aunt might use with a favourite nephew. With gentle guidance, Yammer and others can enhance company culture and the workplace experience. As social networking continues to grow, it's likely the internal version will thrive as well.[26]

DISCUSSION QUESTIONS

1. How does Yammer contribute to a firm's corporate culture?

2. How can Yammer be used as a way to improve productivity?

3. What are some potential pitfalls of Yammer, and how can these pitfalls be avoided?

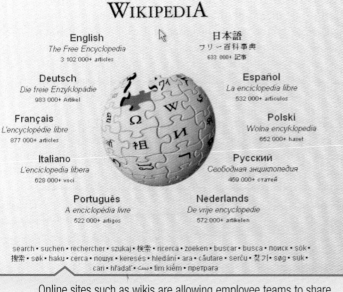

Online sites such as wikis are allowing employee teams to share information and work collaboratively on documents. The most well-known wiki is the online encyclopedia Wikipedia.

communication channels. Grapevines exist in all organizations. Information passed along the grapevine may relate to the job or organization, or it may be gossip and rumours unrelated to either. The accuracy of grapevine information has been of great concern to managers.

Additionally, managers can turn the grapevine to their advantage. Using it as a "sounding device" for possible new policies is one example. Managers can obtain valuable information from the grapevine that could improve decision making. Some organizations use the grapevine to their advantage by floating ideas, soliciting feedback, and reacting accordingly. People love to gossip, and managers need to be aware that grapevines exist in every organization. Managers who understand how the grapevine works also can use it to their advantage by feeding it facts to squelch rumours and incorrect information.

> **"Grapevines exist in all organizations.** Information passed along the grapevine may relate to the job or organization, or it may be gossip **and rumours unrelated to either."**

Monitoring Communications

Technological advances and the increased use of electronic communication in the workplace have made monitoring its use necessary for most companies Many companies require that employees sign and follow a policy on appropriate Internet use. These agreements often require that employees will use corporate computers only for work-related activities. Additionally, several companies use software

> **Grapevine** an informal channel of communication, separate from management's formal, official communication channels

At times, the business will formally require horizontal communication among particular organizational members, as is the case with task forces or project teams.

With more and more companies downsizing and increasing the use of self-managed work teams, many workers are being required to communicate with others in different departments and on different levels to solve problems and coordinate work. When these individuals from different units and organizational levels communicate, it is *diagonal communication.*

Informal Communication Channels

Along with the formal channels of communication shown on an organizational chart, all firms communicate informally as well. Communication between friends, for instance, cuts across department, division, and even management–subordinate boundaries. Such friendships and other non-work social relationships comprise the *informal organization* of a firm, and their impact can be great.

The most significant informal communication occurs through the **grapevine,** an informal channel of communication, separate from management's formal, official

figure 7.8 The Flow of Communication in an Organizational Hierarchy

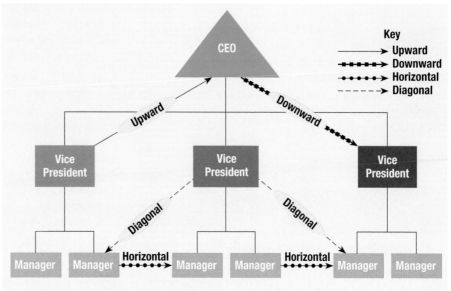

programs to monitor employee computer usage.[27] Instituting practices that show respect for employee privacy but do not abdicate employer responsibility are increasingly necessary in today's workplace. Several websites provide model policies and detailed guidelines for conducting electronic monitoring, including the Guide for Businesses and Organizations, "Your Privacy Responsibilities," on the Privacy Commissioner of Canada site.

TEAM EXERCISE

Assign the responsibility of providing the organizational structure for a company one of your team members has worked for. Was your organization centralized or decentralized in terms of decision making? Would you consider the span of control to be wide or narrow? Were any types of teams, committees, or task forces utilized in the organization? Report your work to the class.

LEARNING OBJECTIVES SUMMARY

LO1 Define organizational structure, and relate how organizational structures develop.

Structure is the arrangement or relationship of positions within an organization; it develops when managers assign work activities to work groups and specific individuals and coordinate the diverse activities required to attain organizational objectives. Organizational structure evolves to accommodate growth, which requires people with specialized skills.

LO2 Describe how specialization and departmentalization help an organization achieve its goals.

Structuring an organization requires that management assign work tasks to specific individuals and groups. Under specialization managers break labour into small, specialized tasks and assign employees to do a single task, fostering efficiency. Departmentalization is the grouping of jobs into working units (departments, units, groups, or divisions). Businesses may departmentalize by function, product, geographic region, or customer, or they may combine two or more of these.

LO3 Determine how organizations assign responsibility for tasks and delegate authority.

Delegation of authority means assigning tasks to employees and giving them the power to make commitments, use resources, and take whatever actions are necessary to accomplish the tasks. It lays responsibility on employees to carry out assigned tasks satisfactorily and holds them accountable to a superior for the proper execution of their assigned work. The extent to which authority is delegated throughout an organization determines its degree of centralization. Span of management refers to the number of subordinates who report to particular manager. A wide span of management occurs in flat organizations; a narrow one exists in tall organizations.

LO4 Compare and contrast some common forms of organizational structure.

Line structures have direct lines of authority that extend from the top manager to employees at the lowest level of the organization. The line-and-staff structure has a traditional line relationship between superiors and subordinates, and specialized staff managers are to assist line managers. A multidivisional structure gathers departments into larger groups called divisions. A matrix, or project-management, structure sets up teams from different departments, thereby creating two or more intersecting lines of authority.

LO5

Distinguish between groups and teams, and identify the types of groups that exist in organizations.

A group is two or more persons who communicate, share a common identity, and have a common goal. A team is a small group whose members have complementary skills, a common purpose, goals, and approach; and who hold themselves mutually accountable. The major distinction is that individual performance is most important in groups, while collective work group performance counts most in teams. Special kinds of groups include task forces, committees, project teams, product-development teams, quality-assurance teams, and self-directed work teams.

LO6

Describe how communication occurs in organizations.

Communication occurs both formally and informally in organizations. Formal communication may be downward, upward, horizontal, and even diagonal. Informal communication takes place through friendships and the grapevine.

KEY TERMS

accountability
centralized organization
committee
customer departmentalization
decentralized organization
delegation of authority
departmentalization
functional departmentalization
geographical departmentalization
grapevine
group
line-and-staff structure
line structure
matrix structure
multidivisional structure

organizational chart
organizational culture
organizational layers
product departmentalization
product-development teams
project teams
quality-assurance teams (or quality circles)
responsibility
self-directed work team (SDWT)
span of management
specialization
structure
task force
team

DESTINATION CEO DISCUSSION QUESTIONS

1. What are the most important factors, according to Cora, contributing to her success?

2. Was marketing or operations most important in preparing Cora for her role as CEO?

3. How does the founder remain involved with her company?

SO YOU WANT A JOB IN GLOBAL BUSINESS
Managing Organizational Culture, Teamwork, and Communication

Jobs dealing with organizational culture and structure are usually at the top of the organization. If you want to be a CEO or high-level manager, you will help shape these areas of business. On the other hand, if you are an entrepreneur or small-business person, you will need to make decisions about assigning tasks, departmentalization, and assigning responsibility. Even managers in small organizations have to make decisions about decentralization, span of management, and forms of organizational structure. While these decisions may be part of your job, there are usually no job titles dealing with these specific areas. Specific jobs that attempt to improve organizational culture could include ethics and compliance positions as well as those who are in charge of communicating memos, manuals, and policies that help establish the culture. These positions will be in communications, human resources, and positions that assist top organizational managers.

Teams are becoming more common in the workplace, and it is possible to become a member of a product-development group or quality-assurance team. There are also human resources positions that encourage teamwork through training activities. The area of corporate communications provides lots of opportunities for specific jobs that facilitate communication systems. Thanks to technology, there are job positions to help disseminate information through online newsletters, intranets, or internal computer networks to increase collaboration. In addition to the many advances using electronic communications, there are technology concerns that create new job opportunities. Monitoring workplace communications such as the use of e-mail and the Internet have created new industries. There have to be internal controls in the organization to make sure that the organization does not engage in any copyright infringement. If this is an area of interest, there are specific jobs that provide an opportunity to use your technological skills to assist in maintaining appropriate standards in communicating and using technology.

If you go to work for a large company with many divisions, you can expect a number of positions dealing with the tasks discussed here. If you go to work for a small company, you will probably engage in most of these tasks as a part of your position. Organizational flexibility requires individual flexibility, and those employees willing to take on new domains and challenges will be the employees who survive and prosper in the future.

BUILD YOUR BUSINESS PLAN

Organization, Teamwork, and Communication

Developing a business plan as a team is a deliberate move of your instructor to encourage you to familiarize yourself with the concept of teamwork. You need to realize that you are going to spend a large part of your professional life working with others. At this point in time you are working on the business plan for a grade, but after graduation you will be "teaming" with co-workers and the success of your endeavour may determine whether or not you get a raise or a bonus. It is important that you be comfortable as soon as possible with working with others and holding them accountable for their contributions.

Some people are natural "leaders" and leaders often feel that if team members are not doing their work, they take it upon themselves to "do it all." This is not leadership, but rather micro-managing.

Leadership means holding members accountable for their responsibilities. Your instructor may provide ideas on how this could be implemented, possibly by utilizing peer reviews. Remember you are not doing a team member a favour by doing their work for them.

If you are a "follower" (someone who takes directions well) rather than a leader, try to get into a team where others are hard workers and you will rise to their level. There is nothing wrong with being a follower; not everyone can be a leader!

Ford is going green with its formation of its all-women renewable materials research team—also known as Ford's Green Team. Debbie Mielewski and her five female colleagues are all engineers looking to make Ford cars more eco-friendly. The idea for the team started when Mielewski was asked to reshape Ford's plastics department. She brought her own green concerns to the job and began researching how to make Ford's cars more sustainable. To date, Mielewski and her team have been awarded ten prize patents for innovations such as soy-filled seats and the blending of traditional plastics with wheat fibres. The group also focuses on reusing damaged materials, rather than throwing them away.

In an industry dominated by men—only one-fourth of auto employees and one-tenth of auto executives are women—Ford's Green Team feels that it has unique skills and insights to contribute. Many members of the team have children, and they bring a passion to protect the environment for future generations to their work. In addition, the six members find that they are able to collaborate well. They tend to divide into teams, rather than working solo, in order to have constant support and feedback. The team emphasizes communication and collective decision making, which they feel has been an important factor in their achievements.

The Green Team has already made an impact on the company. A recent press release states that in one year the company has kept almost 30 million pounds of plastic out of landfills and saved $4.5 million by utilizing recycled materials. Ford plans to replace fibreglass and plastics with sustainable, eco-friendly alternatives, which will lead to a smaller carbon footprint and a reduced use of petroleum. It looks like the Green Team has a winning strategy.[28]

DISCUSSION QUESTIONS

1. Why did Ford form an all-women renewable materials research team to make cars more eco-friendly?

2. Why is collective decision making a benefit to Ford's Green Team?

3. Will Ford's Green Team contribute to consumer loyalty and success?

connect **LEARNSMART** **SMARTBOOK**

For more information on the resources available from McGraw-Hill Ryerson, go to www.mcgrawhill.ca/he/solutions.

DESTINATION CEO

Gary Kusin FedEx Kinko's is a business model that represents a one-stop comprehensive business services operation. Kinko's was known as the copy king but has expanded its services mix and product lines so that it competes with retailers such as Office Depot and Staples.

Gary Kusin, the current CEO of FedEx Kinko's, was profoundly influenced early in his life by Ross Perot. Kusin, like many university and college students during their early academic life, did not have a clear career goal. He did his undergraduate work and after graduating, he looked around and was impressed by successful businesspeople who all seemed to have one thing in common—an M.B.A. from the Harvard Business School. Kusin followed these role models and successfully completed his M.B.A. at Harvard. His work experience took him from working in the family furniture store at age 12 to his successful position as CEO of FedEx Kinko's. Prior to achieving this leadership position, he held the position of Vice President of Sanger Harris in the retail industry. He successfully navigated a merger (Federated Department Stores) with their lead competitor (Laura Mercier), and then the company was finally bought out by Macy's. After his successful career as an executive in the retail sales industry, he assumed the CEO position at FedEx Kinko's.

Introduction

All organizations create products—goods, services, or ideas—for customers. Thus, organizations as diverse as Toyota, Campbell Soup, UPS, and a hospital share a number of similarities relating to how they transform resources into the products we consume. Most hospitals use similar admission procedures, while online social media companies, like Facebook and Twitter, use their technology and operating systems to create social networking opportunities and sell advertising. Such similarities are to be expected. But even organizations in unrelated industries take similar steps in creating goods or services. The check-in procedures of hotels and commercial airlines are comparable, for example. The way Subway assembles a sandwich and the way GMC assembles a truck are similar (both use automation and an assembly line). These similarities are the result of operations management, the focus of this chapter.

Here, we discuss the role of production or operations management in acquiring and managing the resources necessary to create goods and services. Production and operations management involves planning and designing the processes that will transform those resources into finished products, managing the movement of those resources through the transformation process, and ensuring that the products are of the quality expected by customers.

The Nature of Operations Management

Operations management (OM), the development and administration of the activities involved in transforming resources into goods and services, is of critical importance. Operations managers oversee the transformation process and the planning and designing of operations systems, managing logistics, quality, and productivity. Quality and productivity have become fundamental aspects of operations management because a company that cannot make products of the quality desired by consumers, using resources efficiently and effectively, will not be able to remain in business. OM is the "core" of most organizations because it is responsible for the creation of the organization's goods or services.

Historically, operations management has been called "production" or "manufacturing" primarily because of the view that it was limited to the manufacture of physical goods. Its focus was on methods and techniques required to operate a factory efficiently. The change from "production" to " operations" recognizes the increasing importance of organizations that provide services and ideas. Additionally, the term *operations* represents an interest in viewing the operations function as a whole rather than simply as an analysis of inputs and outputs.

Today, OM includes a wide range of organizational activities and situations outside of manufacturing, such as health care, food service, banking, entertainment, education, transportation, and charity. Thus, we use the terms **manufacturing** and **production** interchangeably to represent the activities and processes used in making *tangible* products, whereas we use the broader term **operations** to describe those processes used in the making of *both tangible and intangible products*. Manufacturing provides tangible products such as Hewlett-Packard's latest printer, and operations provides intangibles such as a stay at Wyndham Hotels and Resorts.

The Transformation Process

At the heart of operations management is the transformation process through which **inputs** (resources such as labour, money, materials, and energy) are converted into **outputs** (goods, services, and ideas). The transformation process combines inputs in predetermined ways using different equipment, administrative procedures, and technology to create a product (Figure 8.1). To ensure that this process generates quality products efficiently, operations managers control the process by taking measurements (feedback) at various points in the transformation process and comparing them to previously established standards. If there is any deviation between the actual and desired outputs, the manager may take some sort of corrective action. All adjustments made to create a satisfying product are a part of the transformation process.

Transformation may take place through one or more processes. In a business that manufactures oak furniture, for example, inputs pass through several processes before being turned into the final outputs— furniture that has been designed to meet the desires of customers (Figure 8.2). The furniture maker must first strip the oak trees of their bark and saw them into appropriate sizes—one step in the transformation process. Next, the firm dries the strips of oak lumber, a second form of transformation. Third, the dried wood is routed into its appropriate shape and made smooth. Fourth, workers assemble and treat the wood pieces, then stain or varnish the piece of assembled furniture. Finally, the completed piece of

> **Operations management (OM)** the development and administration of the activities involved in transforming resources into goods and services

> **Manufacturing** the activities and processes used in making tangible products; also called production
>
> **Production** the activities and processes used in making tangible products; also called manufacturing
>
> **Operations** the activities and processes used in making both tangible and intangible products
>
> **Inputs** the resources—such as labour, money, materials, and energy—that are converted into outputs
>
> **Outputs** the goods, services, and ideas that result from the conversion of inputs

figure 8.1 The Transformation Process of Operations Management

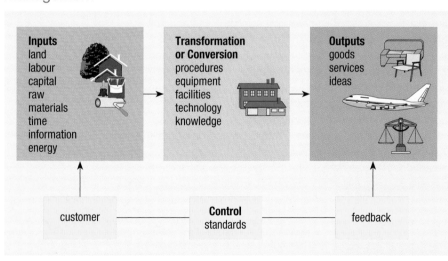

Inputs
land
labour
capital
raw
materials
time
information
energy

Transformation or Conversion
procedures
equipment
facilities
technology
knowledge

Outputs
goods
services
ideas

customer — **Control** standards — feedback

figure 8.2 Inputs, Outputs, and Transformation Processes in the Manufacture of Oak Furniture

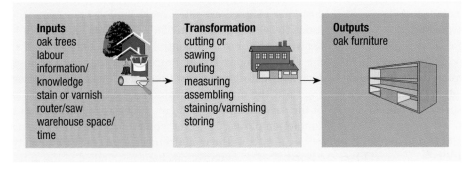

Inputs
oak trees
labour
information/
knowledge
stain or varnish
router/saw
warehouse space/
time

Transformation
cutting or
sawing
routing
measuring
assembling
staining/varnishing
storing

Outputs
oak furniture

furniture is stored until it can be shipped to customers at the appropriate time. Of course, many businesses choose to eliminate some of these stages by purchasing already processed materials—lumber, for example—or outsourcing some tasks to third-party firms with greater expertise.

LO2 Explain how operations management differs in manufacturing and service firms.

Operations Management in Service Businesses

Different types of transformation processes take place in organizations that provide services, such as airlines, universities or colleges, and most nonprofit organizations. An airline transforms inputs such as employees, time, money, and equipment through processes such as booking flights, flying airplanes, maintaining equipment, and training crews. The output of these processes is flying passengers and/or packages to their destinations. In a nonprofit organization like Habitat for Humanity, inputs such as money, materials, information, and volunteer time and labour are used to transform raw materials into homes for needy families. In this setting, transformation processes include fundraising and promoting the cause in order to gain new volunteers and donations of supplies, as well as pouring concrete, raising walls, and setting roofs. Transformation processes occur in all organizations, regardless of their products or their objectives. For most organizations, the ultimate objective is for the produced outputs to be worth more than the combined costs of the inputs.

Unlike tangible goods, services are effectively actions or performances that must be directed toward the consumers who use them. Thus, there is a significant customer-contact component to most services. Examples of high-contact services include health care, real estate, tax preparation, and food service. Low-contact services, such as online auction services like eBay, often have a strong high-tech component. The service sector represents approximately 78 percent of all employment in Canada.[1]

Regardless of the level of customer contact, service businesses strive to provide a standardized process, and technology offers an interface that creates an automatic and structured response. The ideal service provider will be high-tech and high-touch. WestJet, for example, strives to maintain an excellent website; friendly, helpful customer contact; and live satellite TV service at every seat onboard most of the Boeing Next-Generation 737 aircraft. Thus, service organizations must build their operations around good execution, which comes from hiring and training excellent employees, developing flexible systems, customizing services, and maintaining adjustable capacity to deal with fluctuating demand.[2]

Another challenge related to service operations is that the output is generally intangible and even perishable. Few services can be saved, stored, resold, or returned.[3] A seat on an airline or a table in a restaurant, for example, cannot be sold or used at a later date. Because of the perishability of services, it can be extremely difficult for service providers to accurately estimate the demand to match the right supply of a service. If an airline overestimates demand, for example, it will still have to fly each plane even with empty seats. The flight costs the same regardless of whether it is 50 percent full or 100 percent full, but the former will result in much higher costs per passenger. If the airline underestimates demand, the result can be long lines of annoyed customers or even the necessity of bumping some customers off of an overbooked flight.

Although service organizations tend to vary depending on the service provider, businesses strive to standardize operations to ensure a high level of quality. The waitstaff at this hotel wear uniforms and are trained to behave a certain way when interacting with customers.

Businesses that manufacture tangible goods and those that provide services or ideas are similar yet different. For example, both types of organizations must make design and operating decisions. Most goods are manufactured prior to purchase, but most services are performed after purchase. Flight attendants at Air Canada, hotel service personnel, and even the Montreal Canadiens hockey team engage in performances that are a part of the total product. Though manufacturers and service providers often perform similar activities, they also differ in several respects. We can classify these differences in five basic ways.

Nature and Consumption of Output.
First, manufacturers and service providers differ in the nature and consumption of their output. For example, the term *manufacturer* implies a firm that makes tangible products. A service provider, on the other hand, produces more intangible outputs such as Canada Post's delivery of priority mail or a business stay in a Hyatt hotel. As mentioned earlier, the very nature of the service provider's product requires a higher degree of customer contact. Moreover, the actual performance of the service typically occurs at the point of consumption. At the Fairmont Royal York, in Toronto, the business traveller may evaluate in-room communications and the restaurant. Automakers, on the other hand, can separate the production of a

> "The actual performance of the service **typically** occurs at the point of consumption."

car from its actual use. Manufacturing, then, can occur in an isolated environment, away from the customer. On the other hand, service providers, because of their need for customer contact, are often more limited than manufacturers in selecting work methods, assigning jobs, scheduling work, and exercising control over operations. At FedEx, the Quality Improvement Process (QIP) includes sayings such as "Do it right the first time," and "Make the first time you do it the only time anyone has to do it." The quality of the service experience is often controlled by a service contact employee. However, some hospitals are studying the manufacturing processes and quality control mechanisms applied in the automotive industry in an effort to improve their service quality. By analyzing work processes to find unnecessary steps to eliminate and by using teams to identify and address problems as soon as they occur, these hospitals are slashing patient waiting times, decreasing inventories of wheelchairs, readying operating rooms sooner, and generally moving patients through their hospital visit more quickly, with fewer errors, and at a lower cost.

Uniformity of Inputs. A second way to classify differences between manufacturers and service providers has to do with the uniformity of inputs. Manufacturers typically have more control over the amount of variability of the

RESPONDING TO BUSINESS CHALLENGES | Volkswagen's Plan to Rebound in America

Volkswagen (VW) has set forth the lofty goal to surpass Toyota and General Motors to become the world's largest automaker. The company has succeeded in becoming a leader in Europe and is now trying to tackle the U.S. market. Unfortunately, VW has not obtained widespread success in the United States since the 1960s. One of its biggest problems has been that it did not build cars suited for the American market. For instance, VW kept the same transmission gearing for car models sold in the United States as those in Germany, even though roads in Germany allow for faster speeds than U.S. highways. This failure at customization led many American automobile owners to perceive VW cars as being of lower quality.

VW now hopes to change all that. In 2011, the company opened a $1 billion plant in Chattanooga, Tennessee, to produce American versions of the Passat and Jetta. To cut costs, VW is building parts locally and utilizing U.S. suppliers. This time, however, VW is attempting to build more toward American tastes. The company is manufacturing cars with more torque, upgraded features,

and roomier interiors. VW's CEO has even travelled to Florida to ensure that the cars will run smoothly in the more tropical climate conditions of the southern states.

Early reviews of these vehicles are mixed. Prices are reduced—making the cars affordable for a wider audience—but reviewers still cite quality issues, particularly in the interior of the Jetta. Both cars, however, measure up well against the competition. Sales have increased globally, but it remains to be seen whether VW's improvements will propel it to top automaker.[4]

DISCUSSION QUESTIONS

1. Why did Volkswagen fail to succeed in the United States?

2. Describe Volkswagen's new U.S. marketing strategy.

3. Do you feel that Volkswagen has a chance to become the top automaker? Why or why not?

resources they use than do service providers. For example, each customer calling Service Canada is likely to require different services due to differing needs, whereas many of the tasks required to manufacture a Ford Focus are the same across each unit of output. Consequently, the products of service organizations tend to be more "customized" than those of their manufacturing counterparts. Consider, for example, a haircut versus a bottle of shampoo. The haircut is much more likely to incorporate your specific desires (customization) than is the bottle of shampoo.

Uniformity of Output. Manufacturers and service providers also differ in the uniformity of their output, the final product. Because of the human element inherent in providing services, each service tends to be performed differently. Not all grocery checkers, for example, wait on customers in the same way. If a barber or stylist performs 15 haircuts in a day, it is unlikely that any two of them will be exactly the same. Consequently, human and technological elements associated with a service can result in a different day-to-day or even hour-to-hour performance of that service. The service experience can even vary at McDonald's or Burger King despite the fact that the two chains employ very similar procedures and processes. Moreover, no two customers are exactly alike in their perception of the service experience. Health care offers another excellent example of this challenge. Every diagnosis, treatment, and surgery varies because every individual is different. In manufacturing, the high degree of automation available allows manufacturers to generate uniform outputs and, thus, the operations are more effective and efficient. For example, we would expect every Movado or Rolex watch to maintain very high standards of quality and performance.

Labour Required. A fourth point of difference is the amount of labour required to produce an output. Service providers are generally more labour-intensive (require more labour) because of the high level of customer contact, perishability of the output (must be consumed immediately), and high degree of variation of inputs and outputs (customization). For example, Adecco provides temporary support personnel. Each temporary worker's performance determines Adecco's product quality. A manufacturer, on the other hand, is likely to be more capital-intensive because of the machinery and technology used in the mass production of highly similar goods. For instance, it would take a considerable investment for Nokia to make a digital phone that has a battery with longer life.

Measurement of Productivity. The final distinction between service providers and manufacturers involves the measurement of productivity for each output produced. For manufacturers, measuring productivity is fairly straightforward because of the tangibility of the output and its high degree of uniformity. For the service provider, variations in demand (e.g., higher demand for air travel in some seasons

Subway's inputs are sandwich components such as bread, tomatoes, and lettuce, while its outputs are customized sandwiches.

than in others), variations in service requirements from job to job, and the intangibility of the product make productivity measurement more difficult. Consider, for example, how much easier it is to measure the productivity of employees involved in the production of Intel computer processors as opposed to serving the needs of CIBC's clients.

It is convenient and simple to think of organizations as being either manufacturers or service providers as in the preceding discussion. In reality, however, most organizations are a combination of the two, with both tangible and intangible qualities embodied in what they produce. For example, Porsche provides customer services such as toll-free hotlines and warranty protection, while banks may sell cheques and other tangible products that complement their primarily intangible product offering. Thus, we consider "products" to include tangible physical goods as well as intangible service offerings. It is the level of tangibility of its principal product that tends to classify a company as either a manufacturer or a service provider. From an OM standpoint, this level of tangibility greatly influences the nature of the company's operational processes and procedures.

Planning and Designing Operations Systems

Before a company can produce any product, it must first decide what it will produce and for what group of customers. It must then determine what processes it will use to make these products as well as the facilities it needs to produce them. These decisions comprise operations planning. Although planning was once the sole realm of the production and operations department, today's successful companies involve all departments within an organization, particularly marketing and research and development, in these decisions.

Planning the Product

Before making any product, a company first must determine what consumers want and then design a product to satisfy that want. Most companies use marketing research (discussed in Chapter 11) to determine the kinds of goods and services to provide and the features they must possess. Twitter and Facebook provide new opportunities for businesses to discover what consumers want, then design the product accordingly. Marketing research can also help gauge the demand for a product and how much consumers are willing to pay for it.

Developing a product can be a lengthy, expensive process. For example, in the automobile industry, developing the new technology for night vision, bumper-mounted sonar systems that make parking easier, and a satellite service that locates and analyzes car problems has been a lengthy, expensive process. Most companies work to reduce development time and costs. For example, through Web collaboration, faucet manufacturer Moen has reduced the time required to take an idea to a finished product in stores to just 16 months, a drop of 33 percent.[5] Once management has developed an idea for a product that customers will buy, it must then plan how to produce the product.

Within a company, the engineering or research and development department is charged with turning a product idea into a workable design that can be produced economically. In smaller companies, a single individual (perhaps the owner) may be solely responsible for this crucial activity. Regardless of who is responsible for product design, planning does not stop with a blueprint for a product or a description of a service; it must also work out efficient production of the product to ensure that enough is available to satisfy consumer demand. How does a lawn mower company transform steel, aluminum, and other materials into a mower design that satisfies consumer and environmental requirements? Operations managers must plan for the types and quantities of materials needed to produce the

product, the skills and quantity of people needed to make the product, and the actual processes through which the inputs must pass in their transformation to outputs.

Designing the Operations Processes

Before a firm can begin production, it must first determine the appropriate method of transforming resources into the desired product. Often, consumers' specific needs and desires dictate a process. Customer needs, for example, require that all 3/4-inch bolts have the same basic thread size, function, and quality; if they did not, engineers and builders could not rely on 3/4-inch bolts in their construction projects. A bolt manufacturer, then, will likely use a standardized process so that every 3/4-inch bolt produced is like every other one. On the other hand, a bridge often must be customized so that it is appropriate for the site and expected load; furthermore, the bridge must be constructed on site rather than in a factory. Typically, products are designed to be manufactured by one of three processes: standardization, modular design, or customization.

Standardization. Most firms that manufacture products in large quantities for many customers have found that they can make them more quickly and at lower cost by standardizing designs. **Standardization** is making identical, interchangeable components or even complete products. With standardization, a customer may not get exactly what he or she wants, but the product generally costs less than a custom-designed product. Television sets, ballpoint pens, and tortilla chips are standardized products; most are manufactured on an assembly line. Standardization speeds up production and quality control and reduces production costs. And, as in the example of the 3/4-inch bolts, standardization provides consistency so that customers who need certain products to function uniformly all the time will get a product that meets their expectations. As a result of its entry into the World Trade Organization, China promoted the standardization of agricultural production across the country, resulting in increased agricultural production.

Modular Design. **Modular design** involves building an item in self-contained units, or modules, that can be combined or interchanged to create different products. Personal computers, for example, are generally composed of a number of components—CPU case, motherboard, RAM chips, hard drives, floppy drives, graphics card, etc.—that can be installed in different configurations to meet the customer's needs. Because many modular components are produced as integrated units, the failure of any portion of a modular component usually means replacing the entire component. Modular design allows products to be repaired quickly, thus reducing the cost of labour, but the component

Standardization the making of identical interchangeable components or products

Modular design the creation of an item in self-contained units, or modules, that can be combined or interchanged to create different products

itself is expensive, raising the cost of repair materials. Many automobile manufacturers use modular design in the production process. Manufactured homes are built on a modular design and often cost about one-fourth the cost of a conventionally built house.

Customization. **Customization** is making products to meet a particular customer's needs or wants. Products produced in this way are generally unique. Such products include repair services, photocopy services, custom artwork, jewellery, and furniture, as well as large-scale products such as bridges, ships, and computer software. Custom designs are used in communications and service products. Ship design is another industry that uses customization. Builders generally design and build each ship to meet the needs of the customer who will use it. Orca Houseboats, for example, custom-builds each houseboat to the customer's exact specifications and preferences for things like fireplaces, hot tubs, spiral staircases, and water slides. The Vancouver-based company has delivered houseboats up to 23 metres long.[7] Mass customization relates to making products that meet the needs or wants of a large number of individual customers. The customer can select the model, size, colour, style, or design of the product. Dell

can customize a computer with the exact configuration that fits a customer's needs. Services such as fitness programs and travel packages can also be custom designed for a large number of individual customers. For both goods and services, customers get to make choices and have options to determine the final product.

Planning Capacity

Planning the operational processes for the organization involves two important areas: capacity planning and facilities planning. The term **capacity** basically refers to the maximum load that an organizational unit can carry or operate. The unit of measurement may be a worker or machine, a department, a branch, or even an entire plant. Maximum capacity can be stated in terms of the inputs or outputs provided. For example, an electric plant might state plant capacity in terms of the maximum number of kilowatt-hours that can be produced without causing a power outage, while a restaurant might state capacity in terms of the maximum number of customers who

Customization making products to meet a particular customer's needs or wants

Capacity the maximum load that an organizational unit can carry or operate

---

ENTREPRENEURSHIP IN ACTION | Roads Less Travelled

Tony and Maureen Wheeler

Business: Lonely Planet

Founded: Early 1970s

Success: A sense of adventure led to Lonely Planet with offices in Melbourne, London, and Oakland, 500 staff members and 300 authors.

Tony and Maureen met on a park bench in London, England, and married a year later. For their honeymoon, they decided to attempt what few people thought possible—crossing Europe and Asia overland, all the way to Australia. It took them several months and all the money they could earn, beg, or borrow, but they made it. It was too amazing an experience to keep to themselves. Urged on by their friends, they stayed up nights at their kitchen table writing, typing, and stapling together their very first travel guide, *Across Asia on the Cheap*. Within a week they had sold 1,500 copies and Lonely Planet was born. They wrote their second book, *South-East Asia on a Shoestring*, in a backstreet hotel in Singapore, which led to books on Nepal, Australia, Africa, and India. Maureen and Tony decided to settle in Australia where

Maureen went to La Trobe University in Melbourne and received a Bachelor's degree in social work. Faced with a choice between her social work and travelling, she chose to make travel her career. Travelling with children became a way of life for the Wheelers after the births of their children. This prompted Maureen to write a guidebook about it, *Travel With Children*, which is the result of years of experience on the road with the kids. As Lonely Planet became a globally loved brand, Tony and Maureen received several offers for the company. But it was not until 2007 that they found a partner whom they trusted to remain true to Lonely Planet's principles. In October of that year, BBC Worldwide acquired a 75 percent share in Lonely Planet, pledging to uphold Lonely Planet's commitment to independent travel, trustworthy advice, and editorial independence. Tony and Maureen are still actively involved with Lonely Planet. They are travelling more often than ever, and they are devoting their spare time to charitable projects. And the company is still driven by the philosophy in *Across Asia on the Cheap*: "All you've got to do is decide to go and the hardest part is over. So go!"[6]

can be effectively—comfortably and courteously—served at any one particular time.

Efficiently planning the organization's capacity needs is an important process for the operations manager. Capacity levels that fall short can result in unmet demand, and consequently, lost customers. On the other hand, when there is more capacity available than needed, operating costs are driven up needlessly due to unused and often expensive resources. To avoid such situations, organizations must accurately forecast demand and then plan capacity based on these forecasts. Another reason for the importance of efficient capacity planning has to do with long-term commitment of resources. Often, once a capacity decision—such as factory size—has been implemented, it is very difficult to change the decision without incurring substantial costs.

Planning Facilities

Once a company knows what process it will use to create its products, it then can design and build an appropriate facility in which to make them. Many products are manufactured in factories, but others are produced in stores, at home, or where the product ultimately will be used. Companies must decide where to locate their operations facilities, what layout is best for producing their particular product, and even what technology to apply to the transformation process.

Many firms are developing both a traditional organization for customer contact and a virtual organization. RBC Financial Group maintains traditional branches and has developed complete telephone and Internet services for customers. Through its website, clients can obtain banking services and trade securities without leaving their home or office.

Facility Location. Where to locate a firm's facilities is a significant question because, once the decision has been made and implemented, the firm must live with it due to the high costs involved. When a company decides to relocate or open a facility at a new location, it must pay careful attention to factors such as proximity to market, availability of raw materials, availability of transportation, availability of power, climatic influences, availability of labour, community characteristics (quality of life), and taxes and inducements. Inducements and tax reductions have become an increasingly important criterion in recent years. When selecting a site for a contact centre to serve customers throughout Canada and the Americas, Dell chose Edmonton for a good quality of life, highly skilled workers, and world-class training programs. eBay chose to locate its new customer-support centre in Burnaby, B.C., out of 100 other communities who were vying for the centre, because of the combination of the educated workforce, quality of life, and easy access to eBay's headquarters in San Jose, California.[9] The facility-location decision is complex because it involves the evaluation of many factors, some of which cannot be measured with precision. Because of the long-term impact of the decision, however, it is one that cannot be taken lightly.

Apple stores are designed to make the most efficient use of space. The layout of the stores allows customers to test Apple's products before purchasing.

Facility Layout. Arranging the physical layout of a facility is a complex, highly technical task. Some industrial architects specialize in the design and layout of certain types of businesses. There are three basic layouts: fixed-position, process, and product.

A company using a **fixed-position layout** brings all resources required to create the product to a central location. The product—perhaps an office building, house, hydro-electric plant, or bridge—does not move. A company using a fixed-position layout may be called a **project organization** because it is typically involved in large, complex projects such as construction or exploration. Project organizations generally make a unique product, rely on highly skilled labour, produce very few units, and have high production costs per unit.

Firms that use a **process layout** organize the transformation process into departments that group related processes. A metal fabrication plant, for example, may have a cutting department, a drilling department, and a polishing department. A hospital may have an X-ray unit, an obstetrics unit, and so on. These types of organizations are sometimes called **intermittent organizations,** which deal with products of a lesser magnitude than do project organizations, and their products are not necessarily unique but possess a significant number of differences. Doctors, makers of custom-made cabinets, commercial printers, and advertising agencies are intermittent organizations because

Fixed-position layout a layout that brings all resources required to create the product to a central location

Project organization a company using a fixed-position layout because it is typically involved in large, complex projects such as construction or exploration

Process layout a layout that organizes the transformation process into departments that group related processes

Intermittent organizations organizations that deal with products of a lesser magnitude than do project organizations; their products are not necessarily unique but possess a significant number of differences

they tend to create products to customers' specifications and produce relatively few units of each product. Because of the low level of output, the cost per unit of product is generally high.

The **product layout** requires that production be broken down into relatively simple tasks assigned to workers, who are usually positioned along an assembly line. Workers remain in one location, and the product moves from one worker to another. Each person in turn performs his or her required tasks or activities. Companies that use assembly lines are usually known as **continuous manufacturing organizations,** so named because once they are set up, they run continuously, creating products with many similar characteristics. Examples of products produced on assembly lines are automobiles, television sets, vacuum cleaners, toothpaste, and meals from a cafeteria. Continuous manufacturing organizations using a product layout are characterized by the standardized product they produce, the large number of units produced, and the relatively low unit cost of production.

Many companies actually use a combination of layout designs. For example, an automobile manufacturer may rely on an assembly line (product layout) but may also use a process layout to manufacture parts.

Technology. Every industry has a basic, underlying technology that dictates the nature of its transformation process. The steel industry continually tries to improve steelmaking techniques. The health care industry performs research into medical technologies and pharmaceuticals to improve the quality of health care service. Two developments that have strongly influenced the operations of many businesses are computers and robotics.

Computers have been used for decades and on a relatively large scale since IBM introduced its 650 series in the late 1950s. The operations function makes great use of computers in all phases of the transformation process. **Computer-assisted design (CAD),** for example, helps engineers design components, products, and processes on the computer instead of on paper. **Computer-assisted manufacturing (CAM)** goes a step further, employing specialized computer systems

"Every industry has a basic, underlying technology that dictates the nature of its transformation process."

to actually guide and control the transformation processes. Such systems can monitor the transformation process, gathering information about the equipment used to produce the products and about the product itself as it goes from one stage of the transformation process to the next. The computer provides information to an operator who may, if necessary, take corrective action. In some highly automated systems, the computer itself can take corrective action. At Dell's OptiPlex Plant, electronic instructions are sent to double-decker conveyor belts that speed computer components to assembly stations. Two-member teams are told by computers which PC or server to build, with initial assembly taking only three to four minutes. Then more electronic commands move the products (more than 20,000 machines on a typical day) to a finishing area to be customized, boxed, and sent to waiting delivery trucks. Although the plant covers over 18,500 square metres, enough to enclose 23 football fields, it is managed almost entirely by a network of computers.[10]

Using **flexible manufacturing,** computers can direct machinery to adapt to different versions of similar operations. For example, with instructions from a computer, one machine can be programmed to carry out its function for several different versions of an engine without shutting down the production line for refitting.

Robots are also becoming increasingly useful in the transformation process. These "steel-collar" workers have become particularly important in industries

such as nuclear power, hazardous-waste disposal, ocean research, and space construction and maintenance, in which human lives would otherwise be at risk. Robots are used in numerous applications by companies around the world. Many assembly operations—cars, television sets, telephones, stereo equipment, and numerous other products—depend on industrial robots. Researchers continue to create more sophisticated robots, and some speculate that in the future robots will not be limited to space programs and production and operations, but will also be able to engage in farming, laboratory research, and even household activities. Moreover, robotics is increasingly being used in the medical field. Voice-activated robotic arms operate video cameras for surgeons. Similar technology assists with biopsies, as well as heart, spine, and nervous system procedures. A heart surgeon at London Health Science Centre in Ontario uses a surgical robot to perform bypass operations on patients without opening their chests, except for five tiny incisions, while their hearts continue beating. More than 400 surgeons around the world currently use surgical robots with far fewer postoperative complications than encountered in conventional operations.[11] There are an estimated 1 million robots being used in manufacturing around the world, most of them in high-tech industries.

When all these technologies—CAD/CAM, flexible manufacturing, robotics, computer systems, and more—are

The outdoor clothing company Patagonia is always looking for a greener way to design, produce, and recycle its products. The company's mission statement: Build the best product, cause no unnecessary harm, and use business to inspire and implement solutions to the environmental crisis.

Computer-integrated manufacturing (CIM) a complete system that designs products, manages machines and materials, and controls the operations function

integrated, the result is **computer-integrated manufacturing (CIM),** a complete system that designs products, manages machines and materials, and controls the operations function. Companies adopt CIM to boost productivity and quality and reduce costs. Such technology, and computers in particular, will continue to make strong inroads into operations on two fronts—dealing with the technology involved in manufacturing, and dealing with the administrative functions and processes used by operations managers. The operations manager must be willing to work with computers and other forms of technology and to develop a high degree of computer literacy.

Sustainability and Manufacturing

Manufacturing and operations systems are moving quickly to establish environmental sustainability and minimize negative impact on the natural environment. Sustainability deals with reducing the consumption of resources and the long-term well-being of the planet, including natural entities and the interactions of individuals, organizations, and businesses. Sustainability issues are becoming increasingly important to stakeholders and consumers, as they pertain to the future health of the planet. Some sustainability issues include pollution of the land, air, and water, climate change, waste management, deforestation, urban sprawl, protection of biodiversity, and genetically modified foods.

For example, Walmart is working to make its stores and products more environmentally friendly. Walmart has created a series of broad environmental goals, striving to eventually create zero waste, to run entirely on renewable energy, and to sell sustainable products. The company works with suppliers to reduce cardboard and plastic packaging. Walmart already increased the efficiency of its truck fleet by 38 percent and intends to double its efficiency by October 2015. Walmart is also changing its lighting and

other electrical use for maximum efficiency. All of these initiatives relate to making operations greener, contributing to environmental sustainability, providing savings, and being a role model for other businesses.[12]

Walmart and other companies demonstrate that reducing waste, recycling, conserving, and using renewable energy not only protect the environment, but can also gain the support of stakeholders. Green operations and manufacturing can improve a firm's reputation along with customer and employee loyalty, leading to improved profits.

Much of the movement to green manufacturing and operations is the belief that global warming and climate change must decline. The McKinsey Global Institute (MGI) says that just by investing in existing technologies, the world's energy use could be reduced by 50 percent by the year 2020. Just creating green buildings and higher mileage cars could yield $900 billion in savings per year by 2020.[13] Companies like General Motors are adapting to stakeholder demands for greater sustainability by producing smaller and more fuel-efficient cars. For example, the Chevy Volt can run for up to 65 kilometres on one overnight charge before switching to a gas-powered generator. The Volt is also a FlexFuel vehicle, which means that it can use either traditional gasoline or E85 ethanol, which some people believe to be better for the environment.[14] Green products produced through green operations and manufacturing are our future. A report authored by the Center for American Progress cites ways that cities and local governments can play a role. For example, Los Angeles plans to save the city utility costs by retrofitting hundreds of city buildings while creating a green careers training program for low-income residents. Newark, New Jersey, and Richmond, California, also have green jobs training programs. Albuquerque, New Mexico, was the first city to sign on to a pledge to build a green economy as part of its efforts to create green jobs to stimulate the city's economy.[15] Government initiatives provide space for businesses to innovate their green operations and manufacturing.

LO4 Specify some techniques managers may use to manage the logistics of transforming inputs into finished products.

Managing the Supply Chain

A major function of operations is **supply chain management,** which refers to connecting and integrating all parties or members of the distribution system to satisfy customers.[16] Also called logistics, supply chain management includes all the activities involved in obtaining and managing raw materials and component parts, managing finished products, packaging them, and getting them to customers. Sunny Delight had to quickly re-create its supply

Supply chain management connecting and integrating all parties or members of the distribution system in order to satisfy customers

chain after spinning off from Procter & Gamble. This means it had to develop ordering, shipping, billing, and warehouse management systems as well as transportation, so it could focus on growing and managing the Sunny Delight brand.[17] The supply chain integrates firms such as raw material suppliers, manufacturers, retailers, and ultimate consumers into a seamless flow of information and products.[18] Some aspects of logistics (warehousing, packaging, distributing) are so closely linked with marketing that we will discuss them in Chapter 12. In this section, we look at purchasing, managing inventory, outsourcing, and scheduling, which are vital tasks in the transformation of raw materials into finished goods. To illustrate logistics, consider a hypothetical small business—we'll call it Rushing Water Canoes Inc.—that manufactures aluminum canoes, which it sells primarily to sporting goods stores and river-rafting expeditions. Our company also makes paddles and helmets, but the focus of the following discussion is the manufacture of the company's quality canoes as they proceed through the logistics process.

Purchasing

Purchasing, also known as procurement, is the buying of all the materials needed by the organization. The purchasing department aims to obtain items of the desired quality in the right quantities at the lowest possible cost. Rushing Water Canoes, for example, must procure not only aluminum and other raw materials, and various canoe parts and components, but also machines and equipment, manufacturing supplies (oil, electricity, and so on), and office supplies to make its canoes. People in the purchasing department locate and evaluate suppliers of these items. They must constantly be on the lookout for new materials or parts that will do a better job or cost less than those currently being used. The purchasing function can be quite complex and is one area made much easier and more efficient by technological advances.

> **Purchasing** the buying of all the materials needed by the organization; also called procurement

Not all companies purchase all the materials needed to create their products. Oftentimes, they can make some components more economically and efficiently than can an outside supplier. Coors, for example, manufactures its own cans at a subsidiary plant. On the other hand, firms sometimes find that it is uneconomical to make or purchase an item, and instead arrange to lease it from another organization. Some airlines, for example, lease airplanes rather than

> "A major function of operations is supply chain management, which refers to connecting and integrating all parties or members of the distribution system in order to satisfy customers."

buy them. Whether to purchase, make, or lease a needed item generally depends on cost, as well as on product availability and supplier reliability.

Managing Inventory

Once the items needed to create a product have been procured, some provision has to be made for storing them until they are needed. Every raw material, component, completed or partially completed product, and piece of equipment a firm uses—its **inventory**—must be accounted for, or controlled. There are three basic types of inventory. *Finished-goods inventory* includes those products that are ready for sale, such as a fully assembled automobile ready to ship to a dealer. *Work-in-process inventory* consists of those products that are partly completed or are in some stage of the transformation process. At McDonald's, a cooking hamburger represents work-in-process inventory because it must go through several more stages before it can be sold to a customer. *Raw materials inventory* includes all the materials that have been

> **Inventory** all raw materials, components, completed or partially completed products, and pieces of equipment a firm uses

When you think about UPS, you usually think of the brown trucks with the drivers in brown uniforms who deliver packages around the world. In this ad, UPS promotes its "Supply Chain Solutions," its ability to solve logistics and distribution issues for companies, synchronizing "the movement of goods, information, and funds."

purchased to be used as inputs for making other products. Nuts and bolts are raw materials for an automobile manufacturer, while hamburger patties, vegetables, and buns are raw materials for the fast-food restaurant. Our fictional Rushing Water Canoes has an inventory of materials for making canoes, paddles, and helmets, as well as its inventory of finished products for sale to consumers. **Inventory control** is the process of determining how many supplies and goods are needed and keeping track of quantities on hand, where each item is, and who is responsible for it.

Operations management must be closely coordinated with inventory control. The production of televisions, for example, cannot be planned without some knowledge of the availability of all the necessary materials—the chassis, picture tubes, colour guns, and so forth. Also, each item held in inventory—any type of inventory—carries with it a cost. For example, storing fully assembled televisions in a warehouse to sell to a dealer at a future date requires not only the use of space, but also the purchase of insurance to cover any losses that might occur due to fire or other unforeseen events.

Managing inventory involves finding the right balance between excess inventory and not enough inventory. While too much inventory will increase storage costs, companies that have an inventory shortage miss out on additional sales.

Inventory managers spend a great deal of time trying to determine the proper inventory level for each item. The answer to the question of how many units to hold in inventory depends on variables such as the usage rate of the item, the cost of maintaining the item in inventory, the cost of paperwork and other procedures associated with ordering or making the item, and the cost of the item itself. For example, the price of copper has fluctuated between $1.50 and $4 per pound over the last five years. Firms using copper wiring for construction or copper pipes for plumbing, and other industries requiring copper, have to analyze the trade-offs between inventory costs and expected changes in the price of copper. Several approaches may be used to determine how many units of a given item should be procured at one time and when that procurement should take place.

The Economic Order Quantity Model.

To control the number of items maintained in inventory, managers need to determine how much of any given item they should order. One popular approach is the **economic order quantity (EOQ) model,** which identifies the optimum number of items to order to minimize the costs of managing (ordering, storing, and using) them.

Just-In-Time Inventory Management.

An increasingly popular technique is **just-in-time (JIT) inventory management,** which eliminates waste by using smaller quantities of materials that arrive "just in time" for use in the transformation process and therefore require less storage space and other inventory management expense. JIT minimizes inventory by providing an almost continuous flow of items from suppliers to the production facility. While first used by Toyota, many companies now, including IBM, Hewlett-Packard, and Harley-Davidson, have adopted JIT to reduce costs and boost efficiency.

Let's say that Rushing Water Canoes uses 20 units of aluminum from a supplier per day. Traditionally, its inventory manager might order enough for one month at a time: 440 units per order (20 units per day times 22 workdays per month). The expense of such a large inventory could be considerable because of the cost of insurance coverage, recordkeeping, rented storage space, and so on. The just-in-time approach would reduce these costs because aluminum would be purchased in smaller quantities, perhaps in lot sizes of 20, which the supplier would deliver once a day. Of course, for such an approach to be effective, the supplier must be extremely reliable and relatively close to the production facility.

Material-Requirements Planning.

Another inventory management technique is **material-requirements planning (MRP),** a planning system that schedules the precise quantity of materials needed to make the product. The basic components of MRP are a master production schedule, a bill of materials, and an inventory status file. At Rushing Water Canoes, for example, the inventory-control manager will look at the production schedule to determine how many canoes the company plans to make. He or she will then prepare a bill of materials—a list of all the materials needed to make that quantity of canoes. Next, the manager will determine the quantity of these items that RWC already holds in inventory (to avoid ordering excess materials) and then develop a schedule for ordering and accepting delivery

---

Inventory control the process of determining how many supplies and goods are needed and keeping track of quantities on hand, where each item is, and who is responsible for it

Economic order quantity (EOQ) model a model that identifies the optimum number of items to order to minimize the costs of managing (ordering, storing, and using) them

Just-in-time (JIT) inventory management a technique using smaller quantities of materials that arrive "just in time" for use in the transformation process and therefore require less storage space and other inventory management expense

Material-requirements planning (MRP) a planning system that schedules the precise quantity of materials needed to make the product

UPS is doing more with less. In 2010, the company increased its package volume by 1.8 percent. Normally, such an increase requires more resources, but not so at UPS; the company actually reduced its fuel consumption by 3.3 percent for each package. It also decreased its absolute water consumption in the United States by 11 percent. UPS hired Scott Wicker to be its corporate sustainability officer (CSO) to oversee its initiatives and embed sustainability into its operations. According to Wicker, "Sustainability means we operate not only for the present, but for the future as well."

How has UPS been able to increase its productivity and sustainability at the same time? UPS uses technology and data measurements to calculate the resources it consumes and determine ways to be more efficient. For instance, the company has been investing in more fuel-efficient vehicles for years. Additionally, UPS has made slight changes in operations, such as reducing the number of stops and only making right turns to decrease driving time and save fuel. Although these methods may not seem like much, UPS was able to cut more than 11.5 million litres of fuel and 68,000 tonnes of emissions from its logistics operations. The company is also targeting eco-minded consumers with services such as a carbon neutral service for U.S. deliveries. UPS is creating a competitive advantage by becoming expert at incorporating green practices into all facets of its operations.[21]

DISCUSSION QUESTIONS

1. How is UPS using sustainability to cut costs?

2. Which stakeholders have the ability to benefit from UPS's green practices?

3. How can UPS's green practices act as a model for other companies to improve their operations?

of the right quantity of materials to satisfy the firm's needs. Because of the large number of parts and materials that go into a typical production process, MRP must be done on a computer. It can be, and often is, used in conjunction with just-in-time inventory management.

Outsourcing

Increasingly, outsourcing has become a component of supply chain management in operations. As we mentioned in Chapter 3, outsourcing refers to the contracting of manufacturing or other tasks to independent companies, often overseas. Many companies elect to outsource some aspects of their operations to companies that can provide these products more efficiently, at a lower cost, and with greater customer satisfaction. Many high-tech firms have outsourced the production of memory chips, computers, and telecom equipment to Asian companies.[19] The hourly labour costs in countries such as China, India, and Vietnam are far less than in Canada, Europe, or even Mexico. These developing countries have improved their manufacturing capabilities, infrastructure, and technical and business skills, making them more attractive regions for global sourcing. On the other hand, the cost of outsourcing halfway around the world must be considered in decisions.[20] While information technology is often outsourced today, transportation, human resources, services, and even marketing functions can be outsourced. Our hypothetical Rushing Water Canoes might contract with a local janitorial service to clean its offices and with a local accountant to handle routine bookkeeping and tax-preparation functions.

Outsourcing, once used primarily as a cost-cutting tactic, has increasingly been linked with the development of competitive advantage through improved product quality, speeding up the time it takes products to get to the customer, and overall supply-chain efficiencies. Table 8.1

table 8.1 The World's Top Five Outsourcing Providers

Company	Services*
Accenture	Human resource management; information and communication technology management; financial management
Infosys Technologies	Information technology consulting; product engineering; software development; IT solutions
Sodexo	Real estate and asset management; facility services; service vouchers and cards
Wipro Technologies	Information technology management; business and process solutions
IBM	Customer relationship management; human resource management; information technology; strategic consulting

*The services section was provided by the authors.

SOURCES: "IAOP Announces 2010 Rankings for The World's Best Outsourcing Providers and Advisors," International Association of Outsourcing Professionals, https://www.iaop.org/content/23/196/2043/, (accessed January 12, 2011); "About Us," Infosys, www.infosys.com/about/what-we-do/pages/index.aspx (accessed January 12, 2011).

> "Many executives view outsourcing as an innovative way to boost productivity and remain competitive against low-wage offshore factories."

provides the world's top five outsourcing providers that assist mainly in information technology. Outsourcing allows companies to free up time and resources to focus on what they do best and to create better opportunities to focus on customer satisfaction. Many executives view outsourcing as an innovative way to boost productivity and remain competitive against low-wage offshore factories. However, outsourcing may create conflict with labour and negative public opinion when it results in North American workers being replaced by lower-cost workers in other countries.

Many athletic shoe manufacturers such as Nike outsource production to China and Vietnam to take advantage of lower labour costs.

Routing and Scheduling

After all materials have been procured and their use determined, managers must then consider the **routing,** or sequence of operations through which the product must pass. For example, before employees at Rushing Water Canoes can form aluminum sheets into a canoe, the aluminum must be cut to size. Likewise, the canoe's flotation material must be installed before workers can secure the wooden seats. The sequence depends on the product specifications developed by the engineering department of the company.

Once management knows the routing, the actual work

> **Routing** the sequence of operations through which the product must pass
>
> **Scheduling** the assignment of required tasks to departments or even specific machines, workers, or teams

can be scheduled. **Scheduling** assigns the tasks to be done to departments or even specific machines, workers, or teams. At Rushing Water, cutting aluminum for the company's canoes might be scheduled to be done by the "cutting and finishing" department on machines designed especially for that purpose.

Many approaches to scheduling have been developed, ranging from simple trial and error to highly sophisticated computer programs. One popular method is the *Program Evaluation and Review Technique (PERT),* which identifies all the major activities or events required to complete a project, arranges them in a sequence or path, determines the critical path, and estimates the time required for each event. Producing a McDonald's Big Mac, for example, involves removing meat, cheese, sauce, and vegetables from the refrigerator; grilling the hamburger patties; assembling

figure 8.3 A Hypothetical PERT Diagram for a McDonald's Big Mac

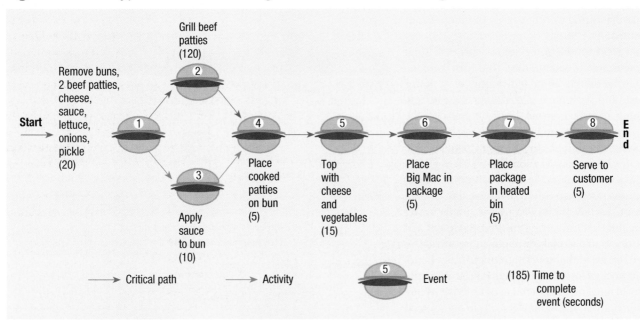

the ingredients; placing the completed Big Mac in its package; and serving it to the customer (Figure 8.3). The cheese, pickles, onions, and sauce cannot be put on before the hamburger patty is completely grilled and placed on the bun. The path that requires the longest time from start to finish is called the *critical path* because it determines the minimum amount of time in which the process can be completed. If any of the activities on the critical path for production of the Big Mac fall behind schedule, the sandwich will not be completed on time, causing customers to wait longer than they usually would.

| LO5 | Assess the importance of quality in operations management. |

Managing Quality

Quality, like cost and efficiency, is a critical element of operations management, for defective products can quickly ruin a firm. Quality reflects the degree to which a good or service meets the demands and requirements of customers. Customers are increasingly dissatisfied with the quality of service provided by many airlines. There are thousands of air travel complaints every year. Determining quality can be difficult because it depends on customers' perceptions of how well the product meets or exceeds their expectations. For example, customer satisfaction on airlines can vary wildly depending on individual customers' perspectives. However, the airline industry is notorious for its dissatisfied customers. Flight delays are a common subject of complaints from airline passengers; 20 percent of all flights arrive more than 15 minutes late. However, most passengers do not select an airline based on how often flights arrive on time.[22]

The fuel economy of an automobile or its reliability (defined in terms of frequency of repairs) can be measured with some degree of precision. Although automakers rely on their own measures of vehicle quality, they also look to independent sources such as the J. D. Power & Associates annual initial quality survey for confirmation of their quality assessment as well as consumer perceptions of quality, as indicated in Figure 8.4. No one was surprised when J. D. Power dropped Toyota from 6th place in 2009 to 21st in 2010. The Initial Quality Study tracks complaints during the first 90 days that a consumer owned the car. Toyota's sudden-acceleration crisis—which forced the once-heralded carmaker to recall more than 8 million vehicles over the past year—resulted in its worst-ever performance in the survey. Consumers complained in the survey about brake and floormat problems, which is what the recalls were mostly about. In 2009, Toyota brand vehicles had 101 problems per 100 vehicles. In 2010, it rose to 117, no big surprise given the massive number of cars recalled.[23] However, it is more difficult to measure psychological characteristics such as design, colour, or status.

It is especially difficult to measure these characteristics when the product is a service. A company has to decide exactly which quality characteristics it considers important and then define those characteristics in terms that can be measured.

The Malcolm Baldrige National Quality Award is given each year to companies that meet rigorous standards of quality. The Baldrige criteria are (1) leadership, (2) information and analysis, (3) strategic planning, (4) human resource development and management, (5) process management, (6) business results, and (7) customer focus and satisfaction. The criteria have become a worldwide framework for driving business improvement.

Quality is so important that we need to examine it in the context of operations management. **Quality control** refers to the processes an organization uses to maintain its established quality standards. Best Buy's Geek Squad helps reduce returns of PCs by 40 percent when they deliver and set up a computer. This demonstrates that measuring perceived quality relates to more than just technical defects of a product, but also to other characteristics.[24] Quality has become a major concern in many organizations, particularly in light of intense foreign competition and increasingly demanding customers. To regain a competitive edge, a number of firms have adopted a total quality management approach. **Total quality management (TQM)** is a philosophy that uniform commitment to quality in all areas of the organization will promote a culture that meets customers' perceptions of quality. It involves coordinating efforts to improve customer satisfaction, increase employee participation and empowerment, form and strengthen supplier partnerships, and foster an organizational culture of continuous quality improvement. TQM requires continuous quality improvement and employee empowerment.

> **Quality control** the processes an organization uses to maintain its established quality standards
>
> **Total quality management (TQM)** a philosophy that uniform commitment to quality in all areas of an organization will promote a culture that meets customers' perceptions of quality

Continuous improvement of an organization's goods and services is built around the notion that quality is free; by contrast, *not* having high-quality goods and services can be very expensive, especially in terms of dissatisfied customers.[25] A primary tool of the continuous improvement process is *benchmarking*, the measuring and evaluating of the quality of the organization's goods, services, or processes as compared with the quality produced by the best-performing companies in the industry.[26] Benchmarking lets the organization know where it stands competitively in its industry, thus giving it a goal to aim for over time. Now that online digital media are becoming more important in businesses, companies such as Compuware Gomez offer benchmarking tools so companies can monitor and compare the success of their websites. Such tools allow companies to track traffic to the site

figure 8.4 J. D. Power & Associates Initial Automobile Quality Study

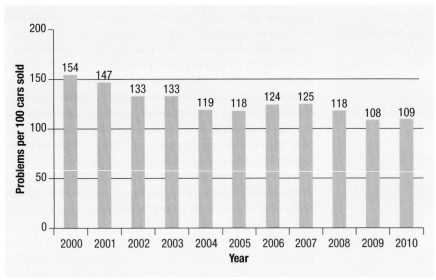

SOURCES: J.D. Power and Associates 2009 Initial Quality Study, http://businesscenter.jdpower.com/news/pressrelease.aspx?ID=2009108 (accessed February 16, 2010); J.D. Power and Associates 2010 Initial Quality Study, June 17, 2010, http://businesscenter.jdpower.com/news/pressrelease.aspx?ID=2010099 (accessed January 12, 2011).

versus competitors' sites. Studies have shown a direct link between website performance and online sales, meaning this type of benchmarking is important.[27]

Companies employing total quality management (TQM) programs know that quality control should be incorporated throughout the transformation process, from the initial plans to develop a specific product through the product and production facility design processes to the actual manufacture of the product. In other words, they view quality control as an element of the product itself, rather than as simply a function of the operations process. When a company makes the product correctly from the outset, it eliminates the need to rework defective products, expedites the transformation process itself, and allows employees to make better use of their time and materials. One method through which many companies have tried to improve quality is **statistical process control,** a system in which management collects and analyzes information about the production process to pinpoint quality problems in the production system.

Establishing Standards— ISO 9000

Regardless of whether a company has a TQM program for quality control, it must first determine what standard of quality it desires and then assess whether its products meet that standard. Product specifications and quality standards must be set so the company can create a product that will compete in the marketplace. Rushing Water Canoes, for example, may specify that each of its canoes has aluminum walls of a specified uniform thickness, that the front and back of each canoe be reinforced with a specified level of steel, and that each canoe contain a specified amount of flotation material for safety. Production facilities must be designed that can build products with the desired specifications.

Quality standards can be incorporated into service businesses as well. A hamburger chain, for example, may establish standards relating to how long it takes to cook an order and serve it to customers, how many fries are in each order, how thick the burgers are, or how many customer complaints might be acceptable. Once the desired quality characteristics, specifications, and standards have been stated

> **Statistical process control** a system in which management collects and analyzes information about the production process to pinpoint quality problems in the production system

Consider the Following: Stella & Chewy's: The Food Dogs Love

After being told that her dog Chewy was deathly ill, Marie Moody's only chance of saving him was to change his diet. She began purchasing organic meat and vegetables to create her own dog food. Almost immediately, Chewy's health improved. Moody began feeding her other dog, Stella, the same mixture and noticed positive results in her as well. Stella & Chewy's dog food, consisting of fresh meats and organic produce, was born.

Moody began in her apartment kitchen and later expanded manufacturing. She developed partnerships with organic and antibiotic-free meat producers and hired animal scientists to help create technology to keep the food pathogen-free. Today, Stella & Chewy's uses hydrostatic high pressure to pasteurize without removing nutrients and taste. The company has a third party test each batch of food. Maintaining quality is critical to a raw food diet and for building a product that consumers trust. Stella & Chewy's has flourished, becoming the dog food of choice for many pet lovers.[28]

in measurable terms, the next step is inspection.

The International Organization for Standardization (ISO) has created a series of quality management standards—**ISO 9000**—designed to ensure the customer's quality standards are met. The standards provide a framework for documenting how a certified business keeps records, trains employees, tests products, and fixes defects. To obtain ISO 9000 certification, an independent auditor must verify that a business's factory, laboratory, or office meets the quality standards spelled out by the International Organization for Standardization. The certification process can require significant investment, but for many companies, the process is essential to being able to compete. Thousands of North American firms have been certified, and many more are working to meet the standards. Certification has become a virtual necessity for doing business in Europe in some high-technology businesses. ISO 9002 certification was established for service providers.

ISO 14000 is a comprehensive set of environmental standards that encourages a cleaner and safer world. ISO 14000 is a valuable standard because, currently, considerable variation exists between the regulations in different nations, and even regions within a nation. These variations make it difficult for organizations committed to sustainability to find acceptable global solutions to problems. The goal of the ISO 14000 standards is to promote a more uniform approach to environmental management and to help companies attain and measure improvements in their environmental performance.

Inspection

Inspection reveals whether a product meets quality standards. Some product characteristics may be discerned by fairly simple inspection techniques—weighing the contents of cereal boxes or measuring the time it takes for a customer to receive a hamburger. As part of the ongoing quality assurance program at Hershey Foods, all wrapped Hershey Kisses are checked, and all imperfectly wrapped kisses are rejected.[29] Other inspection techniques are more elaborate. Automobile manufacturers use automated machines to open and close car doors to test the durability of latches and hinges. The food-processing and pharmaceutical industries use various chemical tests to determine the quality of their output. Rushing Water Canoes might use a special device that can precisely measure the thickness of each canoe wall to ensure that it meets the company's specifications.

Organizations normally inspect purchased items, work-in-process, and finished items. The inspection of purchased items and finished items takes place after the fact; the inspection of work-in-process is preventive. In other words, the purpose of inspection of purchased items and finished items is to determine what the quality level is. For items that are being worked on—an automobile moving down the assembly line or a canoe being assembled—the purpose of the inspection is to find defects before the product is completed so that necessary corrections can be made.

Sampling

An important question relating to inspection is how many items should be inspected. Should all canoes produced by Rushing Water be inspected or just some of them? Whether to inspect 100 percent of the output or only part of it is related to the cost of the inspection process, the destructiveness of the inspection process (some tests last until the product fails), and the potential cost of product flaws in terms of human lives and safety.

Some inspection procedures are quite expensive, use elaborate testing equipment, destroy products, and/or require a significant number of hours to complete. In such cases, it is usually desirable to test only a sample of the output. If the sample passes inspection, the inspector may assume that all the items in the lot from which the sample was drawn would also pass inspection. By using principles of statistical inference, management can employ sampling techniques that assure a relatively high probability of reaching the right conclusion—that is, rejecting a lot that does not meet standards and accepting a lot that does. Nevertheless, there will always be a risk of making an incorrect conclusion—accepting a population that *does not* meet standards (because the sample was satisfactory) or rejecting a population that *does* meet standards (because the sample contained too many defective items).

The ISO 9000 standards are international standards that relate to quality management. ISO 14000 standards relate to environmental management—managing businesses to minimize harmful effects to the environment.

Sampling is likely to be used when inspection tests are destructive. Determining the life expectancy of light-bulbs by turning them on and recording how long they last would be foolish: There is no market for burned-out light-bulbs. Instead, a generalization based on the quality of a sample would be applied to the entire population of light-bulbs from which the sample was drawn. However, human life and safety often depend on the proper functioning of specific items, such as the navigational systems installed in commercial airliners. For such items, even though the inspection process is costly, the potential cost of flawed systems—in human lives and safety—is too great not to inspect 100 percent of the output.

TEAM EXERCISE

Form groups and assign the responsibility of finding companies that outsource their production to other countries. What are the key advantages of this outsourcing decision? Do you see any drawbacks or weaknesses in this approach? Why would a company not outsource when such a tactic can be undertaken to cut manufacturing costs? Report your findings to the class.

LEARNING OBJECTIVES SUMMARY

LO1 Define operations management and differentiate between operations and manufacturing.

Operations management (OM) is the development and administration of the activities involved in transforming resources into goods and services. Operations managers oversee the transformation process and the planning and designing of operations systems, managing logistics, quality, and productivity. The terms *manufacturing* and *production* are used interchangeably to describe the activities and processes used in making tangible products, whereas *operations* is a broader term used to describe the process of making both tangible and intangible products.

LO2 Explain how operations management differs in manufacturing and service firms.

Manufacturers and service firms both transform inputs into outputs, but service providers differ from manufacturers in several ways: They have greater customer contact because the service typically occurs at the point of consumption; their inputs and outputs are more variable than manufacturers', largely because of the human element; service providers are generally more labour intensive; and their productivity measurement is more complex.

LO3 Describe the elements involved in planning and designing an operations system.

Operations planning relates to decisions about what product(s) to make, for whom, and what processes and facilities are needed to produce them. OM is often joined by marketing and research and development in these decisions. Common facility layouts include fixed-position layouts, process layouts, or product layouts. Where to locate operations facilities is a crucial decision that depends on proximity to the market, availability of raw materials, availability of transportation, availability of power, climatic influences, availability of labour, and community characteristics. Technology is also vital to operations, particularly computer-assisted design (CAD), computer-assisted manufacturing (CAM), flexible manufacturing, robotics, and computer-integrated manufacturing (CIM).

LO4 Specify some techniques managers may use to manage the logistics of transforming inputs into finished products.

Logistics, or supply chain management, includes all the activities involved in obtaining and managing raw materials and component parts, managing finished products, packaging them, and getting them to customers. The organization must first make or purchase (procure) all the materials it needs. Next, it must control its inventory by determining how many supplies and goods it needs and keeping track of every raw material, component, completed or partially completed product, and piece of equipment, how many of each are on hand, where they are, and who has responsibility for them. Common approaches to inventory control include the economic order quantity (EOQ) model, the just-in-time (JIT) inventory concept, and material-requirements planning (MRP). Logistics also includes routing and scheduling processes and activities to complete products.

LO5 Assess the importance of quality in operations management.

Quality is a critical element of OM because low-quality products can hurt people and harm the business. Quality control refers to the processes an organization uses to maintain its established quality standards. To control quality, a company must establish what standard of quality it desires and then determine whether its products meet that standard through inspection.

KEY TERMS

capacity
computer-assisted design (CAD)
computer-assisted manufacturing (CAM)
computer-integrated manufacturing (CIM)
continuous manufacturing organizations
customization
economic order quantity (EOQ) model
fixed-position layout
flexible manufacturing
inputs
intermittent organizations
inventory
inventory control
ISO 9000
ISO 14000
just-in-time (JIT) inventory management
manufacturing

material-requirements planning (MRP)
modular design
operations
operations management (OM)
outputs
process layout
product layout
production
project organization
purchasing
quality control
routing
scheduling
standardization
statistical process control
supply chain management
total quality management (TQM)

DESTINATION CEO DISCUSSION QUESTIONS

1. What are the key competitive advantages of FedEx Kinko's?

2. What is the common thread that runs through Gary Kusin's career path?

3. Who was Gary Kusin's earliest role model?

While you might not have been familiar with terms such as *supply chain* or *logistics* or *total quality management* before taking this course, careers abound in the operations management field. You will find these careers in a wide variety of organizations—manufacturers, retailers, transportation companies, third-party logistics firms, government agencies, and service firms. Closely managing how a company's inputs and outputs flow from raw materials to the end consumer is vital to a firm's success. Successful companies also need to ensure that quality is measured and actively managed at each step.

Supply chain managers have a tremendous impact on the success of an organization. These managers are engaged in every facet of the business process, including planning, purchasing, production, transportation, storage and distribution, customer service, and more. Their performance helps organizations control expenses, boost sales, and maximize profits.

Warehouse managers are a vital part of manufacturing operations. A typical warehouse manager's duties include overseeing and recording deliveries and pickups, maintaining inventory records and the product tracking system, and adjusting inventory levels to reflect receipts and disbursements. Warehouse managers also have to consider customer service and employee issues. Warehouse managers can earn up to $60,000 in some cases.

Operations management is also required in service businesses. With more than 80 percent of the North American economy in services, jobs exist for services operations. Many service contact operations require standardized processes that often use technology to provide an interface that provides an automatic quality performance. Consider jobs in health care, the travel industry, fast food, and entertainment. Think of any job or task that is a part of the final product in these industries. Even an online retailer such as Amazon.ca has a transformation process that includes information technology and human activities that facilitate a transaction. These services have a standardized process and can be evaluated based on their level of achieved service quality.

Total quality management is becoming a key attribute for companies to ensure that quality pervades all aspects of the organization. Quality-assurance managers may make salaries in the $55,000 to $65,000 range. These managers monitor and advise on how a company's quality management system is performing and publish data and reports regarding company performance in both manufacturing and service industries.

BUILD YOUR BUSINESS PLAN

Managing Service and Manufacturing Operations

For your business you need to determine if you are providing raw materials that will be used in further production, or you are a reseller of goods and services, known as a retailer. If you are the former, you need to determine what processes you go through in making your product.

The text provides ideas of breaking the process into inputs, transformation processes, and outputs. If you are a provider of a service or a link in the supply chain, you need to know exactly what your customer expectations are. Services are intangible so it is all the more important to better understand what exactly the customer is looking for in resolving a problem or filling a need.

Royal Dutch Shell PLC has partnered with the Middle Eastern emirate of Qatar to create a $19 billion refinery that may bring the company to the forefront of sustainability. The plant, Pearl GTL (gas-to-liquids), is designed to transform natural gas into odour-free, pollutant-free fuel. The venture, which is the largest GTL project to date, has the potential for high returns in a flooded natural gas market. More importantly, the development of a new transformation process has the potential to create a new natural gas.

Shell has been working with GTL for almost four decades and believes it can succeed with Pearl. Lower natural gas prices will likely spur demand, particularly as GTL fuel is roughly half the cost of crude oil. GTL fuel is also purer than traditional crude, appealing to more environmentally conscious consumers and businesses.

Yet despite the benefits of GTL fuel, some have criticized the process. For instance, the GTL process is extremely expensive. Critics feel that alternative procedures are more cost-effective. In addition, the GTL process consumes a great deal of energy, calling into question its environmental sustainability. Others argue that GTL is profitable only when oil prices are high and that Shell has an equal chance of winning or losing on the venture.

However, Shell is optimistic. Not only does it feel that Pearl will pay itself off in five years, but it also has the added bonus of experience. Shell has operated a smaller GTL plant in Malaysia since 1993 and has already worked through many of the glitches in the GTL process. Finally, Qatar is rich in labour and energy reserves; if this partnership proves fruitful, Shell may have access to more profitable relationships in the future. Creating a more sustainable future for energy products can be a significant contribution to society.[30]

DISCUSSION QUESTIONS

1. Why is the development of the new transformation process GTL (gas-to-liquids) so important?

2. What are some of the production or operational barriers that Shell must overcome in order to make GTL successful?

3. Should Shell continue the GTL project if it fails to pay off in five years?

connect **LEARNSMART** **SMARTBOOK**

For more information on the resources available from McGraw-Hill Ryerson, go to www.mcgrawhill.ca/he/solutions.

LEARNING OBJECTIVES

LO1 Define human relations, and determine why its study is important.

LO2 Summarize early studies that laid the groundwork for understanding employee motivation.

LO3 Compare and contrast the human-relations theories of Abraham Maslow and Frederick Herzberg.

LO4 Investigate various theories of motivation, including Theories X, Y, and Z; equity theory; and expectancy theory.

LO5 Describe some of the strategies that managers use to motivate employees.

DESTINATION CEO

Jim Pattison, owner of the Jim Pattison Group, one of Canada's largest firms, is estimated to be worth nearly $4 billion and takes a very direct approach to sales. Pattison, whose first entrepreneurial venture was a car dealership, is known for his toughness in appraising performance.

Pattison's early approach was to fire the worst-performing salesperson every month and to reward the top sales staff. Pattison recalls, "The first guy I ever fired, he cried and I cried," but Pattison insists that he was actually doing the salesman a favour by moving him on toward a job to which he was more suited. "He was a nice fellow, but he wasn't selling cars." Pattison continued with this strategy as he expanded his business, pushing people to perform; if they didn't—one way or the other—they left. "What we do is keep moving non-productive assets out of the company," Pattison says. He is asked, "Does that mean personnel?" "Oh, of course," he replies.[1]

Pattison would no doubt agree with Andrew Wall, owner of the Milton, Ontario, franchise known as Sandler Training, a sales-management training firm. Wall states that successful sales managers shouldn't try to manage unproductive people as it is a waste of time.

Introduction

Because employees do the actual work of the business and influence whether the firm achieves its objectives, most top managers agree that employees are an organization's most valuable resource. To achieve organizational objectives, employees must have the motivation, ability (appropriate knowledge and skills), and tools (proper training and equipment) to perform their jobs. Chapter 10 covers topics related to managing human resources, such as those listed earlier. This chapter focuses on how to motivate employees.

We examine employees' needs and motivation, managers' views of workers, and several strategies for motivating employees. Managers who understand the needs of their employees can help them reach higher levels of productivity and thus contribute to the achievement of organizational goals.

Nature of Human Relations

What motivates employees to perform on the job is the focus of **human relations,** the study of the behaviour of individuals and groups in organizational settings. In business, human relations involves motivating employees to achieve organizational objectives efficiently and effectively. The field of human relations has become increasingly important over the years as businesses strive to understand how to boost workplace morale, maximize employees' productivity and creativity, and motivate their ever more diverse employees to be more effective.

Human relations the study of the behaviour of individuals and groups in organizational settings

Motivation an inner drive that directs a person's behaviour toward goals

Motivation is an inner drive that directs a person's behaviour toward goals. A goal is the satisfaction of some need, and a need is the difference between a desired state and an actual state. Both needs and goals can be motivating. Motivation explains why people behave as they do; similarly, a lack of motivation explains, at times, why people avoid doing what they should do. Motivating employees to do the wrong things or for the wrong reasons can be problematic, however. Encouraging employees to take excessive risks through high compensation, for example, is not a good idea and can lead to ethical misconduct disasters for a corporation. The most recent financial crisis resulted from firms allowing or encouraging excessive risk taking in order to achieve financial rewards. A person who recognizes or feels a need is motivated to take action to satisfy the need and achieve a goal (Figure 9.1). Consider a person who takes a job in sales. If his or her performance is far below other salespeople's, he or she will likely recognize a need to increase sales. To satisfy that need and achieve success, the person may try to acquire new insights from successful salespeople or obtain additional training to improve sales skills. In addition, a sales manager might try different means to motivate the salesperson to work harder and improve his or her skills. Human relations is concerned with the needs of employees, their goals and how they try to achieve them, and the impact of those needs and goals on job performance.

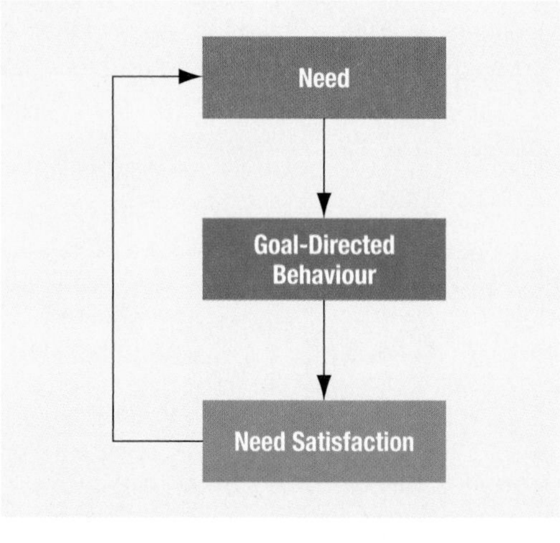

Effectively motivating employees helps keep them engaged in their work. Engagement involves emotional involvement and commitment. Being engaged results in carrying out the expectations and obligations of employment. Many employees are actively engaged in their jobs, while others are not. Some employees do the minimum amount of work required to get by, and some employees are completely disengaged. Motivating employees to stay engaged is a key responsibility of management. For example, to test if his onsite production managers were fully engaged in their jobs, former Van Halen frontman David Lee Roth placed a line in the band's rider asking for a bowl of M&Ms with the brown ones removed. It was a means for the band to test local stage production crews' attention to detail. Because Van Halen's shows were highly technical, Roth would demand a complete recheck of everything if he found brown M&Ms in the bowl.[3]

One prominent aspect of human relations is **morale**—an employee's attitude toward his or her job, employer, and colleagues. High morale contributes to high levels of productivity, high returns to stakeholders, and employee loyalty. Conversely, low morale may cause high rates of absenteeism and turnover (when employees quit or are fired and must be replaced by new employees). Google recognizes the value of happy, committed employees and strives to engage in practices that will minimize turnover. Employees have the opportunity to have a massage every other week; onsite laundry service; free all-you-can-eat gourmet meals and snacks; and the "20% a week" rule, which allows engineers to work on whatever project they want for one day each week.[4]

Employees are motivated by their perceptions of extrinsic and intrinsic rewards. An **intrinsic reward** is the personal satisfaction and enjoyment that you feel from attaining a goal. For example, in this class you may feel personal enjoyment in learning how business works and aspire to have a career in business or to operate your own business one day. An **extrinsic reward** is a benefit and/or recognition that you receive from someone else. In this class, your grade is extrinsic recognition of your efforts and success in the class. In business, praise and recognition, pay increases, and bonuses are extrinsic rewards. If you believe that your job provides an opportunity to contribute to society or the

Morale an employee's attitude toward his or her job, employer, and colleagues

Intrinsic reward the personal satisfaction and enjoyment felt from attaining a goal

Extrinsic reward a benefit and/or recognition received from someone else

DID YOU KNOW?

Absenteeism costs a typical large company more than $3 million a year.[2]

figure 9.1 The Motivation Process

Need

↓

Goal-Directed Behaviour

↓

Need Satisfaction

environment, then that aspect would represent an intrinsic reward. Both intrinsic and extrinsic rewards contribute to motivation that stimulates employees to do their best in contributing to business goals.

Respect, involvement, appreciation, adequate compensation, promotions, a pleasant work environment, and a positive organizational culture are all morale boosters. Table 9.1 lists some ways to retain good employees. Nike seeks to provide a comprehensive compensation and

table 9.1 Top 10 Ways to Retain Great Employees

1. Satisfied employees know clearly what is expected from them every day at work.
2. The quality of the supervision an employee receives is critical to employee retention.
3. The ability of the employee to speak his or her mind freely within the organization is another key factor in employee retention.
4. Talent and skill utilization is another environmental factor your key employees seek in your workplace.
5. The perception of fairness and equitable treatment is important in employee retention.
6. Employees must have the tools, time, and training necessary to do their jobs well—or they will move to an employer who provides them.
7. The best employees, those employees you want to retain, seek frequent opportunities to learn and grow in their careers, knowledge, and skill.
8. Take time to meet with new employees to learn about their talents, abilities, and skills. Meet with each employee periodically.
9. No matter the circumstances, never, never, ever threaten an employee's job or income.
10. Staff members must feel rewarded, recognized, and appreciated.

SOURCE: Susan M. Heathfield, "Top Ten Ways to Retain Your Great Employees," *About.com*, http://humanresources.about.com/od/retention/a/more_retention.htm (accessed February 18, 2010).

Many companies offer onsite day care as a benefit for employees who have children. Company benefits such as these tend to increase employee satisfaction and motivation.

benefits package, which includes traditional elements such as medical, dental, vision, life and disability insurance, paid holidays and time off, sabbaticals, and team as well as individual compensation plans. More comprehensive benefits include employee discounts on Nike products, scholarships for children of employees, employee assistance plans, tuition assistance, group legal plans, and matching gift programs. At their world headquarters in the United States, Nike employees may take advantage of onsite day care and fitness centres, onsite cafés and restaurants, an onsite hair and nail salon, discounted annual transit passes, and several other work-life resources.[5] At WestJet, which is frequently recognized for having the most admired corporate culture in Canada, over 80 percent of its employees are shareholders and its profit-sharing plan provides employees with an extra 25 to 33 percent in earnings each year.[6] Many companies offer a diverse array of benefits designed to improve the quality of employees' lives and increase their morale and satisfaction. Some of the best companies to work for offer onsite day care, concierge services (e.g., dry cleaning, shoe repair, prescription renewal), and fully paid sabbaticals. Table 9.2 offers suggestions as to how leaders can motivate employees on a daily basis.

LO2 Summarize early studies that laid the groundwork for understanding employee motivation.

Historical Perspectives on Employee Motivation

Throughout the 20th century, researchers have conducted numerous studies to try to identify ways to motivate workers and increase productivity. From these studies have come theories that have been applied to workers with varying

table 9.2 You Can Make Their Day: Tips for the Leader About Employee Motivation

1. Use simple, powerful words.
2. Make sure people know what you expect.
3. Provide regular feedback.
4. People need positive and not so positive consequences.
5. It's about discipline, not magic.
6. Continue learning and trying out new ideas for employee motivation.
7. Make time for people.
8. Focus on the development of people.
9. Share the goals and the context: communicate.

SOURCE: Susan M. Heathfield, "You Can Make Their Day: Ten Tips for the Leader About Employee Motivation," *About.com*, http://humanresources.about.com/od/motivationsucces3/a/lead_motivation.htm (accessed February 18, 2010).

Even small symbols of recognition, such as an "Employee of the Month" parking space, can serve as strong motivators for employees.

degrees of success. A brief discussion of two of these theories—the classical theory of motivation and the Hawthorne studies—provides a background for understanding the present state of human relations.

Classical Theory of Motivation

The birth of the study of human relations can be traced to time and motion studies conducted at the turn of the century by Frederick W. Taylor and Frank and Lillian Gilbreth. Their studies analyzed how workers perform specific work tasks in an effort to improve the employees' productivity. These efforts led to the application of scientific principles to management.

According to the **classical theory of motivation,** money is the sole motivator for workers. Taylor suggested that workers who were paid more would produce more, an idea that would benefit both companies and workers. To improve productivity, Taylor thought that managers should break down each job into its component tasks (specialization), determine the best way to perform each task, and specify the output to be achieved by a worker performing the task. Taylor also believed that incentives would motivate employees to be more productive. Thus, he suggested that managers link workers' pay directly to their output. He developed the piece-rate system, under which employees were paid a certain amount for each unit they produced; those who

> "Taylor believed that satisfactory pay and job security would motivate employees to work hard. However, later studies showed that other factors are also important in motivating workers."

Classical theory of motivation theory suggesting that money is the sole motivator for workers

exceeded their quota were paid a higher rate per unit for all the units they produced.

We can still see Taylor's ideas in practice today in the use of mathematical models, statistics, and incentives. Moreover, companies are increasingly striving to relate pay to performance at both the hourly and managerial level. Incentive planners choose an individual incentive to motivate and reward their employees. In contrast, team incentives are used to generate partnership and collaboration to accomplish organizational goals. Boeing develops sales teams for most of its products, including commercial airplanes. The team dedicated to each product shares in the sales incentive program.

More and more corporations are tying pay to performance in order to motivate—even up to the CEO level. The topic of executive pay has become controversial in recent years, and many corporate boards of directors have taken steps to link executive compensation more closely to corporate performance. Despite these changes, many top executives still receive large compensation packages. Michael Pearson, head of Montreal-based Valeant Pharmaceuticals International Inc., is one of the highest paid executives in Canada, with total compensation of $36.3 million.[8]

Like most managers of the early 20th century, Taylor believed that satisfactory pay and job security would motivate employees to work hard. However, later studies showed that other factors are also important in motivating workers.

The Hawthorne Studies

Elton Mayo and a team of researchers from Harvard University wanted to determine what physical conditions in the workplace—such as light and noise levels—would stimulate employees to be most productive. From 1924 to 1932, they studied a group of workers at the Hawthorne Works Plant of the Western Electric Company and measured their productivity under various physical conditions.

What the researchers discovered was quite unexpected and very puzzling: Productivity increased regardless of the physical conditions. This phenomenon has been labelled the Hawthorne effect. When questioned about their behaviour, the employees expressed satisfaction because their co-workers in the experiments were friendly and, more importantly, because their supervisors had asked for their help and cooperation in the study. In other words, they were responding to the attention they received, not the changing physical work conditions. The researchers concluded that social and psychological factors could significantly affect productivity and morale. Medtronic, often called the "Microsoft of the medical-device industry," has a built-in psychological factor that influences employee morale. The company makes life-saving medical devices, such as

Whole Foods is well known for being a customer-centric organization that sells organic and natural produce. The company is 100 percent powered by renewable energy and ranked among Forbes' "America's Greenest Companies." Whole Foods also works hard to create an inviting, informative store environment for the customer.

However, truly creating a quality store experience requires dedication from the company's in-store employees. For this reason, Whole Foods employees are empowered to make decisions that will achieve the company's goals. Employees often work in small self-directed teams to discuss issues and develop solutions to improve the company's operations. Additionally, Whole Foods wants its employees to feel like they are an important component of the company's success. Employees therefore have access to all the company's books, including the compensation report. Whole Foods also implemented a voluntary program to encourage employees

to stay healthy. Employees already receive a 20 percent discount on Whole Foods products, and under the Whole Foods Healthy Living Challenge, employees are eligible to receive an additional 10 percent discount. Its support for employee empowerment, sustainability, and healthy living has earned Whole Foods a place on Fortune's "100 Best Companies to Work For" for 14 consecutive years.[7]

DISCUSSION QUESTIONS

1. How does Whole Foods use teams to improve its operations?

2. What are some ways that Whole Foods empowers its employees?

3. What are some of the benefits of the Whole Foods Healthy Living Challenge?

---

pacemakers, neurostimulators, and stents. New hires at Medtronic receive medallions inscribed with a portion of the firm's mission statement, "alleviate pain, restore health, and extend life." There is an annual party where people whose bodies function thanks to Medtronic devices give testimonials.[9] Obviously, Medtronic employees feel a sense of satisfaction in their jobs. Figure 9.2 indicates what

executives consider to be most valuable in maintaining an effective work–life balance.

The Hawthorne experiments marked the beginning of a concern for human relations in the workplace. They revealed that human factors do influence workers' behaviour and that managers who understand the needs, beliefs, and expectations of people have the greatest success in motivating their workers.

Working conditions are important. However, the Hawthorne studies, which were carried out at the electric company shown here beginning in the 1920s, found that the workers became more productive because of the attention they received—regardless of their working conditions.

figure 9.2 Value of Employer Work-Life Concessions

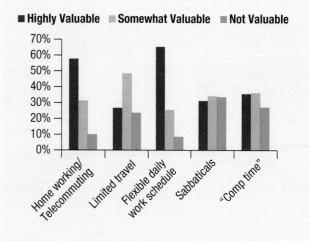

SOURCE: "BlueSteps 2010 Executive Work-Life Balance Survey," http://viewswire.eiu.com/report_dl.asp?mode=fi&fi=757215260.PDF (accessed January 13, 2011).

Theories of Employee Motivation

The research of Taylor, Mayo, and many others has led to the development of a number of theories that attempt to describe what motivates employees to perform. In this section, we will discuss some of the most important of these theories. The successful implementation of ideas based on these theories will vary, of course, depending on the company, its management, and its employees. It should be noted, too, that what worked in the past may no longer work today. Good managers must have the ability to adapt their ideas to an ever-changing, diverse group of employees.

Maslow's Hierarchy of Needs

Psychologist Abraham Maslow theorized that people have five basic needs: physiological, security, social, esteem, and self-actualization. **Maslow's hierarchy** arranges these needs into the order in which people strive to satisfy them (Figure 9.3).

Physiological needs, the most basic and first needs to be satisfied, are the essentials for living—water, food, shelter, and clothing. According to Maslow, humans devote all their efforts to satisfying physiological needs until they are met. Only when these needs are met can people focus their attention on satisfying the next level of needs—security.

Security needs relate to protecting yourself from physical and economic harm.

Actions that may be taken to achieve security include reporting a dangerous workplace condition to management, maintaining safety equipment, and purchasing insurance with income protection in the event you become unable to work. Once security needs have been satisfied, people may strive for social goals.

Social needs are the need for love, companionship, and friendship—the desire for acceptance by others. To fulfill social needs, a person may try many things: making friends with a co-worker, joining a group, volunteering at a hospital, or throwing a party. Once their social needs have been satisfied, people attempt to satisfy their need for esteem.

Esteem needs relate to respect—both self-respect and respect from others. One aspect of esteem needs is competition—the need to feel that you can do something better than anyone else. Competition often motivates people to increase their productivity. Esteem needs are not as easily satisfied as the needs at lower levels in Maslow's hierarchy because they do not always provide tangible evidence of success.

Maslow's hierarchy a theory that arranges the five basic needs of people—physiological, security, social, esteem, and self-actualization—into the order in which people strive to satisfy them

Physiological needs the most basic human needs to be satisfied— water, food, shelter, and clothing

Security needs needs to protect oneself from physical and economic harm

Social needs needs for love, companionship, and friendship—the desire for acceptance by others

Esteem needs needs for respect—both self-respect and respect from others

figure 9.3 Maslow's Hierarchy of Needs

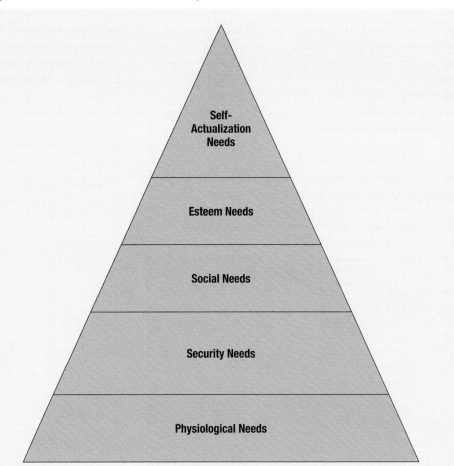

SOURCE: Adapted from Abraham H. Maslow, "A Theory of Human Motivation," *Psychology Review* 50 (1943), pp. 370–396. American Psychology Association.

However, these needs can be realized through rewards and increased involvement in organizational activities. Until esteem needs are met, people focus their attention on achieving respect. When they feel they have achieved some measure of respect, self-actualization becomes the major goal of life.

Self-actualization needs, at the top of Maslow's hierarchy, mean being the best you can be. Self-actualization involves maximizing your potential. A self-actualized person feels that she or he is living life to its fullest in every way. For author Stephen King, self-actualization might mean being praised as the best fiction writer in the world; for actress Halle Berry, it might mean winning an Oscar.

Maslow's theory maintains that the more basic needs at the bottom of the hierarchy must be satisfied before higher-level goals can be pursued. Thus, people who are hungry and homeless are not concerned with obtaining respect from their colleagues. Only when physiological, security, and social needs have been more or less satisfied do people seek esteem. Maslow's theory also suggests that if a low-level need is suddenly reactivated, the individual will try to satisfy that need rather than higher-level needs. Many laid-off workers probably shift their focus from high-level esteem needs to the need

> **"Maslow's theory maintains that the more basic needs at the bottom of the hierarchy must be satisfied before higher-level goals can be pursued."**

for security. When unemployment reached 8.3 percent during the last recession and the job market appeared increasingly insecure, many employees, particularly those in manufacturing, banking, and finance, felt they had to shift their focus back to security needs. Managers should learn from Maslow's hierarchy that employees will be motivated to contribute to organizational goals only if they are able to first satisfy their physiological, security, and social needs through their work.

Herzberg's Two-Factor Theory

In the 1950s, psychologist Frederick Herzberg proposed a theory of motivation that focuses on the job and on the environment where work is done. Herzberg studied various factors relating to the job and their relation to employee motivation and concluded that they can be divided into hygiene factors and motivational factors (Table 9.3).

Consider the Following: Ursula Burns Motivates Employees

In 2009 Ursula Burns became the first black female CEO of a *Fortune* 500 corporation when she took over the top position at Xerox. Burns credits her rise from intern to CEO to hard work. While she admits that Xerox's support of diversity probably helped her at the beginning of her career, Burns's straightforward style and strong work ethic helped her rise to the top.

Raised in poverty by a single mother who worked hard so that her children could attend private school, Burns learned the value of hard work at an early age. She first went to work at Xerox as an intern in 1980 and never left the company. Burns was quickly promoted, eventually becoming president in 2007. Thanks to her no-nonsense management style, Burns helped Xerox find success by improving efficiency and customer service.

According to her peers, Burns has all the skills necessary to successfully lead Xerox as the company's top manager: technical expertise and conceptual, analytical, and human relations skills. Burns will need these skills in coming years. During the last economic recession, Xerox faced losses as customers purchased less and product prices fell. People and businesses are also beginning to use less paper as they move from copies

to e-mail to share information. However, Burns has a strong history of innovation and is making plans to expand Xerox's capabilities.

One of her strategies is to adjust the company's corporate culture. She hopes to use the downturn as a time to encourage her employees worldwide to become more independent and self-managing. Her goal is to establish trust between herself and her workers, empowering them to make the right decisions on their own. Burns's shared commitment to both employees and innovation may be just what Xerox needs to point the company in a new direction.[10]

DISCUSSION QUESTIONS

1. Why do you think Ursula Burns is so successful?

2. What kinds of skills do you think are most useful to Ursula Burns as CEO of Xerox?

3. How do you think Ursula Burns's early life prepared her for her current position at Xerox?

Hygiene factors, which relate to the work setting and not to the content of the work, include adequate wages, comfortable and safe working conditions, fair company policies, and job security. These factors do not necessarily motivate employees to excel, but their absence may be a potential source of dissatisfaction and high turnover. Employee safety and comfort are clearly hygiene factors.

Many people feel that a good salary is one of the most important job factors, even more important than job security and the chance to use one's mind and abilities. Salary and security, two of the hygiene factors identified by Herzberg, make it possible for employees to satisfy the physiological and security needs identified by Maslow. However, the presence of hygiene factors is unlikely to motivate employees to work harder.

Motivational factors, which relate to the content of the work itself, include achievement, recognition, involvement, responsibility, and advancement. The absence of motivational factors may not result in dissatisfaction, but their presence is likely to motivate employees to excel. Many companies are beginning to employ methods to give employees more responsibility and control and to involve them more in their work, which serves to

Hygiene factors aspects of Herzberg's theory of motivation that focus on the work setting and not the content of the work; these aspects include adequate wages, comfortable and safe working conditions, fair company policies, and job security

Motivational factors aspects of Herzberg's theory of motivation that focus on the content of the work itself; these aspects include achievement, recognition, involvement, responsibility, and advancement

The Dirty Jobs television series recognizes individuals who take on society's undesirable, but essential, jobs.

motivate them to higher levels of productivity and quality. For example, Mississauga-based Closing the Gap Healthcare Group founder Connie Clerici allows employees including nurses, occupational therapists, and other health professionals to set their own schedules and determine how long they want to stay with each patient. Clerici says, "We don't micromanage, we trust our workforce to decide what's best for clients." It is not uncommon for Clerici's employees to go above and beyond in making customers happy. Recently one employee not only accompanied a patient to the hospital but stayed with him until he saw a doctor, and another

Consider the Following: Rewarding Performers With Time Off

During the most recent recession, several organizations decided to decrease employee incentives (perks) due to the difficult financial environment. Although incentives are rising again, there are still fewer employee perks than there were pre-recession. However, some employers are taking an unusual approach by offering more time off as a reward—even for part-time workers. Indeed, a survey of companies in the Washington, DC/Baltimore area revealed that 73 percent of surveyed employers now offer paid time off to part-time workers rather than creating full-time positions, which come with their own share of costs.

Three companies that reward employees with extra time off include Travelzoo (a global travel deal website), Bluewolf, Inc. (an IT consulting firm), and Patagonia (an outdoor gear and clothing company). At Bluewolf, emphasis is placed on outcome rather than time spent at a desk, enabling its 175 employees to take unlimited time off to

travel, volunteer, and more. Travelzoo offers its employees of more than one year an annual $1,500–$32,000 with three extra vacation days and the chance to snatch up a deal listed on its site. In return, employees are merely required to submit pictures and brief write-ups to the company's subscriber newsletter. After one year of employment, Patagonia covers up to 60 days' worth of an employee's salary to allow the employee to volunteer with a grassroots organization. Like those at Travelzoo, employees are asked to report back about their experiences.

Studies have suggested that these types of incentives boost bottom-line profits and enhance employee retention. Points of Light Foundation claims that over 80 percent of companies feel that volunteering raises profits. This may be due to the fact that consumers are increasingly doing business with socially responsible companies. Employees also become committed to companies that give back to communities and appreciate their efforts.[11]

table 9.3 Herzberg's Hygiene and Motivational Factors

Hygiene Factors	Motivational Factors
Company policies	Achievement
Supervision	Recognition
Working conditions	Work itself
Relationships with peers, supervisors, and subordinates	Responsibility
Salary	Advancement
Security	Personal growth

employee moved patient furniture including dismantling a bed in order to create a room the patient could use after undergoing surgery.[12]

Herzberg's motivational factors and Maslow's esteem and self-actualization needs are similar. Workers' low-level needs (physiological and security) have largely been satisfied by minimum-wage laws and occupational-safety standards set by various government agencies and are therefore not motivators. Consequently, to improve productivity, management should focus on satisfying workers' higher-level needs (motivational factors) by providing opportunities for achievement, involvement, and advancement and by recognizing good performance.

LO4 Investigate various theories of motivation, including Theories X, Y, and Z; equity theory; and expectancy theory.

McGregor's Theory X and Theory Y

In *The Human Side of Enterprise*, Douglas McGregor related Maslow's ideas about personal needs to management. McGregor contrasted two views of management—the traditional view, which he called Theory X, and a humanistic view, which he called Theory Y.

Theory X McGregor's traditional view of management whereby it is assumed that workers generally dislike work and must be forced to do their jobs

According to McGregor, managers adopting **Theory X** assume that workers generally dislike work and must be forced to do their jobs. They believe that the following statements are true of workers:

1. The average person naturally dislikes work and will avoid it when possible.

2. Most workers must be coerced, controlled, directed, or threatened with punishment to get them to work toward the achievement of organizational objectives.

3. The average worker prefers to be directed and to avoid responsibility, has relatively little ambition, and wants security.[13]

Managers who subscribe to the Theory X view maintain tight control over workers, provide almost constant supervision, try to motivate through fear, and make decisions in an autocratic fashion, eliciting little or no input from their subordinates. The Theory X style of management focuses on physiological and security needs and virtually ignores the higher needs discussed by Maslow.

The Theory X view of management does not take into account people's needs for companionship, esteem, and personal growth, whereas Theory Y, the contrasting view of management, does. Managers subscribing to the **Theory Y** view assume that workers like to work and that under proper conditions employees will seek out responsibility in an attempt to satisfy their social, esteem, and self-actualization needs. McGregor describes the assumptions behind Theory Y in the following way:

Theory Y McGregor's humanistic view of management whereby it is assumed that workers like to work and that under proper conditions employees will seek out responsibility in an attempt to satisfy their social, esteem, and self-actualization needs

1. The expenditure of physical and mental effort in work is as natural as play or rest.

2. People will exercise self-direction and self-control to achieve objectives to which they are committed.

3. People will commit to objectives when they realize that the achievement of those goals will bring them personal reward.

4. The average person will accept and seek responsibility.

5. Imagination, ingenuity, and creativity can help solve organizational problems, but most organizations do not make adequate use of these characteristics in their employees.

6. Organizations today do not make full use of workers' intellectual potential.[14]

Obviously, managers subscribing to the Theory Y philosophy have a management style very different from managers subscribing to the Theory X philosophy. Theory Y managers maintain less control and supervision, do not use fear as the primary motivator, and are more democratic in decision making, allowing subordinates to participate in the process. Theory Y managers address the high-level needs in Maslow's hierarchy as well as physiological and security needs. Today, Theory Y enjoys widespread support and may have displaced Theory X.

"Theory Y managers maintain less control and supervision, do not use fear as the primary motivator, and are more democratic in decision making."

Theory Z

Theory Z is a management philosophy that stresses employee participation in all aspects of company decision making. It was first described by William Ouchi in his book *Theory Z—How American Business Can Meet the Japanese Challenge*. Theory Z incorporates many elements associated with the Japanese approach to management, such as trust and intimacy, but Japanese ideas have been adapted for use in North America. In a Theory Z organization, managers and workers share responsibilities; the management style is participative; and employment is long term and often lifelong. Japan has faced a significant period of slowing economic progress and competition from China and other Asian nations. This has led to experts questioning Theory Z, particularly at firms such as Sony and Toyota. Theory Z results in employees feeling organizational ownership. Research has found that such feelings of ownership may produce positive attitudinal and behavioural effects for employees.[14] In a Theory Y organization, managers focus on assumptions about the nature of the worker. The two theories can be seen as complementary. Table 9.4 compares the traditional American management style, the Japanese management style, and Theory Z (the modified Japanese management style).

> **Theory Z** a management philosophy that stresses employee participation in all aspects of company decision making

Variations on Theory Z

Theory Z has been adapted and modified for use in a number of Canadian companies. One adaptation involves workers in decisions through quality circles. Quality circles (also called quality-assurance teams) are small, usually having five to eight members who discuss ways to reduce waste, eliminate problems, and improve quality, communication, and work satisfaction. Such quality teams are a common technique for harnessing the knowledge and creativity of hourly employees to solve problems in companies. As Theory Z has questioned the use of quality circles, their prevalence has declined. Quality circles have been replaced with quality methods.

Even more involved than quality circles are programs that operate under names such as *participative management, employee involvement,* or *self-directed work teams*. Regardless of the term used to describe such programs, they strive to give employees more control over their jobs while making them more responsible for the outcome of their efforts. Such programs often organize employees into work teams of 5 to 15 members who are responsible for producing an entire product item. Team members are cross-trained and can therefore move from job to job within the team. Each team essentially manages itself and is responsible for its quality, scheduling, ordering and use of materials, and problem solving. Many firms have successfully employed work teams to boost morale, productivity, quality, and competitiveness.

Equity Theory

According to **equity theory,** how much people are willing to contribute to an organization depends on their assessment of the fairness, or equity, of the rewards they will receive in exchange. In a fair situation, a person receives rewards proportional to the contribution he or she makes to the organization. However, in practice, equity is a subjective notion. Each worker regularly develops a personal input–output ratio by taking stock of his or her contributions (inputs) to the organization in time, effort, skills, and experience and assessing the rewards (outputs) offered by the organization in pay, benefits, recognition, and promotions. The worker compares his or her ratio to the input–output ratio of some other person—a "comparison other," who may be a co-worker, a friend working in another organization, or an "average" of several people working in the organization. If the

> **Equity theory** an assumption that how much people are willing to contribute to an organization depends on their assessment of the fairness, or equity, of the rewards they will receive in exchange

table 9.4 Comparison of North American, Japanese, and Theory Z Management Styles

	North American	Japanese	Theory Z
Duration of employment	Relatively short term; workers subject to layoffs when business slows	Lifelong; no layoffs	Long term; layoffs rare
Rate of promotion	Rapid	Slow	Slow
Amount of specialization	Considerable; worker develops expertise in one area only	Minimal; worker develops expertise in all aspects of the organization	Moderate; worker learns all aspects of the organization
Decision making	Individual	Consensual; input from all concerned parties is considered	Consensual; emphasis on quality
Responsibility	Assigned to the individual	Shared by the group	Assigned to the individual
Control	Explicit and formal	Less explicit and less formal	Informal but with explicit performance measures
Concern for workers	Focus is on work only	Focus extends to worker's whole life	Focus includes worker's life and family

SOURCE: Adapted from William Ouchi, *Theory Z—How American Business Can Meet the Japanese Challenge*, p. 58. © 1981 by Addison-Wesley Publishing Company, Inc. Reprinted by permission of Perseus Books Publishers, a member of Perseus Books, L.L.C.

two ratios are close, the individual will feel that he or she is being treated equitably.

Let's say you have a high-school education and earn $25,000 a year. When you compare your input–output ratio with that of a co-worker who has a college degree and makes $35,000 a year, you will probably feel that you are being paid fairly. However, if you perceive that your personal input–output ratio is lower than that of your college-educated co-worker, you may feel that you are being treated unfairly and be motivated to seek change. But, if you learn that the co-worker who makes $35,000 has only a high-school diploma, you may feel cheated by your employer. To achieve equity, you could try to increase your outputs by asking for a raise or promotion. You could also try to have your co-worker's inputs increased or his or her outputs decreased. Failing to achieve equity, you may be motivated to look for a job at a different company or in a different city. Table 9.5 shows the top Canadian cities to work in from a strictly economic perspective.

Because almost all the issues involved in equity theory are subjective, they can be problematic. Author Archie Carroll has argued that feelings of inequity may underlie some unethical or illegal behaviour in business, such as the $3.6 billion a year stolen from companies by their own employees.[15] Shoplifting alone is the cause of more than $10 billion a year in company losses.[16] Carroll believes that employees who do not feel they are being treated equitably may be motivated to equalize the situation by lying, cheating, or otherwise "improving" their pay, perhaps by stealing.[17] Managers should try to avoid equity problems by ensuring that rewards are distributed on the basis of performance and that all employees clearly understand the basis for their pay and benefits.

Expectancy Theory

Psychologist Victor Vroom described **expectancy theory,** which states that motivation depends not only on how much a person wants something but also on the person's perception of how likely he or she is to get it. A person who wants something and has reason to be optimistic will be strongly motivated. For example, say you really want a promotion. And, let's say because you have taken some night classes to improve your skills, and moreover, have just made a large, significant sale, you feel confident that you are qualified and able to handle the new position. Therefore, you are motivated to try to get the promotion. In contrast, if you do not believe you are likely to get what you want, you may not be motivated to try to get it, even though you really want it.

LO5 Describe some of the strategies that managers use to motivate employees.

Strategies for Motivating Employees

Based on the various theories that attempt to explain what motivates employees, businesses have developed several strategies for motivating their employees and boosting morale and productivity. Some of these techniques include behaviour modification and job design, as well as the already described employee involvement programs and work teams.

Behaviour Modification

Behaviour modification involves changing behaviour and encouraging appropriate actions by relating the consequences of behaviour to the behaviour itself. The concept of behaviour modification was developed by psychologist B. F. Skinner, who showed that there are two types of consequences that can

table 9.5 Best Places to Find a Job in Canada

Note: Numbers represent ranking out of 190 cities.

Overall Rank	City	Average House Price	Household Income	Discretionary Income	Pop. Growth	Unemployment	Transit	Hospitals & Schools
1	Strathcona County	152	4	13	85	17	69	3
2	Red Deer	119	31	11	17	17	64	2
3	St. Albert	173	9	10	31	22	48	3
4	Calgary	164	8	7	95	42	11	3
5	Edmonton	134	40	22	68	33	23	3
6	Regina	104	43	81	1	9	57	3
7	Lethbridge	94	61	20	71	10	92	3
8	Burlington	153	20	29	17	38	37	3
9	Canmore	186	6	3	110	5	158	2
10	Grande Prairie	112	11	14	152	28	109	2

SOURCE: "Best Places for Jobs – 2012," *MoneySense,* http://list.moneysense.ca/rankings/best-places-to-live/2012/for-jobs/Default.aspx?sc1=0&d1=a&sp2=1&eh=ch, (accessed January 16, 2013). © 2001–2013 Rogers Media. All rights reserved.

modify behaviour—reward and punishment. Skinner found that behaviour that is rewarded will tend to be repeated, while behaviour that is punished will tend to be eliminated. For example, employees who know that they will receive a bonus, such as an expensive restaurant meal, for making a sale over $2,000 may be more motivated to make sales. Workers who know they will be punished for being tardy are likely to make a greater effort to get to work on time.

However, the two strategies may not be equally effective. Punishing unacceptable behaviour may provide quick results but may lead to undesirable long-term side effects, such as employee dissatisfaction and increased turnover. In general, rewarding appropriate behaviour is a more effective way to modify behaviour.

Job Design

Herzberg identified the job itself as a motivational factor. Managers have several strategies that they can use to design jobs to help improve employee motivation. These include job rotation, job enlargement, job enrichment, and flexible scheduling strategies. Justin Barker, general manager at a small GM dealership in Nova Scotia, believes that small companies can engage in all of these motivational strategies as well. He states that while other car dealers are struggling across Canada, his

dealership has had some of its best months in terms of sales. Barker attributes much of this to his motivated workforce and they in turn attribute much of their motivation to Barker's human resource practices that allow employees to participate in job-sharing, job rotation, and telecommunicating.[18]

Job Rotation. **Job rotation** allows employees to move from one job to another in an effort to relieve the boredom that is often associated with job specialization. Businesses often turn to specialization in hopes

> **Job rotation** movement of employees from one job to another in an effort to relieve the boredom often associated with job specialization

of increasing productivity, but there is a negative side effect to this type of job design: Employees become bored and dissatisfied, and productivity declines. Job rotation reduces this boredom by allowing workers to undertake a greater variety of tasks and by giving them the opportunity to learn new skills. With job rotation, an employee spends a specified amount of time performing one job and then moves on to another, different job. The worker eventually returns to the initial job and begins the cycle again.

Job rotation is a good idea, but it has one major drawback. Because employees may eventually become bored with all the jobs in the cycle, job rotation does not totally eliminate

---

Consider the Following: Motivating for Global Success

Growth in the chemical industry means expansion into developing countries for the Eastman Chemical Company. Failed overseas employee assignments represent a financial loss to the company and can also prove devastating to the employee—and often, the employee's family. When selecting employees for overseas assignments, Eastman focuses on the employee's family members—their interest in relocation and their adaptability to other cultures—as well as the employee's technical skills and qualifications. Eastman's preparation program is so thorough and effective that 99 percent of participating employees successfully complete their two- to five-year term in a foreign country.

How does Eastman motivate for global success? Potential overseas employees and their families meet with a counsellor to determine the family's cultural adaptivity. Also, Eastman offers cultural orientation for the family, including language training, a house-hunting trip, and counselling to prepare the family for life in a new culture. Financial recognition is offered through the Dual Earnings Family Compensation Plan for those spouses who give up a career to move with an Eastman employee. Employees also can choose not to accept an overseas assignment without risk to their careers with Eastman.

Once a family has relocated overseas, counselling is available locally, and hometown newspapers and company newsletters are sent. Family members also have access to a local contact person to help them adjust to their new surroundings. Employees returning home following an overseas assignment provide information to the human resources management group that helps make future assignments more effective for the company and easier for future families.[19]

PriceWaterhouseCoopers recommends six make or break rules for relocation overseas:

1. Find the right candidate, technically, and address the soft issues such as family as well.
2. Offer a set of benefits that supports the transition; be flexible and consider taxes.
3. Provide cultural orientation and language training for the family.
4. Provide support after the move including security and even shopping locations.
5. Address spousal work issues; most households are now dual income so help both persons.
6. Plan for repatriation; help them reintegrate when they return.[20]

---

the problem of boredom. Job rotation is extremely useful, however, in situations where a person is being trained for a position that requires an understanding of various units in an organization. For example, McCain Foods uses job rotation to train both management trainees and potential senior managers in all aspects of the company. The management trainee program at McCain has employees switching jobs or divisions every four to six months for the first couple of years in the company prior to the employer and employee agreeing to a more permanent set of duties and placement in the company. Eli Lilly is a strong believer in the benefits of job rotation. The company leaves employees in their current jobs and asks them to take on short-term assignments outside their field of expertise or interest. The results of the process have been positive, and Nokia is trying the same process with similar outcomes.[21] Many executive training programs require trainees to spend time learning a variety of specialized jobs. Job rotation is also used to cross-train today's self-directed work teams.

Interestingly, some firms are taking the concept of job rotation to a whole new level as larger Canadian companies are starting to engage in a practice called *life swapping*. Essentially colleagues trade not only jobs, but residences and often friends for a period of time. Firms such as PricewaterhouseCoopers believe the program allows it to retain star employees and groom them for bigger opportunities in the firm. Alan Levy, a human resource specialist, notes that, "Organizations need to be creative in their human resources and have progressive retention practices processes. Gen X and Y have greater commitments to their careers than they do to the corporation."[22]

Job Enlargement. **Job enlargement** adds more tasks to a job instead of treating each task as separate. Like job rotation, job enlargement was developed to overcome the boredom associated with specialization. The rationale behind this strategy is that jobs are more satisfying as the number of tasks performed by an individual increases. Employees sometimes enlarge, or craft, their jobs by noticing what needs to be done and then changing tasks and relationship boundaries to adjust. Individual orientation and motivation shape opportunities to craft new jobs and job relationships.[23] Job enlargement strategies have been more successful in increasing job satisfaction than have job rotation strategies.

Job Enrichment. **Job enrichment** incorporates motivational factors, such as opportunity for achievement, recognition, responsibility, and advancement, into a job. It gives workers not only more tasks within the job but more control and authority over the job. Job enrichment programs enhance a worker's feeling of responsibility and provide opportunities for growth and advancement when the worker is able to take on the more challenging tasks. For example, Statistics Canada allows employees who have been with the firm for four years a chance to request "career broadening" where they request an assignment in another department to build their skill set.[24] The potential benefits of job enrichment are great, but it requires careful planning and execution.

Flexible Scheduling Strategies. Many Canadians work a traditional 40-hour workweek consisting of five 8-hour days with fixed starting and ending times. Facing problems of poor morale and high absenteeism as well as a diverse workforce with changing needs, many managers have turned to flexible scheduling strategies such as flextime, compressed workweeks, job sharing, part-time work, and telecommuting. A survey by CareerBuilder.com showed that 40 percent of working fathers were offered flexible work schedules versus 53 percent of working mothers.[25]

Flextime is a program that allows employees to choose their starting and ending times, as long as they are at work during a specified core period (Figure 9.4). It does not reduce the total number of hours that employees work; instead, it gives employees more flexibility in choosing which hours they work. A firm may specify that employees must be present from 10:00 a.m. to 3:00 p.m. One employee may choose to come in at 7:00 a.m. and leave at the end of the core time, perhaps to attend classes at a nearby college after work. Another employee, a mother who lives in the suburbs, may come in at 9:00 a.m. to have time to drop off her children at a day care centre and commute by public transportation to her job. Flextime provides many benefits, including improved ability to recruit and retain workers who wish to balance work and home life. Customers can be better served by allowing more coverage of customers over longer hours, workstations and facilities can be better utilized by staggering employee use, and rush hour traffic may be reduced. In addition, flexible schedules have been associated with an increase in

figure 9.4 Flextime, Showing Core and Flexible Hours

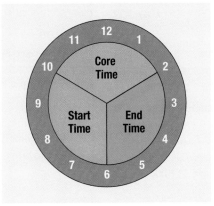

"Flextime provides many benefits, including improved ability to recruit and retain workers who wish to balance work and home life."

healthy behaviours on the part of employees. More flexible schedules are associated with healthier lifestyle choices such as increased physical activity and healthier sleep habits.[26] For example, the engineering firm Terrestrial Ecologist Golder Associates based in Calgary has recently been recognized as one of the top employers in Canada. Employees such as Darrin Nielsen state that the firm's flexible schedule is appreciated by its employees and helps the company retain staff. "They are very accommodating about work/life balance," says Nielsen. "If staff, say, work out in the field for 10 days in a row, they will want to reconnect with their families, and they likely will not have to keep regular office hours when they return."[27]

Related to flextime are the scheduling strategies of the compressed workweek and job sharing. The **compressed workweek** is a four-day (or shorter) period in which an employee works 40 hours. Under such a plan, employees typically work 10 hours per day for four days and have a three-day weekend. The compressed workweek reduces the company's operating expenses because its actual hours of operation are reduced. It is also sometimes used by parents who want to have more days off to spend with their families. The Bank of Montreal, Bell Canada, and Emera all use some variation of a reduced workweek.

> **Compressed workweek**
> a four-day (or shorter) period during which an employee works 40 hours

Job sharing occurs when two people do one job. One person may work from 8:00 a.m. to 12:30 p.m.; the second person comes in at 12:30 p.m. and works until 5:00 p.m. Job sharing gives both people the opportunity to work as well as time to fulfill other obligations, such as parenting or school. With job sharing, the company has the benefit of the skills of two people for one job, often at a lower total cost for salaries and benefits than one person working eight hours a day would be paid.

> **Job sharing** performance of one full-time job by two people on part-time hours

Two other flexible scheduling strategies attaining wider use include allowing full-time workers to work part time for a certain period and allowing workers to work at home either full or part time. Employees at some firms may be permitted to work part time for several months in order to care for a new baby or an elderly parent or just to slow down for a little while to "recharge their batteries." When the employees return to full-time work, they are usually given a position comparable to their original full-time position. Other firms are allowing employees to telecommute or telework (work at home a few days of the week), staying connected via computers, modems, and telephones. Today, 11.2 million Canadians are teleworkers, working most often from home.[29]

Although many employees ask for the option of working at home to ease the responsibilities of caring for family members, some have discovered that they are more productive at home

Consider the Following:
Enhancing Productivity: What's Mine is Yours and What's Yours is Mine

They share a desk, a telephone, a mailing address, and the single full-time position of coordinator for the Diagnostic Evaluation Center at North Shore Children's Hospital. Margot Kaczynski and Joanne Bartlett each work 20 hours a week, scheduling appointments, processing treatment referrals, and billing insurance companies. Both women want to work, but not full time. Kaczynski works Monday and Wednesday. Bartlett works Tuesday and Friday, and they split Thursday. The arrangement began when the hospital was downsizing and sought to combine two positions.

The two are typical of most job sharers—they are women in administrative positions who, for varying personal reasons, do not want full-time work. Job sharing is a small, but important part of the changes being made in the way people work in corporate North America. Flexibility is the key word and the number one priority for an increasing number of employees who are trying to mesh careers with personal lives. More and more employers are viewing flexibility as a necessity and realizing it can be used as a benefit to attract and retain satisfied employees. Keeping employees happy and

loyal to a company can go right to the bottom line. Studies show that employee loyalty correlates to customer loyalty which correlates to greater profits and growth. A firm may actually get greater output from two part-time successful job sharers than one full-time employee. Job sharers are diligent, often focusing intently on the job and maximizing the hours while there.

The arrangement works well for Kaczynski and Bartlett and their employer is pleased with the results. Today, not only must employers attract top talent, but they must work to retain it. To do that, organizations must create environments that support employees' family and lifestyle issues.[28]

DISCUSSION QUESTIONS

1. What jobs would lend themselves to this kind of arrangement? Which would not?

2. What limitations are there to this type of arrangement? To the organization? To the employee?

without the distractions of the workplace. An assessment of 12 company telecommuting programs, including Apple, AT&T, and the state of California, found that positive productivity changes occurred. Traveler's Insurance Company reports its telecommuters to be 20 percent more productive than its traditional employees.[30] Other employees, however, have discovered that they are not suited for working at home. Human resource management executives are split as to whether telecommuting helps or hurts employees' careers. Thirty percent feel telecommuting helps their careers, while 25 percent feel that it hurts, whereas 39 percent feel it does neither.[31] Still, work-at-home programs do help reduce overhead costs for businesses. For example, some companies used to maintain a surplus of office space but have reduced the surplus through employee telecommuting, "hoteling" (being assigned to a desk through a reservation system), and "hot-desking" (several people using the same desk but at different times).

Companies are turning to flexible work schedules to provide more options for employees who are trying to juggle their work duties with other responsibilities and needs. Preliminary results indicated that flexible scheduling plans increase job satisfaction, which, in turn, leads to increases in productivity. Some recent research, however, has indicated there are potential problems with telecommuting. Some managers are reluctant to adopt the practice because the pace of change in today's workplace is faster than ever, and telecommuters may be left behind or actually cause managers more work in helping them stay abreast of changes. Some employers also worry that telecommuting workers create a security risk by creating more opportunities for computer hackers or equipment

Single working-parent families face a tough challenge in balancing work and home life. For single parents, business travel and other routine demands of a corporate career—including overtime and interoffice transfers—can turn life upside down. Sometimes single parents decline promotions or high-profile assignments to preserve time with their children. In some organizations, experts say, it may be assumed single-mom staffers can't handle new duties because of the responsibilities they're shouldering at home.

thieves. Some employees have found that working outside the office may hurt career advancement opportunities, and some report that instead of helping them balance work and family responsibilities, telecommuting increases the strain by blurring the barriers between the office and home. Co-workers call at all hours, and telecommuters are apt to continue to work when they are not supposed to (after regular business hours or during vacation time).[32]

RESPONDING TO BUSINESS CHALLENGES | Bad Moods Contribute to Decreased Productivity

There is no getting around it: Bad moods produce bad results. Employees who come to work unhappy tend to carry that unhappiness throughout the day. Until recently, just how much bad moods affect the work environment was not clear. However, a study by business professor Steffanie Wilk found that employees who start the day in a bad mood can see their productivity levels reduced by more than 10 percent. Additionally, bad moods tend to be contagious, affecting other employees and customers and reducing the bottom line.

This does not bode well for companies in the current work climate. The Gallup-Healthways Well-Being Index reveals that employees are becoming unhappier with their jobs. Much of this can be attributed to economic uncertainty. With businesses cutting back, employees are often expected to take on greater roles with fewer benefits. As a result, employees experience more dissatisfaction with their jobs and a less positive relationship with their employers. The upshot is that managers can take steps to improve employees' moods in simple ways.

Some companies offer very small incentives that make employees feel appreciated.

3M, for instance, gives its employees time to pursue their own projects, an act that not only increases employee morale but has also yielded some of 3M's greatest product ideas. Employers might also encourage short periods of socialization among employees, which can improve moods and build cohesiveness. It seems like carrots, not sticks, are the key to creating a more productive work environment.[33]

DISCUSSION QUESTIONS

1. Why might an uncertain economic climate contribute to decreased productivity?

2. Why do employee bad moods have such a negative effect on an organization?

3. What can employers do to improve the moods of their employees?

Businesses have come up with different ways to motivate employees, including rewards such as trophies and plaques to show the company's appreciation.

need to cut jobs. In the most recent recession, many workers feared losing their jobs and increased the amount they were saving. The firm may have to work harder to keep good employees and to motivate all employees to work to overcome obstacles. In good economic times, employees may be more demanding and be on the lookout for better opportunities. New rewards or incentives may help motivate workers in such economies. Motivation tools, then, must be varied as well. Managers can further nurture motivation by being honest, supportive, empathetic, accessible, fair, and open. Motivating employees to increase satisfaction and productivity is an important concern for organizations seeking to remain competitive in the global marketplace.

Importance of Motivational Strategies

Motivation is more than a tool that managers can use to foster employee loyalty and boost productivity. It is a process that affects all the relationships within an organization and influences many areas such as pay, promotion, job design, training opportunities, and reporting relationships. Employees are motivated by the nature of the relationships they have with their supervisors, by the nature of their jobs, and by characteristics of the organization. Table 9.6 shows the top 10 Canadian companies to work for according to the *Financial Post*. Even the economic environment can change an employee's motivation. In a slow growth or recession economy, sales can flatten or decrease and morale can drop because of the

table 9.6 Best Companies to Work For

Bombardier Inc.
Cameco Corporation
Digital Extremes Ltd.
Golder Associates Ltd.
Ledcor Group of Companies
Nuance Communications Canada Inc.
OpenText Corporation
Shaw Communications Inc.
Suncor Energy Inc.
TD Bank Group

SOURCE: Financial Post's Ten Best Companies to Work For, 2013 Winners, *Financial Post*, http://www.canadastop100.com/fp10/fp10_2013.pdf (accessed February 6, 2013).

TEAM EXERCISE

Form groups and outline a compensation package that you would consider ideal in motivating an employee, recognizing performance, and assisting the company in attaining its cost-to-performance objectives. Think about the impact of intrinsic and extrinsic motivation and recognition. How can flexible scheduling strategies be used effectively to motivate employees? Report your compensation package to the class.

LEARNING OBJECTIVES SUMMARY

LO1	Define human relations, and determine why its study is important.

Human relations is the study of the behaviour of individuals and groups in organizational settings. Its focus is what motivates employees to perform on the job. Human relations is important because businesses need to understand how to motivate their increasingly diverse employees to be more effective, boost workplace morale, and maximize employees' productivity and creativity.

LO2 Summarize early studies that laid the groundwork for understanding employee motivation.

Time and motion studies by Frederick Taylor and others helped them analyze how employees perform specific work tasks in an effort to improve their productivity. Taylor and the early practitioners of the classical theory of motivation felt that money and job security were the primary motivators of employees. However, the Hawthorne studies revealed that human factors also influence workers' behaviour.

LO3 Compare and contrast the human-relations theories of Abraham Maslow and Frederick Herzberg.

Abraham Maslow defined five basic needs of all people and arranged them in the order in which they must be satisfied: physiological, security, social, esteem, and self-actualization. Frederick Herzberg divided characteristics of the job into hygiene factors and motivational factors. Hygiene factors relate to the work environment and must be present for employees to remain in a job. Motivational factors—recognition, responsibility, and advancement—relate to the work itself. They encourage employees to be productive. Herzberg's hygiene factors can be compared to Maslow's physiological and security needs; motivational factors may include Maslow's social, esteem, and self-actualization needs.

LO4 Investigate various theories of motivation, including Theories X, Y, and Z; equity theory; and expectancy theory.

Douglas McGregor contrasted two views of management: Theory X (traditional) suggests workers dislike work, while Theory Y (humanistic) suggests that workers not only like work but seek out responsibility to satisfy their higher-order needs. Theory Z stresses employee participation in all aspects of company decision making, often through participative management programs and self-directed work teams. According to equity theory, how much people are willing to contribute to an organization depends on their assessment of the fairness, or equity, of the rewards they will receive in exchange. Expectancy theory states that motivation depends not only on how much a person wants something but also on the person's perception of how likely he or she is to get it.

LO5 Describe some of the strategies that managers use to motivate employees.

Strategies for motivating workers include behaviour modification (changing behaviour and encouraging appropriate actions by relating the consequences of behaviour to the behaviour itself) and job design. Among the job design strategies businesses use are job rotation (allowing employees to move from one job to another to try to relieve the boredom associated with job specialization), job enlargement (adding tasks to a job instead of treating each task as a separate job), job enrichment (incorporating motivational factors into a job situation), and flexible scheduling strategies (flextime, compressed workweeks, job sharing, part-time work, and telecommuting).

KEY TERMS

behaviour modification
classical theory of motivation
compressed workweek
equity theory
esteem needs
expectancy theory
extrinsic reward
flextime
human relations
hygiene factors
intrinsic reward
job enlargement
job enrichment

job rotation
job sharing
Maslow's hierarchy
morale
motivation
motivational factors
physiological needs
security needs
self-actualization needs
social needs
Theory X
Theory Y
Theory Z

1. What are the pros and cons of Jim Pattison's and Andrew Wall's strategy of investing in star employees and quickly firing underperforming employees?

2. Imagine you are one of Jim Pattison's employees. Would you enjoy working there?

3. Is it ethical to fire people who have one bad year? Do companies have a moral obligation to help people succeed at their jobs?

SO YOU THINK *You May Be Good at Motivating a Workforce*

If you are good at mediation, can smooth over conflict, and have a good understanding of motivation and human relations theories, then you might be a good leader, human resource manager, or training expert. Most organizations, especially as they grow, will need to implement human relations programs. These are necessary to teach employees about sensitivity to other cultures, religions, and beliefs, as well as for teaching the workforce about the organization so that they understand how they fit in the larger picture. Employees need to appreciate the benefits of working together to make the firm run smoothly, and they also need to understand how their contributions help the firm. To stay motivated, most employees need to feel like what they do each day contributes something of value to the firm. Disclosing information and including employees in decision-making processes will also help employees feel valuable and wanted within the firm.

There are many different ways employers can reward and encourage employees. However, employers must be careful when considering what kinds of incentives to use. Different cultures value different kinds of incentives more highly than others. For example, a Japanese worker would probably not like it if she were singled out from the group and given a large cash bonus as a reward for her work. Japanese workers tend to be more group oriented, and therefore anything that singles out individuals would not be an effective way of rewarding and motivating. Canadian workers, on the other hand, are very individualistic, and a raise and public praise might be more effective. However, what might motivate a younger employee (bonuses, raises, and perks) may not be the same as what motivates a more seasoned, experienced, and financially successful employee (recognition, opportunity for greater influence, and increased training). Motivation is not an easy thing to understand, especially as firms become more global and more diverse.

Another important part of motivation is enjoying where you work and your career opportunities. Review Table 9.5 for the "Best Places to Find a Job in Canada." Chances are, workers in these places have encountered fewer frustrations than those in places at the bottom of the list and, therefore, would probably be more content with where they work.

BUILD YOUR BUSINESS PLAN

Motivating the Workforce

As you determine the size of your workforce, you are going to face the reality that you cannot provide the level of financial compensation that you would like to your employees, especially when you are starting your business.

Many employees are motivated by other things than money. Knowing that they are appreciated and doing a good job can bring great satisfaction to employees. Known as "stroking," it can provide employees with internal gratification that can be valued even more than financial incentives. Listening to employees' suggestions, involving them in discussions about future growth, and valuing their input can go a long way toward building loyal employees and reducing employee turnover.

Think about what you could do in your business to motivate your employees without spending much money. Maybe you will have lunch brought in once a week or offer tickets to a local sporting event to the employee with the most sales. Whatever you elect to do, you must be consistent and fair with all your employees.

In an age in which companies are cutting back health care benefits due to a sluggish economy, many employers are turning to low-cost perks to keep workers happy. In addition to perks such as gym and spa facilities and weight-loss programs, an increasing number of companies are actually allowing employees to bring their pets to work. A recent survey conducted by Dogster (an online dog forum) and Simply Hired indicates that two-thirds of all dog owners surveyed would work longer hours if allowed to bring their dogs to work. One-third claimed they would accept a 5 percent pay deduction if allowed to bring their dogs to work. Maybe this is because another survey indicated that 69 percent of dog owners view their dog as part of the family.

Having dogs and cats in the workplace can provide many benefits, including a more relaxed and flexible atmosphere, increased staff morale, and even increased employee retention. One company's spokesperson indicated that its pet policy gives employees individual flexibility and shows that the company respects employees enough to let them make choices about their work environment. The American Psychological Association has even honoured companies such as Small Dog Electronics, a computer merchant with 27 employees, as psychologically healthy workplaces in part because of their pet-friendly policies. At this time, many pet-friendly companies have 50 or fewer employees, although a few *Fortune* 500 companies such as Amazon and Google have pet-friendly policies. At Planet Dog, a company allowing pets in the office daily, the company consists, so to speak, of 16 employees and 14 dogs.

A pet-friendly workplace can be a definite advantage in recruiting and retaining employees. Small Dog Electronics, for example, has boasted an employee turnover rate of 1 percent compared with its industry average of 11 percent. Even non–pet owners often appreciate the informal, flexible environments that characterize workplaces with pets. To some extent, being pet-friendly helps define a corporate culture—as it does at AutoDesk, a software provider. A Pet Products Manufacturers Association survey revealed that 73 percent of surveyed companies believed allowing pets at work increased productivity—compared with a 42 percent productivity increase due to business development or management training. Even when it is not possible for employees to bring pets to work every day, some companies allow them to bring their pets to work occasionally for short periods of time.

Many small businesses, particularly retailers, established pet-friendly policies out of personal necessity. Indeed many small retailers, such as antique dealers and bookstore owners, often have "store cats" or "store dogs" that are appreciated as much by customers as by employees. Although legislation prohibits allowing pets in restaurants in Canada and the United States, many European restaurants allow customers to have their dogs right at their tables where food is served.

While bringing your pet to work can definitely improve morale, there are a few challenges. People with allergies or who are afraid of animals may get distracted from their jobs. Of course, there may be the concern that a dog may bite a person or another dog. However, research by attorneys at Ralston Purina found that lawsuits related to pets in the work environment are quite rare. As long as good judgment is used, allowing animals in the workplace appears to be a great move.[34]

DISCUSSION QUESTIONS

1. Why can a nonfinancial benefit such as being able to bring your dog to work motivate employees?

2. What types of businesses are appropriate for a pet-friendly workplace policy?

3. How do you personally feel about having other people's pets in an office where you work or store where you shop?

LEARNING OBJECTIVES

LO1 Define human resources management, and explain its significance.

LO2 Summarize the processes of recruiting and selecting human resources for a company.

LO3 Discuss how workers are trained and their performance appraised.

LO4 Identify the types of turnover companies may experience, and explain why turnover is an important issue.

LO5 Specify the various ways a worker may be compensated.

LO6 Discuss some of the issues associated with unionized employees, including collective bargaining and dispute resolution.

LO7 Describe the importance of diversity in the workforce.

DESTINATION CEO

Jack Welch For two decades, Jack Welch was at the helm of the most admired company in the world—GE. Now that he is retired, he and his wife, Suzy, have written the book *Winning*.

Welch's secret for success, he says, is recruiting and hiring people who are smarter than he is and who have a lot of energy, those with an edge and who can be energized to pursue the goals of the company. Welch describes three categories of employees—the top performers, the middle 70 percent, and the "others." Success, he says, is about maintaining the energy of the top performers. When asked how he motivates the middle 70 percent, he says that his approach is controversial. Welch maintains that it is important for that group to know what it takes for them to move up in the organization. Welch believes that it is important for all members of the organization to know where they stand. As for the "other" group, he says that more often than not, they will move on. Welch firmly believes that the job of the leader is to focus on the followers—not on your own success.

The most exciting thing about being a manager or a leader is helping people to grow and providing them the opportunity to change their lives. The hardest part, he says, is letting people go. Overall, however, it is important that no one in the organization is ever surprised about their performance review. Constant feedback, letting people know where they stand, is the most important role of the manager. In short, Welch says that once you are a manager, "It's about them, not about you."[1]

Introduction

If a business is to achieve success, it must have sufficient numbers of employees who are qualified and motivated to perform the required duties. Thus, managing the quantity (from hiring to firing) and quality (through training, compensating, and so on) of employees is an important business function. Meeting the challenge of managing increasingly diverse human resources effectively can give a company a competitive edge in a global marketplace.

This chapter focuses on the quantity and quality of human resources. First, we look at how human resources managers plan for, recruit, and select qualified employees. Next, we look at training, appraising, and compensating employees, aspects of human resources management designed to retain valued employees. Along the way, we'll also consider the challenges of managing unionized employees and workplace diversity.

The Nature of Human Resources Management

Chapter 1 defined human resources as labour, the physical and mental abilities that people use to produce goods and services. **Human resources management (HRM)** refers to all the activities involved in determining an organization's human resources needs, as well as acquiring, training, and compensating people to fill those needs. Human resources managers are concerned with maximizing the satisfaction of employees and motivating them to meet organizational objectives productively. In some companies, this function is called personnel management.

> **Human resources management (HRM)** all the activities involved in determining an organization's human resources needs, as well as acquiring, training, and compensating people to fill those needs

HRM has increased in importance over the last few decades, in part because managers have developed a better understanding of human relations through the work of Maslow, Herzberg, and others. Moreover, the human resources themselves are changing. Employees today are concerned not only about how much a job pays; they are concerned also with job satisfaction, personal performance, leisure, the environment, and the future. Once dominated by white men, today's workforce includes significantly more women, African Canadians, Chinese Canadians, and other minorities, as well as disabled and older workers. Human resources managers must be aware of these changes and

Today's organizations are more diverse, with a greater range of women, minorities, and older workers.

make the best use of them to increase the productivity of their employees. Every manager practises some of the functions of human resources management at all times.

Planning for Human Resources Needs

When planning and developing strategies for reaching the organization's overall objectives, a company must consider whether it will have the human resources necessary to carry out its plans. After determining how many employees and what skills are needed to satisfy the overall plans, the human resources department (which may range from the owner in a small business to hundreds of people in a large corporation) ascertains how many employees the company currently has and how many will be retiring or otherwise leaving the organization during the planning period. With this information, the human resources manager can then forecast how many more employees the company will need to hire and what qualifications they must have. HRM planning also requires forecasting the availability of people in the workforce who will have the necessary qualifications to meet the organization's future needs. The human resources manager then develops a strategy for satisfying the organization's human resources needs. As organizations strive to increase efficiency through outsourcing, automation, or learning to effectively use temporary workers, hiring needs can change dramatically. With the Baby Boomers entering retirement years, more companies are stating that they are having staffing difficulties. In a recent survey of the fastest-growing companies in Canada, 70 percent of employers noted that their inability to find qualified workers is hindering their ability to grow.[2] Even as unemployment rates rose throughout 2009 and 2010, many employers stated this was only a blip and anticipated increased competition to hire skilled employees in the coming years. In 2006, Manpower chairman and CEO Jeffrey Joerres declared, "In 10 years, we will see many companies fail because they haven't planned ahead and are unable to find people they need to run their businesses."[3] In fact, by 2016 Canada is expected to have a workforce shortage of one million people, which will grow to three million people by 2026.[4] Next, managers analyze the jobs within the organization so that they can match the human resources to the available assignments. **Job analysis** determines, through observation and study, pertinent information about a job—the specific tasks that comprise it; the knowledge, skills, and abilities necessary to perform it; and the environment in which it will be performed. Managers use the information obtained through a job analysis to develop job descriptions and job specifications. For example, Sandra Wilson, founder of British Columbia-based Robeez

> **Job analysis** the determination, through observation and study, of pertinent information about a job—including specific tasks and necessary abilities, knowledge, and skills

Job description a formal, written explanation of a specific job, usually including job title, tasks, relationship with other jobs, physical and mental skills required, duties, responsibilities, and working conditions

Job specification a description of the qualifications necessary for a specific job, in terms of education, experience, and personal and physical characteristics

Recruiting forming a pool of qualified applicants from which management can select employees

Footwear Ltd., completed a job analysis and determined that the firm would need to hire aggressive, self-motivated people if the company was to keep growing in the highly competitive market of children's footwear.[5]

A **job description** is a formal, written explanation of a specific job that usually includes job title, tasks to be performed (for instance, waiting on customers), relationship with other jobs, physical and mental skills required (such as lifting heavy boxes or calculating data), duties, responsibilities, and working conditions. A **job specification** describes the qualifications necessary for a specific job, in terms of education (some jobs require a postsecondary degree), experience, personal characteristics (newspaper ads frequently request outgoing, hardworking persons), and physical characteristics. Both the job description and job specification are used to develop recruiting materials such as newspaper and online advertisements.

LO2 Summarize the processes of recruiting and selecting human resources for a company.

Recruiting and Selecting New Employees

After forecasting the firm's human resources needs and comparing them to existing human resources, the human resources manager should have a general idea of how many new employees the firm needs to hire. With the aid of job analyses, management can then recruit and select employees who are qualified to fill specific job openings.

Recruiting

Recruiting means forming a pool of qualified applicants from which management can select employees. There are two sources from which to develop this pool of applicants—the internal and external environments.

Internal sources of applicants include the organization's current employees. Many firms have a policy of giving first consideration to their own employees—or promoting from within. The cost of hiring current employees to fill job openings is inexpensive when compared with the cost of hiring from external sources, and it is good for employee morale.

External sources consist of advertisements in newspapers and professional journals, employment agencies, colleges, vocational schools, recommendations from current employees, competing firms, unsolicited applications, and online. Internships are also a good way to solicit for potential employees. Many companies hire university students or recent graduates for low-paying internships that give them the opportunity to get hands-on experience on the job. If the intern proves to be a good fit, an organization may then hire the intern as a full-time worker. Figure 10.1 illustrates some of the top benefits of becoming an intern. There are also hundreds of websites where employers can post job openings and job seekers can post their résumés, including Workopolis.com, Monster.com, and CareerBuilder.com. Employers seeking employees for specialized jobs can use more focused sites such as computerwork.com. Increasingly, companies can turn to their own websites for potential candidates. Employers can also use social networking sites such as LinkedIn to post jobs and search for candidates. Figure 10.2 indicates that many consumers believe social networking sites may eventually supplant traditional résumés. Using external sources of applicants is generally more expensive than hiring from within, but it may be necessary if there are no current employees who meet the job specifications or if there are better-qualified people outside of the organization. Recruiting for entry-level managerial and professional positions is often carried out on college and university campuses. For managerial or professional positions above the entry level, companies sometimes depend on employment agencies or executive search firms, sometimes called *headhunters,* which specialize in luring qualified people away from other companies.

As noted above, recruiting is becoming increasingly important to Canadian companies and many firms are starting to use innovative methods to expand the list of qualified employees. For example, Toronto-based I Love Rewards Inc., a business that advises companies on employee

figure 10.1 Benefits of an Internship

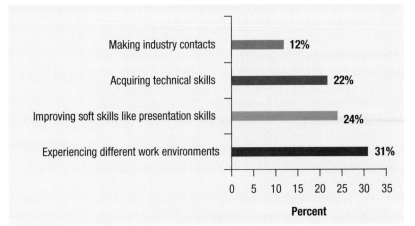

SOURCE: Creative Group Survey of 125 Advertising Executives and 125 Senior Marketing Executives, "'What I did this summer . . . ',' April 15, 2009, http://creativegroup.mediaroom.com/index.php?s=43&item=91 (accessed October 11, 2011).

recognition and incentive programs, recently had to fill 18 positions. Rather than advertise the positions online or in newspapers, or use headhunters, the company's owner Razor Suleman relied on social media sites to find qualified applicants. Suleman had his employees post information about the jobs on their Facebook site, tweet about them, and share the information on LinkedIn. He notes that using these methods saved him thousands as one advertisement in the newspaper would have cost him $5,000 and a headhunter would have charged roughly $260,000 to fill the positions.[6] Larger firms such as FutureShop are also jumping on the bandwagon with plans to staff 5,000 holiday season jobs using Facebook and Twitter as its main posting site. In fact, a recent search on www.tweetmyjobs.com would have found postings from Bombardier, Suncor, and Mercedes-Benz Canada.[7]

Selection

Selection is the process of collecting information about applicants and using that information to decide which ones to hire. It includes the application itself, as well as interviewing, testing, and reference checking. This process can be quite lengthy and expensive. At Procter & Gamble, for example, the steps include application submission, screening and comprehensive interviews, day visits/site visits, and for international applicants, a problem-solving test to ensure that P&G attracts and retains high-quality employees.[8] Such rigorous scrutiny is necessary to find those applicants who can do the work expected and fit into the firm's structure and culture. If an organization finds the "right" employees through its recruiting and selection process, it will not have to spend as much money later in recruiting, selecting, and training replacement employees.

> **Selection** the process of collecting information about applicants and using that information to make hiring decisions

The Application. In the first stage of the selection process, the individual fills out an application form and perhaps has a brief interview. The application form asks for the applicant's name, address, telephone number, education, and previous work experience. The goal of this stage of the selection process is to get acquainted with the applicants and to weed out those who are obviously not qualified for the job. For example, Canada's Wonderland receives roughly 18,000 applications for its 4,000 seasonal jobs. The company relies on résumé screening to eliminate people who do not possess the qualities or experience it looks for in employees.[9] Most companies ask for the following information before contacting a potential candidate: current salary, reason for seeking a new job, years of experience, availability, and level of interest in the position. In addition to identifying obvious qualifications, the application can provide subtle clues about whether a person is appropriate for a particular job. For instance, an applicant who gives unusually creative answers may

be perfect for a position at an advertising agency; a person who turns in a sloppy, hurriedly scrawled application probably would not be appropriate for a technical job requiring precise adjustments. Many companies now accept online applications. The online application at Target is designed not only to collect biographical data but to create a picture of the applicant and how the person might contribute within the company. The completion of the survey takes about 45 minutes, depending on the position. To get a better view of the fit between the applicant and the company, the online application contains a questionnaire that asks applicants for more specific information, from how they might react in a certain situation to personality attributes like self-esteem or ability to interact with people.

The Interview. The next phase of the selection process involves interviewing applicants. Interviews allow management to obtain detailed information about the applicant's experience and skills, reasons for changing jobs, attitudes toward the job, and an idea of whether the person would fit in with the company. Table 10.1 shares some organizational qualities potential employees should evaluate during a visit to the company. Table 10.2 lists some of the most common questions asked by interviewers, while Table 10.3 reveals

figure 10.2 Will Profiles on Networking Sites Replace Traditional Résumés?

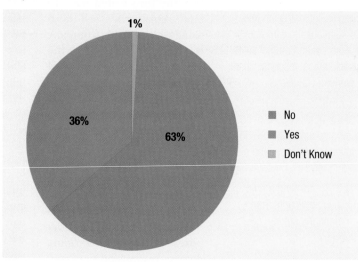

- No
- Yes
- Don't Know

SOURCE: OfficeTeam survey of 500 human resources managers. Reprinted in *USA Today,* March 16, 2011.

table 10.1 Interviewing Tips

1. Evaluate the work environment. Do employees seem to get along and work well in teams?

2. Evaluate the attitude of employees. Are employees happy, tense, or overworked?

3. Are employees enthusiastic and excited about their work?

4. What is the organizational culture, and would you feel comfortable working there?

SOURCE: Adapted from "What to Look for During Office Visits," http://careercenter.tamu.edu/guides/interviews/lookforinoffice.cfm?sn5parents (accessed April 13, 2011).

table 10.2 Top 10 Interview Questions

1. Tell me about yourself.

2. Why should I hire you?

3. Please tell me about your future objectives.

4. Has your education prepared you for your career?

5. Have you been a team player?

6. Did you encounter any conflict with your previous professors or employer? What are the steps that you have taken to resolve this issue?

7. What is your biggest weakness?

8. How would your professors describe you?

9. What are the qualities that a manager should possess?

10. If you could turn back time, what would you change?

SOURCE: "Job Interview Skills Training: Top Ten Interview Questions for College Graduates," February 17, 2010, www.articlesbase.com/business-articles/job-interview-skills-training-top-ten-interview-questions-for-college-graduates-1871741.html (accessed April 13, 2011).

some common mistakes candidates make in interviewing. Furthermore, the interviewer can answer the applicant's questions about the requirements for the job, compensation, working conditions, company policies, organizational culture, and so on. A potential employee's questions may be just as revealing as his or her answers.

Testing. Another step in the selection process is testing. Ability and performance tests are used to determine whether an applicant has the skills necessary for the job. Aptitude, IQ, or personality tests may be used to assess an applicant's potential for a certain kind of work and his or

Some jobs require potential hires to undergo physical examinations such as alcohol tests.

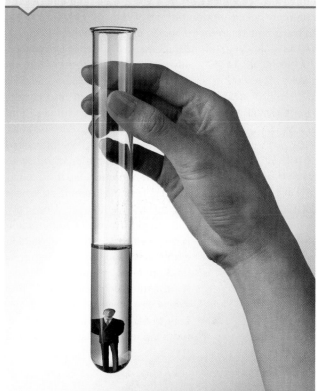

her ability to fit into the organization's culture. One of the most commonly used tests is the Myers-Briggs Type Indicator, which is used more than 2.5 million times each year according to a survey by *Workforce Management*. Although polygraph ("lie detector") tests were once a common technique for evaluating the honesty of applicants, their use has been restricted to specific government jobs and those involving security or access to drugs. Polygraph tests have been replaced by a number of paper-based ethics or honesty tests, which are supposed to screen out unethical candidates without subjecting candidates to the abrasive nature of a polygraph. Applicants may also undergo physical examinations to determine their suitability for some jobs. One difference between Canadian and American human resource practices revolves around the use of drug testing—the practice is no longer legal in Canada (with some exceptions for government positions) but in the United States many companies require applicants to be screened for illegal drug use. More than 40 million drug tests are conducted annually in the U.S. by employers, with less than 5 percent yielding a positive result.[10] In Canada, employers can screen for alcohol but not drugs.[11]

> ## "Ability and performance tests are used to determine whether an applicant has the skills necessary for the job."

Reference Checking. Before making a job offer, the company should always check an applicant's references. Reference checking usually involves verifying educational background and previous work experience. Background checking is important because applicants may misrepresent themselves on their applications or résumés. The star of *Dinner: Impossible* on the Food Network fabricated portions of his résumé, including the claim that he cooked for Britain's

table 10.3 Mistakes Made in Interviewing

1. Not taking the interview seriously.

2. Not dressing appropriately (dressing down).

3. Not appropriately discussing experience, abilities, and education.

4. Being too modest about your accomplishments.

5. Talking too much.

6. Too much concern about compensation.

7. Speaking negatively of a former employer.

8. Not asking enough or appropriate questions.

9. Not showing the proper enthusiasm level.

10. Not engaging in appropriate follow-up to the interview.

SOURCE: "Avoid the Top 10 Job Interview Mistakes," *All Business*, www.allbusiness.com/human-resources/careers-job-interview/1611-1.html (April 13, 2011).

royal family. The Food Network, upon learning of these errors, did not renew Robert Irvine's contract, indicating that viewers place trust in the network and the accuracy of information that it provides and that Irvine "challenged that trust."[12] Irvine had to work for months to apologize and set the record straight about his chef credentials. The Food Network ultimately did rehire him to host *Dinner: Impossible*. As Table 10.4 illustrates, some of the most common types of résumé lies include the faking of credentials, overstatements of skills or accomplishments, lies concerning education/degrees, omissions of past employment, and the falsification of references.[13] Reference checking is a vital, albeit often overlooked, stage in the selection process. Managers charged with hiring should be aware, however, that many organizations will confirm only that an applicant is a former employee, perhaps with beginning and ending work dates, and will not release details about the quality of the employee's work.

Legal Issues in Recruiting and Selecting

Legal constraints and regulations are present in almost every phase of the recruitment and selection process, and a violation of these regulations can result in lawsuits and fines. Therefore, managers should be aware of these restrictions to avoid legal problems. The Charter of Rights and Freedoms guarantees that all people are treated the same way under the law and the Canadian Human Rights Act ensures that all people have equal opportunities for employment.[14] The Human Rights Act is applicable for all federally regulated organizations including banks and airlines. Individual provinces and territories have their own laws to protect workers in non-regulated businesses.[15] Another important law which businesses have to be aware of is the Employment Equity Act, signed in 1986, which ensures that federally regulated employers with more than 100 employees do not disadvantage women, visible minorities, disabled people, and Aboriginals. Furthermore, organizations have to make special accommodations to assist people in these categories in gaining meaningful employment. Additionally, if an employer or organization had a disproportionate number of male employees, then they had to develop a plan to balance out the gender of their employees. The same concept applies to skin colour and/or cultural background.[16] Recently, a new category of workers has gone before Human Rights Boards to fight for their rights. Baby Boomers, who have been forced to retire due to the mandatory retirement age in Canada being set at 65, have successfully challenged the law under the Charter of Rights and Freedoms and mandatory retirement has effectively been abolished in most of Canada as a result.[17]

Developing the Workforce

Once the most qualified applicants have been selected and offered positions, and they have accepted their offers, they must be formally introduced to the organization and trained so they can begin to be productive members of the workforce. **Orientation** familiarizes the newly hired employees with fellow workers, company procedures, and the physical properties of the company. It generally includes a tour of the building; introductions to supervisors, co-workers, and subordinates; and the distribution of organizational manuals describing the organization's policy on vacations, absenteeism, lunch breaks, company benefits, and so on. Orientation also involves socializing the new employee into the ethics and culture of the new company. Many larger companies now show videos of procedures, facilities, and key personnel in the organization to help speed the adjustment process. For example, Canadian Tire now has all Financial Service employees attend Canadian Tire University at the company's Niagara campus, where they learn about all the different divisions, the company's mission and vision statements, and company values.[18]

LO3 Discuss how workers are trained and their performance appraised.

Training and Development

Although recruiting and selection are designed to find employees who have the knowledge, skills, and abilities the company needs, new employees still must undergo **training** to learn how to do their specific job tasks. *On-the-job training* allows workers to learn by actually performing the tasks of the job, while *classroom training* teaches employees with lectures, conferences, videos, case studies, and Web-based training. For instance, McDonald's trains those interested in company operations and leadership development at the Fred L. Turner Training Center, otherwise known as Hamburger University. Hamburger University employs full-time professors to train students in a variety of topics, including crew development, restaurant management, middle management, and executive development. Training includes classroom instruction, hands-on instruction, and

table 10.4 Top 10 Résumé Lies

1. Stretching dates of employment
2. Inflating past accomplishments and skills
3. Enhancing job titles and responsibilities
4. Education exaggeration and fabricating degrees
5. Unexplained gaps and periods of "self employment"
6. Omitting past employment
7. Faking credentials
8. Fabricating reasons for leaving previous job
9. Providing fraudulent references
10. Misrepresenting military record

SOURCE: Christopher T. Marquet and Lisa J. B. Peterson, "Résumé Fraud: The Top 10 Lies," www.marquetinternational.com/pdf/Resume%20 Fraud-Top%20Ten%20Lies.pdf (accessed April 13, 2011).

Development training that augments the skills and knowledge of managers and professionals

computer e-learning, with instruction available in 28 different languages.[19] **Development** is training that augments the skills and knowledge of managers and professionals. Training and development are also used to improve the skills of employees in their present positions and to prepare them for increased responsibility and job promotions. Training is therefore a vital function of human resources management. Use of role-plays, simulations, and online training methods are becoming increasingly popular in employee training. Ron Foxcroft, CEO of Fox 40 International, a Hamilton-based whistle manufacturer, states that training combined with programs to ensure that people are working in the right jobs has boosted employee engagement and profits.[20] Training is therefore a vital function of human resources management. Companies are engaging in more experiential and involvement-oriented training exercises for employees.

Assessing Performance

Assessing an employee's performance—his or her strengths and weaknesses on the job—is one of the most difficult tasks for managers. However, performance appraisal is crucial because it gives employees feedback on how they are doing and what they need to do to improve their performance. It also provides a basis for determining how to compensate and reward employees, and it generates information about the quality of the firm's selection, training, and development activities. Table 10.5 identifies 16 characteristics that may be assessed in a performance review.

Performance appraisals may be objective or subjective. An objective assessment is quantifiable. For example, a Westinghouse employee might be judged by how many circuit boards he typically produces in one day or by how many of his boards have defects. A Century 21 real estate agent might be judged by the number of houses she has shown or the number of sales she has closed. A company can also use tests as an objective method of assessment. Whatever method they use, managers must take into account the work environment when they appraise performance objectively.

When jobs do not lend themselves to objective appraisal, the manager must relate the employee's performance to some other standard. One popular tool used in subjective assessment is the ranking system, which lists various performance factors on which the manager ranks employees against each other. Although used by many large companies, ranking systems are unpopular with many employees. Qualitative criteria, such as teamwork

and communication skills, used to evaluate employees are generally hard to gauge. Such grading systems have triggered employee lawsuits that allege discrimination in grade/ranking assignments. For example, one manager may grade a company's employees one way, while another manager grades a group more harshly depending on the managers' grading style. If layoffs occur, then employees graded by the second manager may be more likely to lose their jobs. Other criticisms of grading systems include unclear wording or inappropriate words that a manager may unintentionally write in a performance evaluation, like *young* or *pretty* to describe an employee's appearance. These liabilities can all be fodder for lawsuits should employees allege that they were treated unfairly. It is therefore crucial that managers use clear language in performance evaluations and be consistent with all employees. Several employee grading computer packages have been developed to make performance evaluations easier for managers and clearer for employees.[21]

Another performance appraisal method used by many companies is the 360-degree feedback system, which provides feedback from a panel that typically includes superiors, peers, and subordinates. Because of the tensions it may cause, peer appraisal appears to be difficult for many. However, companies that have success with 360-degree

table 10.5 General Performance Characteristics

- **Productivity**—rate at which work is regularly produced
- **Quality**—accuracy, professionalism, and deliverability of produced work
- **Job knowledge**—understanding of the objectives, practices, and standards of work
- **Problem solving**—ability to identify and correct problems effectively
- **Communication**—effectiveness in written and verbal exchanges
- **Initiative**—willingness to identify and address opportunities for improvement
- **Adaptability**—ability to become comfortable with change
- **Planning and organization skills**—reflected through the ability to schedule projects, set goals, and maintain organizational systems
- **Teamwork and cooperation**—effectiveness of collaborations with co-workers
- **Judgment**—ability to determine appropriate actions in a timely manner
- **Dependability**—responsiveness, reliability, and conscientiousness demonstrated on the job
- **Creativity**—extent to which resourceful ideas, solutions, and methods for task completion are proposed
- **Sales**—demonstrated through success in selling products, services, yourself, and your company
- **Customer service**—ability to communicate effectively with customers, address problems, and offer solutions that meet or exceed their expectations
- **Leadership**—tendency and ability to serve as a doer, guide, decision maker, and role model
- **Financial management**—appropriateness of cost controls and financial planning within the scope defined by the position

SOURCE: "Performance Characteristics," Performance Review from www.salary.com/Careerresources/docs/related_performance_review_part2_popup.html (accessed June 12, 2001). Used with permission.

feedback tend to be open to learning and willing to experiment and are led by executives who are direct about the expected benefits as well as the challenges.[22] Managers and leaders with a high emotional intelligence (sensitivity to their own as well as others' emotions) assess and reflect upon their interactions with colleagues on a daily basis. In addition, they conduct follow-up analysis on their projects, asking the right questions and listening carefully to responses without getting defensive of their actions.[23] A recent study indicated that roughly one-third of companies in Canada were now using 360-degree performance appraisals.[24]

Whether the assessment is objective or subjective, it is vital that the manager discuss the results with the employee, so that the employee knows how well he or she is doing the job. The results of a performance appraisal become useful only when they are communicated, tactfully, to the employee and presented as a tool to allow the employee to grow and improve in his or her position and beyond. Performance appraisals are also used to determine whether an employee should be promoted, transferred, or terminated from the organization.

> "The results of a performance appraisal become useful only when they are communicated, tactfully, to the employee and presented as a tool to allow the employee to grow and improve in his or her position and beyond."

LO4   Identify the types of turnover companies may experience, and explain why turnover is an important issue.

Turnover

Turnover, which occurs when employees quit, or are fired, promoted, or transferred and must be replaced by new employ-

> **Turnover** occurs when employees quit, or are fired, promoted, or transferred, and must be replaced by new employees

ees, results in lost productivity from the vacancy, fees to recruit replacement employees, management time devoted to interviewing, and training costs for new employees. Some companies are able to manage their employees more effectively to minimize turnover. Costco's turnover rate is 17 percent overall and just 6 percent after one year of employment, costing the company $244 million per year, or $3,628 per employee.[26] On a smaller scale, Karen Flavelle, president of Vancouver-based Purdy's Chocolates, says her loyal employees are paramount to her company's success. Flavelle's employees work nine years on average, which is significant as 50 percent of her employees are frontline staff. Flavelle offers her employees internal promotions, teambuilding activities, and the opportunity to participate in a profit-sharing program. The low turnover has resulted in a reduction in recruitment and training costs and a highly efficient operation.[27] Part of the reason for turnover may be overworked employees as a result of downsizing and a lack of training and advancement opportunities.[28] Of course, turnover is not always an unhappy occasion when it takes the form of a promotion or transfer.

Consider the Following: Morale Among the Survivors

Medallion Corporation manufactures quality carpeting and linoleum. A recession and subsequent downturn in home sales has sharply cut the company's sales. Medallion found itself in the unenviable position of having to lay off hundreds of employees in the home office (the manufacturing facilities) as well as many salespeople. Employees were called in on Friday afternoon and told about their status in individual meetings with their supervisors. The laid-off employees were given one additional month of work and two weeks' severance pay per year of service, along with the opportunity to sign up for classes to help with the transition, including job search tactics and résumé writing.

Several months after the cutbacks, morale was at an all-time low for the company, although productivity had improved. Medallion brought in consultants, who suggested that the leaner, flatter organizational structure would be suitable for more team activities. Medal-

lion therefore set up task forces and teams to deal with employee concerns, but the diversity of the workforce led to conflict and misunderstandings among team members. Medallion is evaluating how to proceed with this new team approach.[25]

DISCUSSION QUESTIONS

1. What did Medallion's HRM department do right in dealing with the employees who were laid off?

2. What are some of the potential problems that must be dealt with after an organization experiences a major trauma such as massive layoffs?

3. What can Medallion do to make the team approach work more smoothly? What role do you think diversity training should play?

For multinational corporations such as McDonald's, employee training and performance assessments might need to be slightly adapted for different cultures.

table 10.6 What to Avoid When Leaving Your Job

1. Do not tell off your boss and co-workers, even if you think they deserve it.

2. Do not damage company property or steal something.

3. Do not forget to ask for a reference.

4. Do not badmouth your employer or any of your co-workers to your replacement.

5. Do not badmouth your employer to a prospective employer when you go on a job interview.

SOURCE: Dawn Rosenberg McKay, "Five Things Not to Do When You Leave Your Job," http://careerplanning.about.com/od/jobseparation/a/leave_mistakes.htm (accessed April 13, 2011).

Job promotion advancement to a higher-level position with increased authority, responsibility, and pay

Transfer a move to another job within the company at essentially the same level and wage

Separations employment changes involving resignation, retirement, termination, or layoff

A **job promotion** is advancement to a higher-level position with increased authority, responsibility, and pay. In some companies and most labour unions, seniority—the length of time a person has been with the company or at a particular job classification—is the key issue in determining who should be promoted. Most managers base promotions on seniority only when they have candidates with equal qualifications: Managers prefer to base promotions on merit.

A **transfer** is a move to another job within the company at essentially the same level and wage. Transfers allow workers to obtain new skills or to find a new position within an organization when their old position has been eliminated because of automation or downsizing.

Separations occur when employees resign, retire, are terminated, or are laid off. Employees may be terminated, or fired, for poor performance, violation of work rules, absenteeism, and so on. Businesses have traditionally been able to fire employees *at will,* that is, for any reason other than for race, religion, sex, or age, or because an employee is a union organizer. However, recent legislation and court decisions now require that companies fire employees fairly, for just cause only. Managers must take care, then, to warn employees when their performance is unacceptable and may lead to dismissal. They should also document all problems and warnings in employees' work records. To avoid the possibility of lawsuits from individuals who may feel they have been fired unfairly, employers should provide clear, business-related reasons for any firing, supported by written documentation if possible. Employee disciplinary procedures should be carefully explained to all employees and should be set forth in employee handbooks. Table 10.6 illustrates what *not* to do when you are terminated.

Many companies have downsized in recent years, laying off tens of thousands of employees in their effort to become more productive and competitive. Chrysler underwent a restructuring plan that cut 3,000 jobs and three models, including the PT Cruiser, Dodge Durango, and Chrysler Aspen. The company also rejected hundreds of car dealership agreements, resulting in significant job losses.[30] Layoffs are sometimes temporary; employees may be brought back when business conditions improve. For instance, after the most recent recession Chrysler began to rehire some of the workers it had been forced to lay off.[31] When layoffs are to be permanent, employers often help employees find other jobs and may extend benefits while the employees search for new employment. Such actions help lessen the trauma of the layoffs. Fortunately, there are several business areas that are choosing not to downsize.

A well-organized human resources department strives to minimize losses due to separations and transfers because recruiting and training new employees is very expensive. For example, Loblaw Cos. Ltd. is shifting more of its employees to full-time work with plans to convert 10,000 part-time positions to full-time work in the coming years. The company says that

Some companies are able to manage their employees more effectively to minimize turnover.

Consider the Following: Human Resources Management Crosses Borders

The proximity of Mexico to the U.S. and Canada and the implementation of the North American Free Trade Agreement have made Mexico an increasingly attractive site for foreign investment. However, the closeness of the three countries can be misleading. Canadian and U.S. companies often assume that their human resources management practices can be transported to Mexico as easily as raw materials. In reality, human resources management in Mexico involves unique challenges, especially in areas of turnover, absenteeism, demographics, employee involvement, and labour unions. The usual tactics for addressing these issues are sometimes unconventional or even not permitted in Canada or the U.S.

Production worker turnover rates in northern Mexico are high, averaging between 7 and 15 percent per month. One factor is the abundance of potential employers. The number of foreign-owned plants in Mexico that export their finished product has risen by 700 in recent years, to approximately 2,700. Some managers consider absenteeism a more severe problem than turnover, with the most frequently given reason for absence being family issues. In general, the Mexican culture gives greater value to family than to work.

To combat the excessive levels of turnover and absenteeism, salaries are competitive and financial incentives are frequently offered. For example, some companies offer bonuses to employees who stay 30 days. Another bonus is given after 60 days and then after 90 days. Bonuses for attendance are standard, and discount coupons, subsidized transportation to and from work, and subsidized lunches encourage employee loyalty. Non-monetary benefits help retention rates too. Parties and picnics are an expected part of the Mexican culture, and it is not uncommon for a job applicant to ask how many parties a company gives each year.

Practices generally viewed as taboo in Canada and the U.S. but frequent in Mexico include the production worker beauty contest, in which employees vote for their plant's most attractive female worker, who then competes against workers from other plants. Gender preference in hiring is legitimate in Mexico, and banners are often seen that say, "Recruiting Female Employees." Because of extensive maternity benefits, however, companies routinely screen job applicants with pregnancy tests. A woman with a positive test may not be hired or may be hired under a short-term contract. This practice is technically illegal in Mexico, but is widespread and tolerated.

It is impossible to transfer all human resources management practices from Canada and the U.S. to other areas. Managing cultural diversity in a global environment requires an assessment of specific management challenges and the identification of approaches for meeting such challenges.[29]

---

the move should reduce staff turnover and improve productivity.[32] Note that a high turnover rate in a company may signal problems either with the selection and training process, the compensation program, or even the type of company. To help reduce turnover, companies have tried a number of strategies, including giving employees more interesting job responsibilities (job enrichment), allowing for increased job flexibility, and providing more employee benefits.

LO5 Specify the various ways a worker may be compensated.

Compensating the Workforce

People generally don't work for free, and how much they are paid for their work is a complicated issue. Also, designing a fair compensation plan is an important task because pay and benefits represent a substantial portion of an organization's expenses. Wages that are too high may result in the company's products being priced too high, making them uncompetitive in the market. Wages that are too low may damage employee morale and result in costly turnover. Remember that compensation is one of the hygiene factors identified by Herzberg.

Designing a fair compensation plan is a difficult task because it involves evaluating the relative worth of all jobs within the business while allowing for individual efforts. Compensation for a specific job is typically determined through a **wage/salary survey**, which tells the company how much compensation comparable firms are paying for specific jobs that the firms have in common. Compensation can also vary amongst employees within the same job category based on productivity.

Wage/salary survey a study that tells a company how much compensation comparable firms are paying for specific jobs that the firms have in common

Wages financial rewards based on the number of hours the employee works or the level of output achieved

Financial Compensation

Financial compensation falls into two general categories—wages and salaries. **Wages** are financial rewards based on the number of hours the employee works or the level of output achieved. Wages based on the number of hours worked are called time wages. A cook at Harvey's, for example, might earn anywhere from $9.27 to $10.25 per hour according to the provincial minimum wage. In Canada the general minimum wage varies by province or territory with a high of $11.00 per hour in Nunavut and a low of $9.95 per hour ($9.05 for liquor servers) in Alberta.[33] Table 10.7 compares the minimum wage across the country. As previously discussed in this chapter, the impending shortage of labour will result in increased levels of compensation especially for skilled workers in Canada.

Time wages are appropriate when employees are continually interrupted and when quality is more important than quantity. Assembly-line workers, clerks, and maintenance personnel are commonly paid on a time-wage basis. The advantage of time wages is the ease of computation. The disadvantage is that time wages provide no incentive to increase productivity. In fact, time wages may encourage employees to be less productive.

To overcome these disadvantages, many companies pay on an incentive system, using piece wages or commissions. Piece wages are based on the level of output achieved. A major advantage of piece wages is that they motivate employees to supervise their own activities and to increase output. Skilled craftworkers are often paid on a piece-wage basis.

The other incentive system, **commission,** pays a fixed amount or a percentage of the employee's sales. John Mulvihill is an automobile salesperson at a General Motors dealership in Sydney, Nova Scotia He earns $250–$300 for every GM and $350–$500 for every Cadillac he sells.[34] This method motivates employees to sell as much as they can. Some companies combine payment based on commission with time wages or salaries.

A **salary** is a financial reward calculated on a weekly, monthly, or annual basis. Salaries are associated with white-collar workers such as office personnel, executives, and professional employees. Although a salary provides a stable stream of income, salaried workers may be required to work beyond usual hours without additional financial compensation.

In addition to the basic wages or salaries paid to employees, a company may offer **bonuses** for exceptional performance as an incentive to increase productivity further. Many workers receive a bonus as a "thank you" for good work and

Commission an incentive system that pays a fixed amount or a percentage of the employee's sales

Salary a financial reward calculated on a weekly, monthly, or annual basis

Bonuses monetary rewards offered by companies for exceptional performance as incentives to further increase productivity

table 10.7 Provincial/Territorial Minimum Wage, September 2013

Jurisdiction	Wage (C$)	Effective Date	Comments
Alberta	9.95	Sept. 1, 2013	$9.05 for liquor servers. Any further increases will be set on a yearly basis using the Consumer Price Index as well as average weekly earnings in Alberta.
British Columbia	10.25	May 1, 2012	$9.00 for liquor servers.
Manitoba	10.25	Oct. 1, 2012	Workers involved in construction have a higher starting minimum wage.
New Brunswick*; Newfoundland and Labrador†; Northwest Territories*; Prince Edward Island*; Saskatchewan	10.00	Apr. 1, 2012*; Jul. 1, 2010†; Dec. 1, 2012	
Nova Scotia	10.30	Apr. 1, 2013	$9.80 for inexperienced workers (less than three months employed in the type of work they are hired to do). Annual increase on Apr. 1 to reflect changes in Statistics Canada's Low Income Cut-Off figures for the previous year.
Nunavut	11.00	Jan. 1, 2011	Highest in Canada
Ontario	10.25	Mar. 31, 2010	Students (under age 18, working ≤ 28 hrs/wk while school is in session or during a school break): $9.60. Liquor servers: $8.90. Homeworkers (includes students and overrides the student wage): $11.28.
Québec	10.15	May 1, 2013	Workers receiving gratuities receive $8.75.
Yukon	10.54	April 1, 2013	Yukon currently pegs annual increases (every April 1) to its minimum wage using the Consumer Price Index.

SOURCE: "Minimum Wage in Canada", September 2013, http://en.wikipedia.org/wiki/Minimum_wage_in_Canada (accessed September 20, 2013).

an incentive to continue working hard. Many owners and managers are recognizing that simple bonuses and perks foster happier employees and reduce turnover. For example, RBC offers employees a number of incentives including shares in the company for meeting and/or exceeding performance goals. Rob Lachowiez, a RBC mortgage broker, has received free trips for meeting annual sales goals. Atlantic Canada-based Maritime Travel offers employees free trips and other travel rewards if they meet their sales targets.[35]

> **Profit sharing** a form of compensation whereby a percentage of company profits is distributed to the employees whose work helped to generate them

Another form of compensation is **profit sharing,** which distributes a percentage of company profits to the employees whose work helped to generate those profits. Some profit-sharing plans involve distributing shares of company stock to employees. Usually referred to as *ESOPs*—employee stock ownership plans—they have been gaining popularity in recent years. One reason for the popularity of ESOPs is the sense of partnership that they create between the organization and employees. Profit sharing can also motivate employees to work hard, because increased productivity and sales mean that the profits or the stock dividends will increase. WestJet management attributes much of its success to the fact that approximately 85 percent of its employees own shares in the company. Senior management has noted that employees who own shares in the business have a vested interest in the company succeeding and they will often go the extra mile to ensure that customers are happy.[36] Many organizations offer

Larger companies such as Google will sometimes offer onsite gyms or workout facilities as an employee benefit.

employees a stake in the company through stock purchase plans, ESOPs, or stock investments through RRSP plans. Almost every large company in Canada, including RBC and Onex, and many small businesses such as LifeofSports.com, are creating opportunities for employees to become shareholders in their business. Employees below senior management levels rarely received stock options, until recently. Companies are adopting broad-based stock option plans to build a stronger link between employees' interests and the organization's interests. ESOPs have met with enormous success over the years, and employee-owned stock has even outperformed the stock market during certain periods. Many businesses have found employee stock options a great way to boost productivity and increase morale.

GOING GREEN | Google Rewards Employees for Being Sustainable

For employees at Google, it pays to be green. Google employees can save money, donate to charities, and receive discounts on eco-friendly technology by taking advantage of the company's green incentives. For instance, employees can save fuel costs by riding to work on Google's biodiesel shuttles. They can also use Google's GFleet car-sharing program, GBikes, or taxi service GRide for travelling across the company campus or attending meetings offsite. For employees who choose to bike, walk, or pogo to work, the company provides them with digital stamps, which can be redeemed for company donations to the employee's favourite charity.

Many of Google's green initiatives help both employees and society. In 2011, Google announced that it was creating a $280 million fund for SolarCity in a partnership to support the installation of solar panels on residential homes. While it may be difficult to convince the average consumer to adopt solar technology, Google offers its employees discounts. The company also created the largest corporate electronic-vehicle charging station in the country, not only to support the electric vehicles in its GFleet but also to inspire employees to purchase their own. Google seeks to make a difference in the field of sustainability—starting with its employees.[37]

DISCUSSION QUESTIONS

1. Describe some of Google's green initiatives.

2. How is Google rewarding employees for adopting greener behaviours?

3. Why do you think it might be beneficial for Google to subsidize the cost of installing solar panels on employee houses, even if it costs the company money?

Benefits

Benefits are nonfinancial forms of compensation provided to employees, such as pension plans for retirement; health, disability, and life insurance; holidays and paid days off for vacation or illness; credit union membership; health programs; child care; elder care; assistance with adoption; and more. According to Statistics Canada the total cost of employee benefits has risen faster than wages with costs to employers increasing two to three times the rate of inflation. Legally required benefits—Canadian Pension Plan, workers' compensation, and Employment Insurance—account for some of the increase in costs, but increases in nonmandatory benefits such as health and dental plans account for the majority of the increase.[38] Such benefits increase employee security and, to a certain extent, morale and motivation.

Table 10.8 lists some of the benefits Internet search engine Google offers its employees. Although health insurance is a common benefit for full-time employees, rising health care costs have forced a growing number of employers to trim this benefit. Even government workers, whose wages and benefits used to be virtually guaranteed safe, have seen reductions in health care and other benefits.

As benefits continue to rise some companies are coming up with measures to keep costs down. Bell Canada, for instance, started the process of discontinuing its post-retirement benefits program in 2012.[39] Many companies are introducing or changing their benefits plan to share the cost burden with employees. Additionally, flexible benefit plans where employees choose the benefits that they want are growing in popularity. Under flex plans the employer provides employees with a dollar amount that it will contribute to employee benefits and employees can choose from options that suit their lifestyle. If employees want additional benefit coverage they make up the cost difference out of their own pockets. Employers like these types of plans as they allow employees to have access to a variety of benefit options and employees often share the costs.

A benefit increasingly offered is the employee assistance program (EAP). Each company's EAP is different, but most offer counselling for and assistance with those employees' personal problems that might hurt their job performance if not addressed. The most common counselling services offered include drug and alcohol-abuse treatment programs, fitness programs, smoking cessation clinics, stress-management clinics, financial counselling, family counselling, and career counselling. EAPs help reduce costs associated with poor productivity, absenteeism, and other workplace issues by helping employees deal with personal problems that contribute to these issues. For example, exercise and fitness programs reduce health insurance costs by helping employees stay healthy. Family counselling may help workers trying to cope with a divorce or other personal problems better focus on their jobs.

Companies try to provide the benefits they believe their employees want, but diverse people may want different things. In recent years, some single workers have felt that co-workers with spouses and children seem to get "special breaks" and extra time off to deal with family issues. Some companies use flexible benefit programs to allow employees to choose the benefits they would like, up to a specified amount.

Fringe benefits include sick leave, vacation pay, pension plans, health plans, and any other extra compensation. Soft benefits include perks that help balance life and work. They include onsite child care, spas, food service, and even laundry services and hair salons. These soft benefits motivate employees and give them more time to focus on their jobs.

> "The most common counselling services offered include drug and alcohol-abuse treatment programs, fitness programs, smoking cessation clinics, stress-management clinics, financial counselling, family counselling, and career counselling."

table 10.8 Google's Employee Benefits

- Health insurance:
  – Dental insurance
  – Vision insurance
- Vacation (15 days per year for one to three years' employment; 20 days off for four to five years' employment; 25 days for more than six years' employment)
- Twelve paid holidays/year
- Savings plans
- Disability and life insurance
- Employee assistance program
- Free lunches and snacks
- Massages, gym membership, hair stylist, fitness class, and bike repair
- Weekly activities
- Maternity leave
- Adoption assistance
- Tuition reimbursement
- Employee referral plan
- On-site doctor
- Backup child care
- Holiday parties, health fair, credit union, roller hockey, outdoor volleyball court, discounts for local attractions

SOURCE: "Google Benefits," www.google.com/intl/en/jobs/lifeatgoogle/benefits (accessed April 13, 2011).

Cafeteria benefit plans provide a financial amount to employees so that they can select the specific benefits that fit their needs. The key is making benefits flexible, rather than giving employees identical benefits. As firms go global, the need for cafeteria or flexible benefit plans becomes even more important. For some employees, benefits are a greater motivator and differentiator in jobs than wages.

Over the last two decades, the list of fringe benefits has grown dramatically, and new benefits are being added every year.

LO6 Discuss some of the issues associated with unionized employees, including collective bargaining and dispute resolution.

Managing Unionized Employees

Employees who are dissatisfied with their working conditions or compensation have to negotiate with management to bring about change. Dealing with management on an individual basis is not always effective, however, so employees may organize themselves into **labour unions** to deal with employers and to achieve better pay, hours, and working conditions. Organized employees are backed by the power of a large group that can hire specialists to represent the entire union in its dealings with management. The Canadian Auto Workers, for example, has considerable power in its negotiations with Ford Motor Company and General Motors. Unionized blue-collar workers make 54 percent more than their non-unionized counterparts and are twice as likely to have health insurance and pension plans.[40]

However, union growth has slowed in recent years, and prospects for improvement do not look good. One reason is that most blue-collar workers, the traditional members of unions, have already been organized. Factories have become more automated and need fewer blue-collar workers. Canada has shifted from a manufacturing to a service economy, further reducing the demand for blue-collar workers. Moreover, in response to foreign competition, Canadian companies are scrambling to find ways to become more productive and cost efficient. Job enrichment programs and participative management have blurred the line between management and workers. Because workers' say in the way plants are run is increasing, their need for union protection is decreasing.

Nonetheless, labour unions have been successful in organizing blue-collar manufacturing, government, and health care workers, as well as smaller percentages of employees in other industries. In fact, approximately 30 percent of all employed Canadians are represented by a union.[41] Consequently, significant aspects of HRM, particularly compensation, are dictated to a large degree by union contracts at many companies. Therefore, we'll take a brief look at collective bargaining and dispute resolution in this section.

Collective Bargaining

Collective bargaining is the negotiation process through which management and unions reach an agreement about compensation, working hours, and working conditions for the bargaining unit (Figure 10.3). The objective of negotiations is to reach agreement about a **labour contract**, the formal, written

figure 10.3 The Collective Bargaining Process

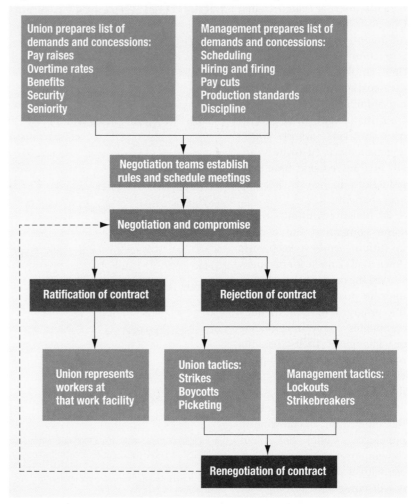

document that spells out the relationship between the union and management for a specified period of time, usually two or three years.

In collective bargaining, each side tries to negotiate an agreement that meets its demands; compromise is frequently necessary. Management tries to negotiate a labour contract that permits the company to retain control over things like work schedules; the hiring and firing of workers; production standards; promotions, transfers, and separations; the span of management in each department; and discipline. Unions tend to focus on contract issues such as magnitude of wages; better pay rates for overtime, holidays, and undesirable shifts; scheduling of pay increases; and benefits. These issues will be spelled out in the labour contract, which union members will vote to either accept (and abide by) or reject.

Many labour contracts contain a *cost-of-living allowance (COLA)*, or cost-of-living escalator clause, which calls for automatic wage increases during periods of inflation to protect the "real" income of the employees. During tough economic times, unions may be forced to accept *givebacks*—wage and benefit concessions made to employers to allow them to remain competitive or, in some cases, to survive and continue to provide jobs for union workers.

Resolving Disputes

Sometimes, management and labour simply cannot agree on a contract. Most labour disputes are handled through collective bargaining or through grievance procedures. When these processes break down, however, either side may resort to more drastic measures to achieve its objectives.

Labour Tactics. **Picketing** is a public protest against management practices and involves union members marching (often waving anti-management signs and placards) at the employer's plant. Picketing workers hope that their signs will arouse sympathy for their demands from the public and from other unions. Picketing may occur as a protest or in conjunction with a strike.

Strikes (employee walkouts) are one of the most effective weapons labour has. By striking, a union makes carrying out the normal operations of a business difficult at best and impossible at worst. Strikes receive widespread publicity, but they remain a weapon of last resort. For example, after the French government announced plans to overhaul pensions and raise the retirement age from 60 to 62, citizens engaged in a nationwide strike to protest the changes. The strikes shut down schools and delayed rail and flight services.[42] The threat of a strike is often enough to get management to back down. In fact, the number of worker-days actually lost to strikes is less than the amount lost to the common cold.

A **boycott** is an attempt to keep people from purchasing the products of a company. In a boycott, union members are asked not to do business with the boycotted organization. Some unions may even impose fines on members who ignore the boycott. To gain further support for their objectives, a union involved in a boycott may also ask the public—through picketing and advertising—not to purchase the products of the picketed firm.

Management Tactics. Management's version of a strike is the **lockout;** management actually closes a worksite so that employees cannot go to work. Lockouts are used, as a general rule, only when a union strike has partially shut down a plant and it seems less expensive for the plant to close completely.

Strikebreakers, called "scabs" by striking union members, are people hired by management to replace striking employees. Managers hire strikebreakers to continue operations and reduce the losses associated with strikes—and to show the unions that they will not bow to their demands. Strikebreaking is generally a last-resort measure for management because it does great damage to the relationship between management and labour.

Outside Resolution. Management and union members normally reach mutually agreeable decisions without outside assistance. Sometimes though, even after lengthy negotiations, strikes, lockouts, and other tactics, management and labour still cannot resolve a contract dispute. In such cases, they have three choices: conciliation, mediation, and arbitration. **Conciliation** brings in a neutral third party to keep labour and management talking. The conciliator has no formal power over union representatives or over management. The conciliator's goal is to get both parties to focus on the issues and to prevent negotiations from breaking down. Like conciliation, **mediation** involves bringing in a neutral third party, but the mediator's role is to suggest or propose a solution to the problem. Mediators have no formal power over either labour or management. With **arbitration,** a neutral third party is brought in to settle the dispute, but the arbitrator's solution is legally binding and enforceable. Generally, arbitration takes place on a voluntary basis—management and labour must agree to it, and they usually split the cost (the arbitrator's fee and expenses) between them. Occasionally, management and labour submit to *compulsory arbitration,* in which an outside party (usually the federal government) requests arbitration as a means of eliminating a prolonged strike that threatens to disrupt the economy.

LO7 Describe the importance of diversity in the workforce.

The Importance of Workforce Diversity

Customers, employees, suppliers—all the participants in the world of business—come in different ages, genders, races, ethnicities, nationalities, and abilities, a truth that business has come to label **diversity.** Understanding this diversity means recognizing and accepting differences as well as valuing the unique perspectives such differences can bring to the workplace.

> **Diversity** the participation of different ages, genders, races, ethnicities, nationalities, and abilities in the workplace

The Characteristics of Diversity

When managers speak of diverse workforces, they typically mean differences in gender and race. While gender and race are important characteristics of diversity, others are also important. We can divide these differences into primary and secondary characteristics of diversity. In the lower segment of Figure 10.4, age, gender, race, ethnicity, abilities, and sexual orientation represent *primary characteristics* of diversity which are inborn and cannot be changed. In the upper section of Figure 10.4 are eight *secondary characteristics* of diversity— work background, income, marital status, military experience, religious beliefs, geographic location, parental status, and education—which *can* be changed. We acquire, change, and discard them as we progress through our lives.

Defining characteristics of diversity as either primary or secondary enhances our understanding, but we must remember that each person is defined by the inter-relation of all characteristics. In dealing with diversity in the workforce, managers must consider the complete person—not one or a few of a person's differences.

Why Is Diversity Important?

The Canadian workforce is becoming increasingly diverse. Once dominated by white men, today's workforce includes significantly more women, Aboriginals,

"Once dominated by white men, today's workforce includes significantly more women, Aboriginals, disabled, and other minority groups."

disabled, and other minority groups. In fact, as of 2010, women, Aboriginals, visible minorities, and the disabled make up over 60 percent of Canada's workforce.[43] These groups have traditionally faced discrimination and higher unemployment rates and have been denied opportunities to assume leadership roles in corporate Canada. Consequently, more and more companies are trying to improve HRM programs to recruit, develop, and retain more diverse employees to better serve their diverse customers. Some firms are providing special programs such as sponsored affinity groups, mentoring programs, and special career development opportunities. Corporate Canada is also aware of the upcoming labour shortage and is becoming increasingly aware that eliminating barriers to potential employees could eliminate part of this problem. In fact, a recent study completed by RBC found that eliminating age, gender, and cultural barriers could bring an additional 1.6 million Canadians to the workforce.[44] Table 10.9 shows the top 20 companies for minorities according to a study by *Fortune.* Effectively managing diversity in the workforce involves cultivating and valuing its benefits and minimizing its problems. Companies that are championing diversity are also becoming aware of the impact a diverse workforce can have on their financial performance.

figure 10.4 Characteristics of Diversity

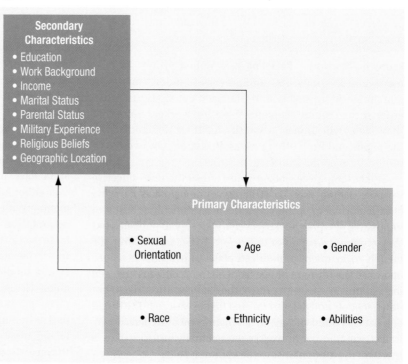

SOURCE: Marilyn Loden and Judy B. Rosener, *Workforce America! Managing Employee Diversity as a Vital Resource,* 1991, p. 20. Used with permission. Copyright © 1991 The McGraw-Hill Companies.

Value Diversity: Her Rise to the Top. The Bank of Montreal is a good example of an organization that took the notion of diversity management seriously. Finding that women held 91 percent of the bank's non-management jobs but only 9 percent of the executive positions, the bank made an early attempt to tap the vast potential of its female workforce. The bank established a Task Force on the Advancement of Women to identify the constraints facing women who wanted career advancement in the bank. Clear goals and action plans were established to eliminate these hurdles. Surveys, focus groups, and intense interviews were carried out to find solutions so that women could progress faster to executive careers.

Apart from the financial benefits it received by tapping a hitherto forgotten resource, the bank also received numerous awards for its success in improving the work climate of women, Aboriginals, and people with disabilities. The Catalyst Award from a New York think tank, the Distinction Award from the YWCA, and Catalyst: Mercury Awards from the International Communications Academy of Arts and Sciences in New York are particularly noteworthy in this context.

By 2006, over 67 percent of BMO's employees were women and 51 percent of the managers were also women. Twenty percent of employees and managers were visible minorities.[45]

The closing of the gender gap has resulted in women holding top-ranking positions in many Canadian companies. The presidents of Canada Post, Indigo/Chapters/ Coles, Linamar Technologies, and Home Depot Canada are all women.

Some of the major benefits of diversity include a wider range of employee perspectives, greater innovation and creativity, and the ability to target a diverse customer base more effectively.

table 10.9 Top 20 Companies for Diversity

1. Sodexo
2. PricewaterhouseCoopers
3. Kaiser Permanente
4. Ernst & Young
5. MasterCard Worldwide
6. Novartis Pharmaceuticals Corp.
7. Procter & Gamble
8. Prudential Financial
9. Accenture
10. Johnson & Johnson
11. Deloitte
12. Merck & Co.
13. AT&T
14. Abbott
15. Cummins
16. Marriott International
17. Medtronic
18. Kraft Foods
19. Aetna
20. Target

SOURCE: "The 2013 DiversityInc Top 50 List," *DiversityInc*, April 24, 2013, www.diversityinc.com/ the-diversityinc-top-50-companies-for-diversity-2013/ (accessed July 8, 2013).

Clearly, operating a large or small business to the benefit of the companies, their customers, and the communities in which they operate can be done by women or men.

The Benefits of Workforce Diversity

There are a number of benefits to fostering and valuing workforce diversity, including the following:

1. More productive use of a company's human resources.

2. Reduced conflict among employees of different ethnicities, races, religions, and sexual orientations as they learn to respect each other's differences.

3. More productive working relationships among diverse employees as they learn more about and accept each other.

4. Increased commitment to and sharing of organizational goals among diverse employees at all organizational levels.

5. Increased innovation and creativity as diverse employees bring new, unique perspectives to decision-making and problem-solving tasks.

6. Increased ability to serve the needs of an increasingly diverse customer base.[46]

Companies that do not value their diverse employees are likely to experience greater conflict, as well as prejudice and discrimination. Among individual employees, for example, racial slurs and gestures, sexist comments, and other behaviours by co-workers harm the individuals at whom such behaviour is directed. The victims of such behaviour may feel hurt, depressed, or even threatened and suffer from lowered self-esteem, all of which harm their productivity and morale. In such cases, women and minority employees may simply leave the firm, wasting the time, money, and other resources spent on hiring and training them. When discrimination comes from a supervisor, employees may also fear for their jobs. A discriminatory atmosphere not only can harm productivity and increase turnover, but may also subject a firm to costly lawsuits and negative publicity.

Astute business leaders recognize that they need to modify their human resources management programs

"Companies that do not value their diverse employees are likely to experience greater conflict, as well as prejudice and discrimination."

to target the needs of *all* their diverse employees as well as the needs of the firm itself. They realize that the benefits of diversity are long term in nature and come only to those organizations willing to make the commitment. Most importantly, as workforce diversity becomes a valued organizational asset, companies spend less time managing conflict and more time accomplishing tasks and satisfying customers, which is, after all, the purpose of business.

Employment Equity

Employee equity emerged in Canada in 1986. The Employment Equity Act is designed to ensure that women, Aboriginals, the disabled, and visible minorities receive the same employment opportunities as all Canadians.

TEAM EXERCISE

Form groups and go to monster.com and look up job descriptions for positions in business (account executive in advertising, marketing manager, human resources director, production supervisor, financial analyst, bank teller, etc). What are the key requirements for the position that you have been assigned (education, work experience, language/computer skills, etc.)? Does the position announcement provide a thorough understanding of the job? Was any key information omitted that you would have expected to see? Report your findings to the class.

LEARNING OBJECTIVES SUMMARY

LO1 Define human resources management, and explain its significance.

Human resources, or personnel, management refers to all the activities involved in determining an organization's human resources needs and acquiring, training, and compensating people to fill those needs. It is concerned with maximizing the satisfaction of employees and improving their efficiency to meet organizational objectives.

LO2 Summarize the processes of recruiting and selecting human resources for a company.

First, the human resources manager must determine the firm's future human resources needs and develop a strategy to meet them. Recruiting is the formation of a pool of qualified applicants from which management will select employees; it takes place both internally and externally. Selection is the process of collecting information about applicants and using that information to decide which ones to hire; it includes the application, interviewing, testing, and reference checking.

LO3 Discuss how workers are trained and their performance appraised.

Training teaches employees how to do their specific job tasks; development is training that augments the skills and knowledge of managers and professionals, as well as current employees. Appraising performance involves identifying an employee's strengths and weaknesses on the job. Performance appraisals may be subjective or objective.

LO4 Identify the types of turnover companies may experience, and explain why turnover is an important issue.

A promotion is an advancement to a higher-level job with increased authority, responsibility, and pay. A transfer is a move to another job within the company at essentially the same level and wage. Separations occur when employees resign, retire, are terminated, or are laid off. Turnovers due to separation are expensive because of the time, money, and effort required to select, train, and manage new employees.

LO5 Specify the various ways a worker may be compensated.

Wages are financial compensation based on the number of hours worked (time wages) or the number of units produced (piece wages). Commissions are a fixed amount or a percentage of a sale paid as compensation. Salaries are compensation calculated on a weekly, monthly, or annual basis, regardless of the number of hours worked or the number of items produced. Bonuses and profit sharing are types of financial incentives. Benefits are nonfinancial forms of compensation, such as vacation, insurance, and sick leave.

LO6 Discuss some of the issues associated with unionized employees, including collective bargaining and dispute resolution.

Collective bargaining is the negotiation process through which management and unions reach an agreement on a labour contract—the formal, written document that spells out the relationship between the union and management. If labour and management cannot agree on a contract, labour union members may picket, strike, or boycott the firm, while management may lock out striking employees, hire strikebreakers, or form employers' associations. In a deadlock, labour disputes may be resolved by a third party—a conciliator, mediator, or arbitrator.

LO7 Describe the importance of diversity in the workforce.

When companies value and effectively manage their diverse workforces, they experience more productive use of human resources, reduced conflict, better work relationships among workers, increased commitment to and sharing of organizational goals, increased innovation and creativity, and enhanced ability to serve diverse customers.

KEY TERMS

arbitration
benefits
bonuses
boycott
collective bargaining
commission
conciliation
development
diversity
human resources management (HRM)
job analysis
job description
job promotion
job specification
labour contract
labour unions

lockout
mediation
orientation
picketing
profit sharing
recruiting
salary
selection
separations
strikebreakers
strikes
training
transfer
turnover
wage/salary survey
wages

DESTINATION CEO DISCUSSION QUESTIONS

1. According to Jack Welch, what is the most important aspect of being a leader?

2. How does Welch deal with the bottom group of employees in an organization?

3. What is the most exciting thing about being a boss, according to Welch?

Managing human resources is a challenging and creative facet of a business. It is the department that handles the recruiting, hiring, training, and firing of employees. Because of the diligence and detail required in hiring and the sensitivity required in firing, human resources managers have a broad skill set. Human resources, therefore, is vital to the overall functioning of the business because without the right staff a firm will not be able to effectively carry out its plans. Like in basketball, a team is only as strong as its individual players, and those players must be able to work together and to enhance strengths and downplay weaknesses. In addition, a good human resources manager can anticipate upcoming needs and changes in the business, hiring in line with the dynamics of the market and organization.

Once a good workforce is in place, human resources managers must ensure that employees are properly trained and oriented and that they clearly understand some elements of what the organization expects. Hiring new people is expensive, time-consuming, and turbulent; thus, it is imperative that all employees are carefully selected, trained, and motivated so that they will remain committed and loyal to the company. This is not an easy task, but it is one of the responsibilities of the human resources manager. Even with references, a résumé, background checks, and an interview, it can be hard to tell how a person will fit into the organization; the HR manager needs to be able to anticipate how every individual will "fit in." Human resources jobs include compensation, labour relations, benefits, training, ethics, and compliance managers. All of the tasks associated with the interface with hiring, developing, and maintaining employee motivation come into play in human resources management. Jobs are diverse and salaries will depend on responsibilities, education, and experience.

One of the major considerations for an HR manager is workforce diversity. A multicultural, multiethnic workforce consisting of men and women will help bring a variety of viewpoints and improve the quality and creativity of organizational decision making. Diversity is an asset and can help a company from having blindspots or too much harmony in thought, background, and perspective, which stifles good team decisions. However, a diverse workforce can present some management challenges. Human resources management is often responsible for managing diversity training and compliance to make sure employees do not violate the ethical culture of the organization or break the law. Different people have different goals, motivations, and ways of thinking about issues that are informed by their culture, religion, and the people closest to them. No one way of thinking is more right or more wrong than others, and they are all valuable. A human resources manager's job can become very complicated, however, because of diversity. To be good at human resources, you should be aware of the value of differences, strive to be culturally sensitive, and ideally should have a strong understanding of and appreciation for different cultures and religions. Human resources managers' ability to manage diversity and those differences will affect their overall career success.

BUILD YOUR BUSINESS PLAN

Managing Human Resources

Now is the time to start thinking about the employees you will need to hire to implement your business plan. What kinds of background/skills are you going to look for in potential employees? Are you going to require a certain amount of work experience?

When you are starting a business you are often only able to hire part-time employees because you cannot afford to pay the benefits for a full-time employee. Remember at the end of the last chapter we discussed how important it is to think of ways to motivate your employees when you cannot afford to pay them what you would like.

You need to consider how you are going to recruit your employees. When you are first starting your business, it is often a good idea to ask people you respect (and not necessarily members of your family) for any recommendations of potential employees they might have. You probably won't be able to afford to advertise in the classifieds, so announcements in sources such as church bulletins or community bulletin boards or on social networking sites should be considered as an excellent way to attract potential candidates with little, if any, investment.

Finally, you need to think about hiring employees from diverse backgrounds—especially if you are considering targeting diverse consumer segments. The more diverse your employees, the greater the chance you will be able to draw in diverse customers.

Working from home may sound like a dream. Yet when that dream comes true, employees find some downsides that they did not expect. Perhaps the greatest challenge is that of balancing work and home life. In a traditional job setting, work occurs in the office while leisure occurs at home. However, those who work at home lack this clear boundary. Lack of office space, family distractions, and sticking to set schedules are additional challenges work-at-home employees face.

These challenges are not going away anytime soon. According to Statistics Canada, in 2008, just under 1.8 million Canadians worked from home, representing 11.2 percent of all paid employees. The situation has led experts to recommend methods to help work-at-home employees.

First, employees working at home should have a clear work space, even if it is only a desk on which work materials reside. Maintaining a schedule of strict hours devoted to work and then communicating these hours to family and friends is important. Additionally, for some workers who crave socialization, working alone might be difficult. However, thanks to technology, employees can often work in social settings like coffee shops or libraries.

Those who can't get past these challenges have pursued other creative alternatives. Some freelancers and entrepreneurs have begun renting office space at work areas designed to accommodate the self-employed. These spaces have a more relaxed atmosphere than a normal work environment; one of these "work spaces," for instance, is located in a Victorian home. Other work-at-home entrepreneurs opt to form weekly work gatherings, where individuals can work on their laptops while being able to socialize with others. For many self-motivated individuals, the rewards of working away from the office outweigh the sacrifices.[47]

DISCUSSION QUESTIONS

1. Why is working from home a challenge to many employees?

2. How does one create a boundary between work and home life when working from home?

3. Would you be more productive working from home or renting space at an out-of-home work area?

connect **LEARNSMART** **SMARTBOOK**

For more information on the resources available from McGraw-Hill Ryerson, go to www.mcgrawhill.ca/he/solutions.

LEARNING OBJECTIVES

LO1 Define marketing and describe the exchange process.

LO2 Specify the functions of marketing.

LO3 Explain the marketing concept and its implications for developing marketing strategies.

LO4 Examine the development of a marketing strategy, including market segmentation and marketing mix.

LO5 Investigate how marketers conduct marketing research, and study buying behaviour.

LO6 Summarize the environmental forces that influence marketing decisions.

DESTINATION CEO

Ronnen Harary and Anton Rabie are living what for many would be a childhood dream. The close friends are co-CEOs of their own toy company—Spin Master Toys. The 40-something Canadians have taken the toy world by storm over the last 15 years with such hot items as *Bakugan*, Moshi Monsters; Air Hogs, planes that fly on air power; Doctor Dreadful Aliens; and the fashionable and stylish La Dee Da dolls. In addition, they have signed partnership agreements with some of the biggest companies in North America, including Disney and McDonald's, to develop such toys as the SpongeBob SquarePants-inspired Bounce 'Rounds (inflatable, portable play gyms) and a McDonald's McFlurry Maker. The company has reached $650 million in sales. One of the first and most common questions people ask after hearing the accomplishments of the two entrepreneurs is, "How did they break into a North American toy market that is characterized by large operators with equally large product development and marketing budgets?" The answer is somewhat surprising. They relied on ingenuity and a combination of public relations (PR) and grassroots marketing.

The company's first product was Earth Buddy, a small head constructed of pantyhose and filled with grass seed that would sprout grass when watered. With no money for a major marketing campaign, the entrepreneurs set out to spread their story using non-traditional marketing and PR, selling the product and their story to anyone who would listen. The product was a huge success and they were on their way. They followed the product with Devil Sticks, a game for children, and they managed to sell 250,000 units in six months without using any traditional promotional campaigns. Instead they hired college and university students to demonstrate the game at playgrounds, local events, and malls, which created a huge demand for the product.

With Devil Sticks becoming a commercial success, the company received its biggest break when it was approached by two inventors with the idea of an air-powered airplane. The concept was simple enough: Children pump the plane full of air and then launch it, watching it soar upward of 15 metres. The result was a flying plane called Air Hogs. Rather than launch a massive retail and marketing campaign, Spin Master decided to focus on selling the product to specialty educational toy stores and through the Sears catalogue, using what they did well: PR and unconventional marketing methods. They built a suitcase to serve as a press kit and filled it with not only the plane but also a plastic airline cup, a bag of peanuts, and a barf bag, sending it out to numerous writers and editors. The campaign worked wonders; both *Time* and *Popular Science* magazines wrote stories on the airplane, with *Popular Science* calling it one of the best products of the year. Spin Master again hired students to travel from air show to air show demonstrating the product and creating a buzz among airplane enthusiasts. Sales were starting to boom. But the best was yet to come as the PR team at Spin Master managed to get the product on NBC's *Today* and Rosie O'Donnell's talk show, creating major demand. The following year the company was ready to launch Air Hogs in traditional retailers and the toy became a runaway hit.

From here the company has continued to create magic using a mix of ingenuity and PR and has become the third-largest toy company in North America.[1]

Introduction

Marketing involves planning and executing the development, pricing, promotion, and distribution of ideas, goods, and services to create exchanges that satisfy individual and organizational goals. These activities ensure that the products consumers want to buy are available at a price they are willing to pay and that consumers are provided with information about product features and availability. Organizations of all sizes and objectives engage in these activities.

In this chapter, we focus on the basic principles of marketing. First we define and examine the nature of marketing. Then we look at how marketers develop marketing strategies to satisfy the needs and wants of their customers. Next we discuss buying behaviour and how marketers use research to determine what consumers want to buy and why. Finally we explore the impact of the environment on marketing activities.

LO1 Define marketing and describe the exchange process.

Nature of Marketing

A vital part of any business undertaking, **marketing** is a group of activities designed to expedite transactions by creating, distributing, pricing, and promoting goods, services, and ideas. These activities create value by allowing individuals and organizations to obtain what they need and want. A business cannot achieve its objectives unless it provides something that customers value. McDonald's, for example, introduced an adult "Happy Meal" with a premium salad, water, exercise booklet, and a "stepometer" to satisfy adult consumers' desires to improve their eating habits and health.[2] EastLink, an Atlantic Canada Communications company, recently introduced cell and smartphone service to its Internet, cable, and telephone business to accomodate customers who wanted to purchase all of their communication services with one carrier.[3] Tim Hortons introduced breakfast sandwiches to accommodate people who wanted a hot breakfast with their morning coffee.[4] But just creating an innovative product that meets many users' needs isn't sufficient in today's volatile global marketplace. Products must be conveniently available, competitively priced, and uniquely promoted.

Of all the business concepts covered in this text, marketing may be the hardest for organizations to master. Businesses try to respond to consumer wants and needs and to anticipate changes in the marketplace. Unfortunately, it is difficult to understand and predict what consumers want. Businesses have found that by using market research (studies of consumers' needs and wants) they can improve their ability to predict consumers' ever-changing desires.

It is important to note what marketing is not: It is not manipulating consumers to get them to buy products they don't want. It is not just selling and advertising. It is a systematic approach to satisfying consumers. Marketing focuses on the many activities—planning, pricing, promoting, and distributing products—that foster exchanges.

> **Marketing** a group of activities designed to expedite transactions by creating, distributing, pricing, and promoting goods, services, and ideas

> **Exchange** the act of giving up one thing (money, credit, labour, goods) in return for something else (goods, services, or ideas)

The Exchange Relationship

At the heart of all business is the **exchange,** the act of giving up one thing (money, credit, labour, goods) in return for something else (goods, services, or ideas). Businesses exchange their goods, services, or ideas for money or credit supplied by customers in a voluntary *exchange relationship,* illustrated in Figure 11.1. The buyer must feel good about the purchase, or the exchange will not continue. If your local dry cleaner cleans your nice suit properly, on time, and without damage, you will probably feel good about using its services. But if your suit is damaged or isn't ready on time, you will probably use another dry cleaner next time.

For an exchange to occur, certain conditions are required. As indicated by the arrows in Figure 11.1, buyers and sellers must be able to communicate about the "something of value" available to each. An exchange does not necessarily take place just because buyers and sellers have something of value to exchange. Each participant must be willing to give up his or her respective "something of value" to receive the "something" held by the other. You are willing to exchange your "something of value"—your money or credit—for the latest technological gadgets, soft drinks, hockey tickets, or new shoes because you

> "A business cannot achieve its objectives unless it provides something that customers value."

figure 11.1 The Exchange Process: Giving Up One Thing in Return for Another

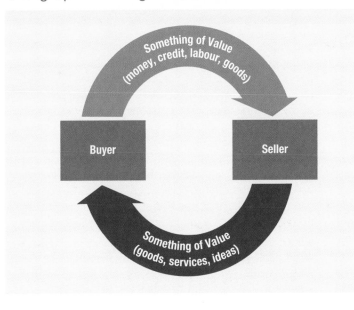

consider those products more valuable or more important than holding on to your cash or credit potential.

When you think of marketing products, you may think of tangible things—cars, stereo systems, or tablets, for example. What most consumers want, however, is a way to get a job done, solve a problem, or gain some enjoyment. You may purchase a Booster Juice drink—not because you want a fruit smoothie, but because you are thirsty and want some nourishment. Second Cup provides coffee drinks at a premium price, providing convenience, quality, and an inviting environment. Therefore, the tangible product itself may not be as important as the image or the benefits associated with the product. This intangible "something of value" may be capability gained from using a product or the image evoked by it, such as "7 for All Mankind" jeans, which can sell for nearly $300.

LO2 Specify the functions of marketing.

Functions of Marketing

Marketing focuses on a complex set of activities that must be performed to accomplish objectives and generate exchanges. These activities include buying, selling, transporting, storing, grading, financing, marketing research, and risk taking.

Buying. Everyone who shops for products (consumers, stores, businesses, governments) decides whether and what to buy. A marketer must understand buyers' needs and desires to determine what products to make available.

Selling. The exchange process is expedited through selling. Marketers usually view selling as a persuasive activity that is accomplished through promotion (advertising, personal

selling, sales promotion, publicity, and packaging). For example, when Jim Balsillie—former co-CEO of Research In Motion (now renamed BlackBerry after its proprietary smartphone)—first introduced the product to the marketplace, he travelled across corporate circles personally selling businesspeople on the virtues of the product.

Transporting. Transporting is the process of moving products from the seller to the buyer. Marketers focus on transportation costs and services.

Storing. Like transporting, storing is part of the physical distribution of products and includes warehousing goods. Warehouses hold some products for lengthy periods in order to create time utility. Consumers want frozen orange juice year-round, for example, although the production season for oranges is only a few months out of the year. This means that sellers must arrange cold storage for frozen orange juice concentrate all year.

Grading. Grading refers to standardizing products and displaying and labelling them so that consumers clearly understand their nature and quality. Many products, such as meat, steel, and fruit, are graded according to a set of standards that often are established by the federal or provincial government.

Financing. For many products, especially large items such as automobiles, refrigerators, and new homes, the marketer arranges credit to expedite the purchase.

Marketing Research. Through research, marketers ascertain the need for new goods and services. By gathering information regularly, marketers can detect new trends and changes in consumer tastes.

Risk Taking. Risk is the chance of loss associated with marketing decisions. Developing a new product creates a chance of loss if consumers do not like it enough to buy it. Spending money to hire a sales force or to conduct marketing research also involves risk. The implication of risk is that most marketing decisions result in either success or failure.

LO3 Explain the marketing concept and its implications for developing marketing strategies.

The Marketing Concept

A basic philosophy that guides all marketing activities is the **marketing concept,** the idea that an organization should try to satisfy customers' needs through coordinated activities that also

> **Marketing concept** the idea that an organization should try to satisfy customers' needs through coordinated activities that also allow it to achieve its own goals

Joel Boblit

Business: BigBadToyStore Inc.

Founded: 1999

Success: Joel Boblit has been able to turn a childhood hobby of collecting action figures into a $4 million business.

After seeing how much Transformers (robot action figures from the 1980s) were selling for online, Joel Boblit began selling various nostalgic action figures himself. Selling action figures began as a hobby during college, but once Boblit graduated he began selling in earnest. BigBadToyStore.com was founded in 1999. The store specializes in vintage items such as figurines from the Star Wars movies and Teenage Mutant Ninja Turtles. Recently, Boblit has also begun selling numerous comic

and movie items. Boblit attributes much of the success of BigBadToyStore.com to his parents, who financed his business and, in the beginning, put in more than 100 hours of work per week. Much of Boblit's success can be linked to the care he takes with customer service. Committed collectors of action figures value the packaging as much as the figures themselves; therefore, Boblit uses a grading system to identify the quality of the packaging. He also provides a premium packing service, promising an item will receive the utmost care when shipped. Customers can also make use of the "Pile of Loot" function—storing purchased items in a virtual storage bin until customers choose to have the items shipped; this reduces shipping costs for customers. With customers around the world and plans to begin distributing to approved retailers, BigBadToyStore.com appears to be a huge success.[5]

allow it to achieve its own goals. According to the marketing concept, a business must find out what consumers need and want and then develop the good, service, or idea that fulfills those needs or wants. The business must then get the product to the customer. In addition, the business must continually alter, adapt, and develop products to keep pace with changing consumer needs and wants. This is sometimes referred to as relationship marketing or customer relationship management—where the company aims to build a mutually beneficial relationship with a customer that lasts a lifetime. Rather than focus on one sale, a company aims to determine a customer's ever-changing needs and meet those needs over the consumer's lifetime. Art Wilson, a sales consultant, states that firms of all sizes can compete effectively as long as they focus on building relations with customers. Walter Hachborn, President Emeritus and co-founder of Home Hardware, which operates over 1,000 stores across Canada, states that "... retailing is all about customer relationships ... recognize customers, give customers what they want, and stand behind your products."[6] Simons, the Quebec-based retailer that has recently expanded to Alberta and is eyeing locations in Toronto, is hoping its commitment to customer relations and dedication to knowing its customers' needs and wants will allow the company to successfully expand across

Canada.[7] McDonald's, as already mentioned, faces increasing pressure to provide more healthful fast-food choices; in addition to introducing its Go Active! Happy Meal, the company has eliminated supersized fries and soft drinks from its menu to address these concerns.[8] McDonald's was also the first fast-food chain to put nutritional information on its food packaging.[9] Over the years, the fast-food giant has experimented with healthier fare, but consumers often rejected these items. To remain competitive, the company must be prepared to add to or adapt its menu to satisfy customers' desires for new fads or changes in eating habits. Each business must determine how best to implement the marketing concept, given its own goals and resources.

Although customer satisfaction is the goal of the marketing concept, a business must also achieve its own objectives, such as boosting productivity, reducing costs, or

> **"According to the marketing concept, a business must find out** what consumers need and want and then develop the good, service, or idea **that fulfills those needs or wants."**

Did Apple, with its iPod and iTunes, "build a better concept"?

achieving a percentage of a specific market. If it does not, it will not survive. For example, Bell Canada could sell smartphones for five dollars and give customers a lifetime guarantee, which would be great for customers but not so great for Bell. Obviously, the company must strike a balance between achieving organizational objectives and satisfying customer needs and wants. Doug Kerr, founder and CEO of Vancouver-based Kerr Construction, embraced the marketing concept when he faced a slowing construction market in that city. Rather than give up, Kerr surveyed his customers to better understand their wants and needs and increased his marketing efforts. During this slow period, 75 percent of his business came from previous clients. Kerr increased his focus on customer service to earn even more repeat business, which allowed Kerr Construction to post annual growth rates of 20 to 25 percent while many competitors went out of business.[10]

To implement the marketing concept, a firm must have good information about what consumers want, adopt a consumer orientation, and coordinate its efforts throughout the entire organization; otherwise, it may be awash with goods, services, and ideas that consumers do not want or need. Robb Chase, CEO of London, Ontario-based Herbal Magic, says, "It's always critical to know what customers' needs are … You need to have a monitoring, information-gathering, and communication system to understand what those needs are and if they change you need to be able to adapt your value proposition."[11] It may be getting easier to learn what customers' needs are according to *Profit* magazine, which is aimed at Canadian entrepreneurs and managers. The publication recently noted that customers now expect to be heard and companies must let them know that they are listening. Minh Ngo, CEO of Memory Express Computer Products Inc., a Calgary-based retailer, allows customers to post comments on products directly on his website, much like Canadian Tire and Sears. Ngo, like other marketing managers, knows that companies can gain valuable information from customer comments including their thoughts on product quality, price, and after-sale service. Companies are also actively monitoring third-party customer review sites such as Yelp, TripAdvisor, Angie's List, ConsumerSearch, and Epinions and social media sites such as Facebook, Twitter, and Pinterest to determine if customers are satisfied and to identify future consumer wants and needs. In fact, businesses are starting to consider it essential to monitor social media sites to understand their customers and identify opportunities, with 42 percent of companies considering social media monitoring one of their top three priorities for 2013.[12] As a result, a number of new businesses have emerged. Meltwater Group has created products such as Meltwater Buzz, a digital private investigator that scans thousands of sites to determine what people are saying about specific issues or companies. Businesses can use the information from Buzz to see if consumers are satisfied or

> "42 percent of companies consider social media monitoring one of their top three priorities for 2013."

not, spot developing trends, and address changes in public opinions. Canadian-based HootSuite, much like Buzz, offers companies a vast array of reports and information it gleans from monitoring social media sites.

Successfully implementing the marketing concept requires that a business view customer value as the ultimate measure of work performance and improving value, and the rate at which this is done as the measure of success.[13] Everyone in the organization who interacts with customers—*all* customer-contact employees—must know what customers want. They are selling ideas, benefits, philosophies, and experiences—not just goods and services. For example, Calgary-based Print Audit, which develops software to track and reduce printing costs, separates itself from the competition by focusing on customer relationships. CEO and founder John MacInnes requires that employees do everything possible to satisfy customers and if the customer remains unsatisfied they get a refund, no questions asked. MacInnes's firm also surveys clients 15 days after they purchased his products and 15 days later to determine if they are happy. In addition each employee has access to flower and gift accounts to send thank-you gifts to customers or to mark key events in their lives.[14]

Someone once said that if you build a better mousetrap, the world will beat a path to your door. Suppose you do build a better mousetrap. What will happen? Actually, consumers are not likely to beat a path to your door because the market is too competitive. A coordinated effort by everyone involved with the mousetrap is needed to sell the product. Your company must reach out to customers and tell them about your mousetrap, especially how your mousetrap works better than those offered by competitors. If you do not make the benefits of your product widely known, in most cases, it will not be successful. Consider Apple's retail stores, which market computers and electronics in a way unlike any other computer manufacturer or retail store. The upscale stores, located in high-rent shopping districts, show off Apple's products in sparse, stylish settings to encourage consumers to try new things—like making a movie on a computer. The stores also offer special events like concerts and classes to give customers ideas on how to maximize their use of Apple's products.[15] You must also find—or create—stores willing to sell your mousetrap to consumers. You must implement the marketing concept by making a product with satisfying benefits and making it available and visible.

Orville Wright said that an airplane is "a group of separate parts flying in close formation." This is what most companies are trying to accomplish: They are striving for a team effort to deliver the right good or service to customers. A breakdown at any point in the organization—whether it be in production, purchasing, sales, distribution, or advertising—can result in lost sales, lost revenue, dissatisfied customers. Dissatisfied customers lead directly to lost sales as reported by Toronto-based research firm Ipsos-Reid, which has found that 84 percent of Canadians will stop making purchases from a company after just one negative experience.[16]

Evolution of the Marketing Concept

The marketing concept may seem like the obvious approach to running a business and building relationships with customers. However, businesspeople are not always focused on customers when they create and operate businesses. Many companies fail to grasp the importance of customer relationships and fail to implement customer strategies. A recent survey indicated that only 46 percent of executives believe that their firm is committed to customers, but 67 percent of executives frequently meet with customers.[17] Our society and economic system have changed over time, and marketing has become more important as markets have become more competitive.

The Production Orientation.   During the second half of the 19th century, the Industrial Revolution was well under way in Canada. New technologies, such as electricity, railroads, internal combustion engines, and mass-production techniques, made it possible to manufacture goods with ever increasing efficiency. Together with new management ideas and ways of using labour, products poured into the marketplace, where demand for manufactured goods was strong.

The Sales Orientation.   By the early part of the 20th century, supply caught up with and then exceeded demand, and businesspeople began to realize they would have to "sell" products to buyers. During the first half of the 20th century, businesspeople viewed sales as the major means of increasing profits, and this period came to have a sales orientation. They believed the most important marketing activities were personal selling and advertising. Today some people still inaccurately equate marketing with a sales orientation.

The Marketing Orientation.   By the 1950s, some businesspeople began to recognize that even efficient production and extensive promotion did not guarantee sales. These businesses, and many others since, found that they must first determine what customers want and then produce it rather than making the products first and then trying to persuade customers that they need them. Managers at General Electric first suggested that the marketing concept was a company-wide philosophy of doing business. As more organizations realized the importance of satisfying customers' needs, Canadian and U.S. businesses entered the marketing era, one of marketing orientation.

A **marketing orientation** requires organizations to gather information about customer needs, share that information throughout the entire firm, and use that information to help build

Marketing orientation an approach requiring organizations to gather information about customer needs, share that information throughout the firm, and use that information to help build long-term relationships with customers

long-term relationships with customers. Top executives, marketing managers, nonmarketing managers (those in production, finance, human resources, and so on), and customers all become mutually dependent and cooperate in developing and carrying out a marketing orientation. Nonmarketing managers must communicate with marketing managers to share information important to understanding the customer. Consider Tim Hortons; the coffee chain started out by selling coffee and doughnuts. Based on market research and feedback from customers, managers expanded the menu to include cookies, bagels, and sandwiches. Recently the company started to offer breakfast sandwiches as the one-time coffee shop has transformed itself into a restaurant that specializes in coffee, breakfast, and lunch.

Trying to assess what customers want is difficult to begin with, and is further complicated by the rate at which trends, fashions, and tastes can change. Businesses today want to satisfy customers and build meaningful long-term relationships with them. It is more efficient to retain existing customers and even increase the amount of business each customer provides the organization than to find new customers. As discussed above, Vancouver-based Kerr Construction at one time was securing over 75 percent of its sales from repeat customers. Most companies' success depends on increasing the amount of repeat business, and many companies are turning to technologies associated with customer-relationship management to help build relationships and boost business with existing customers.

> **"Businesses today want to** satisfy customers and build meaningful long-term relationships **with them."**

Communication remains a major element of any strategy to develop and manage long-term customer relationships. By providing multiple points of interaction with customers—that is, websites, telephone, fax, e-mail, and personal contact—companies can personalize customer relationships.[18] Like many online retailers, Chapters.ca collects, stores, and analyzes purchase data to understand each customer's interests. This information helps the retailer improve its ability to satisfy individual customers and thereby increase sales of books, music, movies, and other products to each customer. The ability to identify individual customers allows marketers to shift their focus from targeting groups of similar customers to increasing their share of an individual customer's purchases. Regardless of the medium through which communication occurs, customers should ultimately be the drivers of marketing strategy because they understand what they want. Customer relationship management systems should ensure that marketers listen to customers to respond to their needs and concerns and build long-term relationships.

Social Media Era

While the marketing orientation era is not over, some would argue that it is slowly being replaced or complemented by the social media era. Social media is redefining marketing, as it allows for the building of online communities, which encourage participation and communication among members. Consumers can communicate in real time with companies, share information with their associates and friends, and search for unbiased product opinions online. The results have been significant as Facebook, Twitter, LinkedIn, YouTube, blogs, wikis, and podcasts have become both communication and business tools. Some entrepreneurs, like Ryan Holmes, founder of HootSuite, think that social media is creating a new type of economy, and businesses will have to adapt as social media is vastly changing how business is conducted.[19] Others are less convinced that social media represents a new era in marketing and view social media as a tool, one that complements marketing orientation concepts. After all, social media allows companies to communicate with customers and learn about their wants and needs, and offers another means to establish a long-term relationship with clients—these are some of the major characteristics associated with a marketing orientation.

LO4 Examine the development of a marketing strategy, including market segmentation and marketing mix.

Developing a Marketing Strategy

To implement the marketing concept and customer relationship management, a business needs to develop and maintain a **marketing strategy,** a plan of action for developing, pricing, distributing, and promoting products that meet the needs of specific customers. This definition has two major components: selecting a target market and developing an appropriate marketing mix to satisfy that target market.

Selecting a Target Market

A **market** is a group of people who have a need, purchasing power, and the desire and authority to spend money on

> **Marketing strategy** a plan of action for developing, pricing, distributing, and promoting products that meet the needs of specific customers
>
> **Market** a group of people who have a need, purchasing power, and the desire and authority to spend money on goods, services, and ideas

---

RESPONDING TO BUSINESS CHALLENGES | Walmart Battles Target for the Same Customers

The original title of this piece read, "Walmart Battles Target for the Same Target Customers," but upon reflection the authors thought it may be too confusing even though it is accurate.

The trendy discount retailer Target has arrived in Canada, and much like in the U.S., the company is targeting middle-, upper–middle, and high-income earners with its trendy merchandise. In the U.S., Target stands somewhat alone, a price leader in what is trendy, a retailer for "aspirational and affluent" customers to shop at albeit at a low price. Interestingly enough, Walmart has been successfully targeting the same group of customers in Canada for 18 years.

The Canadian retail environment is different from the U.S., something that Walmart has learned over the course of nearly 20 years in the country. In fact, Walmart stocks very little (less than 25 percent) of its merchandise from the U.S. in Canada. In America, Walmart is considered to be a discount retailer, with a target market consisting of primarily middle- and lower-income earners. In Canada, almost everyone shops at Walmart, and there is no stigma associated with entering the stores. Walmart Canada CEO Shelley Broader states, "This (Canada) is a very complex market, that's why foreign retailers come here and are often unsuccessful."

Many retail analysts are wondering if there is room in the Canadian marketplace for two discount chains going after the same group of customers. They question if Target will succeed in Canada in the long term. After all, Target naysayers point out, Walmart has superior customer knowledge, 371 locations compared to Target's 124, and a history of selling to consumers that Target would normally have an advantage with in the U.S. Others wonder whether Canadian consumers have only been shopping at Walmart because Target was not an option.[23]

DISCUSSION QUESTIONS

1. Do you think Target will be successful in Canada? Why or why not?

2. Were you surprised to read that Walmart's Canadian merchandise is different from what you would find in the U.S.? Why do you think this is the case?

3. How loyal do you think longtime Walmart shoppers will be now that Target has arrived?

goods, services, and ideas. A **target market** is a more specific group of consumers on whose needs and wants a company focuses its marketing efforts. Nike, for example, introduced a new line of golf clubs targeted at recreational golfers.[20] Marketing managers may define a target market as a relatively small number of people, or they may define it as the total market (Figure 11.2). Rolls-Royce, for example, targets its products at a small, very exclusive, high-income market—people who want the ultimate in prestige in an automobile. General Motors, on the other hand, manufactures vehicles ranging from the Aveo to Cadillac to GMC trucks in an attempt to appeal to varied tastes, needs, and desires. Likewise, Reitmans Canada Ltd., which has grown to include over 950 stores nationwide, operates under seven divisions: Reitmans, Smart-Set, RW & CO., Penningtons 14+, Thyme Maternity, Addition-Elle 14+, and Cassis, and uses different store concepts to appeal to different target markets. Effective managers realize that selecting a target market can ultimately determine the success of a company. The Hudson's Bay Company is in the midst of a business turnaround that began in 2009 and has been attributed to the work of recently retired retail expert, Jeff Sherman. Sherman notes that the key to running a successful retail store is, "a maniacal focus on your target customers."[21] Under Sherman's leadership, Bonnie Brooks was hired as president and CEO of The Bay, and spent several months reviewing data from over 7,000 shopper interviews before determining that the retailer would focus on fashion customers who want high-end labels, pragmatists who want good-quality apparel, and value-shoppers who want the best price. The Bay's target market selection then influenced store design, allocation of advertising dollars, and product selection.[22] The approach at The Bay is no different than the one taken by another Canadian retailer, Shoppers Drug Mart, which had experienced similar business woes over a decade ago. Shoppers spent considerable resources on segmenting and redefining its target markets. The move has paid off and Shoppers is a Canadian retail success story.

Some firms use a **total-market approach,** in which they try to appeal to everyone and assume that all buyers have similar needs and wants. Sellers of salt, sugar, and many agricultural products use a total-market approach because everyone is a potential consumer

of these products. Most firms, though, use **market segmentation** and divide the total market into groups of people who have relatively similar product needs. A **market segment** is a collection of individuals, groups, or organizations who share one or more characteristics and thus have relatively similar product needs and desires. Prior to selecting its three target markets, The Bay had broken Canada into 12 distinct consumer groups. The Bay then looked internally at its own resources. Women are the largest market segment, with 51 percent of the Canadian population. At the household level, segmentation can unlock each woman's social and cultural characteristics and stage in life to determine preferences and needs.[24] One market segment that many marketers are focusing on is the growing immigrant population. As immigration rates rise, more and more companies are altering their products or promotion to appeal

figure 11.2 Target Market Strategies

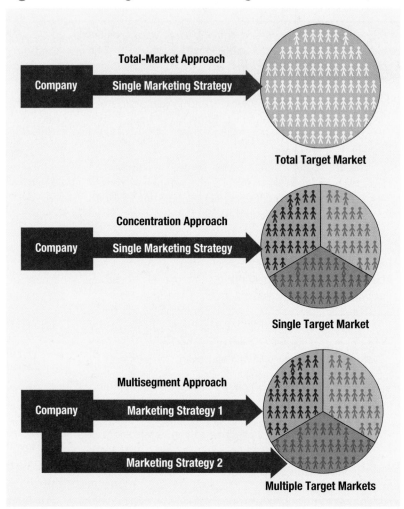

to this important group. For example, Oakville, Ontario-based FlightNetwork.com hires recent immigrants to speak to customers in their native language such as Swahili, Russian, and German. The company notes that many of its top call centre agents have the poorest English skills.[25] Another example is Staples, which has gained a footing in the immigrant market with a program aimed at helping immigrant entrepreneurs succeed. The seminar program teaches immigrants about accounting, taxes, and running a small business.[26] Companies use market segmentation to focus their efforts and resources on specific target markets so that they can develop a productive marketing strategy. Two common approaches to segmenting markets are the concentration approach and the multisegment approach.

> ## "One market segment that many marketers are focusing on is the growing immigrant population."

Market Segmentation Approaches.   In the **concentration approach,** a company develops one marketing strategy for a single market segment. The concentration approach allows a firm to specialize, focusing all its efforts on the one market segment. Porsche, for example, focuses all its marketing efforts toward high-income individuals who want to own high-performance vehicles. A firm can generate a large sales volume by penetrating a single market segment deeply. The concentration approach may be especially effective when a firm can identify and develop products for a particular segment ignored by other companies in the industry.

Concentration approach a market segmentation approach whereby a company develops one marketing strategy for a single market segment

Multisegment approach a market segmentation approach whereby the marketer aims its efforts at two or more segments, developing a marketing strategy for each

In the **multisegment approach,** the marketer aims its marketing efforts at two or more segments, developing a marketing strategy for each. Many firms use a multisegment approach that includes different advertising messages for different segments. RBC targets many different segments including teens, university students and recent grads, families, Baby Boomers, and retirees. The bank has products such as mortgages, which appeal to families, RRSPs that appeal to people saving for their retirement, and student accounts. RBC also targets its promotional efforts to appeal to various customers by communicating through social media, offering services such as Internet banking, and promoting specific products through various commercials. BlackBerry used to focus primarily on the corporate segment when advertising and selling its smartphones. Now, with competition in the marketplace, particularly from Apple with its iPhone, BlackBerry has increased the number of segments it is targeting to include teenagers and university students. Recent advertisements for the company feature teenagers, rock bands, and youth. The company's new message is that BlackBerry is for everyone.

Niche marketing is a narrow market segment that focuses efforts on one small, well-defined segment that has a unique, specific set of needs. To cater to ice cream "addicts" and people who crave new, exotic flavours, several companies are selling ice cream on the Internet. This niche represents only a fraction of the $20.3 billion per year ice cream business, but online sales at some of the biggest makers increased 30 percent in just one year. Some of the firms focusing on this market are IceCreamSource.com, Nuts About Ice Cream, and Graeter's.[27] Another example is HTT Technologies Inc., a St-Eustache, Quebec-based car manufacturing company that builds the Pléthore—a super high-end car aimed at the luxury market. The car currently retails for a special promotional price of $450,000, but HTT plans on raising the price to $750,000, typical for cars in this marketplace.[28]

For a firm to successfully use a concentration or multisegment approach to market segmentation, several requirements must be met:

1. Consumers' needs for the product must be heterogeneous.

2. The segments must be identifiable and divisible.

3. The total market must be divided in a way that allows estimated sales potential, cost, and profits of the segments to be compared.

4. At least one segment must have enough profit potential to justify developing and maintaining a special marketing strategy.

5. The firm must be able to reach the chosen market segment with a particular market strategy.

Bases for Segmenting Markets.   Companies segment markets on the basis of several variables:

1. *Demographic*—age, sex, race, ethnicity, income, education, occupation, family size, religion, social class. These characteristics are often closely related to customers' product needs and purchasing behaviour, and they can be readily measured. Some demographers such as Canada's David Foot, author of *Boom Bust and Echo,* argue that simple demographics can explain upwards of two-thirds of consumer decisions. Foot states that if you know the number of people in each age category you can make reliable decisions about what products will be popular now and in the future. For example, Baby Boomers or people born between 1946 and 1966 make up approximately 33 percent of Canada's population and are responsible for the recent rise in spending on cosmetic surgery and nostalgia products such as the Dodge Dart. The next-largest group of people in Canada is known as the Echo generation and they are the children of Baby Boomers. This group born between 1980 and 1995 is responsible for a renewed interest in child care and kindergarten as they are starting to have their own children.[30]

Samantha Daniels

Business: Samantha's Table

Founded: 2001

Success: Daniels earns between $25,000 and $50,000 per client, plus a hefty bonus if the client marries as the result of her matching skills. She provides services to a niche market of clients who are willing to pay more to meet that special someone.

Originally a divorce attorney, Samantha Daniels changed course to become a high-end matchmaker for wealthy singles. While Daniels remains single, she has had great success finding love for some of the country's richest and most influential individuals. To differentiate herself from online dating services, Daniels takes a much more hands-on approach. She also does not limit her search to paying clients, but rather considers everyone she knows in her vast network of singles. Daniels says that her number-one concern is finding the right match for her clients, regardless of whether the other

party has paid for her services or not. She strategically matches individuals based on what she knows of them and brings together potential matches over drinks, at exclusive events, or trendy venues. Daniels does not reveal names of clients but has disclosed that she has been employed by famous actors, athletes, and those involved in high-profile professional companies. In case you're wondering how this setup works, a potential client pays around $500 for a two-hour initial consultation. She likes to conduct initial meetings in public to better observe clients' behavioural patterns in social situations. Each client is asked to supply information about ex-spouses, homes, and finances and to fill out a prepared questionnaire. Should the deal go further, Daniels charges anywhere from $25,000 to $50,000 to provide dates, coaching, personal shopping, and styling advice. If a match ends in marriage, Daniels usually gets a sizable bonus as well. While this might sound like a strange way to find love, Daniels says that business is booming, with around 200 requests for help daily.[29]

2. *Geographic*—climate, terrain, natural resources, population density, subcultural values. These influence consumers' needs and product usage. Climate, for example, influences consumers' purchases of clothing, automobiles, heating and air conditioning equipment, and leisure activity equipment.

3. *Psychographic*—personality characteristics, motives, lifestyles. For example, Canadian smoothie operator Booster Juice presents its products in bright glasses with illustrations of healthy fruit to appeal to customers who want not only to eat healthy but to be seen eating healthy.

RBC targets many different segments with different products and methods of product promotion, as well as different means of communicating with customers.

4. *Behaviouristic*—some characteristic of the consumer's behaviour toward the product. These characteristics commonly involve some aspect of product use. The three major issues in this category are what benefits consumers are seeking; consumers' rate of use; and how they use and purchase products.

Developing a Marketing Mix

The second step in developing a marketing strategy is to create and maintain a satisfying marketing mix. The **marketing mix** refers to four marketing activities—product, price, distribution, and promotion—that the firm can control to achieve specific goals within a dynamic marketing environment (Figure 11.3). The buyer or the target market is the central focus of all marketing activities.

Product. A product—whether a good, a service, an idea, or some combination—is a complex mix of tangible and intangible attributes that provide satisfaction and benefits. A *good* is a physical entity you can touch. A Porsche Cayenne, Lululemon pants, RONA lumber, and a kitten available for adoption at an animal shelter are examples of goods. A *service* is the application of human and mechanical efforts to people or objects to provide intangible benefits to customers. Air travel on West-Jet or Air Canada, haircuts

> **Marketing mix** the four marketing activities—product, price, promotion, and distribution—that the firm can control to achieve specific goals within a dynamic marketing environment

at SuperCuts, banking at CIBC, and/or insurance from Manulife are examples of services.

A product has emotional and psychological as well as physical characteristics and includes everything that the buyer receives from an exchange. This definition includes supporting services such as installation, guarantees, product information, and promises of repair. Products usually have both favourable and unfavourable attributes; therefore, almost every purchase or exchange involves trade-offs as consumers try to maximize their benefits and satisfaction and minimize unfavourable attributes. For example, a consumer trying to choose between a BlackBerry and an iPhone may have to trade off the superior e-mail service offered by a BlackBerry in order to purchase the iPhone, which offers more apps and a better Web browser.

figure 11.3 The Marketing Mix: Product, Price, Promotion, and Distribution

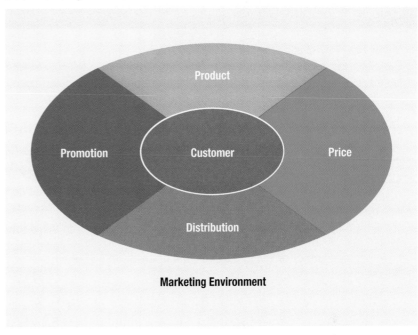

Consider the Following: RBC's Youth Marketing Strategy

As stated above, marketing strategy consists of selecting a target market and designing your marketing mix or your products, price, place, and promotion to appeal to your targeted market and create value compared to your competitors. RBC, Canada's third-largest bank, obviously has many different target markets, which results in the bank managing different marketing mixes. One key target market for the bank is university students and recent graduates. The group is particularly important as they are just starting to form relationships with companies and the bank realizes that if it captures a young customer's business now it may be able to retain the customer for a lifetime. To achieve this result, RBC tries to differentiate itself from the other banks by creating a superior "student focused" marketing mix.

While all the banks in Canada are offering student banking packages, student lines of credit, credit cards for students, and so forth, RBC is attempting to differentiate itself first and foremost by using promotions that appeal to youth. The bank spent upwards of $120 million to sponsor the 2010 Olympics including the "Own the Podium" campaign, which consisted of directing money to athletes who have the best chance to capture an Olympic medal, and the "Torch Relay," a 45,000-kilometre trip across the country that stopped in cities and towns and featured youth-focused entertainment. RBC has

followed up that promotion with a commitment to the "Road to Excellence" program, which replaced "Own the Podium."

In addition, RBC is considered the social media leader among the big banks in Canada. RBC has invested heavily in social media including Twitter, Facebook, blogs, avatars, and online competitions and communities to attract young clients. For example, a recent online contest focused on recent university graduates who were asked to provide the best advice they could to new university students.[31]

DISCUSSION QUESTIONS

1. What markets is RBC targeting with social media?

2. Are there other things RBC could be doing with its marketing mix to appeal to the youth market?

3. Do you think RBC's investment in the Olympics and the Torch Relay was a good idea? Will it improve the bank's market share?

4. Will being a leader in social media translate into more young clients for the bank?

Marketers know that if they are going to be successful in Canada, their goods should appeal to one of two market segments—Baby Boomers, or their children (better known as the Echo generation). Baby Boomers were born between 1946 and 1966, represent approximately one-third of Canada's population, and, as a group, are quite wealthy. Boomers entered the workforce when there were many jobs. They have often been described as materialistic in nature and consider their time to be very valuable. Businesses that appeal to this group include Nurse Next Door, a Vancouver-based homecare company for seniors that Boomers hire to help with their aging parents, and Medicard Finance Inc., an Ontario-based company that offers loans and lines of credit to Boomers who are interested in cosmetic surgery.

From a marketer's perspective, the best innovation or creation by the Baby Boomers may be the Echo generation. This group is the second-largest segment in the population and represents people born from 1980 to 1995. The well-educated Echo generation is interested in the environment and technology and expect to be successful, much like their parents. This generation is starting to buy their first homes, get married, and have children. The result—many products and services that fell out of favour as the Baby Boomers aged will become popular again.[32]

DISCUSSION QUESTIONS

1. What other products or industries should do well as Baby Boomers continue to age?

2. What do you think are the best ways to promote products or services to Baby Boomers?

3. What other products or industries should do well as the Echo generation starts to have families?

4. What do you think are the best ways to promote products or services to the Echo generation?

5. Do some research and determine the size of the Baby Boomer and Echo segments.

6. Do you think companies would be wise to consider marketing their products to other groups? Why or why not? What products or industries are aimed at other groups?

> **Price** a value placed on an object exchanged between a buyer and a seller

Products are among a firm's most visible contacts with consumers. If they do not meet consumer needs and expectations, sales will be difficult, and product life spans will be brief. The product is an important variable—often the central focus—of the marketing mix; the other variables (price, promotion, and distribution) must be coordinated with product decisions.

Price. Almost anything can be assessed by a **price,** a value placed on an object exchanged between a buyer and a seller. Although the seller usually establishes the price, it may be negotiated between buyer and seller. The buyer usually exchanges purchasing power—income, credit, wealth—for the satisfaction or utility associated with a product. Because financial price is the measure of value commonly used in an exchange, it quantifies value and is the basis of most market exchanges.

Marketers view price as much more than a means of assessing value, however. It is a key element of the marketing mix because it relates directly to the generation of revenue and profits. Prices can also be changed quickly to stimulate demand or respond to competitors' actions. For example, WestJet will usually drop its prices quickly in response to similar price drops by Air Canada, and Tim Hortons introduced an English muffin version of its breakfast sandwich, priced lower than McDonald's Egg McMuffin, to generate sales. Recently, the big Canadian banks have started using pricing as a way to generate more sales. BMO has twice offered five-year mortgage rates at 2.99 percent and other banks have dropped their mortgage rates as a result. Finance Minister Jim Flaherty actually urged the banks to be cautious about such low interest rates as he is fearful consumers may borrow beyond their means and won't be able to repay their mortgage if and when interest rates rise.[33]

Place/Distribution. **Place/distribution** is making products available to customers in the location and the quantities desired. The Internet and online sales have greatly impacted the place/distribution category as more and more shoppers are looking to make purchases and receive services online. For example, a number of banks including CIBC have recently introduced a smartphone app for online banking service. The app was introduced to appeal to the vast number of youth who want to bank over their smartphone. Almost every product and service can now be purchased on the Internet,

> **Place/distribution** making products available to customers in the quantities desired

including airline tickets from Air Canada and WestJet and sporting goods from SportChek.[34] Via Vegan Ltd., a Montreal-based designer of women's and men's handbags made out of recycled plastic bottles, has used exporting to reach consumers throughout the world as the environmentally friendly nature of the product has resulted in global demand. The company sells handbags in such high-end department stores as Saks Fifth Avenue in the United States and Selfridges & Co. in the United Kingdom.[35] In fact, global distribution is becoming increasingly important to Canadian companies. The top 71 exporters identified by *Profit* magazine as the top 100 growth companies sold $17 billion abroad last year.[36]

> "Global distribution is becoming increasingly important to Canadian companies. The top 71 exporters identified by *Profit* magazine as the top 100 growth companies sold $17 billion abroad last year."

In addition to making products available in the locations and quantities customers want, place also refers to creating a location that consumers find desirable. For example, Dollarama, a Quebec-based chain, became a billion-dollar retailer by offering consumers not just 594-plus locations to shop at, but by creating a location that customers wanted to visit. Dollarama's stores are organized, clean, and attractive, unlike many mom-and-pop dollar stores, which are often characterized by their unkempt aisles. Some retailers are now opting to build smaller stores as a way to reduce overhead, focus on items that consumers want, and create a more intimate shopping experience. Rona has recently announced the creation of 11 smaller satellite stores that, according to the company, will have a neighbourhood feel to them. Future Shop is testing 5,000 square foot stores, one-fifth the size of the average Future Shop, offering 1,000 of its best-selling items. The store will also have computer kiosks where customers can access the company's other 59,000 products for delivery to the store or their home.[37] Fast-food giant McDonald's has expanded distribution by opening restaurants in Walmart stores, and Starbucks is selling its specialty coffee in Targets throughout Canada and the U.S. This practice permits the food and coffee giants to share costs with their partners and to reach more customers when and where hunger strikes.[38]

Intermediaries, usually wholesalers and retailers, perform many of the activities required to move products efficiently from producers to consumers or industrial buyers. These activities involve transporting, warehousing, materials handling, and inventory control, as well as packaging and communication. For example, Dr. Abdullah Kirumira, founder of Nova Scotia-based biomedical company BioMedical Diagnostic Inc., which developed the world's first rapid HIV test and "lab in a box" diagnostic tools, notes that marketing and distribution were never his strengths. BioMedical relies on a number of distributors to transport and sell his products throughout the world, which allows him to focus on the development of new drugs and medical applications.[39]

Critics who suggest that eliminating wholesalers and other middlemen would result in lower prices for consumers do not recognize that eliminating intermediaries would not do away with the need for their services. Other institutions would have to perform those services, and consumers would still have to pay for them. For example, Mississauga-based Solutions 2 GO Inc. has achieved approximately $750 million in annual sales by relieving video game manufacturers of the task of getting their games onto the shelves of thousands of stores all on the same day. The company serves as a master distributor for many major game manufacturers and some of its top sellers include New Super Mario Brothers, Call of Duty: Modern Warfare 2, and Final Fantasy XIII. In addition, in the absence of wholesalers, all producers would have to deal directly with retailers or customers, keeping voluminous records and hiring people to deal with customers.[40]

Promotion. **Promotion** is a persuasive form of communication that attempts to expedite a marketing exchange by influencing individuals, groups, and organizations to accept goods, services, and ideas. Promotion includes advertising, personal selling, social media, publicity, and sales promotion, all of which we will look at more closely in Chapter 12. One aspect of promotion that has been growing rapidly in recent years is the use of non-traditional marketing to achieve corporate goals. Lululemon, for example, once offered customers free clothing if they would wait in line naked at a store's grand opening. The result was national media coverage of the store's opening and extended coverage in the media about the corporation's edgy promotions.[41] Another example is Tim Hortons' successful Roll up the Rim to Win contest. The contest has been running for over 20 years and still results in increased sales and publicity for the company.

The aim of promotion is to communicate directly or indirectly with individuals, groups, and organizations to facilitate exchanges. When marketers use advertising and other forms of promotion, they must effectively manage their promotional resources and understand product and target-market characteristics to ensure that these promotional activities contribute to the firm's objectives.

> **Promotion** a persuasive form of communication that attempts to expedite a marketing exchange by influencing individuals, groups, and organizations to accept goods, services, and ideas

> "The aim of promotion is to communicate directly or indirectly with individuals, groups, and organizations to facilitate exchanges."

For example, Tim Hortons is using television advertising to appeal to Canadians across the country who want a fresh cup of coffee in a friendly atmosphere. Tim Hortons' advertisements highlight the fact that every 20 minutes there is a new pot of coffee being brewed. Also, as previously noted, both CIBC with its smartphone app and RBC with its reliance on social media are attempting to reach the under-30 market segment with their products and services.

Tim Hortons' market research revealed customers wanted larger cups of coffee.

> **LO5** Investigate how marketers conduct marketing research, and study buying behaviour.

Marketing Research and Information Systems

Before marketers can develop a marketing mix, they must collect in-depth, up-to-date information about customer needs. **Marketing research** is a systematic, objective process of getting information about potential customers to guide marketing decisions. For example, when Simple Audiobook, an Oakville, Ontario company, was contemplating whether to enter the United States market, the company relied on market research to determine if the strategy made sense. CEO Sean Neville says that firms can't guess if there is a market—they need to do research and determine if a market exists, the size of that market, and if customers will purchase the company's product.[42] Janet and Greta Podleski, authors of two best-selling Canadian cookbooks, *Looneyspoons* and *Crazy Plates,* along with partner David Chilton discovered the dangers of not doing any market research. They decided to turn some of their favourite recipes into frozen dinners, but were initially quite unsuccessful. Chilton said that almost all of the errors came because they didn't properly research the market. They were making a product for families of four or five priced between $13 and $14 ... what they found out later is that most people want frozen dinners to feed one or two people and they want to pay much less for them.[43] Since the group had produced a product no one wanted, they were left to repurchase the product from store shelves and re-enter the marketplace only after conducting the necessary market research.

Market research might include data about the age, income, ethnicity, gender, and educational level of people in the target market, their preferences for product features, their attitudes toward competitors' products, and the frequency with which they use the product. For example, Tim Hortons' market research revealed customers wanted larger cups of coffee. As a direct result, the stores are now selling extra-large 24-ounce cups.[44] Toyota's marketing research about Generation Y drivers (born between 1977

> **Marketing research** a systematic, objective process of getting information about potential customers to guide marketing decisions

and 1994) found that they practically live in their cars, and many even keep a change of clothes handy in their vehicles. As a result of this research, Toyota designed its Scion as a "home on wheels" with a 15-volt outlet for plugging in a computer, reclining front seats for napping, and a powerful audio system for listening to MP3 music files, all for a $12,500 price tag.[45] Les Mandelbaum, founder of Umbra, a Toronto-based company that is known as one of the world's top designers of products, states that Umbra is very disciplined when it comes to entering the marketplace with new products and spends considerable time analyzing market research including what customers want, what products are already in stores, and what competitors are offering.[46]

Marketing research is vital because the marketing concept cannot be implemented without information about customers. As evident in this chapter's discussion about the revival at The Bay, market research is essential to making decisions for companies. As discussed above, The Bay's senior executives spent several months reviewing data from thousands of interviews prior to making decisions about target markets and store layout. Canadian Tire uses the massive amount of customer information it gathers when customers use their Canadian Tire card to assist in making decisions on a variety of issues including prices, new product ideas, store layout, and promotional campaigns.

The market research process consists of the following steps:

1. *Define the problem or objective.* Objectives could include whether potential customers will buy a product or what price they are willing to pay for a service.

2. *Collect data.* Researchers will normally start their search for information from pre-existing sources known as secondary sources or secondary data. **Secondary data** are

> **Secondary data** information that is compiled inside or outside an organization for some purpose other than changing the current situation

12 Dimensions of Marketing Strategy

compiled inside or outside the organization for some purpose other than changing the current situation. Marketers typically use information compiled by Statistics Canada, business development centres, and other government agencies; databases created by marketing research firms; as well as sales and other internal reports to gain information about customers. To stay on top of consumer demands and emerging trends Somerset Entertainment Ltd., a Toronto-based music company, hires marketers to read the latest entertainment publications and report back to management. Jason Abbott, founder of Winnipeg-based tour company The Toban Experience, used secondary sources to determine if a market existed for a tour company in his region and if there were any competitors. Abbott relied on secondary data to determine that 6,000 visitors travel through Winnipeg in the summer and spring and no other tour companies were operating in his market.[47]

If there is not enough secondary information available then marketers will often turn to primary research, or the collection of new data that is specific to the problem at hand. **Primary data** is new data or new information. Primary data is usually collected either by observation, where companies watch what consumers do or how consumers react to certain situations; surveys, where people complete a questionnaire; personal interviews; or focus groups, where groups of consumers come together to discuss a product, service, or business. Examples of observation include the use of "mystery shoppers" to visit their retail establishments and report on whether the stores were adhering to the company's standards of service. For example, Tell Us About Us Inc. (TUAU), which was profiled in Chapter 6, is a Winnipeg-based full-service customer feedback company. TUAU offers companies numerous methods including social media monitoring, surveys, and secret shoppers to determine if standards are being met and if consumers are happy and/or would like additional products or services. The province of Nova Scotia used focus groups as part of its effort to develop a formal marketing campaign. Among other things, focus groups suggested the province promote its friendly atmosphere and natural beauty. As noted above, The Bay has used interviews as part of its marketing research efforts and Shoppers Drug Mart has used surveys.

Primary data marketing information that is observed, recorded, or collected directly from respondents

3. *Analyze the research data.* Data results must then be analyzed and interpreted. Researchers may use a number of software and/or online diagnostic tools to generate differentalternatives to a problem.

4. *Choose the best options.* The final step in the research process is determining which alternatives exist and deciding what recommendations to make. For example, when Eryn Green and Tamar Wagman started Sweetpea Baby Food, a Toronto-based fresh-frozen baby food company, they used market research to ensure there was a market for their product. They started with a objective to determine if a market did exist for gourmet baby food. The pair collected data from secondary sources, including Statistics Canada, to determine that while birth rates are declining, the number of mothers in their target group (age 30–35) is rising. The company founders than used primary research and interviewed 50 new moms to see if there was an actual demand for their product. Green and Wagman then analyzed the data and concluded a large market did exist for their business.[48]

A marketing information system (MIS) is a framework for accessing information about customers from sources both inside and outside the organization. Inside the organization, there is a continuous flow of information about prices, sales, and expenses. Outside the organization, data are readily available through private or public reports and census statistics, as well as from many other sources. Computer networking technology provides a framework for companies to connect to useful databases and customers with instantaneous information about product acceptance, sales performance, and buying behaviour. This information is important to planning and marketing strategy development.

The marketing of products and collecting of data about buying behaviour—information on what people

Market research can lead to a whole new market for your product. BMW targets a lower-income consumer than its typical high-end one by selling "certified" used BMWs at a lower cost, but still with the BMW brand recognition and expectation.

actually buy and how they buy it—represents the marketing research of the future. New information technologies are changing the way businesses learn about their customers and market their products. Interactive multimedia research, or *virtual testing,* combines sight, sound, and animation to facilitate the testing of concepts as well as packaging and design features for consumer products. Computerization offers a greater degree of flexibility, shortens the staff time involved in data gathering, and cuts marketing research costs. The evolving development of telecommunications and computer technologies is allowing marketing researchers quick and easy access to a growing number of online services and a vast database of potential respondents. Online research is set to grow from $1.3 billion to $4 billion in the next few years, according to a new report by Cambiar and GMI.[49] Many companies have created private online communities and research panels that bring consumer feedback into the companies 24 hours a day.

Look-Look.com is an online, real-time service that provides accurate and reliable information, research, and news about trendsetting youths aged 14 to 30. With this age group spending an estimated $140 billion a year, many companies are willing to shell out an annual subscription fee of about $20,000 for access to these valuable data. Look-Look pays more than 35,000 hand-picked, prescreened young people from all over the world to e-mail the company information about their styles, trends, opinions, and ideas.[50]

Other companies are finding that quicker, less-expensive online market research is helping them develop products faster and with greater assurance that the products will be successful. The CEO of Stonyfield Farm (maker of higher-priced yogurt) is convinced that Web feedback saved his company from a multimillion-dollar mistake. The online responses from 105 women caused the company to scrap the name originally planned for its new yogurt from YoFemme (which the respondents did not like) to YoSelf (to which the respondents voted yes).[51]

In addition to online market research, and as discussed above, companies are tracking website use, online feedback via blogs, communities, and Facebook and Twitter posts to see how customers are responding to products or messages. This type of activity has resulted in the development of new companies such as Fredericton, New Brunswick-based Radian6, which allows companies to listen to social media by tracking and preparing comprehensive reports about what is being said about the company online, measuring what people are saying about their business and competitors, and analyzing the data to assist companies in making marketing decisions.

Buying Behaviour

Carrying out the marketing concept is impossible unless marketers know what, where, when, and how consumers buy; marketing research into the factors that influence buying behaviour helps marketers develop effective marketing strategies. **Buying behaviour** refers to the decision processes and actions of people who purchase and use products. It includes the behaviour of both consumers purchasing products for personal or household use and organizations buying products for business use. Marketers analyze buying behaviour because a firm's marketing strategy should be guided by an understanding of buyers. People view pets as part of their families, and they want their pets to have the best of everything. Iams, which markets the Iams and Eukanuba pet food brands, recognized this trend and shifted its focus. Today, it markets high-quality pet food, fancy pet treats, sauces, and other

> **Buying behaviour** the decision processes and actions of people who purchase and use products

Polo appeals to people who want to express social roles or identify with a reference group.

items that allow pet lovers to spoil their pets.[52]

Both psychological and social variables are important to an understanding of buying behaviour.

Psychological Variables of Buying Behaviour

Psychological factors include the following:

- **Perception** is the process by which a person selects, organizes, and interprets information received from the senses, as when hearing an advertisement on the radio or touching a product to better understand it.

- Motivation, as we said in Chapter 9, is an inner drive that directs a person's behaviour toward goals. A customer's behaviour is influenced by a set of motives rather than by a single motive. A buyer of a home computer, for example, may be motivated by ease of use, ability to communicate with the office, and price.

- **Learning** brings about changes in a person's behaviour based on information and experience. If a person's actions result in a reward, he or she is likely to behave the same way in similar situations. If a person's actions bring

Consider the Following: Using Technology to Mine Customer Opinions

Successful company marketers take the time to study and understand what they call consumer buying behaviour—in other words, the behaviour of customers buying a company's products for personal or household uses. Marketers pay attention to this behaviour because how customers respond to a company's marketing strategies affects that company's success. They also aim to please customers and undertake research to discover what a company can do to satisfy its customers and keep them coming back. When marketers have a solid grasp on buying behaviour, they can better predict how customers will react to marketing campaigns. A new strategy being used by large companies such as RBC, TD Canada Trust, Johnson & Johnson, Pfizer, and Procter & Gamble is the use of online software to create large-scale focus groups. Companies that sell this software aim to help marketers listen to what their customers want rather than designing marketing campaigns based on generic strategies.

For years, companies have brought people together for traditional, face-to-face focus groups. In other words, a small group of people was brought together in a room to discuss products while people from the company listened (often from another room) to what they had to say. The advantage to the new, large-scale focus groups is that companies can reach a much larger audience—therefore, getting a much wider range of ideas and opinions. Perhaps this may create a more accurate picture of what the general public at large is looking for from a company. For example, for years Lego had been producing the same Lego sets based on feedback from traditional focus groups. The company created an online focus group involving 10,000 people—all Lego customers were invited via e-mail to participate in an online contest regarding new products—and the result was

essentially brainstorming in cyberspace and customers suggesting departures from Lego's traditional toys.

Here is how this software works: In the case of Lego, customers who had received e-mail invitations were part of an online "popularity contest" regarding new-product suggestions. Customers were shown lists of six proposed products at a time. They were asked to rank the toys they liked and, if they chose, offer their own ideas. The customer ideas were then filtered into the mix and sent to other customers to rank against Lego's proposed toys. The software filters the selections shown to customers—those receiving the most votes early on most often appear later, and over time, the most popular ideas rise to the forefront.

Although there are many challenges regarding this new software and its uses (for example, some suggest online research may be skewed toward Internet users), online focus groups are much less expensive than the traditional version. At least for now, this new research method may be a good way to understand more about buying behaviour.[53]

DISCUSSION QUESTIONS

1. How can technology be used to determine consumer beliefs and opinions?

2. Compare face-to-face focus groups with online discussions for understanding consumer behaviour.

3. What are the possible biases from using online research to assess consumer beliefs, opinions, and behaviour?

about a negative result, however—such as feeling ill after eating at a certain restaurant—he or she will probably not repeat that action.

- **Attitude** is knowledge and positive or negative feelings about something. For example, a person who feels strongly about protecting the environment may refuse to buy products that harm the earth and its inhabitants.

- **Personality** refers to the organization of an individual's distinguishing character traits, attitudes, or habits. Although market research on the relationship between personality and buying behaviour has been inconclusive, some marketers believe that the type of car or clothing a person buys reflects his or her personality.

Social Variables of Buying Behaviour

Social factors include **social roles,** which are a set of expectations for individuals based on some position they occupy. A person may have many roles:

mother, wife, student, executive. Each of these roles can influence buying behaviour. Consider a woman choosing an automobile. Her father advises her to buy a safe, gasoline-efficient car, such as a Volvo. Her teenaged daughter wants her to buy a cool car, such as a Honda Civic; her young

---

Consider the Following:
Yelp: Where Consumers Hold the Power

If you want recommendations on a business, Yelp may be just what you need. Founded by Jeremy Stoppelman and Russel Simmons, Yelp.com is a website on which consumers can rate and review businesses. Approximately 30 million users visit the site monthly. Consumers love this site and other online review sites as they provide people with objective third-party opinion. During her stint as marketing director for Yelp Canada, Crystal Henrickson stated that businesses have to be concerned about online review sites as almost 80 percent of regular Internet users consult the Web before making a purchase decision, and roughly 45 percent of all searches on Yelp came from their mobile apps. Mobile users are normally in the process of making a purchase decision and not just conducting research, so their impact on a business could be immediate.

Yet while consumers may love Yelp, the site has a love–hate relationship with many business owners. On the one hand, businesses with loyal customers who post positive reviews on Yelp appreciate the viral nature of the site. A positive review can influence a range of potential customers. For example, Harvard Business School Professor Michael Luca recently conducted a study and determined that a one-star increase in Yelp can positively impact revenue. On the other hand, Yelp makes it easy for consumers to post negative reviews. All a business owner can do is respond either publicly on the site or privately via e-mail to a reviewer. A common complaint from business owners is that responding to complaints can take a significant amount of time. Henrickson's advice is to take the time to respond to consumer comments, as a business would almost always respond to a customer complaining in person. She says a customer complaining online is no different than a complaint in person.

Yelp earns money by selling ad space on the site to represented businesses, but according to co-founder Stoppelman, this does not allow business owners any greater freedom to control review content. What it does give them is the ability to eliminate advertisements of other companies on their pages, the possibility for their ads to appear on other pages, and the opportunity to post photo and video content.

Despite Stoppleman's assurances, businesses have accused Yelp of manipulating reviews either to gain more advertising customers or to punish companies that refuse to advertise through Yelp's paid system. To combat complaints, Yelp has made filtered reviews visible, although they are clearly marked as filtered. Stoppelman continues to support the company's algorithm and claims that Yelp is striving for greater transparency. Whether or not Yelp's actions serve to pacify its detractors, companies are increasingly realizing that the power structure between business and consumer is changing—often in the consumer's favour.[54]

DISCUSSION QUESTIONS

1. What is the benefit of Yelp to consumers?

2. What challenges face businesses that are evaluated on Yelp?

3. Do you think businesses should take the time to respond to customer feedback on Yelp? What are the pros and cons of this strategy?

4. How does Yelp contribute to improving competition and the quality of products?

son wants her to buy a Ford Explorer to take on camping trips. Some of her colleagues at work say she should buy a hybrid Prius to help the environment. Thus, in choosing which car to buy, the woman's buying behaviour may be affected by the opinions and experiences of her family and friends and by her roles as mother, daughter, and employee.

Other social factors include reference groups, social classes, and culture.

- **Reference groups** include families, professional groups, civic organizations, and other groups with whom buyers identify and whose values or attitudes they adopt. A person may use a reference group as a point of comparison or a source of information. A person new to a community may ask other group members to recommend a family doctor, for example.

- **Social classes** are determined by ranking people into higher or lower positions of respect. Criteria vary from one society to another. People within a particular social class may develop common patterns of behaviour. People in the upper-middle class, for example, might buy a Lexus or a Cadillac as a symbol of their social class.

- **Culture** is the integrated, accepted pattern of human behaviour, including thought, speech, beliefs, actions, and artifacts. Culture determines what people wear and eat and where they live and travel. For example, many Atlantic Canadians restrict travel to that particular region of the country because they are less likely to take longer vacations than other groups of Canadians; people in Quebec are more prone to eat baked beans for breakfast and people in Alberta are more prone to purchase trucks.

Understanding Buying Behaviour

Although marketers try to understand buying behaviour, it is extremely difficult to explain exactly why a buyer purchases a particular product. The tools and techniques for analyzing consumers are not exact. Marketers may not be able to determine accurately what is highly satisfying to buyers, but they know that trying to understand consumer wants and needs is the best way to satisfy them. In an attempt to better understand consumer behaviour, Procter & Gamble sent video crews into about 80 households all around the world. The company, maker of Tide, Crest, Pampers, and many other consumer products, hoped to gain insights into the lifestyles and habits of young couples, families with children, and empty nesters. Participants were recorded over a four-day period and were paid about $200–$250 a day. The behaviours caught on video may lead the company to

develop new products or change existing ones to better meet consumers' needs and give the company a competitive advantage over its rivals.[55]

LO6 Summarize the environmental forces that influence marketing decisions.

The Marketing Environment

A number of external forces directly or indirectly influence the development of marketing strategies; the following political, legal, regulatory, social, competitive, economic, and technological forces comprise the marketing environment.

- *Political, legal, and regulatory forces*—laws and regulators' interpretation of laws; law enforcement and regulatory activities; regulatory bodies, legislators and legislation, and political actions of interest groups. Specific laws, for example, require that advertisements be truthful and that all health claims be documented. Changing laws can greatly impact a business. For example, in Nova Scotia the government announced that smoking would only be permitted in bars and restaurants that have a special smoking room. Many businesses spent thousands of dollars building these rooms only to have the government ban smoking altogether a short time later.

- *Social forces*—the public's opinions and attitudes toward issues such as living standards, ethics, the environment, lifestyles, and quality of life. For example, Ontario-based Crystal Head Vodka attempted to sell its vodka in a clear, skull shaped bottle. The response from the Liquor Control Board of Ontario was to ban the booze as it deemed that the message was not appropriate, reflecting society's changing opinion about liquor consumption. Other examples include social concerns which have led marketers to design and market safer toys for children.

- *Competitive and economic forces*—competitive relationships, unemployment, purchasing power, and general economic conditions (prosperity, recession, depression, recovery, product shortages, and inflation).

- *Technological forces*—computers and other technological advances that improve distribution, promotion, and new-product development.

Marketing environment forces can change quickly and radically, which is one reason that marketing requires creativity and a customer focus. For example, *Rolling Stone* magazine did a business analysis before entering the Chinese market. Unfortunately after a successful debut, the Chinese government had concerns about its licence to publish in China. The success of *Rolling Stone* concerned other lifestyle and music magazines, and they informed the authorities that the licence was not appropriate.[56]

Because such environmental forces are interconnected, changes in one may cause changes in others. Consider that because of evidence linking children's consumption of soft drinks and fast foods to health issues such as obesity, diabetes, and osteoporosis, marketers of such products have experienced negative publicity and calls for legislation regulating the sale of soft drinks in public schools. When Morgan Spurlock saw an evening news story about two teenagers who unsuccessfully sued McDonald's for their poor health, he decided to make the movie *Super Size Me*. As director, he went on a supersized diet of fast food and gained 25 pounds, suffered from depression, and experienced heart pain.[57] Some companies have responded to these concerns by reformulating products to make them healthier. Kellogg Company is reformulating many of its popular child-targeted products (which account for 50 percent of its products) to make them more healthy. The goal is to cut sugar and fat to help fight childhood obesity. If brands such as Pop-Tarts, Froot Loops, Apple Jacks, or other products cannot be made more healthy while maintaining their same taste, the products will not be marketed to children under 12.[58] The fast-food industry's frantic race to cook up the first "better-for-you" french fry appears to have been won by Wendy's. The number-three fast-food chain announced that it will dump cooking oil for a blend of nonhydrogenated corn and soy oil containing nearly no artery-clogging trans fats.[59]

Although the forces in the marketing environment are sometimes called uncontrollables, they are not totally so. A marketing manager can influence some environmental variables. For example, businesses can lobby legislators to dissuade them from passing unfavourable legislation. Figure 11.4 shows the variables in the marketing environment that affect the marketing mix and the buyer.

figure 11.4 The Marketing Mix and the Marketing Environment

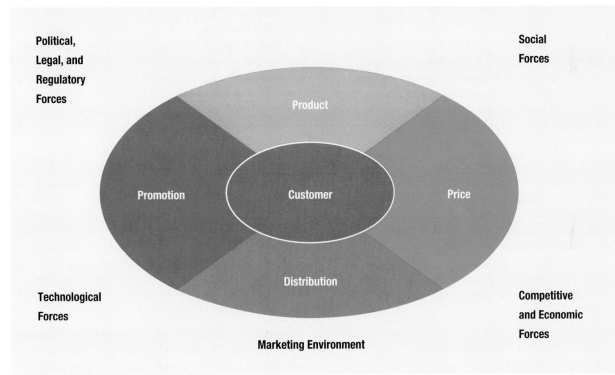

Every year an estimated 500 billion to 1 trillion plastic bags are consumed globally. In the United States alone, 88.5 billion plastic bags were consumed in 2007, and less than 1 percent were recycled. The average American family of four consumes about 1,460 plastic bags every year, the production of which requires 12 million barrels of oil annually. Plastic bags take more than 1,000 years to fully photo-degrade and are a toxic threat for all of that time, representing a pollution crisis of global magnitude.

Responding to this problem, a number of environmentally conscious designers have been promoting high-fashion reusable totes. In 2007, Anya Hindmarch developed a stylish canvas tote embroidered with the phrase "I'm not a plastic bag." The limited edition $15 shoulder bag was in such high demand that people lined up in front of the department stores where they were offered in hopes of obtaining one before they ran out. Anita Ahuja, also known as the "bag lady," is the head of the profit/not-for-profit Conserve, an organization that takes used plastic grocery bags and other trash and recycles them into new, stylish, and low-priced handbags. Based in Delhi, India, Ahuja provides gainful employment to garbage pickers, who not only give her material for her bags but also provide a service by cleaning up the streets of Delhi. Ahuja's products are sold in stores in the United Kingdom, France, Canada, and the United States in chains such as Whole Foods. Anita donates some of her profits to charities, such as starting a school for the children of the ragpickers she employs, and she is trying to get her footing in the world of Parisian fashion.

Haute couture designers are also concerned with running eco-responsible businesses. Stella McCartney, the British designer and daughter of Paul McCartney, is a vegetarian and has been involved in promoting organics for years. Recently, she created a canvas shopping bag, retail $495, as a part of an organic clothing line sold in her shops. Celebrities such as Reese Witherspoon and Alicia Silverstone have been photographed carrying the Stella McCartney tote, spurring sales. Hermès, the brand famous for its silk scarves, has joined the high-fashion totes scene by adding a $960 tote to its line. A Louis Vuitton canvas tote retails for an astounding $1,740. These high-end, fashionable bags are providing the inspiration and driving the sales of lower-priced versions by making canvas grocery bags fashionable, while contributing to the effort to reduce global plastic bag consumption. Designers like Anya Hindmarch and Louis Vuitton are doing their part to lend an air of exclusivity and desirability to being eco-friendly—making it cool for everyone to carry reusable shopping bags.[60]

DISCUSSION QUESTIONS

1. What kinds of consumers are the designers discussed targeting?

2. What might be some good marketing strategies to further encourage the use of reusable bags?

3. What other green fashion movements could benefit from the promotional efforts of these canvas bag designers?

TEAM EXERCISE

Form groups and assign the responsibility of finding examples of companies that excel in one dimension of the marketing mix (price, product, promotion, and distribution). Provide several company and product examples, and defend why this would be an exemplary case. Present your research to the class.

LO1 Define marketing and describe the exchange process.

Marketing is a group of activities designed to expedite transactions by creating, distributing, pricing, and promoting goods, services and ideas. Marketing facilitates the exchange, the act of giving up one thing in return for something else. The central focus of marketing is to satisfy needs.

LO2 Specify the functions of marketing.

Marketing includes many varied and interrelated activities: buying, selling, transporting, storing, grading, financing, marketing research, and risk taking.

LO3 Explain the marketing concept and its implications for developing marketing strategies.

The marketing concept is the idea that an organization should try to satisfy customers' needs through coordinated activities that also allow it to achieve its goals. If a company does not implement the marketing concept, by providing products that consumers need and want while achieving its own objectives, it will not survive.

LO4 Examine the development of a marketing strategy, including market segmentation and marketing mix.

A marketing strategy is a plan of action for creating a marketing mix (product, price, distribution, promotion) for a specific target market (a specific group of consumers on whose needs and wants a company focuses its marketing efforts). Some firms use a total-market approach, designat-ing everyone as the target market. Most firms divide the total market into segments of people who have relatively similar product needs. A company using a concentration approach develops one marketing strategy for a single market segment, whereas a multisegment approach aims marketing efforts at two or more segments, developing a different marketing strategy for each.

LO5 Investigate how marketers conduct marketing research, and study buying behaviour.

Carrying out the marketing concept is impossible unless marketers know what, where, when, and how consumers buy: marketing research into the factors that influence buying behaviour helps marketers develop effective marketing strategies. Marketing research is a systematic, objective process of getting information about potential customers to guide marketing decisions. Buying behaviour is the decision processes and actions of people who purchase and use products.

LO6 Summarize the environmental forces that influence marketing decisions.

There are several forces that influence marketing activities: political, legal, regulatory, social, competitive, economic, and technological.

KEY TERMS

attitude
buying behaviour
concentration approach
culture
exchange
learning
market
market segment
market segmentation
marketing
marketing concept
marketing mix
marketing orientation
marketing research

marketing strategy
multisegment approach
perception
personality
place/distribution
price
primary data
promotion
reference groups
secondary data
social classes
social roles
target market
total-market approach

DESTINATION CEO DISCUSSION QUESTIONS

1. Why is Spin Master Toys successful?

2. What are some of the advantages of non-traditional marketing? What are some of the potential pitfalls?

3. Would non-traditional marketing work in all industries? Why or why not?

SO YOU WANT A JOB *in Marketing*

You probably did not think as a child how great it would be to grow up and become a marketer. That's because often marketing is associated with sales jobs, but opportunities in marketing, public relations, product management, advertising, e-marketing, and customer relationship management and beyond represent almost one-third of all jobs in today's business world. To enter any job in the marketing field, you must balance an awareness of customer needs with business knowledge while mixing in creativity and the ability to obtain useful information to make smart business decisions.

Marketing starts with understanding the customer. Marketing research is a vital aspect in marketing decision making and presents many job opportunities. Market researchers survey customers to determine their habits, preferences, and aspirations. Activities include concept testing, product testing, package testing, test-market research, and new-product research. Salaries vary, depending on the nature and level of the position as well as the type, size, and location of the firm. An entry-level market analyst may make between $24,000 and $50,000, while a market research director may earn from $75,000 to $200,000 or more.

One of the most dynamic areas in marketing is direct marketing, where a seller solicits a response from a consumer using direct communication methods such as telephone, online communications, direct mail, or catalogues. Jobs in direct marketing include buyers, catalogue managers, research/mail-list managers, or order fulfillment managers. Most positions in direct marketing involve planning and market analysis. Some require the use of databases to sort and analyze customer information and sales history.

Use of the Internet for retail sales is growing, and the Internet continues to be very useful for business-to-business sales. E-marketing offers many career opportunities including customer relationship management (CRM). CRM helps companies market to customers through relationships, maintaining customer loyalty. Information technology plays a huge role in such marketing jobs, as you need to combine technical skills and marketing knowledge to effectively communicate with customers. Job titles include e-marketing manager, customer relationship manager, and e-services manager. A CRM customer service manager may receive a salary in the $40,000 to $45,000 range, and experienced individuals in charge of online product offerings may earn up to $100,000.

A job in any of these marketing fields will require a strong sense of the current trends in business and marketing. Customer service is vital to many aspects of marketing so the ability to work with customers and to communicate their needs and wants is important. Marketing is everywhere from the corner grocery or local non-profit organization to the largest multinational corporation, making it a shrewd choice for an ambitious and creative person. We will provide additional job opportunities in marketing in Chapter 12.

BUILD YOUR BUSINESS PLAN

Customer Driven Marketing

The first step is to develop a marketing strategy for your product or service. Who will be the target market you will specifically try to reach? What group(s) of people has the need, ability, and willingness to purchase this product? How will you segment customers within your target market? Segmenting by demographic and geographic variables are often the easiest segmentation strategies to attempt. Remember that you would like to have the customers in your segment be as homogeneous and accessible as possible. You might target several segments if you feel your product or service has broad appeal.

The second step in your marketing strategy is to develop the marketing mix for your product or service. Whether you are dealing with an established product or you are creating your own product or service, you need to think about what differential advantage your product offers. What makes it unique? How should it be priced? Should the product be priced below, above, or at the market? How will you distribute the product? And last but certainly not least, you need to think about the promotional strategy for your product.

What about the uncontrollable variables you need to be aware of? Is your product something that can constantly be technologically advanced? Is your product a luxury that will not be considered by consumers when the economy is in a downturn?

CASE | New "Places" Have Emerged to Sell Wedding Gowns and Rings—Helping Couples Lower Wedding Costs

For years, when the 4Ps were discussed, "Place," which represents the place where items were sold, rarely changed. Food items were sold in grocery stores, computers in small computer boutiques, music and musical instruments in music stores, clothing in department stores, and so forth. This all changed with the emergence of super-centre department stores, discounters, and ultimately the Internet as suddenly products had no traditional "place" of sale. Originally items such as books and computers were products deemed perfect for department stores, discount locations, and eventually online sales as they were mostly straightforward purchases involving little emotion. Naysayers, however, noted that specialty goods such as wedding gowns and engagement rings had too much emotional involvement ever to be sold in non-traditional locations. Most women have been planning their wedding day their whole lives, with a lot of thought going into big ticket items such as the wedding dress and engagement ring. Even into adulthood, many women continue to dream of wearing their fairytale gown and beautiful rings. Consumed by the

vision of a magical, designer-made dress, many women are willing to spend thousands of dollars to purchase it and many grooms and couples will spend countless hours and dollars on an engagement ring. However, such expense is not affordable for most couples. Increasingly, however, alternatives do exist. As the cost of the average Canadian wedding ceremony balloons—up to nearly $28,000 in 2012[61]—more companies, including some online entrants, are seeking to take advantage of a large segment of the market that cannot afford this level of extravagance by offering lower-cost, yet stylish gowns and rings.

In the past 60 years, the bridal industry has reinvented itself numerous times. In the 1950s, most women purchased their wedding dresses in department stores. Then, in the 1960s, small, exclusive, boutique-style wedding shops offering more expensive selections began popping up. Finally, in the 1990s, David's Bridal entered the market, offering affordable gowns ranging from $99 to $1,000. Today, David's Bridal maintains about 30 percent of the wedding dress market. Recognizing this company's success, a number of well-known apparel retailers also now produce low-cost wedding dresses. JC Penney offers a popular wedding gown style for $179.99, Ann Taylor has gowns for $600 to $1,200, and Target features an entire line of Isaac Mizrahi gowns all for under $160. New entrants to the market have also emerged on the Internet as many e-tailers such as TBDress.com and Craibox.ca offer wedding dresses at even deeper discounts, while other sites such as OnceWed.com sell used wedding dresses to brides.

Wedding savings don't end with the dress. More men and couples are using the Internet to cut costs on what is often the most expensive wedding product—the engagement ring. BlueNile.com is the world's largest online retailer of diamonds, with global sales in excess of $400 million and strong revenue growth. The company boasts that buying a diamond should be a simple process, offers customers deep discounts compared to brick and mortar stores, and provides shoppers with online videos, FAQ, and chat features to assist in the process. One of the primary reasons BlueNile can sell rings at such a discount is they do not take possession of the rings until they actually sell them. BlueNile has established relationships with diamond wholesalers throughout the world who will ship the diamonds to BlueNile on demand. While traditionalists may have a problem with not being able to see the diamond before buying it, customers do not. In fact, the average engagement ring sold at BlueNile is $5,500, which is almost twice the industry average, and BlueNile boasts that it sells $20,000–$50,000 rings daily.[62] Other online retailers of wedding rings have popped up, including DiamondPriceGuru.com and Ice.com, that are hoping to duplicate BlueNile's success.

The wedding industry has grown by leaps and bounds and lower-priced alternatives, especially online retailers, are starting to reshape what has been a very traditional industry with consumers benefitting from increased competition and lower prices.

DISCUSSION QUESTIONS

1. Are you surprised that people will purchase wedding dresses and engagement rings from discount or online companies? Would you do this? Why or why not?

2. Wedding dresses and engagement rings were thought to be emotional purchases. Is this still true as discount, department, and online stores have become so successful in selling these products?

3. What are some of the reasons that David's Bridal and BlueNile have been so successful?

4. Online retailers such as BlueNile are often blamed for putting small local stores out of business. Do you think this could be true? Why or why not?

5. Visit BlueNile's website and try out some of the custom apps. After visiting the site and browsing its merchandise, do you feel you are more or less likely to purchase a ring online?

LEARNING OBJECTIVES

LO1 Describe the role of product in the marketing mix, including how products are developed, classified, and identified.

LO2 Define price and discuss its importance in the marketing mix, including various pricing strategies a firm might employ.

LO3 Identify factors affecting distribution decisions, such as marketing channels and intensity of market coverage.

LO4 Specify the activities involved in promotion, as well as promotional strategies and promotional positioning.

DESTINATION CEO

Thorsten Heins, the new CEO of BlackBerry, is dull, or at least his friends say so. *Canadian Business*, the leading national business magazine, summed up critics' views: "Thorsten Heins is a company man without vision," and the wrong choice for a company that is in need of leadership. Supporters of Heins are telling critics to hang on; Heins, while not outgoing, is a determined and focused leader and may be exactly what BlackBerry needs. BlackBerry, formerly Research In Motion (RIM), is being criticized from all corners of the business world. Tech experts are bemoaning the company's inability to meet deadlines for getting new products to market. Marketing experts are claiming that the firm has failed to follow consumer trends, and its products and advertisements are out of touch. Meanwhile, financial experts and investors are wondering if BlackBerry will even exist as a stand-alone company in the coming years.

Heins, who has entered into this fray of problems and criticism, has been quick to respond to business concerns and has left the matter of his personality for the public to judge. Recognizing that the company has had delays in releasing products—including its latest smartphone, the BlackBerry Z10—Heins has instituted a requirement for greater accountability from managers. Additionally, he has placed people on work teams with the instruction to work on one project at a time until completion. BlackBerry then engaged in a very aggressive marketing strategy with the Z10, and released the product one country at a time in order to build up positive reviews and momentum prior to entering the important U.S. market. Social media played a vital role in the aggressive marketing campaign as Facebook and YouTube offered a great deal of build-up prior to the launch of the Z10 and additional marketing when the product hit the shelves. Most consumer and business reviews were positive and Heins says, "We are receiving a very positive response to BlackBerry 10 from our customers, but it's also been attractive for customers coming from other platforms ... we are a little surprised by that.

While initial sales results were strong in Canada and the United Kingdom, results from the all-important American market were weak, as reports indicated that most consumers had written off the company prior to the launch. Additionally, consumer reviews, especially from consumers who spent time with the new Z10 phone, were not favourable. Consumers noticed the Z10 was missing some key functions, lacked apps, and wasn't as fun to use as the iPhone. The result was that consumers returned the phone in droves and BlackBerry recently announced a shocking $1 billion loss. Heins reacted quickly and decisively to the latest problem by announcing he was slashing Z10 prices and selling BlackBerry to Fairfax Financial for $4.7 billion. Fairfax apparently believes Heins's new plan of focusing on corporate clients with the Q10 is worth the investment.[1]

Introduction

Creating an effective marketing strategy is important. Getting just the right mix of product, price, promotion, and distribution is critical if a business is to satisfy its target customers and achieve its own objectives (implement the marketing concept).

In Chapter 11, we introduced the concept of marketing and the various activities important in developing a marketing strategy. In this chapter, we'll take a closer look at the four dimensions of the marketing mix—product, price, distribution, and promotion—used to develop the marketing strategy. The focus of these marketing mix elements is a marketing strategy that builds customer relationships and satisfaction.

The Marketing Mix

The key to developing a marketing strategy is maintaining the right marketing mix that satisfies the target market and creates long-term relationships with customers. To develop meaningful customer relationships, marketers have to develop and manage the dimensions of the marketing mix to give their firm an advantage over competitors. Successful companies offer at least one dimension of value that surpasses all competitors in the marketplace in meeting customer expectations. However, this does not mean that a company can ignore the other dimensions of the marketing mix; it must maintain acceptable and—if possible—distinguishable differences in the other dimensions as well.

Future Shop, for example, emphasizes price ("The lowest price guaranteed"). Rogers Communications and Bell Canada are well known for their product bundles that allow consumers to save money by purchasing their smartphone, home phone, Internet, and TV programming as one package. Bombay Canada is well known for its home décor and mahogany furniture. Domino's Pizza is recognized for its superiority in distribution after developing the largest home delivery pizza company in the world and its innovative new product introductions.

> "The key to developing a marketing strategy is maintaining the right marketing mix that satisfies the target market and creates long-term relationships with customers."

while developing products is a key to the company's success, there are many failures that occur on the way to developing a successful product. The company operated for 10 years prior to developing its first breakthrough product, which was a swing-top plastic trash can. Mandelbaum says he came up with the idea after purchasing a similar toy-sized trash can in a children's shop in Paris. He states that when he brought the product back to Canada his staff doubted it would ever result in a profitable product for the company but pushed forward anyway.[3] Even though new product development can be risky, companies can build a competitive advantage by developing new products. For example, Apple has built a very profitable company by developing the iPad, iPhone, and iPod. Readers should recognize that some success in developing new products does not result in success every time. BlackBerry had built a dominant position in the market by developing what amounted to the world's first smartphone. Recently, the company has failed to deliver products customers want, such as smartphones with advanced browsers and game capabilities, and as a result, the company has fallen on hard times. Even Apple has developed products that have not succeeded commercially, such as the Apple TV.[4] Worldwide giant Nortel Networks declared bankruptcy in 2009, despite being the Canadian leader in investing in new technologies during the previous 10 years.[5] Coca-Cola has, in recent years, created or acquired thousands of new products, including acquiring Glacéau, a maker of vitamin water. New products include Enviga green tea, Vault and Vault Zero energy soda, Full

| LO1 | Describe the role of product in the marketing mix, including how products are developed, classified, and identified. |

Product Strategy

As mentioned previously, the term *product* refers to goods, services, and ideas. Because the product is often the most visible of the marketing mix dimensions, managing product decisions is crucial. In this section, we'll consider product development, classification, mix, life cycle, and identification.

Developing New Products

Each year thousands of products are introduced, but few of them succeed. For example, some estimate that BlackBerry, formerly RIM, lost roughly $1.5 billion trying to develop a tablet computer to compete with Apple's iPad.[2] Umbra, a Toronto-based leader in original designs for the home, sells its products through 25,000 retailers in more than 75 countries. Umbra's co-founder and chairman Les Mandelbaum notes that

Nintendo, the global game company, is an excellent example of a company that invests heavily in new product development with varying degrees of success. The original Nintendo gaming system, Game Boy, and Wii were huge hits with consumers. But the N64 failed miserably. The Wii U is the latest product the company has developed. Do you think it will succeed?

Throttle, and many variations and flavours of Dasani water.[6] A firm can take considerable time to get a product ready for the market: It took more than 20 years for the first photocopier, for example. General Motors has trimmed the time required to develop and introduce a new vehicle model from four years to 18 months. The automaker released 29 new models, many with innovative designs, over a 16-month period.[7] The one-time leader in the automobile industry is hoping innovation, particularly in the area of hybrid technology, will restore the company to greatness. In 2011–12, the company introduced a new hybrid called the Volt that runs only on battery power. *Profit* columnist Rick Spence notes that senior management must employ and support innovators if a company hopes to develop new products and processes. Before introducing a new product, a business must follow a multistep process: idea development, the screening of new ideas, business analysis, product development, test marketing, and commercialization.

Idea Development. New ideas can come from marketing research, engineers, and outside sources such as advertising agencies and management consultants. Microsoft has a separate division—Microsoft Research—where scientists devise the technology of the future. The division has more than 700 full-time employees who work in a university-like research atmosphere. Research teams then present their ideas to Microsoft engineers who are developing specific products.[9] As stated in Chapter 11, ideas sometimes come from customers too. For example, in preparation for the 2010 Winter Olympics at Whistler, Speed Skating Canada relied heavily on feedback from skaters (customers) to develop new skating suits designed to reduce wind traction and improve race times.[10] Kevin Halliday relied on feedback from customers when he started his Calgary-based company, Spindle, Stairs and Railings. Halliday, who had years of experience in the industry, had heard from customers that staircases can be decorative centrepieces in a home. Halliday went on to develop a process of manufacturing winding decorative staircases for smaller homes.[11] Other sources for new products are brainstorming and intracompany incentives or rewards for good ideas. New ideas can even create a company. As discussed in Chapter 4, David Reynolds of Halifax developed the idea for QuickSnap, a shoe fastening device, while waiting impatiently for his friend to tie his shoes. Reynolds, a university student at the time, went on to develop and grow the product into a successful business.

New Idea Screening. The next step in developing a new product is idea screening. In this phase, a marketing manager should look at the organization's resources and objectives and assess the firm's ability to produce and market the product. Important aspects to be considered at this stage are consumer desires, the competition, technological changes, social trends, and political, economic, and environmental considerations. Basically, there are two reasons new

products succeed: They are able to meet a need or solve a problem better than products already available, or they add variety to the product selection currently on the market. For example, Goodyear has developed a tire that will self-inflate as soon as the air pressure in the tire stars to drop. The tire passed through the screening stage as Goodyear obviously has experience manufacturing and marketing innovative tires and management felt there would be a demand for such a product.[12] *Dragons' Den,* a show in which entrepreneurs pitch businesses as well as inventions, usually showcases a number of products that shouldn't have gotten past the screening stage. In the 2010 season, entrepreneurs brought forward fully developed products such as Logo Locs, a hair extension with a button designed for advertisements. Another entrepreneur brought forward a harness to attach a phone to a shirt.[13] If either entrepreneur had screened their idea they would have realized that neither invention was desired by consumers, solved a problem, or improved a current product. Bringing together a team of knowledgeable people including design, engineering, marketing, and customers is a great way to screen ideas. Using the Internet to encourage collaboration is the next sea of innovation for marketers to screen ideas.[14] After many ideas were screened, Heinz Ketchup introduced kid-targeted Silly Squirts with three cool drawing nozzles to keep kids amused and entertained at dinner. In addition, Easy Squeeze upside-down bottles added to convenience.[15] Most new-product ideas are rejected during screening because they seem inappropriate or impractical for the organization, but many, which go on to fail, still make it to market. Indeed, GfK Custom Research has established a collection, nicknamed the Museum of Product Failures, just outside Ann Arbor, Michigan. While not open to the public, companies considering a product idea can visit— for a $5,000 entrance fee—this massive physical database of products as a stark reminder of the consequences of poor market research.[16]

Business Analysis. Business analysis is a basic assessment of a product's compatibility in the marketplace and its potential profitability. Both the size of the market and competing products are often studied at this point. The most important question relates to market demand: How will the product affect the firm's sales, costs, and profits?

Product Development. If a product survives the first three steps, it is developed into a prototype that should reveal the intangible attributes it possesses as perceived by the consumer. Product development is often expensive, and few product ideas make it to this stage. New product research and development costs vary. Adding a new colour to an existing item may cost $100,000 to $200,000, but launching a completely new product can cost millions of dollars. For example, Andrew Scott of Vancouver spent over $1 million developing a replacement for traditional parking meters. Scott's parking meters

> **DID YOU KNOW?**
>
> Domino's Pizza delivery drivers cover 9 million miles a week delivering 400 million pizzas a year.[8]

enable remote monitoring by parking enforcement, six locking points to detect theft, full-colour graphic screens, and a wide variety of payment options including coins, bank cards, and credit cards.[17] The Coca-Cola Co. reduced the time and cost of product development research by 50 percent when it created an online panel of 100 teenagers and asked them how to remake its Powerade sports drink.[18] During product development, various elements of the marketing mix must be developed for testing. Copyrights, tentative advertising copy, packaging, labelling, and descriptions of a target market are integrated to develop an overall marketing strategy.

Test Marketing. **Test marketing** is a trial mini-launch of a product in limited areas that represent the potential market. It allows a complete test of the marketing strategy in a natural environment, giving the organization an opportunity to discover weaknesses and eliminate them before the product is fully launched. For example, when Tim Hortons was considering introducing steeped tea, the company first tried the product in Atlantic Canada to determine what the public reaction would be to the product. Recently, when Tim Hortons was considering increasing the size of its coffee cups, it tested the concept in two Ontario markets, Sudbury and Kingston, to gauge customer reaction.[19] Imperial Tobacco Canada ran similar testing marketing for a type of smokeless tobacco called Snus.[20] The company first introduced the powdered tobacco product at 230 retail outlets in Edmonton to determine whether it might be successful with consumers across the country. Best Buy has recently started selling used games in Canada to determine if the strategy will work. Consider Seasons 52, the latest concept restaurant developed by Darden Restaurants Inc., the world's largest casual dining company with such well-known restaurants as Red Lobster and Olive Garden. Seasons 52 boasts a seasonally inspired menu with the freshest goods available served in a casual atmosphere. Seasons 52 targets those who are striving to live fit, active lives and are concerned about the quality and nutrition of their food. All menu items at Seasons 52 have fewer than 475 calories (significantly lower than competing restaurants), are nutritionally balanced, and are not fried. Darden is test marketing this restaurant concept in Florida and Georgia to experiment with variations in menu, advertising, and pricing and to measure the extent of brand

> **Test marketing** a trial mini-launch of a product in limited areas that represent the potential market

awareness, brand switching, and repeat purchases resulting from these alterations in this concept restaurant.[21] ACNielsen assists companies in test-marketing their products. Figure 12.1 shows the permanent sites as well as custom locations for test marketing.

Commercialization. **Commercialization** is the full introduction of a complete marketing strategy and the launch of the product for commercial success. During commercialization, the firm gears up for full-scale production, distribution, and promotion. When Research In Motion introduced Black-Berry Storm, it spent millions on production, distribution, advertising, and publicity for the product. The original product did not catch on with consumers and was replaced by the Storm2 a short time later. A more successful example of a product launch may be Procter & Gamble's introduction of the Fusion razor, when it used its large distribution and retail network and spent more than $6 million for just two Super Bowl ads for the five-blade product. It blanketed stores with 180,000 displays in the first week, coverage that it took a year to achieve with the Mach3 razor in 1998. The Fusion razor commands 30 percent higher prices than Mach3 products, which—at a time when Procter & Gamble cannot increase the prices on Tide or Crest—will boost earnings by $120 million and increase market share to 15 percent.[22] It's often not until commercialization that companies will know if a product is going to be successful.

> **Commercialization** the full introduction of a complete marketing strategy and the launch of the product for commercial success

figure 12.1 ACNielsen Market Decisions

SOURCE: "Test Marketing," ACNielsen (n.d.), www.acnielsen.com/services/testing/test1.htm (accessed June 5, 2004). Reprinted with permission of ACNielsen Market Decisions.

New products slated for release in 2013–14 are Google Glass, TechPet, and Facebook's branded smartphone. Only time will tell if these products will be successful even though the companies have spent countless hours and millions of dollars ensuring that consumers will want to buy them. [23]

Classifying Products

Products are usually classified as either consumer products or business products. **Consumer products** are for household or family use; they are not intended for any purpose other than daily living. They can be further classified as convenience products, shopping products, and specialty products on the basis of consumers' buying behaviour and intentions.

- *Convenience products,* such as eggs, milk, bread, and newspapers, are bought frequently, without a lengthy search, and often for immediate consumption. Consumers spend virtually no time planning where to purchase these products and usually accept whatever brand is available.

- *Shopping products,* such as furniture, audio equipment, clothing, and sporting goods, are purchased after the consumer has compared competitive products and "shopped around." Price, product features, quality, style, service, and image all influence the decision to buy.

- *Specialty products,* such as ethnic foods, designer clothing and shoes, art, and antiques, require even greater research and shopping effort. Consumers know what

Milk is a convenience product. It is bought frequently by consumers for relatively quick consumption without their conducting a lengthy search.

Google GLASS

Google Glass, which is due to be released commercially in 2014, will enable users to surf the Internet through glasses they wear on their face and by using voice commands. Would you purchase these to wear?

they want and go out of their way to find it; they are not willing to accept a substitute.

Business products are used directly or indirectly in the operation or manufacturing processes of businesses. They are usually purchased for the operation of an organization or the production of other products; thus, their purchase is tied to specific goals and objectives. They too can be further classified:

- *Raw materials* are natural products taken from the earth or from the oceans, and recycled solid waste. Iron ore, bauxite, lumber, cotton, and fruits and vegetables are examples.

- *Major equipment* covers large, expensive items used in production. Examples include earth-moving equipment, stamping machines, and robotic equipment used on auto assembly lines.

- *Accessory equipment* includes items used for production, office, or management purposes, which usually do not become part of the final product. Computers, fax machines, calculators, and hand tools are examples.

- *Component parts* are finished items, ready to be assembled into the company's final products. Tires, window glass, batteries, and spark plugs are component parts of automobiles.

- *Processed materials* are things used directly in production or management operations but not readily identifiable as component parts. Varnish, for example, is a processed material for a furniture manufacturer.

- *Supplies* include materials that make production, management, and other operations possible, such as paper, pencils, paint, cleaning supplies, and so on.

- *Industrial services* include financial, legal, marketing research, security, janitorial, and exterminating services. Purchasers decide whether to provide these services internally or to acquire them from an outside supplier.

Levi Strauss & Co. has long been known for its 501s and affordable prices. Recently, the company delved into the premium denim market, dominated by brands such as Earl Jeans, Seven for All Mankind, Citizens for Humanity, and True Religion, by launching its Premium collection. Now, in an attempt to break into yet another hot market, Levi's is going green.

According to the research group Mintel, about 35 million people in the United States regularly purchase "green" products. Consumers are increasingly willing to pay more for earth-friendly products and services. As a result, companies are going to great lengths to prove that they are part of the green movement. Many are switching to earth-friendly packaging or new production methods that conserve energy. Levi's is producing 100 percent organic cotton jeans.

These new jeans, priced at $250 a pair, are made with 100 percent organic cotton, natural dyes, tags composed of recycled paper and soy ink, and recycled rivets. The company is also releasing less expensive lines composed partly of organic and recycled materials.

Although many of us might be willing to switch to green jeans, we may wonder at the price and find it prohibitive. Why is going green sometimes so expensive? In the case of Levi's jeans, it's the organic cotton. The demand for organic cotton is currently much greater than the supply, making it expensive. For cotton to be certified organic, it cannot be genetically modified and must be pesticide and fungicide free. In 2005, more than 50 percent of cotton in the United States was genetically modified. Many companies are turning to farmers overseas, but certification for these farmers can be a challenge. As of 2007, certified organic cotton composed less than 1 percent of the world's

cotton supply. For now, Levi's can only produce a limited number of green jeans, hence the high price.

However, the very issue that drives up prices can be used as a marketing strategy to gain customers. Many people are willing to pay more to support farmers committed to harvesting through organic methods. In fact, at the recent Cannes Lions International Advertising Festival, "eco-marketing" was an extremely popular topic. Consumers are excited about green products and services and companies are spending big bucks to promote their stances on going green. According to TNS Media Intelligence, marketers spent $18 million on green-focused television advertising in a three-month time span.

While going green may seem to some like a current fad, indicators point to a prolonged increase in demand for such products. According to the Organic Trade Association, Canadian organic retail sales have grown every year since 1990. It seems that companies can only benefit from a continued investment in eco-friendly items, and Levi's appears committed to incorporating organic cotton and other eco-friendly materials into its product lines.[24]

DISCUSSION QUESTIONS

1. Why can companies charge a premium price for green products?

2. What else might Levi's do to increase its offering of moderately priced green products?

3. How much more would you be willing to pay for environmentally friendly clothing such as Levi's new green jeans?

Product Line and Product Mix

Product relationships within an organization are of key importance. A **product line** is a group of closely related products that are treated as a unit because of similar marketing strategy. At Colgate-Palmolive, for example, the oral-care product line includes Colgate toothpaste, toothbrushes, and dental floss. A **product mix** is all the products offered by an organization. For example, a product line at Lululemon could be all of the company's yoga gear while its product mix would be its

Product line a group of closely related products that are treated as a unit because of similar marketing strategy, production, or end-use considerations

Product mix all the products offered by an organization

Apple's product mix and its many product lines are visible on the company's website.

figure 12.2 Colgate-Palmolive's Product Mix and Product Lines

Product Mix			
Oral Care	*Personal Care*	*Household Care*	*Pet Nutrition*
Toothpaste	Men's antiperspirant/deodorant	Dishwashing	Science diet
Toothbrushes	Women's antiperspirant/deodorant	Fabric conditioner	Prescription diet
Kids' products	Bar soap	Household cleaners	
Whitening products	Body wash	Institutional products	
Over the counter	Liquid hand wash		
From the dentist	Toiletries for men		

Product Lines (vertical axis label)

SOURCE: Colgate Products, http://www.colgate.com/app/Colgate/US/Corp/Products.cvsp (accessed June 17, 2007).

> "During the *decline stage*, sales continue to fall rapidly. Profits also decline and may even become losses as prices are cut and necessary marketing expenditures are made."

full range of products—clothing, equipment, and accessories. Figure 12.2 displays a sampling of the product mix and product lines of the Colgate-Palmolive Company.

Product Life Cycle

Like people, products are born, grow, mature, and eventually die. Some products have very long lives. Ivory Soap was introduced in 1879 and is still popular. In contrast, a new computer chip is usually outdated within a year because of technological breakthroughs and rapid changes in the computer industry. There are four stages in the life cycle of a product: introduction, growth, maturity, and decline (Figure 12.3). The stage a product is in helps determine marketing strategy.

In the *introductory stage,* consumer awareness and acceptance of the product are limited, sales are zero, and profits are negative. Profits are negative because the firm has spent money on research, development, and marketing to launch the product. During the introductory stage, marketers focus on making consumers aware of the product and its benefits. When Procter & Gamble introduced the Tide Stainbrush to reach the 70 percent of consumers who pretreat stains when doing laundry, it employed press releases as well as television and magazine advertising to make consumers aware of the new product.[25] Sales accelerate as the product enters the growth stage of the life cycle.

In the *growth stage*, sales increase rapidly and profits peak, then start to decline. One reason profits start to decline during the growth stage is that new companies enter the market, driving prices down and increasing marketing expenses. Consider

Apple's iPod, the most popular digital music player with more than 74 percent of the music player market. It sold 32 million iPods in 2005, and its iTunes music store has 83 percent of the North American market share for legal music downloads. iTunes has more than 20 million unique visitors a month.[26] During the growth stage, the firm tries to strengthen its position in the market by emphasizing the product's benefits and identifying market segments that want these benefits.

Sales continue to increase at the beginning of the *maturity stage,* but then the sales curve peaks and starts to decline while profits continue to decline. This stage is characterized by severe competition and heavy expenditures. Automobiles are an example of a mature product; intense competition in the auto industry requires Toyota, GM, and

figure 12.3 Product Life Cycle

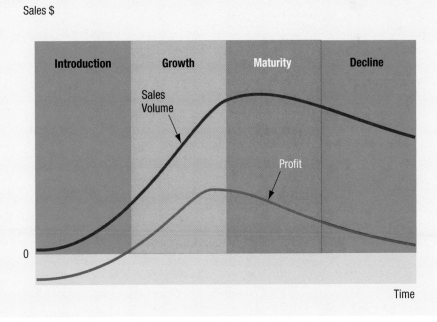

SOURCE: Judann Pollack, "The Endurance Test, 1945–2005: We Map How Four Iconic Brands Have Changed with the Times," *Advertising Age,* November 14, 2005, p. 3.

other automakers to spend huge sums to make their products stand out in a crowded marketplace.

During the *decline stage,* sales continue to fall rapidly. Profits also decline and may even become losses as prices are cut and necessary marketing expenditures are made. As profits drop, firms may eliminate certain models or items. To reduce expenses and squeeze out any remaining profits, marketing expenditures may be cut back, even though such cutbacks accelerate the sales decline. Finally, plans must be made for phasing out the product and introducing new ones to take its place. Unfortunately for Mattel, the 48-year-old Barbie doll has seen her status and sales slide as she has been replaced on retail shelves with more edgy products such as Bratz. Barbie became vulnerable to competition from Bratz and other toys and to the growth of toy sales in stores such as Walmart and Zellers when they chose to allocate shelf space to products they considered more profitable.[27] CanJet airlines, founded in Halifax, Nova Scotia, was pulled from the market after two years after its owner decided the marketplace would not sustain the airline. The company later re-emerged specializing in charter flights and southern destinations.

Identifying Products

Branding, packaging, and labelling can be used to identify or distinguish one product from others. As a result, they are key marketing activities that help position a product appropriately for its target market.

Branding.   **Branding** is the process of naming and identifying products. A *brand* is a name, term, symbol, design, or combination that identifies a product and distinguishes it from other products. Consider that Tim Hortons, Google, and iPod are brand names that are used to identify entire product categories, much like Xerox has become synonymous with photocopying and Kleenex with tissues. Protecting a brand name is important in maintaining a brand identity.[29] Recently a Cape Breton, Nova Scotia-based company, Glenora Distilleries, makers of Glen Breton Whisky, has emerged from a nine-year fight over the right to use the word "Glen" in its brand and on its labels. The Scotch Whisky Association claimed that the use of the name was leading consumers to believe the product was manufactured in Scotland. Throughout the legal proceedings, the Association stated it was protecting the Scottish brand and reputation as the premier manufacturer of whisky and scotch in the world. Lauchie MacLean, owner of Glenora, argued that the company name is derived from the company's home community—Glenville, Cape Breton. After a lengthy dispute, the Supreme Court of Canada found that MacLean could continue to use the name "Glen," which prompted the company to release a new product aptly called, "The Battle of Glen."[30] A new trend has recently emerged in marketing where the CEO or founder of the firm actually

> **Branding** the process of naming and identifying products

Consider the Following:
Silly Bandz: A Flash in the Pan, or Here to Stay?

The title for toy fad in 2010 went to Silly Bandz, the company credited with beginning the U.S. craze for stretchy bracelets. Yet for all of its popularity, it is uncertain whether Silly Bandz is a fad (something that quickly ascends in popularity and just as quickly vanishes) or a trend (something with lasting relevance). Silly Bandz founder Robert Croak is determined to make Silly Bandz last through multiple product lines, licensing deals, and more.

Silly Bandz was born when Croak visited a Chinese trade show and discovered rubber bands shaped like animals. He decided to make a sturdier version into a bracelet. Croak believed that kids would be drawn to collecting and trading these bands. In terms of marketing, Croak claims that everything was done virally via social media sites like Facebook, YouTube, and the Silly Bandz website. Although Croak has no publicist or marketing plan, this hasn't seemed to affect the product's success. In 2009 the company sold 100 packages per week. One year later, it was selling roughly one million packages weekly.

The question is whether this item has a future. Retailers have begun cutting back on Silly Bandz, with 7-Eleven reporting a 97 percent drop in sales since the peak. Croak wants to extend the product's life by introducing related products and improving existing ones. He has signed deals with Marvel Comics and Justin Bieber to represent Marvel's characters and Bieber's likeness in Silly Bandz form. The company has introduced Silly Necklaces, Silly Ringz, and Silly Caribinerz. Croak is also in talks with Zoo Games to develop a videogame. Will these efforts be enough to extend the brand for years to come? Or will Silly Bandz soon become a product beloved only by collectors?[28]

DISCUSSION QUESTIONS

1. Do you think Silly Bandz are a fad or a trend?

2. Why do you think children are drawn to Silly Bandz?

3. Can you think of ways to extend the Silly Bandz brand?

becomes the brand or unique feature that distinguishes the company from its competitors. Heather Reisman from Indigo/Chapters and Galen Weston Jr. from President's Choice and Loblaws are two Canadian examples. While this strategy appears to be becoming more popular, challenges exist if the CEO leaves the company or fails to live up to the brand image, as was the case with Martha Stewart in the U.S. who actually spent time in prison. Students should realize that successful brands can on their own become very valuable and sometimes be worth more than the products that they represent. For example, Polaroid, a brand that was once synonymous with instant cameras, is making a comeback with Lady Gaga as the firm's creative director. The company, which was bought by private investors including Toronto-based Hilco Consumer Capital, is returning to the photo business with a slew of new products including some of its classic instant cameras.[31]

Brand equity refers to the awareness, loyalty, perceived quality, image, and emotions that people feel toward certain brands. Brands that are well established enjoy brand equity, which is the degree to which customers are committed to future purchases of the brand. The world's 10 most valuable brands are shown in Table 12.1 and the 10 most valuable brands in Canada are displayed in Table 12.2. The brand name is the part of the brand that can be spoken and consists of letters, words, and numbers—such as WD-40 lubricant. A *brand mark* is the part of the brand that is a distinctive design, such as the silver star on the hood of a Mercedes or McDonald's golden arches logo. A trademark is a brand that is registered with the Canadian Intellectual Property Office, and is thus legally protected from use by any other firm. Examples of well-known

> **Trademark** a brand that is registered with the Canadian Intellectual Property Office and is thus legally protected from use by any other firm

trademarks include the National Hockey League's logo and the Stanley Cup and the Nike swoosh.

Two major categories of brands are manufacturer brands and private distributor brands. **Manufacturer brands** are brands initiated and owned by the manufacturer to identify products from the point of production to the point of purchase. Bell, Bombardier, Canadian Tire, and Petro-Canada are examples. **Private distributor brands,** which may be less expensive than manufacturer brands, are owned and controlled by a wholesaler or retailer, such as Kenmore

> **Manufacturer brands** brands initiated and owned by the manufacturer to identify products from the point of production to the point of purchase
>
> **Private distributor brands** brands, which may cost less than manufacturer brands, that are owned and controlled by a wholesaler or retailer

table 12.2 The 10 Most Valuable Brands in Canada 2012

Rank	Brand	Brand Value (C$million)
1	Toronto-Dominion Bank	$9,693
2	Thomson Reuters	9,548
3	Royal Bank of Canada	7,929
4	BlackBerry	6,446
5	Scotiabank	3,965
6	Tim Hortons	3,441
7	Lululemon	3,245
8	Shoppers Drug Mart	3,179
9	Bell	3,059
10	Rogers	2,998

SOURCE: "Best Canadian Brands 2012," Interbrand website, http://www.interbrand.com/en/Interbrand-offices/Interbrand-Toronto/Best-Canadian-Brands-2012.aspx (accessed July 30, 2013).

table 12.1 The 10 Most Valuable Brands in the World 2012

Rank	Brand	Brand Value (US$billion)
1	Coca-Cola	$77.839
2	Apple	76.568
3	IBM	75.532
4	Google	69.726
5	Microsoft	57.853
6	GE	43.682
7	McDonald's	40.062
8	Intel	39.385
9	Samsung	32.893
10	Toyota	30.280

SOURCE: Manish Modi, "Coca-Cola Retains Title as World's Most Valuable Brand," Bloomberg website, October 2, 2012, http://www.bloomberg.com/news/2012-10-03/coca-cola-retains-title-as-world-s-most-valuable-brand-table-.html (accessed May 15, 2013).

Polaroid is making a comeback with Lady Gaga as the firm's creative director. The company, which was bought by private investors including Toronto-based Hilco Consumer Capital, is returning to the photo business and even selling some its classic instant cameras.

Generic products like these appeal to consumers who are less concerned about quality and consistency, but want lower prices.

appliances (Sears) and President's Choice grocery products (Loblaws). While private-label brands were once considered cheaper and poor quality, such as Walmart's Ol' Roy dog food, many private-label brands are increasing quality and image and competing with national brands. For example, many President's Choice products are considered to be on par with or superior to branded products. The brand was launched by former Loblaws president Dave Nichol, and his first major success was *The Decadent,* a chocolate chip cookie made with butter and President's Choice-brand *Decadent* chocolate chips, which became Canada's best-selling cookie. Sobeys, in response to President's Choice, has re-launched its own private brand which was originally called *Sobeys,* changing the name to *Our Best* then to *Our Compliments* brand and finally today to *Compliments* or *Sensations by Compliments* for premium products.[32]

Another type of brand that has developed is **generic products**—products with no brand name at all. They often come in plain, simple packages that carry only the generic name of the product—peanut butter, tomato juice, aspirin, dog food, and so on. They appeal to consumers who may be willing to sacrifice quality or product consistency to get a lower price.

Companies use two basic approaches to branding multiple products. In one, a company gives each product within its complete product mix its own brand name. Warner-Lambert, for example, sells many well-known consumer products— Dentyne, Chiclets, Listerine, Halls, Rolaids, and Trident—each individually branded. This branding policy ensures that the name of one product does not affect the names of others, and different brands can be targeted at different segments of the same market, increasing the company's market share (its percentage of the sales for the total market for a product). Another approach to branding is to develop a family of brands with each of the firm's products carrying the same name or at least part of the name. Gillette, Sara Lee, and Dell use this approach.

Packaging. The **packaging,** or external container that holds and describes the product, influences consumers' attitudes and their buying decisions. A survey of over 1,200 consumers found that 40 percent are willing to try a new product based on its packaging.[33] It is estimated that consumers' eyes linger only 2.5 seconds on each product on an average shopping trip; therefore, product packaging should be designed to attract and hold consumers' attention.

A package can perform several functions including protection, economy, convenience, and promotion. Beverage manufacturers have been redesigning their bottles to make them more convenient for consumers and to promote them to certain markets. Scientists videotaped people drinking from different types of bottles and made plaster casts of their hands. They found that the average gulp is 190.45 mL (6.44 ounces) and

that half the population would rather suck liquid through a pop-up top than drink it. Packaging also helps create an overall brand image. Coca-Cola's iconic bottle was transformed for the 2010 Olympics into a canvas for Aboriginal art. In this way, the corporation was able to connect with Canadians and the bottles have become collector's items.[34] Coke engaged in a similar practice for the World Cup by transforming its bottles into the shape of a soccer ball. The soccer ball–shaped bottle was used in association with World Cup meals at McDonald's 1,300 German outlets, and featured pictures of six soccer stars from leading national teams.[35]

Labelling. **Labelling,** the presentation of important information on the package, is closely associated with packaging. The content of labelling, often required by law, may include ingredients or content, nutrition facts (calories, fat, etc.), care instructions, suggestions for use (such as recipes), the manufacturer's address and toll-free number, website, and other useful information. In Canada, all labels must be bilingual. McDonald's introduced packaging that lets consumers know the nutritional value of Big Macs as well as other products. It was the first fast-food chain to adopt the initiative.[36] This information can have a strong impact on sales. The labels of many products, particularly food and drugs, must carry warnings, instructions, certifications, or manufacturers' identifications.

Product Quality. **Quality** reflects the degree to which a good, service, or idea meets the demands and requirements of customers. Quality products are often referred to as reliable, durable, easily maintained, easily used, a good value, or a trusted brand name. The level of quality is the amount of quality that a product possesses, and the consistency of quality depends on the product maintaining the same level of quality over time.

Quality of service is difficult to gauge because it depends on customers' perceptions of how well the service meets

Labelling the presentation of important information on a package

Quality the degree to which a good, service, or idea meets the demands and requirements of customers

Generic products products with no brand name that often come in simple packages and carry only their generic name

Packaging the external container that holds and describes the product

or exceeds their expectations. In other words, service quality is judged by consumers, not the service providers. A bank may define service quality as employing friendly and knowledgeable employees, but the bank's customers may be more concerned with waiting time, ATM access, security, and statement accuracy. Similarly, an airline traveller considers on-time arrival, on-board food service, and satisfaction with the ticketing and boarding process. J.D. Power, a global market information service firm, ranks customer satisfaction in many Canadian and worldwide industries. Below, Figure 12.4 shows Canadians' satisfaction with automobile service, which has been on a steady rise in Canada since 2004.

The quality of services provided by businesses on the Internet can be gauged by consumers on such sites as ConsumerReports.org and BBBOnline. The subscription service offered by ConsumerReports.org provides consumers with a view of e-commerce sites' business, security, and privacy policies. BBBOnline is dedicated to promoting responsibility online. The Web Credibility Project focuses on how health, travel, advocacy, news, and shopping sites disclose business relationships with the companies and products they cover or sell, especially when such relationships pose a potential conflict of interest.[37]

LO2 Define price and discuss its importance in the marketing mix, including various pricing strategies a firm might employ.

Pricing Strategy

Previously, we defined price as the value placed on an object exchanged between a buyer and a seller. Buyers' interest in price stems from their expectations about the usefulness of a product or the satisfaction they may derive from it. Because buyers have limited resources, they must allocate those resources to obtain the products they most desire. They must decide whether the benefits gained in an exchange are worth the buying power sacrificed. Almost anything of value can be assessed by a price. Many factors may influence the evaluation of value, including time constraints,

price levels, perceived quality, and motivations to use available information about prices.[38] Indeed, consumers vary in their response to price: Some focus solely on the lowest price, while others consider quality or the prestige associated with a product and its price. Two of Canada's retail success stories have used very opposing strategies when setting prices for their items. Dollarama has risen to become the largest dollar store in Canada based on its low price policy, while Birks, a high-end jewellery store that has been in business in Canada in one form or another since 1879, is known to charge premium prices for many of its prestigious items.

figure 12.4 Customer Satisfaction With Automobile Service

J.D. Power and Associates
2008 Canadian Customer Commitment Index Study[SM]

Overall Service Experience Satisfaction Index
(Based on a 1,000-point scale)

OK Tire	902
Petro-Canada (Certigard)	886
Autopro	881
Mr. Muffler	873
Firestone Service Centres	872
Saturn/Saab Dealers	871
Toyota/Lexus Dealers	871
Tirecraft	869
Esso	862
Goodyear Service Centres	861
Jiffy Lube	859
KAL Tire	855
Speedy	854
BMW Dealers	853
Hyundai Dealers	853
Acura Dealers	850
Industry Average	850
Fountain Tire	849
Honda Dealers	848
Pennzoil	846
Shell	846
Ford Dealers	845
GM Dealers	844
Ultramar	844
Mazda Dealers	843
VW/Audi Dealers	843
Midas	841
Kia Dealers	839
Nissan/Infiniti Dealers	838
Mr. Lube	837
Suzuki Dealers	836
Chrysler Dealers	831
Ford Fast Lane	831
Subaru Dealers	831
Mitsubishi Dealers	828
Costco	812
Canadian Tire	778
Active Green & Ross	777
Walmart	777
*Independent Repair Shops	884

* "Independent Repair Shops" is a channel as opposed to a branded provider and therefore is not included in the official rankings.

Source: J.D. Power and Associates 2008 Canadian Customer Commitment Index Study[SM]

Charts and graphs extracted from this press release must be accompanied by a statement identifying J.D. Power and Associates as the publisher and the J.D. Power and Associates 2008 Canadian Customer Commitment Index Study[SM] as the source. Rankings are based on numerical scores and not necessarily statistical significance. No advertising or other promotional use can be made of the information in this release or J.D. Power and Associates survey results without the express prior written consent of J.D. Power and Associates.

Coca-Cola's bottle was changed for the 2010 Olympics into a canvas for Aboriginal art.

Pricing Objectives

Pricing objectives specify the role of price in an organization's marketing mix and strategy. They usually are influenced not only by marketing mix decisions but also by finance, accounting, and production factors. Maximizing profits and sales, boosting market share, maintaining the status quo, and survival are four common pricing objectives.

Specific Pricing Strategies

Pricing strategies provide guidelines for achieving the company's pricing objectives and overall marketing strategy. They specify how price will be used as a variable in the marketing mix. Significant pricing strategies relate to price lining, pricing new products, psychological pricing, and price discounting.

Price Lining Price lining occurs when a compay sells multiple products in the same product category. For example, Peoples Jewellers sells three different one-carat diamond rings and has labelled them as good, better, and best. Research indicates people are willing to move up one product/price category if the price difference is not perceived as significant. So if a ring labelled as "good" is priced at $2,000 and cost Peoples $1,200, the company would make $800. But a ring labelled as "better" could sell for $2,500 and cost People's $1,500, resulting in a $1,000 profit. Peoples knows that by creating these labels, consumers will be inclined to jump to the better product description, and as a result Peoples will make more money by selling the ring that is priced slightly higher. As discussed below, Tim Hortons uses a type of product line pricing in its coffee sales to generate additional sales volume and more revenue per cup of coffee sold.

Pricing New Products. Setting the price for a new product is critical: The right price leads to profitability; the wrong price may kill the product. In general, there are two basic strategies to setting the base price for a new product. **Price skimming** is charging the highest possible price that buyers who want the product will pay. The $200 and higher market for jeans is growing rapidly. Companies such as True Religion, Rock & Republic, Citizens of Humanity, and 7 for All Mankind are sold at many independent stores and department stores such as Saks Fifth Avenue and Barneys New York. True Religion experienced a sales increase of 41.8 percent over the previous year.[41] This strategy allows the company to generate much-needed revenue to help offset the costs of research and development. Conversely, a **penetration price** is a low price designed to help a product enter the market and gain market share rapidly. For example, many discount real estate brokers have started to emerge in Canada in recent years. Many of these such as PropertyGuys. ca have been charging much lower fees than traditional real estate agents as a way to break

Price is a key element in the marketing mix because it relates directly to the generation of revenue and profits. Sobeys, for example, has generated more revenue from its premium private label brand *Sensations by Compliments* by charging more for those items than for its regular private label goods—*Compliments*. McDonald's has increased profits with upscale items such as its $4.50 Cobb salad.[39] In large part, the ability to set a price depends on the supply of and demand for a product. For most products, the quantity demanded goes up as the price goes down, and as the price goes up, the quantity demanded goes down. This has been evident in the price of oil and gas in Canada in recent years. When the price per litre has fallen below one dollar, consumers have been much more willing to purchase gas than when the price exceeds one dollar per litre. The change in gas prices has also impacted the sale of other items such as large, less fuel-efficient sport utility vehicles which declined, especially as the price of gas has risen in recent years and stayed above $1.20 per litre. Of course price also depends on the cost to manufacture a good or provide a service or idea.

Changes in buyers' needs, variations in the effectiveness of other marketing mix variables, the presence of substitutes, and dynamic environmental factors can influence demand. A firm may temporarily sell products below cost to match competition, to generate cash flow, or even to increase market share, but in the long run it cannot survive by selling its products below cost. For example many small independent stores in Halifax sold milk well below cost during the early part of 2012 to increase sales of other more profitable items. Sobeys executives have stated that they are not worried about this trend as the practice is not sustainable in the long term.[40]

Price is probably the most flexible variable in the marketing mix. Although it may take years to develop a product, establish channels of distribution, and design and implement promotion, a product's price may be set and changed in a few minutes. Under certain circumstances, of course, the price may not be so flexible, especially if government regulations prevent dealers from controlling prices.

Price skimming charging the highest possible price that buyers who want the product will pay

Penetration price a low price designed to help a product enter the market and gain market share rapidly

into the market. The discount brokers have been dealing with strong resistance from traditional real estate agents who can charge thousands more than discount real estate companies. Examples other than real estate also exist. When Industrias Añaños introduced Kola Real to capitalize on limited supplies of Coca-Cola and Pepsi Cola in Peru, it set an ultra-low penetration price to appeal to the poor who predominate in the region. Kola Real quickly secured one-fifth of the Peruvian market and has since made significant gains in Ecuador, Venezuela, and Mexico, forcing larger soft-drink marketers to cut prices.[42] Penetration pricing is less flexible than price skimming; it is more difficult to raise a penetration price than to lower a skimming price. Penetration pricing is used most often when marketers suspect that competitors will enter the market shortly after the product has been introduced.

Psychological Pricing. **Psychological pricing** encourages purchases based on emotional rather than rational responses to the price. For example, the assumption behind *even/odd pricing* is that people will buy more of a product for $9.99 than $10 because it seems to be a bargain at the odd price. The assumption behind *symbolic/prestige pricing* is that high prices connote high quality. Thus the prices of certain fragrances are set artificially high to give the impression of superior quality. Some over-the-counter drugs are priced high because consumers associate a drug's price with potency.

Price Discounting. Temporary price reductions, or **discounts,** are often employed to boost sales. Although there are many types, quantity, seasonal, and promotional discounts are among the most widely used. Quantity discounts reflect the economies of purchasing in large volume. Seasonal discounts to buyers who purchase goods or services out of season help even out production capacity. Promotional discounts attempt to improve sales by advertising price reductions on selected products to increase customer interest.

Consider the Following: Tim Hortons' Pricing Strategy—Tricking You Into Buying More Coffee or Giving You What You Want?

A recent article in *Canadian Business Week* explains that Canadian icon Tim Hortons is tricking consumers into buying more coffee. The trick, if you want to call it that, is a well-established pricing strategy similiar to product lining. You offer consumers a little more of a product, in this case coffee, while you more than offset the extra product by charging more. In this specific case, Tim Hortons has increased the size of its extra-large coffee to 24 liquid ounces up from 20 ounces, which results in an extra 0.19 cents in profit per cup sold. While 0.19 cents may not seem like a lot, think about the thousands of cups of coffee sold daily in every Tim Hortons' store. Tim Hortons states that the change in cup size had more to do with customer demand than raising profit as marketing research indicated that their old extra-large cup was not large enough. The result of the change was an increase in all cup sizes, as the old extra-large became large, large became medium and medium became small. The original cup size "small" was abandoned. Koert Van Ittersum, a marketing expert in behavioural bias, which leads to overconsumption, says, "Most consumers will continue to order the same size of coffee out of habit and not pay attention to the size difference. The result is consumers will pay more and consume more." Tim Hortons, of course, is not the only restaurant chain to embrace upsizing as a way to increase consumption and profit. Starbucks with its 31-ounce Trenta and 7-Eleven's 32-ounce Big Gulp are still much larger than Tim Hortons' new extra-large offering. Still, health experts are wondering how much bigger drinks and food servings can get, and if consumers won't ultimately say no to bigger and bigger portions.[44]

DISCUSSION QUESTIONS:

1. Are companies acting ethically when they increase the size of their portions as a way to get consumers to consume more and ultimately pay more for a product?

2. What are some of the potential advantages and disadvantages of increasing the size of your products?

3. Do you notice when your favourite restaurant or coffee shop changes the size of its portions? If so does it impact your purchasing behaviour? Why or why not?

4. Using the Internet, do some market research to determine what companies are selling the largest soft drinks and cups of coffee. Has there been any backlash to these extra-large sizes from health experts and consumer advocates? Can you find any incidences where companies reduced the size of their products as a result?

Often promotional pricing is geared to increased profits. On the other hand, many companies such as Walmart, Home Depot, and Toys 'Я' Us have shunned promotional price discounts and, with everyday low pricing, are focusing more on relationships with customers. Polo killed its Polo jeans brand because the price of this product hurt its luxury image.[43] In the airline industry, low-cost airlines like WestJet and Air Canada Tango are competing head-to-head with the major airlines by offering sharply discounted fares. Additionally, websites like iTravel.com, Expedia.ca, Priceline.com, Orbitz.com, and Travelocity.com help flyers find the lowest fares quickly, forcing airlines to become even more price competitive.

LO3 Identify factors affecting distribution decisions, such as marketing channels and intensity of market coverage.

Distribution Strategy

The best products in the world will not be successful unless companies make them available where and when customers want to buy them. In this section, we will explore dimensions of distribution strategy, including the channels through which products are distributed, the intensity of market coverage, and the physical handling of products during distribution.

Marketing Channels

A **marketing channel,** or channel of distribution, is a group of organizations that moves products from their producer to customers. Marketing channels make products available to buyers when and where they desire to purchase them. Organizations that bridge the gap between a product's manufacturer and the ultimate consumer are called *middlemen,* or intermediaries. They create time, place, and ownership utility. Two intermediary organizations are retailers and wholesalers.

Retailers buy products from manufacturers (or other intermediaries) and sell them to consumers for home and household use rather than for resale or for use in producing other products. The Bay, for example, buys products from Spin Master Toys and resells them to consumers. Retailing usually occurs in a store, but the Internet, vending machines, mail-order catalogues, and entertainment, such as going to a Montreal Canadiens hockey game, also provide opportunities for retailing. With more than 20 million Canadians accessing the Internet,

Marketing channel a group of organizations that moves products from their producer to customers; also called a channel of distribution

Retailers intermediaries who buy products from manufacturers (or other intermediaries) and sell them to consumers for home and household use rather than for resale or for use in producing other products

online sales were recently estimated at $62.7 billion.[45] By bringing together an assortment of products from competing producers, retailers create utility. Traditional retailers arrange for products to be moved from producers to a convenient retail establishment (place utility). They maintain hours of operation for their retail stores to make merchandise available when consumers want it (time utility). They also assume the risk of ownership of inventories (ownership utility). New online retailers have altered the landscape as they do not have all the costs associated with operating a retail location and can offer consumers access to products 24 hours a day. However, Internet retailing has given rise to a new term, "showrooming." This is where consumers visit a traditional merchant location to see and touch a product and then purchase it at a savings online. Many traditional retailers, such as Canadian Tire and SportChek, have created online shopping sites to retain customers and compete with online-only retailers. One of the best-known online-only, or cyber, merchants is Amazon. Amazon offers millions of products from which to choose, all from the privacy and convenience of the purchaser's home. In some cases Web merchants offer wide selections, ultra-convenience, superior service, knowledge, and the best products. More detail on the Internet's effect on marketing is presented in Chapter 13.

Table 12.3 describes various types of general merchandise retailers.

Today, competition between retailers in Canada has never been more intense due to the growth in online retailers, Target entering the Canadian market, and upscale retailer Nordstrom following behind. Furthermore, competition

> "Internet retailing has given rise to a new term, 'showrooming.' This is where consumers visit a traditional merchant location to see and touch a product and then purchase it at a savings online."

The creators of the Xbox 360 visual novels use a price skimming strategy. They set the price high when the unit is first introduced, then lower the price significantly to maintain sales.

table 12.3 General Merchandise Retailers

Type of Retailer	Description	Examples
Department store	Large organization offering wide product mix and organized into separate departments	The Bay, Sears
Discount store	Self-service, general merchandise store offering brand name and private brand products at low prices	Dollarama
Supermarket	Self-service store offering complete line of food products and some nonfood products	Sobeys, Loblaws
Superstore	Giant outlet offering all food and nonfood products found in supermarkets, as well as most routinely purchased products	Walmart and Loblaws Real Canadian Superstores
Warehouse club	Large-scale, members-only establishments combining cash-and-carry wholesaling with discount retailing	Costco
Warehouse showroom	Facility in a large, low-cost building with large on-premises inventories and minimum service	Ikea
Catalogue showroom	Type of warehouse showroom where consumers shop from a catalogue and products are stored out of buyers' reach and provided in manufacturer's carton	Sears Catalogue

SOURCE: William M. Pride and O. C. Ferrell, *Marketing: Concepts and Strategies, 2008*, p. 428. Copyright 2008 by Houghton Mifflin Company. Reprinted with permission.

Wholesalers intermediaries who buy from producers or from other wholesalers and sell to retailers

between different types of stores is changing the nature of retailing. Supermarkets compete with specialty food stores, wholesale clubs, and discount stores. Department stores compete with nearly every other type of store including specialty stores, off-price chains, category killers, discount stores, and online retailers.

Wholesalers are intermediaries who buy from producers or from other wholesalers and sell to retailers. They usually do not sell in significant quantities to ultimate consumers. Wholesalers perform the functions listed in Table 12.4.

Wholesalers are extremely important because of the marketing activities they perform, particularly for consumer products. Although it is true that wholesalers can be eliminated, their functions must be passed on to some other entity, such as the producer, another intermediary, or even the customer. Wholesalers help consumers and retailers by buying in large quantities, then selling to retailers in smaller quantities. By stocking an assortment of products, wholesalers match products to demand.

> "Although it is true that wholesalers can be eliminated, their functions must be passed on to some other entity, such as the producer, another intermediary, or even the customer."

Supply Chain Management. In an effort to improve distribution channel relationships among manufacturers and other channel intermediaries, supply chain

table 12.4 Major Wholesaling Functions

Supply Chain Management	Creating Long-Term Partnerships Among Channel Members
Promotion	Providing a sales force, advertising, sales promotion, and publicity
Warehousing, shipping, and product handling	Receiving, storing, and stockkeeping
	Packaging
	Shipping outgoing orders
	Materials handling
	Arranging and making local and long-distance shipments
Inventory control and data processing	Processing orders
	Controlling physical inventory
	Recording transactions
	Tracking sales data for financial analysis
Risk taking	Assuming responsibility for theft, product obsolescence, and excess inventories
Financing and budgeting	Extending credit
	Making capital investments
	Forecasting cash flow
Marketing research and information systems	Providing information about market
	Conducting research studies
	Managing computer networks to facilitate exchanges and relationships

SOURCE: William M. Pride and O. C. Ferrell, *Marketing: Concepts and Strategies*, 2008, p. 389. Copyright 2008 by Houghton Mifflin Company. Reprinted with permission.

management creates alliances between channel members. In Chapter 8, we defined supply chain management as connecting and integrating all parties or members of the distribution system to satisfy customers. It involves long-term partnerships among marketing channel members working together to reduce costs, waste, and unnecessary movement in the entire marketing channel in order to satisfy customers.[46] It goes beyond traditional channel members (producers, wholesalers, retailers, customers) to include *all* organizations involved in moving products from the producer to the ultimate customer. In a survey of business managers, a disruption in the supply chain was viewed as the number-one crisis that could decrease revenue.[47]

The focus shifts from one of selling to the next level in the channel to one of selling products *through* the channel to a satisfied ultimate customer. Information, once provided on a guarded, "as needed" basis, is now open, honest, and ongoing. Perhaps most importantly, the points of contact in the relationship expand from one-on-one at the salesperson–buyer level to multiple interfaces at all levels and in all functional areas of the various organizations.

Channels for Consumer Products. Typical marketing channels for consumer products are shown in Figure 12.5. In Channel A, the product moves from the producer directly to the consumer. Farmers who sell their fruit and vegetables to consumers at roadside stands use a direct-from-producer-to-consumer marketing channel.

In Channel B, the product goes from producer to retailer to consumer. This type of channel is used for products such as textbooks, automobiles, and appliances. In Channel C, the product is handled by a wholesaler and a retailer before it reaches the consumer. Producer-to-wholesaler-to-retailer-to-consumer marketing channels distribute a wide range of products including refrigerators, televisions, soft drinks, cigarettes, clocks, watches, and office products. In Channel D, the product goes to an agent, a wholesaler, and a retailer before going to the consumer. This long channel of distribution is especially useful for convenience products. Candy and some produce are often sold by agents who bring buyers and sellers together.

Services are usually distributed through direct marketing channels because they are generally produced *and* consumed simultaneously. For example, you cannot take a haircut home for later use. Many services require the customer's presence and participation: The sick patient must visit the physician to receive treatment; the child must be at the day care centre to receive care; the tourist must be present to sightsee and consume tourism services.

Channels for Business Products. In contrast to consumer goods, more than half of all business products, especially expensive equipment or technically complex products, are sold through direct marketing channels. Business customers like to communicate directly with producers of such products to gain the technical assistance and personal assurances that only the producer can offer. For this reason, business buyers prefer to purchase expensive and highly complex mainframe computers directly from Dell, HP, and other mainframe producers. Other business products may be distributed through channels employing wholesaling intermediaries such as industrial distributors and/or manufacturer's agents.

Intensity of Market Coverage

A major distribution decision is how widely to distribute a product—that is, how many and what type of outlets should carry it. The intensity of market coverage depends on buyer behaviour, as well as the nature of the target market and the competition. Wholesalers and retailers provide various intensities of market coverage and must be selected carefully to ensure success. Market coverage may be intensive, selective, or exclusive.

Intensive distribution makes a product available in as many

> **Intensive distribution** a form of market coverage whereby a product is made available in as many outlets as possible

figure 12.5 Marketing Channels for Consumer Products

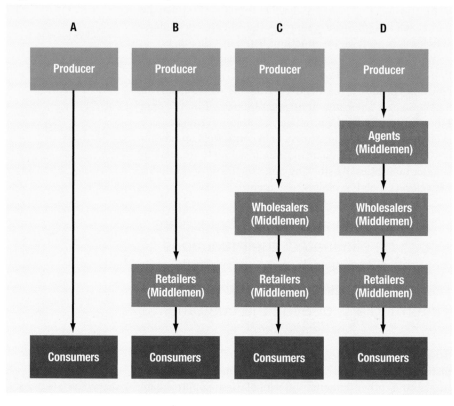

outlets as possible. Because availability is important to purchasers of convenience products such as bread, milk, gasoline, soft drinks, and chewing gum, a nearby location with a minimum of time spent searching and waiting in line is most important to the consumer. To saturate markets intensively, wholesalers and many varied retailers try to make the product available at every location where a consumer might desire to purchase it. For example, to market its one-time-use Max cameras, Eastman Kodak rolled out 10,000 climate-controlled, Internet-connected vending machines. The machines allow credit card transactions and are refrigerated to protect the film. The vending machine's Internet connection allows Kodak to know who bought each camera, where customers live, the specific location of the machine, and the machine's inventory level. The machines are found at zoos, stadiums, parks, hotels, and resorts—all places where consumers typically desire a single-use camera.[48]

Selective distribution uses only a small number of all available outlets to expose products. It is used most often for products that consumers buy only after shopping and comparing price, quality, and style. Many products sold on a selective basis require salesperson assistance, technical advice, warranties, or repair service to maintain consumer satisfaction. Typical products include automobiles, major appliances, clothes, and furniture.

Exclusive distribution exists when a manufacturer gives an intermediary the sole right to sell a product in a defined geographic territory. Such exclusivity provides an incentive for a dealer to handle a product that has a limited market. Exclusive distribution is the opposite of intensive distribution in that products are purchased and consumed over a long period of time, and service or information is required to develop a satisfactory sales relationship. Products distributed on an exclusive basis include high-quality musical instruments, yachts, airplanes, and high-fashion leather goods.

> **Selective distribution** a form of market coverage whereby only a small number of all available outlets are used to expose products

> **Exclusive distribution** the awarding by a manufacturer to an intermediary of the sole right to sell a product in a defined geographic territory

> **Physical distribution** all the activities necessary to move products from producers to customers—inventory control, transportation, warehousing, and materials handling

> **Transportation** the shipment of products to buyers

Physical Distribution

Physical distribution includes all the activities necessary to move products from producers to customers—inventory control, transportation, warehousing, and materials handling. Physical distribution creates time and place utility by making products available when they are wanted, with adequate service and at minimum cost. Walter Hachborn, president of Home Hardware, says that the firm's distribution system is one characteristic that allows it to compete against much larger firms such as Home Depot and RONA. "... We have four warehouses across Canada. We likely have one of the most efficient hardware packing and shipping operations in the world."[49] Both goods and services require physical distribution. Many physical distribution activities are part of supply chain management, which we discussed in Chapter 8; we'll take a brief look at a few more now.

Transportation. **Transportation,** the shipment of products to buyers, creates time and place utility for products, and thus is a key element in the flow of goods and services from producer to consumer. The five major modes of transportation used to move products between cities in Canada are railways, motor vehicles, inland waterways, pipelines, and airways.

Railroads offer the least expensive transportation for many products. Heavy commodities, foodstuffs, raw materials, and coal are examples of products carried by railroads. Trucks have greater flexibility than railroads because they can reach more locations. Trucks handle freight quickly and economically, offer door-to-door service, and are more flexible in their packaging requirements than are ships or airplanes. Air transport offers speed and a high degree of dependability but is the most expensive means of transportation; shipping is the least expensive and slowest form. Pipelines are used to transport petroleum, natural gas,

Most consumer packaged goods companies, such as Pepsi, strive for intensive distribution—they want to be everywhere. But many cosmetics firms use an exclusive distribution strategy by limiting their distribution to a few, select, higher-end retailers in each region.

Timothy Kimber

Business: PlaSmart

Founded: 2003

Success: Timothy Kimber observed children sampling a toy car in an Ottawa mall and turned it into an $11 million business.

Timothy Kimber was walking through an Ottawa mall and saw some children test driving a plastic toy car. Kimber was immediately taken with the toy, which moved when the driver twisted the steering wheel back and forth, and started to investigate the toy's origin. He discovered that while the toy was widely available in China, it was virtually unknown in North America. Kimber proceeded to acquire the North American rights to sell the plastic toy car and started importing them into Canada. At the time, plasma TVs were the latest technology craze, and Kimber opted to call the toy the PlasmaCar. Kimber's initial strategy was to sell the car slowly in Canada, and he took it to several toy and hobby shows where the car was highly acclaimed. The PlasmaCar went on to capture several toy awards and Kimber expanded globally, first into the United States and then into other countries. Kimber notes, "We didn't rush into the U.S. market; we spent two years learning everything we could about the Canadian toy industry first." Kimber eventually diversified into other product lines such as the PlasmaBike, Fun Slides, and Stomp Rocket. Today, the company has revenues in excess of $11 million and the PlasmaCar accounts for 50 percent of sales. Kimber, who is a self-described big kid, loves being in the toy industry. "I've never grown up," he says. "I'm a big kid myself. That is one of my advantages."[50]

semi-liquid coal, wood chips, and certain chemicals. Many products can be moved most efficiently by using more than one mode of transportation.

Factors affecting the selection of a mode of transportation include cost, capability to handle the product, reliability, and availability, and, as suggested, selecting transportation modes requires trade-offs. Unique characteristics of the product and consumer desires often determine the mode selected.

Warehousing. **Warehousing** is the design and operation of facilities to receive, store, and ship products. A warehouse facility receives, identifies, sorts, and dispatches goods to storage; stores them; recalls, selects, or picks goods; assembles the shipment; and finally, dispatches the shipment.

Companies often own and operate their own private warehouses that store, handle, and move their own products. They can also rent storage and related physical distribution services from public warehouses. Regardless of whether a private or a public warehouse is used, warehousing is important because it makes products available for shipment to match demand at different geographic locations.

> **Warehousing** the design and operation of facilities to receive, store, and ship products
>
> **Materials handling** the physical handling and movement of products in warehousing and transportation

Materials Handling. **Materials handling** is the physical handling and movement of products in warehousing and transportation. Handling processes may vary significantly due to product characteristics. Efficient materials-handling procedures increase a warehouse's useful capacity and improve customer service. Well-coordinated loading and movement systems increase efficiency and reduce costs.

Importance of Distribution in a Marketing Strategy

Distribution decisions are among the least flexible marketing mix decisions. Products can be changed over time; prices can be changed quickly; and promotion is usually changed regularly. But distribution decisions often commit resources and establish contractual relationships that are difficult if not impossible to change. As a company attempts to expand into new markets, it may require a complete change in distribution. Moreover, if a firm does not manage its marketing channel in the most efficient manner and provide the best service, then a new competitor will evolve to create a more effective distribution system.

LO4 Specify the activities involved in promotion, as well as promotional strategies and promotional positioning.

Promotion Strategy

The role of promotion is to communicate with individuals, groups, and organizations to facilitate an exchange directly or indirectly. It encourages marketing exchanges by attempting to persuade individuals, groups, and organizations to accept goods, services, and ideas. Promotion is used not only to sell products but also to influence opinions and attitudes toward an organization, person, or cause. The province of Prince Edward Island, for example, has successfully used promotion to educate potential tourists about beautiful beaches and golf courses on the island. The provincial tourism board and the Atlantic Canada Opportunities Agency spent $1 million to bring popular daytime television personalities Regis Philbin and Kelly Ripa to host their show *Live!* from the island for three days. On day one of the show, Prince Edward Island skyrocketed to the number two spot on Google search in the United States.[51] Most people probably equate promotion with advertising, but it also includes personal selling, publicity, and sales promotion. The role that these elements play in a marketing strategy is extremely important.

The Promotion Mix

Advertising, personal selling, publicity, and sales promotion are collectively known as the promotion mix because a strong promotion program results from the careful selection and blending of these elements. The process of coordinating the promotion mix elements and synchronizing promotion as a unified effort is called **integrated marketing communications.** When planning promotional activities, an integrated marketing communications approach results in the desired message for customers. Different elements of the promotion mix are coordinated to play their appropriate roles in delivery of the message on a consistent basis For example, RBC uses TV commercials, social media, Internet marketing, and publicity to reach its target market. The main components of a promotional campaign include:

> **Integrated marketing communications** coordinating the promotion mix elements and synchronizing promotion as a unified effort

1. *Determine objectives.* What are you hoping to accomplish? Objectives must be quantifiable so that they are measurable. Examples include "Increase sales by 2 percent," "Generate 20 leads," "Increase website traffic," and so on.

2. *Define customers.* Whom are you targeting? Are you targeting new customers, current customers, frequent shoppers, holiday shoppers, or some other group?

3. *Determine benchmarks.* Establish measures/controls to measure the effectiveness of a promotion, such as the number of website hits, sales figures, information requests, and so on.

4. *Get the message out.* Determine the method including what you will say to your audience and medium to use: the Internet, TV, radio, direct mail, or some other.

5. *Implement the plan.*

6. *Evaluate the plan.* Look at the controls that you have established and determine if the plan has been successful.

To convince consumers that the S60 model is both safe and sporty, Volvo would use an integrated marketing communication program that included print and broadcast advertising as well as new communication technologies such as social media.

Advertising. Perhaps the best-known form of promotion, **advertising** is a paid form of nonpersonal communication transmitted through a mass medium, such as television commercials, magazine advertisements, or online ads. Commercials featuring celebrities, customers, or unique creations (the e-Trade Baby or the Tim Hortons commercials with Sidney Crosby) serve to grab viewers' attention and pique their interest in a product. Advertisers are doing more and more to make their advertising stand out. Examples include Telus with cute animals, and Molson beer and Coke, which rely on making emotional appeals to Canadians by using advertisements that highlight national pride and hockey. During the recent NHL lockout, both Bauer with its "Own the Moment" advertisements and Nike's "Hockey is Ours" marketing campaign, which went viral, used emotional pitches to connect to viewers. Table 12.5 shows companies that spent between $2 billion and $4 billion on ads in North America in one year.

> **Advertising** a paid form of nonpersonal communication transmitted through a mass medium, such as television commercials or magazine advertisements
>
> **Advertising campaign** designing a series of advertisements and placing them in various media to reach a particular target market

An **advertising campaign** involves designing a series of advertisements and placing them in various media to reach a particular target audience. The basic content and form of an advertising campaign are a function of several factors. A product's features, uses, and benefits affect the content of the campaign message and individual ads. Characteristics of the people in the target audience—gender, age, education, race, income, occupation, lifestyle, and

table 12.5 Top 10 Leading North American Advertisers

Organization	Advertising Expenditures ($ Millions)
1. General Motors	3,997
2. Procter & Gamble	3,920
3. Time Warner	3,283
4. Pfizer	2,957
5. SBC Communications	2,687
6. DaimlerChrysler	2,462
7. Ford Motor Co.	2,458
8. Walt Disney Co.	2,242
9. Verizon Communications	2,197
10. Johnson & Johnson	2,176

SOURCE: "Fact Pack," 4th *Annual Guide to Advertising Marketing, a supplement to Advertising Age*, p. 8.

other attributes—influence both content and form. When Procter & Gamble promotes Crest toothpaste to children, the company emphasizes daily brushing and cavity control, whereas it promotes tartar control and whiter teeth when marketing to adults. To communicate effectively, advertisers use words, symbols, and illustrations that are meaningful, familiar, and attractive to people in the target audience.

An advertising campaign's objectives and platform also affect the content and form of its messages. If a firm's advertising objectives involve large sales increases, the message may include hard-hitting, high-impact language and symbols. When campaign objectives aim at increasing brand awareness, the message may use much repetition of the brand name and words and illustrations associated with it. Thus, the advertising platform is the foundation on which campaign messages are built.

Advertising media are the vehicles or forms of communication used to reach a desired audience. Print media include newspapers, magazines, direct mail, and billboards, and electronic media include television, radio, and cyber ads. Newspapers, television, and direct mail are the most widely used advertising media. The Canadian Marketing Association notes that advertising spending is on the rise and will have increased from $19 billion in 2007 to over $23.3 billion in 2011.[53]

Choice of media influences the content and form of the message. Effective outdoor displays and short broadcast spot announcements require concise, simple messages. Magazine and newspaper advertisements can include considerable detail and long explanations. For example, Oreck Canada, a Winnipeg-based distributor of air purifiers and vacuums, uses two- and 30-minute infomercials to sell its products. The company attributes much of its 820 percent, five-year revenue growth to this form

of promotion, which first informs consumers about these superior products and then effectively closes the sale.[54] Because several kinds of media offer geographic selectivity, a precise message can be tailored to a particular geographic section of the target audience. For example, a company advertising in *Maclean's* might decide to use one message in Ontario and another in the rest of the nation. A company may also choose to advertise in only one region. Such geographic selectivity lets a firm use the same message in different regions at different times.

"Choice of media influences the content and form of the message."

Online Marketing and Social Media. The use of online advertising is increasing as companies are attracted to its wide reach and ability to interact with customers. Businesses are also aware that Canadians are spending more time online than citizens in other countries in the world. Over the last three months, Canadians averaged over 45 hours online, and much of that time was spent on social media sites. In fact, over the three-month period, Canadians

Companies are spending hundreds of millions of dollars sponsoring the Olympics with the hope of building emotional ties with consumers. Do you think this strategy works?

Consider the Following: Sponsoring the Olympics—A Golden Promotional Strategy?

Minutes after Sidney Crosby scored the game-winning goal to capture the 2010 Olympic Gold Medal for Canada in men's hockey, a Coke commercial ran ending with the words, "... now they know it's our game." A scan of the audience at the championship game showed thousands of people, including many Canadian Olympic champions, cheering while they were wearing Olympic clothing branded and sold by The Bay. A short time later, television commercials by RBC, Bell, RONA, McDonald's, Loblaws, Petro-Canada, and GM appeared highlighting their support of Canada's Olympic efforts. If you were to ask Canadians on the day after the games closed who supported the 2010 Olympic Games, most would be able to name some if not all of these companies.

The major question that many executives of these companies will be asking themselves one, three, and likely several years later is whether their $100 million-plus investment was worth the money spent. Top games sponsors such as Bell Canada contributed $200 million to the games and RBC originally committed $110 million but then increased the amount when it was given the opportunity to sponsor the Olympic Torch Relay. What executives may not want to hear is that *Forbes* magazine concluded that companies which sponsored the 2008 Beijing Olympics saw little long-term effect on brand loyalty. Yet others, including RBC chief brand manager Jim Little, differ: "The bank has built a huge list of potential clients and internal surveys show branch staff feel a new sense of pride and involvement in their bank." Senior managers at HBC or The Bay are also telling a much different story. The oldest retailer in Canada, which is trying to write a comeback story of its own, has sold out of almost all of its Olympic clothing, and has created a buzz around the company for the first time in years. Chris Staples, president of Rethink Communications in Vancouver, notes, "This is the first instance of cool stuff at The Bay that I can remember." Furthermore, a report by Charlton Strategic Research indicates that people who bought Olympic goods at The Bay are now more likely to consider making another purchase at the store. The Bay has reported that sales of Olympic apparel have exceeded expectations by 40 to 50 percent and customer numbers have doubled.

The question remains, however: Are The Bay and RBC exceptions to the rule that investing in the Olympics does not make sense, as found by *Forbes* magazine, or is the investment worth the money? In its extensive reporting on the Olympics, *The Globe and Mail* has concluded that The Bay and RBC are obvious short-term winners but have also pegged Loblaws, GM, and Petro-Canada, firms which spent $100 million plus on the 2010 games, as businesses that may have been better off investing their money elsewhere.[52]

DISCUSSION QUESTIONS

1. Do you think it was a worthwhile investment to sponsor the 2010 Olympic Games?

2. Think back to the 2010 Olympic Games—did any of the companies benefit after the torch went out?

3. Besides increased sales, what other benefits would a firm earn by investing in the Olympic Games?

4. If you were the CEO of a large company, would you invest in the Olympics? Why or why not?

---

spent on average the equivalent of 10,000 minutes on Facebook alone. In addition to spending more time online, Canadians are following, if not leading, the global trend of accessing the Internet, especially social media sites using mobile devices such as smartphones and tablets.[55]

Since Chapter 13 discusses the use of social media and digital marketing in greater detail, the coverage here will be condensed. Prior to reading Chapter 13, readers should recognize that the Internet and social media have become a vital part of

"New technology, such as *Behavioural Tracking*, is allowing companies to track user information including demographics, location, and search terms to tailor online advertisements and target their online messages to be more effective and appealing."

most companies' integrated marketing communication plan. Online marketing is growing at a phenomenal rate in Canada, especially since consumers are not only accessing the Internet through computers but are now using smartphones and tablets to stay online when on the move. Additionally, new technology, such as *Behavioural Tracking*, is allowing companies to track user information including demographics, location, and search terms to tailor online advertisements and target their online messages to be more effective and appealing.

- *Company Web Pages:* Websites allow companies to provide stakeholders with a significant amount of information including their entire marketing mix, provide an opportunity for people to make direct purchases, and present significant company information. The sites also allow businesses the chance to interact and communicate with customers using a variety of channels including e-mails, posting reviews, and so forth. A good example of website development and operation is the Chapters/Indigo online bookstore (ChaptersIndigo.ca). The site was developed to keep current customers returning and to provide easy navigation for new visitors. The site stores customer account information to allow for easy processing of payment, provides customer reviews of text, and allows for the tracking of shipping information. In addition, the site contains a search function that allows new users to easily find what they are looking for, provides graphics so that consumers can ensure they are ordering the right material, and allows for immediate feedback so that consumers know whether their order or question has been received. The site is coordinated in both content and graphics with the other marketing divisions of the company, with the front page of the site updated on a weekly basis to draw people in and give them another reason to come back. Some companies also set up special websites to promote specials at their business or to engage consumers. When CBC was looking for a new *Hockey Night in Canada* theme song, it set up a special website which allowed visitors to pitch their ideas and to review other entrants.

- *Working With Search Engines (Search Engine Optimization):* Companies want to be sure that their site will not only appear on the results page when consumers use popular search engines such as Google or Yahoo, but that they appear in the first few results. This is referred to as search engine optimization (SEO), where companies design websites using title tags (also referred to as metatags) that explain the intent of the website, have content pages that use words that relate to the purpose of the site, clearly link all documents, use appropriate external links, update content frequently, and have lots of pages.

- *Pay Per Click Advertising (PPC):* Businesses are now making significant use of PPC advertising. This advertising method allows firms to bid on key words or phrases relevant to their target market. Then, when a consumer enters the phrase or word in the search engine, the company will appear under the results section and their ads will appear on the side of the viewer's screen. The largest PPC advertisers are Google AdWords, Yahoo! Search Marketing, and Microsoft adCenter. For example, Prollenium Medical Technologies, an Aurora, Ontario-based manufacturer of cosmetics, purchased specific search terms using Google AdWorks and Yahoo!. The investment has paid off as the company's $2,000 per month investment has resulted in an increase from 1,000 monthly visitors to 50,000, and PPC now drives 90 percent of the company's sales.[56] The other popular form of PPC advertising is when companies place ads on websites but only have to pay for them when their ad is clicked.

- *Social Media Websites:* Social media sites such as Facebook, LinkedIn, and Pinterest are online communities where people can create and share information. As noted above, Canadians are spending a significant amount of time on these sites, and they are becoming increasingly important to businesses. Facebook is the second-most visited site in Canada, and worldwide boasts over 835 million active viewers of which more than half visit the site daily. Facebook allows companies to create profiles, join online communities, send out flyers, share videos, post pictures, write blogs, encourage people to comment on their wall (bulletin board), join or create discussion groups, and advertise with banner advertisements.[57] For example, TD Bank's Facebook page alerts customers about company news and also answers customer questions posted to its wall. After the earthquake disaster in Haiti, the bank posted and e-mailed all its Facebook friends describing what the bank was doing to help. LinkedIn is often described as a professional Facebook site where professionals can post their résumé, network, and gather information. LinkedIn is often used by professional companies to make and maintain initial contacts with clients and to source opportunities.

  Pinterest is the fastest-growing and third-largest social media website in North America. Pinterest allows users to save and manage images and video content called Pins to an online bulletin board known as a Pinboard. Pinboards can be themed to allow users to easily manage Pins, to share their content, and to search for similiar content or Pins posted by other users. Users can also Pin content they find on the Internet and easily upload it to their Pinboard. Businesses are particularly interested in Pinterest as it allows users to create their own business page, run contests, and engage with consumers. Victoria's Secret and AMC Theatres are using Pinterest to promote their businesses and actively engage with consumers.

Social media sites have become increasingly important to companies in connecting with consumers.

- *Twitter/Tumblr/Blogs:* These are websites where people can voice their opinion on any issue that they see fit to post. Twitter is a special blogger website that limits people to messages, or "tweets," of 140 characters in length and is frequently in the top 10 monthly visited websites by Canadians.[58] Tumblr, much like Twitter, is a social blogging site, though the features in Tumblr are much more advanced. Users do not have any word limits, can easily upload photos, and can manage their information using an online dashboard. Twitter, Tumblr, and other similar blogging sites allow companies to communicate with key stakeholders. Jim Estill, CEO of Symex Canada, notes that he produces a blog to stay in touch with key stakeholders.[59] Michael Jagger, president of Vancouver-based Provident Security and Event Management Corp., dedicates four hours a week to his blog and states that it is part of the company's overall marketing strategy.[60] Jagger feels that his blog allows him to build closer bonds with current customers and generate new sales. David Mandelstam, president and CEO of Markham, Ontario-based Sangoma Technologies Inc., a manufacturer of telephone hardware, takes a different approach to using blogs. His firm identified the most popular blogs on technology and sends the bloggers press releases a few days prior to releasing them to the public. Mandelstam notes that the practice costs very little and the payoff is significant. For example, on days when his firm is mentioned by a blogger it is not uncommon for the company to be contacted by four or five prospective customers and/or potential investors.[61] The advantages of blogging include low costs, ability to reach wide audiences, and ability to reach customers on a personal level.

- *YouTube:* YouTube enables people and companies to share videos with millions of daily visitors. The sites allow participants to load video clips onto their websites and display them for the public to see. The videos can act as mini-commercials or infomercials for a product or service, or can be used to attract prospective employees or as a means to generate PR for your company. For example, Toronto-based I Love Rewards has a four-minute employee recruitment video on YouTube.

- *Direct E-Mail to Customers:* E-mail marketing has an almost unlimited number of uses and can be used to welcome customers (such as the e-mails sent to new clients from RBC CEO Gordon Nixon), encourage people to visit your website (such as the e-mails that David Reynolds sends out from his Halifax office for Quicksnap), and encourage people to buy a product or service (such as the e-mails sent out to past customers by Delta Hotels). In addition, e-mails can convert leads, provide additional information, and/or be used as a mechanism to send videos, blogs, newsletters, and podcasts. E-mails can also be used to supplement other forms of marketing, and research indicates that including e-mail as part of a direct mail campaign increases response rates by 40 percent; when used in conjunction with telemarketing the response rate jumps by 76 percent.[62] It should be noted that e-mail marketing is not spamming, a practice where companies send out e-mails to random lists of people. Rather, it is permission-based marketing.

- *Advertainments:* Advertainments are 6- to 11-minute made-for-the-Web ads. Produced, posted, and promoted by Ford, BMW, Diet Coke, and Absolut vodka, the movies feature a product as the star. One BMW movie features a man who drives difficult passengers (in one film, Madonna stars as a difficult, foul-mouthed celebrity) around in flashy BMWs and gives them the ride of their lives. The Ford advertainments feature a Ford vehicle in three different scenarios—the promise of a Ford Focus to a teenager if he can make the team; a shirtless teen boy lying on a Ford Focus, smoking and eyeing a nearby teen girl; and a young man who drives around in a Ford trying to save his goldfish.[63]

- *Banner Advertisements:* Banner ads are interactive display advertising for the Internet. Just use the Internet and you will see examples of banner advertising by numerous Canadian companies such as Porter Airlines, EastLink, and many of Canada's banks. Banner ad placement has become more effective as companies are using information on consumers' Web usage to create personalized ads that people will find more appealing.

- *Online Classified Advertising Sites:* Sites such as eBay, Kijiji, Backpage, and Craigslist are frequently used by businesses to promote and sell their products and services. eBay is one of the most commonly visited sites in the world, and many small businesses use the site for its global reach. eBay allows businesses to sell individual products as well as maintain a virtual storefront. Canadian eBay Entrepreneur of the Year in 2012, Gatineau's Jean-Francois Lapointe, successfully sells more than $1 million worth of bicycle parts on an annual basis using his digital storefront, Bhdbikestore.[64] Kijiji has become the ninth-most visited site in Canada and businesses are using the site to advertise products and services through individual postings or banner advertisements.[65] Car companies, real estate agents, and landscaping companies are frequent users of Kijiji as they find it to be highly effective in reaching consumers. For example, Chris Neville owns a landscaping business in Nova Scotia and states, "Kijiji is actually my most effective form of advertsing. I use Facebook and other forms of social media but most calls for our services come as a direct result from Kijiji."[66] Craigslist and Backpage work similarly to Kijiji and many companies are promoting their products and services using multiple sites.

- *Online Games:* Many companies are delivering promotional messages during game play or sponsoring games as a way to communicate with consumers.

- *Podcasts:* These online broadcasts use audio and/or video clips that can be downloaded on a wireless device such as an iPod, an MP3 player, or a BlackBerry. Podcasts are increasing in popularity and offer businesses many of the same benefits as posting clips on YouTube or Facebook.

- Other methods of using the Internet for marketing include deal-of-the day websites such as Team Buy and Groupon (see below); affiliate programs where companies post information or links on other companies' sites and do the same in turn; Webinars, which are Web-based seminars where you can engage in a full sales pitch with a customer regardless of their location; online newsletters; contributing to online bulletin boards/message boards; and posting to live online chat rooms.

Businesses are using QR codes like this one to allow consumers to link to additional corporate or product information.

Mobile Marketing. **Mobile marketing** is the use of a mobile device to communicate marketing messages. Given the growth in mobile device usage, especially globally, mobile marketing is expected to grow significantly in coming years. While mobile devices, in particular their Web browsers, can be used for many of the activities discussed above, such as searching the Internet and using social media, this section of the chapter is going to discuss mobile marketing methods that can be used primarily on mobile devices. The most common mobile marketing methods are:

> **Mobile marketing** using a mobile device to communicate marketing messages

- *Apps or Applications:* Companies are now creating applications, or as they are better known, "apps," to be used on smartphones. For example, Yellow Pages offers apps for both the iPhone and BlackBerry where customers can look up addresses, read reviews, and even receive information on discounts. The Score has been a first mover in apps marketing. Their app allows viewers to receive stats, blogs, sports headlines, and real-time updates. CIBC, the first Canadian bank to develop an app, allows customers to complete most of their daily banking on their smartphone and ties into the smartphone's GPS capabilities to assist customers in finding the nearest bank.

- *Text/SMS Messages:* Many companies use smartphones to send quick messages to potential customers. For example, at the recent Youth World Beach Volleyball Championship in Halifax, one of the alcoholic beverage sponsors used text messgaes to alert people about drink specials and opportunities to win prizes. As text messages are normally read within four minutes of receipt, customers are likely to receive them and respond.

- *QR Codes:* These are block bar codes that link print and other forms of media advertising to websites using a mobile device which scans and reads the code. QR codes have become increasingly popular as companies can add them to virtually any form of advertising and consumers can use them to link to additional information. One recent study found that 6.2 percent or 14 million mobile users in the U.S. clicked on a QR code in one month alone. The advertisements with the highest click rates are most often printed in magazines and newspapers.[67] Store owners are also using them at the entrance of their stores to entice people in by offering coupons, links to food items, and additional information that consumers will find attractive.

- *Proximity/Location Based Marketing*: Software embedded or downloaded in a mobile device can allow companies to send out real time advertising and communication to potential customers when they are in close proximity to a business. For example, restaurants located on Spring Garden Road in Halifax, Nova Scotia, would be able to send ads, menus, and/or coupons to potential customers—pedestrians walking in the area—via their mobile device.

Personal Selling. **Personal selling** is direct, two-way communication with buyers and potential buyers. For many products—especially large, expensive ones with specialized uses, such as cars, appliances, and houses—interaction between a salesperson and the customer is probably the most important promotional tool. Robert Herjavec, founder of The Herjavec Group and panelist on *Dragons' Den*, states that the key to building successful firms is to develop a culture that focuses on sales. Herjavec's IT company has amassed millions in sales by having all employees, whether they be frontline workers or salespeople, focus on sales.[68]

Personal selling is the most flexible of the promotional methods because it gives marketers the greatest opportunity to communicate specific information that might trigger a purchase. Only personal selling can zero in on a prospect and attempt to persuade that person to make a purchase. Although personal selling has a lot of advantages, it is one of the most costly forms of promotion. A sales call on an industrial customer can cost as much as $200 or $300. One Canadian firm that has mastered personal selling is Rebecca MacDonald's Energy Saving Plus Income Fund. The company allows people to lock in the price of natural gas for five years at a time using door-to-door salespeople who specialize in cold calls. MacDonald notes that training salespeople is a key to long-term success.[69]

> **Personal selling** direct, two-way communication with buyers and potential buyers

There are three distinct categories of salespersons: order takers (for example, retail sales clerks and route salespeople), creative salespersons (for example, automobile, furniture, and insurance salespeople), and support salespersons (for example, customer educators and goodwill builders who usually do not take orders). For most of these salespeople, personal selling is a six-step process:

1. *Prospecting:* Identifying potential buyers of the product.

2. *Approaching:* Using a referral or calling on a customer without prior notice to determine interest in the product.

3. *Presenting:* Getting the prospect's attention with a product demonstration.

4. *Handling objections:* Countering reasons for not buying the product.

5. *Closing:* Asking the prospect to buy the product.

6. *Following up:* Checking customer satisfaction with the purchased product.

Guerrilla Marketing. Guerrilla marketing is pursuing traditional marketing through unconventional means. Essentially, guerrilla marketing consists of attracting consumer attention to a company using unique and/or creative methods. For example, Montreal-based Lezza Distribution Inc., a high-end manufacturer of countertops and flooring surfaces, is known for its risky marketing efforts. At a recent trade show, the company had barely clothed male models serving drinks, and it has recently started hosting an annual "Seven Sins" party where there are half-naked models and strip poker. Company president Mark Hanna says, "Parties give us a chance to showcase our core values of passion, risk, and creativity and they give us a cool factor that distinguishes us from our competitors."[70] Other examples include Atlantic Lotto's introduction of the Lotto Max game. The company placed large balls onto smashed cars with the words Lotto Max printed on the balls. Other methods include contests or raffles like "Roll up the Rim to Win"; sample giveaways—a strategy successfully used by Swiss Medica Inc., a Mississauga-based company that develops over-the-counter health food products, to compete with much larger drug companies; public demonstrations such as the ones used by Sweetpea, which used new moms as product ambassadors in Vancouver, Calgary, and Montreal to demonstrate organic frozen baby food products at local events; speaking at public events; and so forth. The difference between guerrilla marketing and publicity, which is discussed below, is that guerrilla marketing focuses on creating sales and creating awareness.

Publicity nonpersonal communication transmitted through the mass media but not paid for directly by the firm

Publicity. **Publicity** is nonpersonal communication transmitted through the mass media. Publicity can be free or sometimes paid for directly by the firm. As already discussed,

Prince Edward Island recently paid *Live! With Regis and Kelly* to come to the island and tape three episodes. The investment resulted in strong interest from potential tourists. Sometimes, firms won't pay the media cost for publicity, nor will they be identified as the originator of the message; instead, the message is presented in news story form. Obviously, a company can benefit from publicity by releasing to news sources newsworthy messages about the firm and its involvement with the public. Many companies have *public relations* departments to try to gain favourable publicity and minimize negative publicity for the firm.

Although advertising and publicity are both carried by the mass media, they differ in several major ways. Advertising messages tend to be informative, persuasive, or both; publicity is mainly informative. Advertising is often designed to have an immediate impact or to provide specific information to persuade a person to act; publicity describes what a firm is doing, what products it is launching, or other newsworthy information, but seldom calls for action although action is sometimes implied or is seen by businesses and consumers as the next logical step. For example, Spin Master Toys, Canada's largest private toy company, originally did no advertising at all and relied on PR to increase brand awareness and sell products. When advertising is used, the organization must pay for media time and select the media that will best reach target audiences—this is not always the case with publicity. The mass media often willingly carry publicity because they believe it has general public interest. Advertising can be repeated a number of times; most publicity appears in the mass media once and is not repeated. One of the keys to success in generating positive PR is to create value for all participants.

Advertising, personal selling, and sales promotion are especially useful for influencing an exchange directly. Publicity is extremely important when communication focuses on a company's activities and products and is directed at interest groups, current and potential investors, regulatory agencies, and society in general. Yet, as noted above, companies do expect advertising to result in an increase in sales. Brian Scudamore, CEO of Vancouver-based 1-800-GOT-JUNK?, spent a considerable amount of time and effort getting the company onto the *Oprah* show. While this would be considered publicity, Scudamore knew that the spot would generate sales to customers and increase interest among entrepreneurs who might want to purchase a franchise. In fact, in the days after the spot on *Oprah* aired, the firm received 3,000 calls from customers—up 300 percent from usual—and 500 franchise inquiries.[71]

Linda Hipp, owner of Lija Style Inc., a British Columbia-based company, has been using PR since 2003. Hipp relies on PR to jumpstart sales in new markets rather than spending money on traditional advertising or a sales staff. Prior to entering a market, she blitzes local newspapers and magazines where she almost always generates some publicity with fashion writers. She then passes out free clothes to opinion leaders in the community (ambassador program) in hopes that they will promote the clothes to their colleagues and friends. Only when she establishes her company in the local market does Hipp advertise and hire a salesperson.[72]

Examples of good public relations include the following:

- Develop a press kit
- Write articles for a newspaper, newsletter, or community guide
- Write letters to the editor
- Participate in discussions either online or through traditional mediums
- Host events
- Offer services as a guest speaker

One of the keys to success in generating positive PR is to create value for all participants. Just going to a newspaper and announcing the grand opening of a store or an expansion may not be enough. Furthermore, you do not have to spend a great deal of money to generate positive PR. Publishers are interested in business events and/or ideas that are interesting to their readers.

Sales Promotion. **Sales promotion** involves direct inducements offering added value or some other incentive for buyers to enter into an exchange. The major tools of sales promotion are store displays, premiums, samples and demonstrations, coupons, contests and sweepstakes, refunds, and trade shows. Distribution of coupons increased 10 percent in recent years to more than 3.2 billion coupons, which save Canadians approximately $120 million a year. About 88 percent of these coupons were distributed via weekend newspapers.[76] Recently online deal-of-the day websites, such as Groupon and Team Buy, have been promoting coupons, that will only be redeemable if sales targets are achieved. Consumers who want to purchase the deal

> **Sales promotion** direct inducements offering added value or some other incentive for buyers to enter into an exchange

Consider the Following: Lululemon's Unconventional Marketing

Dennis Wilson founded Vancouver-based Lululemon in 1998 as yoga began to increase in popularity across North America. Wilson opened his first store with the goal of producing products that encourage people to be active and stress free. The first store opened in Vancouver and sales immediately exceeded expectations, fuelled by the popularity of the products and growth in yoga. Today the company operates over 160 stores and sells not only yoga attire but also sports apparel.

A hallmark of the company's success is its unique promotional campaigns, which range from providing local yoga instructors with free clothing, to having customers receive discounts for engaging in wacky activities such as shopping with barely anything on. The company also relies heavily on the Internet and buzz from social media to promote its products. Outgoing CEO Christine Day states, "Our number one goal is to sell to customers where they are at ... we don't do gift-giving and we don't do, like, special promotions, discounts, whatever. That's not our MO, and we don't do big." The company also doesn't engage in market research. Rather, it relies on employees to gather information on customers and Lululemon pays close attention to customer feedback on chalkboards in stores. Unconventional marketing appears to be working as Interbrand recently concluded that Lululemon was the fastest-growing brand of the year as it has increased in value 292 percent to $3.24 billion.[73] Much like anything in life, if you do things unconventionally you are going to get some negative feedback, and Lululemon is no exception.[74] For example, during the 2010 Vancouver Olympic games, Lululemon received some negative reaction to its "Cool Sporting Event That Takes Place in British Columbia Between 2009 & 2011 Edition" promotional campaign for its *Cheer Gear*, which included mitts, toques, and jackets. The company did not sponsor the games and is technically not allowed to use the word *Olympic* in its promotional efforts. Officials at the 2010 Vancouver games felt that while Lululemon did not break the law the company did not follow its spirit, noting the games would not be possible without official sponsors and many paid over $100 million to be associated with the 2010 games.[75]

DISCUSSION QUESTIONS

1. What are the pros and cons of using unconventional marketing campaigns?

2. Do you think customers know that their feedback to employees and on in-store chalkboards is impacting company decisions? Would they appreciate this or feel that to some extent their privacy is being violated?

2. Do you think Lululemon should have produced and sold *Cheer Gear?* Why or why not?

3. What are the long-term consequences to the Olympics if companies produce and sell merchandise without paying any sponsorship dollars?

Push strategy an attempt to motivate intermediaries to push the product down to their customers

will often share information about the coupon with their friends using social media. Companies are taking advantage of these deal-of-the-day sites as they often expose their business to new customers and lower customer acquisition costs. Additionally, businesses don't pay an upfront fee to participate and they can limit how many coupons are sold. One of the challenges of deal-of-the-day sites is the deep discounts companies are expected to offer consumers in order to participate. The normal discount on Groupon and Team Buy is 50 percent off the purchase price, so a $100 lawn care service would be sold for $50. Groupon normally charges 50 percent of the deal's sale price, meaning in this example they would charge the business $25, leaving the business to perform $100 worth of service for $25.

Sales promotion stimulates customer purchasing and increases dealer effectiveness in selling products. It is used to enhance and supplement other forms of promotion. Test drives allow salespersons to demonstrate vehicles, which can help purchase decisions. Sampling a product may also encourage consumers to buy. PepsiCo, for example, used sampling to promote its Sierra Mist soft drink to reach more than 5 million potential consumers at well-travelled sites such as Times Square and Penn Station.[77] In a given year, almost three-fourths of consumer product companies may use sampling.

Sales promotions are generally easier to measure and less expensive than advertising. Although less than 2 percent of the 3.2 billion coupons distributed annually are redeemed, offering them in weekend paper inserts is cheaper than producing a television commercial.

Promotion Strategies: To Push or to Pull

In developing a promotion mix, organizations must decide whether to fashion a mix that pushes or pulls the product (Figure 12.6). A **push strategy** attempts to motivate intermediaries to push the product down to their customers. When a push strategy is used, the company attempts to motivate wholesalers and retailers to make the product available to their customers. Sales personnel may be used to persuade intermediaries to offer the product, distribute promotional materials, and offer special promotional incentives for those who agree to carry the product. A great example of using successful push strategies comes from Jewel Pop, a Dartmouth, Nova Scotia-based

jewellery company which recently reached $3 million in sales. Company founder and president Robert Smith developed a Kameleon jewellery line where beads and silver rings are interchangeable, allowing customers to intermingle and colour-coordinate their outfits and jewellery. After taking samples of the product to an Atlanta gift show, Smith found a number of retailers that were willing to sell the product. But Smith, who has years of experience in the jewellery industry, knows that retailers may offer to sell a product but not push it onto the customers. Smith then devised an incentive plan providing retailers with exclusive territories, free shipping, and other bonuses to push the unique jewellery onto their customers. The strategy is working as Smith notes that some independent retailers are selling in excess of $100,000 a year in jewellery and he hopes to reach $100 million in sales in the next five to six years.[78] On a much larger scale, RIM, now BlackBerry, owes much of its success to its ability to create relationships with national carriers and dealers who in turn push the product onto their customers. BlackBerry provides carriers with unique designs that they can call their own and assists in managing traffic and security on the carrier's network to keep it from overflowing. Chrysler manufacturing plants operate on a push system. They assemble cars according to forecasts of sales demand. Dealers then sell to buyers with the help of incentives and other promotions.[79] A **pull strategy** uses promotion to create consumer demand for a product so that consumers exert pressure on marketing channel members to make it available. For example, when the Coca-Cola Company launched its new hybrid energy soda VAULT, the company gave away samples throughout the United States via sampling teams in VAULT-branded International CXTs, the world's largest production pickup trucks. They distributed ice-cold VAULT

Pull strategy the use of promotion to create consumer demand for a product so that consumers exert pressure on marketing channel members to make it available

figure 12.6 Push and Pull Strategies

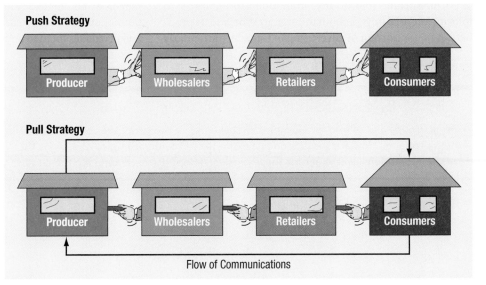

Push Strategy — Producer, Wholesalers, Retailers, Consumers
Pull Strategy — Producer, Wholesalers, Retailers, Consumers
Flow of Communications

at concerts and targeted retail outlets, sporting events, and other locations.[80] Such sampling prior to a product rollout encourages consumers to request the product from their favourite retailer.

A company can use either strategy, or it can use a variation or combination of the two. The exclusive use of advertising indicates a pull strategy. Personal selling to marketing channel members indicates a push strategy. The allocation of promotional resources to various marketing mix elements probably determines which strategy a marketer uses.

Objectives of Promotion

The marketing mix a company uses depends on its objectives. It is important to recognize that promotion is only one element of the marketing strategy and must be tied carefully to the goals of the firm, its overall marketing objectives, and the other elements of the marketing strategy. Firms use promotion for many reasons, but typical objectives are to stimulate demand, to stabilize sales, and to inform, remind, and reinforce customers. For example, Tim Hortons will advertise in Canada to stimulate demand at certain times of the year, but it will also advertise to remind consumers and Canadians that Tim Hortons is a national brand in the country.

Increasing demand for a product is probably the most typical promotional objective. Stimulating demand, often through advertising and sales promotion, is particularly important when a firm is using a pull strategy.

Another goal of promotion is to stabilize sales by maintaining the status quo—that is, the current sales level of the product. During periods of slack or decreasing sales, contests, prizes, vacations, and other sales promotions are sometimes offered to customers to maintain sales goals. Advertising is often used to stabilize sales by making customers aware of slack use periods. For example, both Air Canada and WestJet use Internet advertising to promote air travel and vacation specials during slow times of the year. During the 2010 Olympics, Air Canada announced a new special the day after any Canadian gold medal—most of which were aimed at increasing sales during traditionally slow periods.

An important role of any promotional program is to inform potential buyers about the organization and its products. A major portion of advertising in Canada, particularly in daily newspapers, is informational. Providing information about the availability, price, technology, and features of a product is very important in encouraging a buyer to move toward a purchase decision. Nearly all forms of promotion involve an attempt to help consumers learn more about a product and a company.

Promotion is also used to remind consumers that an established organization is still around and sells certain products that have uses and benefits. Often advertising reminds customers that they may need to use a product more frequently or in certain situations. Canadian Tire, for example, has used a variety of promotions reminding car owners that they need to change their oil every 5,000 kilometres to ensure proper performance of their cars.

Reinforcement promotion attempts to assure current users of the product that they have made the right choice and tells them how to get the most satisfaction from the product. Also, a company could release publicity statements through the news media about a new use for a product. Additionally, firms can have salespeople communicate with current and potential customers about the proper use and maintenance of a product—all in the hope of developing a repeat customer.

Promotional Positioning

Promotional positioning uses promotion to create and maintain an image of a product in buyers' minds. It is a natural result of market segmentation. In both promotional positioning and market segmentation, the firm targets a given product or brand at a portion of the total market. A promotional strategy helps differentiate the product and make it appeal to a particular market segment. For example, VIA Rail advertises ease of boarding and comfort to appeal to consumers who want the freedom to move about as they travel and others who do not want the long security check-ins that are common at airports. Volvo heavily promotes the safety and crashworthiness of Volvo automobiles in its advertising. Volkswagen has done the same thing with its edgy ads showing car crashes. Promotion can be used to change or reinforce an image. Effective promotion influences customers and persuades them to buy.

> **Promotional positioning** the use of promotion to create and maintain an image of a product in buyers' minds

---

TEAM EXERCISE

Form groups and search for examples of convenience products, shopping products, specialty products, and business products. How are these products marketed? Provide examples of any ads that you can find to show examples of the promotional strategies for these products. Report your findings to the class.

LEARNING OBJECTIVES SUMMARY

LO1 Describe the role of product in the marketing mix, including how products are developed, classified, and identified.

Products (goods, services, ideas) are among a firm's most visible contacts with consumers and must meet consumers' needs and expectations to ensure success. New product development is a multi-step process: idea development, the screening of new ideas, business analysis, product development, test marketing, and commercialization. Products are usually classified as either consumer or industrial products. Consumer products can be further classified as convenience, shopping, or specialty products. The industrial product classifications are raw materials, major equipment, accessory equipment, component parts, processed materials, supplies and industrial services. Products also can be classified by the stage of the product life cycle (introduction, growth, maturity and decline). Identifying products includes branding (the process of naming and identifying products); packaging (the product's container); and labelling (information, such as content and warnings, on the package).

LO2 Define price and discuss its importance in the marketing mix, including various pricing strategies a firm might employ.

Price is the value placed on an object exchanged between a buyer and a seller, and is probably the most flexible variable of the marketing mix. Pricing objectives include survival, maximization of profits and sales volume, and maintaining the status quo. When a firm introduces a new product, it may use price skimming or penetration pricing. Psychological pricing and price discounting are other strategies.

LO3 Identify factors affecting distribution decisions, such as marketing channels and intensity of market coverage.

Making products available to customers is facilitated by intermediaries who bridge the gap between the producer of the product and its ultimate user. A marketing channel is a group of marketing organizations that direct the flow of products from producers to consumers. Market coverage relates to the number and variety of outlets that make products available to the customers; it may be intensive, selective, or exclusive. Physical distribution is all the activities necessary to move products from producers to consumers, including inventory planning and control, transportation, warehousing and materials handling.

LO4 Specify the activities involved in promotion, as well as promotional strategies and promotional positioning.

Promotion encourages marketing exchanges by persuading individuals, groups and organizations to accept advertising (a paid form of nonpersonal communication transmitted through a mass medium); personal selling (direct, two-way communication with buyers and potential buyers); publicity (nonpersonal communication transmitted through mass media but not paid for directly by the firm); and sales promotion (direct inducements offering added value or some other incentive for buyers to enter into an exchange). A push strategy attempts to motivate intermediaries to push the product down to their customers, whereas a pull strategy tries to create consumer demand for a product so that consumers exert pressure on marketing channel members to make the product available. Typical promotion objectives are to stimulate demand, stabilize sales, and inform, remind, and reinforce customers. Promotional positioning is the use of promotion to create and maintain in the buyer's mind an image of the product.

KEY TERMS

advertising
advertising campaign
branding
business products
commercialization
consumer products
discounts
exclusive distribution
generic products
integrated marketing communications
intensive distribution
labelling
manufacturer brands
marketing channel
materials handling
mobile marketing
packaging
penetration price
personal selling

physical distribution
price skimming
private distributor brands
product line
product mix
promotional positioning
psychological pricing
publicity
pull strategy
push strategy
quality
retailers
sales promotion
selective distribution
test marketing
trademark
transportation
warehousing
wholesalers

DESTINATION CEO DISCUSSION QUESTIONS

1. Why do you think BlackBerry placed such a heavy reliance on social media in promoting its products?

2. BlackBerry was obviously hoping to resurrect the company with the Z10. Given what you know now, what could the company have done differently?

3. Why do you think Heins's plan for the Z10 failed?

4. Do you think Heins is acting too quickly in selling the company, given that BlackBerry still controls valuable patents and has billions in cash?

5. Would you buy a BlackBerry? Why or why not?

Many jobs in marketing are closely tied to the marketing mix functions: distribution, product, promotion, and price. Often the job titles could be sales manager, distribution or supply chain manager, advertising account executive, or store manager.

A distribution manager arranges for transportation of goods within firms and through marketing channels. Transportation can be costly, and time is always an important factor, so minimizing their effects is vital to the success of a firm. Distribution managers must choose one or a combination of transportation modes from a vast array of options, taking into account local, federal, and international regulations for different freight classifications; the weight, size, and fragility of products to be shipped; time schedules; and loss and damage ratios. Manufacturing firms are the largest employers of distribution managers.

A product manager is responsible for the success or failure of a product line. This requires a general knowledge of advertising, transportation modes, inventory control, selling and sales management, promotion, marketing research, packaging, and pricing. Frequently, several years of selling and sales management experience are prerequisites for such a position as well as college training in business administration. Being a product manager can be rewarding both financially and psychologically.

Some of the most creative roles in the business world are in the area of advertising. Advertising pervades our daily lives, as businesses and other organizations try to grab our attention and tell us about what they have to offer. Copywriters, artists, and account executives in advertising must have creativity, imagination, artistic talent, and expertise in expression and persuasion. Advertising is an area of business in which a wide variety of educational backgrounds may be useful, from degrees in advertising itself, to journalism or liberal arts degrees. Common entry-level positions in an advertising agency are found in the traffic department, account service (account coordinator), or the media department (media assistant). Advertising jobs are also available in many manufacturing or retail firms, nonprofit organizations, banks, professional associations, utility companies, and other arenas outside of an advertising agency.

Although a career in retailing may begin in sales, there is much more to retailing than simply selling. Many retail personnel occupy management positions, focusing on selecting and ordering merchandise, promotional activities, inventory control, customer credit operations, accounting, personnel, and store security. Many specific examples of retailing jobs can be found in large department stores. A section manager coordinates inventory and promotions and interacts with buyers, salespeople, and consumers. The buyer's job is fast-paced, often involving much travel and pressure. Buyers must be open-minded and forward-looking in their hunt for new, potentially successful items. Regional managers coordinate the activities of several retail stores within a specific geographic area, usually monitoring and supporting sales, promotions, and general procedures. Retail management can be exciting and challenging. Growth in retailing is expected to accompany the growth in population and is likely to create substantial opportunities in the coming years.

While a career in marketing can be very rewarding, marketers today agree that the job is getting tougher. Many advertising and marketing executives say the job has gotten much more demanding in the past 10 years, viewing their number-one challenge as balancing work and personal obligations. Other challenges include staying current on industry trends or technologies, keeping motivated/inspired on the job, and measuring success. If you are up to the challenge, you may find that a career in marketing is just right for you to utilize your business knowledge while exercising your creative side as well.

Dimensions of Marketing Strategy

If you think your product/business is truly new to or unique to the market, you need to substantiate your claim. After a thorough exploration on the Web, you want to make sure there has not been a similar business/service recently launched in your community. Check with your Chamber of Commerce or Economic Development Office, which might be able to provide you with a history of recent business failures. If you are not confident about the ability or willingness of customers to try your new product or service, collecting your own primary data to ascertain demand is highly advisable.

The decision of where to initially set your prices is a critical one. If there are currently similar products in the market, you need to be aware of competitors' prices before you determine yours. If your product/service is new to the market, you can price it high (market skimming strategy) as long as you realize that the high price will probably attract competitors to the market more quickly (they will think they can make the same product for less), which will force you to drop your prices sooner than you would like. Another strategy to consider is market penetration pricing, a strategy that sets prices lower and discourages competition from entering the market as quickly. Whatever strategy you decide to use, don't forget to examine your product/service's elasticity.

At this time, you need to start thinking about how to promote your product. Why do you feel your product/service is different or new to the market? How do you want to position your product/service so customers view it favourably? Remember: this is all occurring *within the consumer's mind.*

CASE | Finding the Real Green Products

What makes a green product green? This question is actually quite complicated. The growing popularity of eco-friendly products is encouraging businesses to create and sell more green items. Nancy Wright, vice-president of Vancouver's Globe Foundation, states that the green industry in Canada is flourishing as 70 percent of consumers say they are willing to spend up to 20 percent more for environmentally friendly items. She describes sales of "green" products and services as flourishing. However, some businesses are cutting corners by touting their products as green when they really aren't—a form of misconduct known as greenwashing. Greenwashers make unjustifiable green claims about their products to appeal to the eco-friendly consumer. In fact, a recent study by Terra Choice Environmental Marketing found that 99.9 percent of so-called green products make false, misleading, or unsubstantiated claims. As a result, 40 percent of consumers claim that they don't know how to ensure that a company is really eco-friendly.

One common way that companies engage in greenwashing is by sustainably sourcing one product ingredient while the other ingredients remain unsustainable. This might be akin to a company claiming that its product is green since one of the ingredients is organic cotton, while simultaneously glossing over the fact that the product also consists of nonrecyclable plastics or chemicals. Unfortunately, the subjective nature of greenwashing makes it harder to detect, as consumers themselves differ on what is green and what is greenwashing. For instance, the Fur Council of Canada (FCC) launched its "Fur is Green" campaign a few years ago, advocating that fur is a green product and industry that does more good for society than harm. The Fur Council of Canada maintains a website, www.FurIsGreen.com, that states, "fur is [a] natural, renewable resource ... in nature, each plant and animal species generally produces more offspring than the land can support to maturity. Like other species, we live by making use of part of this surplus that nature creates." As a result of the campaign, companies like Canada Goose added a "Green" label to their clothing. Others including animal rights advocates were shocked that people would consider the fur industry to be green or eco-friendly. Other examples include the number of consumers who posted on social media sites that they felt misled by Cascade Farm's logo of a small idyllic farm after they discovered that the brand is actually owned by General Mills. Others are unconcerned as long as the brand's organic claims are true. The topic of greenwashing has become so pervasive that it is prompting government intervention. Canada's Competition Bureau, along with the Canadian Standards Association, has established standards to cut down on greenwashing with a set guidelines that prohibit vague or misleading environmental claims on products and services. Critics of the Competition Bureau note that these are not laws, only guidelines, and there is nothing to legally prevent a company from claiming a product is green. For now consumers must investigate green claims for themselves. Such an investigation could include looking for third-party certification of a product's "greenness," paying attention to ingredient lists, and looking for information on trustworthy websites. However, until more stringent guidelines are created, the term *green* is likely to remain steeped in subjectivity.[81]

DISCUSSION QUESTIONS

1. Are you more inclined to purchase products because they are labelled as "green"? Would you pay more for such products? Why or why not?

2. Do you feel confident that you can determine if a product is really "green"?

3. Do you think the fur industry is a "green" industry? Why or why not?

4. Are you concerned whether Cascade Farms, owned by General Mills, is making valid organic claims?

5. What will happen to companies and their products if consumers find their green claims to be false?

connect **LEARNSMART** **SMARTBOOK**

For more information on the resources available from McGraw-Hill Ryerson, go to www.mcgrawhill.ca/he/solutions.

LO1 Define digital media and digital marketing and recognize their increasing value in strategic planning.

LO2 Understand the characteristics of digital media and how they differentiate these methods from traditional marketing activities.

LO3 Demonstrate the role of digital marketing and social networking in today's business environment.

LO4 Show how digital media affect the marketing mix.

LO5 Define social networking and illustrate how businesses can use different types of social networking media.

LO6 Identify legal and ethical considerations in digital media.

DESTINATION CEO

Arlene Dickinson is living proof that the Canadian dream is possible.

Dickinson, a star of CBC's *Dragons' Den*, is also the owner of Venture Communications, one of the largest marketing and communications companies in the country. She also has an ownership stake in over 50 businesses, and has won numerous business awards, including being recognized as one of Canada's Most Powerful Women, Top 100 Hall of Fame, and *PROFIT* and *Chatelaine* magazines' Top 100 Business Owners. She was awarded the Pinnacle Award for Entrepreneurial Excellence, Ad Rodeo's Lifetime Achievement Award, and McGill University's Management Achievement Award. She was even recognized as Global Television's Woman of Vision. Today, Dickinson's net worth is estimated to be in excess of $80 million.

Dickinson immigrated to Canada with her parents who, by the time they arrived here from South Africa, only had $50 left to support the family of five. Dickinson's family struggled so much during their early years in Canada that her mother had to sell her engagement ring as their car broke down moving from Edmonton to Calgary and the family had no money to fix the car or buy a replacement. Things improved in Calgary, and Dickinson graduated from high school at the age of 16, but didn't have an interest in pursuing anything that resembled a career. Her main goal was to have a family, which started when she married at the young age of 19. Dickinson soon became a working mother, paying her husband's way through teacher's college. The marriage was very rocky, and Dickinson divorced her husband at the age at 27, leaving her with four children and no job. At this point, Dickinson had her first break when she was offered a job selling advertising for a TV station. While she had no experience in sales, she excelled at the position and spent 18 months working on what she assumed was a new career. Unfortunately, the station went through a cost-cutting program and Dickinson lost her job. One of Dickinson's co-workers had recently started a company called Venture Communications and he inquired if Dickinson would like to become a partner. According to Dickinson, becoming a partner meant working for no pay and hoping that the company became successful. Dickinson says, "I joined the company with no income and we barely scraped by the first few years living off credit cards and whatever money I could scrape together."

The partners eventually received a break. Bob Morrisette wanted a national campaign to be developed for hair salons across the country and asked Venture if they could come to Vancouver and present their ideas to 1,200 hairdressers. Describing the situation, Dickinson says, "...they (Bob Morrisette) could not pay us for the proposal...we couldn't afford to fly to Vancouver or even stay at a hotel. We flew out using points and had to sleep on a friend's boat." The day of the presentation, Dickinson's hair dryer actually stopped working and she arrived to present before 1,200 hairdressers with her hair windblown and a mess; in Dickinson's words, "I looked like Orphan Annie." But the partners did something right as the hairdressers loved their presentation and Venture Communications received its first large contract. The firm continued to grow, and in 1998 Dickinson took over as owner of the company. Today,

Venture Communications is one of the largest marketing and communications firms in Canada, with estimated annual gross sales in excess of $45 million.

While Dickinson is considered an expert in digital media, she believes in doing business a little differently than what you may think. In today's digital world, Dickinson still wants to meet clients face-to-face; she wants to talk to them and understand not only what story they are trying to convey in their marketing plan but also their personal and business story. Dickinson states, "You still have to build relationships; you have to get to know people. E-mail is great for content but if you want to emotionally connect with clients you have to meet them. By connecting with people you can become a better storyteller and do a better job." Dickinson also believes in being nice. On *Dragons' Den*, Arlene is known to be the socially responsible and supportive Dragon. She frequently invests in companies that are developing environmentally friendly businesses and often argues with her co-star Kevin O'Leary that the way people conduct business is changing for the better. As Dickinson says, "You can be successful and nice."[1]

Introduction[2]

The Internet and information technology have dramatically changed the environment for business. Marketers' new ability to convert all types of communications into digital media has created efficient, inexpensive ways of connecting businesses and consumers and has improved the flow and the usefulness of information. Businesses have the information they need to make more informed decisions, and consumers have access to a greater variety of products and more information about choices and quality.

The defining characteristic of information technology in the 21st century is accelerating change. New systems and applications advance so rapidly that it is almost impossible to keep up with the latest developments. Start-up companies emerge that quickly overtake existing approaches to digital media. When Google first arrived on the scene, a number of search engines were fighting for dominance, including Excite, Infoseek, Lycos, and WebCrawler. With its fast, easy-to-use search engine, Google became number one and is now challenging many industries, including advertising, newspapers, mobile phones, and book publishing. Despite its victory, Google is constantly being challenged itself by competitors like Yahoo and Baidu. The Chinese search engine Baidu represents a particular threat as it is the fifth-largest "pure-play" Internet company (after Google, Amazon.com, Tencent, and eBay) and has the majority of the Chinese Internet market. Google is also being challenged by social networks, which most observers believe will dominate digital communication in the future.[3] Today, people spend more time on social networking sites, such as Facebook, than they spend on e-mail.

In this chapter we first provide some key definitions related to digital marketing and social networking. Next we discuss using digital media in business and marketing. We look at marketing mix considerations when using digital media and pay special attention to social networking. Then we focus on digital marketing strategies—particularly new communication channels like social networks—and consider how consumers are changing their information searches and consumption behaviour to fit emerging technologies and trends. Finally, we examine the legal and social issues associated with information technology, digital media, and e-business.

LO1 Define digital media and digital marketing and recognize their increasing value in strategic planning.

> **E-business** carrying out the goals of business through utilization of the Internet
>
> **Digital media** electronic media that function using digital codes via computers, cellular phones, smartphones, and other digital devices that have been released in recent years

What Is Digital Marketing?

Let's start with a clear understanding of our focus in this chapter. First, we can distinguish **e-business** from traditional business by noting that conducting e-business means carrying out the goals of business through the use of the Internet. **Digital media** are electronic media that function using digital codes—when we refer to digital media, we mean media available via computers and other digital devices, including mobile and wireless ones like cell phones and smartphones.

Digital marketing uses all digital media, including the Internet and mobile and interactive channels, to develop communication and exchanges with customers. *Digital marketing* is a term we will use often because we are interested in all types of digital communications, regardless of the electronic channel that transmits the data.

> **Digital marketing** uses all digital media, including the Internet and mobile and interactive channels, to develop communication and exchanges with customers

Growth and Benefits of Digital Communication

The Internet has created tremendous opportunities for businesses to forge relationships with consumers and business customers, target markets more precisely, and even reach previously inaccessible markets at home and around the world. The Internet also facilitates business transactions, allowing companies to network with manufacturers, wholesalers, retailers, suppliers, and outsource firms to serve customers more quickly and more efficiently. The telecommunication opportunities created by the Internet have set the stage for digital marketing's development and growth.

Digital communication offers a completely new dimension in connecting with others. Some of the characteristics that distinguish digital from traditional communication are addressability, interactivity, accessibility, connectivity, and control. Let's look at what these mean and how they enhance marketing.

The ability of a business to identify customers before they make a purchase is **addressability.** Digital media make it possible for visitors on a website like Amazon.ca and Chapters.ca to provide information about their needs and wants before they buy. A social network such as Facebook lets users create a profile to keep in touch or to build a network of identified contacts including friends, colleagues, and businesses. Companies such as Porter Airlines, Canada's third-largest airline, use social networks such as Facebook to announce new promotions and share company news, collect customer feedback, and answer questions. Porter uses Twitter primarily to answer questions from customers and YouTube to share videos about the company.

Interactivity allows customers to express their needs and wants directly to the firm in response to its communications. In traditional one-way forms of communication, such as television advertising, the customer must contact the company by phone or other means. Interactivity relies on digital media that can make a conversation between the firm and the customer happen without any delay; thus, real relationships become possible. Digital media such as blogs and

Porter uses Facebook, Twitter and YouTube in its digital marketing strategy. Porter's online strategy has been successful as it actively encourages consumers to ask questions and engage in conversations with the company.

social networks allow marketers to engage with customers, shape their expectations and perceptions, and benefit from broader market reach at lower cost. As mentioned above, Porter Airlines uses social media sites to communicate with customers in real time. Customers can ask questions about promotions, flight times, and so forth and Porter will respond. Other customers who may not be directly involved in the interaction can also read and benefit from the information. Ken Tencer, a branding and innovation expert, states that conversations with customers are better than a strong communication strategy. Tencer uses the example of Fluevog, a Vancouver-based specialty shoe and accessory store with 14 North American locations. According to Tencer, Fluevog's website and digital strategy have been successful because they engage the customers and ask them to participate in a conversation about products and the brand.[5]

Accessibility allows consumers to find information about competing products, prices, and reviews and become more informed about a firm and the relative value of its products. Mobile devices—including smartphones, mobile computing devices like the iPad, and PDAs—allow customers to leave their desktops and access digital networks from anywhere. Thanks to the popularity of the iPhone and BlackBerry, businesses and their customers can stay in constant touch. Benjamin Moore & Co. has an iPhone app (application) that allows customers to match anything, such as their own home-decorating colour samples and photographs, with shades of Benjamin Moore paint. Many companies are adopting a digital media philosophy of open communication with customers; for example, a firm can go to a site such as GeniusRocket.com, a

> ## DID YOU KNOW?
> The average Canadian sits in front of a computer for 45.3 hours a month, taking in content from some 98 websites.[4]

Addressability the ability of a business to identify customers before they make purchases

Interactivity allows customers to express their needs and wants directly to the firm in response to its communications

Accessibility allows consumers to find information about competing products, prices, and reviews and become more informed about a firm and the relative value of its products

marketing firm that provides customized services linking businesses with customers, to request ideas for new products.

Connectivity keeps customers, employees, and businesses connected with each other. It involves the use of digital networks to provide linkages between information providers and users. Social networking is a key form of connectivity made easier on a global scale by Facebook, Myspace, LinkedIn, Twitter, Tumblr, Pinterest, and other networking sites. Facebook has a larger audience than any television network that has ever existed. Firms can also target precise markets through local social networking sites such as Orkut, a Google-owned service operating in India and Brazil.

Control refers to consumers' ability to regulate the information they receive via the Internet, and the rate and sequence of their exposure to that information. Consumers choose the websites they view, the blogs they follow, and the social networking sites to which they belong. This trend toward a consumer-controlled market requires marketers to approach their jobs in a different way than they did in traditional marketing.

LO3 Demonstrate the role of digital marketing and social networking in today's business environment.

Using Digital Media in Business

The phenomenal growth of digital media has provided new ways of conducting business. Given almost instant communication with precisely defined consumer groups, firms can use real-time exchanges to stimulate interactive communication, forge closer relationships, and learn more accurately about consumer and supplier needs. Consider that Amazon, one of the most successful e-businesses, ranked number 100 on the *Fortune* 500 list of America's largest corporations.[6] Amazon is a true global e-business, and was one of the early success stories in the industry, getting 50 percent of its revenue from international sales.[7] Many of you may not remember a world before Amazon because it has completely transformed how many people shop. Previously, consumers had to travel store to store in order to find goods and compare prices.

Because it is fast and inexpensive, digital communication is making it easier for businesses to conduct marketing research, provide and obtain price and product information, and advertise, as well as to fulfill their business goals by selling goods and services online. Even the government engages in digital marketing activities—marketing

everything from bonds and other financial instruments to oil-drilling leases and surplus equipment. Lululemon uses social media—including over 500,000 Facebook fans, 175,000 Twitter followers, almost 18,000 LinkedIn followers, and hundreds of videos on YouTube and Tumblr, Foursquare, Instagram, Zite, and Pinterest—to create links with customers, get immediate feedback on products, and promote both products and its brand. By getting feedback online, the company can save significant time and money in determining what products are likely to appeal to different segments of the marketplace.

New businesses and even industries are evolving that would not exist without digital media. YouTube is a video website that lets consumers watch a broad collection of videos, anytime and from anywhere. In the U.S., Hulu has emerged as a site that allows users to watch videos from 260 content partners–anywhere and anytime. The company has partnered with several companies to advertise on their sites, including Johnson & Johnson and Best Buy.[8] Rumours persist that Hulu is coming to Canada in 2014 but nothing has been announced as of yet.

The reality, however, is that Internet markets are more similar to traditional markets than they are different. Thus, successful e-business strategies, like traditional business strategies, focus on creating products that customers need or want, not merely developing a brand name or reducing the costs associated with online transactions. Instead of changing all industries, e-business has had much more impact in certain industries where the cost of business and customer transactions has been very high. For example, investment trading is less expensive online because customers can buy and sell investments, such as stocks and mutual funds, on their own. Firms such as TD Waterhouse, the biggest online brokerage firm, have been innovators in promoting online trading. As a result, traditional brokers such as Nesbitt Burns have had to follow with online trading for their customers.

Because the Internet lowers the cost of communication, it can contribute significantly to any industry or activity that depends on the flow of digital information such as entertainment, health care, government services, education, and computer services like software development. The publishing industry is transitioning away from print newspapers, magazines, and books as more consumers purchase e-readers, like the Kobo or iPad, or read the news online. For example, *Fifty Shades of Grey* has been downloaded millions of times over the past few years. Even your textbook is available electronically. Because publishers save money on paper, ink, and shipping, many times electronic versions of books are cheaper than their paper counterparts.

Digital media can also improve communication within and between businesses. In the future, most significant gains will come from productivity improvements within businesses. Communication is a key business function, and improving the speed and clarity of communication can help businesses save time and improve employee problem-solving abilities. Digital media can be a communications backbone that helps to store knowledge, information, and records in management information systems so co-workers can access it when faced with a problem to solve. A well-designed management information system that utilizes digital technology can, therefore, help reduce confusion, improve organization and efficiency, and facilitate clear communication. Given the crucial role of communication and information in business, the long-term impact of digital media on economic growth is substantial, and it will inevitably grow over time.

Firms also need to control access to their digital communication systems to ensure worker productivity. This can be a challenge. For example, in companies across Canada and the United States, employees are surfing the Internet for as much as an hour during each workday. Many firms are trying to curb this practice by limiting employees' access to instant messaging services, streaming music, and websites with adult content.[9] "Digital communication offers a completely new dimension in connecting with others."

LO4 Show how digital media affect the marketing mix.

Digital Media and the Marketing Mix

While digital marketing shares some similarities with conventional marketing techniques, a few valuable differences stand out. First, digital media make customer communications faster and interactive. Second, digital media help companies reach new target markets more easily, affordably, and quickly than ever before. Finally, digital media help marketers utilize new resources in seeking out and communicating with customers. One of the most important benefits of digital marketing is the ability of marketers and customers to easily share information. Through websites, social networks, and other digital media, consumers can learn about everything they consume and use in their lives, ask questions, voice complaints, indicate preferences, and otherwise communicate about their needs and desires. Many marketers use e-mail, mobile phones, social networking, wikis, video sharing, podcasts, blogs, videoconferencing, and other technologies to coordinate activities and communicate with employees, customers, and suppliers. Twitter, considered both a social network and a micro blog, illustrates how these digital technologies can combine to create new communication opportunities.

Nielsen Marketing Research revealed that consumers now spend more time on social networking sites than they do on e-mail, and social network use is still growing. In Canada, 42 percent of Canadians log into social media sites daily and the number increases to 59 percent on a weekly basis.[10] Globally, researchers disagree on which country's citizens spend the most time using the social networks but Australians, British, Italians, Americans, and Canadians are considered heavy users of social media.[11] With digital media, even small businesses can reach new markets through these inexpensive communication channels. For example, FreshBooks, a Toronto-based accounting service for small companies, has expanded to reach five million users in 120 countries. FreshBooks uses social media to communicate with customers and promote its products and services. Brick-and-mortar companies like Canadian Tire and Future Shop utilize online catalogues and company websites and blogs to supplement their retail stores. Internet companies like Amazon and BlueNile, which lack physical stores, let customers post reviews of their purchases on their websites, creating company-sponsored communities.

One aspect of marketing that has not changed with digital media is the importance of achieving the right marketing mix. Product, distribution, promotion, and pricing are as important as ever for successful online marketing strategies. More than one-fourth of the world's population now uses the Internet.[12] That means it is essential for businesses large and small to use digital media effectively, not only to grab or maintain market share but also to streamline their organizations and offer customers entirely new benefits and convenience. Let's look at how businesses are using digital media to create effective marketing strategies on the Web.

Product Considerations. Like traditional marketers, digital marketers must anticipate consumer needs and preferences, tailor their products and services to meet these needs, and continually upgrade them to remain competitive. The connectivity created by digital media provide the opportunity for adding services and can enhance product benefits. Some products—such as online games, applications, and virtual worlds—are only available via digital media. Netflix offers a much wider array of movies and games than the average movie rental stores, along with a two-week free trial, quick delivery and easy returns, online video streaming of some movies, and no late fees. Netflix also prides itself on its recommendation engine, which recommends movies for users based on their previous rental history and how they rate movies they have seen. As Netflix demonstrates, the Internet can make it much easier to anticipate consumer

Amazingly, almost 60 percent of Canadians visit a social media/networking site once a week.

needs. However, fierce competition makes quality product and service offerings more important than ever.[13]

Distribution Considerations.

The Internet is a new distribution channel for making products available at the right time, at the right place, and in the right quantities. Marketers' ability to process orders electronically and increase the speed of communication via the Internet reduces inefficiencies, costs, and redundancies while increasing speed throughout the marketing channel. Shipping times and costs have become an important consideration in attracting customers, prompting many companies to offer consumers low shipping costs or next-day delivery. For example Coastal Contacts, which operates as Clearly Contacts in Canada, is successfully taking customers away from traditional optometrists and eyeglass retailers. The company, which was founded in 2000, is expected to have revenue in excess of $250 million this year.[14] Coastal Contacts is thriving as it sells contacts and glasses at a cheaper price than traditional retailers and is often considered more convenient by consumers. Rather than visit a retailer, consumers can order contacts or glasses online and have them arrive at their home within 48 hours. Coastal has also established an automatic refill program where contact lenses are shipped automatically at a predetermined time. Costco Canada is attempting to take market share away from e-marketers like Amazon by reducing delivery time and creating a "site to store" system so consumers can get a product shipped to their house or, for faster delivery, to a store. This offer has the increased benefit of getting customers into the store, where they might make add-on purchases. Walmart is trying a similar strategy in the U.S. where it is not charging consumers shipping costs if items are delivered to stores. Walmart has even tested a new distribution concept to complement store pick-ups: a drive-through window that allows customers to pick up the products they ordered through Walmart's website. Through even more sophisticated distribution systems, Walmart hopes to overtake online retailers to become the biggest online merchant.[15]

Promotion Considerations.

Perhaps one of the best ways businesses can utilize digital media is for promotion purposes—whether they are increasing brand awareness, connecting with consumers, or taking advantage of social networks or virtual worlds (discussed later) to form relationships and generate positive publicity or "buzz" about their products. Thanks to online promotion, consumers can be more informed than ever, including reading customer-generated content before making purchasing decisions. Consumer consumption patterns are radically changing, and marketers must adapt their promotional efforts to meet them. For example, more and more travellers are using the Internet to purchase flights and to compare prices when planning a trip. WestJet has gone to great lengths to make it easy for consumers to buy airline tickets online using its website, and it relies on digital marketing to promote sales and special events, and to stay connected with customers.

These effects are not limited to the Western world. In a revolutionary shift in China, where online shopping had not been widely adopted by consumers, businesses are now realizing the benefits of marketing online. One of the first adopters of Internet selling was the Chinese company Taobao, a consumer auction site that also features sections for Chinese brands and retailers. Taobao provides online promotion of retailers and products featured on its site. The majority of online sales in China take place on Taobao.[16] Consumer trends like these demonstrate that the shift to digital media promotion is well under way worldwide.

Pricing Considerations.

Price is the most flexible element of the marketing mix. Digital marketing can enhance the value of products by providing extra benefits such as service, information, and convenience. Through digital media, discounts and other promotions can be quickly communicated. As consumers have become better informed about their options, the demand for low-priced products has grown, leading to the creation of deal sites where consumers can directly compare prices. Expedia, for instance, provides consumers with a wealth of travel

---

ENTREPRENEURSHIP IN ACTION | Mobovivo Allows Consumers Legal Access to TV and Movies on Mobile Devices

Trevor Doerksen

Business: Mobovivo

Founded: 1999

Success: Trevor Doerksen's company offered legal downloads of TV shows for iPods faster than Apple.

Mobovivo is a Canadian-based company that enables video content producers (think TV and movies) to distribute their shows on mobile devices. The company, founded by Trevor Doerksen, managed to be the first

legal provider of TV shows to the iPod in 2006, beating even Apple. The company has grown using strategic partnerships with content providers such as the BBC Worldwide and Cinram. The partnership with the BBC allows Mobovivo to distribute such hit shows as *The Tudors*, while its alliance with Cinram, a company which takes content and places it on DVDs and Blu-Ray discs for production studios, will have Mobovivo enable all its discs for mobile devices such as smartphones and tablets.[17]

information about everything from flights to hotels that lets them compare benefits and prices. Many marketers offer buying incentives like online coupons or free samples to generate consumer demand for their products.

Social Networking

A **social network** is "a web-based meeting place for friends, family, co-workers and peers that lets users create a profile and connect with other users for purposes that range from getting acquainted, to keeping in touch, to building a work related network."[18] Social networks are a valued part of marketing because they are changing the way consumers communicate with each other and with firms. Sites such as Facebook, Myspace, Twitter, LinkedIn, Tumblr and Pinterest have emerged as opportunities for marketers to build communities, provide product information, and learn about consumer needs. By the time you read this, it is possible there will be new social network sites that continue to advance digital communication and opportunities for marketers.

You might be surprised to know that social networks have existed in some form or other for 40 years. The precursors of today's social networks began in the 1970s as online bulletin boards that allowed users with common interests to interact with one another. The first modern social network was Six Degrees.com, launched in 1997. This system permitted users to create a profile and connect with friends—the core attributes of today's networks.[19] Although Six Degrees eventually shut down for lack of interest, the seed of networking had been planted.[20] Other social networks followed, with each new generation becoming increasingly sophisticated. Today's sites offer a multitude of consumer benefits, including the ability to download music, games, and applications; upload photos and videos; join groups; find and chat with friends; comment on friends' posts; and post and update status messages. Table 13.1 lists some popular social networks in different countries.

As the number of social network users increases, interactive marketers are finding opportunities to reach out to consumers in new target markets. MyYearBook.com is a social networking site that offers teenagers a forum in which to write about particular subjects important to them, including sensitive topics facing today's younger generation. Its popularity with teenagers is rising; the site's traffic has increased 36 percent annually, with most users coming from North America. For advertisers, the site is an opportunity to connect with teens and young adults, a demographic that is difficult to reach with traditional marketing. Advertisers from Nikon and Paramount Pictures have both made deals to advertise

> "Social networks are a valued part of marketing because they are changing the way consumers communicate with each other and with firms."

table 13.1 Popular Social Networking Sites in Different Countries

South Korea	Cyworld
Netherlands	Hyves
Japan	Mixi
Brazil	Orkut
China	QZone
France	SkyRock
Germany	StudiVZ
Spain	Tuenti
Russia	Vkontakte
United Kingdom	Bebo
United States	Facebook

SOURCE: "Nine Extremely Successful Non-English Social Networking Sites," Pingdom, September 9, 2009, http://royal.pingdom.com/2009/09/09/nine-extremely-successful-non-english-social-networking-sites/ (accessed March 25, 2010); Sorav Jain, "40 Most Popular Social Networking Sites of the World," Social Media Today, http://socialmediatoday.com/index.php?q=soravjain/195917/40-most-popular-social-networking-sites-world (accessed January 17, 2011).

through MyYearBook.com.[21] We'll have more to say about how marketers utilize social networks later in this chapter.

An important question relates to how social media sites are adding value to the economy. Marketers at companies like BlackBerry and Ford Canada, for instance, are using social media to promote products and build consumer relationships. Most corporations are supporting Facebook pages and Yammer accounts for employees to communicate across departments and divisions. Professionals such as professors, doctors, and engineers also share ideas on a regular basis. Even staffing organizations use social media, bypassing traditional e-mail and telephone channels. While billions of dollars in investments are being funnelled into social media, it may be too early to assess the exact economic contribution of social media to the entire economy.[22]

LO5 Define social networking and illustrate how businesses can use different types of social networking media.

Types of Consumer-Generated Marketing and Digital Media

While digital marketing has generated exciting opportunities for companies to interact with their customers, digital media are also more consumer-driven than traditional

Social network a Web-based meeting place for friends, family, co-workers, and peers that lets users create a profile and connect with other users for a wide range of purposes

media. Internet users are creating and reading consumer-generated content as never before and are having a profound effect on marketing in the process.

Two factors have sparked the rise of consumer-generated information:

1. The increased tendency of consumers to publish their own thoughts, opinions, reviews, and product discussions through blogs or digital media.

2. Consumers' tendencies to trust other consumers over corporations. Consumers often rely on the recommendations of friends, family, and fellow consumers when making purchasing decisions.

Marketers who know where online users are likely to express their thoughts and opinions can use these forums to interact with them, address problems, and promote their companies. Types of digital media in which Internet users are likely to participate include blogs, wikis, video sharing sites, podcasts, social networking sites, virtual reality sites, and mobile applications. Let's look a little more closely at each.

Blogs and Wikis

Today's marketers must recognize that the impact of consumer-generated material like blogs and wikis and their significance to online consumers have increased a great deal. **Blogs** (short for Web logs) are Web-based journals in which writers can editorialize and interact with other Internet users. Two-thirds of Internet users read blogs, and more than half of bloggers say they blog about topics and brands about which they feel strongly.[23] The blogging phenomenon is not limited to North America. In South Korea, for example, more than two-thirds of the online population creates blogs or similar material.[24]

> **Blog** a Web-based journal in which a writer can editorialize and interact with other Internet users

Blogs give consumers power, sometimes more than companies would like. Bloggers can post whatever they like about a company or its products, whether their opinions are positive or negative, true or false. When a Korean Dunkin' Donuts worker created a blog alleging that a company factory had unsanitary conditions, the company forced him to delete the blog. However, readers had already created copies of it and spread it across the Internet after the original's removal.[26] In other cases, a positive review of a product or service posted on a popular blog can result in large increases in sales. Thus, blogs can represent a potent threat or opportunity to marketers.

Rather than trying to eliminate blogs that cast their companies in a negative light, some firms are using their own blogs, or employee blogs, to answer consumer concerns or defend their corporate reputations. For example, when Electronic Arts's recently launched SimCity game failed to work properly the company used blogs to respond to consumer complaints and questions. Electronic Arts also used blogs to highlight some of the company's news and promotions.[27] As blogging changes the face of media, smart companies are using it to build enthusiasm for their products and create relationships with consumers. As noted in Chapter 12, many CEOs, such as Jim Estill, CEO of Symex Canada, are using blogs to reach out and connect with consumers and provide information that customers find relevant and interesting. **Wikis** are websites where users can add to or edit the content of posted articles. One of the best known is Wikipedia, an online encyclopedia with over 17 million entries in over 250 languages on nearly every subject imaginable (*Encyclopedia Britannica* only has 120,000 entries).[28] Wikipedia is one of the 10 most popular sites on the Web, and because much of its content can be edited by anyone, it is easy for online consumers to add detail and supporting evidence and to correct inaccuracies in content. Wikipedia used to be completely open to editing, but in order to stop vandalism, the site had to make some topics off-limits that are now editable only by a small group of experts.

> **Wiki** software that creates an interface that enables users to add or edit the content of some types of websites

Like all digital media, wikis have advantages and disadvantages for companies. Wikis about controversial companies like Walmart and Nike often contain negative publicity, such as about workers' rights violations. However, monitoring relevant wikis can provide companies with a better idea of how consumers feel about the company or brand. Some companies have also begun to use wikis as internal tools for teams working on projects that require a great deal of documentation.[29] There is too much at stake financially for marketers to ignore wikis and blogs. Despite this fact, less than one-fifth of *Fortune* 500 companies have a blog.[30] Marketers who want to form better customer relationships and promote their company's products must not underestimate the power of these two media outlets.

Video Sharing

Video sharing sites allow virtually anybody to upload videos, from professional marketers at *Fortune* 500 corporations to the average Internet user. Some of the most popular video sharing sites include YouTube, Video, Yahoo.com, Metacafe.com, and Hulu. Video sharing sites give companies the opportunity to upload ads and informational videos about their products. YouTube use in Canada and

DID YOU KNOW?
Searching is the most popular online activity, while social networking and blogging are fourth.[25]

globally is significant and YouTube has recently released the following statistics about traffic to its site:

- 1 billion unique users visit the site monthly
- 100 hours of video are uploaded to YouTube every minute.
- YouTube is localized in 56 countries and across 61 languages
- Over 6 billion hours of video are watched each month on YouTube.[31]

Video sharing sites are increasingly being used as a low-cost promotional method to educate and entertain potential consumers. Almost all major Canadian companies such as TELUS and Rogers Communications make use of YouTube, and many small organizations are using the video sharing site as well. For example, many schools—such as Mount Saint Vincent University with 4,500 students—are using YouTube to create promotional videos about student experiences and to showcase campus events on the Internet. Ontario-based Roger Neilson's Hockey Camp is using YouTube to advertise annual hockey camps and highlight some of the instruction that occurs in its programs. Global pop sensation Justin Bieber actually owes a lot of his fame and fortune to YouTube and other social media sites. After finishing second in a local singing contest, Bieber started posting videos on both YouTube and Myspace. This eventually led to his being noticed by his first music contact.

A few videos become viral at any given time, and although many of these gain popularity because they are unusual in some way, others reach viral status because people find them entertaining. **Viral marketing** occurs when a message gets sent from person to person to person. It can be an extremely effective tool for marketers—particularly on the Internet, where one click can send a message to dozens or hundreds of people simultaneously. However, viral marketing often requires marketers to develop an offbeat sense of humour and creativity in order to catch the viewer's attention—something with which some marketers may not be comfortable. For instance, April Fool's Day has become a day when Canadian companies try to generate some added attention to their company and products by offering some offbeat ads and often fake products. Recently, WestJet, Lululemon, and Boston Pizza all offered gag products on April Fool's Day in Canada. WestJet used April Fool's Day to promote a "new policy" where any animal including pet bears are allowed on airplanes; Lululemon introduced the mock product Lululeather including Cowabunga leather yoga pants; and Boston Pizza announced that it was banning all buns from the store and creating new products with pizza dough such as pizza salad, pizza beer, and pizza cake. Such campaigns can be successful as WestJet's gag "Child-Free Cabins" promotion video had 600,000

Justin Bieber's singing career actually started on YouTube with videos he created himself. Bieber's videos were eventually discovered and he has gone on to sing numerous number one hits and star in his own movie.

hits on YouTube and boosted the company's rank in search engines. Other times, when consumers do not know they are being tricked, the gag can backfire. While most of Lululemon's loyal followers recognized leather yoga pants were an April Fool's Day prank, the company did such a good job making the announcements that some consumers thought the product was in fact real and expressed displeasure with the company on its website.[32] Companies such as IBM have created an entire video series to generate publicity for the company. IBM's six videos, called "The Art of the Sale," present three attributes of the company's mainframe computer in a humorous format reminiscent of episodes of *The Office*. Though some wrote off the videos as a forced attempt at humorous marketing, they received hundreds of thousands of hits on YouTube.[33]

Businesses have also begun to utilize consumer-generated video content, saving money they would have spent on hiring advertising firms to develop professional advertising campaigns. For example, many universities and colleges throughout Canada are creating their own content with students and staff, and running video contests to promote their school or a particular field of academic study. The Ontario government has recently started using a similar

Viral marketing a marketing tool that uses the Internet, particularly social networking and video sharing sites, to spread a message and create brand awareness

strategy asking people to create their own videos stressing job safety in the "It's Your Job" video contest.[34] Perhaps the most successful campaign in recent years is Frito Lay's "Crash the Super Bowl" contest, where the company invites customers to create ads which may be selected for broadcast during the football game. The most recent winner created an ad featuring a grandmother using a child's Jolly Jumper to slingshot a baby to steal a bag of Doritos. The advertisement was widely considered to be the best commercial played during the Super Bowl and created significant attention from social and mainstream media.[35] Marketers believe consumer videos appear more authentic and create enthusiasm for the product among consumer participants.

Google is so confident that video sharing sites will revolutionize online marketing that it purchased YouTube for $1.65 billion in 2006.[36] If Google is correct in its predictions, then online videos clips—both corporate-sponsored and consumer-generated—are likely to revolutionize the marketing industry.

Photo Sharing

Photo sharing sites allow users to upload and share their photos and short videos with the world. Well-known photo sharing sites include Instagram, SmugMug, Webshots, Photobucket, and Flickr. Flickr is owned by Yahoo and

Consider the Following: Going Viral

As social media increases in importance more and more companies are relying on the public to create a buzz for their products and/or their online promotions. Companies are often hoping that their online advertisements will "go viral," meaning that the public will become so interested in an ad campaign or product that they will share it within their own online social networks, thus spreading the company's brand, products, or advertisement to thousands if not millions of computers. As discussed in Chapter 12, both Bauer's "Own the Moment" and Nike's "Hockey is Ours" campaigns went viral, as the ads connected with Canadians during the NHL lockout. Other Canadian examples include Mike Evans and Nick de Pencier's healthy living YouTube video which has been seen by over two million North Americans and shared throughout the globe. Old Spice had a viral hit on its hands with the "Old Spice Guy" advertisements. The ads, which were originally intended only for TV use, resonated with viewers and became a YouTube sensation. Old Spice supported the campaign by releasing hundreds of videos on YouTube and has the actor in the commercials answering questions using the popular video sharing network and Twitter. The campaign has spread like wildfire on the Internet as consumers are using Facebook, Twitter, and other social media sites to promote the advertisements to their networks. TeamBuy, a Toronto-based company, is relying on social media and going viral as a business model. The company founded by Chris Nyguen and Lee Liu is an online social buying website where people sign up to receive e-mails promoting "deals of the day." Interested consumers agree to purchase the product using their credit card but no sales occur until a minimum number of buyers are reached and the deal is unlocked. If the minimum number of buyers is not reached then the deal is withdrawn. Since customers want the deal, they

usually share it with their social networks using Facebook, Twitter, and YouTube. Participating companies like the concept as they acquire customers at low cost and increase the number of people who know about their company. Consumers like the idea as they get to purchase products at substantial savings. TeamBuy's biggest challenge may not be getting customers and companies to participate, but dealing with competitors including the giant in the online social buying world—Groupon Inc.—which is constantly expanding.[37]

DISCUSSION QUESTIONS

1. Do you think companies' sales benefit from viral ads such as the ones discussed above and throughout this chapter? Why or why not?

2. Do you think advertising with a strong emotional appeal is effective?

3. Given that firms are intentionally trying to generate viral campaigns such as creating mock ads on April Fool's Day, do you think consumers will eventually grow tired of such campaigns?

4. Given the increasing number of "deal of the day" coupon sites, do you think they will lose their effectiveness as an advertising tool?

5. Companies who participate in "deal of the day" sites often have to perform services or offer products well below costs. For example, restaurants which offer coupons for $100 worth of food for $50 normally only receive $25 after paying all the fees to the coupon site. Do you think this is a worthwhile investment for the restaurant? Why or why not?

was the most popular photo sharing site on the Internet. A Flickr user can upload images, edit them, classify the images, create photo albums, and share photos with friends without having to e-mail bulky image files or send photos through the mail. Flickr is still popular and the site experiences thousands of new image uploads every minute. Most users have free accounts that allow them to upload two videos and 100 MB of photos per month, but for around $25 a year, users can open an unlimited Pro account.[38] Photo sharing represents an opportunity for companies to market themselves visually by displaying snapshots of company events, company staff, and/or company products. Companies can direct viewers to their photostreams (their sets of photographs) by marking their pictures with the appropriate keywords, or tags.[39] Tags are essential for marketing on Flickr as they help direct traffic to the corporate photostreams.

Many businesses with pictures on Flickr have a link connecting their Flickr photostreams to their corporate websites.[40] Suncor Energy, for example, a Canadian oil and gas company, uses Flickr to showcase its work and important events. One of Flickr's rivals is Picasa Web Albums, a Google photo sharing site that developed out of Google's photo-editing program Picasa. The program has grown rapidly and is growing in popularity, as it provides more features than Flickr and other major photo sharing websites. Picasa Web Albums is free, and generates revenues through ads shown on the site. If users want to use more than 1 GB of storage space, they can rent additional space up to 16 TB.

Flickr has recently been surpassed in popularity by two new photo sharing sites that have a much stronger social networking element to them. Pinterest (see below) is actually now the third-largest social media site in the world. Instagram, which has 100 million monthly users, allows people to post photos onto their site using their smartphones as the primary camera and to share the photos using other social networking sites. Instagram is especially popular among people under the age of 24 and has very few users older than 35. Many younger celebrities frequently use Instagram to post pictures of their daily routine, including Canadian star Justin Bieber. Businesses have been using Instagram to post pictures of their products to get customer feedback or to tell a story about their brand. Pinterest is described below and the focus is not just on posting business or personal pictures, but on building Pinboards with similar content. Pinterest's users tend to be more female and cover a much broader demographic compared to Instagram. Pinterest has less peer-to-peer communication compared to Instagram but offers businesses more peer-to-social network communication.

As one Web marketer puts it, companies that use photo sharing "add a personal touch to their businesses."[41] Although it is too early to gauge the effects of marketing through photo sharing sites, more and more marketers will likely use the sites as an inexpensive way to reach their audience.

> "Podcasting offers the benefit of convenience, **giving users the ability to listen to or view content when and where they choose.**"

Podcasting

Podcasts are audio or video files that can be downloaded from the Internet via a subscription that automatically delivers new content to listening devices or personal computers. Podcasting offers the benefit of convenience, giving users the ability to listen to or view content when and where they choose.

Podcasting is rapidly gaining in popularity. Dozens of online programs, such as Apple's iPodderX and Podcast Studio or Android's dPod, offer podcasting services. Other companies, such as Yodio, combine podcasting with photos to create customized online greeting card–style messages. It is estimated that by 2013, more than 37 million North American consumers will be downloading podcasts every month. Most current podcast users are between 18 and 29 years of age, making podcasts a good marketing tool for reaching this demographic.[43]

As podcasting continues to catch on, radio stations and television networks like CBC Radio, NPR, MSNBC, and PBS are creating podcasts of their shows to profit from this growing trend. Many companies hope to use podcasts to create brand awareness, promote their products, and encourage customer loyalty.

Social Networks

It is estimated that two-thirds of consumers in the United States have visited social networks or blogs.[44] One in three South Korean and one in five Japanese Internet users participate in social networks.[45] As social networks evolve, both marketers and the owners of social networking sites are realizing the opportunities such networks offer—an influx of advertising dollars for site owners and a large reach for the advertiser. As a result, marketers have begun investigating and experimenting with promotion on social networks. Some of the most prominent sites are Facebook, LinkedIn, Twitter, Myspace, Pinterest, and Tumblr.

Myspace. Myspace could be classified as the first social networking site and during its prominence was one of the most visited sites in North America. Myspace offers users the chance to create a profile and connect with other Myspace members across the world. Users can invite people to be their friends, watch videos, listen to and promote music, instant message their friends, write on various

> **Podcast** an audio or video file that can be downloaded from the Internet with a subscription that automatically delivers new content to listening devices or personal computers

As discussed in Chapter 12, Pinterest is the fastest-growing, and third-largest, social media website in North America. In a very short time, the company has overtaken Flickr as the number one photo sharing site by combining photo sharing with elements of social media.

Pinterest allows users to manage pictures and videos named Pins to an online bulletin board known as a Pinboard. Themed Pinboards allow users to easily manage Pins, to share their content and to search Pins posted by other users. Users can also Pin content they find on the Internet and easily upload it to their Pinboard. Pinboard users take great pride in creating attractive Pinboards to share.

According to experts, Pinterest's success can be attributed to many subtle differences compared to traditional photo sharing sites. Pinterest is, first and foremost, free and its focus is on social networking. The site refers to users as friends and lets you know when friends are logged on to Twitter and Facebook. Additionally, the company allows you to follow others, comment on their Pinboard, and quickly load embedded photos to an attractive website. These subtle differences stand out when compared to Flickr, the previous leader in the online photo sharing industry. Flickr, while allowing for some free sharing of photos, charges for a premium account, does not alert you when contacts are online, and, while having a social network element, has stayed fairly rigid in its business model. Charlotte Henry, an online journalist, says Pinterest has clearly won the battle for online photo sharing. "In terms of advertising and building an online presence the choice is simple. The ability to categorise images, the deep social interaction, not to mention the attractive interface, make Pinterest the clear winner. You can really build a brand image on Pinterest, and display your products. Flickr remains important to photographers, but has been overtaken by Pinterest by almost every other kind of user."[42]

DISCUSSION QUESTIONS

1. Why do you think Pinterest has replaced Flickr as the number one photo sharing site?

2. Do you think Flickr charging for a premium account has hindered its ability to grow?

3. Flickr has recently added some additional social networking elements to its website. Do you think it will be able to re-establish itself as the leader in photo sharing?

4. Given what you have learned about Pinterest, Flickr, and Instagram, which photo sharing site would you recommend for a company to use if it were trying to appeal to young women between the ages of 25 and 40 with a new product? Why?

topics (called forums), network with friends and colleagues, and play games. Since 2006, Myspace has been accessible in a variety of languages, including Swedish, Chinese, Spanish, Portuguese, and Turkish. Alternate versions also exist depending on the locality.[46]

Myspace, while being one of the first social network sites, could not maintain its first-mover advantage in the face of competition from the likes of Facebook and Twitter. Additional factors influencing Myspace's decline have been attributed to its practice of pushing content onto users and a lack of features that allow members to communicate with one another.

Facebook. In April 2008, the social networking site Facebook surpassed Myspace in its number of members, becoming the most popular social networking site in the world.[47] It is estimated that nearly one-third of Internet users have visited the site.[48] Facebook users create profiles, which they can make public or private, and then search the network for people with whom to connect. Users often must be a "friend" of the person whose profile they are trying to view before they can see that user's personal information. Facebook appeals to a broad demographic, attracting parents and grandparents as well as teens and college students.[49] In fact, the fastest-growing group on Facebook is women 55 and over.[50] For this reason, many marketers are turning to Facebook to market products, interact with consumers, and gain publicity. It is possible for a consumer to become a "fan" of a major company like Starbucks by clicking on the "Like" icon on the coffee retailer's Facebook page. Companies are also using Facebook to generate awareness about themselves and encourage repeat visits. Many companies such as RBC and CBC have online contests to keep people coming back to their social media sites. CBC, for example, held a national

> "Many marketers are turning to Facebook to market products, interact with consumers, and gain publicity."

contest that was heavily promoted on social media sites including Facebook to come up with a new theme song for *Hockey Night in Canada*.[51] Facebook, like other social networking sites, is also allowing companies to sell goods directly to users; this is known as F-commerce when talking purely about Facebook and as social commerce when discussing this new emerging trend.

Social networking sites are also useful for small businesses. Vines restaurant in Halifax, Nova Scotia, uses interactive marketing on a social networking outlet to drum up more business. The company provides users with coupons, special seating, and updates on new menu items on Facebook and other social media sites.[52] Some small businesses are actually abandoning traditional websites and just maintain a Facebook page.

Other companies that have utilized relationship marketing to help consumers feel more connected to their products are Pepsi and Walt Disney Co. The Pepsi Refresh Project (PRP) invites consumers to suggest local charities that are making a positive impact. Consumers vote for their favourites, and Pepsi donates money to the winning causes. The company utilized Facebook, Twitter, and blogging to spread the word about PRP.[55] The Walt Disney Co. has created many different Facebook pages, which have succeeded in generating over 100 million Facebook fans. Some of its success is attributed to the Disney Pages promotion tab on its main Disney Facebook page. The tab allows users to access promotional content without having to navigate away from Facebook. In many ways, Facebook is becoming an e-commerce platform whereby companies can sell products through the site. DigiSynd, Disney's social media agency, was able to use a platform on Facebook called Disney Tickets Together that allowed fans to purchase tickets for movies like *Toy Story 3*. These new opportunities for businesses demonstrate the evolution of Facebook into a marketing destination.[56]

LinkedIn. LinkedIn is a social networking site geared toward professionals from all over the world. With 120 million professional members, including executives from all the *Fortune* 500 companies, it is the fourth-largest social networking site and logs several million visitors a month.[57] A LinkedIn profile resembles a résumé. It contains information about past and current job experiences, qualifications, goals, and educational background. Like all social networking sites, it lets users locate and connect with other members and join groups, which are often professional

organizations. LinkedIn facilitates job searches and allows companies to search the network for potential employees with the necessary skills. Scotiabank, Delta Hotels, Microsoft, Target, eBay, and Netflix have all used the LinkedIn network to recruit new employees.[58] Employees are also using LinkedIn to search for potential employers. Approximately 28 percent of college students have indicated that they plan to use LinkedIn to search for employment opportunities.[59] Although a professional networking site like LinkedIn seems more like a recruiting site than a marketing tool, companies do use it to familiarize users with their business. In addition to listing job openings, most company LinkedIn profiles also offer a link to the company website, some background on the business, links to news updates on company activities and products, and stock information. Procter & Gamble has a LinkedIn page that allows users to locate professionals, research careers, and get updates about the company. LinkedIn Groups—a feature on the site that highlights particular industries—is a useful tool for companies that want to describe their expertise and activities. Organizations can also build a group on LinkedIn based around their company or industry for no charge.[60] Smart marketers can use LinkedIn to reach professionals not only for recruiting purposes, but also to spread information about and interest in the company.

Twitter. Twitter is a hybrid of a social networking site and a micro-blogging site that asks users one simple question: "What are you doing?" Members can post answers of up to 140 characters, which are then available for their registered "followers" to read. It sounds simple enough, but Twitter's effect on digital media has been immense. The site quickly progressed from a novelty to a social networking staple, attracting millions of viewers each month.[62] About 11 percent of Internet users have used a micro-blogging site like Twitter.[63] The thrill of Twitter is that users get to tell the world about their daily lives in short messages, known as "tweets." These tweets can be mundane, such as "I'm eating a sandwich," to interesting. Prime Minister Stephen Harper uses Twitter to make various announcements and the newly elected leader of the federal Liberal Party, Justin Trudeau, is a frequent Twitter user. Trudeau, unlike Harper, will often respond to questions on Twitter and is more engaged with the social media site. Halfway across the world, Russian president Dmitry Medvedev actually had to rebuke one of his regional governors for tweeting during a government session on educational policy.[64] Twitter has quickly transformed from novelty to serious marketing tool, with the company

By this point in your reading, it should be clear that social media monitoring has become quite important for businesses. Not only do companies want to share information on social media sites, but they want to learn what you are saying about their organizations. Social media dashboards (discussed below) are becoming increasingly common tools to monitor what people are saying about a company on the Internet. Still, other tools exist. For example, Google Alerts notifies a business if its name comes up anywhere online. Businesses such as New Brunswick-based Radian6 identify trends in online communities and assist businesses in dealing with complaints. Other software tools, such as KISSmetrics, have been developed to help businesses identify the behaviour of Web users. Users of KISSmetrics can not only identify who is visiting their site but their

actions as well. This information can be used to tailor offerings and improve sales. Since the company's inception it has tracked the Web use of 4.5 billion people and their 36 billion interactions.[61]

DISCUSSION QUESTIONS

1. Do you think organizations should be able to track who visits their websites and their online behaviour?

2. Do you think it is a worthwhile investment for businesses to monitor and respond to social media discussions about their companies? Why or why not?

announcing plans to generate revenue through sponsored tweets and working to make the service more user-friendly.[65] Although 140 characters may not seem like enough for companies to send an effective message, some have become experts at using Twitter in their marketing strategies. Starbucks Canada has used Twitter in marketing campaigns to promote new store openings, offer coupons, and respond to questions. Twitter and social networks were heavily used by Starbucks when they released their new Blond Roast which was aimed primarily at Canadians.[66] On a small scale many local restaurants have turned to Twitter to share nightly specials, receive customer feedback, and book reservations. Restaurants such as Ryan Duffy's in Halifax use the social media site to promote specials and solicit consumer response.

Like other social networking tools, Twitter is also being used to build customer relationships. Media experts almost universally agree that the most effective use of Twitter involves creating conversation, not just pushing information onto followers. As discussed above, Porter Airlines is a service business that effectively uses Twitter to communicate with followers. Finally, companies are using Twitter to gain a competitive advantage. Microsoft's search engine Bing developed a partnership with Twitter in which Bing sorts the millions of tweets by relevance and the popularity of the person tweeting. By doing a Bing-Twitter search, Twitter fans can get the most important tweets in real time.[67] Firms also have a chance to utilize promoted tweets, promoted accounts, and promoted trends offered on the site. Marketers can pay Twitter to highlight advertisements or company brands to a wider array of users while they search for specific terms or topics.[68] The race is on among companies that want to use Twitter to gain a competitive edge.

Social Media Dashboards

Given the popularity of social networking/media sites, businesses, especially larger businesses, often attempt to maintain an active presence on all the sites. Posting and then managing responses to numerous social networking sites can be time consuming and businesses often simultaneously monitor numerous websites. A recent emerging solution has been social media dashboards, which enable companies to submit information to a central location and then software posts the information onto various social media sites. For example, RBC could enter information about a new promotion into a social media dashboard and the dashboard would then distribute the information to RBC's various social networks such as Facebook, Twitter, Tumblr, and YouTube. The dashboard could then monitor the consumer feedback about the posting and summarize the information for RBC. As previously mentioned in the text, the most common social media dashboard is HootSuite, which is based in British Columbia. HootSuite is popular as it allows companies to post and manage information to multiple sites including Twitter, Facebook, LinkedIn, Google+, Foursquare, Myspace, WordPress, Mixi, Instagram, MailChimp, Reddit, Storify, Tumblr, Vimeo, and YouTube. HootSuite's major competitor, TweetDeck, only allows for companies to work with Twitter and Facebook.[69]

Virtual Worlds

Games and programs allowing viewers to develop avatars that exist in an online virtual world have exploded in popularity in the 21st century. Second Life is a social network with a twist. It is a virtual, three-dimensional game world created by users that features its own economy, its own lands, and residents of every shape and size. Internet users who participate in Second Life choose a fictional persona, called an *avatar*, to communicate with one another, purchase goods with virtual Linden dollars (convertible to real dollars at a rate of around 250 Linden dollars per $1), and even own virtual businesses. For entertainment purposes, residents can shop, attend concerts, or travel to virtual environments—all while spending real money. Farmville provides a similar virtual world experience, except it is limited to life on a farm.

Second Life has the most potential for marketers, given that avatars can purchase property, goods, and services. While the businesses in Second Life are virtual ones, real-world marketers and organizations have been eager to capitalize on the site's popularity. Second Life allows businesses to reach consumers in ways that are creative and fun. For instance, to connect with consumers and build brand loyalty, car companies like Toyota and General Motors began selling virtual cars to Second Life residents.[70] Other businesses are looking toward Second Life to familiarize consumers with their products and services. For instance, large corporations like Best Buy and H&R Block offer support services on Second Life.

Second Life has become so popular that even professors are using it as a way to connect with their students. Ulrike Schultz is a business professor at Southern Methodist University. Students can choose to attend her real-world class, the virtual one, or both. Schultz sees virtual worlds as the next step in communications and feels that they are a great way to connect with young people who are accustomed to being wired for most of their waking hours.[71] Schultz sees opportunities for businesses in virtual environments, not only to promote and sell products, but also to engage in virtual teamwork between physically distant employees and in role-playing exercises. Prestigious universities like the University of Texas, Harvard Law School, Bowling Green State University, and the University of California at Davis all have virtual classrooms in Second Life.

Companies are also using Second Life to encourage residents to participate in company activities. CNN created a virtual news hub and began encouraging residents to submit stories that occur in this virtual world.[72] Such firms are not only creating brand loyalty by connecting with Second Life residents, but are also using consumer knowledge and money to earn virtual and real-world profits. Although the presence of real-world companies in virtual worlds is still in the experimental stages, virtual worlds like Second Life offer a novel way for marketers to interact with consumers.

Mobile Marketing

Digital marketing is becoming increasingly sophisticated as consumers are beginning to utilize mobile devices like smartphones as a highly functional communication

> ### "New businesses and even industries are evolving that would not exist without digital media."

The use of mobile marketing is growing as more and more people are replacing their desktop with a mobile device.

method. The iPhone and BlackBerry have changed the way consumers communicate, and a growing number of travellers are using their smartphones to find online maps, travel guides, and taxis. In industries such as hotels, airlines, and car rental agencies, mobile phones have become a primary method for booking reservations and communicating about services. They can act as airline boarding passes, GPS devices, and even hotel room keys. Travel companies are collecting personal information so they can send consumers relevant updates about travel opportunities. FARELOGIX, a travel software company, is working with a number of airlines to introduce features that allow airlines to sell services such as priority boarding. While airlines already make these services available on their websites, they also want to communicate with travellers who experience unexpected changes on their trips. Other marketing uses of mobile phones include sending shoppers timely messages related to discounts and shopping opportunities.[73]

Marketing over mobile devices has been made possible largely by mobile applications or apps—programs that can be loaded onto certain mobile devices to allow users to perform a variety of functions, from playing games to comparing product prices from different stores. The latter is becoming particularly useful for consumers. The smartphone's ability to find retailers and entertainment and to organize an itinerary is changing the nature of consumer and business relationships. Large hotel chains, such as Delta Hotels, are increasingly using iPhone apps that allow guests to check in early, order room service so food is waiting for them when they arrive, and even specify bed and pillow types.

The most important feature of apps is the convenience and cost savings they offer the consumer. To remain competitive, companies are beginning to use mobile marketing to offer additional customer incentives, with some success. Jiffy Lube offered coupons for one of its franchises over mobile devices. The company estimated that 50 percent of the new customers who came to the franchise did so as a result of its mobile marketing.[74] Another application that marketers are finding useful is the QR scanning app. You might have noticed that black-and-white squares have begun appearing on magazines, posters, storefront displays, and more. These are QR codes, and they contain messages not visible to the naked eye. To read these messages, smartphone users must download the QR scanning application. When they come across a QR code, they simply open their smartphone and scan the black-and-white square. The QR scanning app will recognize the code and open up the link, video, or image on the phone's screen. Marketers are using QR codes to market their companies and offer consumer discounts. As more people adopt smartphones, these apps are likely to add a whole new layer to digital marketing.[75]

Using Digital Media to Reach Consumers

We've seen that customer-generated communications and digital media connect consumers. These connections let consumers share information and experiences without company interference so they get more of the "real story" on a product or company feature. In many ways, these media take some of the professional marketer's power to control and dispense information and place it in the hands of the consumer.

However, this shift does not have to spell doom for marketers, who can choose to utilize the power of the consumer and Internet technology to their advantage. While consumers use digital media to access more product information, marketers can use the same sites to get better and more targeted information about the consumer—often more than they could gather through traditional marketing venues. Marketers increasingly use consumer-generated content to aid their own marketing efforts, even going so far as to incorporate Internet bloggers in their publicity

GOING GREEN | Nestlé Experiences the Dark Side of Social Media

Social media can have an ugly side, as Nestlé found out firsthand after an attack launched by environmental organization Greenpeace. It started after Greenpeace discovered that Nestlé was sourcing a portion of its palm oil (an ingredient used in its chocolate bars) nonsustainably. The problem from Greenpeace's perspective is that many palm oil producers destroy rain forests in order to grow the plants from which the oil is harvested; it is argued that this action increases global warming and threatens orangutan populations.

Greenpeace began its attack by releasing a report, protesting outside Nestlé's headquarters, and launching a video on YouTube. Greenpeace altered Nestlé's Kit Kat logo to read Killer. Although Nestlé forced Greenpeace to pull the video, thousands of protesters had already shared it via their Facebook and Twitter accounts. The commentary on Nestlé's Facebook page and Twitter feed was scathing. Worse yet, the news had gone viral, making it nearly impossible for Nestlé to contain.

Nestlé responded by severing ties with the company in question and promised to do a thorough audit of all third-party suppliers. It made a commitment to source 50 percent of sustainable palm oil by 2011 and 100 percent by 2015. Nestlé also partnered with The Forest Trust to create responsible sourcing guidelines. Despite its response, Nestlé continued to get hammered in the press for its initial handling of protesters.

As this situation demonstrates, the relative newness of social media has left many companies with their guard down. In the future, Nestlé and other businesses should consider using social media not as a way to quench negative publicity, but as a method to address consumer concerns.[76]

DISCUSSION QUESTIONS

1. Do you think consumers of Nestlé's Kit Kat bar would not buy the product if they knew about the palm oil source?

2. Did Nestlé handle the protests appropriately?

3. What should Nestlé do in the future to avoid negative social media publicity?

campaigns. Finally, marketers are using the Internet to track the success of their online marketing campaigns, creating an entirely new way of gathering marketing research.

The challenge for digital media marketers is to constantly adapt to new technologies and changing consumer patterns. Unfortunately, the attrition rate for digital media channels is very high, with some dying off each year as new ones emerge. Social networks are no exception: the earliest ones, like Six Degrees, disappeared when they failed to catch on with the general public, and Friendster, though still active, has been far surpassed by newer networks. As time passes, digital media are becoming more sophisticated so as to reach consumers in more effective ways. Those that are not able to adapt and change eventually fail.

Mastering digital media presents a daunting task for businesses, particularly those used to more traditional means of marketing. For this reason, it is essential that marketers focus on the changing social behaviours of consumers, the ways in which they gather and use information, and the way the Internet is enabling them to get involved in the marketing process.

Charlene Li and Josh Bernoff of Forrester Research, a technology and market research company, emphasize the need for marketers to understand these changing relationships in the online media world. By grouping consumers into different segments based on how they utilize digital media, marketers can gain a better understanding of the online market and how best to proceed.[77] Table 13.2 shows six ways to group consumers based on their Internet activity (or lack thereof). The categories are not mutually exclusive; online consumers can participate in more than one at a time.

Creators are consumers who create their own media outlets, such as blogs, podcasts, consumer-generated videos, and wikis.[78] Consumer-generated media are increasingly important to online marketers as a conduit for addressing consumers directly. The second category, *critics,* consists of people who comment on blogs or post ratings and reviews. Because many online shoppers read ratings and reviews to aid their purchasing decisions, critics should be a primary component in a company's digital marketing strategy. *Collectors* are the most recently recognized category. They collect information and organize content generated by critics and creators.[79] Because collectors are active members of the online community, a company story or site that catches the eye of a collector is likely to be posted, discussed on collector sites, and made available to other online users looking for information.

Joiners include all who become users of Twitter, Facebook, LinkedIn, Pinterest, Tumblr, or other social networking sites. It is not unusual for consumers to be members of several social networking sites at once. Joiners use these sites to connect and network with other users, but as we've seen, marketers too can take significant advantage of these sites to connect with consumers and form customer relationships.[80] The last two segments are Spectators and Inactives. *Spectators,* who read online information but do not join groups or post anywhere, are the largest group in most countries. *Inactives* are online users who do not participate in any digital online media, but their numbers are dwindling.

table 13.2 Social Technographics

Creators	• Publish a blog
	• Publish your own Web pages
	• Upload video you created
	• Upload audio/music you created
	• Write articles or stories and post them
Critics	• Post ratings/reviews of products or services
	• Comment on someone else's blog
	• Contribute to online forums
	• Contribute to/edit articles in a wiki
Collectors	• Use RSS feeds
	• Add tags to Web pages or photos
	• "Vote" for websites online
Joiners	• Maintain profile on a social networking site
	• Visit social networking sites
Spectators	• Read blogs
	• Watch video from other users
	• Listen to podcasts
	• Read online forums
	• Read customer ratings/reviews
Inactives	• None of the activities

SOURCE: Charlene Li and Josh Bernoff, *Groundswell* (Boston: Harvard Business Press, 2008), p. 43.

Marketers who want to capitalize on social and digital media marketing need to consider what proportion of online consumers are creating, rating, collecting, joining, or simply reading online materials. As in traditional marketing efforts, they need to know their target market. For instance, where spectators make up the majority of the online population, companies should post their own corporate messages through blogs and websites promoting their organizations.

Using Digital Media to Learn About Consumers

Marketing research and information systems can use digital media and social networking sites to gather useful information about consumers and their preferences. Sites such as Twitter, Facebook, LinkedIn, Pinterest, and Tumblr can be good substitutes for focus groups. Online surveys can serve as an alternative to mail, telephone, or personal interviews.

Crowdsourcing describes how marketers use digital media to find out the opinions or needs of the crowd (or potential markets). Communities of interested consumers join sites like threadless.com, which designs T-shirts, or crowdspring.com, which creates logos and print and

Web designs. These companies give interested consumers opportunities to contribute and give feedback on product ideas. Crowdsourcing lets companies gather and utilize consumers' ideas in an interactive way when creating new products. There are even sites that crowdsource entire advertising campaigns, like victorandspoils.com. Mobile phone brand LG offered the public more than $80,000 for ideas about what the mobile phone should look like in two, five, or ten years. Barilla, the Italian pasta brand, gets consumers involved in designing new pasta for little expense— far less than the cost of banner ads on websites. The Ottawa-based company Ideavibes has built a crowdsourcing app that will allow companies to engage with consumers in crowdsourcing campaigns. Ideavibes states, "Crowdsourcing can lead to the creation of cool products, which are customer focused and easy to use."[81] Chaordix is another Canadian company that is enabling businesses to use crowdsourcing. The company has built a platform using feedback from a 50,000 member crowd. The platform allows companies to engage crowds online in a user friendly environment.

There is no end to the opportunities to gain information, insights, and new-product ideas from consumers. For instance, Rupert Barksfield developed the Multi-Pet Feeder to end pet feeding-time frenzy when one greedy pet eats the other pet's food. Barksfield paid $99 to post a concept and some drawings at quirky.com, and 30,000 people passed judgment on his idea.[82] Consumer feedback is an important part of the digital media equation. Some of the oldest forms of digital media are online forums, where participants post and respond to messages and discuss specific topics. About one-fifth of U.S. and Japanese Internet users participate in discussion forums, whose topics can range from consumer products to movies. Ratings and reviews have become exceptionally popular; 25 percent of the U.S. online population

reads this type of consumer-generated feedback.[83] Retailers such as Amazon, Netflix, and Priceline allow consumers to post comments on their sites about the books, movies, and travel arrangements they sell. Today, most online shoppers search the Internet for ratings and reviews before making major purchase decisions.

While consumer-generated content about a firm can be either positive or negative, digital media forums do allow businesses to closely monitor what their customers are saying. In the case of negative feedback, businesses can communicate with consumers to address problems or complaints much more easily than through traditional communication channels. Hotels and resorts, for example, have begun monitoring social media sites to see what their guests are saying about them. In some cases, guests who have complained about their rooms using digital media have found themselves upgraded to better rooms that very night.[84] Yet despite the ease and obvious importance of online feedback, many companies do not yet take full advantage of the digital tools at their disposal.

LO6 Identify legal and ethical considerations in digital media.

Legal and Social Issues in Internet Marketing

The extraordinary growth of information technology, the Internet, and e-business has generated many legal and social issues for consumers and businesses. These issues include privacy concerns, the risk of identity theft and online fraud,

Consider the Following: Viewpoints Network Helps Manage Brands Online

As more companies turn toward social media to promote their products, Viewpoints Network is there to help. Founded by entrepreneur Matt Moog in 2006, Viewpoints Network consists of a product review website (the second-largest) and a software suite to help companies use social media to create effective marketing campaigns. Clients include such well-known companies as Procter & Gamble, Sears, and Kraft.

Viewpoints Network utilizes the power of viral marketing with over a million members registered on its website.

When a company hires Viewpoints Network to promote a brand, Viewpoints Network invites members, specifically opinion leaders, to try the product. Members then write product reviews and share them with their friends on sites like Twitter and Facebook. This represents a growing trend where consumers use the feedback of other consumers—many that they've never met—in their purchasing decisions. According to founder Matt Moog, this will require a significant change in marketing: the incorporation of the consumer into the marketing mix.[85]

and the need to protect intellectual property. The major issues related to digital media are privacy, identify theft, online fraud, and intellectual property, which are discussed below.

Privacy

Businesses have long tracked consumers' shopping habits with little controversy. However, observing the contents of a consumer's shopping cart or the process a consumer goes through when choosing a box of cereal generally does not result in the collection of specific, personally identifying data. Although using credit cards, shopping cards, and coupons forces consumers to give up a certain degree of anonymity in the traditional shopping process, they can still choose to remain anonymous by paying cash. Shopping on the Internet, however, allows businesses to track them on a far more personal level, from the contents of their online purchases to the websites they favour. Current technology has made it possible for marketers to amass vast quantities of personal information, often without consumers' knowledge, and to share and sell this information to interested third parties.

How is personal information collected on the Web? Many sites follow users online by storing a "cookie," or an identifying string of text, on users' computers. Cookies permit website operators to track how often a user visits the site, what he or she looks at while there, and in what sequence. They also allow website visitors to customize services, such as virtual shopping carts, as well as the particular content they see when they log onto a Web page. Users have the option of turning off cookies on their machines, but nevertheless the potential for misuse has left many consumers uncomfortable with this technology. The European Union even passed a law that requires companies to get users' consent before using cookies to track their information. Because of this law Yahoo Inc. now allows Internet users in the United Kingdom to choose whether to opt out of having their Internet habits tracked.[87] Some companies have become even more creative when tracking users. Aaron's, a rent to own store, has recently gotten into hot water for installing software in laptops that enables the company to use the computer's Webcam to see what its customers are doing. The software, called PC Rental Agent, has been the subject of a number of consumer complaints as it has been used to capture pictures and video of people in very intimate moments including playing with their children and in some cases having sex.

Even information that consumers willingly post can be used improperly. Facebook in particular has been criticized over the last few years for the mishandling of user information. In 2010, an online security consultant collected public user information from over 100 million Facebook users and placed it in a file for companies to download. This type of "scraping"—where companies offer to collect personal information from social networking sites and other online forums—is becoming increasingly common. Since Internet privacy issues have become such a problem, governments in both Canada and the U.S. are proposing bills to address the issue. One proposed law, called the "do not track" law,

Businesses may be taking online monitoring to a whole new level. PC Rental Agent is software installed on people's laptops that enables the rental agent to capture pictures and video of users.

has been supported by several elected officials in both countries. The "do not track" bill would be an online equivalent of the "do not call" bill for telephones, allowing users to opt out of having their information tracked.[88]

Laws or regulation could pose a significant threat to Web advertisers, who use consumer information to better target advertisements. Such regulations could harm search engines and social networking sites as well. According to Facebook, 80 percent of the world's 100 largest advertisers are on Facebook. As a result of this threat, Google, Facebook, and other Web-based companies are increasing their lobbying efforts to ward off regulation that may be potentially damaging. In one year, Google spent approximately $4 million on lobbying efforts. Self-regulation is another option some Web advertisers are pursuing.[89] On the other hand, certain advertising agencies, networks, and industry trade groups have made the decision to work with Internet-browser makers to create a "do-not-track" system. This represents a major shift for these advertising groups, which until recently have largely opposed such a system. However, although Microsoft and Mozilla have both integrated "do-not-track" features into their browsers, advertisers have a choice as to whether they will respect users' do-not-track requests.[90] Several nonprofit organizations have stepped in to help companies develop privacy policies. Among the best known are TRUSTe and the Better Business Bureau Online. TRUSTe is a nonprofit organization devoted to promoting global trust in Internet technology. Companies that agree to abide by TRUSTe's privacy standards may display a "trustmark" on their websites; thousands of websites currently do so.[91] The BBBOnLine program provides verification, monitoring and review, consumer dispute resolution, a compliance seal, enforcement mechanisms, and an educational component. It is managed by the Council of Better Business Bureaus, an organization with considerable experience in conducting self-regulation and dispute-resolution programs.[92] The hope among online marketers is that widespread adoption of these privacy policies may prevent regulation that could make it more difficult to advertise effectively online.

Identity Theft

Identity theft occurs when criminals obtain personal information that allows them to impersonate someone else in order to use the person's credit to access financial accounts and make purchases. Many of these breaches occur at banks, universities, and other businesses that contain sensitive consumer information.[93] This requires organizations to implement increased security measures to prevent database theft and while these usually work, problems do still occur. For example, the Canadian government recently announced it lost a portable hard drive containing the personal information of over 500,000 people who took out student loans. The lost drive included vast amounts of information including names, Social Insurance Numbers, dates of birth, addresses, and other personal information. The most common complaints about identity theft relate to credit card fraud, followed by utility fraud, bank fraud, employment-related fraud, government document fraud, and loan fraud.[94]

The Internet's relative anonymity and speed make possible both legal and illegal access to databases storing Social Insurance Numbers, driver's licence numbers, dates of birth, mothers' maiden names, and other information that can be used to establish a credit card or bank account in another person's name in order to make fraudulent transactions. One growing scam used to initiate identity theft fraud is the practice of *phishing*, whereby con artists counterfeit a well-known website and send out e-mails directing victims to it. There visitors find instructions to reveal sensitive information such as their credit card numbers. Phishing scams have faked websites for PayPal, AOL, and the Federal Deposit Insurance Corporation.

Some identity theft problems are resolved quickly, while other cases take weeks and hundreds of dollars before a victim's bank balances and credit standings are restored.

Online Fraud

Online fraud includes any attempt to conduct fraudulent activities online, such as by deceiving consumers into releasing personal information. It is becoming a major source of frustration among users of social networking sites, because cybercriminals are finding new ways to use sites like Facebook and Twitter to commit fraudulent activities. For instance, they will create profiles under a company's name to either damage the company's reputation (particularly larger, more controversial companies) or lure that company's customers into releasing personal information the perpetrators can use for monetary gain.

Another tactic is to copy a blog entry from a reputable company and repost it with a link that connects the user to the criminal's own fraudulent site, where he or she attempts to sell the user goods (under the reputable company's name) or collect personal information. For instance, a fraudster may repost a blog written by a professional sport organization with a fraudulent link that connects users to a site that sells unlicensed sporting goods.[95] Criminals may also use social networking sites to pose as charitable institutions. After the 2010 earthquake in Haiti, fraudsters set up fake accounts to scam Facebook users into donating money for the fraudsters' own financial gain.[96] Despite any number of safeguards, the best protection for consumers is to be careful when they divulge information online. The surest way to stay out of trouble is never to give out personal information, like a Social Insurance Number or credit card number, unless it is a site you trust and that you know is legitimate.

Intellectual Property

In addition to protecting personal privacy, Internet users and others want to protect their rights to property they may create, including songs, movies, books, and software. Such intellectual property consists of the ideas and creative materials developed to solve problems, carry out applications, and educate and entertain others.

Although intellectual property is generally protected by patents and copyrights, each year losses from the illegal copying of computer programs, music, movies, compact discs, and books reaches billions of dollars in North America. This has become a particular problem with digital media sites. Chinese search engine Baidu has been accused of offering an MP3 service that allows users to download proprietary songs for free. The recording industry sued Baidu in 2005 for Internet piracy, but the Chinese government sided with Baidu.[97] Another example is YouTube, which has faced lawsuits over its users' possible infringement of other companies' copyrights. In one case, Viacom

Even the government is prone to mistakes in managing people's information as is evident in the announcement that Canada has lost a file containing personal information about 500,000 Canadians.

Identity theft when criminals obtain personal information that allows them to impersonate someone else in order to use their credit to access financial accounts and make purchases

Online fraud any attempt to conduct fraudulent activities online

Inc. sued YouTube's owner, Google, claiming Google had violated its copyrights by allowing users to post protected film clips on YouTube.[98] Although YouTube is responsible for the video content shown on its sites, it can be difficult for Google to monitor and remove all the videos that may contain copyrighted content, given the many millions of clips that are loaded onto YouTube daily.

Illegal sharing of content is another major intellectual property problem. Some consumers rationalize the pirating of software, videogames, movies, and music for a number of reasons. First, many feel they just don't have the money to pay for what they want. Second, because their friends engage in piracy and swap digital content, some users feel influenced to engage in this activity. Others enjoy the thrill of getting away with something with a low risk of consequences. And finally, some people feel being tech-savvy allows them to take advantage of the opportunity to pirate content.[99] There are also a number of consumers who simply do not feel they are doing anything wrong when they share or download software. As discussed in Chapter 2, Gary Fung, founder of Vancouver-based isoHunt, does not think there is anything wrong with sharing TV shows, films, and so forth and has made millions selling advertising to his website. The U.S. courts do not agree with Mr. Fung and have levied a $150 million fine against his company. Fung's argument is his site, much like Google, is a search engine that organizes data. What users do with that data is not for him to control and when asked to remove a movie or TV show due to copyright he complies.

The software industry loses over $50 billion globally each year due to theft and illegal use of software products, according to the Business Software Alliance.[100] About 90 percent of illegal software copying is actually done by businesses. For example, a firm may obtain a licence to install a specific application on 100 of its computers but actually installs it on 300. In some cases, software is illegally made available through the Internet by companies that have taken the software from the producer and set up their own distribution system. Both the Canadian and U.S. governments are pursuing tougher laws against online piracy.

Digital Media's Impact on Marketing

To be successful in business, you need to know much more than how to use a social networking site to communicate with friends. Developing a strategic understanding of how digital marketing can make business more efficient and productive is increasingly necessary. If you are thinking of becoming an entrepreneur, then the digital world can open doors to new resources and customers. Smart phones, mobile broadband, and Webcams are among the tools that can make the most of the online business world, creating greater efficiency at less cost. For example, rather than using traditional phone lines, Skype helps people make and receive calls via the Internet and provides free video calling and text messaging for about 10 percent of the cost of a land line.[101] It is up to businesses and entrepreneurs to develop strategies that achieve business success using existing and future technology, software, and networking opportunities.

Traditional businesses accustomed to using print media can find the transition to digital challenging. New media may require employees with new skills or additional training for current employees. There is often a gap between technical knowledge of how to develop sites and how to develop effective digital marketing strategies to enhance business success. Determining the correct blend of traditional and new media requires careful consideration; the mix will vary depending on the business, its size, and its target market. Future career opportunities will require skills in both traditional and digital media areas so that marketers properly understand and implement marketing strategies that help businesses achieve a competitive advantage.

> "Developing a strategic understanding of how digital marketing can make business more efficient and productive is increasingly necessary."

TEAM EXERCISE

Develop a digital marketing promotion for a local sports team. Use Twitter, Facebook, and other social networking media to promote ticket sales for next season's schedule. In your plan, provide specific details and ideas for the content you would use on the sites. Also, describe how you would encourage fans and potential fans to go to your site. How would you use digital media to motivate sports fans to purchase tickets and merchandise and attend games?

LEARNING OBJECTIVES SUMMARY

LO1 Define digital media and digital marketing and recognize their increasing value in strategic planning.

Digital media are electronic media that function using digital codes via computers, cellular phones, smartphones, and other digital devices that have been released in recent years. Digital marketing uses all digital media, including the Internet and mobile and interactive channels, to develop communication and exchanges with customers.

Because both have impacted strategic planning by allowing for instant communication with precisely defined consumer groups, firms can use real-time exchanges to stimulate interactive communication, forge closer relationships, and learn more accurately about consumer and supplier needs. Thus, firms who use digital media and digital marketing should have a better understanding of consumers, be able to communicate with them more efficiently, and be able to manage their marketing mix to appeal to a broad range of people.

LO2 Understand the characteristics of digital media and how they differentiate these methods from traditional marketing activities.

While digital marketing shares some similarities with conventional marketing techniques, a few valuable differences stand out. First, digital media make customer communications faster and interactive. Second, digital media help companies reach new target markets more easily, affordably, and quickly than ever before. Finally, digital media help marketers utilize new resources in seeking out and communicating with customers.

LO3 Demonstrate the role of digital marketing and social networking in today's business environment.

One of the most important benefits of digital marketing is the ability of marketers and customers to easily share information. Through websites, social networks, and other digital media, consumers can learn about everything they consume and use in their lives, ask questions, voice complaints, indicate preferences, and otherwise communicate about their needs and desires. Many marketers use e-mail, mobile phones, social networking, wikis, video sharing, podcasts, blogs, videoconferencing, and other technologies to coordinate activities and communicate with employees, customers, and suppliers. Twitter, considered both a social network and a micro blog, illustrates how these digital technologies can combine to create new communication opportunities.

LO4 Show how digital media affect the marketing mix.

Product Considerations. Like traditional marketers, digital marketers must anticipate consumer needs and preferences, tailor their products and services to meet these needs, and continually upgrade them to remain competitive. The connectivity created by digital media provide the opportunity for adding services and enhancing product benefits.

Distribution/Place. The Internet is a new distribution channel for making products available at the right time, at the right place, and in the right quantities. Marketers' ability to process orders electronically and increase the speed of communication via the Internet reduces inefficiencies, costs, and redundancies while increasing speed throughout the marketing channel. Shipping times and costs have become an important consideration in attracting customers, prompting many companies to offer consumers low shipping costs or next-day delivery.

Promotion Considerations. Perhaps one of the best ways businesses can utilize digital media is for promotion purposes—whether they are increasing brand awareness, connecting with consumers, or taking advantage of social networks or virtual worlds to form relationships and generate positive publicity or "buzz" about their products. Thanks to online promotion, consumers can be more informed than ever, including reading customer-generated content before making purchasing decisions. Consumer consumption patterns are radically changing, and marketers must adapt their promotional efforts to meet them.

Pricing Considerations. Price is the most flexible element of the marketing mix. Digital marketing can enhance the value of products by providing extra benefits such as service, information, and convenience. Through digital media, discounts and other promotions can be quickly communicated.

LO5 Define social networking and illustrate how businesses can use different types of social networking media.

A social network is "a Web-based meeting place for friends, family, co-workers, and peers that lets users create a profile and connect with other users for purposes that range from getting acquainted, to keeping in touch, to building a work-related network." Social networks are a valued part of marketing because they are changing the way consumers communicate with each other and with firms. Sites such as Facebook, Myspace, Twitter, and LinkedIn have emerged as opportunities for marketers to build communities, provide product information, and learn about consumer needs. By the time you read this, it is possible there will be new social network sites that continue to advance digital communication and opportunities for marketers. The uses of social networking are widespread. Companies can use blogs to answer questions, YouTube to post videos, and social network sites such as Facebook to communicate with customers.

LO6 Identify legal and ethical considerations in digital media.

The major issues related to legal and ethical concerns are privacy, identity theft, online fraud, and intellectual property.

KEY TERMS

accessibility
addressability
blog
connectivity
control
digital marketing
digital media
e-business

identity theft
interactivity
online fraud
podcast
social network
viral marketing
wiki

DESTINATION CEO DISCUSSION QUESTIONS

1. Do you think Arlene Dickinson's approach of getting to know people personally is becoming more difficult in today's business world?

2. Do you think it is essential to get to know people's stories, both business and personal, to serve them successfully in a marketing and communication campaign? Why or why not?

3. Dickinson works for businesses which are heavily reliant on social media and frequently track website usage of consumers. Does this information change your opinion of her, especially given her belief that she acts in a socially responsible manner?

4. Dickinson's company represents businesses that have been charged with harming the environment in Canada's oil sands. Can you be personally ethical if you work for firms in questionable industries?

SO YOU WANT TO BE *a Digital Marketer*

The business world has grown increasingly dependent on digital marketing to maintain communication with stakeholders. Reaching customers is often a major concern, but digital marketing can also be used to communicate with suppliers, concerned community members, and special interest groups about issues related to sustainability, safety practices, and philanthropic activities. Many types of jobs exist: account executive directors of social media and directors of marketing for digital products, as well as digital advertisers, online marketers, global digital marketers, and brand managers are prominently listed on career opportunity websites.

Entrepreneurs are taking advantage of the low cost of digital marketing, building social networking sites to help market their products. In fact, some small businesses such as specialty publishing, personal health and beauty, and other specialty products can use digital marketing as the primary channel for reaching consumers. Many small businesses are posting signs outside their stores with statements such as "Follow us on Twitter" or "Check out our Facebook page."

To utilize digital marketing, especially social networking, requires more than information technology skills related to constructing websites, graphics, videos, podcasts, and so on. Most importantly, one must be able to determine how digital media can be used in implementing a marketing strategy. All marketing starts with identifying a target market and developing a marketing mix to satisfy customers. Digital marketing is just another way to reach customers, provide information, and develop relationships. Therefore, your opportunity for a career in this field is greatly based on understanding the messages, desired level of interactivity, and connectivity that helps achieve marketing objectives.

As social media use skyrockets, digital marketing professionals will be in demand. The experience of many businesses and research indicate digital marketing is a powerful way to increase brand exposure and generate traffic. In fact, a study conducted on Social Media Examiner found that 85 percent of marketers surveyed believe generating exposure for their business is their number-one advantage in Internet marketing. As consumers use social networking for their personal communication, they will be more open to obtaining information about products through this channel. Digital marketing could be the fastest-growing opportunity in business.

To prepare yourself for a digital marketing career, learn not only the technical aspects, but also how social media can be used to maximize marketing performance. A glance at careerbuilder.com indicates that management positions such as account manager, digital marketing manager, and digital product manager can pay from $60,000 to $170,000 or more per year.

BUILD YOUR BUSINESS PLAN

Digital Marketing Strategy

As you are building your business plan, one thing that is virtually certain is that you will need a digital marketing strategy. Digital marketing including social networking sites allows businesses to engage with more consumers, establish a two-way communication relationship with customers, and ultimately should enable a business to be more successful.

The question many new businesses face is not whether they should use online marketing tools, but what tools are most appropriate for their business. As discussed throughout the chapter, there are a number of different online techniques a business can use, and each involves an investment of time and sometimes money. Given that new businesses often have a shortage of both, it is crucial that as an entrepreneur you develop a clear strategy for digital marketing. A successful way to do this is to evaluate each marketing tool in a table or spreadsheet as they relate to your business. Create a table where you assess and highlight the user demographics of the various sites— Facebook, Twitter, and so forth—and how you may use the site in your business. You can start to think about which tools you will use, and which tools would likely not work best for your business. You could then extend the table further and state specifically how you could incorporate these digital marketing sites into your company's overall marketing plan. After completing this analysis you should have a sense of what digital marketing tools would work best with your prospective business.

To advertise on social media sites, or not to advertise? It depends on whom you ask. Users of social media are increasingly coming upon advertisements on their pages, and some are unhappy about it. They feel that social media sites are a place to have fun, not to be subjected to yet more marketing. Marketers, on the other hand, love the added exposure they receive; with over 1.06 billion Facebook users and 500 million Twitter users, these sites offer businesses access to many market segments at once. However, businesses soon learn that marketing their brands on social media sites is not so easy.

One challenge is frequent monitoring of Facebook and Twitter pages. Simply posting ads or creating Facebook fan pages is not enough. As consumers are frequently turning to these social media sites to post complaints or concerns, companies must be vigilant to respond. Additionally, although it contains several features to support company advertisements, Facebook cannot always enforce appropriate ad content. It counts on users to complain when inappropriate ads are posted. This can be a problem for both consumers, who might be exposed to ads they feel are inappropriate, and businesses, who could unintentionally alienate their target market. (Facebook is currently updating its rules and restrictions.)

Businesses must also face the fact that their social media marketing activities can still bomb. Fox found this out the hard way when it began broadcasting live Twitter overlays over reruns of *Fringe* and *Glee.* Viewers found the overlays intrusive and distracting. The campaign was a failure. Other companies have accounts on both Facebook and Twitter, but they simply haven't done anything to make them exciting. These setbacks show that although social media offers exciting new marketing opportunities, campaigns must be carefully thought out and implemented to be successful.[102]

DISCUSSION QUESTIONS

1. Do you think consumers would be willing to pay for the use of social media sites if there were no marketing activities?

2. Why do some marketers post what are considered by some as inappropriate advertisements?

3. What do marketers need to do to make advertising on social media sites acceptable to consumers?

Mc Graw Hill Education connect **Mc Graw Hill Education LEARNSMART** **Mc Graw Hill Education SMARTBOOK**™

For more information on the resources available from McGraw-Hill Ryerson, go to www.mcgrawhill.ca/he/solutions.

14

Accounting and Financial Statements

LEARNING OBJECTIVES

LO1 Define accounting, and describe the different uses of accounting information.

LO2 Demonstrate the accounting process.

LO3 Examine the various components of an income statement to evaluate a firm's "bottom line."

LO4 Interpret a company's balance sheet to determine its current financial position.

LO5 Analyze the statement of cash flow to evaluate the increase and decrease in a company's cash balance.

LO6 Assess a company's financial position using its accounting statements and ratio analysis.

DESTINATION CEO

Clarence Otis About 30 years ago, Clarence Otis changed the name of his restaurant from the Green Frog to the Red Lobster. Today, it is the number-one seafood chain in the country. The same parent corporation, Darden Restaurants, owns the Olive Garden chain. Darden has more than 150,000 employees and nearly 1,500 restaurants.

At an early age, Otis had excellent guidance as his mother had very high expectations for him. His first job was to be a server in a full-service restaurant, where he learned the pressures associated with high expectations of customers. He attended Williams College as an undergraduate. From there, he returned to northern California to attend law school at Stanford. Otis returned to the East Coast, where he practised corporate law in New York City with a focus on mergers and acquisitions. He found that he liked the financial aspects of the business better than the legal side. Otis changed his career and became an investment banker. He moved to Darden in 1995 as treasurer. Eventually Otis became the CFO and advanced to the role of CEO.

Today, he sees a tremendous amount of growth potential for both the Red Lobster and Olive Garden chains. To remain relevant is the key. Both restaurants continue to evolve in concert with the guests' expectations. People who work for the Darden chains must be inspired and understand the corporate philosophy and its goals.

Introduction

Accounting, the financial "language" that organizations use to record, measure, and interpret all of their financial transactions and records, is very important in business. All businesses—from a small family farm to a giant corporation—use the language of accounting to make sure they use their money wisely and to plan for the future. Nonbusiness organizations such as charities and governments also use accounting to demonstrate to donors and taxpayers how well they are using their funds and meeting their stated objectives.

This chapter explores the role of accounting in business and its importance in making business decisions. First, we discuss the uses of accounting information and the accounting process. Then, we briefly look at some simple financial statements and accounting tools that are useful in analyzing organizations worldwide.

KPMG is part of the "Big Four," or the four largest international accounting firms. The other three are PricewaterhouseCoopers, Ernst & Young, and Deloitte Touche Tohmatsu.

The Nature of Accounting

Simply stated, **accounting** is the recording, measurement, and interpretation of financial information. Large numbers of people and institutions, both within and outside businesses, use accounting tools to evaluate organizational operations. The Canadian Institute of Chartered Accountants (CICA) sets the underlying rules of accounting in Canada. These rules are called "generally accepted accounting principles," or GAAP. The Accounting Standards Board (AcSB) is responsible for developing and establishing standards of accounting and reporting by Canadian companies and nonprofit organizations. Public companies must follow the principles and rules set out in the International Financial Reporting Standards (IFRS). Private companies can choose to follow either IFRS or Canadian Accounting Standards for Private Enterprises (ASPE). International Financial Reporting Standards (IFRS) are a single set of high-quality, understandable, and enforceable global standards.[1] Auditors must follow Canadian Auditing Standards (CAS) while planning and performing financial statement audits. Canadian Auditing Standards provide auditors with the required tools, procedures, and guidance they need to carry out high-quality audits.

To better understand the importance of accounting, we must first understand who prepares accounting information and how it is used.

Accountants

Many of the functions of accounting are carried out by public or private accountants.

Accounting the recording, measurement, and interpretation of financial information

Accountant a professional who has met the education, examination, and experience requirements set by the professional society or association—such as the Certified General Accountants Association of Canada, the Canadian Institute of Chartered Accountants (Ordre des comptables agréés in Quebec), and CMA Canada—of which they are a member

Accountants. An **accountant** is a designated professional who has met the education, examination, and experience requirements set by the professional society and association—such as the Certified General Accountants Association of Canada, the Canadian Institute of Chartered Accountants (Ordre des comptables agréés in Quebec), and CMA Canada—of which they are a member. They can be chartered accountants (CAs), certified general accountants (CGAs), or certified management accountants (CMAs).

Many large corporations, government agencies, and other organizations employ their own accountants to prepare and analyze their financial statements. With titles such as controller, tax accountant, or internal auditor, accountants are deeply involved in many of the most important financial decisions of the organizations for which they work. Many accountants are either self-employed or members of large public accounting firms such as Ernst & Young, KPMG, Deloitte Touche Tohmatsu, and PricewaterhouseCoopers, together referred to as "the Big Four." Table 14.1 lists the top seven accounting firms in 2012.

A growing area for public accountants is *forensic accounting*, which involves analyzing financial documents in search of fraudulent entries or financial misconduct. Functioning as much like detectives as accountants, forensic accountants have been used since the 1930s. In the wake of the accounting scandals of the early 2000s, many auditing firms are rapidly adding or expanding forensic or fraud-detection services. Additionally, many forensic accountants root out evidence of "cooked books" for federal agencies like the RCMP. The Association of Certified Fraud Examiners, which certifies accounting professionals as *Certified Fraud Examiners (CFEs)*, has grown to more than 40,000 members with chapters in Canada and around the world.[3]

Accounting or Bookkeeping?

The terms *accounting* and *bookkeeping* are often mistakenly used interchangeably. Much narrower and far more mechanical than accounting, bookkeeping is typically limited to the routine, day-to-day recording of business transactions. Bookkeepers are responsible for obtaining and recording the information that accountants require to analyze a firm's financial position. They generally require less training than accountants. Accountants, on the other hand, usually complete course work beyond their basic four- or five-year accounting degrees. This additional training allows accountants not only to record financial information, but to understand, interpret, and even develop the sophisticated accounting systems necessary to classify and analyze complex financial information.

table 14.1 Leading Accounting Firms

Company	2012 U.S. Revenues ($ Millions)	2012 Partners
"Top Seven Firms"		
Deloitte Touche Tohmatsu	$11,939	2,886
PricewaterhouseCoopers	$8,844	2,290
Ernst & Young	$7,500	2,400
KPMG	$5,391	1,744
McGladrey & Pullen	$1,370.42	708
Grant Thornton	$1,146.12	549
CBIZ/Mayer Hoffman McCann	$597.50	415

SOURCE: Accounting Today, *Top 100 Firms, 2012,* special supplement to *Accounting Today,* p. 15. Published by SourceMedia, http://digital.accountingtoday.com/accountingtoday/2012top100.

The Uses of Accounting Information

Accountants summarize the information from a firm's business transactions in various financial statements (which we'll look at in a later section of this chapter) for a variety of stakeholders, including managers, investors, creditors, and government agencies. Many business failures may be directly linked to ignorance of the information "hidden" inside these financial statements. Likewise, most business successes can be traced to informed managers who understand the consequences of their decisions. While maintaining and even increasing short-run profits is desirable, the failure to plan sufficiently for the future can easily lead an otherwise successful company to insolvency and bankruptcy court.

Basically, managers and owners use financial statements (1) to aid in internal planning and control and (2) for external purposes such as reporting to the Canada Revenue Agency shareholders, creditors, customers, employees, and other interested parties. Figure 14.1 shows some of the users of the accounting information generated by a typical corporation.

Internal Uses. **Managerial accounting** refers to the internal use of accounting statements by managers in planning and directing the organization's activities. Perhaps management's greatest single concern is **cash flow,** the movement of money through an organization over a daily, weekly, monthly, or yearly basis. Obviously, for any business to succeed, it needs to generate enough cash to pay its bills as they fall due. However, it is not at all unusual for

highly successful and rapidly growing companies to struggle to make payments to employees, suppliers, and lenders because of an inadequate cash flow. One common reason for a so-called cash crunch, or shortfall, is poor managerial planning

Managerial accountants also help prepare an organization's **budget,** an internal financial plan that forecasts expenses and income over a set period of time. It is not unusual for an organization to prepare separate daily, weekly, monthly, and yearly budgets. Think of a budget as a financial map, showing how the company expects to move from Point A to Point B over a specific period of time. While most companies prepare *master budgets* for the entire firm, many also prepare budgets for smaller segments of the organization such as divisions, departments, product lines, or projects. "Top-down" master budgets begin at the top and filter down to the individual department level, while "bottom-up" budgets start at the department or project level and are combined at the chief executive's office. Generally, the larger and more rapidly growing an organization, the greater will be the likelihood that it will build its master budget from the ground up.

Regardless of focus, the major value of a budget lies in its breakdown of cash inflows and outflows. Expected operating expenses (cash outflows such as wages, materials costs, and taxes) and operating revenues (cash inflows in the form of payments from

> **Managerial accounting** the internal use of accounting statements by managers in planning and directing the organization's activities
>
> **Cash flow** the movement of money through an organization over a daily, weekly, monthly, or yearly basis
>
> **Budget** an internal financial plan that forecasts expenses and income over a set period of time

figure 14.1 The Users of Accounting Information

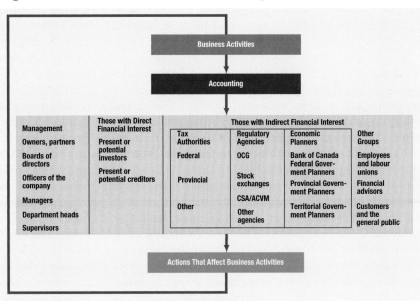

SOURCE: Adapted from Belverd E. Needles, Henry R. Anderson, and James C. Caldwell, *Principles of Accounting*, 4th edition. Copyright © 1990 by Houghton Mifflin Company. Reprinted with permission.

Accounting and sustainability may seem like an unusual combination. After all, the purpose of the accounting profession is handling and reporting financial information, not adopting green practices. However, an increasing emphasis on sustainability has prompted the Canadian Institute of Chartered Accountants, the Chartered Institute of Management Accountants, the American Institute of CPAs (AICPA), and other global organizations to rethink the importance of sustainability to the financial profession.

Studies by these organizations have determined that at least one-third of smaller companies are incorporating sustainability strategies into their businesses, with another quarter indicating that they intend to do the same in the next few years. For instance, organizations such as French firm Esker have begun adopting cloud-based hiring tools to replace traditional paper résumés. For such practices to succeed, managers from all levels of the organization must support these initiatives, particularly company accountants and finance executives. These finance professionals are essential to the process because they are the ones who are in the best position to understand the "big picture." Although sustainability is important, businesses must still succeed financially if they want to survive. Therefore, it is up to financial professionals—who have in-depth knowledge of the company's financial information—to find ways to use sustainability initiatives to improve operations.

Accounting organizations have created recommendations for finance professionals to determine which sustainable strategies to adopt. For instance, finance professionals must link sustainability to profit and find out which initiatives would cut costs and increase efficiency. They must create metrics to measure the success of these initiatives and determine whether changes are needed. Additionally, these organizations recommend that accountants incorporate the company's sustainability efforts into "mainstream reporting" for stakeholders.[4]

DISCUSSION QUESTIONS

1. Why should accountants be involved in a company's decision to incorporate greener business practices?

2. Describe some of the recommendations that accounting organizations have developed regarding sustainability strategies.

3. What could happen if companies arbitrarily adopted sustainability strategies without assessing their impact?

---

customers) over a set period of time are carefully forecasted and subsequently compared with actual results. Deviations between the two serve as a "trip wire" or "feedback loop" to launch more detailed financial analyses in an effort to pinpoint trouble spots and opportunities.

External Uses. Managers also use accounting statements to report the business's financial performance to outsiders. Such statements are used for filing income taxes, obtaining credit from lenders, and reporting results to the firm's shareholders. They become the basis for the information provided in the official corporate **annual report,** a summary of the firm's financial information, products, and growth plans for owners and potential investors. While frequently presented between slick, glossy covers prepared by major advertising firms, the single most important component of an annual report is the signature of a certified public accountant attesting that the required financial statements are an accurate reflection of the underlying financial condition of the firm. Financial statements

Annual report summary of a firm's financial information, products, and growth plans for owners and potential investors

meeting these conditions are termed *audited.* The primary external users of audited accounting information are government agencies, shareholders and potential investors, and lenders, suppliers, and employees.

During the global financial crisis, it turns out that Greece had been engaging in deceptive accounting practices, with the help of U.S. investment banks. Greece was using financial techniques that hid massive amounts of debt from its public balance sheets. Eventually, the markets figured out that the country might not be able to pay off its creditors. The European Union and the International Monetary Fund came up with a plan to give Greece some credit relief, but tied to this was the message to "get your financial house in order." By the middle of 2012, the European problem was often referred to as the PIGS. This referred to Portugal, Italy, Ireland, Greece and Spain—all of which were having debt problems. The PIGS have caused cracks in the European Monetary Union. While Germany demanded austerity, others wanted more growth-oriented strategies. Clearly, the financial crisis will have some lasting effects that need clear accounting solutions.[5]

Financial statements evaluate the return on shareholders' investment and the overall quality of the firm's

Even profitable businesses can become unprofitable if they do not manage their cash flows right.

management team. A corporation's shareholders use financial statements to evaluate the return on their investment and the overall quality of the firm's management team. As a result, poor financial statements often result in changes in top management. Potential investors study the financial statements in a firm's annual report to determine whether the company meets their investment requirements and whether the returns from a given firm are likely to compare favourably with other similar companies.

> "A corporation's shareholders use financial statements to evaluate the return on their investment and the overall quality of the firm's management team."

Banks and other lenders look at financial statements to determine a company's ability to meet current and future debt obligations if a loan or credit is granted. To determine this ability, a short-term lender examines a firm's cash flow to assess its ability to repay a loan quickly with cash generated from sales. A long-term lender is more interested in the company's profitability and indebtedness to other lenders.

Labour unions and employees use financial statements to establish reasonable expectations for salary and other benefit requests. Just as firms experiencing record profits are likely to face added pressure to increase employee

wages, so too are employees unlikely to grant employers wage and benefit concessions without considerable evidence of financial distress.

LO2   Demonstrate the accounting process.

The Accounting Process

Many view accounting as a primary business language. It is of little use, however, unless you know how to "speak" it. Fortunately, the fundamentals—the accounting equation and the double-entry bookkeeping system—are not difficult to learn. These two concepts serve as the starting point for all currently accepted accounting principles.

> "Many view accounting as a primary business language."

The Accounting Equation

Accountants are concerned with reporting an organization's assets, liabilities, and owners' equity. To help illustrate these concepts, consider a hypothetical flower shop called Anna's Flowers, owned by Anna Rodriguez. A firm's economic resources, or items of value that it owns, represent its **assets**—cash, inventory, land, equipment, buildings, and other tangible and intangible things. The assets of Anna's Flowers include counters, refrigerated display cases, flowers, decorations, vases, cards, and other gifts, as well as something known as "goodwill," which in this case is Anna's reputation for preparing and delivering beautiful floral arrangements on a timely basis. **Liabilities,** on the other hand, are debts the firm owes to others. Among the liabilities of Anna's Flowers are a loan from the Small Business Administration and money owed to flower suppliers and other creditors for items purchased. The **owners' equity** category contains all of the money that has ever been contributed to the company that never has to be paid back. The funds can come from investors who have given money or assets to the company, or it can come from past profitable operations. In the case of Anna's Flowers, if Anna were to sell off, or liquidate, her business, any money left over after selling all the shop's assets and paying off its liabilities would comprise her owner's equity. The relationship between assets, liabilities, and owners' equity is a fundamental concept in accounting and is known as the **accounting equation:**

$$\text{Assets} = \text{Liabilities} + \text{Owners' equity}$$

Assets a firm's economic resources, or items of value that it owns, such as cash, inventory, land, equipment, buildings, and other tangible and intangible things

Liabilities debts that a firm owes to others

Owners' equity equals assets minus liabilities and reflects historical values

Accounting equation assets equal liabilities plus owners' equity

A firm's assets include tangible items, as in the case of this restaurant's service tables, equipment, and even the atmosphere created by the wall's artwork.

Double-Entry Bookkeeping

Double-entry bookkeeping is a system of recording and classifying business transactions in separate accounts in order to maintain the balance of the accounting equation. Returning to Anna's Flowers, suppose Anna buys $325 worth of roses on credit from the Antique Rose Emporium to fill a wedding order. When she records this transaction, she will list the $325 as a liability or a debt to a supplier. At the same time, however, she will also record

> **Double-entry bookkeeping**
> a system of recording and classifying business transactions that maintains the balance of the accounting equation

$325 worth of roses as an asset in an account known as "inventory." Because the assets and liabilities are on different sides of the accounting equation, Anna's accounts increase in total size (by $325) but remain in balance:

$$\text{Assets} = \text{Liabilities} + \text{Owners' equity}$$
$$\$325 = \$325$$

Thus, to keep the accounting equation in balance, each business transaction must be recorded in two separate accounts.

In the final analysis, all business transactions are classified as either assets, liabilities, or owners' equity. However, most organizations further break down these three accounts to provide more specific information about a transaction. For example, assets may be broken down into specific categories such as cash, inventory, and equipment, while liabilities may include bank loans, supplier credit, and other debts.

Figure 14.2 shows how Anna used the double-entry bookkeeping system to account for all of the transactions that took place in her first month of business. These transactions include her initial investment of $2,500, the loan from the Small Business Administration, purchases of equipment and inventory, and the purchase of roses on credit. In her first month of business, Anna generated revenues of $2,000 by selling $1,500 worth of inventory. Thus, she deducts, or (in accounting notation that is appropriate for assets) *credits*, $1,500 from inventory and adds, or *debits*, $2,000 to the cash account. The difference between Anna's $2,000 cash inflow and her $1,500 outflow is represented by a credit to owners' equity, because it is money that belongs to her as the owner of the flower shop.

figure 14.2 The Accounting Equation and Double-Entry Bookkeeping for Anna's Flowers

	Assets			= Liabilities		+ Owners' Equity
	Cash	Equipment	Inventory	Debts to suppliers	Loans	Equity
Cash invested by Anna	$2,500.00					$2,500.00
Loan from SBA	$5,000.00				$5,000.00	
Purchase of furnishings	–$3,000.00	$3,000.00				
Purchase of inventory	–$2,000.00		$2,000.00			
Purchase of roses			$325.00	$325.00		
First month sales	$2,000.00		–$1,500.00			$500.00
Totals	$4,500.00	$3,000.00	$825.00	$325.00	$5,000.00	$3,000.00

$8,325 = $5,325 + $3,000

$8,325 Assets = $8,325 Liabilities + Owners' Equity

The Accounting Cycle

In any accounting system, financial data typically pass through a four-step procedure sometimes called the **accounting cycle.** The steps include examining source documents, recording transactions in an accounting journal, posting recorded transactions, and preparing financial statements. Figure 14.3 shows how Anna works through them. Traditionally, all of these steps were performed using paper, pencils, and erasers (lots of erasers!), but today the process is often fully computerized.

Step One: Examine Source Documents. Like all good managers, Anna Rodriguez begins the accounting cycle by gathering and examining source documents— cheques, credit-card receipts, sales slips, and other related evidence concerning specific transactions.

Step Two: Record Transactions. Next, Anna records each financial transaction in a **journal,** which is basically just a time-ordered list of account transactions. While most businesses keep a general journal in which all transactions are recorded, some classify transactions into specialized journals for specific types of transaction accounts.

Step Three: Post Transactions. Anna next transfers the information from her journal into a **ledger,** a book or computer program with separate files for each account. This process is known as *posting.* At the end of the accounting period (usually yearly, but occasionally quarterly or monthly), Anna prepares a *trial balance,* a summary of the balances of all the accounts in the general ledger. If, upon totalling, the trial balance doesn't balance (that is, the accounting equation is not in balance), Anna or her accountant must look for mistakes (typically an error in one or more of the ledger entries) and correct them. If the trial balance is correct, the accountant can then begin to prepare the financial statements.

Step Four: Prepare Financial Statements. The information from the trial balance is also used to prepare the company's financial statements. In the case of public corporations and certain other organizations, a CA must *attest,* or certify, that the organization followed generally accepted accounting principles in preparing the financial statements. When these statements have been completed, the organization's books are "closed," and the accounting cycle begins anew for the next accounting period.

Accounting cycle the four-step procedure of an accounting system: examining source documents, recording transactions in an accounting journal, posting recorded transactions, and preparing financial statements

Journal a time-ordered list of account transactions

Ledger a book or computer file with separate sections for each account

Financial Statements

The end results of the accounting process are a series of financial statements. The income statement, the balance sheet, and the statement of cash flows are the best-known examples of financial statements. These statements are provided to shareholders and potential investors in a firm's annual report as well as to other relevant outsiders such as creditors, government agencies, and the Canada Revenue Agency.

It is important to recognize that not all financial statements follow precisely the same format. The fact that different organizations generate income in different ways suggests that when it comes to financial statements, one size definitely does not fit all. Manufacturing firms, service providers, and nonprofit organizations each use a different set of accounting principles or rules upon which the public accounting profession has agreed. As we have already mentioned, these are sometimes referred to as *generally accepted accounting principles (GAAP).* Each country has a different set of rules that the businesses within that country are required to use for their accounting process and financial statements, however, many countries (including Canada) have adopted International Financial Reporting Standards (IFRS) for listed or large companies so that statutory reporting is comparable across international jurisdictions. Still, as is the case in many other disciplines, certain concepts have more than one name. For example, *sales* and *revenues* are often interchanged, as are *profits, income,* and *earnings.* Table 14.2 lists a few common equivalent terms that should help you decipher their meaning in accounting statements.

LO3 Examine the various components of an income statement to evaluate a firm's "bottom line."

The Income Statement

The question, "What's the bottom line?" derives from the income statement, where the bottom line shows the overall profit or loss of the company after taxes. Thus, the

table 14.2 Equivalent Terms in Accounting

Term	Equivalent Term
Revenues	Sales
	Goods or services sold
Gross profit	Gross income
	Gross earnings
Operating income	Operating profit
	Earnings before interest and taxes (EBIT)
	Income before interest and taxes (IBIT)
Income before taxes (IBT)	Earnings before taxes (EBT)
	Profit before taxes (PBT)
Net income (NI)	Earnings after taxes (EAT)
	Profit after taxes (PAT)
Income available to common shareholders	Earnings available to common shareholders

figure 14.3 The Accounting Process for Anna's Flowers

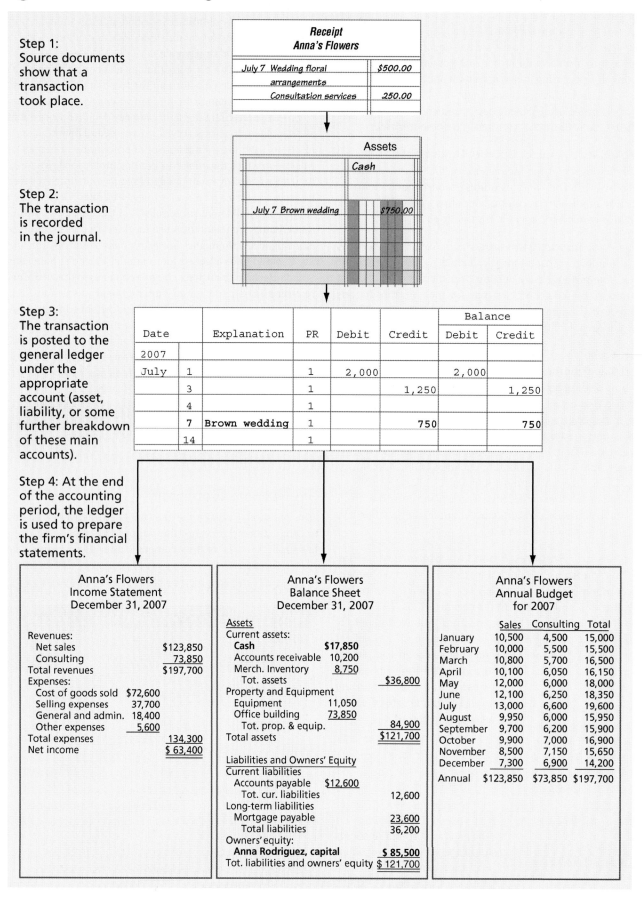

Step 1:
Source documents show that a transaction took place.

Receipt
Anna's Flowers

July 7 Wedding floral arrangements	$500.00
Consultation services	250.00

Step 2:
The transaction is recorded in the journal.

Assets

Cash

July 7 Brown wedding $750.00

Step 3:
The transaction is posted to the general ledger under the appropriate account (asset, liability, or some further breakdown of these main accounts).

					Balance	
Date	Explanation	PR	Debit	Credit	Debit	Credit
2007						
July	1		1	2,000		2,000
	3		1		1,250		1,250
	4		1				
	7	Brown wedding	1		750		750
	14		1				

Step 4: At the end of the accounting period, the ledger is used to prepare the firm's financial statements.

Anna's Flowers
Income Statement
December 31, 2007

Revenues:		
Net sales		$123,850
Consulting		73,850
Total revenues		$197,700
Expenses:		
Cost of goods sold	$72,600	
Selling expenses	37,700	
General and admin.	18,400	
Other expenses	5,600	
Total expenses		134,300
Net income		$ 63,400

Anna's Flowers
Balance Sheet
December 31, 2007

Assets
Current assets:

Cash	**$17,850**	
Accounts receivable	10,200	
Merch. Inventory	8,750	
Tot. assets		$36,800
Property and Equipment		
Equipment	11,050	
Office building	73,850	
Tot. prop. & equip.		84,900
Total assets		$121,700

Liabilities and Owners' Equity
Current liabilities

Accounts payable	$12,600	
Tot. cur. liabilities		12,600
Long-term liabilities		
Mortgage payable		23,600
Total liabilities		36,200
Owners' equity:		
Anna Rodriguez, capital		**$ 85,500**
Tot. liabilities and owners' equity		$ 121,700

Anna's Flowers
Annual Budget
for 2007

	Sales	Consulting	Total
January	10,500	4,500	15,000
February	10,000	5,500	15,500
March	10,800	5,700	16,500
April	10,100	6,050	16,150
May	12,000	6,000	18,000
June	12,100	6,250	18,350
July	13,000	6,600	19,600
August	9,950	6,000	15,950
September	9,700	6,200	15,900
October	9,900	7,000	16,900
November	8,500	7,150	15,650
December	7,300	6,900	14,200
Annual	$123,850	$73,850	$197,700

Income statement a financial report that shows an organization's profitability over a period of time—month, quarter, or year

Revenue the total amount of money received from the sale of goods or services, as well as from related business activities

income statement is a financial report that shows an organization's profitability over a period of time, be that a month, quarter, or year. By its very design, the income statement offers one of the clearest possible pictures of the company's overall revenues and the costs incurred in generating those revenues. Other names for the income statement include profit and loss (P&L) statement or operating statement. A sample income statement with line-by-line explanations is presented in Table 14.3, while Table 14.4 presents the income statement of Tim Hortons. The income statement indicates the firm's profitability or income (the bottom line), which is derived by subtracting the firm's expenses from its revenues.

Revenue. **Revenue** is the total amount of money received (or promised) from the sale of goods or services, as well as

from other business activities such as the rental of property and investments. Nonbusiness entities typically obtain revenues through donations from individuals and/or grants from governments and private foundations. Tim Hortons' income statement (see Table 14.4) shows one main source of income: sales of Tim Hortons' products.

For most manufacturing and retail concerns, the next major item included in the income statement is the **cost of goods sold,** the amount of money the firm spent (or promised to spend) to buy and/or produce the products it sold during the accounting period. This figure may be calculated as follows:

Cost of goods sold the amount of money a firm spent to buy or produce the products it sold during the period to which the income statement applies

$$\text{Cost of goods sold} = \text{Beginning inventory} + \text{Interim purchases} - \text{Ending inventory}$$

table 14.3 Sample Income Statement

The following exhibit presents a sample income statement with all the terms defined and explained.

Company Name for the Year Ended December 31	
Revenues (sales)	Total dollar amount of products sold (includes income from other business services such as rental-lease income and interest income).
Less: Cost of goods sold	The cost of producing the goods and services, including the cost of labour and raw materials as well as other expenses associated with production.
Gross profit	The income available after paying all expenses of production.
Less: Selling and administrative expense	The cost of promoting, advertising, and selling products as well as the overhead costs of managing the company. This includes the cost of management and corporate staff. One non-cash expense included in this category is depreciation, which approximates the decline in the value of plant and equipment assets due to use over time. In most accounting statements, depreciation is not separated from selling and administrative expenses. However, financial analysts usually create statements that include this expense.
Income before interest and taxes (operating income or EBIT)	This line represents all income left over after operating expenses have been deducted. This is sometimes referred to as operating income since it represents all income after the expenses of operations have been accounted for. Occasionally, this is referred to as EBIT, or earnings before interest and taxes.
Less: Interest expense	Interest expense arises as a cost of borrowing money. This is a financial expense rather than an operating expense and is listed separately. As the amount of debt and the cost of debt increase, so will the interest expense. This covers the cost of both short-term and long-term borrowing.
Income before taxes (earnings before taxes—EBT)	The firm will pay a tax on this amount. This is what is left of revenues after subtracting all operating costs, depreciation costs, and interest costs.
Less: Taxes	The tax rate is specified in the federal tax code.
Net income	This is the amount of income left after taxes. The firm may decide to retain all or a portion of the income for reinvestment in new assets. Whatever it decides not to keep it will usually pay out in dividends to its shareholders.
Less: Preferred dividends	If the company has preferred shareholders, they are first in line for dividends. That is one reason why their stock is called "preferred."
Income to common shareholders	This is the income left for the common shareholders. If the company has a good year, there may be a lot of income available for dividends. If the company has a bad year, income could be negative. The common shareholders are the ultimate owners and risk takers. They have the potential for very good or very poor returns since they get whatever is left after all other expenses.
Earnings per share	Earnings per share is found by taking the income available to the common shareholders and dividing by the number of shares of common stock outstanding. This is income generated by the company for each share of common stock.

Let's say that Anna's Flowers began an accounting period with an inventory of goods for which it paid $5,000. During the period, Anna bought another $4,000 worth of goods, giving the shop a total inventory available for sale of $9,000. If, at the end of the accounting period, Anna's inventory was worth $5,500, the cost of goods sold during the period would have been $3,500 ($5,000 + $4,000 − $5,500 = 3,500). If Anna had total revenues of $10,000 over the same period of time, subtracting the cost of goods sold ($3,500) from the total revenues of $10,000 yields the store's **gross income (or profit)** (revenues minus the cost of goods sold required to generate the revenues): $6,500. Notice that Tim Hortons calls it cost of sales, rather than cost of goods sold. This is because Tim Hortons buys raw materials and supplies and produces drinks.

Expenses.   **Expenses** are the costs incurred in the day-to-day operations of an organization. Three common expense accounts shown on income statements are (1) selling, general, and administrative expenses; (2) research, development, and engineering expenses; and (3) interest expenses (remember that the costs directly attributable to selling goods or services are included in the cost of goods sold). Selling expenses include advertising and sales salaries. General and administrative expenses include salaries of executives and their staff and the costs of owning and maintaining the general office. Research and development costs include scientific, engineering, and marketing personnel and the equipment and information used to design and build

prototypes and samples. Interest expenses include the direct costs of borrowing money.

The number and type of expense accounts vary from organization to organization. Included in the general and administrative category is a special type of expense known as **depreciation**, the process of spreading the costs of long-lived assets such as buildings and equipment over the total number of accounting periods in which they are expected to be used. Consider a manufacturer that purchases a $100,000 machine expected to last about 10 years. Rather than showing an expense of $100,000 in the first year and no expense for that equipment over the next nine years, the manufacturer is allowed to report depreciation expenses of $10,000 per year in each of the next 10 years because that better matches the cost of the machine to the years the machine is used. Each time this depreciation is "written off" as an expense, the book value of the machine is also reduced by $10,000. The fact that the equipment has a zero value on the firm's balance sheet when it is fully depreciated (in this case, after 10 years) does not necessarily mean that it can no longer be used or is economically worthless. Indeed, in some industries, machines used every day have been reported as having no book value whatsoever for over 30 years.

Net Income.   **Net income** (or net earnings) is the total profit (or loss) after all expenses including taxes have been deducted from revenue. Generally, accountants

ENTREPRENEURSHIP IN ACTION | Entrepreneurial Success Story Hits a Snag

Mark Zuckerberg, Eduardo Saverin, Dustin Moskovitz, Chris Hughes

Business: Facebook

Founded: 2004

Success: Facebook has become the largest social networking site in the world with an estimated market value of $1.04 billion.

When Mark Zuckerberg decided to exchange computer code writing for managing his start-up in 2006, nobody would have guessed that Facebook would become the biggest social network worldwide. In 2012, Facebook went public. At $38 a share, the social network had the third-largest public offering in U.S. history at $1.6 billion. However, it was not long before Facebook hit a snag.

Facebook's massive growth requires accurate accounting and financial growth forecasts. Everything seemed to go well with its initial public offering (IPO) on the opening day. Yet shortly after the launch, Facebook stock dropped 16 percent from its original price. Investors realized that analysts at Morgan Stanley and other firms had reduced Facebook's earnings estimates prior to the IPO launch. Knowledge of Facebook's decreased earnings projections would likely have reduced the value of Facebook's IPO, yet this information was not made widely available until after the launch. Investors filed a lawsuit against Facebook, Morgan Stanley, and other firms because they felt deceived into paying more for Facebook shares than they were worth. This debacle will likely teach all participants in the IPO the valuable lesson about the importance of transparency and disclosure in accounting.[6]

divide profits into individual sections such as operating income and earnings before interest and taxes. Tim Hortons, for example, lists income before income taxes, net income, and earnings per share of outstanding stock (see Table 14.4). Like most companies, Tim Hortons presents not only the current year's results but also the previous two years' income statements to permit comparison of performance from one period to another.

Temporary Nature of the Income Statement Accounts. Companies record their operational activities in the revenue and expense accounts during an accounting period.

Gross profit, earnings before interest and taxes, and net income are the results of calculations made from the revenue and expense accounts; they are not actual accounts. At the end of each accounting period, the dollar amounts in all the revenue and expense accounts are moved into an account called "Retained Earnings," one of the owners' equity accounts. Revenues increase owners' equity, while expenses decrease it. The resulting change in the owners' equity account is exactly equal to the net income. This shifting of dollar values from the revenue and expense accounts allows the firm to begin the next accounting period with zero balances in those accounts. Zeroing out the balances

table 14.4 Consolidated Statement of Operations for Tim Hortons
(in thousands of Canadian dollars, except per share data)

	2012	2011	2010
Revenues			
Sales	2,225,659	2,012,170	1,755,244
Franchise revenues	894,845	840,796	781,251
Total revenues	3,120,504	2,852,966	2,536,495
Costs and expenses			
Cost of sales	1,959,416	1,774,107	1,527,405
Operating expenses	287,652	259,098	246,335
Franchise fee costs	116,644	104,884	91,743
General and administrative expenses	158,476	161,444	147,300
Equity income	−14,693	−14,354	−14,649
Corporate reorganization expenses	18,874	0	0
Asset impairment and closure costs, net	−372	372	28,298
Other income, net	−18	−2,060	−1,100
Total costs and expenses, net	2,525,979	2,283,491	2,025,332
Gain on sale of interest in Maidstone Bakeries	0	0	361,075
Operating income	594,525	569,475	872,238
Interest expense	−33,709	−30,000	−26,642
Interest income	3,296	4,127	2,462
Income before income taxes	564,112	543,602	848,058
Income taxes	156,346	157,854	200,940
Net income	407,766	385,748	647,118
Net income attributable to noncontrolling interests	4,881	2,936	23,159
Net income attributable to Tim Hortons Inc.	402,885	$382,812	$623,959
Basic earnings per common share attributable to Tim Hortons Inc.	$2.60	$2.36	$3.59
Diluted earnings per common share attributable to Tim Hortons Inc.	$2.59	$2.35	$3.58
Weighted average number of common shares outstanding—Basic (in thousands)	155,160	162,145	174,035
Weighted average number of common shares outstanding—Diluted (in thousands)	155,676	162,597	174,215
Dividends per common share	$0.84	$0.68	$0.52

SOURCE: http://annualreport.timhortons.com/#financial-results/documents (accessed February 19, 2013).

enables a company to count how much it has sold and how many expenses have been incurred during a period of time. The basic accounting equation (assets = liabilities + owners' equity) will not balance until the revenue and expense account balances have been moved or "closed out" to the owners' equity account.

One final note about income statements: You may remember from Chapter 4 that corporations may choose to make cash payments called dividends to shareholders out of their net earnings. When a corporation elects to pay dividends, it decreases the cash account (in the assets category) as well as a capital account (in the owners' equity category). During any period of time, the owners' equity account may change because of the sale of stock (or contributions/withdrawals by owners), the net income or loss, or from the dividends paid.

LO4   Interpret a company's balance sheet to determine its current financial position.

The Balance Sheet

The second basic financial statement is the **balance sheet,** which presents a "snapshot" of an organization's financial position at a given moment. As such, the balance sheet indicates what the organization owns or controls and the various sources of the funds used to pay for these assets, such as bank debt or owners' equity.

The balance sheet takes its name from its reliance on the accounting equation: Assets *must* equal liabilities plus owners' equity. Table 14.5 provides a sample balance sheet with line-by-line explanations. Unlike the income statement, the balance sheet does not represent the result of transactions completed over a specified accounting period. Instead, the balance sheet is, by definition, an accumulation of all financial transactions conducted by an organization since its founding. Following long-established traditions, items on the balance sheet are listed on the basis of their original cost less accumulated depreciation, rather than their present values.

> ### "The balance sheet takes its name from its reliance on the accounting equation: Assets must equal liabilities plus owners' equity."

Balance sheets are often presented in two different formats. The traditional balance sheet format placed the organization's assets on the left side and its liabilities and owners' equity on the right. More recently, a vertical format, with assets on top followed by liabilities and owners' equity, has gained wide acceptance. Tim Hortons' balance sheet for 2011 and 2012 is presented in Table 14.6.

Assets.   All asset accounts are listed in descending order of *liquidity*—that is, how quickly each could be turned into cash. **Current assets,** also called short-term assets, are those that are used or converted into cash within the course of a calendar year. Thus, cash is followed by temporary investments, accounts receivable, and inventory, in that order. **Accounts receivable** refers to money owed the company by its clients or customers who have promised to pay for the products at a later date. Accounts receivable usually includes an allowance for bad debts that management does not expect to collect. The bad-debts adjustment is normally based on historical collections experience and is deducted from the accounts receivable balance to present a more realistic view of the payments likely to be received in the future, called net receivables. Inventory may be held in the form of raw materials, work-in-progress, or finished goods ready for delivery.

Long-term or fixed assets represent a commitment of organizational funds of at least one year. Items classified as fixed include long-term investments, plant and equipment, and intangible assets, such as corporate "goodwill," or reputation, as well as patents and trademarks.

Liabilities.   As seen in the accounting equation, total assets must be financed either through borrowing (liabilities) or through owner investments (owners' equity). **Current liabilities** include a firm's financial obligations to short-term creditors, which must be repaid within one year, while long-term liabilities have longer repayment terms. **Accounts payable** represents amounts owed to suppliers for goods and services purchased

This type of machinery would be considered a long-term asset on the balance sheet.

table 14.5 Sample Balance Sheet

The following exhibit presents a balance sheet in word form with each item defined or explained.

Typical Company December 31

Assets	This is the major category for all physical, monetary, or intangible goods that have some dollar value.
Current assets	Assets that are either cash or are expected to be turned into cash within the next 12 months.
Cash	Cash or chequing accounts.
Marketable securities	Short-term investments in securities that can be converted to cash quickly (liquid assets).
Accounts receivable	Cash due from customers in payment for goods received. These arise from sales made on credit.
Inventory	Finished goods ready for sale, goods in the process of being finished, or raw materials used in the production of goods.
Prepaid expense	A future expense item that has already been paid, such as insurance premiums or rent.
Total current assets	The sum of the above accounts.
Fixed assets	Assets that are long-term in nature and have a minimum life expectancy that exceeds one year.
Investments	Assets held as investments rather than assets owned for the production process. Most often the assets include small ownership interests in other companies.
Gross property, plant, and equipment	Land, buildings, and other fixed assets listed at original cost.
Less: Accumulated depreciation	The accumulated expense deductions applied to all plant and equipment over their life. Land may not be depreciated. The total amount represents in general the decline in value as equipment gets older and wears out. The maximum amount that can be deducted is set by the Canada Revenue Agency (CRA) and varies by type of asset.
Net property, plant, and equipment	Gross property, plant, and equipment minus the accumulated depreciation. This amount reflects the book value of the fixed assets and not their value if sold.
Other assets	Any other asset that is long-term and does not fit into the above categories. It could be patents or trademarks.
Total assets	The sum of all the asset values.
Liabilities and Shareholders' Equity	This is the major category. Liabilities refer to all indebtedness and loans of both a long-term and short-term nature. Shareholders' equity refers to all money that has been contributed to the company over the life of the firm by the owners.
Current liabilities	Short-term debt expected to be paid off within the next 12 months.
Accounts payable	Money owed to suppliers for goods ordered. Firms usually have between 30 and 90 days to pay this account, depending on industry norms.
Wages payable	Money owed to employees for hours worked or salary. If workers receive cheques every two weeks, the amount owed should be no more than two weeks' pay.
Taxes payable	Firms are required to pay corporate taxes quarterly. This refers to taxes owed based on earnings estimates for the quarter.
Notes payable	Short-term loans from banks or other lenders.
Other current liabilities	The other short-term debts that do not fit into the above categories.
Total current liabilities	The sum of the above accounts.
Long-term liabilities	All long-term debt that will not be paid off in the next 12 months.
Long-term debt	Loans of more than one year from banks, pension funds, insurance companies, or other lenders. These loans often take the form of bonds, which are securities that may be bought and sold in bond markets.
Deferred income taxes	This is a liability owed to the government but not due within one year.
Other liabilities	Any other long-term debt that does not fit the above two categories.
Shareholders' equity	The following categories are the owners' investment in the company.
Common stock	The tangible evidence of ownership is a security called common stock. The par value is stated value and does not indicate the company's worth.
Capital in excess of par (a.k.a. contributed capital)	When shares of stock were sold to the owners, they were recorded at the price at the time of the original sale. If the price paid was $10 per share, the extra $9 per share would show up in this account at 100,000 shares times $9 per share, or $900,000.
Retained earnings	The total amount of earnings the company has made during its life and not paid out to its shareholders as dividends. This account represents the owners' reinvestment of earnings into company assets rather than payments of cash dividends. This account does not represent cash.
Total shareholders' equity	This is the sum of the above equity accounts representing the owners' total investment in the company.
Total liabilities and shareholders' equity	The total short-term and long-term debt of the company plus the owners' total investment. This combined amount *must* equal total assets.

table 14.6 Consolidated Balance Sheet for Tim Hortons (in thousands of Canadian dollars)

	2012	2011
ASSETS		
Current assets		
Cash and cash equivalents	$120,139	$126,497
Restricted cash and cash equivalents	150,574	130,613
Accounts receivable, net	171,605	173,667
Notes receivable, net	7,531	10,144
Deferred income taxes	7,142	5,281
Inventories and other, net	107,000	136,999
Advertising fund restricted assets	45,337	37,765
Total current assets	609,328	620,966
Property and equipment, net	1,553,308	1,463,765
Intangible assets, net	3,674	4,544
Notes receivable, net	1,246	3,157
Deferred income taxes	10,559	12,197
Equity investments	41,268	43,014
Other assets	64,796	56,307
Total assets	2,284,179	2,203,950
LIABILITIES AND EQUITY		
Current liabilities		
Accounts payable	169,762	177,918
Accrued liabilities:		
Salaries and wages	21,477	23,531
Taxes	8,391	26,465
Other	197,871	179,315
Deferred income taxes	197	0
Advertising fund liabilities	44,893	59,420
Current portion of long-term obligations	20,781	10,001
Total current liabilities	463,372	476,650
Long-term obligations		
Long-term debt	359,471	352,426
Long-term debt—Advertising Fund	46,849	0
Capital leases	104,383	94,863
Deferred income taxes	10,399	4,608
Other long-term liabilities	109,614	120,970
Total long-term obligations	630,716	572,867
Commitments and contingencies		
EQUITY		
Equity of Tim Hortons Inc.		
Common shares ($2.84 stated value per share). Authorized: unlimited shares. Issued: 153,404,839 and 157,814,980, respectively	435,033	447,558
Common shares held in trust, at cost: 316,923 and 277,189 shares, respectively	−13,356	−10,136
Contributed surplus	10,970	6,375
Retained earnings	893,619	836,968
Accumulated other comprehensive loss	−139,028	−128,217
Total equity of Tim Hortons Inc.	1,187,238	1,152,548
Noncontrolling interests	2,853	1,885
Total equity	1,190,091	1,154,433
Total liabilities and equity	2,284,179	2,203,950

SOURCE: http://annualreport.timhortons.com/#financial-results/documents (accessed February 19, 2013).

with credit. For example, if you buy gas with a Shell credit card, the purchase represents an account payable for you (and an account receivable for Shell). Other liabilities include wages earned by employees but not yet paid and taxes owed to the government. Occasionally, these accounts are consolidated into an **accrued expenses** account, representing all unpaid financial obligations incurred by the organization.

Owners' Equity. Owners' equity includes the owners' contributions to the organization along with income earned by the organization and retained to finance continued growth and development. If the organization were to sell off all of its assets and pay off all of its liabilities, any remaining funds would belong to the owners. Not surprisingly, the accounts listed as owners' equity on a balance sheet may differ dramatically from company to company. As mentioned in Chapter 4, corporations sell stock to investors, who become the owners of the firm. Many corporations issue two, three, or even more different classes of common and preferred stock, each with different dividend payments and/or voting rights. Because each type of stock issued represents a different claim on the organization, each must be represented by a separate owners' equity account, called contributed capital.

L05 Analyze the statement of cash flow to evaluate the increase and decrease in a company's cash balance.

The Statement of Cash Flow

The third primary financial statement is called the **statement of cash flow,** which explains how the company's cash changed from the beginning of the accounting period to the end. Cash, of course, is an asset shown on the balance sheet, which provides a snapshot of the firm's financial position at one point in time. However, many investors and other users of financial statements want more information about the cash flowing into and out of the firm than is provided on the balance sheet to better understand the company's financial health. The statement of cash flow takes the cash balance from one year's balance sheet and compares it to the next while providing detail about how the firm used the cash. Table 14.7 presents Tim Hortons' statement of cash flow.

The change in cash is explained through details in three categories: cash from (used for) operating activities, cash from (used for) investing activities, and cash from (used for) financing activities. *Cash from operating activities* is calculated by combining the changes in the revenue accounts, expense accounts, current asset accounts, and current liability accounts. This category of cash flows includes all the accounts on the balance sheet that relate to computing revenues and expenses for the accounting period. If this amount is a positive number, as it is for Tim Hortons, then the business is making extra cash that it can use to invest in increased long-term capacity or to pay off debts such as loans or bonds. A negative number may indicate a business that is still in a growing stage or one that is in a declining position with regards to operations.

Cash from investing activities is calculated from changes in the long-term or fixed asset accounts. If this amount is negative, as is the case with Tim Hortons, the company is purchasing long-term assets for future growth. A positive figure indicates a business that is selling off existing long-term assets and reducing its capacity for the future.

Finally, *cash from financing activities* is calculated from changes in the long-term liability accounts and the contributed capital accounts in owners' equity. If this amount is negative, the company is likely paying off long-term debt or returning contributed capital to investors. If this amount is positive, the company is either borrowing more money or raising money from investors by selling more shares of stock.

L06 Assess a company's financial position using its accounting statements and ratio analysis.

Ratio Analysis: Analyzing Financial Statements

The income statement shows a company's profit or loss, while the balance sheet itemizes the value of its assets, liabilities, and owners' equity. Together, the two statements provide the means to answer two critical questions: (1) How much did the firm make or lose? and (2) How much is the firm currently worth based on historical values found on the balance sheet? **Ratio analysis,** calculations that measure an organization's financial health, brings the complex information from the income statement and balance sheet into sharper focus so that managers, lenders, owners, and other interested parties can measure and compare the organization's productivity, profitability, and financing mix with other similar entities.

As you know, a ratio is simply one number divided by another, with the result showing the relationship between the two numbers. Financial ratios are used to weigh and evaluate a firm's performance. Interestingly, an absolute value such as earnings of $70,000 or accounts receivable of $200,000 almost never provides as much useful information as a well-constructed ratio. Whether those numbers are good or bad depends on their relation to other numbers. If a company earned $70,000 on $700,000 in sales (a 10 percent return), such an earnings level might be quite satisfactory.

table 14.7 Tim Hortons Consolidated Statement of Cash Flows
(in thousands of Canadian dollars)

	2012	2011	2010
Cash flows provided from (used in) operating activities			
Net income	407,766	385,748	647,118
Adjustments to reconcile net income to net cash provided by operating activities			
Depreciation and amortization	132,167	115,869	118,385
Asset impairment	0	1,850	18,352
Stock-based compensation expense	11,862	17,323	14,263
Deferred income taxes	5,065	−5,433	1,285
Changes in operating assets and liabilities			
Restricted cash and cash equivalents	−20,182	−63,264	−6,920
Accounts receivable	−1,346	2,099	−10,923
Inventories and other	33,415	−32,057	−29,275
Accounts payable and accrued liabilities	6,692	349	104,829
Taxes	−18,065	−39,197	40,715
Gain on sale of interest in Maidstone Bakeries	0	0	−361,075
Other	1,913	8,180	−11,210
Net cash provided from operating activities	559,287	391,467	525,544
Cash flows (used in) provided from investing activities			
Capital expenditures (including Advertising Fund)	−235,808	−181,267	−132,912
Purchase of restricted investments	0	0	−37,832
Proceeds from sale of restricted investments	0	38,000	20,240
Proceeds from sale of interest in Maidstone Bakeries	0	0	475,000
Cash and cash equivalents of Maidstone Bakeries divested	0	0	−30,411
Other investing activities	−6,400	−9,460	1,934
Net cash (used in) provided from investing activities	−242,208	−152,727	296,019
Cash flows (used in) provided from financing activities			
Repurchase of common shares	−225,200	−572,452	−242,595
Dividend payments to common shareholders	−130,509	−110,187	−90,304
Distributions, net to noncontrolling interests	−3,913	−6,692	−22,524
Net proceeds from debt	51,850	3,699	300,823
Principal payments on long-term debt obligations	−7,710	−8,586	−307,023
Other financing activities	−6,885	6,398	−4,005
Net cash used in financing activities	−322,367	−687,820	−365,628
Effect of exchange rate changes on cash	−1,070	1,223	−3,234
(Decrease) Increase in cash and cash equivalents	−6,358	−447,857	452,701
Cash and cash equivalents at beginning of year	126,497	574,354	121,653
Cash and cash equivalents at end of year	120,139	126,497	574,354

SOURCE: http://annualreport.timhortons.com/#financial-results/documents (accessed February 19, 2013).

Profitability ratios ratios that measure the amount of operating income or net income an organization is able to generate relative to its assets, owners' equity, and sales

Profit margin net income divided by sales

Return on assets net income divided by assets

The president of a company earning this same $70,000 on sales of $7 million (a 1 percent return), however, should probably start looking for another job!

Looking at ratios in isolation is probably about as useful and exciting as staring at a blank wall. It is the relationship of the calculated ratios to both prior organizational performance and the performance of the organization's "peers," as well as its stated goals, that really matters. Remember, while the profitability, asset utilization, liquidity, debt ratios, and per share data we'll look at here can be very useful, you will never see the forest by looking only at the trees.

Profitability Ratios

Profitability ratios measure how much operating income or net income an organization is able to generate relative to its assets, owners' equity, and sales. The numerator (top number) used in these examples is always the net income after taxes. Common profitability ratios include profit margin, return on assets, and return on equity. The following examples are based on the 2012 income statement and balance sheet for Tim Hortons as shown in Tables 14.4 and 14.6. Except where specified, all data are expressed in thousands of dollars.

The **profit margin,** computed by dividing net income by sales, shows the overall percentage profits earned by the company. It is based solely upon data obtained from the income statement. The higher the profit margin, the better the cost controls within the company and the higher the return on every dollar of revenue. Tim Hortons' profit margin is calculated as follows:

$$\text{Profit Margin} = \frac{\text{Net income}}{\text{Sales}} = \frac{\$407,766}{\$2,225,659} = 18.32\%$$

Thus, for every $1 in sales, Tim Hortons generated profits of over 18 cents.

Return on assets, net income divided by assets, shows how much income the firm produces for every dollar invested in assets. A company with a low return on assets is probably not using its assets very productively—a key managerial failing. By its construction, the return on assets calculation requires data from both the income statement and the balance sheet.

$$\text{Return on Assets} = \frac{\text{Net income}}{\text{Assets}} = \frac{\$407,766}{\$2,284,179} = 17.85\%$$

In the case of Tim Hortons, every $1 of assets generated a return of 17.85 percent, or profits of almost 18 cents.

Shareholders are always concerned with how much money they will make on their investment, and they frequently use the return on equity ratio as one of their key performance measures. **Return on equity** (also called return on investment [ROI]), calculated by dividing net income by owners' equity, shows how much income is generated by each $1 the owners have invested in the firm. Obviously, a low return on equity means low shareholder returns and may indicate a need for immediate managerial attention. Because some assets may have been financed with debt not contributed by the owners, the value of the owners' equity is usually considerably lower than the total value of the firm's assets. Tim Hortons' return on equity is calculated as follows:

$$\text{Return on Equity} = \frac{\text{Net income}}{\text{Equity}} = \frac{\$407,766}{\$1,187,238} = 34.35\%$$

For every dollar invested by Tim Hortons' shareholders, the company earned a 34.35 percent return, or 34.35 cents per dollar invested.

Return on equity net income divided by owners' equity; also called return on investment (ROI)

Asset utilization ratios ratios that measure how well a firm uses its assets to generate each $1 of sales

Receivables turnover sales divided by accounts receivable

Inventory turnover sales divided by total inventory

> "Profitability ratios measure how much operating income or net income an organization is able to generate relative to its assets, owners' equity, and sales."

Asset Utilization Ratios

Asset utilization ratios measure how well a firm uses its assets to generate each $1 of sales. Obviously, companies using their assets more productively will have higher returns on assets than their less efficient competitors. Similarly, managers can use asset utilization ratios to pinpoint areas of inefficiency in their operations. These ratios (receivables turnover, inventory turnover, and total asset turnover) relate balance sheet assets to sales, which are found on the income statement.

The **receivables turnover,** sales divided by accounts receivable, indicates how many times a firm collects its accounts receivable in one year. It also demonstrates how quickly a firm is able to collect payments on its credit sales. Obviously, no payments mean no profits. Tim Hortons collected its receivables 12.97 times per year.

$$\frac{\text{Receivables}}{\text{Turnover}} = \frac{\text{Sales}}{\text{Receivables}} = \frac{\$2,225,659}{\$171,605} = 12.97\text{ x}$$

Inventory turnover, sales divided by total inventory, indicates how many times a firm sells and replaces its inventory over the course of a year. A high inventory turnover ratio may indicate great efficiency but may also suggest the possibility of lost sales due to insufficient stock levels. Tim

Hortons' inventory turnover indicates that it replaced its inventory nearly 20.80 times per year.

$$\text{Inventory Turnover} = \frac{\text{Sales}}{\text{Inventory}} = \frac{\$2,225,659}{\$107,000} = 20.80 \text{ x}$$

Total asset turnover, sales divided by total assets, measures how well an organization uses all of its assets in creating sales. It indicates whether a company is using its assets productively. Tim Hortons generated $0.97 in sales for every $1 in total corporate assets.

$$\text{Total Asset Turnover} = \frac{\text{Sales}}{\text{Total assets}} = \frac{\$2,225,659}{\$2,284,179} = 0.97 \text{ x}$$

Liquidity Ratios

Liquidity ratios compare current (short-term) assets to current liabilities to indicate the speed with which a company can turn its assets into cash to meet debts as they fall due. High liquidity ratios may satisfy a creditor's need for safety, but ratios that are too high may indicate that the organization is not using its current assets efficiently. Liquidity ratios are generally best examined in conjunction with asset utilization ratios because high turnover ratios imply that cash is flowing through an organization very quickly—a situation that dramatically reduces the need for the type of reserves measured by liquidity ratios.

The **current ratio** is calculated by dividing current assets by current liabilities. Tim Hortons' current ratio indicates that for every $1 of current liabilities, the firm had $1.31 of current assets on hand. They turn over their assets very quickly and are very liquid.

$$\text{Current Ratio} = \frac{\text{Current assets}}{\text{Current liabilities}} = \frac{\$609,328}{\$463,372} = 1.31 \text{ x}$$

The **quick ratio (acid test)** is a far more stringent measure of liquidity because it eliminates inventory, the least liquid current asset. It measures how well an organization can meet its current obligations without resorting to the sale of its inventory. In 2012, Tim Hortons had just $1.08 invested in current assets (after subtracting inventory) for every $1 of current liabilities.

$$\text{Quick Ratio} = \frac{\text{Current assets} - \text{Inventories}}{\text{Current liabilities}}$$

$$= \frac{\$609,328 - 107,000}{\$463,372} = 1.08 \text{ x}$$

Debt Utilization Ratios

Debt utilization ratios provide information about how much debt an organization is using relative to other sources of capital, such as owners' equity. Because the use of debt carries an interest charge that must be paid regularly regardless of profitability, debt financing is much riskier than equity. Unforeseen negative events such as recessions affect heavily indebted firms to a far greater extent than those financed exclusively with owners' equity. Because of this and other factors, the managers of most firms tend to keep debt-to-asset levels below 50 percent. However, firms in very stable and/or regulated industries, such as electric utilities, often are able to carry debt ratios well in excess of 50 percent with no ill effects.

The **debt to total assets ratio** indicates how much of the firm is financed by debt and how much by owners' equity. To find the value of Tim Hortons' total debt, you must add current liabilities to long-term debt and other liabilities.

$$\text{Debt to Total Assets} = \frac{\text{Total debt}}{\text{Total assets}} = \frac{\$1,094,088}{\$2,284,179} = 47.90\%$$

Thus, for every $1 of Tim Hortons' total assets, 48 percent is financed with debt. The remaining 52 percent is provided by owners' equity.

The **times interest earned ratio,** operating income divided by interest expense, is a measure of the safety margin a company has with respect to the interest payments it must make to its creditors. A low times interest earned ratio indicates that even a small decrease in earnings may lead the company into financial straits. We can see that Tim Hortons covered interest expense by income before interest and taxes 17 times.

$$\text{Times Interest Earned} = \frac{\$594,525}{\$33,709} = 17.64\%$$

Per Share Data

Investors may use **per share data** to compare the performance of one company with another on an equal, or per share, basis. Generally, the more shares of stock a company issues, the less income is available for each share.

Earnings per share is calculated by dividing net income or profit by the number of shares of stock outstanding. This ratio is important because yearly changes in earnings per share, in combination with other economywide factors, determine a company's overall stock price. When earnings go up, so does a company's stock price—and so does the wealth of its shareholders.

$$\frac{\text{Earnings}}{\text{Per Share}} = \frac{\text{Net income}}{\text{Number of shares outstanding}} = \frac{\$407,766}{\$155,160} = \$2.63$$

We can see from the income statement and these calculations that Tim Hortons' basic earnings per share increased from $2.36 in 2011 to $2.60 in 2012. You can see from the income statement that diluted earnings per share include more shares than the basic calculation; this is because diluted shares include potential shares that could be issued due to the exercise of stock options or the conversion of certain types of debt into common stock. Investors generally pay more attention to diluted earnings per share than basic earnings per share.

Dividends per share the actual cash received for each share owned

Dividends per share are paid by the corporation to the shareholders for each share owned. The payment is made from earnings after taxes by the corporation but is taxable income to the shareholder. Thus, dividends result in double taxation: The corporation pays tax once on its earnings, and the shareholder pays tax a second time on his or her dividend income.

Industry Analysis

We have used Starbucks as a comparison to Tim Hortons because there are no real national coffee houses that compete with Tim Hortons on the same scale. While Starbucks is almost four times larger than Tim Hortons in terms of sales, Starbucks has a national presence and to some extent competes for the Canadian consumer's dollars. Table 14.8 shows that while Tim Hortons earns more profit per dollar of sales, both Starbucks and Tim Hortons earn about the same dollars per dollar of invested assets. A Tim Hortons coffee shop is about as expensive to build

table 14.8 Industry Analysis

	Tim Hortons	Starbucks
Profit margin	18.32%	10.65%
Return on assets	17.85%	16.92%
Return on equity	34.35%	28.39%
Receivables turnover	12.97 x	30.27 x
Inventory turnover	20.80 x	12.11 x
Total asset turnover	0.97 x	1.59 x
Current ratio	1.31 x	1.83 x
Quick ratio	1.08 x	1.36 x
Debt to total assets	47.90%	40.00%
Times interest earned	17.64 x	51.91 x
Earnings per share	$2.60	$1.62 (US$)
Dividends per share	$0.84	$0.52 (US$)

and operate as a Starbucks. Both companies have little accounts receivable relative to the size of their sales, but Starbucks has a better receivables turnover. Tim Hortons' quick ratio and current ratio are comparable to Starbucks'. Starbucks has a very high times interest earned ratio, significantly higher than Tim Hortons'. Tim Hortons earns more per share than Starbucks and pays a higher dividend. In summary, both companies are in good financial health, and it is hard to say which company is better managed. One thing is for sure: If Starbucks could earn the same profit margin as Tim Hortons, it would improve its other profitability ratios dramatically.

TEAM EXERCISE

You can look at websites such as Yahoo! Finance (http://finance.yahoo.com/), under the company's "key statistics" link, to find many of its financial ratios, such as return on assets and return on equity. Have each member of your team look up a different company, and explain why you think there are differences in the ratio analysis for these two ratios among the selected companies.

LO1 Define accounting and describe the different uses of accounting information.

Accounting is the language businesses and other organizations use to record, measure, and interpret financial transactions. Financial statements are used internally to judge and control an organization's performance and to plan and direct its future activities and measure goal attainment. External organizations such as lenders, governments, customers, suppliers, and the CRA are major consumers of the information generated by the accounting process.

LO2 Demonstrate the accounting process.

Assets are an organization's economic resources; liabilities are debts the organization owes to others; owners' equity is the difference between the value of an organization's assets and its liabilities. This principle can be expressed as the accounting equation: Assets = Liabilities + Owners' equity. The double-entry bookkeeping system is a system of recording and classifying business transactions in accounts that maintains the balance of the accounting equation. The accounting cycle involves examining source documents, recording transactions in a journal, posting transactions, and preparing financial statements on a continuous basis throughout the life of the organization.

LO3 Examine the various components of an income statement to evaluate a firm's "bottom line."

The income statement indicates a company's profitability over a specific period of time. It shows the "bottom line," the total profit (or loss) after all expenses (the costs incurred in the day-to-day operations of the organization) have been deducted from revenue (the total amount of money received from the sale of goods or services and other business activities). The statement of cash flow shows how much cash is moving through the firm and thus adds insight to a firm's "bottom line."

LO4 Interpret a company's balance sheet to determine its current financial position.

The balance sheet, which summarizes the firm's assets, liabilities, and owners' equity since its inception, portrays its financial position as of a particular point in time. Major classifications included in the balance sheet are current assets (assets that can be converted to cash within one calendar year), fixed assets (assets of greater than one year's duration), current liabilities (bills owed by the organization within one calendar year), long-term liabilities (bills due more than one year hence), and owners' equity (the net value of the owners' investment).

LO5 Analyze the statement of cash flow to evaluate the increase and decrease in a company's cash balance.

The statement of cash flows shows how the company's cash changed from the beginning of the accounting period to the end. Cash from operating activities includes all the accounts on the balance sheet that relate to computing revenues and expenses for the accounting period. Cash from investing activities is calculated from changes in the long-term or fixed asset accounts. Cash from financing activities is calculated from changes in the long-term liability accounts and the contributed capital accounts in owners' equity.

LO6 Assess a company's financial position using its accounting statements and ratio analysis.

Ratio analysis is a series of calculations that brings the complex information from the income statement and balance sheet into sharper focus so that managers, lenders, owners, and other interested parties can measure and compare the organization's productivity, profitability, and financing mix with other similar entities. Ratios may be classified in terms of profitability (dollars of return for each dollar of employed assets), asset utilization (how well the organization uses its assets to generate $1 in sales), liquidity (assessing organizational risk by comparing current assets to current liabilities), debt utilization (how much debt the organization is using relative to other sources of capital), and per share data (comparing the performance of one company with another on an equal basis).

accountant
accounting
accounting cycle
accounting equation
accounts payable
accounts receivable
accrued expenses
annual report
asset utilization ratios
assets
balance sheet
budget
cash flow
cost of goods sold
current assets
current liabilities
current ratio
debt to total assets ratio
debt utilization ratios
depreciation
dividends per share
double-entry bookkeeping
earnings per share

expenses
gross income or profit
income statement
inventory turnover
journal
ledger
liabilities
liquidity ratios
managerial accounting
net income
owners' equity
per share data
profit margin
profitability ratios
quick ratio (acid test)
ratio analysis
receivables turnover
return on assets
return on equity
revenue
statement of cash flow
times interest earned ratio
total asset turnover

DESTINATION CEO DISCUSSION QUESTIONS

1. What prepared Clarence Otis for his position as CEO of Darden?

2. How extensive is Darden Restaurants in North America?

3. According to Otis, what is the key area for success for employees at the Darden company?

Do you like numbers and finances? Are you detail oriented, a perfectionist, and highly accountable for your decisions? If so, accounting may be a good field for you. If you are interested in accounting, there are always job opportunities available no matter the state of the economy. Accounting is one of the most secure job options in business. Of course, becoming an accountant is not easy. You will need at least a bachelor's degree in accounting to get a job, and many positions require additional training. If you are really serious about getting into the accounting field, you will probably want to consider getting your master's in accounting and obtaining your accounting designation. The field of accounting can be complicated, and the extra training provided through a master's in accounting program will prove invaluable when you go out looking for a good job. Accounting is a volatile discipline affected by changes in legislative initiatives.

Accountants are needed in the public and the private sectors, in large and small firms, in for-profit and not-for-profit organizations. Accountants in firms are generally in charge of preparing and filing tax forms and financial reports.

Public-sector accountants are responsible for checking the veracity of corporate and personal records in order to prepare tax filings. Basically, any organization that has to deal with money and/or taxes in some way or another will be in need of an accountant, either for in-house service or occasional contract work. The fact that accounting rules and tax filings tend to be complex virtually ensures that the demand for accountants will never decrease.[7]

Accounting rules and regulations are becoming increasingly complex, thereby not only requiring the skills of an accountant but also requiring more time and effort. With industry demand high and increasing, and the number of qualified accountants holding steady or even decreasing, accounting salaries continue to rise from what are already high levels when compared with other business degrees. One reason for this increase is that accountants are continually building upon their traditional reputation as having the best overall qualifications among the financial designations for leadership positions within public accounting, industry, government, and academia. As a result, they are valued highly by the market.[8]

BUILD YOUR BUSINESS PLAN

Accounting and Financial Statements

After you determine your initial *reasonable selling price,* you need to estimate your sales forecasts (in terms of units and dollars of sales) for the first year of operation. Remember to be conservative and set forecasts that are modest.

While customers may initially try your business, many businesses have seasonal patterns. A good budgeting/planning system allows managers to anticipate problems, coordinate activities of the business (so that subunits within the organization are all working toward the common goal of the organization), and control operations (know whether spending is "in line").

The first financial statement you need to prepare is the income statement. Beginning with your estimated sales revenue, determine what expenses will be necessary to generate that level of sales revenue. Refer to Table 14.3 to assist you with this process.

The second financial statement you need to create is your balance sheet. Your balance sheet is a snapshot of your financial position in a moment in time. Refer to Table 14.5 to assist you in listing your assets, liabilities, and owners' equity.

The last financial statement, the statement of cash flow, is the most important one to a bank. It is a measure of your ability to get and repay the loan from the bank. Referring to Table 14.7, be as realistic as possible as you are completing it. Allow yourself enough cash on hand to survive until the point at which the business starts to support itself.

Finance managers became key players as the recent recession forced many companies to alter how they budget. With plummeting revenues, the recessionary business climate seemed to offer few positives. For example, for United Parcel Service (UPS), the recession removed the company's ability to predict the path its finances would take. Management no longer had concrete information with which to make such predictions.

However, instead of seeing this as a liability, UPS Chief Financial Officer Kurt Kuehn and several others saw this as an opportunity to improve the financial function of budgeting. According to Kuehn, UPS was forced to adapt to focus on bare bones costs. Instead of focusing so extensively on absolute targets and measures, managers began to examine the minute details of budgeting. As a result, they created a system that allows them to match spending to changing revenue. This new philosophy was applied to every department. Focus on growth was replaced with an emphasis on balancing gains and losses in revenue with the company's spending costs. A good portion of this focus was turned toward identifying and trimming unnecessary spending.

For UPS, this resulted in a more flexible budget that received periodic reviews. The company is now making a comeback; recent quarterly numbers beat analyst predictions.

Financial consultants have long advocated for this shift and continue to urge CFOs to increase budget revisions. For example, rather than having a budget with set forecasts, managers should continually review the budget and make changes when needed. In addition, consultants are advising companies to plan for a variety of scenarios. Having strategies in place can potentially save a company, and periodic reviews of the budget can help companies identify changing scenarios and develop appropriate strategies. The effects of the recession might just change how finance departments view budgeting—for the better![9]

DISCUSSION QUESTIONS

1. Why did UPS change its budgeting process?

2. What changes did UPS make in its budgeting?

3. Do you think that UPS's new budgeting process would work well during a more prosperous economic period?

connect **LEARNSMART** **SMARTBOOK™**

For more information on the resources available from McGraw-Hill Ryerson, go to www.mcgrawhill.ca/he/solutions.

15

Money and the Financial System

LEARNING OBJECTIVES

LO1 Define money, its functions, and its characteristics.

LO2 Describe various types of money.

LO3 Specify how the Bank of Canada manages the money supply and regulates the Canadian banking system.

LO4 Compare and contrast chartered banks, trust companies, and credit unions/caisses populaires.

LO5 Distinguish among nonbanking institutions such as insurance companies, pension funds, mutual funds, and finance companies.

LO6 Investigate the challenges ahead for the banking industry.

DESTINATION CEO

Jack Dorsey grew up in Missouri and later studied at New York University. He then moved to California where he started a company to dispatch couriers, taxis, and emergency services using the Internet. He co-founded Twitter, Inc. in 2006, alongside Biz Stone and Evan Williams. Now, Dorsey is entering into new territory: the banking industry. Specifically, Dorsey has created a product called Square that he hopes will replace traditional credit card readers. Square is a small credit card swiper that merchants plug into their smart phones. After swiping the card, customers sign on the phone's screen, and within one minute, the transaction is complete. Square also tracks all sales conducted through its readers, creating a useful database.

Dorsey created Square after recognizing the massive unmet demand from less traditional merchants—such as artists—who do not own credit card readers. Square also reduces the number of organizations and fees involved with traditional credit card transactions, charging merchants a flat 2.75 percent and 15 cents for each transaction. *Time* was so impressed with Square that it nominated the product as one of the 50 best inventions of 2010. Despite its promising start, opportunities for credit card fraud will require Square to proactively take measures to ensure safe, convenient transactions.[1]

Introduction

From Bay Street to Main Street—both overseas and at home—money is the one tool used to measure personal and business income and wealth. Not surprisingly, **finance** is the study of money: how it's made, how it's lost, and how it's managed. This chapter introduces you to the role of money and the financial system in the economy. Of course, if you have a chequing account, automobile insurance, a student loan, or a credit card, you already have personal experience with some key players in the financial world.

> **Finance** the study of money; how it's made, how it's lost, and how it's managed

We begin our discussion with a definition of money and then explore some of the many forms money may take. Next, we examine the roles of the Bank of Canada and other major institutions in the financial system. Finally, we explore the future of the finance industry and some of the changes likely to occur over the course of the next several years.

For centuries, people on the Micronesian island of Yap have used giant round stones, like the ones shown here, for currency. The stones aren't moved, but their ownership can change.

Money in the Financial System

Strictly defined, **money** is anything generally accepted in exchange for goods and services. Materials as diverse as salt, cattle, fish, rocks, shells, and cloth, as well as precious metals such as gold, silver, and copper, have long been used by various cultures as money. Most of these materials were limited-supply commodities that had their own value to society (for example, salt can be used as a preservative or as jewellery). The supply of these commodities therefore determined the supply of "money" in that society. The next step was the development of "IOUs," or slips of paper that could be exchanged for a specified supply of the underlying commodity. "Gold" notes, for instance, could be exchanged for gold, and the money supply was tied to the amount of gold available. While paper money was first used in North America in 1685 (and even earlier in Europe), the concept of *fiat money*—a paper money not readily convertible to a precious metal such as gold—did not gain full acceptance until the Great Depression in the 1930s. Canada abandoned its gold-backed currency standard largely in response to the Great Depression and converted to a fiduciary, or fiat, monetary system. In Canada, paper money is really a government "note" or promise, worth the value specified on the note.

> **Money** anything generally accepted in exchange for goods and services

Functions of Money

No matter what a particular society uses for money, its primary purpose is to enable a person or organization to transform a desire into an action. These desires may be for entertainment actions, such as party expenses; operating actions, such as paying for rent, utilities, or employees; investing actions, such as buying property or equipment; or financing actions, such as for starting or growing a business. Money serves three important functions: as a medium of exchange, a measure of value, and a store of value.

Medium of Exchange.   Before fiat money, the trade of goods and services was accomplished through *bartering*—trading one good or service for another of similar value. As any school-age child knows, bartering can become quite inefficient—particularly in the case of complex, three-party transactions involving peanut butter sandwiches, baseball cards, and hair barrettes. There had to be a simpler way, and that was to decide on a single item—money—that can be freely converted to any other good upon agreement between parties.

"No matter what a particular society uses for money, its primary purpose is to enable a person or organization to transform a desire into an action."

Measure of Value.   As a measure of value, money serves as a common standard for the value of goods and services. For example, $2 will buy a dozen large eggs and $25,000 will buy a nice car in Canada. In Japan, where the currency is known as the yen, these same transactions would cost about 185 yen and 2.3 million yen, respectively. Money, then, is a common denominator that allows people to compare the different goods and services that can be consumed on a particular income level. While a star athlete and a "burger-flipper" are paid vastly different wages, each uses money as a measure of the value of yearly earnings and purchases.

Store of Value.   As a store of value, money serves as a way to accumulate wealth (buying power) until it is needed. For example, a person making $500 per week who wants to buy a $500 computer could save $50 per week for each of the next 10 weeks. Unfortunately, the value of stored money is directly dependent on the health of the economy. If, due to rapid inflation, all prices double in one year, then the purchasing power value of the money "stuffed in the mattress" would fall by half. On the other hand, "mattress savings" buy more when prices fall as they did for more than 52 months in Hong Kong between 1999 and 2005.

Characteristics of Money

To be used as a medium of exchange, money must be acceptable, divisible, portable, stable in value, durable, and difficult to counterfeit.

Acceptability.   To be effective, money must be readily acceptable for the purchase of goods and services and for the settlement of debts. Acceptability is probably the most important characteristic of money: If people do not trust the value of money, businesses will not accept it as a payment for goods and services, and consumers will have to find some other means of paying for their purchases.

Divisibility.   Given the widespread use of quarters, dimes, nickels, and pennies in Canada, it is no surprise that the principle of divisibility is an important one. With barter, the lack of divisibility often makes otherwise preferable trades impossible, as would be an attempt to trade a steer for a loaf of bread. For money to serve effectively as a measure of value, all items must be valued in terms of comparable units—dimes for a piece of bubble gum, quarters for laundry machines, and dollars (or dollars and coins) for everything else.

Portability. Clearly, for money to function as a medium of exchange, it must be easily moved from one location to the next. Large coloured rocks could be used as money, but you couldn't carry them around in your wallet. Paper currency and metal coins, on the other hand, are capable of transferring vast purchasing power into small, easily carried (and hidden!) bundles.

Stability. Money must be stable and maintain its declared face value. A $10 bill should purchase the same amount of goods or services from one day to the next. The principle of stability allows people who wish to postpone purchases and save their money to do so without fear that it will decline in value. As mentioned earlier, money declines in value during periods of inflation, when economic conditions cause prices to rise. Thus, the same amount of money buys fewer and fewer goods and services. In some countries, particularly in Latin America, people spend their money as fast as they can in order to keep it from losing any more of its value. Instability destroys confidence in a nation's money and its ability to store value and serve as an effective medium of exchange. Ultimately, people faced with spiralling price increases avoid the increasingly worthless paper money at all costs, storing all of their savings in the form of real assets such as gold and land.

Durability. Money must be durable. The crisp new dollar bills you trade at the music store for the hottest new CD will make their way all around town for about 20 months before being replaced (see Table 15.1). Were the value of an old, faded bill to fall in line with the deterioration of its appearance, the principles of stability and universal acceptability would fail (but, no doubt, fewer bills would pass through the washer!). Although metal coins, due to their much longer useful life, would appear to be an ideal form of money, paper currency is far more portable than metal because of its light weight. Today, coins are used primarily to provide divisibility.

Difficulty to Counterfeit. Finally, to remain stable and enjoy universal acceptance, it almost goes without saying that money must be very difficult to counterfeit— that is, to duplicate illegally. Every country takes steps to make counterfeiting difficult. Most use multicoloured money, and many use specially watermarked papers that

table 15.1 The Life Expectancy of Paper Currency

Denomination of Bill	Life Expectancy (Years)
$ 5	1 – 2
$ 10	1 – 2
$ 20	2 – 4
$100	7 – 9

SOURCE: Adapted from Doug Hanchard, "Polymer to replace cotton in Canadian currency notes," ZDNet, March 9, 2010, http://www.zdnet.com/blog/government/polymer-to-replace-cotton-in-canadian-currency-notes/7537 (accessed September 29, 2010).

are virtually impossible to duplicate. To thwart the problem of counterfeiting, the Bank of Canada has redesigned banknotes, most recently issuing the Polymer series, which uses innovative security features that can be seen in transparent areas on both sides of the notes.[2]

Although counterfeiting is not as much of an issue with coins, metal coins have their own problems. The value of certain coins is less than the money it costs to produce them. Due to the increased price of metals, many countries have removed the one-cent coin from circulation. Canada, for example, eliminated the one-cent coin with an estimated savings of $11 million a year.[3] Australia and New Zealand eliminated both the one-cent and two-cent coins. New Zealand has even stopped issuing the five-cent coin.[4]

The Bank of Canada redesigns currency in order to stay ahead of counterfeiters and protect the public.

As the world's second-largest economy, China is increasing efforts to make the yuan a global currency. China hopes that the yuan will achieve the status of the dollar, euro, and yen as an international currency for trade and investment. In order to encourage the yuan's internationalization, China has begun to allow other countries, including the United States, to trade in the yuan (previously such trade was restricted to the Chinese mainland). An increase in yuan trading and investment would help to buffer China against the dollar's decrease in value. Currently, 60 percent of the world's foreign reserves consist of the U.S. dollar and are used to help stabilize the global economy during economic unrest. A massive decrease in the dollar's value could, therefore, disrupt the world economy.

Making the yuan a global currency could be beneficial for businesses as well. For example, Caterpillar and McDonald's are financing China-based projects using the yuan. According to Caterpillar, this is more efficient and less expensive than having to convert U.S. dollars to yuan first. Despite these possibilities, China has many obstacles to overcome before the yuan can achieve status as a global currency. Demand among foreign businesses for trading and investing in the yuan is not high, and the yuan must be convertible to be used as a major currency in the foreign reserves. Convertibility means that currency must be easily converted into other currencies, which requires the currency to be valued at the current market rate. China was reluctant to do this in the past, keeping its currency rates lower than market value in a highly criticized move. Although China has expressed its intention to make its currency fully convertible, this will create many challenges for China in maintaining its competitive advantage in international trade.

LO2 Describe various types of money.

Types of Money

While paper money and coins are the most visible types of money, the combined value of all of the printed bills and all of the minted coins is actually rather insignificant when compared with the value of money kept in chequing accounts, savings accounts, and other monetary forms.

You probably have a **chequing account** (also called a demand deposit), money stored in an account at a bank or other financial institution that can be withdrawn without advance notice. One way to withdraw funds from your account is by writing a *cheque*, a written order to a bank to pay the indicated individual or business the amount specified on the cheque from money already on deposit. As legal instruments, cheques serve as a substitute for currency and coins and are preferred for many transactions due to their lower risk of loss. If you lose a $100 bill, anyone who finds or steals it can spend it. If you lose a blank cheque, however, the risk of catastrophic loss is quite low. Not only does your bank have a sample of your signature on file to compare with a suspected forged signature, but you can render the cheque immediately worthless by means of a stop-payment order at your bank.

There are several types of chequing accounts, with different features available for different monthly fee levels or specific minimum account balances. Some chequing accounts earn interest (a small percentage of the amount deposited in the account that the bank pays to the depositor). The interest rate paid on such accounts varies with the interest rates available in the economy but is typically quite low (ranging between zero and a little over 1 percent).

Savings accounts (also known as time deposits) are accounts with funds that usually cannot be withdrawn without advance notice and/or have limits on the number of withdrawals per period. While seldom enforced, the "fine print" governing most savings accounts prohibits withdrawals without two or three days' notice. Savings accounts are not generally used for transactions or as a medium of exchange, but their funds can be moved to a chequing account or turned into cash.

Money market accounts are similar to interest-bearing chequing accounts, but with more restrictions. Generally, in exchange for slightly higher interest rates, the owner of a money market account can write only a limited number of cheques each month, and there may be a restriction on the minimum amount of each cheque.

Certificates of deposit (CDs) are savings accounts that guarantee a depositor a set interest rate over a specified interval of

Chequing account money stored in an account at a bank or other financial institution that can be withdrawn without advance notice; also called a demand deposit

Savings accounts accounts with funds that usually cannot be withdrawn without advance notice; also known as time deposits

Money market accounts accounts that offer higher interest rates than standard bank rates but with greater restrictions

Certificates of deposit (CDs) savings accounts that guarantee a depositor a set interest rate over a specified interval as long as the funds are not withdrawn before the end of the period—six months or one year, for example

time as long as the funds are not withdrawn before the end of the interval—six months, one year, or seven years, for example. Money may be withdrawn from these accounts prematurely only after paying a substantial penalty. In general, the longer the term of the CD, the higher the interest rate it earns. As with all interest rates, the rate offered and fixed at the time the account is opened fluctuates according to economic conditions.

Credit cards allow you to promise to pay at a later date by using preapproved lines of credit granted by a bank or finance company. They are a popular substitute for cash payments because of their convenience, easy access to credit, and acceptance by merchants around the world. The institution that issues the credit card guarantees payment of a credit charge to merchants and assumes responsibility for collecting the money from the cardholders. Card issuers charge a transaction fee to the merchants for performing the credit check, guaranteeing the payment, and collecting the payment. The fee is typically between 2 and 5 percent, depending on the type of card. American Express fees are usually higher than Visa and MasterCard.

The original American Express cards require full payment at the end of each month, but American Express now offers credit cards similar to Visa, MasterCard, and Discover that allow cardholders to make installment payments and carry a maximum balance. There is a minimum monthly payment with interest charged on the remaining balance. Some people pay off their credit cards monthly, while others make monthly payments. Charges for unpaid balances can run 18 percent or higher at an annual rate, making credit card debt one of the most expensive ways to borrow money.

Besides the major credit card companies, many stores— Sears, The Bay, and others—have their own branded credit cards. They use credit rating agencies to check the credit of the cardholders and they generally make money on the finance charges. Unlike the major credit cards discussed, these "private label" cards are generally accepted only at stores associated with the issuing company.

New credit card regulations came in force as of January 1, 2010. These regulations are important to all companies and cardholders. Without going into details, the regulations enhance consumers' access to clear information about key details, such as interest rates, fees, and penalty charges. They also strengthen consumers' rights by limiting certain business practices of financial institutions.[5]

A **debit card** looks like a credit card but works like a cheque. The use of a debit card results in a direct, immediate, electronic payment from the cardholder's account to a

High interest rates on credit cards and the most recent recession have led many Canadians to reduce credit card balances for the first time in years.

merchant or other party. While they are convenient to carry and profitable for banks, they lack credit features, offer no purchase "grace period," and provide no hard "paper trail." Debit cards are gaining more acceptance with merchants, and consumers like debit cards because of the ease of getting cash from an increasing number of ATMs. Financial institutions also want consumers to use debit cards because they reduce the number of teller transactions and cheque processing costs.

> ### "Two major credit cards— MasterCard and Visa—represent the vast majority of credit cards held in Canada."

Traveller's cheques, money orders, and cashier's cheques are other common forms of "near money." Although each is slightly different from the others, they all share a common characteristic: A financial institution, bank, credit company, or neighbourhood currency exchange issues them in exchange for cash and guarantees that the purchased note will be honoured and exchanged for cash when it is presented to the institution making the guarantee.

Credit cards means of access to preapproved lines of credit granted by a bank or finance company

Debit card a card that looks like a credit card but works like a cheque; using it results in a direct, immediate, electronic payment from the cardholder's chequing account to a merchant or third party

The Canadian Financial System

The Canadian financial system fuels our economy by storing money, fostering investment opportunities, and making loans for new businesses and business expansion as well as for homes, cars, and postsecondary educations. This amazingly complex system includes banking institutions, nonbanking financial institutions such as finance companies, and systems that provide for the electronic transfer of funds throughout the world. Over the past 20 years, the rate at which money turns over, or changes hands, has increased exponentially. Different cultures place unique values on saving, spending, borrowing, and investing. The combination of this increased turnover rate and increasing interactions with people and organizations from other countries has created a complex money system. First, we need to meet the guardian of this complex system.

> "The Bank of Canada establishes and enforces banking rules that affect monetary policy and the overall level of the competition between different banks. "

The Bank of Canada

The nation's central bank is the **Bank of Canada** (the Bank), a crown corporation of the federal government founded in 1934 "to promote the economic and financial welfare of Canada." The Bank of Canada tries to create a positive economic environment capable of sustaining low inflation, high levels of employment, and long-term economic growth. To this end, the Bank of Canada has four major responsibilities: (1) to conduct monetary policy; (2) to issue Canada's bank notes and be responsible for their design and security, distribution, and replacement; (3) to promote safe, sound, and efficient financial systems; and (4) to provide high-quality, effective, and efficient funds-management services for the federal government, the Bank, and other clients.

Monetary Policy.　The Bank of Canada controls the amount of money available in the economy through **monetary policy.** Without this intervention, the supply of and demand for money might not balance. This could result in either rapid price increases (inflation) because of too little money, or economic recession and a slowdown of price increases (disinflation) because of too little growth in the money supply. In very rare cases (the depression of

Bank of Canada an independent agency of the federal government established in 1934 to regulate the nation's banking and financial industry

Monetary policy means by which the Bank of Canada controls the amount of money available in the economy

the 1930s) Canada has suffered from deflation, where the actual purchasing power of the dollar has increased as prices declined. To effectively control the supply of money in the economy, the Bank of Canada must have a good idea of how much money is in circulation at any given time. This has become increasingly challenging because of the global nature of our economy. Using several different measures of the money supply, the Bank of Canada establishes specific growth targets that, presumably, ensure a close balance between money supply and money demand. The Bank carries out monetary policy by influencing short-term interest rates. It does this by raising and lowering the target for the overnight rate. (The "overnight rate" is the interest rate at which major financial institutions, banks, credit unions, and similar credit-granting organizations borrow and lend one-day funds among themselves. This is different from the "bank rate," which is the midpoint of the range for the overnight rate). There is generally a lag of 6 to 18 months before the effect of these changes shows up in economic activity. As with other central banks, notably those of the European Union and the United States, the Bank of Canada has other tools at its disposal to fine-tune money growth, including open market operations, desired reserves, the bank (discount) rate, and credit controls (see Table 15.2).

　　Open market operations refer to decisions to buy or sell Treasury bills (short-term debt

Open market operations decisions to buy or sell Treasury bills (short-term debt issued by the government) and other investments in the open market

table 15.2 Tools for Regulating the Money Supply

Activity	Effect on the Money Supply and the Economy
Buy government securities	The money supply increases; economic activity increases.
Sell government securities	The money supply decreases; economic activity slows down.
Raise bank rate	Interest rates increase; the money supply decreases; economic activity slows down.
Lower bank rate	Interest rates decrease; the money supply increases; economic activity increases.
Increase reserves	Banks make fewer loans; the money supply declines; economic activity slows down.
Decrease reserves	Banks make more loans; the money supply increases; economic activity increases.
Relax credit controls	More people are encouraged to make major purchases, increasing economic activity.
Restrict credit controls	People are discouraged from making major purchases, decreasing economic activity.

issued by a government; also called T-bills) and other investments in the open market. The actual purchase or sale of the investments is performed by the Bank. This monetary tool, the most commonly employed of all operations, is performed almost daily in an effort to control the money supply.

When the Bank buys securities, it writes a cheque on its own account to the seller of the investments. When the seller of the investments (usually a large bank) deposits the cheque, the Bank transfers the balance from its account into the seller's account, thus increasing the supply of money in the economy and, hopefully, fueling economic growth. The opposite occurs when the Bank sells investments. The buyer writes a cheque to the Bank, and when the funds are transferred out of the purchaser's account, the amount of money in circulation falls, slowing economic growth to a desired level.

The second major monetary policy tool is the requirement of **desired reserves,** the percentage of deposits that banking institutions must hold in reserve ("in the vault," as it were). Funds so held are not available for lending to businesses and consumers. For example, a bank holding $10 million in deposits with a 10 percent desired reserves requirement must have reserves of $1 million. If the Bank of Canada were to reduce the desired reserves requirement to, say, 5 percent, the financial institution would need to keep only $500,000 in reserves. It could then lend to customers the $500,000 difference between the old reserve level and the new lower reserve level, thus increasing the supply of money. Because desired reserves have such a powerful effect on the money supply, the Bank of Canada does not change them very often, relying instead on open market operations most of the time.

The third monetary policy tool, the **bank rate,** is the rate of interest the Bank charges to loan money to any banking institution to meet reserve requirements. The Bank is the lender of last resort for these banks. When a bank borrows from the Bank of Canada, the interest rates charged there are often higher than those charged on loans of comparable risk elsewhere in the economy. This added interest expense, when it exists, serves to discourage banking institutions from borrowing from the Bank. When the Bank wants to expand the money supply, it lowers the bank rate to encourage borrowing. Conversely, when the Bank wants to decrease the money supply, it raises the bank rate. Not surprisingly, economists watch changes in this sensitive interest rate as an indicator of the Bank of Canada's monetary policy.

The final tool in the Bank's arsenal of weapons is **credit controls**—the authority to establish and enforce credit rules for financial institutions and some private investors.

Desired reserves the percentage of deposits that banking institutions hold in reserve

Bank rate the rate of interest the Bank of Canada charges to loan money to any banking institution to meet reserve requirements

Credit controls the authority to establish and enforce credit rules for financial institutions and some private investors

One of the roles of the Bank of Canada is to use its policies to keep money flowing. Money is the lifeblood of the economy. If banks become too protective of their funds and stop lending money, the economy can grind to a halt.

For example, the Bank can determine how large a down payment individuals and businesses must make on credit purchases of expensive items such as automobiles, and how much time they have to finish paying for the purchases. By raising and lowering minimum down payment amounts and payment periods, the Bank can stimulate or discourage credit purchases of "big ticket" items. The Bank also has the authority to set the minimum down payment investors must use for the credit purchases of stock. Buying stock with credit—"buying on margin"—is a popular investment strategy among individual speculators. By altering the margin requirement (commonly set at 50 percent of the price of the purchased stocks), the Bank can effectively control the total amount of credit borrowing in the stock market.

> ## "The Bank of Canada establishes and enforces banking rules that affect monetary policy and the overall level of the competition between different banks."

Bank Notes. Another responsibility of the Bank of Canada is for Canada's bank notes. The Bank of Canada is the country's sole bank note-issuing authority and is responsible for designing, producing, and distributing Canada's bank notes. The Bank of Canada must supply financial institutions with enough bank notes to satisfy public demand. Financial institutions get bank notes through the country's Bank Note Distribution System and return notes that are considered unfit for further circulation to the Bank of Canada. These notes are verified on high-speed, note-processing equipment and then shredded.[6]

The Financial System. The Bank of Canada works to promote safe, sound, and efficient financial systems. A stable financial system is essential to the health of Canada's economy. The Bank of Canada works with other agencies and market participants to promote the safe and efficient operation of the system's key elements. The Bank provides liquidity to the system; gives policy advice to the federal government on the design and development of the financial system; oversees major clearing and settlement systems; provides banking services to these systems and their participants; and collaborates with other domestic and international bodies involved in financial-stability issues.[7]

Funds Management Services. The Bank acts as the "fiscal agent" for the Government of Canada. As a government banker and treasury manager the Bank manages the accounts of the Receiver General, through which almost all money collected and spent by the government flows. The Bank ensures that these accounts have enough cash to meet daily requirements and invests any surpluses in term deposits. The Bank also manages the government's foreign exchange reserves. These reserves promote stability in the Canadian-dollar foreign exchange market. The Bank also provides policy advice to the government on the efficient management of the government debt and sells the securities at auction to financial market distributors and dealers. The main goal of the Bank's debt-management activities is to help provide stable and low-cost funding to the government.[8]

> "Banks are quite diversified **and offer a number of services.**"

LO4	Compare and contrast chartered banks, trust companies, and credit unions/caisses populaires.

Banking Institutions

Banking institutions accept money deposits from and make loans to individual consumers and businesses. Some of the most important banking institutions include chartered banks, trust companies, and credit unions/caisses populaires. Historically, these have all been separate institutions. However, new hybrid forms of banking institutions that perform two or more of these functions have emerged over the last two decades. The following banking institutions all have one thing in common: They are businesses whose objective is to earn money by managing, safeguarding, and lending money to others. Their sales revenues come from the fees and interest that they charge for providing these financial services.

Chartered Banks. The largest and oldest of all financial institutions are **chartered banks,** which perform a variety of financial services. They rely mainly on chequing and savings accounts as their major source of funds and use only a portion of these deposits to make loans to businesses and individuals. Because it is unlikely that all

Chartered banks the largest and oldest of all financial institutions, relying mainly on chequing and savings accounts as sources of funds for loans to businesses and individuals

the depositors of any one bank will want to withdraw all of their funds at the same time, a bank can safely loan out a large percentage of its deposits.

Today, banks are quite diversified and offer a number of services. Chartered banks make loans for virtually any conceivable legal purpose, from vacations to cars, from homes to postsecondary educations. Banks offer *home equity loans,* by which home owners can borrow against the appraised value of their already purchased homes. Banks also issue Visa and MasterCard credit cards and offer CDs and trusts (legal entities set up to hold and manage assets for a beneficiary). Many banks rent safe deposit boxes in bank vaults to customers who want to store jewellery, legal documents, artwork, and other valuables. The banking industry in Canada includes domestic banks, foreign bank subsidiaries, and foreign bank branches. In total, these institutions manage almost $1.8 trillion in assets. The Office of the Superintendent of Financial Institutions, along with the Bank of Canada and the Canada Deposit Insurance Corporation, regulate and supervise federally registered financial institutions.[9] Table 15.3 gives an overview of the Canadian financial system.

Trust Companies. **Trust companies** act as fiduciaries or corporate trustees and operate under either provincial or federal legislation and conduct the same activities as a bank. Like a bank, they operate through a network of branches. However, because of its fiduciary role, a trust company can administer estates, trusts, pension plans, and agency contracts, which banks cannot

Trust companies corporations that act as a trustee and usually also provide banking services

table 15.3 Overview of the Canadian Financial Services Sector

Sector	Number of Active Firms
Banks	78
Trust companies	48
Loan companies	19
Credit unions/caisses populaires	427
Life and health insurance companies	83
Property and casualty insurance companies	186
Mutual fund companies	831
Securities dealers	205
Finance and leasing companies	190

SOURCES: Office of the Superintendent of Financial Institutions, www.osfi-bsif.gc.ca/osfi/index_e.aspx?DetailID=568, ; Credit Union Central of Canada, http://www.cucentral.ca/QuickFacts ; Investment Funds Institute of Canada, https://www.ific.ca/Content/Content.aspx?id=152 ; Investment Dealers Association of Canada, http://www.iiroc.ca/English/About/OurRole/Pages/DealersWeRegulate.aspx,; Canadian Finance & Leasing Association, http://www.cfla-acfl.ca/, (all accessed July 2, 2010).

The World Bank, created in 1944 by delegates from across the world, raises money through donations, bond sales, and shareholder support. This money is then used to provide loans and other financial assistance to developing countries. The loans fund a variety of projects, including education, infrastructure, and public administration. Realizing that funding certain projects could negatively affect the environment, the World Bank adopted policies to assess the sustainability of proposed projects.

Despite these policies, environmental groups have accused the World Bank of funding projects that harm the environment. One project, the Sardar Sarovar Dam in India's River Narmada, was criticized for causing environmental degradation. Yet advocates for the dam argue that it provides irrigation and drinking water. The World Bank must juggle both the human and environmental impacts when determining which projects to fund. As the importance of sustainability grows, the World Bank has taken steps to curb climate change and support renewable energy initiatives. The World Bank partnered with the C40 Cities Climate Leadership Group to reduce global greenhouse gas emissions.

The bank has also increased its loans for renewable energy projects to almost 23 percent of energy loans, including $175 million for a geothermal project in Indonesia. Whether these actions will lead to significant change or whether they are merely window-dressing to reduce criticism remains to be seen.

DISCUSSION QUESTIONS

1. Describe what the World Bank does. Why is it important?

2. Why is sustainability becoming a major issue for the World Bank?

3. Do you feel that the World Bank should make sustainability a priority?

---

do.[10] The Bank Act has allowed regulated federal financial institutions to own trust companies. As a result, and with the acquisition of Canada Trust by the Toronto Dominion Bank, trust companies are a small market segment.

Credit Unions and Caisses Populaires. A **credit union/caisse populaire** (as it is known in Quebec) is a co-operative financial institution that is owned and controlled by its depositors, who usually have a common employer, profession, trade group, or religion. Because the credit union is tied to a common organization, the credit unions are operated democratically and owned by their depositors as members. The members are allowed to vote for directors and share in the credit union's profits in the form of higher interest rates on accounts and/or lower loan rates. While credit unions were originally created to provide depositors with a short-term source of funds for low-interest consumer loans for items such as cars, home appliances, vacations, and postsecondary education, today they offer a wide range of financial services. Generally, the larger the credit union, the more sophisticated its financial service offerings will be. They are subject to provincial regulation and are usually small and locally oriented. This sector is almost exclusively regulated at the provincial level in Canada. However, the Credit Union Central of Canada is chartered and regulated by the federal government.[11]

Credit union/caisse populaire a financial institution owned and controlled by its depositors, who usually have a common employer, profession, trade group, or religion

Insurance for Banking Institutions. The **Canada Deposit Insurance Corporation (CDIC),** a federal crown corporation that insures individual bank accounts, was established in 1967 and insures deposits in banks and trust and loan companies against loss in the event of member failure. It insures eligible deposits up to $100,000 per depositor in each member institution, which must pay premiums to cover CDIC's insurance obligations. Should a member bank fail, its depositors can recover all of their funds, up to $100,000. Deposits of credit unions and caisses populaires are protected under provincial stabilization funds and/or deposit insurance and guarantee corporations. Deposit insurance coverage ranges from $60,000 to unlimited coverage, with the amount varying by province.[12] When they were originally established, the federal government hoped that these insurance funds would make people feel secure about their savings so that they would not panic and withdraw their money when news of a bank failure was announced. During the Great Depression, many banks failed and their depositors lost everything. The fact that large numbers of major financial institutions failed in the 1980s and 1990s—without a single major banking panic—underscores the effectiveness of the current insurance system. While the future may yet bring unfortunate surprises, most depositors go to sleep every night without worrying about the safety of their savings.

Canada Deposit Insurance Corporation (CDIC) a federal crown corporation that insures bank accounts

Distinguish among nonbanking institutions such as insurance companies, pension funds, mutual funds, and finance companies.

Nonbanking Institutions

Nonbank financial institutions offer some financial services, such as short-term loans or investment products, but do not accept deposits. These include insurance companies, pension funds, mutual funds, brokerage firms, nonfinancial firms, and finance companies.

Diversified Firms. Recently, a growing number of traditionally nonfinancial firms have moved onto the financial field. These firms include manufacturing organizations, such as General Motors and General Electric, that traditionally confined their financial activities to financing their customers' purchases. GE was once so successful in the financial arena that its credit subsidiary accounted for more than 40 percent of the company's revenues and earnings. Unfortunately, GE Capital became a liability to GE during the financial crisis, and the stock price fell from $42 per share to less than $8 per share. It is in the process of recovery as GE cuts the size of its finance unit and writes off billions of dollars in bad loans. Other nonfinancial firms have been also been unsuccessful in their financial ventures. Sears, the North American retail giant, once commanded an imposing financial network composed of real estate, credit card, and brokerage companies, but losses of hundreds of millions of dollars forced Sears to dismantle its network. Perhaps the moral of the story for firms like Sears is "stick to what you know."

Insurance Companies. **Insurance companies** are businesses that protect their clients against financial losses from certain specified risks (death, injury, disability, accident, fire, theft, and natural disasters, for example) in exchange for a fee, called a premium. Because insurance premiums flow into the companies regularly, but major insurance losses cannot be timed with great accuracy (although expected risks can be assessed with considerable precision), insurance companies generally have large amounts of excess funds. They typically invest these or make long-term loans, particularly to businesses in the form of commercial real estate loans.

Pension Funds. **Pension funds** are managed investment pools set aside by individuals, corporations, unions, and some nonprofit

> "A growing number of traditionally nonfinancial firms have moved onto the financial field."

Insurance companies businesses that protect their clients against financial losses from certain specified risks (death, accident, and theft, for example)

Pension funds managed investment pools set aside by individuals, corporations, unions, and some nonprofit organizations to provide retirement income for members

organizations to provide retirement income for members. One type of pension fund is the *registered retirement savings plan (RRSP)*, which is established by individuals to provide for their personal retirement needs. RRSPs can be invested in a variety of financial assets, including shares, bonds, mutual funds, and low-risk financial "staples" such as Treasury securities. The choice is up to each person and is dictated solely by individual objectives and tolerance for risk. The interest earned by all of these investments may be deferred tax-free until retirement.

In 2009, the Canadian Minister of Finance announced the creation of a Tax-Free Savings Account (TFSA). Investors may contribute up to a set amount per year (currently $5,500); the money and the contribution are considered an after-tax contribution. When the money is withdrawn at retirement, or at any other time, no tax is paid on the distribution. The TSFA is beneficial to young people who can allow a long time for their money to compound and who may be able to have their parents or grandparents fund the TSFA with gift money.

Most major corporations provide some kind of pension plan for their employees. Many of these are established with bank trust departments or life insurance companies. Money is deposited in a separate account in the name of each individual employee, and when the employee retires, the total amount in the account can be either withdrawn in one lump sum or taken as monthly cash payments over some defined time period (usually for the remaining life of the retiree).

All employed Canadians contribute to either the Canada Pension Plan or the Quebec Pension Plan through payroll deductions. The funds are managed separately from general tax dollars and all the monies generated are used to pay benefits to eligible plan members. The plans offer similar benefits including pensions after age 60, survivor benefits for spouses and dependants, and disability payments.

State Farm Insurance allows users to input their information on its website to receive an auto insurance quote quickly and conveniently.

Mutual Funds. A **mutual fund** pools individual investor dollars and invests them in large numbers of well diversified securities. Individual investors buy shares in a mutual fund in the hope of earning a high rate of return and in much the same way as people buy shares of stock. Because of the large numbers of people investing in any one mutual fund, the funds can afford to invest in hundreds (if not thousands) of securities at any one time, minimizing the risks of any single security that does not do well. Mutual funds provide professional financial management for people who lack the time and/or expertise to invest in particular securities, such as government bonds. While there are no hard-and-fast rules, investments in one or more mutual funds are one way for people to plan for financial independence at the time of retirement.

A special type of mutual fund called a *money market fund* invests specifically in short-term debt securities issued by governments and large corporations. Although they offer services such as cheque-writing privileges and reinvestment of interest income, money market funds differ from the money market accounts offered by banks primarily in that the former represent a pool of funds, while the latter are basically specialized, individual chequing accounts. Money market funds usually offer slightly higher rates of interest than bank money market accounts.

Mutual fund an investment company that pools individual investor dollars and invests them in large numbers of well diversified securities

Brokerage firms firms that buy and sell stocks, bonds, and other securities for their customers and provide other financial services

Brokerage Firms. Brokerage firms buy and sell stocks, bonds, and other securities for their customers and provide other financial services. The largest of the brokerage firms (including RBC Dominion Securities) have developed so many specialized services that they may be considered financial networks—organizations capable of offering virtually all of the services an individual may require.

Most brokerage firms are really part of financial conglomerates that provide many different kinds of services besides buying and selling securities for clients. The investment

Mutual funds are considered an excellent method for investing for retirement.

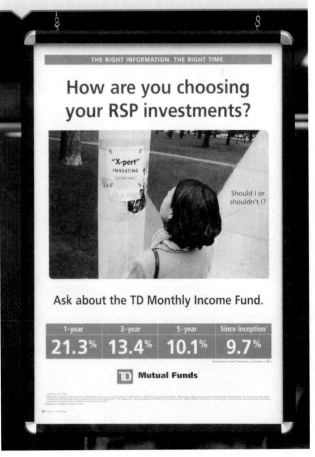

banker underwrites new issues of securities for corporations, states, and municipalities that need to raise money in the capital markets. The new issue market is called a *primary market* because the sale of the securities is for the first time. After the first sale, the securities are traded in the *secondary markets* by brokers. The investment banker advises on the price of the new securities and generally guarantees the sale while overseeing the distribution of the securities through the selling brokerage houses. Investment bankers also act as dealers who make markets in securities. They do this by offering to sell the securities at an asked price (which is a higher rate) and buy the securities at a bid price (which is a lower rate)—the difference in the two prices represents the profit for the dealer.

Finance Companies. **Finance companies** are businesses that offer short-term loans at substantially higher rates of interest than banks. Commercial finance companies make loans to businesses, requiring their borrowers to pledge assets such as equipment, inventories, or unpaid accounts as collateral for the loans. Consumer finance companies make loans to individuals. Like commercial finance companies, these firms require some sort of personal collateral as security against the borrower's possible inability to repay the loans. Because

> **Finance companies** businesses that offer short-term loans at substantially higher rates of interest than banks

of the high interest rates they charge and other factors, finance companies typically are the lender of last resort for individuals and businesses whose credit limits have been exhausted and/or those with poor credit ratings.

Electronic Banking

Since the advent of the computer age, a wide range of technological innovations have made it possible to move money all across the world electronically. Such "paperless" transactions have allowed financial institutions to reduce costs in what has been (and what appears to continue to be) a virtual competitive battlefield. **Electronic funds transfer (EFT)** is any movement of funds by means of an electronic terminal, telephone, computer, or magnetic tape. Such transactions order a particular financial institution to subtract money from one account and add it to another. The most commonly used forms of EFT are automated banking machines and home banking systems.

Automated Banking Machines. Probably the most familiar form of electronic banking is the **automated banking machine (ABM)**, which dispenses cash, accepts

> **Electronic funds transfer (EFT)** any movement of funds by means of an electronic terminal, telephone, computer, or magnetic tape
>
> **Automated banking machine (ABM)** the most familiar form of electronic banking, which dispenses cash, accepts deposits, and allows balance inquiries and cash transfers from one account to another

Consider the Following: Cost of Borrowing Poses a Threat to Brazilian Consumers

Debt is not necessarily a bad thing. Many companies borrow in order to finance projects, which can lead to greater profits. Consumers borrow to obtain objects that they value. The problem arises when businesses or individuals incur so much debt that they cannot pay it off. This is becoming a serious concern for consumers in Brazil.

The Brazilian economy has been booming in recent years, creating a growing middle class. With their newfound wealth, consumers are spending and using credit like never before. Unfortunately, many Brazilian consumers have little experience with credit, which is contributing to widespread consumer borrowing and a rising number of loan defaults. While retail sales rose 9 percent in one year—faster than GDP growth—the default rate on personal loans rose 22 percent in a six-month period.

Consumer spending has become such a problem that the central bank of Brazil has increased interest rates. However, some banks charge even higher rates than the central bank. Credit cards have an annual interest rate of 238 percent on average, whereas the cost of borrowing for personal loans is 85 percent for retailers and 47 percent for banks.

The ethics of charging such high interest rates are questionable. On the one hand, higher interest rates tend to deter spending. Additionally, inflation in Brazil has risen significantly, which in turn increases the cost of borrowing. On the other hand, the lack of knowledge that many Brazilian consumers have of credit puts them at a major disadvantage at understanding the financial dangers of too much debt.

DISCUSSION QUESTIONS

1. Why are Brazilians having difficulty with borrowing and paying back debt?

2. Do you feel that it is ethical for banks to charge such high rates for borrowing?

3. What would you suggest as a way to reduce the debt problems that Brazilian consumers are facing?

deposits, and allows balance inquiries and cash transfers from one account to another. ABMs provide 24-hour banking services—both at home (through a local bank) and far away (via worldwide ABM networks such as Cirrus and Plus). Rapid growth, driven by both strong consumer acceptance and lower transaction costs for banks (about half the cost of teller transactions), has led to the installation of hundreds of thousands of ABMs worldwide. Table 15.4 presents some interesting statistics about banks and technology.

Online Banking. Many banking activities may now be carried out on a computer at home or at work, or through wireless devices such as cell phones and PDAs anywhere there is a wireless "hot point." Consumers and small businesses can now make a bewildering array of financial transactions at home or on the go 24 hours a day. Functioning much like a vast network of personal ABMs, banks allow their customers to make sophisticated banking transactions, buy and sell stocks and bonds, and purchase products and airline tickets without ever leaving home or speaking to another human being. Many banks allow customers to log directly into their accounts to check balances, transfer money between accounts, view their account statements, and pay bills via home computer or other Internet-enabled devices. Computers and advanced telecommunications technology have revolutionized world commerce.

| **LO6** | Investigate the challenges ahead for the banking industry. |

Banking in the Future and the Impact of the Financial Crisis

Rapid advances and innovations in technology are challenging the banking industry and requiring it to change. As we said earlier, more and more banks, both large and small, are offering electronic access to their financial services. ABM technology is rapidly changing, with machines now dispensing more than just cash. Online financial services, ABM technology, and bill presentation are just a few of the areas where rapidly changing technology is causing the banking industry to change as well.

The premise that banks will get bigger over the next 10 years is uncertain. During 2007–08, the financial markets collapsed under the weight of declining housing prices, subprime mortgages (mortgages with low-quality borrowers), and risky securities backed by these subprime mortgages. Because the value of bank assets declined dramatically, most large banks had a shrinking capital base. That is, the amount of debt in relation to their equity was so high that they were below the minimum required capital requirements. This was a financial environment where banks did not trust the counterparties to their loans and asset-backed securities. In this environment, the markets ceased to function in an orderly fashion. To keep the banking system from total collapse, central banks around the world created different programs, like the Troubled Asset Relief Program in the United States.

There have been very few bank failures in Canada, which is widely acknowledged as having one of the safest and soundest financial sectors in the world.[14] In response to technological innovation and globalization, the financial services sector has undergone rapid change. The sector is increasingly competitive as changes to federal laws and regulations have resulted in the entry of new domestic and foreign competitors in the Canadian market. The hunt will continue for other merger partners that will globally expand institutions' customer reach and the services they are able to offer.

Indeed, the recent trend toward ever bigger banks and other financial institutions is not happening by chance alone. Financial services may be an example of a "natural oligopoly," meaning that the industry may be best served by a few very large firms rather than a host of smaller ones. As the largest banks merge into even larger international entities, they will erase the relative competitive advantages now enjoyed by the largest banks. It is by no means implausible that the financial services industry in 2020 will be dominated by 10 or so internationally oriented "megabanks."

table 15.4 Bank Fact Sheet

Number of cash dispensing machines in Canada (2011)	17.6 million
Number of online banking transactions completed with the six largest banks in Canada in 2011	561 million
Number of transactions logged at bank-owned ABMs in Canada (2011)	889 million
Amount six largest Canadian banks spent on technology in 2011	$7 billion
Amount six largest Canadian banks have spent on technology during 1996–2011	$69.6 billion

SOURCES: www.cba.ca/contents/files/statistics/stat_abmnum_db247_en.pdf; www.cba.ca/en/component/content/category/53-quick-facts

LEARNING OBJECTIVES SUMMARY

LO1 Define money, its functions, and its characteristics.

Money is anything generally accepted as a means of payment for goods and services. Money serves as a medium of exchange, a measure of value, and a store of wealth. To serve effectively in these functions, money must be acceptable, divisible, portable, durable, stable in value, and difficult to counterfeit.

LO2 Describe various types of money.

Money may take the form of currency, chequing accounts, or other accounts. Chequing accounts are funds left in an account in a financial institution that can be withdrawn (usually by writing a cheque) without advance notice. Other types of accounts include savings accounts (funds left in an interest-earning account that usually cannot be withdrawn without advance notice), money market accounts (an interest-bearing chequing account that is invested in short-term debt instruments), certificates of deposit (deposits left in an institution for a specified period of time at a specified interest rate), credit cards (access to a preapproved line of credit granted by a bank or company), and debit cards (means of instant cash transfers between customer and merchant accounts), as well as traveller's cheques, money orders, and cashier's cheques.

LO3 Specify how the Bank of Canada manages the money supply and regulates the Canadian banking system.

The Bank of Canada manages the money supply indirectly through its influence on the target overnight rate. Increases in interest rates reduce the demand for loans and lead to debtors paying down existing debt. This results in slower growth or even a reduction in money supply. The Bank's other activities include the issuance of Canadian bank notes, provision of banking services for the federal government, and promotion of a safe financial system. Other central bank tools for the conduct of monetary policy are buying and selling government securities, raising or lowering the bank rate (the rate of interest at which banks may borrow cash reserves from the central bank), raising or lowering bank reserve requirements (the percentage of funds on deposit at a bank that must be held to cover expected depositor withdrawals), and adjusting down payment and repayment terms for credit purchases.

LO4 Compare and contrast chartered banks, trust companies, and credit unions/caisses populaires.

Chartered banks are federally regulated under the Bank Act. They take and hold deposits in accounts and make loans to individuals and businesses. Trust companies may be incorporated federally or provincially. Trust companies accept and hold deposits in accounts and make loans to individuals but are restricted in commercial lending. Only trust companies can offer trustee services. Credit unions/caisses populaires are provincially regulated co-operatives. Both offer deposit accounts and loan services to their members.

LO5 Distinguish among nonbanking institutions such as insurance companies, pension funds, mutual funds, and finance companies.

Insurance companies are businesses that protect their clients against financial losses due to certain circumstances, in exchange for a fee. Pension funds are investments set aside by organizations or individuals to meet retirement needs. Mutual funds pool investors' money and invest in large numbers of different types of securities. Brokerage firms buy and sell stocks and bonds for investors. Finance companies make short-term loans at higher interest rates than do banks.

LO6 Investigate the challenges ahead for the banking industry.

Future changes in financial regulations are likely to result in fewer but larger banks and other financial institutions.

KEY TERMS

automated banking machine (ABM)
Bank of Canada
bank rate
brokerage firms
Canada Deposit Insurance Corporation (CDIC)
certificates of deposit (CDs)
chartered banks
chequing account
credit cards
credit controls
credit union/caisse populaire
debit card
desired reserves

electronic funds transfer (EFT)
finance
finance companies
insurance companies
monetary policy
money
money market accounts
mutual fund
open market operations
pension funds
savings accounts
trust companies

DESTINATION CEO DISCUSSION QUESTIONS

1. Why do you think Jack Dorsey was successful as an inventor?

2. What are expansion opportunities for Square?

3. How does technology play a role in the success of Square?

Economics is the science of money and its interaction within the general economy. Economists study the ways a society uses scarce resources such as land, labour, raw materials, machinery, and money to produce goods and services. Employed by most major companies and virtually all government agencies, economists conduct research, collect and analyze data, monitor economic trends, and develop forecasts concerning a wide range of economic factors and issues. Within private industry, economists are asked to make predictions concerning the likely economic consequences of various government and/or competitor policies, as well as those of the employing firm.

Chartered banks and other financial institutions are major employers of economists. Indeed, the economic forecasts generated by internal economists play a key role in hosts of financial decisions, from those involving changes in loan rates to the likely future direction of the stock and bond markets, to reasoned conjectures about the direction and impact of expected changes in the money supply and/or government tax policy. While economists can't actually see into the future, their estimates about it are frequently so accurate as to suggest otherwise.

BUILD YOUR BUSINESS PLAN

Money and the Financial System

This chapter provides you with the opportunity to think about money and the financial system and just how many new businesses fail every year. In some industries the failure rate is as high as 80 percent. One reason for such a high failure rate is the inability to manage the finances of the organization. From the start of the business, financial planning plays a key role. Try getting a loan without an accompanying budget/forecast of earnings and cash flow.

While obtaining a loan from a family member may be the easiest way to fund your business, it may cause more problems for you later on if you are unable to pay the money back as scheduled. Before heading to a lending officer at a bank, contact your local SBA centre to see what assistance they might provide.

Is it time to ditch the bank for the credit union? After the most recent financial crisis led to the closure of several banks, credit unions began looking better and better. Credit unions have several advantages over banks. Because they are nonprofit institutions, and therefore do not have to pay shares or executive salaries, the money that credit unions earn goes back to members in the form of dividends. The lack of pressure to make a profit also allows credit unions to offer more attractive rates on items like GICs, mortgages, credit cards, and car loans. For example, in May 2010 credit unions charged an average 5.73 percent for a four-year new-car loan, while banks charged an average of 6.98 percent.

Some consumers also feel that credit unions offer more quality services, such as taking the time to help customers set up financial plans. Additionally, most credit unions offer free chequing and lower penalty fees than banks. With 5.3 million members, credit unions are becoming a popular alternative to traditional banking. In Canada, one in three residents of B.C. belong to a credit union; in Ontario it is one in ten.

Of course, credit unions have their downsides as well. Unlike banks, consumers must meet requirements to become members of credit unions and in Canada, they must pay a small fee to join. Banks also offer more diverse products and services than many credit unions do. These downsides have led analysts to recommend that consumers carefully investigate financial institutions, be it bank or credit union, before investing. However, for those consumers who constantly get frustrated with their banks, credit unions might be the way to go.[15]

DISCUSSION QUESTIONS

1. What are the advantages of credit unions over banks?

2. What are the disadvantages of credit unions over banks?

3. Given a choice, would you rather deal with a bank or a credit union?

connect **LEARNSMART** **SMARTBOOK**™

For more information on the resources available from McGraw-Hill Ryerson, go to www.mcgrawhill.ca/he/solutions.

LO1 Describe some common methods of managing current assets.

LO2 Identify some sources of short-term financing (current liabilities).

LO3 Summarize the importance of long-term assets and capital budgeting.

LO4 Specify how companies finance their operations and manage fixed assets with long-term liabilities, particularly bonds.

LO5 Discuss how corporations can use equity financing by issuing stock through an investment banker.

LO6 Describe the various securities markets in Canada.

DESTINATION CEO

Michael Lee-Chin has a Coke story. If an investor had bought one share of Coke for $26 back in 1919, it would be worth $4.3 million today. If 100 people had bought the stock at that time, only one investor would remain because the other 99 investors would have sold the stock because of price fluctuations. Lee-Chin built his company, AIC Advantage Mutual Fund, by applying this investment principle: "Buy. Hold. And prosper." His approach has worked. AIC was the 15th-largest mutual fund in Canada, and Lee-Chin has a reported net worth of $1.1 billion. His wealth makes him one of the world's richest men and one of three confirmed black billionaires in North America.

Fifty years ago, Lee-Chin was a poor kid from Port Antonio, Jamaica. He was one of nine children born to a Chinese and Jamaican father and a Jamaican mother, both of whom worked as grocery clerks. Lee-Chin graduated from McMaster University in Hamilton with a degree in Civil Engineering, and later returned to Jamaica to work as an engineer. In 1976, he moved back to Ontario where he took a job as a bouncer at McMaster University's pub bar. While working at the bar, a friend told him of the commissions he made as a financial advisor. That conversation changed Lee-Chin's life forever. He landed a job at Investors Group, talked to investment professionals, and read every book and publication on investing he could find. After working for Investors Group and building a solid track record over a nine-year period, Lee-Chin became interested in portfolio management and in running his own firm. In 1986, he purchased a small financial services company for $132,000 that had a mutual fund and $526,000 in assets. That company was AIC.

In 2006, Michael Lee-Chin stepped down as head of the mutual fund firm. AIC has been plagued by lower-than-average returns and investor withdrawals had cut assets under management nearly in half. The company had faced a regulatory probe of industry trading in 2004 in which the firm ended up paying a fine of almost $60 million. In addition, AIC's investment strategy, which includes holding companies like banks, fund firms, and large retail stocks for the long term, also meant it was not able to match the big returns from red-hot sectors including income trusts and commodities. The financial crisis of 2008 hurt AIC and by the end of July 2009, its assets had shrunk to $3.8 billion. In 2009, Lee-Chin's Portland Holdings Inc. sold AIC Ltd.'s Canadian retail mutual-fund business to Manulife Financial Corp. Portland continues to serve as sub-advisor for about $2.2 billion in assets for the insurance giant and Lee-Chin is lead portfolio manager of the Advantage AIC fund.[1]

Introduction

While it's certainly true that money makes the world go 'round, financial management is the discipline that makes the world turn more smoothly. Indeed, without effective management of assets, liabilities, and owners' equity, all business organizations are doomed to fail—regardless of the quality and innovation of their products. Financial management is the field that addresses the issues of obtaining and managing the funds and resources necessary to run a business successfully. It is not limited to business organizations: All organizations, from the corner store to the local nonprofit art museum, from giant corporations to county governments, must manage their resources effectively and efficiently if they are to achieve their objectives.

In this chapter, we look at both short- and long-term financial management. First, we discuss the management of short-term assets, which companies use to generate sales and conduct ordinary day-to-day business operations. Next we turn our attention to the management of short-term liabilities, the sources of short-term funds used to finance the business. Then, we discuss the management of long-term assets such as plant and equipment and the long-term liabilities such as stocks and bonds used to finance these important corporate assets. Finally, we look at the securities markets, where stocks and bonds are traded.

LO1 Describe some common methods of managing current assets.

Managing Current Assets and Liabilities

Managing short-term assets and liabilities involves managing the current assets and liabilities on the balance sheet (discussed in Chapter 14). Current assets are short-term resources such as cash, investments, accounts receivable, and inventory. Current liabilities are short-term debts such as accounts payable, accrued salaries, accrued taxes, and short-term bank loans. We use the terms *current* and *short-term* interchangeably because short-term assets and liabilities are usually replaced by new assets and liabilities within three or four months, and always within a year. Managing short-term assets and liabilities is sometimes called **working capital management** because short-term assets and liabilities continually flow through an organization and are thus said to be "working."

Managing Current Assets

The chief goal of financial managers who focus on current assets and liabilities is to maximize the return to the business on cash, temporary investments of idle cash, accounts receivable, and inventory.

Managing Cash. A crucial element facing any financial manager is effectively managing the firm's cash flow. Remember that cash flow is the movement of money through an organization on a daily, weekly, monthly, or yearly basis. Ensuring that sufficient (but not excessive) funds are on hand to meet the company's obligations is one of the single most important facets of financial management.

Idle cash does not make money, and corporate chequing accounts typically do not earn interest. As a result, astute money managers try to keep just enough cash on hand, called **transaction balances,** to pay bills—such as employee wages, supplies, and utilities— as they fall due. To manage the firm's cash and ensure that enough cash flows through the organization quickly and efficiently, companies try to speed up cash collections from customers.

> **Transaction balances** cash kept on hand by a firm to pay normal daily expenses, such as employee wages and bills for supplies and utilities
>
> **Lockbox** an address, usually a commercial bank, at which a company receives payments in order to speed collections from customers

To facilitate collection, some companies have customers send their payments to a **lockbox,** which is simply an address for receiving payments, instead of directly to the company's main address. The manager of the lockbox, usually a commercial bank, collects payments directly from the lockbox several times a day and deposits them into the company's bank account. The bank can then start clearing the cheques and get the money into the company's chequing account much more quickly than if the payments had been submitted directly to the company. However, there is no free lunch: The costs associated with lockbox systems make them worthwhile only for those companies that receive thousands of cheques from customers each business day.

More and more companies are now using electronic funds transfer systems to pay and collect bills online. It is interesting that companies want to collect cash quickly but pay out cash slowly. When companies use electronic funds transfers between buyers and suppliers, the speed of collections and disbursements increases to one day. Only with the use of cheques can companies delay the payment of cash quickly and have a three- or four-day waiting period until the cheque is presented to their bank and the cash leaves their account.

Investing Idle Cash. As companies sell products, they generate cash on a daily basis, and sometimes cash comes in faster than it is needed to pay bills. Organizations often invest this "extra" cash, for periods as short as one day (overnight)

> **Working capital management** the managing of short-term assets and liabilities

or for as long as one year, until it is needed. Such temporary investments of cash are known as **marketable securities.**

Examples include Treasury bills, Banker's Acceptances, commercial paper (corporate paper), and eurodollar loans. Table 16.1 summarizes a number of different marketable securities used by businesses and some sample interest rates on these investments. The safety rankings are relative. While all of the listed securities are very low risk, the Bank of Canada securities are the safest.

Many large companies invest idle cash in Government of Canada **Treasury bills (T-bills),** which are short-term debt obligations the federal government sells to raise money. Auctioned biweekly by the Bank of Canada, T-bills carry maturities of one week to one year. T-bills are generally considered to be the safest of all investments and are called risk-free because the federal government will not default on its debt.

Commercial certificates of deposit (CDs) are issued by commercial banks and brokerage companies. They are available in minimum amounts of $100,000 but are typically in units of $1 million for large corporations investing excess cash. Unlike consumer CDs (discussed in Chapter 15), which must be held until maturity, commercial CDs may be traded prior to maturity. Should a cash shortage occur, the organization can simply sell the CD on the open market and obtain needed funds.

One of the most popular short-term investments for the largest business organizations is **commercial paper**—a written promise from one company to another to pay a specific amount of money. Because commercial paper is backed only by the name and reputation of the issuing company, sales of commercial paper are restricted to only the largest and most financially stable companies. As commercial paper is frequently bought and sold for durations of as short as one business day, many "players" in the market find themselves buying commercial paper with excess cash on one day and selling it to gain extra money the following day.

Some companies invest idle cash in international markets such as the **eurodollar market,** a market for trading U.S.

dollars in foreign countries. Because the eurodollar market was originally developed by London banks, any dollar-denominated deposit in a non-U.S. bank is called a eurodollar deposit, regardless of whether the issuing bank is actually located in Europe, South America, or anyplace else. For example, if you travel overseas and deposit $1,000 in a German bank, you will have "created" a eurodollar deposit in the amount of $1,000. Since the U.S. dollar is accepted by most countries for international trade, these dollar deposits can be used by international companies to settle their accounts. The market created for trading such investments offers firms with extra dollars a chance to earn a slightly higher rate of return with just a little more risk than they would face by investing in Treasury bills.

Maximizing Accounts Receivable. After cash and marketable securities, the balance sheet lists accounts receivable and inventory. Remember that accounts receivable are money owed to a business by credit customers. For example, if you charge your Shell gasoline purchases, until you actually pay for them with cash or a cheque, they represent an account receivable to Shell. Many businesses make the vast majority of their sales on credit, so managing accounts receivable is an important task.

Each credit sale represents an account receivable for the company, the terms of which typically require customers to pay the full amount due within 30, 60, or even 90 days from the date of the sale. To encourage quick payment, some businesses offer some of their customers discounts of 1 to 2 percent if they pay off their balance within a specified period of time (usually between 10 and 30 days). On the other hand, late payment charges of between 1 and 1.5 percent serve to discourage slow payers from sitting on their bills forever. The larger the early payment discount offered, the faster customers will tend to pay their accounts. Unfortunately, while discounts increase cash flow, they also reduce profitability. Finding the right balance between the added advantages of early cash receipt and the disadvantages of reduced profits is no simple matter. Similarly, determining the optimal balance between the higher sales likely to result from extending credit to customers with less than

table 16.1 Short-Term Investment Possibilities for Idle Cash

Type of Security	Maturity	Issuer of Security	Interest Rate (Jan. 21, 2013)	Safety Level
Treasury Bills	1 month	Bank of Canada	0.88	Excellent
Treasury Bills	3 months	Bank of Canada	0.92	Excellent
Commercial Paper	3 months	Corporations	1.12	Very Good
Certificates of Deposit	12 months	Chartered Banks	0.78	Very Good
Eurodollars	3 months	European Commercial Banks	0.29	Very Good

SOURCES: Adapted from Bank of Canada, www.bankofcanada.ca/rates/interest-rates/t-bill-yields/; www.bankofcanada.ca/rates/interest-rates/canadian-interest-rates/; and "Selected Interest Rates," *Federal Reserve Statistical Release*, January 22, 2013, www.federalreserve.gov/releases/h15/current/ (accessed January 22, 2013).

The Canadian Bankers Association developed the YourMoney seminars as part of its commitment to improving financial literacy among Canadians.

sterling credit ratings and the higher bad-debt losses likely to result from a more lenient credit policy is also challenging. Information on company credit ratings is provided by local credit bureaus, national credit-rating agencies such as Dun and Bradstreet, and industry trade groups.

Optimizing Inventory. While the inventory that a firm holds is controlled by both production needs and marketing considerations, the financial manager has to coordinate inventory purchases to manage cash flows. The object is to minimize the firm's investment in inventory without experiencing production cutbacks as a result of critical materials shortfalls or lost sales due to insufficient finished goods inventories. Every dollar invested in inventory is a dollar unavailable for investment in some other area of the organization. Optimal inventory levels are determined, in large part, by the method of production. If a firm attempts to produce its goods just in time to meet sales demand, the level of inventory will be relatively low. If, on the other hand, the firm produces materials in a constant, level pattern, inventory increases when sales decrease and decreases when sales increase. One way that companies are attempting to optimize inventory is through the use of radio frequency identification (RFID) technology. Companies such as Walmart are attempting to better manage their inventories by using RFID tags. An RFID tag, which contains a silicon chip and an antenna, allows a company to use radio waves to track and identify the products to which the tags are attached. These tags are primarily used to track inventory shipments from the manufacturer to the buyer's warehouses and then to the individual stores.

The automobile industry is an excellent example of an industry driven almost solely by inventory levels. Because it is inefficient to continually lay off workers in slow times and call them back in better times, Ford, General Motors, and Chrysler try to set and stick to quarterly production quotas. Automakers typically try to keep a 60-day supply of unsold cars. During particularly slow periods, however, it is not unusual for inventories to exceed 100 days of sales.

Although less publicized, inventory shortages can be as much of a drag on potential profits as too much inventory. Not having an item on hand may send the customer to a competitor—forever. Complex computer inventory models are frequently employed to determine the optimum level of inventory a firm should hold to support a given level of sales. Such models can indicate how and when parts inventories should be ordered so that they are available exactly when required—and not a day before. Developing and maintaining such an intricate production and inventory system is difficult, but it can often prove to be the difference between experiencing average profits and achieving spectacular ones.

LO2 Identify some sources of short-term financing (current liabilities).

Managing Current Liabilities

While having extra cash on hand is a delightful surprise, the opposite situation—a temporary cash shortfall—can be a crisis. The good news is that there are several potential sources of short-term funds. Suppliers often serve as an important source through credit sales practices. Also, banks, finance companies, and other organizations offer short-term funds through loans and other business operations.

Companies such as Walmart are attempting to better manage their inventories by using radio-frequency-identification (RFID) tags. An RFID tag, which contains a silicon chip and an antenna, allows a company to use radio waves to track and identify the products to which the tags are attached—even after the products have left the store.

Accounts Payable.   Remember from Chapter 14 that accounts payable consist of money an organization owes to suppliers for goods and services. Just as accounts receivable must be actively managed to ensure proper cash collections, so too must accounts payable be managed to make the best use of this important liability.

The most widely used source of short-term financing, and therefore the most important account payable, is **trade credit**—credit extended by suppliers for the purchase of their goods and services. While varying in formality, depending on both the organizations involved and the value of the items purchased, most trade credit agreements offer discounts to organizations that pay their bills early. A supplier, for example, may offer trade terms of "1/10 net 30," meaning that the purchasing organization may take a 1 percent discount from the invoice amount if it makes payment by the 10th day after receiving the bill. Otherwise, the entire amount is due within 30 days. For example, pretend that you are the financial manager in charge of payables. You owe Ajax Company $10,000, and it offers trade terms of 2/10 net 30. By paying the amount due within 10 days, you can save 2 percent of $10,000, or $200. Assume you place orders with Ajax once per month and have 12 bills of $10,000 each per year. By taking the discount every time, you will save 12 times $200, or $2,400, per year. Now assume you are the financial manager of Gigantic Corp., and it has monthly payables of $100 million per month. Two percent of $100 million is $2 million per month. Failure to take advantage of such trade discounts can, in many cases, add up to large opportunity losses over the span of a year.

Bank Loans.   Virtually all organizations—large and small—obtain short-term funds for operations from banks. In most instances, the credit services granted these firms take the form of a line of credit or fixed dollar loan. A **line of credit** is an arrangement by which a bank agrees to lend a specified amount of money to the organization upon request—provided that the bank has the required funds to make the loan. In general, a business line of credit is very

> **Line of credit**   an arrangement by which a bank agrees to lend a specified amount of money to an organization upon request

> **Trade credit**   credit extended by suppliers for the purchase of their goods and services

similar to a consumer credit card, with the exception that the preset credit limit can amount to millions of dollars.

In addition to credit lines, banks also make **secured loans**—loans backed by collateral that the bank can claim if the borrowers do not repay the loans—and **unsecured loans**—loans backed only by the borrowers' good reputation and previous credit rating. Both individuals and businesses build their credit rating from their history of borrowing and repaying borrowed funds on time and in full. The three national credit-rating services are Equifax, TransUnion, and Experian. A lack of credit history or a poor credit history can make it difficult to get loans from financial institutions. The *principal* is the amount of money borrowed; *interest* is a percentage of the principal that the bank charges for use of its money. As we mentioned in Chapter 15, banks also pay depositors interest on savings accounts and some chequing accounts. Thus, banks charge borrowers interest for loans and pay interest to depositors for the use of their money. In addition, these loans may include origination fees.

The **prime rate** is the interest rate commercial banks charge their best customers (usually large corporations) for short-term loans. While, for many years, loans at the prime rate represented funds at the lowest possible cost, the rapid development of the market for commercial paper has dramatically reduced the importance of commercial banks as a source of short-term loans. Today, most "prime" borrowers are actually small and medium-sized businesses.

Nonbank Liabilities. Banks are not the only source of short-term funds for businesses. Indeed, virtually all financial institutions, from insurance companies to pension funds, from money market funds to finance companies, make short-term loans to many organizations. The largest companies also actively engage in borrowing money from the eurodollar and commercial paper markets. As noted earlier, both of these funds' sources are typically slightly less expensive than bank loans.

In some instances, businesses actually sell their accounts receivable to a finance company known as a **factor,** which gives the selling organizations cash and assumes responsibility for collecting the accounts. For example, a factor might pay $60,000 for receivables with a total face value of $100,000 (60 percent of the total). The factor profits if it can collect more than what it paid for the accounts. Because the selling organization's customers send their payments to a lockbox, they may have no idea that a factor has bought their receivables.

Additional nonbank liabilities that must be efficiently managed to ensure maximum profitability are taxes owed to the government and wages owed to employees. Clearly, businesses are responsible for many different types of taxes and similar payments, including federal, provincial, and municipal income taxes, property taxes, mineral rights taxes, unemployment insurance, CPP contributions, workers' compensation taxes, excise taxes, and even more! While the public tends to think that the only relevant taxes are on income and sales, many industries must pay other taxes that far exceed those levied against their income. Taxes and employees' wages represent debt obligations of the firm, which the financial manager must plan to meet as they fall due.

LO3 Summarize the importance of long-term assets and capital budgeting.

Managing Fixed Assets

Up to this point, we have focused on the short-term aspects of financial management. While most business failures are the result of poor short-term planning, successful ventures must also consider the long-term financial consequences of their actions. Managing the long-term assets and liabilities and the owners' equity portion of the balance sheet is important for the long-term health of the business.

Long-term (fixed) assets are expected to last for many years—production facilities (plants), offices, equipment, heavy machinery, furniture, automobiles, and so on. In today's fast-paced world, companies need

the most technologically advanced, modern facilities and equipment they can afford. Automobile, oil refining, and transportation companies are dependent on fixed assets.

Modern and high-tech equipment carries high price tags, and the financial arrangements required to support these investments are by no means trivial. Leasing is just one approach to financing. Obtaining major long-term financing can be challenging for even the most profitable organizations. For less successful firms, such challenges can prove nearly impossible. One approach is leasing assets such as equipment, machines, and buildings. In the case of leasing or not taking ownership but paying a fee for usage, potential long-term assets can be taken off the balance sheet as a debt. Still, the company has the asset and an obligation to pay money that is a contractual obligation. We'll take a closer look at long-term financing in a moment, but first let's address some issues associated with fixed assets, including capital budgeting, risk assessment, and the costs of financing fixed assets.

Capital Budgeting and Project Selection

One of the most important jobs performed by the financial manager is to decide what fixed assets, projects, and investments will earn profits for the firm beyond the costs necessary to fund them. The process of analyzing the needs of the business and selecting the assets that will maximize its value is called **capital budgeting,** and the capital budget is the amount of money budgeted for investment in such long-term assets. But capital budgeting does not end with the selection and purchase of a particular piece of land, equipment, or major investment. All assets and projects must be continually re-evaluated to ensure their compatibility with the organization's needs. If a particular asset does not live up to expectations, then management must determine why and take necessary corrective action. Budgeting is not an exact process, and managers must be flexible when new information is available.

> "All assets and projects must be continually re-evaluated to ensure their compatibility with the organization's needs."

Capital budgeting the process of analyzing the needs of the business and selecting the assets that will maximize its value

Assessing Risk

Every investment carries some risk. Figure 16.1 ranks potential investment projects according to estimated risk. When considering investments overseas, risk assessments must include the political climate and economic stability of a region. The decision to introduce a product or build a manufacturing facility in England would be much less risky than a decision to build one in the Middle East, for example.

Not apparent from Figure 16.1 are the risks associated with time. The longer a project or asset is expected to last,

the greater its potential risk because it is hard to predict whether a piece of equipment will wear out or become obsolete in 5 or 10 years. Predicting cash flows one year down the road is difficult, but projecting them over the span of a 10-year project is a gamble.

The level of a project's risk is also affected by the stability and competitive nature of the marketplace and the world economy as a whole. IBM's latest high-technology computer product is far more likely to become obsolete overnight than is a similar $10 million investment in a manufacturing plant. Dramatic changes in the marketplace are not uncommon. Indeed, uncertainty created by the rapid devaluation of Asian currencies in the late 1990s wrecked a host of assumptions in literally hundreds of projects worldwide. Financial managers must constantly consider such issues when making long-term decisions about the purchase of fixed assets.

figure 16.1 Qualitative Assessment of Capital Budgeting Risk

Highest Risk

Introduce a New Product in Foreign Markets (risk depends on stability of country)

Expand Into a New Market

Introduce a New Product in a Familiar Area

Add to a Product Line

Buy New Equipment for an Established Market

Repair Old Machinery

Lowest Risk

Although pharmaceutical manufacturers may want to undertake many projects, the costs involved require them to use capital budgeting to determine which projects will lead to the greatest profits. The company Allergan used capital budgeting to determine the potential profitability of the eye medication Restasis.

Pricing Long-Term Money

The ultimate profitability of any project depends not only on accurate assumptions of how much cash it will generate but also on its financing costs. Because a business must pay interest on money it borrows, the returns from any project must cover not only the costs of operating the project but also the interest expenses for the debt used to finance its construction. Unless an organization can effectively cover all of its costs—both financial and operating—it will eventually fail.

Clearly, only a limited supply of funds is available for investment in any given enterprise. The most efficient and profitable companies can attract the lowest-cost funds because they typically offer reasonable financial returns at very low relative risks. Newer and less prosperous firms must pay higher costs to attract capital because these companies tend to be quite risky. One of the strongest motivations for companies to manage their financial resources wisely is that they will, over time, be able to reduce the costs of their funds and in so doing increase their overall profitability.

In our free-enterprise economy, new firms tend to enter industries that offer the greatest potential rewards for success. However, as more and more companies enter an industry, competition intensifies, eventually driving profits down to average levels. The digital music player market of the early 2000s provides an excellent example of the changes in profitability that typically accompany increasing competition. The sign of a successful capital budgeting program is that the new products create higher than normal profits and drive sales and the stock price up. This has certainly been true for Apple. It introduced the first iPod in 2001, and after many enhancements it continued to sell 8.3 million iPods in 2007. Its sales have grown from $6.2 billion in 2003 to $65.2 billion in 2010, while its earnings per share have increased from $0.10 per share to $15.25 during the same time frame. From a low price of $6.36 per share in 2003, its stocks rose to a high of $350 on April, 8, 2011. Note that $1,000 invested in Apple at

its low point in 2003 would be worth approximately $55,000 on April, 8, 2011, at $350 per share.[3]

The success of the iPod and iTunes was followed up with the introduction of the iPhone in 2007. The iPhone was followed by the successful introduction of the iPad tablet in April 2010. The combination of these products and the ease of synchronization with the iMac computers caused a complementary sales effect for Apple computers. Even with a well-planned capital budgeting program, it may be difficult for Apple to stay ahead of the competition because it is difficult to maintain market dominance in the consumer electronics industry for extended periods of time.

> **LO4** Specify how companies finance their operations and manage fixed assets with long-term liabilities, particularly bonds.

Financing With Long-Term Liabilities

As we said earlier, long-term assets do not come cheap, and few companies have the cash on hand to open a new store across town, build a new manufacturing facility, research and develop a new life-saving drug, or launch a new product worldwide. To develop such fixed assets, companies need to raise low-cost, long-term funds to finance them. Two common choices for raising these funds are attracting new owners (*equity financing*), which we'll look at in a moment, and taking on long-term liabilities (*debt financing*), which we'll look at now.

Long-term liabilities are debts that will be repaid over a number of years, such as long-term bank loans and bond issues. These take many different forms, but in the end, the key word is *debt*. Companies may raise money by borrowing it from commercial banks or other financial institutions in the form of lines of credit, short-term loans, or long-term loans. Many corporations acquire debt by borrowing money from pension funds, mutual funds, or life-insurance funds.

Companies that rely too heavily on debt can get into serious trouble should the economy falter; during these times, they may not earn enough operating income to make the required interest payments (remember the times interest earned ratio in Chapter 14). In severe cases when the problem persists too long, creditors will not restructure loans but will instead sue for the interest and principal owed and force the company into bankruptcy.

Bonds: Corporate IOUs

Aside from loans, much long-term debt takes the form of **bonds,** which are debt instruments that larger companies sell to raise long-term funds. In essence, the buyers of bonds (bondholders) loan the issuer of

> **Long-term liabilities** debts that will be repaid over a number of years, such as long-term loans and bond issues
>
> **Bonds** debt instruments that larger companies sell to raise long-term funds

As a public corporation, one way in which Dell takes on long-term debt is in the form of bonds. The company sells bonds to raise long-term funds.

the bonds cash in exchange for regular interest payments until the loan is repaid on or before the specified maturity date. The bond itself is a certificate, much like an IOU, that represents the company's debt to the bondholder. Bonds are issued by a wide variety of entities, including corporations; federal, provincial, and local governments; public utilities; and nonprofit corporations. Most bondholders need not hold their bonds until maturity; rather, the existence of active secondary markets of brokers and dealers allows for the quick and efficient transfer of bonds from owner to owner.

The bond contract, or *indenture*, specifies all of the terms of the agreement between the bondholders and the issuing organization. The indenture, which can run more than 100 pages, specifies the basic terms of the bond, such as its face value, maturity date, and annual interest rate. Table 16.2 briefly explains how to determine these and more things about a bond from a bond quote, as it might appear in the *National Post*. The face value of the bond, its initial sales price, is typically $1,000. After this, however, the price of the bond on the open market will fluctuate along with changes in the economy (particularly, changes in interest rates) and in the creditworthiness of the issuer. Bondholders receive the face value of the bond along with the final interest payment on the maturity date. The annual interest rate (often called the *coupon rate*) is the guaranteed percentage of face value that the company will pay to the bond owner every year. For example, a $1,000 bond with a coupon rate of 7 percent would pay $70 per year in interest. In most cases, bond indentures specify that interest payments be made every six months. In the preceding example, the $70 annual payment would be divided into two semiannual payments of $35.

In addition to the terms of interest payments and maturity date, the bond indenture typically covers other important areas, such as repayment methods, interest payment dates, procedures to be followed in case the organization fails to make the interest payments, conditions for the early repayment of the bonds, and any conditions requiring the pledging of assets as collateral.

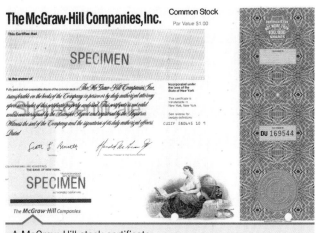

A McGraw-Hill stock certificate.

Types of Bonds

Not surprisingly, there are a great many different types of bonds. Most are **unsecured bonds,** meaning that they are not backed by specific collateral; such bonds are termed *debentures*. **Secured bonds,** on the other hand, are backed by specific collateral that must be forfeited in the event that the issuing firm defaults. Whether secured or unsecured, bonds may be repaid in one lump sum or with many payments spread out over a period of time.

Unsecured bonds debentures, or bonds that are not backed by specific collateral

Secured bonds bonds that are backed by specific collateral that must be forfeited in the event that the issuing firm defaults

Serial bonds a sequence of small bond issues of progressively longer maturity

Floating-rate bonds bonds with interest rates that change with current interest rates otherwise available in the economy

Serial bonds, which are different from secured bonds, are actually a sequence of small bond issues of progressively longer maturity. The firm pays off each of the serial bonds as they mature. **Floating-rate bonds** do not have fixed interest payments; instead, the interest rate changes with current

table 16.2 A Basic Bond Quote

Issuer (1)	Coupon (2)	Maturity Date (3)	Bid $ (4)	Yield % (5)
Loblaw	5.220	June 18/20	113.05	3.22

(1) Issuer—the name or abbreviation of the name of the company issuing the bond; in this case, Loblaw.

(2) Coupon—the annual percentage rate specified on the bond certificate: Loblaw's is 5.22 percent so a $1,000 bond will earn $52.20 per year in interest.

(3) Maturity Date—the bond's maturity date; the year in which the issuer will repay bondholders the face value of each bond; 2020.

(4) Bid $—the closing price; 113.05 percent of $1,000 per value or $1,130.50 per bond.

(5) Yield %—yield to maturity; the percentage return based on the closing price; if you buy a bond with a $1,000 par value at today's closing price of 113.05 ($1,130.50) and receive $52.20 per year to maturity, your return will be 3.22 percent.

SOURCE: Data from *Financial Post,* Canadian Bonds on January 21, 2013, http://www.financialpost.com/markets/market-data/bonds-canadian.html.

Chris DeWolfe and Tom Anderson

Business: Myspace.com

Founded: 2003

Success: DeWolfe and Anderson sold Myspace.com to News Corp. for $580 million in 2005.

Myspace.com is still a popular cyber-location for socializing. In October 2005, it was the fourth most viewed website on the Internet. When Chris DeWolfe and Tom Anderson created Myspace.com in 2003, they aimed the site at the music industry—hoping to create a site on which musicians could post bios, songs, and gig dates/locations and on which they could network. Although many musicians still use the site today, it also enjoyed popularity with the teenage/young adult crowd. Myspace works like this: You create a profile and then begin to acquire "friends"—people who join your networking group via your approval. Although no longer the primary focus, music is still a large part of Myspace culture. Popular bands such as Nine Inch Nails and R.E.M. used Myspace to promote new music directly to fans. Recently, bands such as Hawthorne Heights and Hollywood Undead have launched successful careers, thanks in part to Myspace and the bands' "friends." In 2005, DeWolfe and Anderson sold Myspace to News Corporation/Rupert Murdoch for $580 million—an incredible sum for a two-year-old company. News Corp. has international interest in media outlets, including FOX TV, *The New York Post*, HarperCollins book publishing, and DirecTV. A News Corp. official was quoted as saying that Myspace.com is expected to bring the company a healthy profit of a few million dollars annually. Although they no longer own the company, DeWolfe and Anderson remain with the company as CEO and president, respectively.[4]

> **Junk bonds** a special type of high interest-rate bond that carries higher inherent risks

interest rates otherwise available in the economy.

In recent years, a special type of high-interest-rate bond has attracted considerable attention (usually negative) in the financial press. High-interest bonds, or **junk bonds** as they are popularly known, offer relatively high rates of interest because they have higher inherent risks. Historically, junk bonds have been associated with companies in poor financial health and/or start-up firms with limited track records. In the mid-1980s, however, junk bonds became a very attractive method of financing corporate mergers; they remain popular today with many investors as a result of their very high relative interest rates. But higher risks are associated with those higher returns (upward of 12 percent per year in some cases) and the average investor would be well-advised to heed those famous words: Look before you leap!

LO5 | Discuss how corporations can use equity financing by issuing stock through an investment banker.

Financing With Owners' Equity

A second means of long-term financing is through equity. Remember from Chapter 14 that owners' equity refers to the owners' investment in an organization. Sole proprietors and partners own all or a part of their businesses outright, and their equity includes the money and assets they have brought into their ventures. Corporate owners, on the other hand, own stock or shares of their companies, which they hope will provide them with a return on their investment. Shareholders' equity includes common stock, preferred stock, and retained earnings.

"A second means of long-term financing is through equity."

Common stock (introduced in Chapter 4) is the single most important source of capital for most new companies. On the balance sheet, the common stock account is separated into two basic parts—common stock at par and capital in excess of par. The *par value* of a stock is simply the dollar amount printed on the stock certificate and has no relation to actual *market value*—the price at which the common stock is currently trading. The difference between a stock's par value and its offering price is called *capital in excess of par*. Except in the case of some very low-priced stocks, the capital in excess of par account is significantly larger than the par value account. Table 16.3 briefly explains how to gather important information from a stock quote, as it might appear in financial newspapers.

Preferred stock was defined in Chapter 14 as corporate ownership that gives the shareholder preference in the distribution of the company's profits but not the voting and control rights accorded to common shareholders. Thus, the primary advantage of owning preferred stock is that it is a safer investment than common stock.

table 16.3 A Basic Stock Quote

Stock (1)	Ticker (2)	Close (3)	Net Chg (4)	Volume (5)	Day High/ Low (6)	% Yld (7)	52-Week High/Low (8)
Tim Hortons	THI	50.13	+$0.29	773,603	50.49/49.84	1.661	57.91/45.11

(1) Stock—the name of the issuing company.

(2) Ticker—the ticker tape symbol for the stock; for Tim Hortons, THI.

(3) Close—the last sale of the day; for Tim Hortons, $50.13.

(4) Net Change—the difference between the previous day's close and the close on the day being reported; Tim Hortons was up 29 cents.

(5) Volume—the number of shares traded on this day; for Tim Hortons, 773,603.

(6) Day High/Low—the highest and lowest prices, respectively, paid for the stock during the day; for Tim Hortons, the highest was $50.49 and the lowest price, $49.84.

(7) Percent Yield—the dividend return on one share of common stock; 1.661%.

(8) 52-Week High/Low—the highest and lowest prices, respectively, paid for the stock in the last year; for Tim Hortons' stock, the highest was $57.91 and the lowest price, $45.11.

SOURCE: Data from *The Globe and Mail*, Jan 22, 2013, www.theglobeandmail.com/globe-investor/markets/stocks/summary/?q=thi-T

Retained earnings earnings after expenses and taxes that are reinvested in the assets of the firm and belong to the owners in the form of equity

Dividend yield the dividend per share divided by the stock price

All businesses exist to earn profits for their owners. Without the possibility of profit, there can be no incentive to risk investors' capital and succeed. When a corporation has profits left over after paying all of its expenses and taxes, it has the choice of retaining all or a portion of its earnings and/or paying them out to its shareholders in the form of dividends. **Retained earnings** are reinvested in the assets of the firm and belong to the owners in the form of equity. Retained earnings are an important source of funds and are, in fact, the only long-term funds that the company can generate internally.

When the board of directors distributes some of a corporation's profits to the owners, it issues them as cash dividend payments. But not all firms pay dividends.

Many fast-growing firms retain all of their earnings because they can earn high rates of return on the earnings they reinvest. Companies with fewer growth opportunities typically pay out large proportions of their earnings in the form of dividends, thereby allowing their shareholders to reinvest their dividend payments in higher-growth companies. Table 16.4 presents a sample of companies and the dividend each paid on a single share of stock. As shown in the table, when the dividend is divided by the price, the result is the **dividend yield.** The dividend yield is the cash return as a percentage of the price but does not reflect the total return an investor earns on the individual stock. If the dividend yield is 1.3 percent on a company and the stock price increases by 10 percent, then the total return would be 11.3 percent. It is not clear that stocks with high dividend yields will be preferred by investors to those with little or no dividends. Most large companies pay their shareholders dividends on a quarterly basis.

Investment Banking

A company that needs more money to expand or take advantage of opportunities may be able to obtain financing by issuing stock. The first-time sale of stocks and bonds directly to the public is called a *new issue*. Companies that already have stocks or bonds outstanding may offer a new issue of stock to raise additional funds for specific projects. When a company offers its stock to the public for the very first time, it is said to be "going public," and the sale is called an *initial public offering*.

New issues of stocks and bonds are sold directly to the public and to institutions in what is known as the **primary market**—the market where firms raise financial capital. The primary market differs from **secondary markets,** which are stock exchanges and over-the-counter markets where investors can trade their securities with other investors rather than the company that issued the stock or bonds. Primary market transactions actually raise cash for the issuing corporations, while secondary market transactions do not.

Investment banking, the sale of stocks and bonds for corporations, helps such companies raise funds by matching people and institutions who have money to invest with corporations in need of resources to exploit new opportunities. Corporations usually employ an investment banking firm to help sell their securities in the primary market. An investment banker helps firms establish appropriate offering prices for their securities. In addition, the investment banker takes care of the myriad details and

Primary market the market where firms raise financial capital

Secondary markets stock exchanges and over-the-counter markets where investors can trade their securities with others

Investment banking the sale of stocks and bonds for corporations

table 16.4 Estimated Common Stock Price–Earnings Ratios and Dividends for Selected Companies

Ticker Symbol	Company Name	Price Per Share	Dividend Per Share	Dividend Yield	Earnings Per Share	P–E Ratio
THI	Tim Hortons	50.42	0.84	1.661	2.60	19.427
SU	Suncor	34.08	0.52	1.524	3.06	11.15

SOURCE: Data from *National Post*, January 22, 2013, www.theglobeandmail.com/globe investor/markets/stocks/summary/?q=thi-T

securities regulations involved in any sale of securities to the public.

Just as large corporations such as BCE, Bombardier, and Microsoft have a client relationship with a law firm and an accounting firm, they also have a client relationship with an investment banking firm. An investment banking firm such as CIBC World Markets can provide advice about financing plans, dividend policy, or stock repurchases, as well as advice on mergers and acquisitions. Many now offer additional banking services, making them "one-stop shopping" banking centres. When companies merge, they often use investment bankers to help them value the transaction. Each firm will want an outside opinion about what it is worth to the other. Sometimes mergers fall apart because the companies cannot agree on the price each company is worth or the structure of management after the merger. The advising investment banker, working with management, often irons out these details. Of course, investment bankers do not provide these services for free. They usually charge a fee of between 1 and 1.5 percent of the transaction. A $20 billion merger can generate between $200 and $300 million in investment banking fees. The merger mania of the late 1990s allowed top investment bankers to earn huge sums. Unfortunately, this type of fee income is dependent on healthy stock markets, which seem to stimulate the merger fever among corporate executives.

DID YOU KNOW?

If you bought one share of Microsoft stock when the company went public in 1986, it would be worth almost $8,000 today, after allowing for stock splits and adjustments.[5]

LO6   Describe the various securities markets in Canada.

The Securities Markets

Securities markets provide a mechanism for buying and selling securities. They make it possible for owners to sell their stocks and bonds to other investors. Thus, in the broadest sense, stocks and bonds markets may be thought of as providers of liquidity—the ability to turn security holdings into cash quickly and

Securities markets the mechanism for buying and selling securities

at minimal expense and effort. Without liquid securities markets, many potential investors would sit on the sidelines rather than invest their hard-earned savings in securities. Indeed, the ability to sell securities at well-established market prices is one of the very pillars of the capitalistic society that has developed over the years in Canada.

Unlike the primary market, in which corporations sell stocks directly to the public, secondary markets permit the trading of previously issued securities. There are many different secondary markets for both stocks and bonds. If you want to purchase 100 shares of Tim Hortons common stock, for example, you must purchase this stock from another investor or institution. It is the active buying and selling by many thousands of investors that establishes the prices of all financial securities. Secondary market trades may take place on organized exchanges or in what is known as the over-the-counter market. Many brokerage houses exist to help investors with financial decisions, and many offer their services through the Internet. One such broker is TD Waterhouse. Its site offers a wealth of information and provides educational material to individual investors.

Stock Markets

Stock markets exist around the world in New York, Toronto, Tokyo, London, Frankfurt, Paris, and other world locations. The TSX Group operates Canada's two national stock exchanges, the Toronto Stock Exchange serving the senior equity market and the TSX Venture Exchange serving the public venture equity market. The Montréal Exchange is Canada's oldest exchange and has leadership in the financial derivatives market. The two biggest stock markets in the United States are the New York Stock Exchange (NYSE) and the NASDAQ.

Exchanges used to be divided into organized exchanges and over-the-counter markets, but during the last several years, dramatic changes have occurred. The TSX, NYSE, and NASDAQ became publicly traded companies. They were previously not-for-profit organizations but are now for-profit companies. Additionally exchanges have bought or merged with electronic exchanges, for example, the NYSE with Archipelago and the NASDAQ with Instinet. Electronic trading is faster and less expensive than floor trading (where brokers meet to transact business) and now accounts for most of the stock trading done worldwide.

In an attempt to expand their markets, NASDAQ acquired the OMX, a Nordic stock exchange headquartered in Sweden, and the New York Stock Exchange merged with Euronext, a large European electronic exchange that trades options and futures contracts as well as common stock. Both the NYSE and NASDAQ have expanded their reach, their product line, and their ability to trade around the world. What we are witnessing is the globalization of the world's financial markets.

Traditionally, the NASDAQ market has been an electronics market, and many of the large technology companies such as Microsoft and Apple Computer trade on it. The NASDAQ operates through dealers who buy and sell common stock (inventory) for their own accounts. The TSX has traditionally been a floor-traded market, where brokers meet at trading posts on the floor of the Toronto Stock Exchange to buy and sell common stock. The brokers act as agents for their clients and do not own their own inventory. This traditional division between the two markets is becoming less significant as the exchanges become electronic.

The Over-the-Counter Market

Unlike the organized exchanges, the **over-the-counter (OTC) market** is a network of dealers all over the country linked by computers, telephones, and Teletype machines. It has no central location. While many very small new companies are traded on the OTC market, many very large and well-known concerns trade there as well. Indeed, thousands of shares of the stocks of companies such as Apple Computer, Intel, and Microsoft are traded on the OTC market every day. Further, because most corporate bonds and all U.S. securities are traded over the counter, the OTC market regularly accounts for the largest total dollar value of all of the secondary markets.

> **Over-the-counter (OTC) market** a network of dealers all over the country linked by computers, telephones, and Teletype machines

Measuring Market Performance

Investors, especially professional money managers, want to know how well their investments are performing relative to the market as a whole. Financial managers also need to know how their companies' securities are performing when compared with their competitors'. Thus, performance

---

RESPONDING TO BUSINESS CHALLENGES | Advancing Gender Diversity in Finance

While more than half of accounting majors in university undergraduate programs are women, only 12 percent of CFOs at major companies are female. This discrepancy is a concern to companies that are trying to emphasize diversity in management. Although sexual discrimination is still a problem, studies suggest that other factors contribute to this low percentage.

One theory is that women do not have as many connections with higher-level finance executives as men. According to a former portfolio consultant, because female employees do not often connect as well with male supervisors, they may inadvertently be passed up for future management opportunities. The support of senior executives is often essential for career advancement because these executives can more successfully advocate on behalf of the employee.

A solution that some companies have implemented is formal mentorship programs for women, but even these efforts have not seemed very successful. Instead, certain businesses have created programs to encourage female executives to form long-lasting relationships with female finance employees. In one such program, female finance executives agree to

spend a year mentoring employees who have been recommended by their managers. It is believed that this longer time period will enable the executive and the employee to form a closer relationship; this in turn could result in more female employees being sponsored for financial leadership positions. Another example is a program at the financial institution Goldman Sachs, which has created a six-month Women's Career Strategies Initiative. The initiative pairs potential sponsees with sponsors and seeks to help women form contacts by introducing them to executives throughout the organization.[6]

DISCUSSION QUESTIONS

1. Why do you think there are so few female CFOs?

2. Describe some ways that companies are trying to promote management positions to female finance employees.

3. Do you feel that a mentorship program will help close the gap?

table 16.5 Top 10 Constituents by Market Capitalization on the S&P/TSX 60 (as of September 10, 2012)

Constituent	Symbol	GICS® Sector	Price (C$)
Royal Bank of Canada	RY	Financials	56.44
Toronto-Dominion Bank	TD	Financials	82.24
Bank of Nova Scotia Halifax	BNS	Financials	52.88
Suncor Energy Inc	SU	Energy	32.54
Canadian National Railway	CNR	Industrials	90.35
Barrick Gold Corp	ABX	Materials	38.53
Bank of Montreal	BMO	Financials	58.00
Potash Corp of Saskatchewan	POT	Materials	41.97
Canadian Natural Resources	CNQ	Energy	31.63
BCE Inc	BCE	Telecommunication Services	44.26

SOURCE: www.standardandpoors.com/indices/sp-tsx-60/en/us/?indexId=spcadntx--caduf--p-ca-l (accessed January 22, 2013).

measures—averages and indexes—are very important to many different people. They not only indicate the performance of a particular securities market but also provide a measure of the overall health of the economy.

Indexes and averages are used to measure stock prices. An *index* compares current stock prices with those in a specified base period, such as 1944, 1967, or 1977. An *average* is the average of certain stock prices. The averages used are usually not simple calculations, however. Some stock market averages (such as the S&P/TSX Composite Index) are weighted averages, where the weights employed are the total market values of each stock in the index (in this case 500). The Dow Jones Industrial Average is a price-weighted average. Regardless of how constructed, all market averages of stocks move closely together over time.

Many investors follow the activity of stock indexes like the S&P/TSX or the Dow Jones Industrial Average very closely to see whether the stock market has gone up or down. Table 16.5 lists the top 10 constituents that currently make up the S&P/TSX 60.

The numbers listed in an index or average that tracks the performance of a stock market are expressed not as dollars but as a number on a fixed scale. A period of large increases in stock prices is known as a *bull market,* with the bull symbolizing an aggressive, charging market and rising stock prices. A declining stock market is known as a *bear market,* with the bear symbolizing sluggish, retreating activity. When stock prices decline very rapidly, the market is said to *crash.* Figure 16.2 graphically displays the long-term performance of the Canadian stock market.

For investors to make sound financial decisions, it is important that they stay in touch with business news, markets, and indexes. Of course, business and investment magazines, such as the *Financial Post,* the *Report on Business,* and *Money,* offer this type of information. Many Internet sites—including the *CNN/Money, Globe Investor,* and other online newspapers, as well as *PR Newswire*—offer this information as well. Many sites offer searchable databases of information by topic, company, or keyword. However investors choose to receive and review business news, doing so is a necessity in today's market.

"Many investors follow the activity of the S&P/TSX to see whether the stock market has gone up or down."

figure 16.2 Long-Term Performance of the Canadian Stock Market

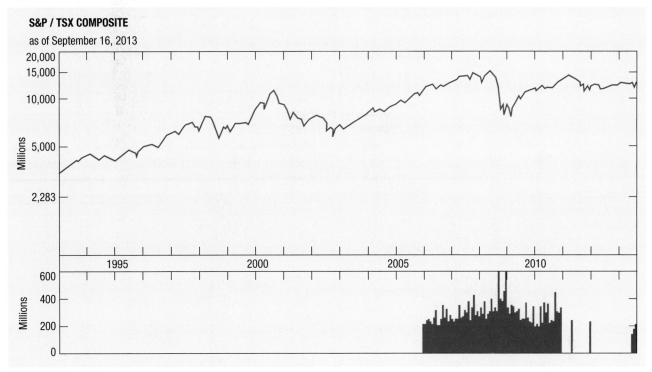

S&P / TSX COMPOSITE
as of September 16, 2013

TEAM EXERCISE

Compare and contrast financing with long-term liabilities such as bonds versus financing with owners' equity, typically retained earnings, common stock, and preferred stock. Form groups and suggest a good mix of long-term liabilities and owners' equity for a new firm that makes wind turbines for generating alternative energy and that would like to grow quickly.

LO1 Describe some common methods of managing current assets.

Current assets are short-term resources such as cash, investments, accounts receivable, and inventory, which can be converted to cash within a year. Financial managers focus on minimizing the amount of cash kept on hand and increasing the speed of collections through lockboxes and electronic funds transfer and investing in marketable securities. Marketable securities include Treasury bills, certificates of deposit, commercial paper, and money market funds. Managing accounts receivable requires judging customer creditworthiness and creating credit terms that encourage prompt payment. Inventory management focuses on determining optimum inventory levels that minimize the cost of storing and ordering inventory without sacrificing too many lost sales due to stockouts.

LO2 Identify some sources of short-term financing (current liabilities).

Current liabilities are short-term debt obligations that must be repaid within one year, such as accounts payable, taxes payable, and notes (loans) payable. Trade credit is extended by suppliers for the purchase of their goods and services. A line of credit is an arrangement by which a bank agrees to lend a specified amount of money to a business whenever the business needs it. Secured loans are backed by collateral; unsecured loans are backed only by the borrower's good reputation.

LO3 Summarize the importance of long-term assets and capital budgeting.

Long-term, or fixed, assets are expected to last for many years, such as production facilities (plants), offices, and equipment. Businesses need modern, up-to-date equipment to succeed in today's competitive environment. Capital budgeting is the process of analyzing company needs and selecting the assets that will maximize its value; a capital budget is the amount of money budgeted for the purchase of fixed assets. Every investment in fixed assets carries some risk.

LO4 Specify how companies finance their operations and manage fixed assets with long-term liabilities, particularly bonds.

Two common choices for financing are equity financing (attracting new owners) and debt financing (taking on long-term liabilities). Long-term liabilities are debts that will be repaid over a number of years, such as long-term bank loans and bond issues. A bond is a long-term debt security that an organization sells to raise money. The bond indenture specifies the provisions of the bond contract—maturity date, coupon rate, repayment methods, and others.

LO5 Discuss how corporations can use equity financing by issuing stock through an investment banker.

Owners' equity represents what owners have contributed to the company and includes common stock, preferred stock, and retained earnings (profits that have been reinvested in the assets of the firm). To finance operations, companies can issue new common and preferred stock through an investment banker that sells stocks and bonds for corporations.

LO6 Describe the various securities markets in Canada.

Securities markets provide the mechanism for buying and selling stocks and bonds. Primary markets allow companies to raise capital by selling new stock directly to investors through investment bankers. Secondary markets allow the buyers of previously issued shares of stock to sell them to other owners. The major secondary market is the S&P/TSX Composite Index in Canada. Investors measure stock market performance by watching stock market averages and indexes such as the S&P/TSX Composite Index and the Dow Jones Industrial Average.

KEY TERMS

bonds
capital budgeting
commercial certificates of deposit (CDs)
commercial paper
dividend yield
eurodollar market
factor
floating-rate bonds
investment banking
junk bonds
line of credit
lockbox
long-term (fixed) assets
long-term liabilities
marketable securities

over-the-counter (OTC) market
primary market
prime rate
retained earnings
secondary markets
secured bonds
secured loans
securities markets
serial bonds
trade credit
transaction balances
Treasury bills (T-bills)
unsecured bonds
unsecured loans
working capital management

DESTINATION CEO DISCUSSION QUESTIONS

1. What was the key for AIC's initial success?

2. What is the relative size of AIC as a company?

3. Discuss the recent problems at AIC.

SO YOU WANT TO WORK *in Financial Management or Securities*

Taking classes in financial and securities management can provide many career options, from managing a small firm's accounts receivable to handling charitable giving for a multinational to investment banking to stock brokerage. We have entered into a less certain period for finance and securities jobs, however. In the world of investment banking, the past few years have been especially challenging. Tens of thousands of employees around the world have lost their jobs. This type of phenomenon is not isolated to the finance sector. In the early 2000s, the tech sector experienced a similar downturn, from which it has subsequently largely recovered. Undoubtedly, markets will bounce back and job creation in finance and securities will increase again—but until that happens the atmosphere across finance and securities will be more competitive than it has been in the past. However, this does not mean that there are no jobs. All firms need financial analysts to determine whether a project should be implemented, when to issue stocks or bonds, or when to initiate loans. These and other forward-looking questions such as how to invest excess cash must be addressed by financial managers. Economic uncertainty in the financial and securities market has made for more difficulty in finding the most desirable jobs.

Why this sudden downturn in financial industry prospects? A lot of these job cuts came in response to the financial crises. All of these people who lost their jobs will be looking for new jobs in new organizations, increasing the competitive level in a lot of different employment areas. For young job seekers with relatively little experience, this may result in a great deal of frustration. On the other hand, by the time you graduate, the job market for finance majors could be in recovery and rebuilding with new employees. Uncertainty results in hiring freezes and layoffs, but leaves firms lean and ready to grow when the cycle turns around, resulting in hiring from the bottom up.

Many different industries require people with finance skills. So do not despair if you have a difficult time finding a job in exactly the right firm. Most students switch companies a number of times over the course of their careers. Many organizations require individuals trained in forecasting, statistics, economics, and finance. Even unlikely places like museums, aquariums, and zoos need people who are good at numbers. It may require some creativity, but if you are committed to a career in finance, look to less obvious sources—not just the large financial firms.

Financial Management and Securities Market

This chapter helps you realize that once you are making money, you need to be careful in determining how to invest it. Meanwhile, your team should consider the pros and cons of establishing a line of credit at the bank.

Remember that the key to building your business plan is to be realistic!!

CASE | Hershey Foods: Melts in Your Mouth and May Melt Your Heart

Hershey Foods is the leading North American producer of quality chocolate and candy products, including much-loved brands such as Hershey's milk chocolate bar, Hershey's syrup, Hershey's cocoa, Almond Joy, Mr. Goodbar, Hershey's Kisses, Kit Kat, and Reese's peanut butter cups. A century after its founding, the company continues to operate by the values of its founder. Milton Hershey was born in 1857 and was of Pennsylvania Dutch descent. He became an apprentice to a candy maker in 1872, at age 15. By age 30, he had founded the Lancaster Caramel Company. After visiting the Chicago Exhibition in 1893, he became interested in a new chocolate-making machine. He sold his caramel factory and built a large chocolate factory in Derry Church, Pennsylvania, in 1905; the city was renamed Hershey in 1906. Hershey pioneered modern confectionery mass-production techniques by developing much of the machinery for making and packaging his milk chocolate products. The Hershey Foods Corporation as it exists today was organized under the laws of the state of Delaware on October 24, 1927, as a successor to the original business founded in 1894 by Milton Hershey. The company's stock was first publicly traded on December 1, 1927, and investors can still purchase shares today.

Milton Hershey was not only interested in innovative candy making; he also wanted to help the members of his community. An example of his concern for the community was the founding of a home and school for orphan children, the Hershey Industrial School (now called the Milton Hershey School) in 1909. Many of the children who attended the school became Hershey employees, including former Hershey chairman William Dearden (1976–1984). Today, the 10,000-acre campus houses and provides education for nearly 1,300 financially and socially disadvantaged children. Although Hershey remains a public corporation, the Milton Hershey School Trust, which financially supports the school, owns about 30 percent of Hershey Foods' total equity. The Milton Hershey School Trust also owns 100 percent of the Hershey Entertainment and Resort Company, which operates a number of Hershey's nonchocolate properties, including the Hershey Park theme park, the Dutch Wonderland theme park for younger children, the Hershey Hotel, the Hershey Lodge and Convention Center, the Hershey Bears minor league hockey team, Hershey's zoo, a four-course golf club, an outdoor sports stadium, and an indoor sports arena. Because of Milton Hershey's original funding and the wise investment management by the trust managers, the assets of the Milton Hershey School Trust have grown to a value of more than $7 billion. Milton Hershey was a visionary in terms of using a public corporation to support his philanthropic dreams.[7]

DISCUSSION QUESTIONS

1. Do you think that Milton Hershey made the right decision in leaving his foundation the controlling voting interest in the Hershey Foods Corporation?

2. Is Hershey Foods' example of founders willing stock for philanthropic purposes something that you believe that companies could do today? Why or why not?

3. Knowing that a large share of Hershey's profits support philanthropic causes, would you be more likely to purchase the company's stock?

connect **LEARNSMART** **SMARTBOOK**™

For more information on the resources available from McGraw-Hill Ryerson, go to www.mcgrawhill.ca/he/solutions.

ENDNOTES

Chapter 1

1. Timothy Taylor, "CEO of the Year: Christine Day of Lululemon," *Report on Business* Magazine, *The Globe and Mail*, November 24, 2011, **http://www.theglobeandmail.com/report-on-business/rob-magazine/ceo-of-the-year-christine-day-of-lululemon/article4252293/**; Stefania Moretti, "Lululemon's Christine Day named CEO of the year," Canoe.ca, November 23, 2011, **http://cnews.canoe.ca/CNEWS/Canada/2011/11/23/19008561.html.**

2. Ibid; "Lululemon Athletica," wikipedia.org, accessed January 11, 2013, **http://en.wikipedia.org/wiki/Lululemon_Athletica.**

3. Jim Reid, presenter, Business & Tourism Conference 2009, Mount Saint Vincent University, Halifax, Nova Scotia.

4. "Streettohome Foundation Receives Support for Supportive Housing for Homeless Youth and Adults," November 4, 2012, StreetToHome website, **http://streetohome.org/news-events/news-release/2012/apr-11/streetohome-foundation-receives-support-supportive-housing-home.**

5. "Seeing is Believing Tour Explores Innovative Solutions to Homelessness in Lower Mainland," Canadian Business for Social Responsibility, accessed July 17, 2010, **http://www.cbsr.ca/node/245.**

6. Ibid.

7. Hurricane Sandy Corporate Aid Tracker, Business Civic Leadership Centre, accessed March 14, 2013, **http://bclc.uschamber.com/site-page/hurricane-sandy-corporate-aid-tracker.**

8. "Aboriginal Community Partnerships," Suncor Energy, Petro-Canada 2009 Report on Sustainability, accessed July 17, 2010, **http://sustainability.suncor.com/2009/en/responsible/1104.aspx.**

9. "Talisman Energy—2005 Corporate Responsibility Report: Local Benefits," Talisman Energy, accessed July 17, 2010, **http://www.talisman-energy.com/cr_online/2005/social-local_benefits.html.**

10. Jeff Beer, "Saving Face: Bombardier's CSeries Will Take Off," *Canadian Business*, February 18, 2013, p. 57.

11. Nathan Vanderklippe, "Gearing up for a new labour crunch," Diamond Global Recruitment Group website, **http://www.diamondglobal.ca/Gearing-up-for-a-new-labour-crunch.html.**

12. Canadian Business for Social Responsibility, accessed July 17, 2010, **www.cbsr.ca.**

13. Robert D. Hisrich, Michael P. Peters, Dean A. Shepherd, and Peter Mombourquette, *Entrepreneurship* (2nd Canadian edition), (Toronto: McGraw-Hill Ryerson Ltd., 2009), p. 186.

14. Ron Joyce, *The Untold Story of Tim Hortons by the Man Who Created a Canadian Empire*, (Toronto: Harper Collins Publisher's Ltd., 2006), p. 180; Adam Lauzon, "Can I get a Large Double-Double, Please?", accessed July 17, 2010, **http://adamlauzon.wordpress.com/.**

15. Zenn Motor Company, **www.zenncars.com/**; "Zenn Motor Company," Wikipedia, **http://en.wikipedia.org/wiki/ZENN**; Nick Waddell, "Who killed the Zenn Motors car?", *Cantech Letter*, May 1, 2013, **http://www.cantechletter.com/2013/05/who-killed-the-zenn-motors-car0501/**; Tim Kiladze, "Zenn raises $2-million, without its electric car," *Report on Business*, April 19, 2012, **http://www.theglobeandmail.com/report-on-business/streetwise/zenn-raises-2-million-without-its-electric-car/article4101209/.**

16. "Canadian Public Companies' Dead Cash May Be A Myth: Analysis," *The Huffington Post* online, May 9, 2012, **http://www.huffingtonpost.ca/2012/09/05/canadas-public-companies-dead-cash-stockpile_n_1859479.html.**

17. "Why So Much Cash?" *Canadian Business*, February 18, 2013, p. 49.

18. Matthew McClearn, "The Tipping Point," *Canadian Business*, February 18, 2013, p. 61.

19. "Clock ticking on Teck debt," *The Globe and Mail* Blog Post, November 12, 2008, **http://www.theglobeandmail.com/globe-investor/investment-ideas/streetwise/article714385.ece**; Yahoo Canada Finance, Teck Resources Limited (TCK), accessed July 17, 2010, **http://ca.finance.yahoo.com/q?s=TCK.**

20. "RBC—Corporate Responsibility," RBC, accessed July 17, 2010, **http://www.rbc.com/responsibility/community/index.html**; "Canada's biggest charitable donations," *CBC News* online, October 30, 2006, **www.cbc.ca/news/background/wealth/charitable-donations.html**; "Vibrant Communities: RBC 2011 Donations Report," **http://www.rbc.com/community-sustainability/_assets-custom/pdf/RBC-Donation-List-2011.pdf.**

21. Wayne Gretzky Foundation, accessed July 17, 2010, w**ww.gretzky.com/foundation/.**

22. Michael McCullough, "Oil Nation," *Canadian Business*, March 5, 2012, pp. 46–51; Joanna Pachner, "Canada Takes on the World," *Canadian Business*, March 19, 2012, pp. 20–25.

23. Nathan VanderKlippe, "Canada home to a century's worth of natural gas," *CTV News* online, accessed May 2010, **http://www.ctv.ca/generic/generated/static/business/article1566425.html.**

24. Jen Gerson, "What the #!%*? is the 'Dutch disease' exactly and does Canada have it?" *National Post*, May 18, 2012, **http://news.nationalpost.com/2012/05/18/what-the-is-the-dutch-disease-exactly-and-does-canada-have-it/**; Barrie McKenna, "Is Canada Grappling With Dutch Disease?", *The Globe and Mail*, May 16, 2012, **http://www.theglobeandmail.com/report-on-business/economy/manufacturing/is-canada-grappling-with-dutch-disease/article4184569/**; David Frum, " If It's Dutch Disease, Mulcair, Then Harper Has the Cure," *The Huffington Post* online, May 28, 2012, **http://www.huffingtonpost.ca/david-frum/if-its-dutch-disease-mulc_b_1548731.html** (all accessed June 18, 2013).

25. "Nortel," Wikipedia, accessed July 17, 2010, **http://en.wikipedia.org/wiki/Nortel**; Ian Austen, "Nortel Seeks Bankruptcy Protection," *The New York Times*, January 14, 2009, **http://www.nytimes.com/2009/01/15/technology/companies/15nortel.html.**

26. James R. Healey, "Gasoline Supplies Likely to Shrink, Prices Rise," *USA Today*, February 26, 2004, p. 1B.

27. Michael McCarthy and Theresa Howard, "Universal Music Slashes CD, Cassette Prices," *USA Today*, September 4, 2003, p. 1B.

28. Canadian Intellectual Property Office, "Patent Applications Filed By Language, 2011–2012," (Table 8), CIPO website, accessed June 13, 2013, **http://www.cipo.ic.gc.ca/eic/site/cipointernet-internetopic.nsf/eng/wr03599.html**

29. "Inflation Rate: Country List," Trading Economics website, **http://www.tradingeconomics.com/country-list/inflation-rate**.

30. "Canada GDP Growth Rate," Trading Economics website, accessed March 13, 2013, **http://www.tradingeconomics.com/canada/gdp-growth**.

31. "Canada's debt to jump to $630B in 5 years: TD Bank," *CBC News* online, June 2, 2009, **http://www.cbc.ca/money/story/2009/06/02/td-forecast-canada-fiscal.html#ixzz11OXjv7zN**.

32. "Women in the Labor Force, 1900–2002" (n.d.), InfoPlease, accessed March 9, 2004, **www.infoplease.com/ipa/A0104673.html**.

33. "Canada's debt to jump to $630B in 5 years: TD Bank," *CBC News* online, June 2, 2009, **http://www.cbc.ca/money/story/2009/06/02/td-forecast-canada-fiscal.html#ixzz11OXjv7zN**.

34. Terry Long, "The History of New France: The First European Settlers in Canada," Suite101.com, May 31, 2009, **http://www.suite101.com/content/the-history-of-new-france-a121662**.

35. John E. Foster, "Merger of the North West and Hudson's Bay Companies," *The Canadian Encyclopedia* online, accessed July 17, 2010, **http://www.thecanadianencyclopedia.com/index.cfm?PgNm=TCE&Params=a1ARTA0003112**.

36. "Hudson's Bay Company ends its fur trade," CBC Digital Archives, accessed July 17, 2010, **http://archives.cbc.ca/economy_business/consumer_goods/clips/2740/**. Original Broadcast date January 30, 1991.

37. Tom McNichol, "Building a Wiki World," Business 2.0, March 2007, pp. 102–108; Jonathan Dee, "All the News That's Fit to Print Out," *The New York Times*, July 1, 2007, **http://www.nytimes.com/2007/07/01/magazine/01WIKIPEDIA-t.html?ex=1189828800 &en=b2e607ab370a06f8&ei=5070**; Daniel Terdiman, "Growing Pains for Wikipedia," News.com, December 7, 2005, **http://www.news.com/2102-1025_3-5981119 .html?tag=st.util.print**.

38. Ian M. Drummond, "Economic History," *The Canadian Encyclopedia* online, accessed July 17, 2010, **http://www.thecanadianencyclopedia.com/index.cfm?PgNm=TCE&Params=A1ARTA0002512**.

39. Peter J. Nicholson, "The Growth Story: Canada's Long-run Economic Performance and Prospects," *International Productivity Monitor, 2003*, **www.csls.ca/ipm/7/nicholson-e.pdf**, pp. 3–23.

40. Someshwar Rao, Andrew Sharpe, and Jianmin Tang, "Productivity Growth in Service Industries: A Canadian Success Story," *CSLS Research Report*, February 2004, **http://www.csls.ca/reports/ProdServiceIndustries.pdf**, p. 14.

41. Enactus Canada website, **www.enactus.ca** (accessed June 19, 2013); Metro Lyrics website, **http://www.metrolyrics.com/about.html** (accessed March 13, 2013).

42. Jenny Lee, "Kicking Horse Coffee Makes Sweet Deal," *Vancouver Sun*, November 28, 2012, **http://www.vancouversun.com/business/Kicking+Horse+Coffee+makes+sweet+deal/7620169/story.html**; *Kootenay* Business, January/February 2013, Vol 29, no.1, p. 39, **http://www.kickinghorsecoffee.com/files/2013_Feb_Kootenay_Business.pdf**; Kicking Horse Coffee website, accessed March 13, 2013, **http://www.kickinghorsecoffee.com/en/story**; Jim McElgunn, "Staying on a Kicking Horse," *Profit*, Vol. 25, 5, p. 57; "Fair-Trade Champions Win BDC's Young Entrepreneur Award for British Columbia," *Canada News Wire*, October 20, 2003, p. 1; "Thrifty Foods Bucking Downward Sales Trend," *Canadian Grocer*, August 2002, Vol. 116, 6, p. S10; **www.kickinghorsecoffee.com**.

43. "Stewart Convicted on All Charges," CNNMoney, March 5, 2004, **www.money.cnn.com**; "Martha Stewart Settles with SEC on Civil Charges," *The Wall Street Journal* online, August 8, 2006, accessed May 31, 2007, **http://online.wsj.com/article/SB115496196167028712.html?mod=home_whats_news_us**.

44. Just Us! Coffee Roasters Co-op, accessed July 7, 2010, **http://www.justuscoffee.com/**.

45. Ronald Alsop, "Corporate Scandals Hit Home," *The Wall Street Journal*, February 18, 2004, **http://online.wsj.com**.

46. Tim Shufelt, "How low will house prices go?" *Canadian Business*, February 18, 2013, pp. 52–53.

Chapter 2

1. "Most Wanted," Global Exchange website, **http://www.globalexchange.org/corporateHRviolators#TransCanada** (accessed June 18, 2013).

2. Daniela Minicucci, "Pros and cons of the Keystone XL pipeline project," Communications, Energy and Paperworkers Union of Canada website, September 26, 2011, **http://www.cep.ca/en/news/in-the-news/pros-and-cons-keystone-xl-pipeline-project** (accessed June 17, 2013).

3. Sheldon Alberts, "An Interview with TransCanada CEO Russell Girling on the Keystone XL Pipeline," ocanada.com, October 9, 2011, **http://o.canada.com/2011/10/09/an-interview-with-transcanada-ceo-russ-girling-on-the-keystone-xl-pipeline/** (accessed June 17, 2013).

4. Ibid.

5. Campbell Clark, "Ericsson, RIM to face off over Nortel," *The Globe and Mail* online, August 5, 2009, **http://www.theglobeandmail.com/news/technology/ericsson-rim-to-face-off-over-nortel/article1242512/**; "Canada Won't Intervene to Block Nortel Sale," *The New York Times* online, August 12, 2009, **http://dealbook.blogs.nytimes.com/2009/08/12/canada-chief-wont-block-nortel-sale-to-ericsson/**.

6. "A timeline of auto sector layoffs," *CBC News* online, February 9, 2009, **http://www.cbc.ca/canada/story/2008/10/21/f-auto-layoffs.html**.

7. Greg Farrell, "Lay, Skilling Found Guilty," *USA Today*, May 26, 2006, pp. A1, B1; *The New York Times* coverage of the Enron trial, accessed May 18, 2006, **www.nytimes.com/business/businessspecial3/index.html?adxnnl=1&adxnnlx=1147986237-z56Vd16RUkp6eHnHTTXBHw**; "RCMP charge former Nortel CEO, 2 other execs," *CBC News* online, June 19, 2008, **http://**

www.cbc.ca/money/story/2008/06/19/nortel-rcmp.html#ixzz11ROltiTM; Marguerite Reardon, "Former Nortel execs face criminal charges," *cnet News* online, June 19, 2008, http://news.cnet.com/8301-10784_3-9973257-7.html#ixzz 11RQKFGJr; "Enron," *Wikipedia*, accessed July 17, 2010, http://en.wikipedia.org/wiki/Enron.

8. "Firm Profile—Going Green Program," Stikeman Elliott, accessed July 17, 2010, http://www.stikeman.com/cps/rde/xchg/se-en/hs.xsl/11097.htm.

9. Katie Engelhart, "The Green 30: From the bottom up," *Canadian Business* magazine online, May 10, 2010, http://www.canadianbusiness.com/innovation/article.jsp?content=20100510_10024_10024.

10. Ibid.

11. "Sarbanes-Oxley Act," *Wikipedia*, accessed July 17, 2010, http://en.wikipedia.org/wiki/Sarbanes%E2%80%93Oxley_Act.

12. Simon Houpt, "Telus sues Rogers over ad claims," *The Globe and Mail* online, November 18, 2009, http://www.theglobeandmail.com/news/technology/telus-sues-rogers-over-ad-claims/article1368486/; "Rogers stands behind its Internet advertising as fastest and most reliable," *The Cape Breton Post* online, February 17, 2010, http://www.capebretonpost.com/Living/Technologies/2010-02-17/article-837486/Rogers-stands-behind-its-Internet-advertising-as-fastest-and-most-reliable/1.

13. O. C. Ferrell, John Fraedrich, Linda Ferrell, *Business Ethics: Ethical Decision Making and Cases,* 6th ed. (Boston: Houghton Mifflin, 2005), p. 7.

14. David Callahan, as quoted in Archie Carroll, "Carroll: Do We Live in a Cheating Culture?", *Athens Banner-Herald,* February 21, 2004, www.onlineathens.com/stores/022204/bus_20040222028.shtml.

15. Devon Leonard, "The Curse of Pooh," *Fortune,* January 20, 2003, pp. 85–92; "Pooh Suit against Disney Dismissed," *CNN* online, March 29, 2004, www.cnn.com.

16. "Auditor General investigating MLA expense irregularities," *CBC News* online, February 12, 2010, http://www.cbc.ca/canada/nova-scotia/story/2010/02/12/auditor-general-forensic-investigation-spending.html#ixzz11RZCX6Kt.

17. "Another MLA Expenses Case Referred to RCMP," Government of Nova Scotia, June 3, 2010, http://www.gov.ns.ca/news/details.asp?id=20100603004.

18. Tina Comeau, "Yarmouth MLA Richard Hurlburt resigns," *NovaNewsNow.com*, February 9, 2010, http://www.novanewsnow.com/Natural-resources/2010-02-09/article-809272/Yarmouth-MLA-Richard-Hurlburt-resigns/1.

19. John Lyman, "Who Is Scooter Libby?", *Center for American Progress,* October 28, 2005, http://www.americanprogress.org/issues/2005/10/b109719.html.

20. "Hwang Woo-suk," *Wikipedia*, accessed May 23, 2006, http://en.wikipedia.org/wiki/Hwang_Woo-suk.

21. "Colorado Places Barnett on Administrative Leave," *SI.com,* February 19, 2004, http://sportsillustrated.cnn.com/.

22. Mark Long, "Jimmy Johnson's Crew Chief Thrown out of Daytona 500," *StarTribune.com,* February 13, 2006, www.startribune.com/694/story/244568.html.

23. Ferrell, Fraedrich, and Ferrell, *Business Ethics*, p. 21

24. Adrian Humphreys, "Canada's organic food certification system 'little more than an extortion racket' report says," *National Post* online, November 24, 2012, http://news.nationalpost.com/2012/11/24/canadas-organic-food-certification-system-little-more-than-an-extortion-racket-report-says/; Mischa Popoff and Patrick Moore, "Canada's Organic Nightmare," Frontier Centre Policy Series, http://mobi.fcpp.org/publication.php/4361; Mischa Popoff, "Opinions and Editorials," Is It Organic? website, http://isitorganic.ca/opinions_and_editorials (accessed June 19, 2013).

25. "National Business Ethics Survey 2005," "Survey Documents State of Ethics in the Workplace," and "Misconduct" (n.d.), Ethics Resource Center, accessed April 11, 2006, www.ethics.org/nbes/2005/release.html.

26. Thomas Watson, "Ashley Madison: Abandoned at the altar," *Canadian Business* magazine, March 1, 2010, http://www.canadianbusiness.com/managing/strategy/article.jsp?content=20100301_10022_10022; "Noel Biderman Created the Most Controversial Website since Napster in Ashley Madison," *Jewish Business Magazine* online, May 11, 2010, http://jewishbusinessmagazine.com/jewish-business-news/noel-biderman-ashley-madison-infidelity-cheating-dating-website/#; "Noel Biderman: Making a fortune promoting adultery," *Money Week* online, May 29, 2009, http://www.moneyweek.com/news-and-charts/noel-biderman-making-a-fortune-promoting-adultery-43732.aspx.

27. Peter Lattman, "Boeing's Top Lawyer Spotlights Company's Ethical Lapses," *The Wall Street Journal: Law Blog*, January 30, 2006, accessed March 31, 2006, http://blogs.wsj.com/law/2006/01/31/boeings-top-lawyer-rips-into-his-company.

28. Janet Guyon, "Jack Grubman Is Back. Just Ask Him," *Fortune,* May 16, 2005, pp. 119–26.

29. Karen MacGregor, "Acres International convicted in African bribery case," *Probe International,* September 18, 2002, http://www.probeinternational.org/odious-debts/acres-intl-convicted-african-bribery-case.

30. Greg McArthur, "NIKO Resources: Ottawa's corruption test case," *Report on Business* online, August 25, 2011, http://www.theglobeandmail.com/report-on-business/rob-magazine/niko-resources-ottawas-corruption-test-case/article542842/ (accessed June 18, 2013).

31. Canadian Competition Bureau, June 13, 2003, http://www.competitionbureau.gc.ca/eic/site/cb-bc.nsf/eng/01863.html, and July 6, 2004, http://www.competitionbureau.gc.ca/eic/site/cb-bc.nsf/eng/01863.html.

32. "Pens and Post-Its Among Most Pilfered Office Supplies, Says New Vault Survey," *Vault*, November 16, 2005, accessed June 2, 2006, www.vault.com/nr/newsmain.jsp?nr_page=3&ch_id=420&article_id=25720773.

33. David Whelan, "Only the Paranoid Resurge," *Forbes,* April 10, 2006, http://www.forbes.com/forbes/2006/0410/042.html (accessed June 19, 2013).

34. "Maple Leaf Foods plant linked to Listeria outbreak," *CTV News* online, August 23, 2008, http://www.ctv.ca/CTVNews/EdmontonHome/20080823/recall_listeria_080823/; Sarah Schmidt and Mike De Souza, "Maple Leaf CEO says food industry must improve safety regime," *National Post* online, April 20, 2009, http://www.nationalpost.com/news/canada/story.html?id=1516299; *Our Journey to Safe*

Leadership (Maple Leaf blog), accessed July 17, 2010, **http://blog.mapleleaf.com/**.

35. "6 automakers part of massive recall of 3.4 million airbags," CBC News online, April 11, 2013, **http://www.cbc.ca/news/business/story/2013/04/11/vehicle-airbag-recall-honda-nissan-toyota.html** (accessed June 18, 2013); Tim Shufelt, "Toyota moves fast on recall," *Financial Post* online, August 26, 2010, **http://www.financialpost.com/news/Toyota+moves+fast+recall/3445963/story.html**.

36. Renata D'Aliesio, "XL owners giants in the beef business," *The Globe and Mail* online, October 13, 2012, **http://www.theglobeandmail.com/news/national/xl-owners-giants-in-the-beef-business/article4611119/** (accessed June 18, 2013), "XL Foods E. coli recall preventable, probe finds," CBC News online, June 5, 2013, **http://www.cbc.ca/news/politics/story/2013/06/05/pol-e-coli-xl-foods-report.html** (accessed June 18, 2013); Todd Zaun, "Mitsubishi Motors seeks damages from ex-officials," *The New York Times* online, March 31, 2005, **http://www.nytimes.com/2005/03/31/business/ worldbusiness/31mitsubishi.html?ref=katsuhiko_kawasoe**; Yuri Kageyama, "Mitsubishi Motors Says Massive Defect Cover-ups Were Intentional," *Boston Globe,* August 22, 2000, **www.boston.com**; "Mitsubishi Cover-up May Bring Charges," *Detroit News,* August 23, 2000, **www.det-news.com/2000/autos/0008/23/b03-109584.htm**.

37. Transparency International, **http://www.transparency.org/** (accessed July 17, 2010).

38. "Music sales in Canada fall 4 percent in 2005," CRIA, March 2, 2006, **http://www.cria.ca/news/020306a_n.php**.

39. "RIAA Releases 2003 Consumer Profile: *Online Music Purchasing Expands*," April 30, 2004, accessed July 27, 2010, **http://www.riaa.com/newsitem.php?news_month_filter=&news_year_ filter=& resultpage=49&id=1D5364BF-B187-A206-C3B8-94B7424E50F4.**

40. Gary Fung, "There is no way you can shut file-sharing down," periodicfitness website, **http://www.periodfitness.com/tag/gary-fung/** (accessed June 19, 2013); Ernesto, "BitTorrent Behind the Scenes: isoHunt," TorrentFreak website, **http://torrentfreak.com/bittorrent-behind-the-scenes-isohunt-090729/** (accessed June 19, 2013); and "isoHunt," Wikipedia website, **http://en.wikipedia.org/wiki/IsoHunt** (accessed June 19, 2013).

41. Alex Gillis, "Cheating themselves," University Affairs online, March 12, 2007, **http://www.universityaffairs.ca/cheating-themselves.aspx**.

42. "Teens Respect Good Business Ethics," *USA Today,* Snapshots, December 12, 2005, p. 13-1.

43. Marianne Jennings, "An Ethical Breach by Any Other Name," *College of Business Master Teacher Initiative, Colorado State University,* January/February 2006 **http://www.biz.colostate.edu/MTI/TeachingTips/Academic_Integrity/Ethical Breach.aspx.**

44. Matthew McClearn, "Probiotics: Yogurt's secret ingredient," *Canadian Business* website, November 1, 2012, **http://www.canadianbusiness.com/lifestyle/probiotics-yogurts-secret-ingredient/** (accessed June 19, 2013).

45. Erica Johnson, "Questioning the Magic at Herbal Magic," *CBC.ca Marketplace Blog,* February 5, 2010, **http://www.cbc.ca/marketplace/blog/2010/02/questioning-the-magic-at-herbal-magic.html**.

46. "Tracking a diet scam," *CTV News* online, February 22, 2002, **http://www.ctv.ca/CTVNews/SpecialEvent1/20020222/ctvnews836330/**.

47. "Mexico, United States, Canada Combat Weight Loss Fraud," U.S. Food and Drug Administration, October 24, 2005, **http://www.fda.gov/NewsEvents/Newsroom/PressAnnouncements/2005/ucm108504.htm**.

48. "Campaign Warns about Drugs from Canada," *CNN,* February 5, 2004, **www.cnn.com**; Gardiner Harris and Monica Davey, "FDA Begins Push to End Drug Imports," *The New York Times,* January 23, 2004, p. C1.

49. "Briefing: Tobacco Packaging and Labelling," Information Resource Center, accessed July 31, 2006, **http://infolink.cancerresearchuk.org/publicpolicy/briefings/prevention/tobacco**.

50. Food and Consumer Products of Canada, Consumer Products Safety, accessed July 18, 2010, **http://www.fcpc.ca/issues/safety/index.html**

51. Nestor E. Arellano. "Toronto firm fined for unlicensed software use," IT World Canada, October 4, 2006, accessed July 17, 2010, **http://www.itworldcanada.com/news/toronto-firm-fined-for-unlicensed-software-use/100124**.

52. "WestJet to sue Air Canada for corporate spying," *CTV News* online, June 30, 2004, **http://www.ctv.ca/CTVNews/Canada/20040630/westjet_suesaircanada_20040629/**; "WestJet apologizes to Air Canada for snooping," *National Post* online, May 30, 2006, **http://www.canada.com/topics/technology/story.html?p=1&k=30762&id=6138fbd4-c3db-44ca-83a7-bfb6bcc0cbdb**; "Air Canada, WestJet settle spying lawsuit," *CBC News* online, May 30, 2006, **http://www.cbc.ca/money/story/2006/05/29/westjet-aircansettle.html**.

53. Susan Pullman, "Ordered to Commit Fraud, A Staffer Balked, Then Caved," *The Wall Street Journal,* June 23, 2003, **http://online.wsj.com**.

54. CTVNews.ca staff, "Corporate espionage costing billions each year," *CTV News* online, November 29, 2011, **http://www.ctvnews.ca/corporate-espionage-costing-billions-each-year-1.732885** (accessed June 19, 2013).

55. Blake Morrison, "Ex-USA Today Reporter Faked Major Stories," *USA Today,* March 19, 2004, **www.usatoday.com/**.

56. Thomas M. Jones, "Ethical Decision Making by Individuals in Organizations: An Issue-Contingent Model," *Academy of Management Review* 2 (April 1991), pp. 371–73.

57. Sir Adrian Cadbury, "Ethical Managers Make Their Own Rules," *Harvard Business Review* 65 (September–October 1987), p. 72.

58. Ferrell, Fraedrich, and Ferrell, *Business Ethics,* pp. 174–75.

59. Ethics Resource Center, "Misconduct" (n.d.), accessed April 11, 2006, **www.ethics.org/nbes/2005/release.html**.

60. Ethics Resource Center, "2005 National Business Ethics Survey: Executive Summary" (n.d.), accessed July 17, 2010, **www.ethic.org/nbes2005/2005nbes_summary.html**, p. 29.

61. "Whistleblower legislation: Bill C-25, Disclosure Protection," CBC News Online, April 28, 2004, accessed July 27, 2010, **http://www.cbc.ca/news/background/whistleblower/**.

62. Ferrell, Fraedrich, and Ferrell, *Business Ethics,* p. 13.

63. John Galvin, "The New Business Ethics," *SmartBusinessMag. com,* June 2000, p. 99.

64. Archie B. Carroll, "The Pyramid of Corporate Social Responsibility: Toward the Moral Management of Organizational Stakeholders," *Business Horizons* 34 (July/August 1991), p. 42.

65. Steve Brearton, "50 Best Employers in Canada," *ROB Magazine, The Globe and Mail* online, December 29, 2009, **http://www.theglobeandmail.com/report-on-business/rob-magazine/50-best-employers-in-canada/article1413413/**.

66. "About Us," Nexen Inc., accessed July 17, 2010, **http://www.nexeninc.com/en/AboutUs.aspx**.

67. Corporate Knights, accessed July 17, 2010, **http://www.corporateknights.ca/**.

68. Ferrell, Fraedrich, and Ferrell, *Business Ethics*, pp. 13–19.

69. "Canadian Auto Workers," *Wikipedia,* accessed July 17, 2010, **http://en.wikipedia.org/wiki/Canadian_Auto_Workers**; "Deadline passes with no deal between CAW, GM," *CBC News* online, May 16, 2009, **http://www.cbc.ca/canada/story/2009/05/15/gm-canada-caw-talks497.html**.

70. "WestJet Airlines Ltd.—Company Profile, Information, Business Description, History, Background Information on WestJet Airlines Ltd.," accessed July 17, 2010, **http://www.referenceforbusiness.com/history2/70/WestJet-Airlines-Ltd.html**; Richard Yerema and R. Caballero, "Employer Review: Royal Bank of Canada," Mediacorp Canada Inc., November 2, 2009, **http://www.eluta.ca/top-employer-rbc**.

71. "Nestlé Boss Starts an African Crusade," *The Sunday Times,* March 13, 2005, **www.timesonline.co.uk/article/0,,2095-1522290,00.html**; "The Nestlé Coffee Report," *Faces of Coffee,* Nestlé S.A., Public Affairs, March 2004, **www.nestle.com/NR/rdonlyres/4F893E04-4129-4E4C-92F1-91AF4C8C4738/0/2003_Coffee_Report.pdf**; "The Nestlé Commitment to Africa," Africa Report, Nestlé, **www.nestle.com/Our_Responsibility/Africa+Report/Overview/Africa+Report.htm** (all accessed November 7, 2005).

72. Wendy Zellner, "No Way to Treat a Lady?", *BusinessWeek,* March 3, 2003, pp. 63–66.

73. Chad Terhune, "Jury Says Home Depot Must Pay Customer Hurt by Falling Merchandise $1.5 Million," *The Wall Street Journal,* July 16, 2001, p. A14.

74. "About Us," Office of Consumer Affairs, accessed June 28, 2010, **http://www.ic.gc.ca/eic/site/oca-bc.nsf/eng/ca00038.html**.

75. Loren Drummond, "EU representative condemns seal hunt after Canada visit," The Humane Society of the United States, March 28, 2007, **http://www.hsus.org/marine_mammals/marine_mammals_news/eu_representative_condemns_hunt.html**; "Seal hunting," *Wikipedia,* accessed July 17, 2010, **http://en.wikipedia.org/wiki/Seal_hunting**; "Bring on the seal war, fisheries minister tells activists," *CBC News* online, September 7, 2006, **http://www.cbc.ca/canada/newfoundland-labrador/story/2006/09/07/seal-war.html**; "FAQs: The Atlantic seal hunt," *CBC News* online, July 27, 2009, **http://www.cbc.ca/canada/story/2009/05/05/f-seal-hunt.html**.

76. "FAQs: The Atlantic seal hunt," *CBC News* online, July 27, 2009, accessed July 27, 2010, **http://www.cbc.ca/canada/story/2009/05/05/f-seal-hunt.html**.

77. Campbell Robertson and Clifford Krauss, "Gulf Spill Is the Largest of Its Kind, Scientists Say," *The New York Times,* August 2, 2010, accessed September 3, 2010, **http://www.nytimes.com/2010/08/03/us/03spill.html?_r=1&fta=y**; "Deepwater Horizon oil spill," *Wikipedia,* accessed July 17, 2010, **http://en.wikipedia.org/wiki/Deepwater_Horizon_oil_spill**.

78. Anne Hayden, "Will One Gulf's Tragedy Affect Drilling in Another?", *Gulf of Maine Times* online, June 30, 2010, **http://www.gulfofmaine.org/gomt/?p=392**; Kevin Jess, "Oil drilling moratorium on Georges Bank extended," *Digital Journal,* May 18, 2010, **http://www.digitaljournal.com/article/292182**.

79. "Drinking Water Legislation," Ministry of the Environment: Drinking Water Ontario, July 27, 2010, **http://www.ontario.ca/ONT/portal61/drinkingwater/General?docId=STEL01_046858&breadcrumbLevel=1&lang=en** (accessed Sept 16, 2010); "Safe Drinking Water Act, 2002" Government of Ontario, **http://www.e-laws.gov.on.ca/html/statutes/english/elaws_statutes_02s32_e.htm** (accessed July 16, 2010).

80. "China's Energy Crunch," Asia Economic Institute, accessed July 17, 2010, **http://www.asiaecon.org/exclusives/ex_read/9**; Bradsher, K., 2009, "China Outpaces U.S. in Cleaner Coal-Fired Plants," *The New York Times* online, May 10, accessed June 13, 2010, **http://www.nytimes.com/2009/05/11/world/asia/11coal.html**.

81. John Yaukey, "Discarded Computers Create Waste Problem" (n.d.), *USA Today,* accessed October 13, 2000, **www.usatoday.com/news/ndsmon14.htm**.

82. Dell Inc., "WEEE recycling," accessed July 18, 2010, **http://www1.euro.dell.com/content/topics/topic.aspx/emea/topics/services/weee_directive?c=eu&l=en**.

83. Cahal Milmo "The biggest environmental crime in history," *The Independent Close.* accessed July 18, 2010, **http://www.independent.co.uk/environment/the-biggest-environmental-crime-in-history-764102.html**.

84. Laura Judy, "Green from the Ground Up," *Atlanta Home Improvement,* January 2006, **www.homeimprovementmag.com/Articles/2006/06Jan_ground_up.html** (accessed June 15, 2007); Earthcraft House, **www.earthcrafthouse.com** (accessed October 5, 2007); "Earthcraft House Program," "Green Fast Facts: Did You Know...," **www.atlantahomebuilders.com/education/earthcraft.cfm** (accessed October 5, 2007); Melanie Lindner, "Living Green" EarthCraft House," *Atlanta Intown Newspaper,* January 2007, **www.atlantaintownpaper.com/features/EarthCraftHouseJAN07.php** (accessed October 5, 2007).

85. Alan K. Reichert, Marion S. Webb, and Edward G. Thomas, "Corporate Support for Ethical and Environmental Policies: A Financial Management Perspective," *Journal of Business Ethics* 25 (2000), pp. 53–64.

86. "Trend Watch," *Business Ethics,* March/April 2001, p. 8.

87. David J. Lynch, "Corporate America Warms to Fight Against Global Warming," *USA Today,* June 1, 2006, p. B1.

88. Laurie Goldstein, "Marriott Meetings Go Green," Marriott News, July 22, 2008, accessed July 16, 2010, **http://www.marriott.com/news/detail.mi?marrArticle=347592**.

89. Lush Fresh Handmade Cosmetics, accessed July 27, 2010, **http://www.lush.ca/shop/about-lush/articles/our-green-initiatives/packaging.html**.

90. "Certification" (n.d.), Home Depot, accessed April 6, 2004, **www.homedepot.com/HDUS/EN_US/corporate/corp_respon/certification.shtml**.

91. "Yes, We Have No Bananas: Rainforest Alliance Certifies Chiquita Bananas" (n.d.), *Ag Journal*, accessed April 6, 2004, **www.agjournal.com/story.cfm?story_id_1047**.

92. David Leonhardt, "Spillonomics: Underestimating Risk," *The New York Times*, May 31, 2010, **www.nytimes.com/2010/06/06/magazine/06fob-wwln-t.html** (accessed June 22, 2010); Robert Mackey, "Rig Worker Says BP Was Told of Leak in Emergency System Before Explosion," June 21, 2010, *The New York Times*, **http://thelede.blogs.nytimes.com/2010/06/21/rig-worker-claims-bp-knew-of-leak-in-emergency-system-before-explosion/?scp=5&sq=BP&st=cse** (accessed June 22, 2010); "BP and the Gulf of Mexico Alliance Announce Implementation of BP's $500 Million Independent Research Initiative," BP, September 29, 2010, **www.bp.com/genericarticle.do?categoryId=2012968&contentId=7065262** (accessed October 27, 2010); "BP Pledges Collateral for Gulf of Mexico Oil Spill Trust," BP, October 1, 2010, **www.bp.com/genericarticle.do?categoryId=2012968&contentId=7065280** (accessed October 27, 2010); Russell Gold and Tom McGinty, "BP Relied on Cheaper Wells," *The Wall Street Journal*, June 19, 2010, **http://online.wsj.com/article/NA_WSJ_PUB:SB10001424052748704289504575313010283981200.html** (accessed October 27, 2010); Joel K. Bourne, Jr., "The Deep Dilemma," *National Geographic*, October 2010, pp. 40–53.

93. "Delta Hotels and Resorts Wraps Up Cross-Canada Tour to Build Stronger Communities," Habitat for Humanity Canada, accessed Nov. 3, 2010, **http://habitat.ca/deltap4088.php**; MADD Canada, accessed Nov 3. 2010, **http://www.madd.ca/english/donating/sponsors_complete.html**; "CMHA Corporate Donors," Canadian Mental Health Association, accessed November 3, 2010, **http://www.cmha.ca/bins/content_page.asp?cid=7-19**.

94. "Federal government, Ontario agree on $3.3B auto bailout package," *CBC News* online, December 12, 2008, **http://www.cbc.ca/canada/story/2008/12/12/flaherty-deficit.html**; Greg Keenan, Steven Chase, Karen Howlett, and Shawn McCarthy, "Auto bailout costs soar," *The Globe and Mail* online, May 28, 2009, **http://www.theglobeandmail.com/report-on-business/auto-bailout-costs-soar/article1156756/**; "No bailout for Nortel, industry minister says," *CTV News* online, June 18, 2009, **http://www.ctv.ca/CTVNews/TopStories/20090618/Nortel_CEO_090618/**.

95. "Who Really Pays for CSR Initiatives," *Environmental Leader,* February 15, 2008, **www.environmentalleader.com/2008/02/15/who-really-paysfor-csr-initiatives/** (accessed February 25, 2010); "Global Fund," **www.joinred.com/globalfund** (accessed February 25, 2010); Reena Jana, "The Business of Going Green," *BusinessWeek Online,* June 22, 2007, **www.businessweek.com/innovate/content/jun2007/id20070622_491833.htm?chan=search** (accessed June 19, 2008).

96. Mark Zuckerberg, "Six years of making connections," February 4, 2010, **http://blog.facebook.com/blog.php?post=287542162130**; Personal interview with Dr. Amy Thurlow, professor, Mount Saint Vincent University, May 2009.

97. Dana Matiolli, "At Kodak, Patents Hold the Key to the Future," *The Wall Street Journal*, April 20, 2010, p. B8; Grant Gross, ITC to Investigate Apple's Patent Complaint Against Kodak," *ComputerWorld*, May 14, 2010, **www.computerworld.com/s/article/9176792/ITC_to_investigate_Apple_s_patent_complaint_against_Kodak** (accessed June 15, 2010); Franklin Paul, "UPDATE3-Kodak Growth Concerns Overshadow Patent Riches," *Reuters*, April 29, 2010, **www.reuters.com/article/idUSN2923844820100429** (accessed June 15, 2010), United States Patent and Trademark Office, **www.uspto.gov** (accessed October 15, 2010), Geoff Duncan, Samsung and Kodak Reach Patent Settlement," *Digital Trends*, December 23, 2009, **www.digitaltrends.com/mobile/samsung-and-kodak-reach-patent-settlement/** (accessed October 16, 2010).

Chapter 3

1. Boston Pizza (n.d.), **http://www.bostonpizza.com/**.

2. "Julie Jargon, "Subway Runs Past McDonald's Chain," *The Wall Street Journal*, March 9, 2011, p. B4.

3. Bruce Horowitz and Howard Schultz, "Starbucks Hits 40 Feeling Perky," *USA Today*, March 7, 2011, pp. 1B, 3B.

4. Ellen Byron, "Febreze Joins P&G's $1 Billion Club," *The Wall Street Journal*, March 9, 2011, **http://online.wsj.com/article/SB10001424052748704076804576180683371307932.html** (accessed January 7, 2013).

5. Elisabeth A. Sullivan, "Choose Your Words Wisely," *Marketing News*, February 15, 2007, Vol. 42 Issue 3, p. 22.

6. Michelle Yun and Kathy Chu, "Philippines May Answer Call," *USA Today*, January 10, 2011, pp. 1B-2B.

7. Adapted from Statistics Canada, "Imports, exports and trade balance of goods on a balance-of-payments basis, by country or country grouping," **http://www.statcan.gc.ca/tables-tableaux/sum-som/l01/cst01/gblec02a-eng.htm** (accessed January 7, 2013).

8. Adapted from Statistics Canada, "Imports, exports and trade balance of goods on a balance-of-payments basis, by country or country grouping," **http://www.statcan.gc.ca/tables-tableaux/sum-som/l01/cst01/gblec02a-eng.htm** (accessed January 7, 2013).

9. Adapted from Statistics Canada, "Canadian international merchandise trade: Annual review, 2011," **http://www.statcan.gc.ca/daily-quotidien/120404/dq120404a-eng.htm** (accessed January 7, 2013).

10. Adapted from Statistics Canada, "Canadian international merchandise trade," *The Daily*, February 11, 2009, **http://www.statcan.gc.ca/daily-quotidien/090211/dq090211a-eng.htm** (accessed August 17, 2009).

11. Jeanne Whalen, "Novartis Invests in Chinese Vaccines," *The Wall Street Journal*, November 5, 2009, p. B2.

12. Calum MacLeod, "Pollution Fogs China's Future," USA Today, September 13, 2011, 6A; Keith Bradsher, "China Fears Consumer Impact on Global Warming," July 4, 2010, **www.nytimes.com/2010/07/05/business/global/05warm.html?pagewanted=all** (accessed October 6, 2011); "China Leading Global Race to Make Clean Energy," *The New York Times*, January 30, 2010, **www.nytimes.com/2010/01/31/business/energy-environment/31renew.html** (accessed October 6, 2011); Michael Scherer, "The Solyndra Syndrome," *Time*, October 10, 2011, 42–45; "Taxing Times Ahead," *The Economist*, October 29, 2011, p. 77.

13. Summer Said, "Pact Keeps BlackBerrys Running," *The Wall Street Journal*, August 9, 2010, p. B3; "Forbidden Telecoms Fuit," *The Economist*, August 7, 2010, pp. 46-47; "Indonesia Joins Countries Mulling BlackBerry Ban," *CBS News*, Auguist 4, 2010, **http://www.cbsnews.com/stories/2010/08/04/ tech/main6742774.shtml (accessed January 7, 2013)**; "United Arab Emirates Will Not Ban Blackberries," *BBC News* online, October 8, 2010, **www.bbc.co.uk/news/technology-11499755** (accessed January 7, 2013).

14. "Goods from Canada: A Handy Guide for Exporters. Why you have to report your exports," **www.cbsa-asfc.gc.ca/publications/ pub/bsf5081-eng.html** (accessed August 17, 2009).

15. "The Restricted Zone in Mexico," Penner & Associates—Mexico Law Firm and Business Consulting for Mexico, **www.mexicolaw. com/LawInfo17.htm** (accessed January 10, 2011).

16. "Sixth Annual BSA and IDC Global Software Piracy Study," Business Software Alliance, May 2009, **http://global.bsa.org/ globalpiracy2008/index.html** (accessed February 20, 2010).

17. Jose De Cordoba and Nicholas Casey. "Cuba Unveils Huge Layoffs in Tilt toward Free Market," *The Wall Street Journal*, September 14, 2010, pp. A1, A15; Tim Padgett, "Cuba's Big Layoffs: What to Do with the Unemployed?" *Time*, September 14, 2010, **www.time.com/time/world/article/ 0,8599,2019225,00.html** (accessed September 20, 2010); WSJ Staff Reporter, "Cubans Dip a Toe in Capitalist Waters," *The Wall Street Journal*, October 6, 2010, p. A18.

18. Steven Chase, "New Zealand disputes Harper's stand on tariff walls," *The Globe and Mail*, September, 6 2012, **http://m. theglobeandmail.com/news/politics/new-zealand-disputes-harpers-stand-on-tariff-walls/article 4184159/?service=mobile** (accessed January 7, 2013).

19. Foreign Affairs and International Trade Canada Web site, **www.international.gc.ca/controls-controles/about-a_propos/impor/importing-importation.aspx** (accessed August 17, 2009).

20. Kitty Bean Yancey and Laura Bly, "Door May Be Inching Open for Tourism," *USA Today*, February 20, 2008, p. A5; Sue Kirchhoff and Chris Woodyard, "Cuba Trade Gets 'New Opportunity,'" *USA Today*, February 20, 2008, p. B1.

21. Keith Bradsher, "China Files W.T.O. Case Against Europe," *The New York Times*, November 5, 2012, **http://www.nytimes. com/2012/11/06/business/global/china-retaliates-in-trade-dispute-with-europe.html?_r=0** (accessed January 7, 2013).

22. Julie Bennett, "Product Pitfalls Proliferate in Global Cultural Maze," *The Wall Street Journal*, May 14, 2001, p. B11.

23. Greg Botelho, "2003 Global Influentials: Selling to the World," *CNN*, December 9, 2003, **www.cnn.com.**

24. Slogans Gone Bad, **www.joe-ks.com/archives_apr2004/ slogans_gone_bad.htm** (accessed June 6, 2006).

25. David Ricks, *Blunders in International Business*, 4th ed. (Malden, MA: Blackwell Publishing, 2006), p. 70. Downloaded from Google Books, **http://books.google.com/ books?id=S4L3ntwgs-8C&pg=PA68&lpg=PA68&dq=Mou ntain+Bell+company,+Saudi+advertisement&source=bl &ots=9apNX6s3hy&sig=Z5BEVaLe4-2p39kNYMlBd5sOX-GA&hl=en&ei=XJGFS6rfNpPKsAODk5zEDw&sa=X&oi=b ook_result&ct=result&resnum=5&ved=0CBcQ6AEwBA#v =onepage&q=airline&f=false** (accessed February 24, 2010).

26. J. Bonasia, "For Web, Global Reach Is Beauty—and Challenge," *Investor's Business Daily*, June 13, 2001, p. A6.

27. Matthew Wilkins, "Dell Retakes Second Rank in Global PC Market as Acer Stumbles," iSuppli, September 2, 2010, **www. isuppli.com/Home-and-Consumer-Electronics/News/ Pages/Dell-Retakes-Second-Rank-in-Global-PC-Market-as-Acer-Stumbles.aspx** (accessed January 10, 2011).

28. "Our Approach, Sanergy, **http://saner.gy/ourapproach/** (accessed October 20, 2011); Patrick Clark, "Innovator: Cleaning Up," *BusinessWeek*, October 12, 2011, **www. businessweek.com/magazine/cleaning-up-david-auerbachs-sanergy-10132011.html** (accessed October 20, 2011); Jennifer Chu, "Waste-Conversion Startup Sanergy Bowls over Competition," *MITNews* online, May 12, 2011, **http://web. mit.edu/newsoffice/2011/100k-competition-0512.html** (accessed October 20, 2011).

29. "World trade talks end in collapse," *BBC News* online, July 29, 2008, **http://news.bbc.co.uk/go/pr/fr/-/2/hi/ business/7531099.stm**.

30. "What Is the WTO," World Trade Organization (n.d.), **www. wto.org** (accessed February 25, 2004).

31. Bao Chang, "Steel Fastener Makers Hope EU Sales Can Recover on WTO Ruling," China Daily, December 7, 2010, **www.china daily.com.cn/bizchina/2010-12/07/content_11662675. htm** (accessed January 10, 2011).

32. CIA—The World Factbook, **https://www.cia.gov/library/ publications/the-world-factbook/geos/us.html**.

33. "Trade in Goods (Imports, Exports and Trade Balance) with Canada," U.S. Census Bureau, **www.census.gov/foreign-trade/balance/c1220.html** (accessed February 24, 2010); "North America: Canada," *CIA—World Factbook*, **https:// www.cia.gov/library/publications/the-world-factbook/ geos/ca.html** (accessed February 24, 2010).

34. "America's Biggest Partners," *CNBC.com*, **www.cnbc.com/ id/31064179?slide=11** (accessed February 24, 2010).

35. "North America: Mexico," *CIA World Factbook*, **https://www. cia.gov/library/publications/the-world-factbook/geos/ mx.html** (February 24, 2010); International Monetary Fund, **www.imf.org/external/pubs/ft/weo/2010/02/weodata/ weorept.aspx?sy=2008&ey=2015&scsm=1&ssd=1&sort= country&ds=.&br=1&c=273&s=PPPGDP%2CPPPPC&gr p=0&a=&pr.x=67&pr.y=136** (accessed January 10, 2011).

36. "Country Comparison: GDP (purchasing power parity)," *CIA—World Factbook*, **https://www.cia.gov/library/ publications/the-worldfactbook/rankorder/2001rank. html?countryName=United%20States&countryCode=us &regionCode=na&rank=2#us** (accessed February 3, 2010).

37. "A Tale of Two Mexicos: North and South," *The Economist*, April 26, 2008, pp. 53–54.

38. "Antecedents of the FTAA Process," Free Trade Area of the Americas (n.d.), **www.ftaa-alca.org/View_e.asp** (accessed February 25, 2004); "FTAA Fact Sheet," Market Access and Compliance, U.S. Department of Commerce (n.d.), **www. mac.doc.gov/ftaa2005/ftaa_fact_sheet.html** (accessed November 3, 2003).

39. Pete Engardio and Geri Smith, "Business Is Standing Its Ground," *BusinessWeek*, April 20, 2009, pp. 34–39.

40. "Europe in 12 Lessons," The Official EU Web site, **http://europa.eu/abc/12lessons/lesson_2/index_en.htm** (accessed June 7, 2007).

41. Stanley Reed, with Ariane Sains, David Fairlamb, and Carol Matlack, "The Euro: How Damaging a Hit?" *BusinessWeek*, September 29, 2003, p. 63; "The Single Currency," *CNN* (n.d.), **www.cnn.com/SPECIALS/2000/eurounion/story/currency/** (accessed July 3, 2001).

42. Abigail Moses, "Greek Contagion Concern Spurs European Sovereign Default Risk to Record," *Bloomberg*, April 26, 2010, **www.bloomberg.com/news/2010-04-26/greek-contagion-concern-spurs-european-sovereign-default-risk-to-record.html** (accessed March 18, 2011).

43. James G. Neuger and Joe Brennan, "Ireland Weighs Aid as EU Spars Over Debt-Crisis Remedy," *Bloomberg*, **www.bloomberg.com/news/2010-11-16/ireland-discusses-financial-bailout-as-eu-struggles-to-defuse-debt-crisis.html** (accessed March 18, 2011).

44. "Spreading Infection," *The Economist*, March 3, 2011, **www.bloomberg.com/news/2010-04-26/greek-contagion-concern-spurs-european-sovereign-default-risk-to-record.html** (accessed March 18, 2011).

45. "About EFSF," EFSF, **www.efsf.europa.eu/about/index.htm** (accessed March 18, 2011).

46. "About APEC," Asia-Pacific Economic Cooperation, **www.apec.org/apec/about_apec.html** (accessed February 25, 2010).

47. Smith and Lindblad, "Mexico: Was NAFTA Worth It?"

48. "China Economic Growth Accelerates," *BBC News*, October 22, 2009, **http://news.bbc.co.uk/2/hi/business/8319706.stm** (accessed February 25, 2010).

49. Kathy Chu and Michelle Yun, "Workers Are Finding Their Voice in China," *USA Today*, November 19, 2010, pp. 1B–2B; Elizabeth Holmes, "U.S. Apparel Retailers Turn Their Gaze Beyond China," *The Wall Street Journal*, June 16, 2010, p. B1.

50. James T. Areddy, James Hookway, John Lyons, and Marcus Walker, "U.S. Slump Takes Toll Across Globe," *The Wall Street Journal*, April 3, 2008, p. A1; Pam Woodall, "The New Champions," *The Economist*, November 15, 2008, p. 55; Matt Jenkins, "A Really Inconvenient Truth," *Miller-McCune*, April/May 2008, p. 42.

51. Holmes, "U.S. Apparel Retailers Turn Their Gaze Beyond China," p. B1.

52. Lauren Pollock, "Starbucks Adds Division Focused on Asia," *The Wall Street Journal*, July 11, 2011, **http://online.wsj.com/article/SB10001424052702303678704576440292712481616.html** (accessed July 15, 2011); Matt Hodges, "Schultz Brews Up Major Push in China," *China Daily*, June 10–11, 2011, 5; "Starbucks Company Profile," **http://assets.starbucks.com/assets/aboutuscompanyprofileq12011final13111.pdf** (accessed July 15, 2011); Mariko Sanchanta, "Starbucks Plans Big Expansion in China," *The Wall Street Journal*, April 14, 2010, B10; "Asia Pacific," Starbucks Newsroom, **http://news.starbucks.com/about+starbucks/starbucks+coffee+international/asia+pacific/** (accessed July 19, 2011); David Teather, "Starbucks Legend Delivers Recovery by Thinking Smaller," *The Guardian*, January 21, 2010, **www.guardian.co.uk/business/2010/jan/21/starbucks-howard-schultz** (accessed July 19, 2011); "How Starbucks Colonised the World," *The Sunday Times*, February 17, 2008, **http://business.timesonline.co.uk/tol/business/industry_sectors/leisure/article3381092.ece** (accessed July 19, 2011); "Greater China," Starbucks Newsroom, **http://news.starbucks.com/about+starbucks/starbucks+coffee+international/greater+china** (accessed July 19, 2011).

53. Rebecca Christie, "IMF Says Greek Program Doing Well, Approves New Loan Payment," *Bloomberg BusinessWeek*, December 17, 2010, **www.businessweek.com/news/2010-12-17/imf-says-greek-program-doing-well-approves-new-loan-payment.html** (accessed January 10, 2011); Bruno Waterfield, "Ireland Forced to Take EU and IMF Bail-Out Package," *The Telegraph*, November 22, 2010, **www.telegraph.co.uk/finance/financetopics/financialcrisis/8150137/Ireland-forced-to-take-EU-and-IMF-bail-out-package.html** (accessed January 10, 2011).

54. David J. Lynch, "The IMF Is Tired ... Fund Struggles to Reinvent Itself," *USA Today*, April 19, 2006. p. B1.

55. Ilan Brat and Paul Kiernan, "Heinz Seeks to Tap Mexico's Taste for Ketchup," *The Wall Street Journal*, November 24, 2009, pp. B1–B2.

56. Canadian Commercial Corporation (n.d), **www.ccc.ca/eng/home.cfm**.

57. Export Development Canada (n.d.), **www.edc.ca/english/corporate. htm**.

58. Ben Worthen, "The Crazy World of Outsourcing," *WSJ.com*, February 25, 2008. **http://blogs.wsj.com/biztech/2008/02/25/the-crazy-world-ofoutsourcing/?mod=relevancy** (accessed May 6, 2008).

59. Nick Heath, "Banks: Offshoring, Not Outsourcing," *BusinessWeek*, March 10, 2009, **www.businessweek.com/globalbiz/content/mar2009/gb20090310_619247.htm** (accessed February 25, 2010); Coomi Kapoor, "What Now after the Satyam Fraud?" *Asia News Network*, December 1, 2009, **www.asianewsnet.net/news.php?id= 3368&sec=3&t=** (accessed February 25, 2010).

60. Barclays Wealth, **www.census.gov/hhes/www/cpstables/032009/hhinc/new01_009.htm** (accessed March 3, 2010); Heath, "Banks: Offshoring, Not Outsourcing."

61. "About Us," Carrefour: Arab Republic of Egypt, **www.carrefour.com.eg/aboutus.aspx** (accessed February 25, 2010).

62. Matt O'Sullivan, "Virgin Blue mines fly-in, fly-out boom," *The Sydney Morning Herald*, January 10, 2011, **www.smh.com.au/business/virgin-blue-mines-flyin-flyout-boom-20110110-19kb3.html** (accessed January 10, 2011); Matt O'Sullivan, "Virgin Blue hooks up with regional Skywest," *The Sydney Morning Herald*, January 11, 2011, **www.smh.com.au/business/virgin-blue-hooks-up-with-regional-skywest-20110110-19l7d.html** (accessed January 11, 2011).

63. Sharon Silk Carty, "Ford Plans to Park Jaguar, Land Rover with Tata Motors," *USA Today*, March 26, 2008, p. B1.

64. O. C. Ferrell, John Fraedrich, and Linda Ferrell, *Business Ethics*, 6th ed. (Boston: Houghton Mifflin, 2005), pp. 227–30.

65. Canadian Trade Commissioner (n.d.), **http://www.tradecommissioner. gc.ca/eng/services.jsp**.

66. Keith B. Richburg, "Chinese films look to team up with Hollywood," *The Washington Post*, September 6, 2010, **www.washingtonpost.com/wp-dyn/content/article/2010/09/03/AR2010090302853_2.html?sid= ST2010090305799** (accessed

October 29, 2010); Jonathan Watts, "Chinese film industry aims to challenge Hollywood," *The Guardian*, September 13, 2010, **www.guardian.co.uk/world/2010/sep/13/chinese-film-industry-rival-hollywood** (accessed October 29, 2010); Ronald Grover and Michael White, "Hollywood Looks to China for Movie Money," *BusinessWeek*, October 14, 2010, **www.business week.com/magazine/content/10_43/b4200023890594.htm** (accessed October 29, 2010).

Chapter 4

1. Anne Kingston, "Heather's Fix," *Maclean's* online, January 6, 2012, **http://www2.macleans.ca/2012/01/06/heathers-fix/**; "Heather Reisman," *Wikipedia* website, **http://en.wikipedia.org/wiki/Heather_Reisman**; "Our Company—Management," Indigo website, **http://www.chapters.indigo.ca/our-company/management/** (all accessed July 15, 2013).

2. "Stride Rite buys Robeez Footwear," *Boston Business Journal*, September 6, 2006, **http://www.bizjournals.com/boston/stories/2006/09/04/daily12.html**.

3. Maggie Overfelt, "Start-Me-Up: The California Garage," *Fortune Small Business*, July/Aug. 2003, **www.fortune.com/fortune/smallbusiness/articles/0,15114,475872,00.html**.

4. "1: Digital Artists Agency," *Business 2.0*, April 2004, p. 90.

5. "Facts & History," Kiva, **www.kiva.org/about/facts** (accessed March 18, 2011); David M. Ewalt, "Low-Dose Capitalism," *Forbes*, November 2, 2009, p. 40; Leena Rao, "Kiva Brings Microlending Home to U.S. Entrepreneurs in Need," *TechCrunch*, June 10, 2009, **www.techcrunch.com/2009/06/10/kiva-brings-microlending-home-tous-entrepreneurs-in-need** (accessed December 19, 2009); Peter Greer and Phil Smith, *The Poor Will Be Glad* (Grand Rapids, MI: Zondervan, 2009), pp. 99, 107.

6. "5 Smart Strategies of Super Startups," Kim Shiffman, PROFIT: Your Guide to Business Success, July 12, 2007, **http://www.profit guide.com/search?q=Dekalam%20Hire%20Learning%2C**.

7. Daryl-Lynn Carlson, "QuickSnap Invention Clicks … ," *Financial Post*, December 11, 2008, **http://www.financialpost.com/story.html?id=1067682** (accessed September 13, 2010).

8. Linda Tischles, "Join the Circus," *Fast Company*, July 2005, pp. 53–58.

9. "Mike Lazaridis," *PROFITguide* online, September 1, 2009, **http://www.profitguide.com/article/4359--mike-lazaridis**.

10. Rick Spence, "Dragons' Den: The Magic Touch," *PROFITguide* online, October 1, 2008, **http://www.profitguide.com/article/4487--dragons-146-den-the-magic-touch**.

11. Alexis Muellner, "Marlins Partners in Dispute, Still Want Rings," *South Florida Business Journal*, February 27, 2004, **www.bizjournals.com/southflorida/stories/2004/03/01/story5.html**.

12. "Harrison McCain, 76, King Of the Frozen French Fry," Sabrina Tavernise, *The New York Times*, March 21, 2004, **http://www.nytimes.com/2004/03/21/world/harrison-mccain-76-king-of-the-frozen-french-fry.html**

13. "How Tim Hortons will take over the world," Dawn Calleja, *The Globe and Mail*, September 23, 2010, **http://www.theglobe andmail.com/report-on-business/rob-magazine/how-tim-hortons-will-take-over-the-world/article1718843/singlepage/**.

14. "List of Largest Public Companies in Canada by Profit," *Wikipedia* website, **http://en.wikipedia.org/wiki/List_of_largest_public_companies_in_Canada_by_profit** (accessed July 15, 2013).

15. Kevin J. Delaney and Robin Sidel, "Google IPO Aims to Change the Rules," *The Wall Street Journal*, April 30, 2004, **http://online.wsj.com**.

16. Lee Spears and Sarah Frier, "Facebook Set for Public Debut After IPO Seals $104 Billion Value," *Bloomberg* online, May 18, 2012, **http://www.bloomberg.com/news/2012-05-18/facebook-set-for-public-debut-after-ipo-seals-104-billion-value.html**; Dave Copeland, "The Only Facebook Number That Matters: $104.2 Billion," *readwrite* online, May 18, 2012, **http://readwrite.com/2012/05/18/the-only-facebook-number-that-matters-1042-billion#awesm=~obB2JI6oR Q7zht**; Natasha Chandel, "Mark Zuckerberg's Big Week: $19 Billion and a Wedding," *MTV News*, **http://www.mtv.com/news/articles/1685452/facebook-mark-zuckerberg-married.jhtml** (all accessed July 14, 2013).

17. Merissa Marr, "Video Chain CEO to Take Company Private in Buyout," *The Wall Street Journal*, March 30, 2004, **http://online.wsj.com**.

18. O. C. Ferrell, John Fraedrich, and Linda Ferrell, *Business Ethics: Ethical Decision Making and Cases*, 6th ed. (Boston: Houghton Mifflin, 2005), p. 84.

19. "*Report to the Congress*: Increased Penalties under the Sarbanes-Oxley Act of 2002," **http://www.ussc.gov/r_congress/s-oreport.pdf**.

20. Matt Krantz, "Web of Board Members Ties Together Corporate America," *USA Today*, November 23, 2002, pp. 1B, 3B.

21. Emily Thornton and Aaron Pressman, "Phil Purcell's Credibility Crisis," *BusinessWeek*, March 21, 2005.

22. Krantz, "Web of Board Members."

23. "His way or the highway: Frank Stronach is God's gift to shareholders. Don't believe it? Just ask him," Thomas Watson, *Canadian Business* online, May 23, 2005, **http://www.canadian business.com/managing/strategy/article.jsp?cont ent=20060109_103241_4508**.

24. "RBC, Canada's biggest company, has revenue equal to the GDP of Latvia," Sarah Efron, FP Magazine Daily, June 02, 2009, **http://network.nationalpost.com/np/blogs/fpmagazine daily/archive/2009/06/02/rbc-canada-s-biggest-company-has-revenue-equal-to-the-gdp-of-latvia.aspx**.

25. Eleanor Beaton, "The lure of ESOPs," *PROFITguide* online, May 31, 2007, **http://www.profitguide.com/manage-grow/strategy-operations/the-lure-of-esops-29171** (accessed June 20, 2013).

26. Ron Ruggless, "Cold Stone, Tim Hortons expand co-branding," *Nation's Restaurant News*, February 6, 2009; Robin Hilmantel, "Tim Hortons and Cold Stone Will Team Up in 100 Stores," *QSR* online, **http://www2.qsrmagazine.com/articles/exclusives/0209/timhortons-1.phtml** (accessed July 15, 2013).

27. Marina Strauss, "Loblaw's Joe Fresh Hooks Up with J.C. Penney," *The Globe and Mail* online, July 25, 2012, **http://www.theglobeandmail.com/globe-investor/loblaws-joe-fresh-hooks-up-with-jc-penney/article4439978/** (accessed July 15, 2013).

28. Eric J. Savitz, "Movie Madness," *Barron's*, February 23, 2004, **http://online.wsj.com/barrons/**.

29. "What Is Community Supported Agriculture and How Does It Work?" Local Harvest, **www.localharvest.org/csa.jsp** (accessed February 18, 2008); "Community Supported Agriculture at Indian Line Farm," Indian Line Farm, **http://www.indianlinefarm.com/csa.html** (accessed February 25, 2008).

30. "Farmers Offering up Beef in a Can," CNN, March 22, 2004, **www.cnn.com/2004/US/Midwest/03/22/canned.beef.asp**; Him Suhr, "Farmers Form Canned-Beef Co-op," *Courier-Journal*, March 28, 2004, **www.courier-journal.com/business/news2004/03/28/E7-beefcan28-4323.html**; Jim Suhr, "Livestock Farmer Hopes Canned Beef Will Catch On," *The Fort Collins Coloradoan*, March 28, 2004, p. E2; Erica Coble, "Trading on Tradition," March 2005, **www.rurdev.usda.gov/rbs/pub/mar05/value.htm** (accessed March 1, 2006); **www.heartlandfarmfoods.com;www.heartlandfarmfoods.com/Company.htm**; **www.heartlandfarmfoods.com/Catalog_Page%201.htm; www.heartlandfarmfoods.com/Producers.htm** (all accessed March 1, 2006).

31. Devin Leonard, "How Disney Bought Lucasfilm—and Its Plans for 'Star Wars'," *Bloomberg Businessweek* online, March 7, 2013, **http://www.businessweek.com/articles/2013-03-07/how-disney-bought-lucasfilm-and-its-plans-for-star-wars** (accessed July 15, 2013).

32. Grant Robertson, "With Ally Assets, RBC Becomes Top Player in Auto Financing," *The Globe and Mail* online, February 20, 2013, **http://www.theglobeandmail.com/globe-investor/with-ally-assets-rbc-becomes-top-player-in-auto-financing/article4630654/?service=mobile** (accessed July 15, 2013).

33. "TD Pays $6B for Target's Retail Credit Card Unit," *CBC News* online, October 23, 2012, **http://www.cbc.ca/news/business/story/2012/10/23/td-target.html** (accessed July 15, 2013).

34. "Scotiabank Completes the Acquisition of ING Direct Canada," Scotiabank website, **http://www.scotiabank.com/ca/en/0,,5504,00.html** (accessed July 15, 2013).

35. "CRTC Rejects Bell-Astral Merger," *The Canadia Business Journal* online, October 18, 2012, **http://www.cbj.ca/business_news/canadian_business_news/crtc_rejects_bell-astral_merger.html** (accessed July 15, 2013).

36. Derek DeCloet, "Canadians should stop worrying about foreign takeovers," *The Globe and Mail* online, August 29, 2012, **http://www.theglobeandmail.com/report-on-business/rob-magazine/canadians-should-stop-worrying-about-foreign-takeovers/article4507568/** (accessed June 20, 2013).

37. "Will Your PC Kill the Video Store?: Blockbuster sizes up online movie rentals and adopts the advantages for its own service," Liane Cassavoy, *PCWorld*, Mar 10, 2004, **http://www.pcworld.com/article/115160/will_your_pc_kill_the_video_store.html**.

38. "Aventis Accepts Higher, Friendly Sanofi Bid," Dow Jones Newswire, April 26, 2004, via *The Wall Street Journal*, **http://online.wsj.com**.

39. J. Connelly, "Premier Brad Wall Warns of Potash Hostile Takeover," *Business Review Canada* online, October 25, 2010, **http://www.businessreviewcanada.ca/sectors/premier-brad-wall-warns-potash-hostile-takeover** (accessed July 15, 2013).

40. Shawn McCarthy and Steven Chase, "Ottawa Approves Nexen, Progress Foreign Takeovers," *The Globe and Mail* online, December 7, 2012, **http://www.theglobeandmail.com/globe-investor/ottawa-approves-nexen-progress-foreign-takeovers/article6107548/** (accessed July 15, 2013).

41. David Aiken, "Feds Wrestle with China's Oilsands Takeover," *Toronto Sun* online, August 8, 2012, **http://www.torontosun.com/2012/08/08/feds-wrestle-with-chinas-oilsands-takeover**; Aaron Wherry, "Harper Government Approves CNOOC and Petronas Deals," *Maclean's* online, December 7, 2012, **http://www2.macleans.ca/2012/12/07/harper-government-approves-cnooc-and-petronas-deals/** (accessed July 15, 2013).

Chapter 5

1. Brainy Quote website, **http://www.brainyquote.com/quotes/authors/k/kevin_oleary_2. html#CSEhoaluBliJ8UOU.99** (accessed June 24, 2013).

2. Brainy Quote website, **http://www.brainyquote.com/quotes authors/k/kevin_oleary. html#2MjRIMbVCJPyESK8.99** (accessed June 24, 2013).

3. "Speaking Points—The Honourable Tony Clement, PC, MP, Minister of Industry—Business Development Bank of Canada Funding Announcement," Industry Canada Site, June 15, 2009, **http://www.ic.gc.ca/eic/site/ic1.nsf/eng/04758.html**.

4. Ian Portsmouth (Ed.), *Profit*, March 2013, **http://www.pdfmagazines.org/magazines/business/44338-profit-march-2013.html**.

5. "The Power of Innovation," *Inc. State of Small Business*, 23, no. 7 (2001), p. 103.

6. Scott Allen, "Entrepreneur Success Story: Brian Scudamore of 1-800-GOT-JUNK?", *About.com: Entrepreneurs*, **http://entrepreneurs.about.com/od/casestudies/a/1800gotjunk.htm (accessed July 17, 2010)**.

7. Robert D. Hisrich, Michael P. Peters, Dean A. Shepherd, and Peter Mombourquette, *Entrepreneurship* (2nd Canadian edition), (Toronto: McGraw-Hill Ryerson Ltd., 2009), p. 75.

8. "U of T student named 2010 Student Entrepreneur Ontario Champion," ACE, February 17, 2010, **http://www.acecanada.ca/news/newsItem.cfm?cms_news_id=372**.

9. Tony Martin, "Profit Hot 50: Simple ways to sell more," *PROFITguide* online, September 1, 2009, **http://www.profitguide.com/article/4360--profit-hot-50-simple-ways-to-sell-more**.

10. "Survey on Financing of Small and Medium Enterprises," Statistics Canada, March 11, 2009, **http://www.statcan.gc.ca/cgi-bin/imdb/p2SV.pl?Function=getSurvey&SDDS=2941&lang=en&id=imdb&adm=8&dis=2**.

11. Canadian Federation of Independent Business, **www.cfib.ca/** (accessed July 17, 2010).

12. "Key Small Business Statistics," Industry Canada: Small Business and Tourism Branch, July 2009, **https://www.safec.ca/userfiles/file/%C3%89tudes%20indicateurs%20%C3%A9conomiques/%C3%89tudes%202009%20AN/Key%20Small%20Business%20Statistics%20-%20July%202009.pdf**.

13. Exportsavvy International Projects Development for Medium and Small Business, Export Development, **http://www.exportsavvy.com/ (accessed July 17, 2010)**.

14. Yves Robichaud, Jean-Charles Cachon, and Rana Haq, "Motives, Success Factors, and Barriers among Canadian Female Entrepreneurs: The Case of Greater Sudbury," *Entrepreneurial Practice Review* 1(2), winter 2010, **http://www.entryerson.com/epr/index.php/jep/article/viewFile/49/27**.

15. "Sleep Country Canada gets $356M takeover offer," *Toronto Star* online, August 14, 2008, **http://www.thestar.com/article/478312.**

16. "FAQs: Frequently Asked Questions," U.S. Small Business Administration, **http://web.sba.gov/faqs/faqIndexAll.cfm?areaid=24 (accessed June 1, 2006).**

17. Row House Publishing Services, **http://rhps.ca/** (accessed July 17, 2010).

18. "Innovation in Large and Small Firms," Zoltan J. Acs and David B. Andretsch, *The American Economic Review* © 1988 **http://www.jstor.org/action/showPublisher?publisherCode=aea**%, p. 678.

19. Hisrich, Peters, Shepherd, Mombourquette, *Entrepreneurship*, pp. 57–58; Margot Hornblower, "In a Hurry to Prove the 'Pistonheads' Wrong," *TIME* magazine, March 8, 1999, **www.time.com/time/reports/environment/heroes/heroesgallery/0,2967,ballard,00.html;** and Leonard Brody and David Raffa, *Everything I Needed to Know about Business... I Learned from a Canadian* (Toronto: John Wiley & Sons Canada Ltd., 2005), p. 14.

20. Diane Disse, "The Birth of IMAX," **http://www.ieee.ca/millennium/imax/imax_birth.html** (accessed July 17, 2010).

21. Trevor Melanson, "Is HootSuite Canada's Next Billion-Dollar Tech Titan?", *Canadian Business*, Winter 2012/13, **http://www.canadianbusiness.com/technology-news/is-hootsuite-canadas-next-tech-titan/**.

22. Ron Joyce, *Always Fresh: The Untold Story of Tim Hortons by the Man Who Created a Canadian Empire* (Toronto: Harper Collins Publishers Ltd., 2006).

23. Beth Carney, "Dyson Magic Carpet Ride," *BusinessWeek online*, April 1, 2005, **www.businessweek.com/bwdaily/dnflash/apr2005/nf2005041_8000_db016.htm?campaign_id=search** (accessed June 3, 2006); Dyson Official Site, **www.dyson.com/** and **www.dyson.com/nav/inpageframe.asp?id=DYSON/HIST/MUSEUMS** (accessed June 3, 2006).

24. Hisrich, Peters, Shepherd, Mombourquette, *Entrepreneurship*, p. 77; "eBay Canada Recognizes Top e-Business Owners," October 12, 2007, **http://p.s.ebay.ca/aboutebay/thecompany/2007-12.html;** Fourth annual entrepreneur of the year awards (2008): "Last Year's Winner": **http://pages.ebay.ca/entrepreneurs;** "eBay Canada Recognizes Top e-Business Owners," *CNW*, October 12, 2007, **http://www.newswire.ca/en/releases/archive/October2007/12/c3188.html.**

25. Jerry Langton, "Canine couture," *Toronto Star* online, November 17, 2008, **http://www.thestar.com/Business/Small Business/article/538014.**

26. Douglas Quenqua, "To Create Its Hits, a Company Takes Its Toys on Tour," *The New York Times* online, June 9, 2008, **http://www.nytimes.com/2008/06/09/business/media/09spin.html.**

27. Ibid.

28. Peter Svensson, "U.S. Economy Grows at a Slower Pace," *The Washington Post* online, June 5, 2006, **www.washingtonpost.com/wp-dyn/content/article/2006/06/05/AR2006060500376.html** (accessed June 5, 2006).

29. Jim McElgunn, "Canada's Fastest-Growing Companies," *PROFITguide* online, June 1, 2011, **http://www.profitguide.com/opportunity/canadas-fastest-growing-companies-3-30175** (accessed July 15, 2013).

30. "22nd Annual Profit 100: Canada's Fastest-Growing Companies," *PROFITguide* online, **http://www.profitguide.com/awards/profit100** (accessed July 17, 2010); "Profit Hot 50," *Canadian Business* online, 2009, **http://list.canadianbusiness.com/rankings/hot50/2009/include/PROFIT_HOT_50_2009.xls** (accessed July 17, 2010).

31. Jerry Langton, "Saving people drowning in debt," *Toronto Star* online, January 19, 2009, **http://www.thestar.com/business/smallbusiness/article/573203.**

32. "Profit Hot 50," *Canadian Business* online, 2009, **http://list.canadianbusiness.com/rankings/hot50/2009/include/PROFIT_HOT_50_2009.xls** (accessed July 17, 2010).

33. "21st Annual Profit 100: Canada's Fastest-Growing Companies," *Canadian Business* online, **http://list.canadianbusiness.com/rankings/profit100/2009/Default.aspx?sc1=1&d1=a&sp2=1&ech=ch** (accessed July 17, 2010).

34. XMG website, "About," **http://www.xmg.com/about/** (accessed June 24, 2013).

35. "Dell at a Glance" (n.d.), Dell, **www1.us.dell.com/content/topics/global.aspx/corp/background/en/facts?c=us&l=en&s=corp&section=000&ck=mn** (accessed May 4, 2004); **www.hoouess.com/dell/--ID_13193-/free-co-factsheet.xhtml** (accessed June 5, 2006).

36. "The Evolution of Apple...," October 10, 1995, **http://www2.cs.uregina.ca/~rbm/cs100/timeline.html.**

37. Robin Wauters, "Disney Online Buys Kaboose Assets for $18.4 Million," *TechCrunch*, April 2009, **http://techcrunch.com/2009/04/01/disney-online-buys-kaboose-assets-for-184-million/** (accessed September 20, 2010).

38. "Small Business Statistics" (n.d.), Small Business Administration, **www.sba.gov/aboutsba/sbastats.html** (accessed March 16, 2004).

39. "Skoll Foundation," *Wikipedia* website, **http://en.wikipedia.org/wiki/Skoll_Foundation** (accessed July 18, 2013).

40. **http://www.avisonyoung.com/Our_Professionals/Halifax/Bio/MacDonald~Kenzie/.**

41. Andrea Gordon, "Mompreneurs boom," *Toronto Star* online, April 4, 2008, **http://www.thestar.com/article/409934.**

42. Colin MacDonald, guest speaker, Mount Saint Vincent University's 35th Annual Business and Tourism Conference, October 2009, Halifax, NS.

43. "Entrepreneur Success Story," Canadian Youth Business Foundation, September 2009, **http://www.cybf.ca/story-gallery/success-stories/bc/Rocky%20Point%20Kayak.pdf.**

44. Andy Holloway, "Problem Solvers: To boldly grow ... carefully, that is," *Profit*, **http://list.canadianbusiness.com/rankings/profit100/2009/growth/article.aspx?id=20090601_30010_30010,** (accessed July 18, 2010).

45. Kym Wolfe, "The Sound of Success," *Alumni Gazette* (University of Western Ontario), September 7, 2010, **http://communications. uwo.ca/com/alumni_gazette/alumni_gazetteprofiles/ the_sound_of_success_20100907446732/.**

46. Laura Pratt, "PROFIT HOT 50: Safer Passage," *PROFIT*, October 2009, p. 36.

47. Ibid.

48. Dana Knight, "Big Headed Guy Gets a Big Idea for Sunglasses Business," *USA Today,* March 21, 2006, p. 4B; Fatheadz Eyewear, **www.fatheadz.com** (accessed June 5, 2006).

49. "CEO Michael Gokturk interviewed on BNN," VersaPay, January 27, 2010, **http://www.versapay.com/video/ceo-mike-gokturk-interviewed-on-bnn/;** Jennifer Myers, "The Little Shop with a Big Friend," *PROFIT*, October 2009, pp. 28–30.

50. "Burpee Seeds and Plants," **http://www.burpee.com/** (accessed July 17, 2010).

51. "You're Not the Boss of Me Now," *Weekend Today*, October 21, 2005, **www.msnbc.msn.com/id/9762771/** (accessed June 5, 2006).

52. "Small Business Resource," **www.2-small-business.com** (accessed June 5, 2006).

53. Peter Mombourquette, May 2010, interview with Dan Young.

54. Hisrich, Peters, Shepherd, Mombourquette, *Entrepreneurship,* p. 542.

55. Hisrich, Peters, Shepherd, Mombourquette, *Entrepreneurship*, p. 543; Jennifer Myers, "To Boldly Grow," *PROFITguide* online, October/November 2003, **www.profitguide.com/ w100/2003/article.asp?ID=1276&p.=1.**

56. "The man with the Midas touch," Jennifer Myers, *Profit*, April 2005, **http://www.canadianbusiness.com/entrepreneur/ managing/article.jsp?content=20050407_004729_4968& page=3** (accessed July 18, 2010).

57. Rodney Tanake, "Clothier a Favorite of Vegans, PETA Honors Pasadena 'Animal-Friendly' Firm," *Pasadena Star-News*, **www.pasadenastarnews.com/** (accessed January 14, 2006); "About Us," Alternative Outfitters, **www.alternative outfitters.com/index.asp?PageAction=COMPANY;** "Alternative Outfitters News," **www.alternativeoutfitters.com/ index.asp?PageAction=Custom&ID=10;** "Pasadena-based Alternative Outfitters Wins Second Straight National PETA Award," **www.alternativeoutfitters.com/index. asp?PageAction=Custom&ID=45;** "The 2005 Veggie Awards," **www.vegnews.com/veggieawards_2005.html** (all accessed January 12, 2006).

58. Nickels, McHugh, McHugh, Cossa, Sproule, *Understanding Canadian Business*, Seventh Canadian Edition, p. 168, McGraw-Hill Ryerson, 2009.

59. Centre for Entrepreneurship, Education & Development, **http://www.ceed.ca/default.asp?id=190&pagesize=1 &sfield=content.id&search=919&mn=1.212.256.305** (accessed July 18, 2010).

60. Wency Leung, "Kimchi on Wheels: Food Truck Trend Gears Up In Canada," *The Globe and Mail*, June 14, 2011, **http:// www.theglobeandmail.com/life/food-and-wine/food-trends/kimchi-on-wheels-food-truck-trend-gears-up-in-canada/article4261217/** (accessed June 24, 2013).

61. Kim Hart Macneill, "An Apple for the Tutor," *PROFITguide* online, February 11, 2013, **http://www.profitguide.com/ opportunity/an-apple-for-the-tutor-48089** (accessed June 24, 2013).

62. Nova Scotia Business Inc., **http://www.nsbi.ca/next/kiru. shtml** (accessed July 18, 2010).

63. Adapted from Carol Kinsey Gorman, *Creativity in Business: A Practical Guide for Creative Thinking*, Crisp Publications Inc., 1989, pp. 5–6. © Crisp Publications Inc., 1200 Hamilton Court, Menlo Park, CA 94025.

64. Nitasha Tiku, "Making the Most of a Brush with Fame," *Inc.*, August 2007, p. 19; Recycline, **http://www.recycline.com/** (accessed May 4, 2008); "Recycline: Sitting on Mainstream's Doorstep," Sustainable Is Good, **http://www.sustainable isgood.com/blog/2007/03/recycline_produ.html** (accessed May 4, 2008).

65. Will Moniz, "Young Entrepreneur Profile: NotableTV's Julian Brass," *TalentEgg*, August 5, 2009, **http://talentegg. ca/incubator/2009/08/05/young-entrepreneur-profile-notabletvs-julian-brass/.**

66. Patrick Maloney, "Make your banker say yes," *PROFITguide* online, November 7, 2001, **www.profitguide.com/maximize/ article.jsp?content=694.**

67. **http://www.bostonpizza.com/en/about/PressKit.aspx** (accessed July 18, 2010).

68. Hisrich, Peters, Shepherd, Mombourquette, *Entrepreneurship*, p. 381; "Ask the Legends," *PROFIT*, March 2008, p. 72.

69. Rebecca Gardiner, "PROFIT 100 Fundraising Secrets," *Canadian Business Online*, May 12, 2005, **http://www.canadian business.com/entrepreneur/financing/article.jsp?cont ent=20050511_120413_4152.**

70. Ibid.

71. Rick Spence, "Sweetpea Baby Food: Stuck in the middle," *Profit*, October 2007, **http://www.canadianbusiness. com/entrepreneur/sales_marketing/article.jsp?cont ent=20071002_12233_122337.**

72. Hisrich, Peters, Shepherd, Mombourquette, *Entrepreneurship*, pp. 397–398.

73. Alex Halperin, "A Virtual World Targets Teens," *Business-Week*, May 15, 2006, **www.businessweek.com/technology/ content/may2006/tc20060515_945235.htm?campaign_ id=search** (accessed June 5, 2006).

74. Hisrich, Peters, Shepherd, Mombourquette, *Entrepreneurship*, pp. 397–398; Kerry Gold, "Dragons' Den success stories," MSN, December 7, 2009, **http://money. ca.msn.com/small-business/gallery/gallery.aspx?cp-documentid=22789615&page=1;** Rick Spence, "Dragons' Den: The magic touch," *PROFITguide* online, October 1, 2008, **http://www.profitguide.com/article/4487--dragons-146-den-the-magic-touch.**

75. Hisrich, Peters, Shepherd, Mombourquette, *Entrepreneurship*, p. 372; Outpost, **www.outpostmagazine.com;** W.S. Good, *Building a Dream* (6th ed.) (Toronto: McGraw-Hill Ryerson Ltd., 2005), p. 277.

76. John Baldwin, Lin Bian, Richard Dupuy, and Guy Gellatly, "Failure Rates for New Canadian Firms: New Perspectives on Entry and Exit," Statistics Canada, 2000, p. 7.

77. "The Success of Crowdfunding," The Brooklyn Warehouse website, February 26, 2013, **http://brooklynwarehouse. ca/theblog/2013/2/26/the-success-of-crowdfunding** (accessed July 15, 2013).

78. Douglas How and Ralph Costello, *K.C.: The Biography of K.C. Irving* (Toronto: Key Porter Books Ltd., 1993).

79. Hisrich, Peters, Shepherd, Mombourquette, *Entrepreneurship*, pp. 589, 592; Susanne Ruder, "A Tale of Two Brothers," *PROFIT*, March 2007.

80. Thomas W. Zimmerer and Norman M. Scarborough, *Essentials of Entrepreneurship and Small Business Management* (4th ed.) (Upper Saddle River, NJ: Pearson Prentice Hall, 2005), pp. 118–24.

81. Ibid.

82. Peter Mombourquette, March 2010, in-class interview.

83. Adapted from "Tomorrow's Entrepreneur," *Inc. State of Small Business*, 23, no. 7 (2001), pp. 80–104.

84. David K. Foot, *Boom, Bust & Echo: How to profit from the coming demographic shift* (Toronto: Macfarlane Walter & Ross, 1996).

85. Comfort Life, Masterpiece Retirement Communities, **http:// www.comfortlife.ca/masterpiece-retirement-communities. php** (accessed July 18, 2010).

86. Melissa Campeau, "Companies Anticipate Business Growth and Skills Shortage," *PROFITguide* online, January 10, 2013, **http://www.profitguide.com/news/companies-anticipate-business-growth-and-skills-shortages-in-2013-46839** (accessed July15, 2013).

87. Foot, *Boom, Bust & Echo*.

88. "Facts about Canada," Business Immigration, **http://www. businessimmigrationtocanada.ca/businessimmigration canadaquebecinvestorimmigrationvisa.htm** (accessed July 17, 2010).

89. **http://www.careerbuilder.com/Jobs/Company/ C8C0SC719RSDTDZTZP6/Walmart-Field-Operations/** (accessed July 18, 2010).

90. Kevin Swayze, "Cost-cutting ideas shrinking Cambridge hospital's deficit still mostly secret," *Cambridge Reporter*, August 21, 2009, **http://cambridgereporter.com/news/ article/185850**.

91. Gifford Pinchott III, *Intrapreneuring* (New York: Harper & Row, 1985), p. 34.

92. Paul Brown, "How to Cope With Hard Times," *The New York Times*, June 10, 2008.

93. Hisrich, Peters, Shepherd, Mombourquette, *Entrepreneurship*, pp. 130, 217, 522; "Lija puts a new spin on golfwear," *PROFITguide* online, July 28, 2005, **http://www.profitguide.com/ article/4406--lija-puts-a-new-spin-on-golfwear**; "Lija by Linda Hipp Named One of British Columbia's 50 Fastest Growing Companies," press release (2004), **www.lijastyle. com/press.html**; Karen VanKampen, "Golfers looking hip, stylish and colourful, too," CanWest News Services, June 21, 2005; Kim Shiffman, "Canada's Fastest Growing Companies," *PROFIT*, June 2005, p. 38; A. Holloway, "The Right Way to Tee Off," *PROFIT* (December/January 2007), p. 69; Hal Quinn, "Lady of Lija," *Canadian Business Online*, April 25, 2005, **http://www.canadianbusiness.com/managing/article. jsp?content=20050425_66971_66971**.

Chapter 6

1. Dave Michaels (moderator), "Walk a Mile in Her Holeys," online discussion forum, *The Globe and Mail*, August 23, 2012 (updated), **http://m.theglobeandmail.com/report-on-business/small-business/sb-digital/innovation/walk-a-mile-in-her-holeys/article4301366/?service=mobile.**

2. Ibid.

3. "Growth Becomes Her," *Profit*, Oct. 2006, Vol. 25 (4), p. 55; Joanne Sasvari, "Crazy For Crocs: The Ugliest Shoes You'll Ever Fall In Love With," *Edmonton Journal*, Jan. 31, 2006, p. E2; Rebecca Addelman, "Foaming At The Feet," *Maclean's*, Jun. 5, 2006, Vol.119 (23), p. 31; Paul Brent, "Plan Lands Holey Soles Firmly On Its Feet," *National Post*, Mar 5. 2007, p. EN4; **http:// holeysoles.com** (accessed August 25, 2009).

4. John Lorinc, "The Golden Goose," *PROFITguide* online, October 17, 2012, **http://www.profitguide.com/manage-grow/ strategy-operations/the-golden-goose-42172/2**.

5. "About Us," Magnotta website, **http://www.magnotta.com/ About.aspx** (accessed June 24, 2013).

6. Canadian Press, "Dollarama speeds up expansion plans, could add up to 70 new stores this year," *Financial Post*, December 9, 2012, **http://business.financialpost.com/2012/09/12/ dollarama-speeds-up-expansion-plans-could-add-up-to-70-new-stores-this-year/** (accessed June 24, 2013).

7. Marc Gunther, "Yoga…Soy…McDonald's," *Fortune*, May 17, 2006, **http://money.cnn.com/2006/05/17/news/companies/ pluggedin_fortune/index.htm** (accessed June 12, 2006); **www.mcdonalds.com/corp/news/corppr/2004/ cpr_11222004.html** McDonald's Press Release, November 22, 2004 (accessed June 12, 2006).

8. "Community & Corporate Responsibility: Our Strategy & Our Values," Telus website, **www.telus.ca** (accessed June 24, 2013).

9. "Our Mission," Celestial Seasonings website, **www.celestial seasonings.com/whoweare/corporatehistory/mission. php** (accessed June 12, 2006).

10. "A Tale of Two Brothers," *Canadian Business*, Mar 26, 2007, Vol.80 (7), p. S18; **www.tellusaboutus.com/news_article. asp?KBID=536** (accessed August 25, 2009). **http://www. winnipegfreepress.com/business/customer-feedback-firm-sold-118826334.html.**

11. "Strategic Management," *Wikipedia*, **http://en.wikipedia. org/wiki/Strategic_management** (accessed June 25, 2013).

12. "ImClone Stock Drops on Erbitux Outlook," *New York Business.com*, June 7, 2007, **http://www.newyork business.com/apps/pbcs.dll/article?AID=/20070607/ FREE/70607003/1045/breaking** (accessed June 14, 2007).

13. Canadian Press, "Dollarama speeds up expansion plans…".

14. Joe Castaldo, "New RIM CEO Thorsten Heins's Stay-the Course Plan," *Canadian Business* online, February 14, 2012, **http:// www.canadianbusiness.com/technology-news/new-rim-ceo-thorsten-heinss-stay-the-course-plan/** (accessed July 15, 2013).

15. Omar El Akkad, "Retailers Slash Prices on RIM's Playbook Tablet," *The Globe and Mail* online, September 26, 2011, **http://www.theglobeandmail.com/technology/tech-news/retailers-slash-prices-on-rims-playbook-tablet/ article595740/** (accessed July 15, 2013).

16. CNW Group, "$27 Million Maple Leaf Listeriosis Settlement Approved by Courts: Simple claims submission process begins for largest human food contamination class action in Canadian History," **http://www.newswire.ca/en/releases/archive/May2009/05/c8350.html** (accessed August 25, 2009).

17. Josh Greenberg and Charlene Elliott, "A Cold Cut Crisis: Listeriosis, Maple Leaf Foods, and the Politics of Apology," *Canadian Journal of Communication,* Vol. 34(2), pp. 189–204, retrieved from academia.edu website, **http://www.academia.edu/223591/A_Cold_Cut_Crisis_Listeriosis_Maple_Leaf_Foods_and_the_Politics_of_Apology** (accessed June 24, 2013)

18. *Canadian Business,* November 12, 2012, "What Little We Knew," p. 12.

19. **www2.reuters.com/productsinfo/** (accessed September 9, 2010).

20. Hollie Shaw, "Best Buy to Close 15 Stores in Canada; Lay Off 900 Workers," *Financial Post* online, January 31, 2013, **http://business.financialpost.com/2013/01/31/best-buy-to-close-15-stores-in-canada-lay-off-900-workers/** (accessed July 15, 2013).

21. John Shepler, "Managing After Downsizing."

22. "The Big Picture," *BusinessWeek,* July 16, 2001, p. 12.

23. "Chrysler Group: You Don't Know the Dealers without a Scorecard," *Ward's Dealer Business,* May 31, 2006 **http://wardsdealer.com/dealers_scorecard/** (accessed June 12, 2006).

24. "ASPO-USA Response to Exxon Mobil Peak Oil Advertisement," March 3, 2006, Association for the Study of Peak Oil & Gas-USA, **www.aspo-usa.com/news.cfm?nd=1468** (accessed June 12, 2006).

25. Dan Wilchins and Jonathan Stempel, "Citigroup CEO to Resign: Reports," *Reuters,* November 2, 2007, **www.reuters.com/article/idUSN0233640620071103** (accessed January 12, 2011); Chuck Prince, Citigroup memo, February 14, 2005, **http://specials.ft.com/spdocs/launchmemo14205.pdf** (accessed January 12, 2011).

26. **www.conferenceboard.ca/CPO/membership.asp** (accessed August 25, 2009).

27. "Growing Gap Project," Canadian Centre for Policy Alternatives website, **http://www.policyalternatives.ca/projects/growing-gap** (accessed June 25, 2013).

28. Allison Graham, "Making the case for diversity," *Financial Post,* Mar. 16, 2010, **http://www.financialpost.com/executive/story.html?id=2686724** (accessed April 2, 2010).

29. Tavia Grant, "Canada a laggard in developing women leaders," *Report on Business'* Economy Lab online, March 3, 2011, **http://www.theglobeandmail.com/report-on-business/economy/economy-lab/canada-a-laggard-in-developing-women-leaders/article612208/** (accessed June 24, 2013).

30. Roma Luciw, "Corner Office Headcount: Women, 3; Men, 97. Go Figure," *The Globe and Mail,* Jan. 12, 2007, p. C1.

31. "Developing Colleagues with Passion," *Inbound Logistics,* April 2004, p. 14.

32. "Improved Health of Employees and Financial Bottom Line Demonstrated Through Innovative Pilot Program at Daimler Chrysler Canada's Windsor Assembly Plant," **www.pfizer.ca/en/media-centre/news_releases/article?year=2006&article=194** (accessed July 8, 2010).

33. "10 Employers 2013," *The Financial Post* online, **http://www.canadastop100.com/fp10/fp10_2013.pdf,** pp. 4, 7 (accessed June 25, 2013).

34. "Corporate Information," **www.google.com/corporate/facts.html** (accessed June 12, 2006); "The Google Culture," **www.google.com/corporate/culture.html** (accessed June 12, 2006).

35. Bo Burlington, "Lessons From a Blue-Collar Millionaire," Inc., February 2010, pp. 57–63; **www.nickspizzapub.com** (accessed March 22, 2011); Bo Burlington, "Lessons From a Blue-Collar Millionaire—Addendum," Small Giants Community, February 1, 2010, **www.smallgiants.org/article.php?article_id-2** (accessed March 22, 2011).

36. Jeff Beer, "Q&A: Brian Scudamore, founder/CEO, 1-800-Got-Junk," *Canadian Business* online, May 7, 2012, **http://www.canadianbusiness.com/business-strategy/qa-brian-scudamore-founderceo-1-800-got-junk/** (accessed June 24, 2013).

37. James Kouzes and Barry Posner, *The Leadership Challenge: How to Make Extraordinary Things Happen in Organizations,* (5th edition) (Hoboken, NJ: Jossey-Bass, 2012).

38. "Tougher to Be a Leader," *USA Today* Snapshot, March 6, 2006, p. B1.

39. "The X Factor," **http://www.chiefexecutive.net/ME2/Audiences/dirmod.asp?sid=&nm=&type=Publishing&mod=Publications%3A%3AArticle&mid=8F3A7027421841978F18BE895F87F791&AudID=257093CD337F495B86A6A07046702F8C&tier=4&id=9D8A41A470494615ACF504170EB0A3A8** (accessed July 8, 2010); "Xerox Chairman & CEO Among the Most Powerful Women in Business," **www.xerox.com/go/xrx/template/019b.jsp?view=AwardAnnouncement&id=NR_Award_Fortune_Most_Powerfule_Women_Business&Xcntry=USA&Xlang=en_US** (accessed June 12, 2006).

40. Bruce Horovitz, "CEO Turns the Flame Up," *USA Today,* May 23, 2005; Elaine Walker, "Whopper of a Recovery?" *The Kansas City Star,* September 24, 2005; Kate MacArthur, "Franchisees Turn on Crispin's King," *Advertising Age,* October 24, 2005; "Greg Brenneman, Chairman and Chief Executive Officer, Burger King Corporation," Burger King Corporation, **www.bk.com/CompanyInfo/bk_corporation/executive_team/brenneman.aspx** (accessed November 8, 2005); **http://www.cbc.ca/money/story/2010/09/02/burger-king-sold.html** (accessed September 9, 2010).

41. Hollie Shaw, "Walmart Canada puts expansion plan in high gear to fend off Target," *Financial Post* online, January 22, 2013, **http://business.financialpost.com/2013/01/22/wal-mart-canada-plans-us450-million-expansion-opening-37-super-stores-over-next-year/** (accessed June 24, 2013).

42. Leanne Delap, "Small-box Wal-marts tailored to urban cores," *The Globe and Mail* online, November 12, 2012, **http://www.theglobeandmail.com/report-on-business/industry-news/property-report/small-box-wal-marts-tailored-to-urban-cores/article5214080/** (accessed June 24, 2013).

43. Kerrie Unsworth, "Unpacking Creativity," *Academy of Management Review,* 26 (April 2001), pp. 289–97.

44. *Harvard Business Review* 60 (November–December 1982), p. 160.

45. Kris Maher, "The Jungle," *The Wall Street Journal,* May 29, 2001, p. B16.

46. "The Passion to Perform," The Neirenberg Group, **www.self-marketing.com/about.html** (accessed March 11, 2010).

47. "Salary After Taxes," *Employment Spot,* **www.employmentspot.coméemployment-articles/salary-after-taxes** (accessed March 22, 2011).

48. Ibid.

49. Mae Anderson, "Lululemon says no need for downward dog demo for yoga pants refund," *The Financial Post* online, March 27, 2013, **http://business.financialpost.com/2013/03/27/lululemon-says-no-need-for-downward-dog-demo-for-yoga-pants-refund/**; Lululemon Addict blog, March 19, 2013, **http://www.lululemon.com/media/index.php?id=225** (both accessed June 24, 2013).

50. Scott Simpson, "Lululemon grabs headlines with pants recall," *The Vancouver Sun* online, March 20, 2013, **http://www.vancouversun.com/business/Lululemon+grabs+headlines+with+pants+recall/8124248/story.html** (accessed June 24, 2013).

Chapter 7

1. "About Cora: Our Founder," *Cora Restaurants* website, **http://www.chezcora.com/a/01-belle-histoire/1-0-belle-histoire.htm** (accessed April 2, 2010).

2. Mina Kimes, "What Admired Firms Don't Have in Common," *CNNMoney.com,* March 6, 2009, **http://money.cnn.com/2009/03/06/news/companies/ hay.survey.fortune.index.htm** (accessed March 22, 2011).

3. Adapted from "Best Buy Fights Against Electronic Waste," in O.C. Ferrell, John Fraedrich, and Linda Ferrell, *Business Ethics: Ethical Decision Making and Cases,* 9th ed. (Mason, OH: South-Western Cengage Learning, 2013), pp. 505–15; Aman Singh, "Best Buy Releases 2011 Sustainability Report: Responsibility in a Recession," *Forbes,* July 15, 2011, **www.forbes.com/sites/csr/2011/07/15/best-buy-releases-2011-sustainability-report-responsibility-in-a-recession/** (accessed April 9, 2012).

4. "A New Future for Toms Shoes, Tweed Shire and Room to Read," *Reputation Report,* August 7, 2009, **www.reputationreport.com.au/2009/07/a-new-future-by-toms-shoes-tweed-shire-and-room-to-read/** (accessed March 22, 2011); "Our Movement," TOMS Shoes, **www.tomsshoes.com/content.asp?tid = 271** (accessed March 22, 2011).

5. Kasey Wehrum, "An Office of Rock Stars," *Inc.,* November 2010, pp. 115–116.

6. Joe Light, "Finance and Tech Signal Bold Attitudes on Ethics," *The Wall Street Journal,* March 7, 2011, **http://online.wsj.com/article/SB10001424052747704727004576167671104 2012064.html** (accessed March 21, 2011).

7. Telis Demos, "Cirque du Balancing Act," *Fortune,* June 12, 2006, p. 114.

8. Adam Smith, *Wealth of Nations* (New York: Modern Library, 1937; originally published in 1776).

9. Jyoti Thottam, "When Execs Go Temp," *Time,* April 26, 2004, pp. 40–41.

10. Chris Perttila, "Keep It Simple," *Entrepreneur,* February 2006, pp. 60–64.

11. "Profile: Campbell Soup Company (CPB)," *Reuters,* **www.reuters.com/finance/stocks/companyProfile?symbol=CPB** (accessed March 21, 2011).

12. Ella Ide, "Italy Critics Trash McDonald's Nationalist Food Bid," **http://af.reuters.com/article/oddlyEnoughNews/idAFTRE6143I720100205** (accessed March 22, 2011).

13. Leigh Buchanan, "The Way I Work: 'I Have to Be the Worry-wart So My Son Feels Free to Exercise His Imagination,'" *Inc.,* May 2010, pp. 125–128; Johnny Cupcakes website, **www.johnnycupcakes.com** (accessed July 26, 2010).

14. "Why Work Here?" **www.wholefoodsmarket.com/careers/workhere.php** (accessed March 3, 2010).

15. "PepsiCo Unveils New Organizational Structure, Names CEOs of Three Principal Operating Units," PepsiCo Media, November 5, 2007, **www.pepsico.com/PressRelease/PepsiCo-Unveils-New-Organizational-Structure-Names.html** (accessed March 22, 2011); "The PepsiCo Family," PepsiCo, **www.pepsico.com/Company/The-Pepsico-Family/PepsiCo-Americas-Beverages.html** (accessed January 12, 2011).

16. Jon R. Katzenbach and Douglas K. Smith, "The Discipline of Teams," *Harvard Business Review* 71 (March–April 1993), pp. 111–20.

17. Ibid.

18. Berner and Grow, "Out-Discounting the Discounter."

19. Darryl Haralson and Adrienne Lewis, "USA Today Snapshots," *USA Today,* April 26, 2001, p. B1.

20. "Toyota Motor Corporation President Akio Toyoda Announces Global Quality Task Force," Toyota Newsroom, February 5, 2010, **http://pressroom.toyota.com/pr/tms/toyota-motor-corporation-president-153566.aspx** (accessed March 22, 2011).

21. Jerry Useem, "What's That Spell? TEAMWORK," *Fortune,* June 12, 2006, p. 66.

22. Jia Lynnyang, "The Power of Number 4.6," *Fortune,* June 12, 2006, p. 122.

23. Richard S. Wellins, William C. Byham, and Jeanne M. Wilson, *Empowered Teams: Creating Self-Directed Work Groups That Improve Quality, Productivity, and Participation* (San Francisco: Jossey-Bass Publishers, 1991), p. 5.

24. Matt Krumrie, "Are Meetings a Waste of Time? Survey Says Yes," *Minneapolis Workplace Examiner,* May 12, 2009, **www.examiner.com/workplace-in-minneapolis/are-meetings-a-waste-of-time-survey-says-yes** (accessed March 21, 2011).

25. Ashlee Vance, "Trouble at the Virtual Water Cooler," *Bloomberg Businessweek,* May 2–8, 2011, pp. 31–32; Chris Brogan, "How to Foster Company Culture with Remote Employees," Entrepreneur, May 2011, **www.entrepreneur.com/article/219471** (accessed August 4, 2011); **www.yammer.com** (accessed August 4, 2011); "Yammer Guidelines," **http://blogxero.com/2011/01/yammer-guidelines** (accessed August 5, 2011).

26. "Top 10 Ideas: Making the Most of Your Corporate Intranet," **www.claromentis.com/blog/2009/04/top-10-ideas-**

making-the-most-of-yourcorporate-intranet (accessed March 22, 2011).

27. Kim Komando, "Why You Need a Company Policy on Internet Use," **www.microsoft.com/business/en-us/resources/ management/employee-relations/why-you-need-a-company-policy-on-internet-use.aspx?fbid=abWQUs C20hw#WhyyouneedacompanypolicyonInternetuse** (accessed March 22, 2011).

28. Jenna Goudreau, "Ford's Green Team," *Forbes*, February 9, 2010, **www.forbes.com/2010/02/09/ford-green-technology-forbes-woman-leadership-cars.html** (accessed October 28, 2010); Carol Costello, "Ford's 'Green' Team of Female Engineers," *CNN*, June 1, 2010, **http://am.fix.blogs.cnn. com/2010/06/01/fords-green-team-of-female-engineers** (accessed December 2, 2010); Stephen Calogera, "Ford Making Greener Vehicles by Using Renewable, Recycled Materials," egmCarTech, April 20, 2010, **www. egmcartech.com/2010/04/20/ford-making-greener-vehicles-by-using-renewable-recyclable-materials/** (accessed December 11, 2010).

Chapter 8

1. "Employment by industry and sex," adapted from Statistics Canada, CANSIM, Table 282-0008. Last modified: 2013-01-04, **www.statcan.gc.ca/tables-tableaux/sum-som/l01/cst01/ labor10a-eng.htm** (accessed January 14, 2013).

2. Leonard L. Berry, *Discovering the Soul of Service* (New York: The Free Press, 1999), pp. 86–96.

3. Zeithaml and Bitner, *Services Marketing*, pp. 3, 22.

4. Andreas Cremer and Tim Higgins, "Volkswagen Rediscovers America," *Bloomberg Businessweek*, May 23–29, 2011, pp. 11–12; Paul A. Eisenstein, "VW Is Back in the USA and Aiming High with New Plant," MSNBC, May 26, 2011, **www.msnbc.msn. com/id/43159310/ns/business-autos/t/vw-back-usa-aiming-high-new-plant/** (accessed July 29, 2011); Deepa Seetharaman, "Volkswagen Sees U.S. Plant as Key to Topping Toyota," Reuters, May 24, 2011, **www.reuters.com/article/2011/05/24/ us-volkswagen-idUSTRE74N6RA20110524** (accessed July 29, 2011); "Germany: VW PC Brand Sales Rise 17.2% in July," Automotive World, August 16, 2011, **www.automotiveworld.com/ news/oems-and-markets/88694-germany-vw-pc-brand-sales-rise-17-2-in-july** (accessed August 16, 2011); Tom Mutchler, "First Look Video: 2012 Volkswagen Passat," *Consumer Reports*, August 5, 2011, **http://news.consumerreports.org/ cars/2011/08/first-look-video-2012-volkswagen-passat. html** (accessed August 16, 2011).

5. Faith Keenan, "Opening the Spigot," *BusinessWeek e.biz*, June 4, 2001, **www.businessweek.com/magazine/content/01_23/ b3735616.htm.**

6. Lonely Planet, **www.lonelyplanet.com/about/** (accessed July 2, 2010).

7. **www.orcahouseboats.com.**

8. "Making Chocolate," Hershey's, **www.hersheys.com/ discover/tour_printv.htm** (accessed January 12, 2011).

9. "Why Leading Executives Choose Canada," **www.location canada.com/art_5.htm.**

10. Stacy Perman, "Automate or Die," *eCompany*, July 2001, p. 62.

11. David Noonan, "The Ultimate Remote Control," *Newsweek*, via **www.msnbc.com/news/588560.asp** (accessed July 18, 2001).

12. "Sustainability," Walmart, **http://walmartstores.com/ sustainability** (accessed March 22, 2011).

13. Bryan Walsh, "Why Green Is the New Red, White and Blue," *Time*, April 28, 2008, p. 53.

14. "Introducing Chevrolet Volt," Chevrolet, **www.chevrolet. com/pages/open/default/future/volt.do** (accessed March 22, 2011).

15. Megan Kamerick, "How to Go Green," *New Mexico Business Weekly*, May 23–29, 2008, p. 3.

16. O. C. Ferrell and Michael D. Hartline, *Marketing Strategy* (Mason, OH: South-Western, 2005), p. 215.

17. John Edwards, "Orange Seeks Agent," *Inband Logistics*, January 2006, pp. 239–242.

18. Ferrell and Hartline, *Marketing Strategy*, p. 215.

19. Bruce Nussbaum, "Where Are the Jobs?" *BusinessWeek*, March 22, 2004, pp. 36–37.

20. Lisa H. Harington, "Balancing on the Rim," *Inband Logistics*, January 2006, pp. 168–170.

21. John O'Mahony, "The Future Is Now," Special Advertising Section, *Bloomberg Businessweek*, pp. S1–S11; "Recycling & Conservation," UPS, **http://responsibility.ups.com/ Environment/Recycling 1 and 1 Conservation** (accessed October 18, 2011); Rebecca Treacy-Lenda, "Sustainability Is…" UPS, July 28, 2011, **http://blog.ups.com/2011/07/28/ sustainability-is/** (accessed October 18, 2011); Heather Clancy, "Sustainability Update: UPS Squeezes Out More Fuel Consumption," SmartPlanet, July 28, 2011, **www.smartplanet. com/blog/business-brains/sustainability-update-ups-squeezes-out-more-fuel-consumption/17597** (accessed October 18, 2011).

22. Susan Carey, "Airlines Play Up Improvements in On-Time Performance," *The Wall Street Journal*, February 10, 2010, p. B6.

23. David Welch, "J.D. Power's Quality Survey: Toyota Tumbles, GM Disappoints," *BusinessWeek*, **www.businessweek.com/ autos/autobeat/archives/2010/06/jd_powers_quality_ survey_toyota_tumbles_gm_disappoints.html** (accessed July 2, 2010).

24. Christopher Lawton, "The War on Product Returns," *The Wall Street Journal*, May 8, 2008, p. D1.

25. Philip B. Crosby, *Quality Is Free: The Art of Making Quality Certain* (New York: McGraw-Hill, 1979), pp. 9–10.

26. Nigel F. Piercy, *Market-Led Strategic Change* (Newton, MA: Butterworth-Heinemann, 1992), pp. 374–385.

27. "Compuware Gomez Introduces Free Web Performance Benchmarking Tool," Gomez, February 16, 2010, **www. gomez.com/compuware-gomez-introduces-free-web-performance-benchmarking-tool/** (accessed March 22, 2011).

28. K.W., "The Dog Lover," *Inc.*, October 2010, pp. 68–70; Rebecca Konya, "Marie Moody: Women of Influence 2010," *The Business Journal*, 2010, **www2.bizjournals.com/ milwaukee/events/2010/women_of_influence/marie_ moody_women_of_influence_2010.html** (accessed October 19, 2010); **www.stellaandchewys.com** (accessed October 19, 2010).

29. Hershey, "Hershey's Chocolate Kisses."

30. Guy Chazan, "Clean-Fuels Refinery Rises in Desert," *The Wall Street Journal*, April 16, 2010, p. B8; Stanley Reed & Robert Tuttle, "Shell Aims for 'New Nigeria' as Qatari Plant Starts (update 2)," *Bloomberg Businessweek*, March 4, 2010, **www.businessweek.com/news/2010-03-04/shell-aims-for-new-nigeria-as-qatari-plant-starts-update1-.html** (accessed June 9, 2010).

Chapter 9

1. Peter Kennedy, "At 74, Jimmy Pattison focuses on long term," *The Globe and Mail*, June 2, 2003.

2. "The Flip Side of Productivity," *Ceredian*, newsletter, Spring 2004, **www.ceredian.com/myceredian/article/1,2481,11337-=3923,00.html** (accessed July 11, 2010).

3. Dan Heath and Chip Heath, "Business Advice from Van Halen," *Fast Company*, March 1, 2010, **www.fastcompany.com/magazine/143/made-to-stick-thetelltale-brown-mampm.html** (accessed March 11, 2010).

4. "100 Best Companies to Work For 2010," *Fortune*, **http://money.cnn.com/magazines/fortune/bestcompanies/2010/snapshots/4.html** (accessed February 18, 2010); "Benefits," Google Jobs, **www.google.com/support/jobs/bin/static.py?page= benefits.html** (accessed February 18, 2010).

5. "Careers," Nikebiz.com, **www.nikebiz.com/careers/benefits/other/whq_campus.html** (accessed February 9, 2010).

6. "WestJet brings its culture and lessons of success to Ivey," *Inside@Ivey*, The University of Western Ontario, May 14, 2009, **http://www.ivey.uwo.ca/inside/mba_speakers.htm** (accessed July 16, 2010).

7. "Why Work Here," **www.wholefoodsmarket.com/careers/workhere.php** (accessed November 9,2011); "Best Companies to Work For Rankings," **www.wholefoodsmarket.com/careers/fortune100.php** (accessed November 9, 2011); "Whole Food Market's Core Values," **www.wholefoodsmarket.com/values/corevalues.php#supporting** (accessed November 9, 2011); "100 Best Companies to Work For: Whole Foods Market," CNNMoney, **http://money.cnn.com/magazines/fortune/bestcompanies/2011/snapshots/24.html** (accessed November 9, 2011); Kerry A. Dolan, "America's Greenest Companies 2011," Forbes, April 18, 2011, **www.forbes.com/2011/04/18/americas-greenest-companies.html** (accessed November 9, 2011); Joseph Brownstein, "Is Whole Foods' Get Healthy Plan Fair?" ABC News, January 29, 2010, **http://abcnews.go.com/Health/w_DietAndFitnessNews/foods-incentives-make-employees-healthier/story?id 5 9680047** (accessed November 9, 2011); Deborah Dunham, "At Whole Foods Thinner Employees Get Fatter Discounts," *That's Fit*, January 27, 2010, **www.thatsfit.com/2010/01/27/whole-foods-thin-employees-get-discounts/** (accessed November 9, 2011).

8. Dana Flavelle, "Top 100 CEOs in Canada earned $7.7 million on average," *the star.com*, December 31, 2012, **www.thestar.com/business/article/1308766--top-100-ceos-in-canada-earned-7-7-million-on-average** (accessed January 16, 2012).

9. Medtronic, **http://www.medtronic.com/** (accessed July 17, 2010).

10. Jon L. Pierce, Tatiana Kostova, and Kurt T. Kirks, "Toward a Theory of Psychological Ownership in Organizations," *Academy of Management Review* 26, no. 2 (2001), p. 298.

11. Charisse Jones, "Great Work. Now Hit the Road—on Us," *USA Today*, May 12, 2010, pp. 1B–2B; V. Dion Haynes, Washington-Baltimore Benefits Survey: Part-Timers Getting More Perks," *The Washington Post*, June 8, 2010, **www.washingtonpost.com/wp-dyn/content/article/2010/06/07/AR2010060704513.html** (accessed June 10, 2010); Kim Covert, "Travel Perks One Way to Keep Employees Engaged," *The Vancouver Sun*, April 27, 2010, **www.vancouversun.com/life/Travel+perks+keep+employees+engaged/2956071/story.html** (accessed June 10, 2010); **www.pointsoflight.org** (accessed May 2, 2010); "Best Places to Work 2009," crain's, **www.crainsnewyork.com/apps/pbcs.dll/gallery?Site=CN&Date=20091207&Category=GALLERIES&ArtNo=120209998&Ref=PH&Params=Itemnr=31** (accessed May 2, 2010); **www.patagonia.com** (accessed July 10, 2010).

12. Jennifer Myers, "Company culture: Invisible weapon," *PROFITguide* online, July 28, 2010, **http://www.profitguide.com/article/4728--company-culture-invisible-weapon** (accessed August 12, 2010).

13. Douglas McGregor, *The Human Side of Enterprise* (New York: McGraw-Hill, 1960), pp. 33–34.

14. Ibid, pp. 47–48.

15. Archie Carroll, "Carroll: Do We Live in a Cheating Culture?", *Athens Banner-Herald*, February 21, 2004, **www.onlineathens.com/stories/022204/bus_20040222028.shtml**.

16. "The Shoplifting Issue," The National Association for Shoplifting Prevention, **www.shopliftingprevention.org/TheIssue.htm** (accessed June 2, 2006).

17. Carroll, "Carroll: Do We Live in a Cheating Culture?"

18. Robert Martin, "Family Ties," *Progress*, July 2009, Vol. 16 (4), **http://www.progressmedia.ca/article/2009/07/family-ties** (accessed July 11, 2010).

19. "Going Global, Eastman Chemical Company's Expatriate Program," **www.hemnet.com/body_globalissues.htm**, September 1, 1998.

20. PricewaterhouseCoopers, **www.pwcglobal.com/ie/eng/ins-sol/spec-int/globalhr/steeprise.html** (accessed July 11, 2010).

21. Geoff Colvin, "How Top Companies Breed Stars," September 20, 2007, **http://money.cnn.com/magazines/fortune/fortune_archive/2007/10/01/100351829/index.htm** (accessed March 12, 2010).

22. Julia Belluz, "'Life-swapping' with colleagues from around the world," *CBOnline*, March 15, 2010, **http://www.canadianbusiness.com/managing/employees/article.jsp?content=20100315_10028_10028** (accessed July 12, 2010).

23. Amy Wrzesniewski and Jen E. Dutton, "Crafting a Job: Revisioning Employees as Active Crafters of Their Work," *Academy of Management Review* 26, no. 2 (2001), p. 179.

24. **http://www.careerbuilder.com/Jobs/Company/C8D7BN6GV5F6ZYT9WDZ/Hyatt-Hotels/** ; **http://www.generalmills.com/en/Responsibility/Community_Engagement/Grants/Minneapolis_area/Communities_of_color/grant_recipients_2006.aspx**; "Seminar on Human Resources and Training Session I," Conference of European

Statisticians, United Nations Economic and Social Council, June 2006, **http://www.unescap.org/stat/apex/2/APEX2_S.1_Human_Resources&Training_Canada.pdf**

25. My Guides, USA.com, "Which Jobs Offer Flexible Work Schedules?" **http://jobs.myguidesusa.com/answers-to-myquestions/which-jobs-offer-flexiblework-schedules?/** (accessed March 12, 2010).

26. Robert Preidt, "Workplace Flexibility Can Boost Healthy Behaviors," Wake Forest University Baptist Medical Center, news release, December 10, 2007, via **http://yourtotalhealth.ivillage.com/workplaceflexibility-can-boost-healthy-behaviors.html** (accessed March 12, 2010).

27. Brearton, Friesen, and Brooker, "50 Best Employers in Canada."

28. Michael Cohen, "Share and Share Alike...," *Boston Business Journal,* July 13, 1998.

29. Statistics Canada, "Working at home: An update," December 7, 2010, **http://www.statcan.gc.ca/pub/11-008-x/2011001/article/11366-eng.htm#a13** (accessed January 16, 2013).

30. "Telecommuting Benefits," **http://www.telecommutect.com/employees/benefits.php**, Telecommute Connecticut! (accessed June 21, 2006); Nicole Demerath, "Telecommuting in the 21st century: Benefits, issues, and leadership model which will work," *AllBusiness.com*, April 1, 2002, **http://www.allbusiness.com/buying_exiting_businesses/3503510-1.html;** Fran Irwin, "Gaining the Air Quality and Climate Benefit from Telework," January 2004, **http://pdf.wri.org/teleworkguide.pdf;** "The State of California Telecommuting Pilot Project: Final Report Executive Summary," JALA Associates Inc., June 1990, **http://www.jala.com/caexecsumm.pdf.**

31. "HR Executives Split on Telecommuting," *USA Today*, March 1, 2006, p. B1.

32. Stephanie Armour, "Telecommuting Gets Stuck in the Slow Lane," *USA Today,* June 25, 2001, pp. 1A, 2A.

33. Nancy Rothbard, "Put on a Happy Face. Seriously." *The Wall Street Journal*, October 24, 2011, p. R2; "How 3M Gave Everyone Days Off and Created an Innovation Dynamo," February 1, 2011, **www.fastcodesign.com/1663137/how-3m-gave-everyone-days-off-and-created-aninnovation-dynamo** (accessed October 31, 2011); "Americans Increasingly Unhappy at Work," *BusinessNewsDaily,* March 10, 2011, **www.businessnewsdaily.com/work-wellness-index-1073**/ (accessed October 31, 2011); "Employee Mood Impacts Bottom Line," *BusinessNewsDaily* April 5, 2011, **www.businessnewsdaily.com/employee-mood-customer-service-1152/** (accessed October 31, 2011).

34. "Employers Reap Awards and Rewards for Psychologically Healthy Workplaces," *Employee Benefit News*, April 15, 2004, **www.benefitnews.com/pfv.cfm?id=5832;** Susan McCullough, "Pets Go to the Office," *HR Magazine* 43 (June 1998), pp. 162–68; "Pets Provide Relief to Workplace Stress," *BenefitNews Connect*, July 1, 2003, **www.benefitnews.com/detail.cfm?id=4736;** "Taking Your Best Friend to Work," *Toronto Star*, December 13, 2004, p. C11; "Working Like a Dog—Survey of Owners Reveals They Would Work More Hours or for Less Pay if They Could Bring Their Pooch to Work," *CNNMoney.com,* January 24, 2006, **http://money.cnn.com/2006/01/24/news/funny/dog_work/index.htm?cnn=yes** (accessed January 27, 2006); "Every Day Is 'Take Your Dog to Work Day'" at Planet Dog," Press Releases, **www.planetdog.com/Press.asp?id=6** (accessed January 27, 2006); Best Friends Survey taken March 27, and 30, 2006, of 1,000 registered voters, "All in the Family," *USA Today Snapshots*, June 21, 2006.

Chapter 10

1. Jack Welch, *Winning*, (New York: Harper Business, 2005).

2. Robert D. Hisrich, Michael P. Peters, Dean A. Shepherd, and Peter Mombourquette, *Entrepreneurship* (2nd Canadian edition), (Toronto: McGraw-Hill Ryerson Ltd., 2009), p. 253.

3. Allan Britnell, "The ultimate guide to hiring today's best employees: The new rules of recruiting," *PROFIT/Canadian Business* online, October 2006, **http://www.canadianbusiness.com/entrepreneur/human_resources/article.jsp?content=20061019_145640_5628** (accessed June 21, 2010).

4. Report: The Aging Workforce and Human Resources Development Implications for Sector Councils: Prepared for the Alliance Sector Councils, Prepared by R.A. Malatest & Associates, February 2002, **http://www.cpsc-ccsp.ca/PDFS/Aging%20Workforce%20Final%20Report.pdf** (accessed July 17, 2010).

5. Eleanor Beaton, "The ultimate guide to hiring today's best employees: Tactics of talent magnets," *PROFIT/Canadian Business* online, October 2006, **http://www.canadianbusiness.com/entrepreneur/human_resources/article.jsp?content=20061019_145652_1204** (accessed September 5, 2010).

6. Tavia Grant, "Employers sidestep recruiters to tap social media," *The Globe and Mail* online, November 10, 2009, **http://www.theglobeandmail.com/report-on-business/employers-sidestep-recruiters-to-tap-social-media/article1359961/** (accessed May 15, 2010).

7. Grant, "Employers sidestep recruiters to tap social media"; TweetMyJOBS, **http://tweetmyjobs.com/** (accessed July 17, 2010).

8. Procter & Gamble, "U.S. Recruiting process," **www.pg.com/jobs/jobs_us/recruitblue/recprocess.jhtml** (accessed July 5, 2006); "The Recruitment Process," Procter & Gamble, **http://www.pg.com/en_CA/careers/view_jobs/index.shtml** (accessed June 4, 2010).

9. "Important Employment Information," Canada's Wonderland, **http://www.canadaswonderland.com/jobs/jobs_benefits.cfm?et_id=1** (accessed July 2, 2010).

10. Adam Geller, "Cheating Is Employed in Worker Drug Tests," *Detroit News,* March 28, 2004, **www.detnews.com/2004/business/0403/29/c04-105176.htm.**

11. "Canadian Human Rights Commission Policy on Alcohol and Drug Testing," Canadian Human Rights Commission, **http://www.chrc-ccdp.ca/pdf/poldrgalceng.pdf** (accessed May 17, 2010).

12. Associated Press, "Food Network Chef Fired After Resume Fraud," *USA Today*, March 3, 2008, **www.usatoday.com/news/nation/2008-03-03-chef-fired_N.htm** (accessed April 14, 2011).

13. Christopher T. Marquet and Lisa J.B. Peterson, "Résumé Fraud: The Top Ten Lies," Marquet International, Ltd., **www.marquetinternational.com/pdf/Resume%20Fraud-Top%20Ten%20Lies.pdf** (accessed April 14, 2011).

14. The Canadian Charter of Rights and Freedoms, Canadian Heritage, **http://dsp-psd.pwgsc.gc.ca/Collection/CH37-4-3-2002E.pdf** (accessed July 17, 2010).

15. Canadian Human Rights Act, **http://www.efc.ca/pages/law/canada/canada.H-6.head.html** (accessed July 17, 2010).

16. "Overview," Canadian Human Rights Commission (n.d.), **http://www.chrc-ccdp.ca/about/icm_page2_gci-eng.aspx** (accessed July 17, 2010).

17. George Waggott and Lang Michener, "Mandatory Retirement: 65 or Not?", Supreme Court Law, **http://www.supremecourtlaw.ca/default_e.asp?id=68** (accessed July 17, 2010).

18. "Canadian Tire University," Canadian Tire Dealers' Association (n.d.), **http://www.ctda.ca/docs/public%20view%20side/7-customer%20service%20excellence/01-how%20do%20i%20get%20involved.pdf** (accessed July 17, 2010).

19. "Our Curriculum," Hamburger University, **www.aboutmcdonalds.com/mcd/careers/hamburger_university/our_curriculum.html** (accessed April 14, 2011).

20. Beaton, "The ultimate guide to hiring today's best employees: Tactics of talent magnets."

21. Doug Stewart, "Employee-Appraisal Software," *Inc.,* **www.inc.com/magazine/19940615/3288_pagen_2.html** (accessed April 14, 2011).

22. Maury A. Peiperl, "Getting 360-Degree Feedback Right," *Harvard Business Review,* January 2001, pp. 142–48.

23. Chris Musselwhite, "Self Awareness and the Effective Leader," *Inc.com,* October 1, 2007, **www.inc.com/resources/leadership/articles/20071001/musselwhite.html** (accessed April 14, 2011).

24. Ron Robertson, "Who Will Lead? Twelve Canadian Organizations Discuss How to Assess Executive Talent," *Ivey Business Journal,* July/August 2010 (accessed July 17, 2010).

25. O.C. Ferrell, Geoffrey Hirt, Rick Bates, Elliott Currie, *Business: A Changing World, Second Canadian Edition,* p. 258.

26. "High Cost for Treating Employees Poorly," *InfoWorld,* December 17, 2006, **http://weblog.infoworld.com/openresource/archives/2006/12/high_cost_for_t.html** (accessed June 16, 2007).

27. Hisrich, Peters, Shepherd, and Mombourquette, *Entrepreneurship,* pp. 256–258; Susanne Bailler-Ruder, "Sweetly Devoted Employees," *PROFITguide* online, December 2004, **www.profitguide.com/great-place/article.jsp?content=20041203_144250_1852.**

28. Marcia Zidle, "Employee Turnover: Seven Reasons Why People Quit Their Jobs," **http://ezinearticles.com/?Employee-Turnover:-Seven-Reasons-Why-People-Quit-Their-Jobs&id=42531** (accessed April 14, 2011).

29. Lisa H. Pelled, "So Close and Yet So Far: Human Resource Management in Northern Mexico," *Marshall,* Spring 1998, pp. 35–39.

30. "GM, Chrysler to Cut 50,000 Jobs," *CBC News,* February 17, 2009, **www.cbc.ca/money/story/2009/02/17/carbailout.html** (accessed April 14, 2011); "2009 Chrysler Will Shed 789 Dealers," **www.carpictures.com/vehicle/09EDD063625060.html** (accessed April 14, 2011).

31. "Chrysler to Rehire 376 Workers at Kokomo Plants," *The Seattle Times,* May 11, 2010, **http://seattletimes.nwsource.com/html/businesstechnology/2011835839_apuschryslerkokomo.html?syndication=rss** (accessed January 13, 2011).

32. Tavia Grant, "Canada's job market in deep freeze," *The Globe and Mail* online, November 6, 2009, **http://www.theglobeandmail.com/report-on-business/economy/canadas-job-market-in-deep-freeze/article1354678/** (accessed November 3, 2010).

33. "Hourly Minimum Wages in Canada for Adult Workers," Human Resources and Skills Development Canada, **http://srv116.services.gc.ca/dimt-wid/sm-mw/rpt2.aspx?lang=eng&dec=5** (accessed January 16, 2013).

34. Personal interview with John Mulvihill, Sydney, N.S., March 2010.

35. Robert Lachowiez, presenter, Business & Tourism Conference 2009, Mount Saint Vincent University, Halifax, Nova Scotia.

36. "WestJet Airlines' winning strategy for engagement," *Internal Comms Hub,* 1(8), December/January 2008, **http://www.bridgesconsultancy.com/newsroom/articles/youve_got_the%20strategy.pdf**, pp. 10–11.

37. Alison van Diggelen, "Working@Google: Green Carrots & Pogo Sticks," Fresh Dialogues, **www.freshdialogues.com/** (accessed November 9, 2011); "Can We Commute Carbon-Free," Google Green, **www.google.com/green/operations/commuting-carbon-free.html** (accessed November 9, 2011); Tiffany Hsu, "Google Creates $280-Million Solar Power Fund," *Los Angeles Times,* June 14, 2011, **http://articles.latimes.com/2011/jun/14/business/la-fi-google-solar-20110614** (accessed November 9, 2011).

38. Perspectives on Labour and Income, The Online Edition, "Benefits of the Job," Katherine Marshall, May 2003, Vol. 4, No. 5, **http://www.statcan.gc.ca/pub/75-001-x/00503/6515-eng.html** (accessed July 17, 2010).

39. Janet McFarland, "Bell takes the axe to future retirement benefits," *The Globe and Mail* online, March 27, 2007, **http://www.theglobeandmail.com/report-on-business/article749077.ece** (accessed July 17, 2010).

40. Michelle Conlin and Aaron Bernstein, "Working ... and Poor," *Business Week,* May 31, 2004, **www.businessweek.com/.**

41. "Union Membership in Canada—2008," Human Resources and Skills Development Canada, **http://www.rhdcc-hrsdc.gc.ca/eng/labour/labour_relations/info_analysis/union_membership/index.shtml** (accessed September 27, 2010).

42. "Pension Rallies Hit French Cities," *BBC News,* September 7, 2010, **www.bbc.co.uk/news/world-europe-11204528** (accessed April 14, 2011).

43. Human Resources and Skills Development Canada, "Pan-Canadian Study of First Year College Students, December 2008," June 12, 2009, **http://www.hrsdc.gc.ca/eng/publications_resources/learning_policy/sp_890_12_08/page03.shtml** (accessed November 3, 2010).

44. **http://www.rbc.com/diversity/research.html** (accessed November 3, 2010).

45. Richard W. Yerema, "Canada's Top 100 Employers 2006," © 2006, Mediacorp Canada Inc.; Michell Neely Martinez, "Equality Effort Sharpens Bank's Edge," *HR Magazine,* January 1995, pp. 38–43.

46. Taylor H. Cox, Jr., "The Multicultural Organization," *Academy of Management Executives* 5 (May 1991), pp. 34–47; Marilyn Loden and Judy B. Rosener, *Workforce America! Managing Employee Diversity as a Vital Resource* (Homewood, IL: Business One Irwin, 1991).

47. Statistics Canada, "Study: Working at Home," **http://www.statcan.gc.ca/daily-quotidien/101207/dq101207b-eng.htm** (accessed September 20, 2013); Sharon Jayson, "Working at Home: Family-friendly?," *USA Today*, April 15, 2010, p. 1A; "Is Working from Home the New Calling in Sick?," *msnbc*, March 2, 2010, **www.msnbc.msn.com/id/35676647/ns/business-careers** (accessed April 14, 2011); Emili Vesilind, "The Home Office Is Humming," *Entrepreneur*, June 2010, **www.entrepreneur.com/magazine/entrepreneur/2010/june/206662.html** (accessed April 14, 2011); Max Chafkin, "The Office Is Dead. Long Live the Office; The Case, and the Plan, for the Virtual Company," *Inc.*, April 2010, pp. 62–73; Joel Stein, "Where the Copy Machine Never Jams...," *Bloomberg Businessweek*, June 28–July 4, 2010, pp. 73–75; Anna Jane Grossman, "Freelancers Forgo Office Space for Casual Coworking," *WIRED*, July 20, 2007, **www.wired.com/techbiz/people/news/2007/07/coworking** (accessed April 14, 2011); Carrie Sloan, "Office Space for the Self-Employed: Working Away from Home Helps Freelancers, Entrepreneurs Succeed," *NY Daily News*, July 13, 2009, **www.nydailynews.com/money/2009/07/13/2009-07-13_office_space_for_the_selfemployed_working_away_ from_home_helps_freelancers_entre.html** (accessed April 14, 2011).

Chapter 11

1. Company Overview, Spin Master Toys website, **http://www.spinmaster.com/company-overview.php** (accessed July 9, 2013); Kate Rockwood, "How Spin Master Mixes Tech and Toys and Keeps Mattel Looking Over Its Shoulder," *Fast Company* online, April 1, 2010, **http://www.fastcompany.com/1579439/how-spin-master-mixes-tech-and-toys%E2%80%94and-keeps-mattel-looking-over-its-shoulder** (accessed July 9, 2013).

2. "McDonald's Adult Happy Meal Arrives," *CNN/Money*, May 11, 2004, **http://money.cnn.com/** (accessed June 6, 2006).

3. "Wireless," EastLink website, **http://www.eastlink.ca/Wireless.aspx** (accessed July 9, 2013).

4. "In Our Restaurant: Breakfast," Tim Hortons website, **http://www.timhortons.com/ca/en/menu/breakfast-sandwich.html** (accessed July 9, 2013).

5. April Y. Pennington, "Not Just for Kids; Who Says Business Can't Be Fun? Not These Specialty Toy E-tailers," *Entrepreneur Magazine*, **www.entrepreneur.com/article/0,4621,325141,00.html** (accessed January 18, 2006); "Joel Boblit—Big Bad Toy Store (01–2005)," *The Allspark*, **www.allspark.com/modules.php?name=Content&pa=showpage&pid=12** (accessed January 18, 2006).

6. Tony Martin, "Ask the Legends: Walter Hachborn," *CBOnline*, March 2009, **http://www.canadianbusiness.com/article.jsp?content=20090201_30016_30017** (accessed July 7, 2010)

7. Jennifer Kwan, "Quebec's Simons Eyes Toronto Sears Locations," *Yahoo! Finance* online, June 17, 2013, **http://ca.finance.yahoo.com/blogs/insight/quebec-simons-eyes-toronto-sears-locations-180217911.html** (accessed July 9, 2013).

8. "McDonald's Adult Happy Meal Arrives."

9. Marguerite Higgins, "McDonalds Labels Nutrition," *Washington Times*, October 26, 2005, **www.washingtontimes.com/business/20051025-102731-2213r.htm** (accessed June 16, 2006).

10. Jamie Beliveau, "Does Size Matter When You Want to Hire a Construction Company?", Kerr Construction, **http://www.kerrconstruction.ca/articles.html** (accessed July 7, 2010).

11. "Success of Herbal Magic Franchise," The Franchise Mall, June 18, 2008, **http://www.thefranchisemall.com/news/articles/21579-0.htm** (accessed July 7, 2010)

12. Avi Dan, "When It Comes to Social Media Consumers Tell Brands to Speak Only When Spoken To," *Forbes* online, March 31, 2013, **http://www.forbes.com/sites/avidan/2013/03/31/when-it-comes-to-social-media-consumers-tell-brands-to-speak-only-when-spoken-to/** (accessed July 9, 2013).

13. Michael Treacy and Fred Wiersema, *The Discipline of Market Leaders* (Reading, MA: Addison Wesley, 1995), p. 176.

14. "Print Audit," ASTech Awards, **http://www.printaudit.com/downloads/pdf/ASTech_Profile.pdf** (accessed July 6, 2010).

15. Apple Annual Report 10-k, 2005.

16. Ipsos-Reid, **http://www.ipsos-na.com/news-polls/searchresults.aspx?search=negativek** (accessed July 7, 2010).

17. "Customer Is King—Says Who," *Advertising Age*, April 15, 2006, p. 4.

18. Venky Shankar, "Multiple Touch Point Marketing," American Marketing Association Faculty Consortium on Electronic Commerce, Texas A&M University, July 14–17, 2001.

19. Trevor Melanson, "Is HootSuite Canada's Next Billion-Dollar Titan?", *Canadian Business* online, January 9, 2013, **http://www.canadianbusiness.com/technology-news/is-hootsuite-canadas-next-tech-titan/** (accessed August 5, 2013).

20. Stephanie Kang, "The Swoosh Finds Its Swing, Targeting Weekend Golfers," *The Wall Street Journal*, April 8, 2004, p. B1.

21. "About the Company," Reitmans, **http://www.reitmans.com/en/company/** (accessed September 1, 2010).

22. Hollie Shaw, "Hudson's Bay CEO Lost in Space," *Financial Post*, **http://www.nationalpost.com/life/health/Hudson+lost+space/857928/story.html** (accessed July 7, 2010).

23. Marina Strauss and Susan Krashinsky, "The Target Invasion: How Pricing Will be Key to Canadian Success," *The Globe and Mail* online, January 19, 2013, **http://www.theglobeandmail.com/globe-investor/the-target-invasion-how-pricing-will-be-key-to-canadian-success/article7550145/?page=all**; Joanna Pachner, "Shelly Broader: Walmart Canada's New Secret Weapon," *Canadian Business* online, September 26, 2102, **http://www.canadianbusiness.com/business-strategy/shelley-broader-walmart-canadas-new-secret-weapon/**; and Linda Nguyen, "Walmart Canada vs. Target Canada: Retailers to Fight It Out with Major Expansion Plans," *The Huffington Post* online, January 22, 2013, **http://www.huffingtonpost.ca/2013/01/22/walmart-canada-target-locations_n_2525319.html** (all accessed July 9, 2013).

24. Allison Marr, "Household-Level Research Gives Clearer Picture," *Marketing News*, April 15, 2006, p. 18.

25. Kara Aaserud, "How to Really Listen to Your Customers," *PROFIT guide* online, September 13, 2010, **http://www.profitguide.com/manage-grow/sales-marketing/how-to-really-listen-to-your-customers-29921** (accessed August 5, 2013).

26. Mya Frazier, "Staples Gains Footing in Hispanic Market," *Advertising Age*, April 3, 2006, p. 58.

27. Charles Passy, "Your Scoop Is in the Mail," *The Wall Street Journal*, May 25, 2001, pp. W1, W6; Allysa Bikowski, Sam Bryant, Sarah Crossin et. al., "Research In Motion: Case Study Report," October 22, 2009, **http://zenportfolios.com/theresa/files/2009/11/mktg-RIM-case.pdf**.

28. Bryan Borzykowski, "Business Plan: Can a Canadian Company Make the Next Bugatti?", *PROFITguide* online, June 2, 2010, **http://www.profitguide.com/manage-grow/success-stories/business-plan-can-a-canadian-company-make-the-next-bugatti-29744** (accessed August 5, 2013).

29. Matthew Miller, "Playing Cupid to the Rich and Famous," *Forbes*, May 30, 2007, **http://www.forbes.com/entrepreneurs/management/2007/05/30/matchmaking-small-business-ent-manage-cx_mm_0530match.html?feed=rss_entrepreneurs_entremgmt** (accessed February 4, 2008); Samantha's Table, **www.samanthastable.com** (accessed February 5, 2008).

30. David Foot, *Boom Bust and Echo* (Toronto: Macfarlane Walter & Ross, 1998).

31. RBC Financial Group Sponsorship, **http://www.rbc.com/sponsorship/ownthepodium.html** (accessed July 7, 2010).

32. Nurse Next Door, **http://www.nursenextdoor.com/index.php** (accessed September 1, 2010); Medicard Finance Inc., **http://www.medicard.com/** (accessed September 1, 2010).

33. "Under Attack, Jim Flaherty Defends Mortgage Meddling," CTVNews online, March 20, 2013, **http://www.ctvnews.ca/canada/under-attack-jim-flaherty-defends-mortgage-meddling-1.1203361** (accessed August 5, 2013).

34. "CIBC becomes first major Canadian bank to offer a Mobile Banking App for iPhone," *CNW*, February 2, 2010, **http://www.newswire.ca/en/releases/archive/February2010/02/c6153.html** (accessed September 1, 2010).

35. "Growth is in the Bag," Canada Export Achievement Awards, **http://www.exportawards.ca/exportawards/quebec.html** (accessed September 1, 2010).

36. Kim Shiffman, "Overview: Role models for the recovery," *PROFITguide* online, May 28, 2010, **http://www.profitguide.com/article/4686--overview-role-models-for-the-recovery** (accessed September 28, 2010).

37. Marina Strauss, "Rona's Big Bet on Small Stores," *The Globe and Mail* online, September 21, 2012, **http://www.theglobeandmail.com/globe-investor/ronas-big-bet-on-small-stores/article4560618/**; Sarah Barmak, "Retailers Bring E-Shopping In-Store," *Canadian Business* online, December 8, 2012, **http://www.canadianbusiness.com/companies-and-industries/retailers-bring-e-shopping-in-store/** (both accessed August 5, 2013).

38. "McDonald's Franchisee's Jobs," CareerBuilder.com, **http://www.careerbuilder.com/Jobs/Company/C8E5975ZLC66B4JB4D4/McDonalds-Franchisees/** (accessed July 7, 2010); "AboutMcDonalds," **http://www.mcdonalds.com/corp/about.html** (accessed June 17, 2007).

39. Dr. Abdullah Kirumira, BioMedical Diagnostic Inc., in a personal interview with Peter Mombourquette, 2010. Information reconfirmed 2013.

40. Eleanor Beaton, "Gabrielle Chevalier, COO and grandmother, has turned Solutions 2 Go Inc. into the market leader," *PROFIT guide* online, October 13, 2010, **http://www.profitguide.com/article/6520--gabrielle-chevalier-coo-and-grandmother-has-turned-solutions-2-go-inc-into-the-market-leader**; Solutions 2 Go Inc., **http://www.solutions2go.ca/** (accessed September 1, 2010).

41. "Lululemon: Building the Brand From the Ground—Yoga Mat—Up," Strategyonline.ca, January 13, 2003, **http://strategyonline.ca/2003/01/13/lululemon-20030113/ (accessed August 5, 2013)**.

42. Ellen Roseman, "Blockbuster of Books," thestar.com, **http://www.thestar.com/article/269013** (accessed July 7, 2010).

43. Lee Oliver, "Appetite for resurrection," *CBOnline*, October 2003, **http://www.canadianbusiness.com/profit_magazine/article.jsp?content=20031020_142029_3976&page=1**.

44. Wency Leung, "Tim Hortons' Extra-Large Coffee to Get Even Larger," *The Globe and Mail* online, January 16, 2012, **http://www.theglobeandmail.com/life/food-and-wine/food-trends/tim-hortons-extra-large-coffee-to-get-even-larger/article1358604/** (accessed August 5, 2013).

45. Michael J. Weiss, "To Be About to Be," *American Demographics* 25 (September 2003), pp. 29–36.

46. "Ask the Legends: Les Mandelbaum," *CBOnline*, December 2009, **http://www.canadianbusiness.com/entrepreneur/managing/article.jsp?content=20091130_145811_9872**.

47. Rasha Mourtada, "Tour business," *The Globe and Mail* online, August 29, 2007, **http://www.theglobeandmail.com/report-on-business/tourbusiness/article778331/singlepage/#articlecontent**.

48. Rick Spence, "Sweetpea Baby Food: Stuck in the Middle," *CBOnline*, October 2007, **http://www.canadianbusiness.com/entrepreneur/sales_marketing/article.jsp?content=20071002_12233_12233&page=1**.

49. "Online Research Spending Predicted to Grow to $4 Billion," GMI, June 14, 2005, **www.gmi-mr.com/press/release.php?p=2005–06–14** (accessed June 16, 2006).

50. Look-Look, **www.look-look.com** (accessed June 16, 2006).

51. Faith Keenan, "Friendly Spies on the Net," *BW Online*, July 9, 2001, **http://www.businessweek.com/magazine/content/01_28/b3740624.htm**.

52. Diane Brady, "Pets Are People, Too, You Know," *BusinessWeek*, November 28, 2005, p. 114.

53. Allison Fass, "Collective Opinion, Forget the Up-Close Focus Group. Newfangled Software Lets Lego, Procter & Gamble and Others Mine Ideas from Tens of Thousands of Opinionated Customers," *Forbes*, November 28, 2005, pp. 76–79; "About Us," **www.informative.com/aboutUs.html**; "Solutions and Services," **www.informative.com/solutionsServices.html**; "Customer Communities," **www.communispace.com/customer_c.htm**; "The Communispace Difference," **www.communispace.com/difference.htm**; "Technology and Services," **www.communispace.com/technology.htm** (all accessed December 10, 2005).

54. Chris Griffiths, "A Pro's Guide to Managing Your Reputation Online," *The Globe and Mail* online, November 6, 2012, **http://www.theglobeandmail.com/report-on-business/small-business/sb-digital/biz-categories-technology/a-pros-guide-to-managing-your-reputation-online/article4887679/**; and Harvey Schacter, "What's the Real Impact of Online Reviews?", *The Globe and Mail* online, October 10, 2011, **http://www.theglobeandmail.com/report-on-business/careers/management/whats-the-real-impact-of-online-reviews/article618142/** (both accessed July 9, 2013); Yelp website, **www.yelp.com** (accessed August 10, 2010); "Yelp Adds a Tiny Bit of Transparency...And Inches Away from Pay for Placement," The Entrepreneur's Corner, TechDirt, **ww.techdirt.com/blog/entrepreneurs/articles/20100330/1539268795.shtml** (accessed August 20, 2010); Peter Burrows & Joseph Galante, "Yelp: Advertise or Else?," *Bloomberg Businessweek*, March 3, 2010, **www.businessweek.com/magazine/content/10_11/b4170027355708.htm** (accessed August 10, 2010); Jeremy, YELP CEO, "Additional Thoughts on Last Week's Lawsuit, or How a Conspiracy Theory Is Born," Yelp Web Log, **http://officialblog.yelp.com/2010/03/additional-thoughts-on-last-weeks-lawsuit-or-how-a-conspiracy-theory-is-born-.html** (accessed August 10, 2010); Kermit Pattison, "Talking to the Chief of Yelp, the Site That Businesses Love to Hate," *The New York Times*, March 24, 2010, **www.nytimes.com/2010/03/25/business/smallbusiness/25sbiz.html** (accessed August 10, 2010); Bill Chappell, "Yelp Goes Unfiltered. Let the Arguments Begin," all tech CONSIDERED, NPR, April 6, 2010, **www.npr.org/blogs/alltechconsidered/2010/04/06/125631274/yelp-goes-unfiltered—let-the-arguments-begin** (accessed August 10, 2010); Jessica Guynn, "Restaurant Review Site Yelp and Reservation Booking Site OpenTable Team Up," *The Los Angeles Times*, June 3, 2010, **http://latimesblogs.latimes.com/technology/2010/06/restaurant-review-site-yelp-and-reservationbooking-site-opentable-team-up.html** (accessed August 10, 2010).

55. Emily Nelson, "P&G Checks Out Real Life," *The Wall Street Journal*, May 17, 2001, p. B1.

56. Normandy Madden, "'Rolling Stone' Smacks into Great Wall of China," *Advertising Age*, April 3, 2006, p. 8.

57. Karen Valby, "The Man Who Ate Too Much," *Entertainment Weekly*, May 21, 2004, p. 45.

58. Anjali Cordeiro, "Kelloggs Retreats on Ads to Kids," June 14, 2007, **http://online.wsj.com/article/SB118177043343134415-search.html?KEYWORDS=obesity& COLLECTION=wsjie/6month** (accessed June 17, 2007).

59. Bruce Horovitz, "Wendy's Will Be 1st Foodie with Healthier Oil," *USA Today*, June 8, 2006, p. 1A.

60. Lisa McLaughlin, "Paper, Plastic or Prada?," *Time*, August 13, 2007, pp. 49–51; Megha Bahree, "Bag Lady," *Forbes*, November 26, 2007, **http://members.forbes.com/forbes/2007/1126/109.html** (accessed December 4, 2007).

61. "Beauty Queen," *People*, May 10, 2004, p. 187.

62. "Blue Nile, Inc.," *Wikipedia*, **http://en.wikipedia.org/wiki/Blue_Nile_Inc.** (accessed August 5, 2013).

Chapter 12

1. Joe Castaldo, "New RIM CEO Thorsten Heins's Stay-the-Course Plan," *Canadian Business* online, February 14, 2012, ht**tp://**www.canadianbusiness.com/technology-news/new-rim-ceo-thorsten-heinss-stay-the-course-plan; Iain Marlow "Your RIM Questions Answered: Thorsten Heins Responds," *The Globe and Mail* online, June 6, 2012, **http://www.theglobeandmail.com/technology/your-rim-questions-answered-ceo-thorsten-heins-responds/article4395605/?page=all**; Manuel Baigorri and Hugo Miller, Bloomberg News, "BlackBerry Z10 Winning Converts, Heins says, as Shares Rise," *Financial Post* online, March 6, 2013, **http://business.financialpost.com/2013/03/06/blackberry-z10-winning-converts-heins-says-as-shares-rise/?__lsa=47c3-71a0**; Iain Marlow, "BlackBerry 10 Puts Research in Motion Back in the Black," *The Globe and Mail* online, March 28, 2013, **http://www.theglobeandmail.com/globe-investor/blackberry-10-puts-research-in-motion-back-in-the-black/article10478674/** (all accessed July 11, 2013).

2. Charles Arthur, "PlayBook Writeoff means RIM's Tablet Has Been a $1.5bn Mistake," *The Guardian* online, December 5, 2011, **http://www.guardian.co.uk/technology/blog/2011/dec/05/playbook-writeoff-rim-tablet-mistake** (accessed July 11, 2013).

3. Umbra, **http://www.umbra.com/**; "Ask the Legends: Les Mandelbaum," *Canadian Business* online, December 2009, **http://www.canadianbusiness.com/entrepreneur/managing/article.jsp?content=20091130_145811_9872** (accessed September 1, 2010).

4. Galen Gruman, "*Rotten Apple: Apple's 12 Biggest Failures*," *CIO* online, **http://www.cio.com/article/507483/Rotten_Apple_Apple_s_12_Biggest_Failures?page=13#slideshow** (accessed July 11, 2013).

5. "Nortel," *Wikipedia* website, **http://en.wikipedia.org/wiki/Nortel** (accessed July 11, 2013).

6. "New Products," The Coca Cola Company, **www.thecocacolacompany.com/presscenter/newproducts.html** (accessed June 17, 2007).

7. Steve Rosenbush, "At GM, Tech Is Steering," *BusinessWeek*, May 27, 2004, **www.businessweek.com/**.

8. **www.dominos.com/Public-EN/site+Content/secondary/inside+dominos/pizza+particulars/** (accessed June 14, 2006).

9. "About Microsoft Research," Microsoft Research, **http://research.microsoft.com/en-us/about/default.aspx** (accessed September 1, 2010).

10. "Karen Crouse, "A Fashion Statement Designed to Grab Gold," *NYTimes.com*, February 11, 2010, **http://www.nytimes.com/2010/02/12/sports/olympics/12speedsuits.html**.

11. "About Us," Spindle, Stairs and Railings, **http://www.greatstairs.com/aboutus.cfm** (accessed June 17, 2010).

12. "Best Inventions of the Year 2012: Self-Inflating Tires," *TIME* online, October 31, 2012, **http://techland.time.com/2012/11/01/best-inventions-of-the-year-2012/slide/self-inflating-tires/** (accessed July 11, 2013).

13. "*Dragons' Den*—Pitches," CBC Television, **http://www.cbc.ca/dragonsden/s5.html#ep2** (accessed June 17, 2010).

14. Brett Shevack, "Open Up to a New Way to Develop Better Ideas," *Point*, June 2006, p. 8.

15. Judann Pollack, "The Endurance Test, Heinz Ketchup," *Advertising Age*, November 14, 2005, p. 39.

16. Oliver Burkman, "Happiness is a Glass Half-Empty," *The Guardian* online, June 15, 2012, **http://www.guardian.co.uk/lifeandstyle/2012/jun/15/happiness-is-being-a-loser-burkeman**; Dan Gould, "The Museum of Product Failures," *PSFK* online, August 12, 2008, **http://techland.time.com/2012/11/01/best-inventions-of-the-year-2012/slide/self-inflating-tires/** (both accessed July 11, 2013).

17. "Digital Payment Technologies Named to Deloitte's 2010 Technology Fast 500™ in North America," Digital Payment Technologies, October 25, 2010, **http://www.digitalpaytech.com/news/press_releases/2010/101025_Fast_500.pdf** (accessed November 17, 2010).

18. Faith Keenan, "Friendly Spies on the Net," *BW Online*, July 9, 2001, **http://www.businessweek.com/magazine/content/01_28/b3740624.htm**.

19. James Cowan, "Tim Hortons' New Coffee Cup: Why the Supersize?", *Canadian Business* online, February 14, 2012, **http://www.canadianbusiness.com/business-strategy/tim-hortons-new-coffee-cup-why-the-supersize/** (accessed July 11, 2013); "Tim Horton's tempest in a tea cup," *CBC News* online, November 26, 2001, **http://www.cbc.ca/news/story/2001/11/23/TimmysTea_011123.html** (accessed June 15, 2006).

20. "Jan 24—Imperial Tobacco Canada Expands Harm Reduction program with start of a Snus market in Ottawa," Imperial Tobacco Canada, January 24, 2008, **http://www.imperialtobaccocanada.com/groupca/sites/IMP_7VSH6J.nsf/vwPagesWebLive/DO7WNJHL?opendocument&SKN=1** (accessed November 17, 2010).

21. Seasons 52, **www.seasons52.com** (accessed June 15, 2006).

22. William C. Symonds, "Gillette's New Edge: P&G Is Helping Pump Up the Fusion Razor," *BusinessWeek*, February 6, 2006, p. 44.

23. "Best Inventions of the Year 2012: Techpet," *TIME* online, October 31, 2012, **http://techland.time.com/2012/11/01/best-inventions-of-the-year-2012/slide/techpet**; "Best Inventions of the Year 2012: Google Glass," *TIME* online, October 31, 2012, **http://techland.time.com/2012/11/01/best-inventions-of-the-year-2012/slide/google-glass** (accessed July 11, 2013).

24. Reena Jana, "Green Threads for the Eco Chic," *BusinessWeek*, September 27, 2006, **www.businessweek.com/print/innovate/content/sep2006/id20060927_111136.htm** (accessed June 20, 2007); Laura Petrecca and Theresa Howard, "Eco-marketing a Hot Topic for Advertisers at Cannes," *USA Today*, June 22, 2007, **www.usatoday.com/money/advertising/2007-06-22-cannes-green-usat_N.htm?csp=34** (accessed June 23, 2007); Laura McClure, "Green Jeans," *Reader's Digest*, June 2007, p. 213; "Levi's Brand Launches 100% Organic Cotton Jeans," **www.levistrauss.com**, July 5, 2006, **http://www.levistrauss.com/News/PressReleaseDetail.aspx?pid=784** (accessed June 20, 2007).

25. "Tide Unveils Milestone in Fabric Care with New Tide Stainbrush," Procter & Gamble, press release, February 13, 2004, **www.pg.com/news/**.

26. Allison Enright, "The Urge to Merge," *Marketing News*, March 15, 2006, pp. 9–10.

27. T. L. Stanley, "Barbie Hits the Skids," *Advertising Age*, October 31, 2005, pp. 1, 33.

28. Susan Berfield, "The Man Behind The Bandz," *Bloomberg Businessweek*, June 14–20, 2010, pp. 62–67; Emily Maltby, "Silly Bandz Seek to Stretch Popularity," *The Wall Street Journal*, July 8, 2010, **http://online.wsj.com/article/SB10001424052748703636404575353306049729790.html** (accessed July 4, 2010); "Silly Bandz Could Be 'Hottest Toy of the Year,'" *Chicago Sun Times*, July 2, 2010, **www.suntimes.com/business/2456678,CST-NWS-bandz02.article** (accessed July 4, 2010); "Brand Central Joins the Craze with Silly Bandz," The Licensing Blog, **http://licensingblog.com/brand-central-joins-the-craze-with-sillybandz** (accessed July 6, 2010); Bruce Horovitz, "Silly Bandz Stretch into a Trend as Copycat Rivals Hop on Board," *USA Today*, July 1, 2010, **www.usatoday.com/money/smallbusiness/2010-07-01-sillybandz01_CV_N.htm** (accessed July 30, 2010); **www.crazyfads.com** (accessed August 10, 2010); "Beanie Babies," Wikipedia, **http://en.wikipedia.org/wiki/Beanie_Baby** (accessed August 10, 2010); Bruce Horovitz, "Silly Bandz Fad Fades Out," *USA Today*, December 17, 2010, p. B1.

29. Eric Wellweg, "Test Time for TiVo," *Business2.0*, May 24, 2004, **www.business2.com/**.

30. "Glenora Distillers," *Wikipedia* website, **http://en.wikipedia.org/wiki/Glenora_Distillers**; The Glenora Inn & Distillery website, **http://www.glenoradistillery.com/glen.html** (accessed July 11, 2013).

31. David Goldman and Julianne Pepitone, "Lady Gaga is the new face of Polaroid," *CNN Money*, January 8 2010, **http://money.cnn.com/2010/01/06/news/companies/lady_gaga_polaroid/** (accessed June 17, 2010); Jason Kirby, "Polaroid goes Gaga," *CBOnline*, February 15, 2010, **http://www.canadianbusiness.com/managing/strategy/article.jsp?content=20100113_10010_10010** (accessed June 17, 2010).

32. "Loblaw Companies," **http://en.wikipedia.org/wiki/Loblaw_Companies** (accessed June 17, 2010); "Sobey's," **http://en.wikipedia.org/wiki/Sobeys** (accessed June 17, 2010).

33. Alessandra Galloni, "Advertising," *The Wall Street Journal*, June 1, 2001, p. B6.

34. Madhuri Katti, "Coke Displays Aboriginal Art on Bottles at Vancouver Winter Olympics 2010," Trends Updates, February 18, 2010, **http://trendsupdates.com/coke-displays-aboriginal-art-on-bottles-at-vancouver-winter-olympics-2010/** (accessed June 17, 2010).

35. Dagmar Mussey, "Coke Bottle Shape-Shifts for World Cup in Germany," *Advertising Age*, May 29, 2006, p. 12.

36. Pallavi Gogoi, "McDonald's New Wrap," *BusinessWeek*, February 17, 2006, **www.businessweek.com/print/bwdaily/dnflash/feb2006/nf20060217_8329_db016.htm?chan=db** (accessed February 2006).

37. Stephanie Miles, "Consumer Groups Want to Rate the Web," *The Wall Street Journal*, June 21, 2001, p. B13.

38. Rajneesh Suri and Kent B. Monroe, "The Effects of Time Constraints on Consumers' Judgments of Prices and Products," *Journal of Consumer Research* 30 (June 2003), pp. 92 +.

39. Steven Gray, "McDonald's Menu Upgrade Boosts Meal Prices and Results," *The Wall Street Journal*, February 18, 2006, p. A1.

40. Craig Sutherland, in a personal interview with Peter Mombourquette, August 4, 2010. Information reconfirmed 2013.

41. Reena Jana, "Riding Hip Jeans into New Luxury Market," January 22, 2007, **http://www.businessweek.com/innovate/**

content/jan2007/id20070122_366747.htm?chan=search (accessed June 17, 2007).

42. David Luhnow and Chad Terhune, "Latin Pop: A Low-Budget Cola Shakes Up Markets South of the Border," *The Wall Street Journal*, October 27, 2003, pp. A1, A18.

43. Stephanie Thompson, "Polo Jeans Thrown in the Hamper," *Advertising Age*, June 5, 2006, p. 3.

44. "Tim Hortons Changing Cup Sizes Across the Country," *CTV* online, January 16, 2012, **http://www.ctvnews.ca/tim-hortons-changing-cup-sizes-across-the-country-1.75466**; Wency Leung, "Tim Hortons' Extra-Large Coffee to Get Even Larger," *The Globe and Mail* online, January 16, 2012, **http://www.theglobeandmail.com/life/food-and-wine/food-trends/tim-hortons-extra-large-coffee-to-get-even-larger/article1358604**; Emily Jackson, "Tim Hortons Supersizes Its Coffee Cups," *Toronto Star* online, January 16, 2012, **http://www.thestar.com/business/2012/01/16/tim_hortons_super sizes_its_coffee_cups.html**; James Cowan, "Tim Hortons' New Coffee Cup: Why the Supersize?" (all accessed July 11, 2013).

45. "Electronic Commerce and Technology," *The Daily*, Statistics Canada, April 24, 2008, **http://www.statcan.gc.ca/daily-quotidien/080424/dq080424a-eng.htm** (accessed June 17, 2010); Mark Iype, "Internet usage rising, 80% of Canadians online," *National Post* online, May 10, 2010, **http://www.nationalpost.com/news/story.html?id=3008492** (accessed June 17, 2010).

46. O. C. Ferrell and Michael D. Hartline, *Marketing Strategy* (Mason, OH: South-Western, 2005), p. 215.

47. "Top Threats to Revenue," *USA Today*, February 1, 2006, p. A1.

48. Todd Wasserman, "Kodak Rages in Favor of the Machines," *BrandWeek*, February 26, 2001, p. 6.

49. Tony Martin, "Ask the Legends: Walter Hachborn," *CBOnline*, March 2009, **http://www.canadianbusiness.com/article.jsp?content=20090201_30016_30017** (accessed June 17, 2010).

50. "About PlaSmart," PlaSmart website, **http://www.plasmart toys.com/about.html**; "Fastest Growing Companies: #7—PlaSmart," *Ottawa Business Journal* online, April 22, 2009, **http://www.obj.ca/Other/Special-Reports/2009-04-22/article-303847/FASTEST-GROWING-COMPANIES%3A-%237---PlaSmart-Inc./** (both accessed July 11, 2013).

51. Amber MacArthur, "PEI's (million dollar) Google juice," *The Globe and Mail* online, July 14, 2010, **http://www.theglobe andmail.com/news/technology/trending-tech/peis-million-dollar-google-juice/article1639896/** (accessed August 3, 2010).

52. Andrew Willis, "How the torch lit the way for RBC," *The Globe and Mail* online, February 9, 2010, **http://www.theglobe andmail.com/globe-investor/investment-ideas/street wise/how-the-torch-lit-the-way-for-rbc/article1460954/** (accessed June 17, 2010); Marina Strauss, "HBC tries to build on Olympic momentum," *The Globe and Mail* online, February 26, 2010, **http://www.theglobeandmail.com/report-on-business/hbc-tries-to-build-on-olympic-momentum/article1483478/** (accessed June 17, 2010); Michael Brush, "Less gold for Olympic sponsors?" *MSN Money*, February 9, 2010, **http://articles.moneycentral.msn.com/Investing/CompanyFocus/less-gold-for-olympic-sponsors.aspx** (accessed June 17, 2010).

53. Terry Poulton, "Canadian ad spend on the rise in the next five years: CMA," Media In Canada, November 13, 2007, **http://www.mediaincanada.com/articles/mic/20071113/adspend.html?__b=yes** (accessed June 17, 2010).

54. "22nd Annual Profit 100: Canada's Fastest Growing Companies," *Canadian Business* online, 2010, **http://list.canadian business.com/rankings/profit100/2010/include/Profit-100-Next-100-downloadable.xls** (accessed June 17, 2010).

55. "Canadians Lead in Time Spent Online," CBC News website, March 2, 2012, **http://www.cbc.ca/news/canada/story/2012/03/02/canadians-more-time-online.html** (accessed July 14, 2013).

56. Eleanor Beaton, "Sales & Marketing: How to sell more, more, more," *PROFITguide* online, May 28, 2010, **http://www.profit guide.com/article/4689--sales-marketing-how-to-sell-more-more-more** (accessed June 17, 2010).

57. Derek Thompson, "The Profit Network: Facebook and Its 835-Million Man Workforce," *The Atlantic* online, February 2, 2012, **http://www.theatlantic.com/business/archive/2012/02/the-profit-network-facebook-and-its-835-million-man-workforce/252473/** (accessed July 30, 2013).

58. "Top Sites in Canada," Alexa website, **http://www.alexa.com/topsites/countries/CA** (both accessed July 30, 2013).

59. Tony Martin, "They blog, therefore they are ... better CEOs," March 15, 2008, *GlobeAdvisor.com*, **http://www.globeadvisor.com/servlet/ArticleNews/story/gam/20080315/RWORK OUT15** (accessed June 17, 2010); Grant Robertson, "CEO blogs: The new company 'water cooler,'" *The Globe and Mail* online, February 6, 2006, **http://www.theglobeandmail.com/news/technology/ceo-blogs-the-new-company-water-cooler/article810687/singlepage/** (accessed June 17, 2010).

60. Kara Aaserud, "Bonding by Blogging," Provident Security Press, October 1, 2006, **http://www.providentsecurity.ca/press/31** (accessed June 17, 2010).

61. Beaton, "Sales & Marketing: How to sell more, more, more."

62. "Direct Mail," Answers.com, **http://www.answers.com/topic/direct-marketing** (accessed June 17, 2010).

63. Jefferson Graham, "Web Pitches, That's 'Advertiament,'" *USA Today*, June 26, 2001, p. 3D.

64. "Meet eBay Canada's Entrepreneur of the Year," *Tech-Vibes* online, October 4, 2012, **http://www.techvibes.com/blog/meet-ebay-canadas-entrepreneur-of-the-year-2012-10-04** (accessed July 14, 2013).

65. "Top Sites in Canada," Alexa website.

66. Chris Neville, in a personal interview with Peter Mombour-quette, February 14, 2013.

67. Paul Skeldon, "14 Million Americans Scanned QR and Barcodes with Their Mobiles in June 2011," *Internet Retailing* online, August 16, 2011, **http://www.internetretailing.net/2011/08/14m-americans-scanned-qr-and-bar-codes-with-their-mobiles-in-june-2011** (accessed July14, 2013).

68. Chris Atchison, "Entrepreneurial success: Masters of one," *CBOnline*, May 2009, **http://www.canadianbusiness.com/entrepreneur/sales_marketing/article.jsp?cont ent=20090501_30008_30008**.

69. Jim McElgunn and Kim Shiffman, "Canada's Entrepreneurs of the Decade," *CBOnline*, December 2009, **http://www.canadian**

business.com/entrepreneur/managing/article.jsp?con tent=20091201_30044_30044; Just Energy Income Fund, **http://www.je-un.ca/SiteResources/ViewContent.asp?Do cID=3&v1ID=&RevID=730&lang=1** (accessed July 17, 2010).

70. Beaton, "Sales & Marketing: How to sell more, more, more."

71. Susanne Baillie and Kim Shiffman, "How to get on Oprah," *Canadian Business* online, February 2004, **http://www.canadian business.com/entrepreneur/sales_marketing/article.jsp?c ontent=20040213_155625_4316** (accessed June 17, 2010).

72. Andy Holloway, "The right way to tee off," *Canadian Business* online, December 2006, **http://www.canadianbusiness. com/entrepreneur/sales_marketing/article.jsp?content= 20061201_152142_5592**.

73. "Lululemon Canada's Fastest Growing Brand, as TD, RIM Still Top List: Study," *Financial Post*, June 7, 2012, **http://business. financialpost.com/2012/06/07/lululemon-canadas-fast est-growing-brand-as-td-rim-still-top-list-study** (accessed July 14, 2013).

74. Disruptive Dave, "Meeting Customers Where They Are At," My Disruption Blog, October 2, 2012, **http://mydisruption. wordpress.com/2012/10/02/meeting-customers-where- they-are-at** (accessed July14, 2013).

75. "VANOC accuses Lululemon of bad sportsmanship," *Marketing*, December 16, 2009, **http://www.marketing mag.ca/english/news/marketer/article.jsp?content= 20091216_150310_9752** (accessed June 17, 2010); "Lululemon Athletica," **http://en.wikipedia.org/wiki/Lululemon_Athletica**, (accessed June 17, 2010).

76. Donna Montaldo, "2005 Coupon Usage and Trends," About. com, **http://couponing.about.com/od/groceryzone/ a/2005cp_usage.htm** (accessed June 17, 2010).

77. Kate MacArthur, "Sierra Mist: Cie Nicholson," *Advertising Age*, November 17, 2003, p. S-2.

78. "A tale of two customers," Canada Export Achievement Awards, **http://www.exportawards.ca/exportawards/ atlantic.html** (accessed June 17, 2010).

79. Michelle Maynard, "Amid the Turmoil, A Rare Success at DaimlerChrysler," *Fortune*, January 22, 2001, p. 112.

80. "Coca-Cola North America Announces the Launch of VAULT," February 17, 2006, **www2.coca-cola.com/presscenter/ newproducts_vault.html** (accessed June 16, 2006).

81. "Don't Be Fooled by Greenwashing," *The Vancouver Province* online, February 24, 2008, **http://www.canada.com/story. html?id=92a3d1cc-596c-4c10-9f69-f89c879768fa**; "Ques- tions and Answers about Fur," **http://www.furisgreen.com/ questions_about_fur.aspx** and "Fur, a Renewable Resource," Fur Is Green website, **http://www.furisgreen.com/renew able.aspx**; Shannon Kornelsen, "The Only Thing Green About Fur is Profit," *The Huffington Post; The Blog*, February 25, 2013, **http://www.huffingtonpost.ca/shannon-kornelsen/fur- isnt-green_b_2755972.html** (all accessed July 14, 2013); **http://www.canadianlawyermag.com/Watch-out-for- green-washing.html**; Laura Petrecca and Christine Dugas, "Going Truly Green Might Require Detective Work," *USA Today*, April 22, 2010, pp. 1B–2B; Laura Petrecca and Christina Dugas, "Groups Help Consumers Find 'Real' Green Products," *USA Today*, April 22, 2010, p. 2B; Julie Deardorff, "How to Spot Green- washing," *Chicago Tribune*, May 7, 2010, **http://featuresblogs. chicagotribune.com/features_julieshealthclub/2010/05/**

how-to-spot-greenwashing.html (accessed June 13, 2010); Sarah Mahoney, "H&M Introduces Its First Organic Skin- care," MarketingDaily, March 3, 2010, **www.mediapost.com/ publications/?fa=Articles.showArticle&art_aid=123424** (accessed June 13, 2010); Leslie Berkman, "Efforts Spread to Verify Claims of Businesses Who Market Themselves as Envi- ronmentally Friendly," *The Press-Enterprise*, January 31, 2010, **www.pe.com/business/local/stories/PE_New_Local_W_ green01.46c7f14.html** (accessed June 13, 2010); **www.green washingindex.com** (accessed June 13, 2010); Julie Deardorff, "Eco-friendly Claims: When Is 'Green' Really Green?," *Chicago Tribune*, May 7, 2010, **http://featuresblogs.chicagotribune .com/features_julieshealthclub/2010/05/ecofriendly- claims-when-is-green-really-green.html** (accessed Decem- ber 12, 2010).

Chapter 13

1. "Bio," Arlene Dickinson website, **http://arlenedickinson.com/ bio/**; Angus Gillespie, "Power of Persuasion—The Inspirational Life Story of Arlene Dickinson," *The Canadian Business Jour- nal* online, **http://www.cbj.ca/features/may_12_features/ power_of_persuasion_the_inspirational_life_story_of_ arlene_dicki.html** (both accessed July 16, 2013).

2. The material in this chapter is reserved for use in the authors' other textbooks and teaching materials.

3. Brad Stone and Bruce Einhorn, "Baidu China," *Bloomberg Businessweek*, November 15–21, 2010, pp. 60–67; Loretta Chao, "China's Baidu Brings App Craze to Web," *The Wall Street Journal*, September 3, 2010, p. B8.

4. Steve Ladurantaye, "Canada Tops Globe in Internet Usage," *The Globe and Mail* online, March 1, 2012, **http://www. theglobeandmail.com/technology/tech-news/canada- tops-globe-in-internet-usage/article551593/** (accessed July 16, 2013).

5. Ken Tencer, "What's Better than a Great Communication Strat- egy? Conversation," *The Globe and Mail* online, March 13, 2013, **http://www.theglobeandmail.com/report-on-business/ small-business/sb-digital/innovation/whats-better-than- a-great-communication-strategy-conversation/arti- cle9600803/** (accessed July 16, 2013).

6. "Fortune 500," CNNMoney, **http://money.cnn.com/maga- zines/fortune/fortune500/2010/full_list/** (accessed Janu- ary 17, 2011).

7. "Fortune 500: Amazon.com," *Fortune*, 2009, **http://money. cnn.com/magazines/fortune/fortune500/ 2009/snap- shots/10810.html** (accessed April 13, 2011); Josh Quitter, "How Jeff Bezos Rules the Retail Space," *Fortune*, May 5, 2008, pp. 127–132.

8. "Media Info," Hulu, **www.hulu.com/about** (accessed April 13, 2011).

9. Bobby White, "The New Workplace Rules: No Video-Watch- ing," *The Wall Street Journal*, March 4, 2008, p. B1.

10. Bertrand Marotte, "Most Canadians Still Shy Away From Social Media for Shopping: Report," *The Globe and Mail* online, January 28, 2013, **http://www.theglobeandmail.com/ technology/digital-culture/social-web/most-canadians- still-shy-away-from-social-media-for-shopping-report/ article7903948/** (accessed July 17, 2013).

11. "A World of Connections," *The Economist,* January 28, 2010, **www.economist.com/node/15351002** (accessed January 27, 2011).

12. "Internet Usage Statistics," Internet World Stats, **www.Internet worldstats.com/stats.htm** (accessed April 13, 2011).

13. Michael V. Copeland. "Tapping Tech's Beautiful Mind," *Fortune,* October 12, 2009, pp. 35–36.

14. Jacqueline Nelson, "Business without Borders: Coastal Contacts," *Canadian Business* online, March 13, 2012, **http://www.cana dianbusiness.com/business-news/industries/consumer-goods/business-without-borders-coastal-contacts/** (accessed July 30, 2013).

15. Miguel Bustillo and Geoffrey A. Fowler, "Walmart Uses Its Stores to Get an Edge Online," *The Wall Street Journal,* December 15, 2009, p. B1.

16. Aaron Back, "China's Big Brands Tackle Web Sales," *The Wall Street Journal,* December 1, 2009, p. B2.

17. "About Us," Mobovivo website, **http://www.mobovivo.com/about-us/team.html** (accessed July 16, 2013).

18. "2009 Digital Handbook," *Marketing News,* April 30, 2009, p. 13.

19. Cameron Chapman, "The History and Evolution of Social Media." *WebDesigner Depot,* October 7, 2009, **www.web designerdepot.com/2009/10/the-history-and-evolution-of-social-media/** (accessed April 19, 2011).

20. Danah M. Boyd and Nicole B. Ellison, "Social Network Sites: Definition, History, and Scholarship," *Journal of Computer-Mediated Education,* 2007, **http://jcmc.indiana.edu/vol13/issue1/boyd.ellison.html** (accessed April 19, 2011).

21. Emily Schmall, "Growing Pains," *Forbes,* August 11, 2008, pp. 60–63.

22. Zachary Karabell, "To Tweet or Not to Tweet," April 12, 2011, *Time,* p. 24.

23. "2009 Digital Handbook," p. 11.

24. Charlene Li and Josh Bernoff, *Groundswell* (Boston: Harvard Business Press, 2008), p. 43.

25. A.C. Nielsen, "Global Faces and Networked Places: A Nielsen Report on Social Networking's New Global Footprint," March 2009, **http://blog.nielsen.com/nielsenwire/wp-content/uploads/2009/03/nielsen_globalfaces_mar09.pdf** (accessed April 19, 2011).

26. "Couldn't Stop the Spread of the Conversation in Reactions from Other Bloggers," from Hyejin Kim's May 4, 2007, blog post "Korea: Bloggers and Donuts" on the blog Global Voices at **http://groundswell.forrester.com/site1-16** (accessed April 19, 2011).

27. Mia Pearson, "Why Corporate Blogging is on the Rebound," *The Globe and Mail* online, March 21, 2103, **http://www.the globeandmail.com/report-on-business/small-business/sb-digital/biz-categories-technology/why-corporate-blogging-is-on-the-rebound/article10003057/** (accessed July 17, 2013).

28. Drake Bennett, "Assessing Wikipedia, Wiki-Style, on Its 10th Anniversary," *Bloomberg Businessweek,* January 10–16, 2011, pp. 57–61.

29. Li and Bernoff, *Groundswell,* pp. 25–26.

30. "2009 Digital Handbook," p. 11.

31. "Statistics," YouTube Press, **http://www.youtube.com/yt/press/statistics.html**; Jeff Bullas, "30 Mind-Numbing YouTube Facts, Figures, and Statistics," jeffbullas.com, **http://www.jeffbullas.com/2012/05/23/35-mind-numbing-youtube-facts-figures-and-statistics-infographic/** (both accessed July 30, 2013).

32. "WestJet Introduces Child-Free Cabins," WestJet website, **http://www.westjet.com/guest/en/deals/promo-code/april-fools.shtml**; "Lululemon's April Fool's Prank: Introducing Lulu Leather," *The Huffington Post* online, April 1, 2013, **http://www.huffingtonpost.ca/2013/04/01/lululemon-lululeather_n_2994378.html**; "April Fool's 'lululeather' prank disgusts some yoga fans," CBC News online, **http://www.cbc.ca/news/canada/british-columbia/story/2013/04/01/bc-lululemon-companies-april-fools.html** (both accessed July 17, 2013).

33. David Meerman Scott, *The New Rules of Marketing & PR* (Hoboken, NJ: John Wiley & Sons, Inc., 2009), p. 224; "Mainframe: The Art of the Sales, Lesson One," YouTube, **www.youtube.com/watch?v= MSqXKp-00Hm**; Ryan Rhodes, "The Mainframe: It's Like a Barn," IBM Systems, March–April 2007, **www.ibmsystemsmag.com/mainframe/marchapril07/stoprun/11984p1.aspx** (both accessed April 13, 2011).

34. "It's Your Job Video Contest," Ontario Ministry of Labour, **http://www.labour.gov.on.ca/english/contest/index.php** (accessed July 30, 2013).

35. "Crash the Superbowl Winners and Finalists," Frito Lay Facebook page, **https://apps.facebook.com/crashthe superbowl/**; "Crash the Superbowl," *Wikipedia,* **http://en.wikipedia.org/wiki/Crash_the_Super_Bowl** (both accessed July 30, 2013).

36. "Search Giant Google to Buy YouTube for $1.65B," *FoxNews .com,* October 10, 2006, **www.foxnews.com/story/0,2933,218921,00.html** (accessed April 13, 2011).

37. Ryan Caligiuri, "Can small businesses harness that Old Spice magic?", *The Globe and Mail* online, August 20, 2010, **http://www.theglobeandmail.com/report-on-business/your-business/grow/ryan-caligiuri/can-small-businesses-harness-that-old-spice-magic/article1679081/**; TeamSave, **www.teamsave.com/**; Becky Reuber, "Startup picks fight with social-buying giant Groupon," *The Globe and Mail* online, September 17, 2010, **http://www.theglobeandmail.com/report-on-business/your-business/grow/customer-experience/startup-picks-fight-with-social-buying-giant-groupon/article1710446/** (both accessed July 17, 2010).

38. Zeke Camusio, "Flickr Marketing—6 Awesome Tactics to Promote Your Website on Flickr," The Outsourcing Company, February 19, 2009, **www.theoutsourcingcompany.com/blog/social-media-marketing/flickr-marketing-6-awe some-tactics-to-promote-your-website-on-flickr/** (accessed April 19, 2011).

39. Bianca Male, "How to Promote Your Business on Flickr," *The Business Insider,* December 1, 2009, **www.business insider.com/how-to-promote-your-business-on-flickr-2009-12?utm_source=feedburner&utm_medium= feed&utm_campaign=Feed%3A+businessinsider+(The+Business+Insider)** (accessed on April 13, 2011).

40. "How to Market on Flickr," Small Business Search Marketing, **www.smallbusinesssem.com/articles/marketing-on-flickr/#ixzz0cLlpJUTW** (accessed April 13, 2011).

41. Sage Lewis, "Using Flickr for Marketing," YouTube, uploaded February 13, 2007, **www.youtube.com/watch?v= u2Xyzkfzlug** (accessed January 11, 2010).

42. Charlotte Henry, "Pinterest vs. Flickr: the Battle for Photo Dominance," *The Wall* website, March 6, 2013, **http://wall blog.co.uk/2013/03/06/pinterest-vs-flickr-the-battle-for-photo-dominance/** (accessed July 17, 2013).

43. "2009 Digital Handbook," p. 14.

44. "2009 Digital Handbook," p. 13.

45. Li and Bernoff, *Groundswell*, p. 22.

46. "2009 Digital Handbook," p. 13.

47. "Facebook: Largest, Fastest Growing Social Network," *Tech Tree*, August 13, 2008, **www.techtree.com/India/News/Facebook_Largest_Fastest_Growing_Social_Network/551-92134-643.html** (accessed April 13, 2011).

48. "2009 Digital Handbook," p. 13.

49. Nick Summers, "Heated Rivalries:#9 Facebook vs. MySpace," *Newsweek*, **www.2010.newsweek.com/top-10/heated-rival ries/facebook-vs-myspace.html** (accessed April 13, 2011).

50. "2009 Digital Handbook," p. 13.

51. "Hockey Night in Canada theme contest opens," CBC News online, June 19, 2008, **http://www.cbc.ca/sports/hockey/story/2008/06/19/hockey-song-contest.html** (accessed July 17, 2013).

52. "Canada Facebook Statistics," Socialbakers website, **http://www.socialbakers.com/facebook-statistics/canada** (accessed July 17, 2013).

53. Steve Ladurantaye, "Inside a New Facebook: the Good, the Bad, and the Creepy," *The Globe and Mail* online, January 16, 2013, **http://www.theglobeandmail.com/technology/digital-culture/social-web/inside-a-new-facebook-search-the-good-the-bad-and-the-creepy/article7406282/** (accessed July 17, 2013).

54. Vines Pasta Grill website, **www.vinespastagrill.com** (accessed July 30, 2013).

55. "Pepsi Refresh Project," **www.refresheverything.com/index** (accessed April 13, 2011); Stuart Elliot, "Pepsi Invites the Public to Do Good," *The New York Times*, January 31, 2010, **www.nytimes.com/2010/02/01/business/media/01adco.html** (accessed April 13, 2011).

56. "Facebook Needs to Be a Marketing Destination, Not Just a Conduit," *Marketing News*, March 15, 2011, p. 12.

57. "2009 Digital Handbook," p. 13; "Top 15 Most Popular Social Networking Websites," *eBizMBA*, April 2011, **www.ebizmba.com/articles/social-networking-websites** (accessed April 13, 2011).

58. Alison Doyle, "LinkedIn and Your Job Search," *About.com*, **http://jobsearch.about.com/od/networking/a/linkedin.htm** (accessed April 13, 2011).

59. Laura Petrecca, "More Grads Use Social Media to Job Hunt," *USA Today*, April 5, 2011, p. 3B.

60. "LinkedIn's Newest Features Allow for Corporate Networking and Business Promotion," *Marketing News*, March 15, 2011, p. 12.

61. "Neil Patel (entrepreneur)," *Wikipedia*, **http://en.wikipedia.org/wiki/Neil_Patel_%28entrepreneur%29** (accessed July 17, 2013).

62. Jefferson Graham, "Cake Decorator Finds Twitter a Tweet Recipe for Success," *USA Today*, April 1, 2009, p. 5B.

63. "2009 Digital Handbook," p. 11.

64. Gregory L. White, "Medvedev Sets Kremlin Atwitter," *The Wall Street Journal*, September 1, 2010, p. A12.

65. Claire Cain Miller, "Twitter Loses Its Scrappy Start-Up Status," *The New York Times*, April 15, 2010, **www.nytimes.com/2010/04/16/technology/16twitter.html** (accessed April 13, 2011).

66. **https://twitter.com/@StarbucksCanada** and **https://twitter.com/Starbucks/status/304274571845054465** (accessed July 17, 2013).

67. Josh Tyrangiel, "Bing vs. Google: The Conquest of Twitter," *Time*, October 22, 2009, **www.time.com/time/business/article/0,8599,1931532,00.html** (accessed April 13, 2011).

68. "As Twitter Grows and Evolves, More Manpower Is Needed," *Marketing News*, March 15, 2011, p. 13.

69. Daniel Zeevi, "10 Best Social Media Management Tools," Dashburst website, April 8, 2013, **http://dashburst.com/best-social-media-management-tools/** (accessed July 17, 2013).

70. "Real Cars Drive into Second Life," *CNNMoney.com*, November 18, 2006, **http://money.cnn.com/2006/11/17/autos/2nd_life_cars/index.htm** (accessed April 13, 2011)

71. Alice Truong, "Q&A: A Real Study of Virtual Worlds," *The Wall Street Journal*, May 4, 2010, **http://blogs.wsj.com/digits/2010/05/04/qa-a-real-study-ofvirtual-worlds/** (accessed May 6, 2010).

72. "CNN Enters the Virtual World of Second Life," November 12, 2007, *CNN.com*, **www.cnn.com/2007/TECH/11/12/second.life.irpt/index.html** (accessed April 13, 2011).

73. Roger Yu, "Smartphones Help Make Bon Voyages," *USA Today*, March 5, 2010, p. B1.

74. Mickey Alam Khan, "Jiffy Lube Mobile Coupons Bring 50 Percent New Households," *Mobile Marketer*, January 30, 2009, **www.mobilemarketer.com/cms/news/commerce/2551.html** (accessed April 13, 2011).

75. Umika Pidaparthy, "Marketers Embracing QR Codes, for Better or Worse," *CNN Tech*, March 28, 2011, **http://articles.cnn.com/2011-03-28/tech/qr.codes.marketing_1_qr-smartphone-users-symbian?_s= PM:TECH** (accessed April 11, 2011).

76. Emily Steel, "Nestlé Takes a Beating on Social-Media Sites," *The Wall Street Journal*, March 29, 2010, p. B5; "World's Most Admired Companies 2010," *Fortune*, **http://money.cnn.com/magazines/fortune/mostadmired/2010/full_list**; Augie Ray, "Seven Things Your Organization Must Do Because of Social Media," Forrester, May 11, 2010, **http://blogs.forrester.com/augie_ray/10-05-11-seven_things_your_organi zation_must_do_because_social_media**; Jennifer Van Grove, "Nestle Meets Greenpeace's Demand Following Social Media Backlash," mashable, May 2010, **http://mashable.com/2010/05/17/nestle-social-media-fallout**; Caroline McCarthy, "Nestle Mess Shows Sticky Side of Facebook Pages," cnet news, March 9, 2010, **http://news.cnet.com/8301-13577_3-20000805-36.html** (all accessed April 13, 2011).

77. Li and Bernoff, *Groundswell*, p. 41.

78. Ibid., pp. 41–42.

79. Ibid., p. 44.

80. Ibid., pp. 44–45.

81. Rebecca MacLary, "New Canadian User Friendly Crowdfunding and Crowdsourcing Apps," Daily Crowdsource website, **http://dailycrowdsource.com/crowdsourcing/company-reviews/341-new-canadian-user-friendly-crowdfunding-and-crowdsourcing-apps** (accessed July 17, 2013).

82. Mya Frazier, "CrowdSourcing," *Delta Sky Mag,* February 2010, p. 70.

83. Li and Bernoff, *Groundswell,* pp. 26–27.

84. Sarah Nassauer, "'I Hate My Room,' The Traveler Tweeted. Ka-Boom! An Upgrade!" *The Wall Street Journal,* June 24, 2010, p. D1.

85. Melissa Harris, "Viewpoints Network Snags Client, Enhances Its Long-Term Outlook," *Chicago Tribune,* May 23, 2010, **http://articles.chicagotribune.com/2010-05-23/business/ct-biz-0523-confidential-viewpoints-20100523_1_autistic-adults-business-plan-venture-capitalists** (accessed April 13, 2011); Michael Krauss, "Moog Synthesizes Social Media," *Marketing News,* September 30, 2010, pp. 10.

86. "Why Social Media Marketing?", Digital Visitor website, **http://www.digitalvisitor.com/why-social-media-marketing/** (accessed July 30, 2013).

87. John W. Miller, "Yahoo Cookie Plan in Place," *The Wall Street Journal,* March 19, 2011, **http://online.wsj.com/article/SB10001424052748703512404576208700813815570.html** (accessed April 11, 2011).

88. Jon Swartz, "Facebook Changes Its Status in Washington," *USA Today,* January 13, 2011, pp. 1B–2B; "Details of 100 Million Facebook Users Published Online," *MSNBC.com,* July 29, 2010, **www.msnbc.msn.com/id/38463013/ns/technology_and_science/?GT1=43001** (accessed July 29, 2010); Julia Angwin and Steve Stecklow, "'Scrapers' Dig Deep for Data on Web," *The Wall Street Journal,* October 12, 2010, pp. A1, A18.

89. Quentin Hardy, "In Mark We Trust," *Forbes,* October 11, 2010, pp. 81–86; Swartz, "Facebook Changes Its Status in Washington," pp. 1B–2B.

90. Jennifer Valentino-DeVries, "Ad Industry Takes Another Look At 'Do-Not-Track' in Browsers," *The Wall Street Journal,* March 31, 2011, p. B5.

91. "About TRUSTe," TRUSTe website, **www.truste.com/about_TRUSTe/index.html** (accessed April 13, 2011).

92. Better Business Bureau Online, **www.bbbonline.org/** (accessed April 13, 2011).

93. Larry Barrett, "Data Breach Costs Surge in 2009: Study," *eSecurityPlanet,* January 26, 2010, **www.esecurityplanet.com/features/article.php/3860811/Data-Breach-Costs-Surgein-2009-Study.htm** (accessed April 13, 2011).

94. Steve Rennie, "Government Faces Class-Action Lawsuits Over Student Loan Borrowers' Lost Data," *The Globe and Mail* online, January 17, 2013, **http://www.theglobeandmail.com/news/politics/government-faces-class-action-lawsuits-over-student-loan-borrowers-lost-data/article7492261/** (accessed July 30, 2013).

95. Sarah E. Needleman, "Social-Media Con Game," *The Wall Street Journal,* October 12, 2009, p. R4.

96. "Facebook Takes Strong Stance Against Haiti Fraud," *Media Street,* January 19, 2010, **www.www.media-street.co.uk/blog/facebook-takes-strong-stance-against-haiti-fraud** (accessed April 19, 2011).

97. Brad Stone and Bruce Einhorn, "Baidu China," *Bloomberg Businessweek,* November 15–21, 2010, pp. 60–67.

98. Abigail Field, "Viacom v. YouTube/Google: A Piracy Case in Their Own Words," *Daily Finance,* March 21, 2010, **www.dailyfinance.com/story/company-news/viacom-v-youtube-google-a-piracy-case-in-their-ownwords/19407896/** (accessed April 13, 2011).

99. Kevin Shanahan and Mike Hyman "Motivators and Enablers of SCOURing," *Journal of Business Research* 63 (September–October 2010), pp. 1095–1102.

100. Seventh Annual BSA and IDC Global Software Piracy Study," BSA, **http://portal.bsa.org/globalpiracy2009/index.html** (accessed April 13, 2011).

101. Max Chafkin, "The Case, and the Plan, for the Virtual Company," *Inc.,* April 2010, p. 68.

102. Dan Macsai and Zachary Wilson, "When Brands Go Social," *Fast Company,* December 2009/January 2010, p. 77; Brad Stone, "Ads Posted on Facebook Strike Some as Off-Key," *The New York Times,* March 3, 2010, **www.nytimes.com/2010/03/04/technology/04facebook.html**; Emily Bryson York, "McDonald's to Use Facebook's Upcoming Location Feature," *AdvertisingAge,* May 6, 2010, **http://adage.com/digital/article?article_id=143742**; Benny Evangelista, "Twitter Puts Ads in Mix of Tweets," Sfgate, April 14, 2010, **http://articles.sfgate.com/2010-04-14/business/20848338_1_twitter-users-tweets-biz-stone**; John Yates, "Using Twitter, Facebook to Submit Consumer Complaints," *Chicago Tribune,* April 23, 2010, **http://newsblogs.chicagotribune.com/the-problem-solver/2010/04/social-media-as-a-consumercomplaint-avenue.html**; Kit Eaton, "Fox's Twitter TV Experiment Tweets Its Way to Epic Failure," *Fast Company,* September 4, 2009, **http://www.fastcompany.com/1347437/foxs-twitter-tv-experiment-tweets-its-way-epic-failure**; "Twitter Snags over 100 Million Users, Eyes Money-Making," *The Economic Times,* April 15, 2010, **http://economictimes.indiatimes.com/infotech/internet/Twitter-snags-over-100-million-users-eyes-money-making/articleshow/5808927.cms** (all accessed April 13, 2011); "Hello World," April 13, 2010, **http://blog.twitter.com/2010/04/hello-world.html** (accessed June 4, 2010).

Chapter 14

1. Source: Adapted from Financial & Assurance Standards Canada, **http://www.frascanada.ca/index.aspx** (accessed January 22, 2013).

2. *Report to the Nations: 2010 Global Fraud Study,* **www.acfe.com/rttn/rttn-2010.pdf** (accessed April 26, 2011).

3. **www.acfe.com/about/press-release-04-25-2007.asp; http://eweb.acfe.com/eweb/DynamicPage.aspx?Site=ACFE&WebCode=ChapterList** (accessed August 20, 2009); About—Association of Certified Fraud Examiners, **http://www.acfe.com/about/about.asp** (accessed June 18, 2007).

4. "Sustainability," Chartered Accountants of Canada website, **http://www.cica.ca/focus-on-practice-areas/sustainability/item61279.aspx**; "CIMA, AICPA and CICA release

global survey findings on accounting for sustainability practices" Chartered Institute of Management Accountants," December 16, 2010, **http://www.cimaglobal.com/About-us/Press-office/Press-releases/2010/December-2010/CIMA-AICPA-and-CICA-release-global-survey-findings-on-accounting-for-sustainability-practices/**; "Sustainability, Reporting and Assurance," American Institute of CPAs (AICPA) website, **http://www.aicpa.org/INTERESTAREAS/BUSINESSINDUSTRYANDGOVERNMENT/RESOURCES/SUSTAINABILITY/Pages/Sustainability%20Accounting,%20Reporting,%20Assurance%20and%20Other%20Services.aspx** (all accessed July 18, 2013).

5. *Report to the Nations: 2010 Global Fraud Study,* **www.acfe.com/rttn/rttn-2010.pdf** (accessed April 26, 2011).

6. Evelyn M. Rusli and Peter Eavis, "Facebook Raises $16 Billion in I.P.O.," *The New York Times,* May 17, 2012, **http://dealbook.nytimes.com/2012/05/17/facebook-raises-16-billion-in-i-p-o-/?hp** (accessed May 25, 2012); Brad Stone and Douglas MacMillan, "How Zuck Hacked the Valley," *Bloomberg Businessweek,* May 21–May 27, 2012, pp. 60–67; Facebook Newsroom, **http://newsroom.fb.com/content/default.aspx?NewsAreaId=22** (accessed May 25, 2012); "Facebook IPO Fallout Continues," The Washington Post, May 24, 2012, **www.washingtonpost.com/business/economy/facebook-ipo-fallout-continues/2012/05/24/gJQAJcTxnU_story.html** (accessed May 25, 2012); Brett Philbin and David Benoit, "Morgan Stanley Revisits Facebook Trades; Investors File Suit," *The Wall Street Journal,* **http://online.wsj.com/article/SB10001424052702304707604577422063685311108.html?KEYWORDS=Investors+File+Suit+Against+Facebook** (accessed May 25, 2012).

7. Bureau of Labor Statistics, "Accountants and Auditors," Occupational Outlook Handbook 2010–2011, **www.bls.gov/oco/ocos001.htm** (accessed April 26, 2011).

8. Adapted from: **www.icao.on.ca/CA/CompensationSurvey/page4862.aspx** (accessed August 20, 2009).

9. Kate O'Sullivan, "From Adversity, Better Budgets," *CFO Magazine,* June 2010, pp. 45–47; Jack Sweeny, "UPS CFO Spies a Silver Lining," *Business Finance,* March 10, 2010, **www.businessfinancemag.com/article/ups-cfo-spies-silver-lining-0310** (accessed October 8, 2010).

Chapter 15

1. Michael Lev-Ram, "A Twitter Guy Takes on Banks," *Fortune,* February 7, 2011, pp. 37–42; Jason Tanz, "Twitter Cofounder Shakes Up the Credit Card Biz," *Wired,* May 17, 2011, **www.wired.com/magazine/2011/05/mf_qadorsey/all/1**; Dan Fletcher, "The 50 Best Inventions of 2010," *Time,* November 11, 2010, **www.time.com/time/specials/packages/article/0,28804,2029497_2030652_2029712,00.html** (both accessed November 2, 2011); Karsten Strauss, "The New Billionaire Behind Twitter And Square: Jack Dorsey," *Forbes* online, July 25, 2012, **www.forbes.com/sites/karstenstrauss/2012/07/25/the-new-billionaire-behind-twitter-and-square-jack-dorsey/** (accessed July 18, 2013); **http://en.wikipedia.org/wiki/Jack_Dorsey** (accessed January 21, 2012).

2. Bank of Canada, **"Polymer Series (2011),"** **www.bankofcanada.ca/banknotes/bank-note-series/polymer/** (accessed January 21, 2012).

3. Royal Canadian Mint, "Phasing out the Penny," **www.mint.ca/store/mint/learn/phasing-out-the-penny-6900002**, (accessed January 21, 2012).

4. **www.desjardins.com/en/a_propos/etudes_economiques/actualites/point_vue_economique/pve70215.pdf** (accessed August 20, 2009).

5. Financial Consumer Agency of Canada, "New Credit Card Rules," **www.fcac-acfc.gc.ca/eng/partners/campaign/rulescc/index-eng.asp** (accessed January 21, 2012).

6. **www.bankofcanada.ca/en/about/currency.html** (accessed August 20, 2009).

7. **www.bankofcanada.ca/en/financial/financial_system.html** (accessed August 20, 2009).

8. **www.bankofcanada.ca/en/about/funds.html** (accessed August 20, 2009).

9. **www.cba.ca/en/section.asp?fl=2&sl=204&tl=&docid** (accessed August 20, 2009).

10. **http://www.fin.gc.ca/toc/2005/fact-cfss-eng.asp** (accessed August 9, 2010).

11. **http://www.fin.gc.ca/toc/2005/fact-cfss-eng.asp** (accessed August 9, 2010).

12. **www.cdic.ca/1/2/1/8/index1.shtml** (accessed August 20, 2009).

13. Sarah Kessler, "For Sale: A Young Entrepreneur's Future Income," *Inc.,* May 2010, p. 23; **www.thrustfund.com**; Kim-Mai Cutler, "Entrepreneurs Offer Their Life's Future Earnings for an Investment," Deals & More, March 3, 2010, **deals.venturebeat.com/2010/03/03/life-investment**; Marcia Stepanek, "Three Social Entrepreneurs Sell Shares in Selves to Scale," Stanford Social Innovation, January 14, 2010, **www.ssireview.org/opinion/entry/three_social_entrepreneurs_sell_shares_in_selves_to_scale**; Saul Garlick, "Invest in Me, Take My Equity," social edge, January 2010, **www.socialedge.org/discussions/funding/invest-in-me-take-my-equity** (all accessed April 26, 2011).

14. **www.fin.gc.ca/toce/1999/banke.html** (accessed August 20, 2009).

15. Laura Kane, "Why Credit Unions Could Gain from Shrinking Direct Banking Market," *Toronto Star* online, March 24, 2013, **http://www.thestar.com/business/personal_finance/2013/03/24/why_credit_unions_could_gain_from_shrinking_direct_banking_market.html** (accessed July 18, 2013); Jane J. Kim, "Credit Unions: A Better Bet Than Banks?" *The Wall Street Journal,* June 5–6, 2010, p. B8; Bankrate.com, "Are Credit Unions Better Than Banks?" Bankrate.com, **www.bankrate.com/finance/savings/are-credit-unions-better-than-banks.aspx**; Mark Maremont and Victoria McGrane, "Credit Unions Bailed Out," *The Wall Street Journal,* September 25, 2010, **http://online.wsj.com/article/SB10001424052748703499960457551225 4063682236.html** (both accessed November 15, 2010).

Chapter 16

1. Lori McLeod, "Lee-Chin Steps Aside At Beleaguered AIC," with files from Jonathan Chevreau, CanWest News, Oct 6, 2006, p. 1; Matthew S. Scott, "Buy, Hold, And Prosper," *Black Enterprise,* Aug 2002, Vol. 33 (1), p. 68; Jonathan Ratner, "Michael Lee-Chin on the comeback," *Financial Post,* Friday, Apr. 16, 2010, **http://www.financialpost.com/story.html?id=2913175** (accessed July 13, 2010).

2. **http://ycombinator.com** (accessed September 15, 2010); Ira Sager, Kimberly Weisul, and Spencer Ante, "Tech Investing: How Smart Is the Smart Money?" *Bloomberg Businessweek*, February 2010, **http://images.businessweek.com/ss/10/02/0225_angel_investors/12.htm** (accessed October 7, 2010); Om Malik, "Notes From a Conversation With Y Combinator's Paul Graham," *Gigaom*, February 1, 2010, **http://gigaom.com/2010/02/01/ycombinator-paul-graham/** (accessed September 20, 2010); Paul Graham, "A New Venture Animal," March 2008, **www.paulgraham.com/ycombinator.html** (accessed June 20, 2009); Sean Ellis, "Y Combinator Hatches Brilliant Entrepreneurs," Start Up Marketing Blog by Sean Ellis," December 2, 2008, **http://startup-marketing.com/y-combinator-hatches-brilliant-entrepreneurs/** (accessed June 20, 2009); Andy Louis-Charles, "Ignore Y Combinator at Your Own Risk," *The Motley Fool*, April 28, 2009, **www.fool.com/investing/general/2009/04/28/ignore-y-combinator-at-your-own-risk.aspx** (accessed June 20, 2009); Josh Quittner, "The New Internet Start-Up Boom: Get Rich Slow," *Time*, April 9, 2009, **www.time.com/time/magazine/article/0,9171,1890387-1,00.html** (accessed June 20, 2009).

3. Financial information, Apple, Inc., **http://finance.yahoo.com/q?s = AAPL** (accessed April 8, 2011).

4. "Chris DeWolfe & Tom Anderson, MySpace.com," *Entrepreneurs*, *BusinessWeek*, December 19, 2005, p. 66; Janet Kornblum, "Teens Hang Out at MySpace," *USA Today*, January 8, 2006, **www.usatoday.com/tech/news/2006-01-08-myspace-teens_x.htm** (accessed January 15, 2006); Richard Siklos, "News Corp. to Acquire Owner of MySpace.com," *The New York Times*, July 18, 2005, **www.nytimes.com/2005/07/18/business/18cnd-newscorp.html?ei=5090&en=33422c62f772785c&ex=1279339200&partner=rssuserland&emc=rss&pagewanted=print** (accessed January 15, 2006).

5. Vincent Ryan, "From Wall Street to Main Street," *CFO Magazine*, June 2008, pp. 85–86.

6. David Hall, "The Morning Ledger: Women CFOs Winning Outside Board Seats," *CFO Journal* online, July 16, 2013 **http://blogs.wsj.com/cfo/2013/07/16/the-morning-ledger-women-cfos-winning-outside-board-seats/** (accessed July 18, 2013); Marielle Segarra, "Taking the Next Step," *CFO*, July 15, 2011, **www.cfo.com/article.cfm/14586563?f 5 singlepage** (accessed November 3, 2011); Dan Fitzpatrick and Lisa Rappaport, "Financial Firms' Ceiling," *The Wall Street Journal*, September 8, 2011, **http://online.wsj.com/article/SB1000142405311190410340457655710038402620.html?KEYWORDS5Financial1Firms%275Ceiling** (accessed November 3, 2011); Kyle Stock, "Ranks of Women on Wall Street Thin," *The Wall Street Journal*, September 20, 2010, **http://online.wsj.com/article/SB1000142405274870485830457549807173213670 4.html** (accessed November 3, 2011).

7. Hershey Trust, "About Hershey Trust Company" (n.d.), **www.hersheytrust.com/cornerstones/about.shtml** (accessed March 26, 2006); O. C. Ferrell, "Hershey Foods' Ethics and Social Responsibility," case developed for classroom use, Colorado State University, revised edition, 2004; Hershey Foods, "Frequently Asked Questions," (n.d.), **www.hersheyinvestorrelations.com/ireye/ir_site.zhtml?ticker5HSY&script51801** (accessed June 10, 2004), "Company History," **www.hersheys.com/discover/history/company.asp** (accessed March 27, 2006); William C. Smith, "Seeing to the Business of Fun: Franklin A. Miles Jr., Hershey Entertainment & Resorts Co.," *National Law Journal*, December 22, 2003, p. 8; "Funding the School Trust," **www.hersheys.com/discover/milton/fund_school_trust.asp** (accessed March 27, 2006).

PHOTO CREDITS

GLOSSARY

absolute advantage a monopoly that exists when a country is the only source of an item, the only producer of an item, or the most efficient producer of an item (p. 64)

accessibility allows consumers to find information about competing products, prices, and reviews and become more informed about a firm and the relative value of its products (p. 309)

accountability the principle that employees who accept an assignment and the authority to carry it out are answerable to a superior for the outcome (p. 169)

accountant a professional who has met the education, examination, and experience requirements set by the professional society and association—such as the Certified General Accountants Association of Canada, the Canadian Institute of Chartered Accountants (Ordre des comptables agréés in Quebec), and CMA Canada—of which they are a member (p. 334)

accounting the recording, measurement, and interpretation of financial information (p. 334)

accounting cycle the four-step procedure of an accounting system: examining source documents, recording transactions in an accounting journal, posting recorded transactions, and preparing financial statements (p. 339)

accounting equation assets equal liabilities plus owners' equity (p. 337)

accounts payable the amount a company owes to suppliers for goods and services purchased with credit (p. 344)

accounts receivable money owed a company by its clients or customers who have promised to pay for the products at a later date (p. 344)

accrued expenses an account representing all unpaid financial obligations incurred by the organization (p. 347)

acquisition the purchase of one company by another, usually by buying its shares (p. 102)

addressability the ability of a business to identify customers before they make purchases (p. 309)

administrative managers those who manage an entire business or a major segment of a business; they are not specialists but coordinate the activities of specialized managers (p. 152)

advertising a paid form of nonpersonal communication transmitted through a mass medium, such as television commercials or magazine advertisements (p. 291)

advertising campaign designing a series of advertisements and placing them in various media to reach a particular target market (p. 291)

agenda a calendar, containing both specific and vague items, that covers short-term goals and long-term objectives (p. 158)

analytical skills the ability to identify relevant issues, recognize their importance, understand the relationships between them, and perceive the underlying causes of a situation (p. 155)

angel investors private investors who supply equity financing for businesses (p. 127)

annual report summary of a firm's financial information, products, and growth plans for owners and potential investors (p. 336)

arbitration settlement of a labour/management dispute by a third party whose solution is legally binding and enforceable (p. 239)

Asia-Pacific Economic Cooperation (APEC) community established in 1989 to promote international trade and facilitate business; as of 2013, has 21 member countries (p. 74)

asset utilization ratios ratios that measure how well a firm uses its assets to generate each $1 of sales (p. 349)

assets a firm's economic resources, or items of value that it owns, such as cash, inventory, land, equipment, buildings, and other tangible and intangible things (p. 337)

attitude knowledge and positive or negative feelings about something (p. 264)

automated banking machine (ABM) the most familiar form of electronic banking, which dispenses cash, accepts deposits, and allows balance inquiries and cash transfers from one account to another (p. 368)

balance of payments the difference between the flow of money into and out of a country (p. 65)

balance of trade the difference in value between a nation's exports and its imports (p. 65)

balance sheet a "snapshot" of an organization's financial position at a given moment (p. 344)

Bank of Canada an independent agency of the federal government established in 1934 to regulate the nation's banking and financial industry (p. 362)

bank rate the rate of interest the Bank of Canada charges to loan money to any banking institution to meet reserve requirements (p. 363)

behaviour modification changing behaviour and encouraging appropriate actions by relating the consequences of behaviour to the behaviour itself (p. 215)

benefits nonfinancial forms of compensation provided to employees, such as pension plans, health insurance, paid vacation and holidays, and the like (p. 237)

blog a Web-based journal in which a writer can editorialize and interact with other Internet users (p. 314)

board of directors a group of individuals, elected by the shareholders to oversee the general operation of the corporation, who set the corporation's long-range objectives (p. 97)

bonds debt instruments that larger companies sell to raise long-term funds (p. 382)

bonuses monetary rewards offered by companies for exceptional performance as incentives to further increase productivity (p. 235)

boycott an attempt to keep people from purchasing the products of a company (p. 239)

branding the process of naming and identifying products (p. 280)

bribes payments, gifts, or special favours intended to influence the outcome of a decision (p. 38)

brokerage firms firms that buy and sell stocks, bonds, and other securities for their customers and provide other financial services (p. 367)

budget an internal financial plan that forecasts expenses and income over a set period of time (p. 335)

budget deficit the condition in which a nation spends more than it takes in from taxes (p. 17)

budget surplus the condition in which a nation spends less than it takes in from taxes (p. 17)

business individuals or organizations who try to earn a profit by providing products that satisfy people's needs (p. 4)

business ethics principles and standards that determine acceptable conduct in business (p. 31)

business plan a precise statement of the rationale for a business and a step-by-step explanation of how it will achieve its goals (p. 124)

business products products that are used directly or indirectly in the operation or manufacturing processes of businesses (p. 277)

buying behaviour the decision processes and actions of people who purchase and use products (p. 262)

Canada Deposit Insurance Corporation (CDIC) a federal crown corporation that insures bank accounts (p. 365)

capacity the maximum load that an organizational unit can carry or operate (p. 189)

capital budgeting the process of analyzing the needs of the business and selecting the assets that will maximize its value (p. 381)

capitalism, or free enterprise an economic system in which individuals own and operate the majority of businesses that provide goods and services (p. 12)

cartel a group of firms or nations that agree to act as a monopoly and not compete with each other, in order to generate a competitive advantage in world markets (p. 70)

cash flow the movement of money through an organization over a daily, weekly, monthly, or yearly basis (p. 335)

centralized organization a structure in which authority is concentrated at the top, and very little decision-making authority is delegated to lower levels (p. 170)

certificate of incorporation a legal document that the provincial or federal government issues to a company based on information the company provides in the articles of incorporation (p. 95)

certificates of deposit (CDs) savings accounts that guarantee a depositor a set interest rate over a specified interval as long as the funds are not withdrawn before the end of the period—six months or one year, for example (p. 360)

chartered banks the largest and oldest of all financial institutions, relying mainly on chequing and savings accounts as sources of funds for loans to businesses and individuals (p. 364)

chequing account money stored in an account at a bank or other financial institution that can be withdrawn without advance notice; also called a demand deposit (p. 360)

classical theory of motivation theory suggesting that money is the sole motivator for workers (p. 208)

codes of ethics formalized rules and standards that describe what a company expects of its employees (p. 44)

collective bargaining the negotiation process through which management and unions reach an agreement about compensation, working hours, and working conditions for the bargaining unit (p. 238)

commercial certificates of deposit (CDs) certificates of deposit issued by commercial banks and brokerage companies, available in minimum amounts of $100,000, which may be traded prior to maturity (p. 377)

commercial paper a written promise from one company to another to pay a specific amount of money (p. 377)

commercialization the full introduction of a complete marketing strategy and the launch of the product for commercial success (p. 276)

commission an incentive system that pays a fixed amount or a percentage of the employee's sales (p. 235)

committee a permanent, formal group that performs a specific task (p. 174)

common shares shares whose owners have voting rights in the corporation, yet do not receive preferential treatment regarding dividends (p. 98)

communism first described by Karl Marx as a society in which the people, without regard to class, own all the nation's resources (p. 10)

comparative advantage the basis of most international trade, when a country specializes in products that it can supply more efficiently or at a lower cost than it can produce other items (p. 64)

competition the rivalry among businesses for consumers' dollars (p. 14)

compressed workweek a four-day (or shorter) period during which an employee works 40 hours (p. 218)

computer-assisted design (CAD) the design of components, products, and processes on computers instead of on paper (p. 191)

computer-assisted manufacturing (CAM) manufacturing that employs specialized computer systems to actually guide and control the transformation processes (p. 191)

computer-integrated manufacturing (CIM) a complete system that designs products, manages machines and materials, and controls the operations function (p. 192)

concentration approach a market segmentation approach whereby a company develops one marketing strategy for a single market segment (p. 255)

conceptual skills the ability to think in abstract terms and to see how parts fit together to form the whole (p. 154)

conciliation a method of outside resolution of labour and management differences in which a third party is brought in to keep the two sides talking (p. 239)

connectivity the use of digital networks to provide linkages between information providers and users (p. 310)

consumer products products intended for household or family use (p. 277)

consumerism the activities that independent individuals, groups, and organizations undertake to protect their rights as consumers (p. 48)

continuous manufacturing organizations companies that use continuously running assembly lines, creating products with many similar characteristics (p. 191)

contract manufacturing the hiring of a foreign company to produce a specified volume of the initiating company's product to specification; the final product carries the domestic firm's name (p. 77)

control consumers' ability to regulate the information they receive via the Internet, and the rate and sequence of their exposure to that information (p. 310)

controlling the process of evaluating and correcting activities to keep the organization on course (p. 146)

cooperative or co-op an organization composed of individuals or small businesses that have banded together to reap the benefits of belonging to a larger organization (p. 100)

corporate citizenship the extent to which businesses meet the legal, ethical, economic, and voluntary responsibilities placed on them by their stakeholders (p. 46)

corporation a legal entity, whose assets and liabilities are separate from its owners (p. 94)

cost of goods sold the amount of money a firm spent to buy or produce the products it sold during the period to which the income statement applies (p. 341)

countertrade agreements foreign trade agreements that involve bartering products for other products instead of for currency (p. 76)

credit cards means of access to preapproved lines of credit granted by a bank or finance company (p. 361)

credit controls the authority to establish and enforce credit rules for financial institutions and some private investors (p. 363)

credit union/caisse populaire a financial institution owned and controlled by its depositors, who usually have a common employer, profession, trade group, or religion (p. 365)

crisis management or contingency planning an element in planning that deals with potential disasters such as product tampering, oil spills, fires, earthquakes, computer viruses, or airplane crashes (p. 144)

crown corporations corporations owned and operated by government (federal or provincial) (p. 96)

culture the integrated, accepted pattern of human behaviour, including thought, speech, beliefs, actions, and artifacts (p. 265)

current assets assets that are used or converted into cash within the course of a calendar year (p. 344)

current liabilities a firm's financial obligations to short-term creditors, which must be repaid within one year (p. 344)

current ratio current assets divided by current liabilities (p. 350)

customer departmentalization the arrangement of jobs around the needs of various types of customers (p. 169)

customization making products to meet a particular customer's needs or wants (p. 189)

debit card a card that looks like a credit card but works like a cheque; using it results in a direct, immediate, electronic payment from the cardholder's chequing account to a merchant or third party (p. 361)

debt to total assets ratio a ratio indicating how much of the firm is financed by debt and how much by owners' equity (p. 350)

debt utilization ratios ratios that measure how much debt an organization is using relative to other sources of capital, such as owners' equity (p. 350)

decentralized organization an organization in which decision-making authority is delegated as far down the chain of command as possible (p. 170)

delegation of authority giving employees not only tasks, but also the power to make commitments, use resources, and take whatever actions are necessary to carry out those tasks (p. 169)

demand the number of goods and services that consumers are willing to buy at different prices at a specific time (p. 13)

departmentalization the grouping of jobs into working units usually called departments, units, groups, or divisions (p. 167)

depreciation the process of spreading the costs of long-lived assets such as buildings and equipment over the total number of accounting periods in which they are expected to be used (p. 342)

depression a condition of the economy in which unemployment is very high, consumer spending is low, and business output is sharply reduced (p. 16)

desired reserves the percentage of deposits that banking institutions hold in reserve (p. 363)

development training that augments the skills and knowledge of managers and professionals (p. 231)

digital marketing uses all digital media, including the Internet and mobile and interactive channels, to develop communication and exchanges with customers (p. 308)

digital media electronic media that function using digital codes via computers, cellular phones, smartphones, and other digital devices that have been released in recent years (p. 308)

direct investment the ownership of overseas facilities (p. 78)

directing motivating and leading employees to achieve organizational objectives (p. 146)

discounts temporary price reductions, often employed to boost sales (p. 285)

diversity the participation of different ages, genders, races, ethnicities, nationalities, and abilities in the workplace (p. 240)

dividend yield the dividend per share divided by the stock price (p. 385)

dividends profits of a corporation that are distributed in the form of cash payments to shareholders (p. 94)

dividends per share the actual cash received for each share owned (p. 351)

double-entry bookkeeping a system of recording and classifying business transactions that maintains the balance of the accounting equation (p. 338)

downsizing the elimination of a significant number of employees from an organization (p. 145)

dumping the act of a country or business selling products at less than what it costs to produce them (p. 69)

e-business carrying out the goals of business through utilization of the Internet (p. 308)

earnings per share net income or profit divided by the number of stock shares outstanding (p. 350)

economic contraction a slowdown of the economy characterized by a decline in spending and during which businesses cut back on production and lay off workers (p. 15)

economic expansion the situation that occurs when an economy is growing and people are spending more money; their purchases stimulate the production of goods and services, which in turn stimulates employment (p. 15)

economic order quantity (EOQ) model a model that identifies the optimum number of items to order to minimize the costs of managing (ordering, storing, and using) them (p. 194)

economic system a description of how a particular society distributes its resources to produce goods and services (p. 10)

economics the study of how resources are distributed for the production of goods and services within a social system (p. 9)

electronic funds transfer (EFT) any movement of funds by means of an electronic terminal, telephone, computer, or magnetic tape (p. 368)

embargo a prohibition on trade in a particular product (p. 69)

entrepreneurship the process of creating and managing a business to achieve desired objectives (p. 113)

equilibrium price the price at which the number of products that businesses are willing to supply equals the amount of products that consumers are willing to buy at a specific point in time (p. 13)

equity theory an assumption that how much people are willing to contribute to an organization depends on their assessment of the fairness, or equity, of the rewards they will receive in exchange (p. 214)

esteem needs the need for respect—both self-respect and respect from others (p. 210)

ethical issue an identifiable problem, situation, or opportunity that requires a person to choose from among several actions that may be evaluated as right or wrong, ethical or unethical (p. 35)

eurodollar market a market for trading U.S. dollars in foreign countries (p. 377)

European Union (EU) community established in 1958 to promote trade within Europe; as of 2013, has 27 member countries (p. 73)

exchange the act of giving up one thing (money, credit, labour, goods) in return for something else (goods, services, or ideas) (p. 248)

exchange controls regulations that restrict the amount of currency that can be bought or sold (p. 68)

exchange rate the ratio at which one nation's currency can be exchanged for another nation's currency (p. 66)

exclusive distribution the awarding by a manufacturer to an intermediary of the sole right to sell a product in a defined geographic territory (p. 289)

expectancy theory the assumption that motivation depends not only on how much a person wants something but also on how likely he or she is to get it (p. 215)

expenses the costs incurred in the day-to-day operations of an organization (p. 342)

exporting the sale of goods and services to foreign markets (p. 65)

external shocks unanticipated events that occur in a firm's external environment that hurt the company's business (p. 122)

extrinsic reward benefits and/or recognition received from someone else (p. 206)

factor a finance company to which businesses sell their accounts receivable—usually for a percentage of the total face value (p. 380)

finance the study of money; how it's made, how it's lost, and how it's managed (p. 357)

finance companies businesses that offer short-term loans at substantially higher rates of interest than banks (p. 368)

financial managers those who focus on obtaining needed funds for the successful operation of an organization and using those funds to further organizational goals (p. 149)

financial resources the funds used to acquire the natural and human resources needed to provide products; also called capital (p. 10)

first-line managers those who supervise both workers and the daily operations of an organization (p. 149)

fixed-position layout a layout that brings all resources required to create the product to a central location (p. 190)

flexible manufacturing the direction of machinery by computers to adapt to different versions of similar operations (p. 191)

flextime a program that allows employees to choose their starting and ending times, provided that they are at work during a specified core period (p. 217)

floating-rate bonds bonds with interest rates that change with current interest rates otherwise available in the economy (p. 383)

franchise a licence to sell another's products or to use another's name in business, or both (p. 130)

franchisee the purchaser of a franchise (p. 130)

franchiser the company that sells a franchise (p. 130)

franchising a form of licensing in which a company—the franchiser—agrees to provide a franchisee a name, logo, methods of operation, advertising, products, and other elements associated with a franchiser's business, in return for a financial commitment and the agreement to conduct business in accordance with the franchiser's standard of operations (p. 77)

free-market system pure capitalism, in which all economic decisions are made without government intervention (p. 12)

functional departmentalization the grouping of jobs that perform similar functional activities, such as finance, manufacturing, marketing, and human resources (p. 168)

General Agreement on Tariffs and Trade (GATT) a trade agreement, originally signed by 23 nations in 1947, that provided a forum for tariff negotiations and a place where international trade problems could be discussed and resolved (p. 72)

general partnership a partnership that involves a complete sharing in both the management and the liability of the business (p. 89)

generic products products with no brand name that often come in simple packages and carry only their generic name (p. 282)

geographical departmentalization the grouping of jobs according to geographic location, such as state, region, country, or continent (p. 169)

global strategy (globalization) a strategy that involves standardizing products (and, as much as possible, their promotion and distribution) for the whole world, as if it were a single entity (p. 79)

grapevine an informal channel of communication, separate from management's formal, official communication channels (p. 177)

gross domestic product (GDP) the sum of all goods and services produced in a country during a year (p. 17)

gross income (or profit) revenues minus the cost of goods sold required to generate the revenues (p. 342)

group two or more individuals who communicate with one another, share a common identity, and have a common goal (p. 174)

human relations the study of the behaviour of individuals and groups in organizational settings (p. 206)

human relations skills the ability to deal with people, both inside and outside the organization (p. 155)

human resources the physical and mental abilities that people use to produce goods and services; also called labour (p. 10)

human resources management (HRM) all the activities involved in determining an organization's human resources needs, as well as acquiring, training, and compensating people to fill those needs (p. 226)

human resources managers those who handle the staffing function and deal with employees in a formalized manner (p. 150)

hygiene factors aspects of Herzberg's theory of motivation that focus on the work setting and not the content of the work; these aspects include adequate wages, comfortable and safe working conditions, fair company policies, and job security (p. 212)

identity theft when criminals obtain personal information that allows them to impersonate someone else in order to use their credit to access financial accounts and make purchases (p. 326)

import tariff a tax levied by a nation on goods imported into the country (p. 68)

importing the purchase of goods and services from foreign sources (p. 65)

income statement a financial report that shows an organization's profitability over a period of time—month, quarter, or year (p. 341)

inflation a condition characterized by a continuing rise in prices (p. 15)

information technology (IT) managers those who are responsible for implementing, maintaining, and controlling technology applications in business, such as computer networks (p. 150)

infrastructure the physical facilities that support a country's economic activities, such as railroads, highways, ports, airfields, utilities and power plants, schools, hospitals, communication systems, and commercial distribution systems (p. 66)

initial public offering (IPO) selling a corporation's shares on public markets for the first time (p. 95)

inputs the resources—such as labour, money, materials, and energy—that are converted into outputs (p. 184)

insurance companies businesses that protect their clients against financial losses from certain specified risks (death, accident, and theft, for example) (p. 366)

integrated marketing communications coordinating the promotion mix elements and synchronizing promotion as a unified effort (p. 291)

intensive distribution a form of market coverage whereby a product is made available in as many outlets as possible (p. 288)

interactivity allows customers to express their needs and wants directly to the firm in response to its communications (p. 309)

intermittent organizations organizations that deal with products of a lesser magnitude than do project organizations; their products are not necessarily unique but possess a significant number of differences (p. 190)

international business the buying, selling, and trading of goods and services across national boundaries (p. 64)

International Monetary Fund (IMF) organization established in 1947 to promote trade among member nations by eliminating trade barriers and fostering financial cooperation (p. 74)

intrapreneurs individuals in large firms who take responsibility for the development of innovations within the organizations (p. 134)

intrinsic reward the personal satisfaction and enjoyment felt from attaining a goal (p. 206)

inventory all raw materials, components, completed or partially completed products, and pieces of equipment a firm uses (p. 193)

inventory control the process of determining how many supplies and goods are needed and keeping track of quantities on hand, where each item is, and who is responsible for it (p. 194)

inventory turnover sales divided by total inventory (p. 349)

investment banking the sale of stocks and bonds for corporations (p. 385)

ISO 9000 a series of quality assurance standards designed by the International Organization for Standardization (ISO) to ensure consistent product quality under many conditions (p. 199)

ISO 14000 a comprehensive set of environmental management standards determined by the ISO that help companies attain and measure improvements in their environmental performance (p. 199)

job analysis the determination, through observation and study, of pertinent information about a job—including specific tasks and necessary abilities, knowledge, and skills (p. 226)

job description a formal, written explanation of a specific job, usually including job title, tasks, relationship with other jobs, physical and mental skills required, duties, responsibilities, and working conditions (p. 227)

job enlargement the addition of more tasks to a job instead of treating each task as separate (p. 217)

job enrichment the incorporation of motivational factors, such as opportunity for achievement, recognition, responsibility, and advancement, into a job (p. 217)

job promotion an advancement to a higher-level position with increased authority, responsibility, and pay (p. 233)

job rotation movement of employees from one job to another in an effort to relieve the boredom often associated with job specialization (p. 216)

job sharing performance of one full-time job by two people on part-time hours (p. 218)

job specification a description of the qualifications necessary for a specific job, in terms of education, experience, and personal and physical characteristics (p. 227)

joint venture a partnership established for a specific project or for a limited time involving the sharing of the costs and operation of a business, often between a foreign company and a local partner (pp. 78, 100)

journal a time-ordered list of account transactions (p. 339)

junk bonds a special type of high interest-rate bond that carries higher inherent risks (p. 384)

just-in-time (JIT) inventory management a technique using smaller quantities of materials that arrive "just in time" for use in the transformation process and therefore require less storage space and other inventory management expense (p. 194)

labelling the presentation of important information on a package (p. 282)

labour contract the formal, written document that spells out the relationship between the union and management for a specified period of time—usually two or three years (p. 238)

labour unions employee organizations formed to deal with employers for achieving better pay, hours, and working conditions (p. 238)

leadership the ability to influence employees to work toward organizational goals (p. 152)

learning changes in a person's behaviour based on information and experience (p. 263)

ledger a book or computer file with separate sections for each account (p. 339)

leveraged buyout (LBO) a purchase in which a group of investors borrows money from banks and other institutions to acquire a company (or a division of one), using the assets of the purchased company to guarantee repayment of the loan (p. 104)

liabilities debts that a firm owes to others (p. 337)

licensing a trade agreement in which one company—the licensor—allows another company—the licensee—to use its company name, products, patents, brands, trademarks, raw materials, and/or production processes in exchange for a fee or royalty (p. 76)

limited liability partnership LLP a partnership agreement where partners are not responsible for losses created by other partners (p. 90)

limited partnership a business organization that has at least one general partner, who assumes unlimited liability, and at least one limited partner, whose liability is limited to his or her investment in the business (p. 90)

line of credit an arrangement by which a bank agrees to lend a specified amount of money to an organization upon request (p. 379)

line structure the simplest organizational structure in which direct lines of authority extend from the top manager to the lowest level of the organization (p. 172)

line-and-staff structure a structure having a traditional line relationship between superiors and subordinates and also specialized managers—called staff managers—who are available to assist line managers (p. 172)

liquidity ratios ratios that measure the speed with which a company can turn its assets into cash to meet short-term debt (p. 350)

lockbox an address, usually a commercial bank, at which a company receives payments in order to speed collections from customers (p. 376)

lockout management's version of a strike, wherein a worksite is closed so that employees cannot go to work (p. 239)

long-term (fixed) assets production facilities (plants), offices, and equipment—all of which are expected to last for many years (p. 380)

long-term liabilities debts that will be repaid over a number of years, such as long-term loans and bond issues (p. 382)

management a process designed to achieve an organization's objectives by using its resources effectively and efficiently in a changing environment (p. 140)

managerial accounting the internal use of accounting statements by managers in planning and directing the organization's activities (p. 335)

managers those individuals in organizations who make decisions about the use of resources and who are concerned with planning, organizing, staffing, directing, and controlling the organization's activities to reach its objectives (p. 140)

manufacturer brands brands initiated and owned by the manufacturer to identify products from the point of production to the point of purchase (p. 281)

manufacturing the activities and processes used in making tangible products; also called production (p. 184)

market a group of people who have a need, purchasing power, and the desire and authority to spend money on goods, services, and ideas (p. 253)

market segment a collection of individuals, groups, or organizations who share one or more characteristics and thus have relatively similar product needs and desires (p. 254)

market segmentation a strategy whereby a firm divides the total market into groups of people who have relatively similar product needs (p. 254)

marketable securities temporary investment of "extra" cash by organizations for up to one year in Treasury bills, certificates of deposit, commercial paper, or eurodollar loans (p. 377)

marketing a group of activities designed to expedite transactions by creating, distributing, pricing, and promoting goods, services, and ideas (p. 248)

marketing channel a group of organizations that moves products from their producer to customers; also called a channel of distribution (p. 286)

marketing concept the idea that an organization should try to satisfy customers' needs through coordinated activities that also allow it to achieve its own goals (p. 249)

marketing managers those who are responsible for planning, pricing, and promoting products and making them available to customers (p. 150)

marketing mix the four marketing activities—product, price, promotion, and distribution—that the firm can control to achieve specific goals within a dynamic marketing environment (p. 256)

marketing orientation an approach requiring organizations to gather information about customer needs, share that information throughout the firm, and use that information to help build long-term relationships with customers (p. 252)

marketing research a systematic, objective process of getting information about potential customers to guide marketing decisions (p. 260)

marketing strategy a plan of action for developing, pricing, distributing, and promoting products that meet the needs of specific customers (p. 253)

Maslow's hierarchy a theory that arranges the five basic needs of people—physiological, security, social, esteem, and self-actualization—into the order in which people strive to satisfy them (p. 210)

material-requirements planning (MRP) a planning system that schedules the precise quantity of materials needed to make the product (p. 194)

materials handling the physical handling and movement of products in warehousing and transportation (p. 290)

matrix structure a structure that sets up teams from different departments, thereby creating two or more intersecting lines of authority; also called a project-management structure (p. 173)

mediation a method of outside resolution of labour and management differences in which the third party's role is to suggest or propose a solution to the problem (p. 239)

merger the combination of two companies (usually corporations) to form a new company (p. 102)

middle managers those members of an organization responsible for the tactical planning that implements the general guidelines established by top management (p. 148)

mission the statement of an organization's fundamental purpose and basic philosophy (p. 141)

mixed economies economies made up of elements from more than one economic system (p. 12)

mobile marketing using a mobile device to communicate marketing messages (p. 296)

modular design the creation of an item in self-contained units, or modules, that can be combined or interchanged to create different products (p. 188)

monetary policy means by which the Bank of Canada controls the amount of money available in the economy (p. 362)

money anything generally accepted in exchange for goods and services (p. 358)

money market accounts accounts that offer higher interest rates than standard bank rates but with greater restrictions (p. 360)

monopolistic competition the market structure that exists when there are fewer businesses than in a pure-competition environment and the differences among the goods they sell are small (p. 14)

monopoly the market structure that exists when there is only one business providing a product in a given market (p. 15)

morale an employee's attitude toward his or her job, employer, and colleagues (p. 206)

motivation an inner drive that directs a person's behaviour toward goals (p. 206)

motivational factors aspects of Herzberg's theory of motivation that focus on the content of the work itself; these aspects include achievement, recognition, involvement, responsibility, and advancement (p. 212)

multidivisional structure a structure that organizes departments into larger groups called divisions (p. 173)

multinational corporation (MNC) a corporation that operates on a worldwide scale, without significant ties to any one nation or region (p. 78)

multinational strategy a plan, used by international companies, that involves customizing products, promotion, and distribution according to cultural, technological, regional, and national differences (p. 79)

multisegment approach a market segmentation approach whereby the marketer aims its efforts at two or more segments, developing a marketing strategy for each (p. 255)

mutual fund an investment company that pools individual investor dollars and invests them in large numbers of well diversified securities (p. 367)

natural resources land, forests, minerals, water, and other things that are not made by people (p. 10)

net income (or net earnings) the total profit (or loss) after all expenses including taxes have been deducted from revenue (p. 342)

networking the building of relationships and sharing of information with colleagues who can help managers achieve the items on their agendas (p. 158)

nonprofit corporations corporations that focus on providing a service rather than earning a profit but are not owned by a government entity (p. 96)

nonprofit organizations groups that may provide goods or services but do not have the fundamental purpose of earning profits (p. 4)

North American Free Trade Agreement (NAFTA) agreement that eliminates most tariffs and trade restrictions on agricultural and manufactured products to encourage trade among Canada, the United States, and Mexico (p. 72)

offshoring the relocation of business processes by a company or subsidiary to another country; it differs from outsourcing because the company retains control of the offshored processes (p. 78)

oligopoly the market structure that exists when there are very few businesses selling a product (p. 15)

online fraud any attempt to conduct fraudulent activities online (p. 326)

open market operations decisions to buy or sell Treasury bills (short-term debt issued by the government) and other investments in the open market (p. 362)

operational plans very short-term plans that specify what actions individuals, work groups, or departments need to accomplish in order to achieve the tactical plan and ultimately the strategic plan (p. 144)

operations the activities and processes used in making both tangible and intangible products (p. 184)

operations management (OM) the development and administration of the activities involved in transforming resources into goods and services (p. 184)

organizational chart a visual display of the organizational structure, lines of authority (chain of command), staff relationships, permanent committee arrangements, and lines of communication (p. 165)

organizational culture a firm's shared values, beliefs, traditions, philosophies, rules, and role models for behaviour (p. 164)

organizational layers the levels of management in an organization (p. 171)

organizing the structuring of resources and activities to accomplish objectives in an efficient and effective manner (p. 145)

orientation familiarizing newly hired employees with fellow workers, company procedures, and the physical properties of the company (p. 230)

outputs the goods, services, and ideas that result from the conversion of inputs (p. 184)

outsourcing the transferring of manufacturing or other tasks—such as data processing—to countries where labour and supplies are less expensive (p. 65)

over-the-counter (OTC) market a network of dealers all over the country linked by computers, telephones, and Teletype machines (p. 387)

owners' equity equals assets minus liabilities and reflects historical values (p. 337)

packaging the external container that holds and describes the product (p. 282)

partnership a form of business organization defined as "an association of two or more persons who carry on as co-owners of a business for profit" (p. 89)

partnership agreement document that sets forth the basic agreement between partners (p. 90)

penetration price a low price designed to help a product enter the market and gain market share rapidly (p. 284)

pension funds managed investment pools set aside by individuals, corporations, unions, and some nonprofit organizations to provide retirement income for members (p. 366)

per share data data used by investors to compare the performance of one company with another on an equal, per share basis (p. 350)

perception the process by which a person selects, organizes, and interprets information received from his or her senses (p. 263)

personal selling direct, two-way communication with buyers and potential buyers (p. 296)

personality the organization of an individual's distinguishing character traits, attitudes, or habits (p. 264)

physical distribution all the activities necessary to move products from producers to customers—inventory control, transportation, warehousing, and materials handling (p. 289)

physiological needs the most basic human needs to be satisfied—water, food, shelter, and clothing (p. 210)

picketing a public protest against management practices that involves union members marching and carrying anti-management signs at the employer's plant (p. 239)

place/distribution making products available to customers in the quantities desired (p. 258)

plagiarism the act of taking someone else's work and presenting it as your own without mentioning the source (p. 43)

planning the process of determining the organization's objectives and deciding how to accomplish them; the first function of management (p. 141)

podcast an audio or video file that can be downloaded from the Internet with a subscription that automatically delivers new content to listening devices or personal computers (p. 317)

preferred shares a special type of share whose owners, though not generally having a say in running the company, have a claim to profits before other shareholders do (p. 98)

price a value placed on an object exchanged between a buyer and a seller (p. 258)

price skimming charging the highest possible price that buyers who want the product will pay (p. 284)

primary data marketing information that is observed, recorded, or collected directly from respondents (p. 261)

primary market the market where firms raise financial capital (p. 385)

prime rate the interest rate that commercial banks charge their best customers (usually large corporations) for short-term loans (p. 380)

private corporation a corporation owned by just one or a few people who are closely involved in managing the business (p. 95)

private distributor brands brands, which may cost less than manufacturer brands, that are owned and controlled by a wholesaler or retailer (p. 281)

process layout a layout that organizes the transformation process into departments that group related processes (p. 190)

product a good or service with tangible and intangible characteristics that provide satisfaction and benefits (p. 4)

product departmentalization the organization of jobs in relation to the products of the firm (p. 168)

product-development teams a specific type of project team formed to devise, design, and implement a new product (p. 175)

product layout a layout requiring that production be broken down into relatively simple tasks assigned to workers, who are usually positioned along an assembly line (p. 191)

product line a group of closely related products that are treated as a unit because of similar marketing strategy, production, or end-use considerations (p. 277)

product mix all the products offered by an organization (p. 277)

production the activities and processes used in making tangible products; also called manufacturing (p. 184)

production and operations managers those who develop and administer the activities involved in transforming resources into goods, services, and ideas ready for the marketplace (p. 149)

profit the difference between what it costs to make and sell a product and what a customer pays for it (p. 4)

profit margin net income divided by sales (p. 349)

profit sharing a form of compensation whereby a percentage of company profits is distributed to the employees whose work helped to generate them (p. 236)

profitability ratios ratios that measure the amount of operating income or net income an organization is able to generate relative to its assets, owners' equity, and sales (p. 349)

project organization a company using a fixed-position layout because it is typically involved in large, complex projects such as construction or exploration (p. 190)

project teams groups similar to task forces that normally run their operation and have total control of a specific work project (p. 175)

promotion a persuasive form of communication that attempts to expedite a marketing exchange by influencing individuals, groups, and organizations to accept goods, services, and ideas (p. 259)

promotional positioning the use of promotion to create and maintain an image of a product in buyers' minds (p. 300)

psychological pricing encouraging purchases based on emotional rather than rational responses to the price (p. 285)

public corporation a corporation whose shares anyone may buy, sell, or trade (p. 95)

publicity nonpersonal communication transmitted through the mass media but not paid for directly by the firm (p. 297)

pull strategy the use of promotion to create consumer demand for a product so that consumers exert pressure on marketing channel members to make it available (p. 299)

purchasing the buying of all the materials needed by the organization; also called procurement (p. 193)

pure competition the market structure that exists when there are many small businesses selling one standardized product (p. 14)

push strategy an attempt to motivate intermediaries to push the product down to their customers (p. 299)

quality the degree to which a good, service, or idea meets the demands and requirements of customers (p. 282)

quality-assurance teams (or quality circles) small groups of workers brought together from throughout the organization to solve specific quality, productivity, or service problems (p. 175)

quality control the processes an organization uses to maintain its established quality standards (p. 197)

quick ratio (acid test) a stringent measure of liquidity that eliminates inventory (p. 350)

quota a restriction on the number of units of a particular product that can be imported into a country (p. 69)

ratio analysis calculations that measure an organization's financial health (p. 347)

receivables turnover sales divided by accounts receivable (p. 349)

recession a decline in production, employment, and income (p. 16)

recruiting forming a pool of qualified applicants from which management can select employees (p. 227)

reference groups groups with whom buyers identify and whose values or attitudes they adopt (p. 265)

responsibility the obligation, placed on employees through delegation, to perform assigned tasks satisfactorily and be held accountable for the proper execution of work (p. 169)

retailers intermediaries who buy products from manufacturers (or other intermediaries) and sell them to consumers for home and household use rather than for resale or for use in producing other products (p. 286)

retained earnings earnings after expenses and taxes that are reinvested in the assets of the firm and belong to the owners in the form of equity (p. 385)

return on assets net income divided by assets (p. 349)

return on equity net income divided by owners' equity; also called return on investment (ROI) (p. 349)

revenue the total amount of money received from the sale of goods or services, as well as from related business activities (p. 341)

routing the sequence of operations through which the product must pass (p. 196)

salary a financial reward calculated on a weekly, monthly, or annual basis (p. 235)

sales promotion direct inducements offering added value or some other incentive for buyers to enter into an exchange (p. 298)

savings accounts accounts with funds that usually cannot be withdrawn without advance notice; also known as time deposits (p. 360)

scheduling the assignment of required tasks to departments or even specific machines, workers, or teams (p. 196)

secondary data information that is compiled inside or outside an organization for some purpose other than changing the current situation (p. 260)

secondary markets stock exchanges and over-the-counter markets where investors can trade their securities with others (p. 385)

secured bonds bonds that are backed by specific collateral that must be forfeited in the event that the issuing firm defaults (p. 383)

secured loans loans backed by collateral that the bank can claim if the borrowers do not repay them (p. 380)

securities markets the mechanism for buying and selling securities (p. 386)

security needs the need to protect oneself from physical and economic harm (p. 210)

selection the process of collecting information about applicants and using that information to make hiring decisions (p. 228)

selective distribution a form of market coverage whereby only a small number of all available outlets are used to expose products (p. 289)

self-actualization needs the need to be the best one can be; at the top of Maslow's hierarchy (p. 211)

self-directed work team (SDWT) a group of employees responsible for an entire work process or segment that delivers a product to an internal or external customer (p. 175)

separations employment changes involving resignation, retirement, termination, or layoff (p. 233)

serial bonds a sequence of small bond issues of progressively longer maturity (p. 383)

shares shares of a corporation that may be bought or sold (p. 94)

small business any independently owned and operated business that is not dominant in its competitive area and does not employ more than 500 people (p. 115)

social classes a ranking of people into higher or lower positions of respect (p. 265)

social needs the need for love, companionship, and friendship—the desire for acceptance by others (p. 210)

social network a Web-based meeting place for friends, family, co-workers, and peers that lets users create a profile and connect with other users for a wide range of purposes (p. 313)

social responsibility a business's obligation to maximize its positive impact and minimize its negative impact on society (p. 32)

social roles a set of expectations for individuals based on some position they occupy (p. 264)

socialism an economic system in which the government owns and operates basic industries but individuals own most businesses (p. 11)

sole proprietorships businesses owned and operated by one individual; the most common form of business organization in Canada (p. 86)

span of management the number of subordinates who report to a particular manager (p. 170)

specialization the division of labour into small, specific tasks and the assignment of employees to do a single task (p. 167)

staffing the hiring of people to carry out the work of the organization (p. 145)

stakeholders groups that have a stake in the success and outcomes of a business (p. 4)

standardization the making of identical interchangeable components or products (p. 188)

statement of cash flow explains how the company's cash changed from the beginning of the accounting period to the end (p. 347)

statistical process control a system in which management collects and analyzes information about the production process to pinpoint quality problems in the production system (p. 198)

strategic alliance a partnership formed to create competitive advantage on a worldwide basis (p. 78)

strategic plans those plans that establish the long-range objectives and overall strategy or course of action by which a firm fulfills its mission (p. 142)

strikebreakers people hired by management to replace striking employees; called "scabs" by striking union members (p. 239)

strikes employee walkouts; one of the most effective weapons labour has (p. 239)

structure the arrangement or relationship of positions within an organization (p. 165)

supply the number of products—goods and services—that businesses are willing to sell at different prices at a specific time (p. 13)

supply chain management connecting and integrating all parties or members of the distribution system in order to satisfy customers (p. 192)

tactical plans short-range plans designed to implement the activities and objectives specified in the strategic plan (p. 143)

target market a specific group of consumers on whose needs and wants a company focuses its marketing efforts (p. 254)

task force a temporary group of employees responsible for bringing about a particular change (p. 174)

team a small group whose members have complementary skills; have a common purpose, goal, and approach; and hold themselves mutually accountable (p. 174)

technical expertise the specialized knowledge and training needed to perform jobs that are related to particular areas of management (p. 153)

test marketing a trial mini-launch of a product in limited areas that represent the potential market (p. 276)

Theory X McGregor's traditional view of management whereby it is assumed that workers generally dislike work and must be forced to do their jobs (p. 213)

Theory Y McGregor's humanistic view of management whereby it is assumed that workers like to work and that under proper conditions employees will seek out responsibility in an attempt to satisfy their social, esteem, and self-actualization needs (p. 213)

Theory Z a management philosophy that stresses employee participation in all aspects of company decision making (p. 214)

times interest earned ratio operating income divided by interest expense (p. 350)

top managers the president and other top executives of a business, such as the chief executive officer (CEO), chief financial officer (CFO), chief operations officer (COO) and, more recently, chief privacy officer (CPO), who have overall responsibility for the organization (p. 147)

total asset turnover sales divided by total assets (p. 350)

total-market approach an approach whereby a firm tries to appeal to everyone and assumes that all buyers have similar needs (p. 254)

total quality management (TQM) a philosophy that uniform commitment to quality in all areas of an organization will promote a culture that meets customers' perceptions of quality (p. 197)

trade credit credit extended by suppliers for the purchase of their goods and services (p. 379)

trade deficit a nation's negative balance of trade, which exists when that country imports more products than it exports (p. 65)

trademark a brand that is registered with the Canadian Intellectual Property Office and is thus legally protected from use by any other firm (p. 281)

trading company a firm that buys goods in one country and sells them to buyers in another country (p. 76)

training teaching employees to do specific job tasks through either classroom development or on-the-job experience (p. 230)

transaction balances cash kept on hand by a firm to pay normal daily expenses, such as employee wages and bills for supplies and utilities (p. 376)

transfer a move to another job within the company at essentially the same level and wage (p. 233)

transportation the shipment of products to buyers (p. 289)

Treasury bills (T-bills) short-term debt obligations the Canadian government sells to raise money (p. 377)

trust companies corporations that act as a trustee and usually also provide banking services (p. 364)

turnover occurs when employees quit, are fired, promoted, or transferred and must be replaced by new employees (p. 232)

undercapitalization the lack of funds to operate a business normally (p. 122)

unemployment the condition in which a percentage of the population wants to work but is unable to find jobs (p. 16)

unsecured bonds debentures, or bonds that are not backed by specific collateral (p. 383)

unsecured loans loans backed only by the borrowers' good reputation and previous credit rating (p. 380)

values guiding principles that direct an organization's decisions (p. 141)

venture capitalists persons or organizations that agree to provide some funds for a new business in exchange for an ownership interest or stock (p. 127)

viral marketing a marketing tool that uses the Internet, particularly social networking and video sharing sites, to spread a message and create brand awareness (p. 315)

vision statement the statement that explains why an organization exists and discusses its long-range goals (p. 141)

wage/salary survey a study that tells a company how much compensation comparable firms are paying for specific jobs that the firms have in common (p. 234)

wages financial rewards based on the number of hours the employee works or the level of output achieved (p. 234)

warehousing the design and operation of facilities to receive, store, and ship products (p. 290)

whistleblowing the act of an employee exposing an employer's wrongdoing to outsiders, such as the media or government regulatory agencies (p. 45)

wholesalers intermediaries who buy from producers or from other wholesalers and sell to retailers (p. 287)

wiki software that creates an interface that enables users to add or edit the content of some types of websites (p. 314)

working capital management the managing of short-term assets and liabilities (p. 376)

World Bank an organization established by the industrialized nations in 1946 to loan money to underdeveloped and developing countries; formally known as the International Bank for Reconstruction and Development (p. 74)

World Trade Organization (WTO) international organization dealing with the rules of trade between nations (p. 72)

INDEX

tangibility
    manufacturing vs. service business,
        186–187
    operations management (OM), 184
Taobao, 312
Target, 228, 241, 253, 271
target market, 254
Targray Technology International Inc., 120
task force, 174–175
taxation
    corporation, 99
    partnership, 93
    sole proprietorships, 87, 89
Tax-Free Savings Account (TFSA), 366
Taylor, Frederick W., 208
TBDress.com, 271
T-bills, 362–363, 377
TD Bank, 94, 294
TD Bank Group, 220
TD Canada Trust, 103
team, 174
TeamBuy, 316
technical expertise, 153–154
technology
    computer-assisted design (CAD), 191
    computer-assisted manufacturing
        (CAM), 191
    computer-integrated manufacturing
        (CIM), 192
    flexible manufacturing, 191
Teck Cominco Limited, 103
Teck Resources, 8, 94
telecommuting, 218–219
Tell Us About Us Inc., 143, 261
TELUS, 32, 142
Tencer, Ken, 309
termination, 233
Terrestrial Ecologist Golder Associates,
    218
Tesovic, Milun, 20
test marketing, 276
testing, selection, 229
The Dirty Jobs, 212
The Forzani Group, 39
The Human Side of Enterprise, 213
The Lang and O'Leary Exchange, 111
The Learning Centre (TLC), 111
The New York Times, 29
The Wealth of Nations (1776), 12, 167
Theory X, 213
Theory Y, 213
Theory Z, 214
*Theory Z—How American Business Can
    Meet the Japanese Challenge*, 214
Thompson, Jim, 156
360-degree feedback, 231–232
3M, 219
Thrust Fund, 367
Thurlow, Amy, 57

Tim Hortons, 8, 77, 93, 100, 116, 143, 248,
        252, 259, 260, 276, 285, 300
    balance sheet, 346
    industry analysis, 351
    profitability ratios, 349–351
    statement of cash flow, 348
    statement of operations, 343
time wage, 235
Time Warner, 292
times interest earned ratio, 350
Tobin, Brian, 97
TOMS Shoes, 164, 165
top managers, 147–148
"Top Seven Firms," 335
Toronto-Dominion Bank, 365, 388
tort, 59
total asset turnover, 350
Total Debt Freedom Inc., 118
total quality management (TQM),
    197–198
total-market approach, 254
Toyota, 40, 79, 175, 260, 281
trade. *See* international business; interna-
    tional trade barriers
trade balance, 18
trade barriers. *See* international trade
    barriers
trade credit, 379
trade deficit, 65
trademark, 61, 281
trading company, 76
transaction balances, 376
TransCanada Corporation, 29–30
transfer, 233
transformation process, 184–485
transportation, 289–290
Travel With Children, 189
Traveler's Insurance Company, 219
traveller's cheques, 361
Travelzoo, 212
Treasury bills (T-bills), 362–363, 377
Treliving, Jim, 63, 126, 128–129
trip wire, 336
Trudeau, Justin, 319
trust companies, 364
TRUSTe, 325
TSX Group, 386
Tuenti, 313
Tumblr, 295
Turner, Victoria, 118
turnover, 232–234
    job promotion, 233
    separations, 233
    transfer, 233
Twitter
    digital media, 309, 310
    monitoring, 331
    online fraud, 326
    online marketing, 295
    social media monitoring, 251
    social network, 319–320

U

Umbra, 274
undercapitalization, 122
unemployment, 16
unemployment rate, 16, 17, 18
unionized employees
    collective bargaining, 238–239
    dispute resolution, 239–240
United States, 72, 77
Universal Music Group, 14
University Poker Championship, 86
unsecured bonds, 383
unsecured loans, 380
UPS, 193, 195, 355
upward communication, 176
Uruguay Round, 72
USA Today, 44

V

Valeant Pharmaceuticals, 15, 103
Vallabhaneni, Ani, 71
values, 141–142
Van Ittersum, Koert, 285
Varadi, Ben, 117
Vault.com, 40
venture capitalists, 127
Venture Communications, 307–308
Verizon Communications, 292
VersaPay Corp., 121
vertical merger, 104
Via Vegan Ltd., 259
ViaRail, 300
Victoria's Secret, 294
video sharing, 314–316
Vietnam, 74
Viewpoints Network, 324
Vinson, Betty, 43
viral marketing, 315, 316
Virgin Blue, 78
virtual teams, 174
virtual testing, 262
virtual worlds, 320–321
Visa, 361
vision statement, 141–142
Vkontakte, 313
Volkswagen (VW), 186, 300
voluntary agreement, 59
Volvo, 291, 300
VOM FASS, 77

W

W. Atlee Burpee and Co., 121
W5, 42
wages, 234–235
wage/salary survey, 234
Wagman, Tamar, 7–8, 127, 261